MCTS
Microsoft® SharePoint®
2010 Configuration
Study Guide

MCTS
Microsoft® SharePoint® 2010 Configuration
Study Guide

James Pyles

WILEY
Wiley Publishing, Inc.

Acquisitions Editor: Jeff Kellum
Development Editor: Kim Beaudet
Technical Editor: Marilyn Miller-White
Production Editor: Eric Charbonneau
Copy Editor: Kim Wimpsett
Editorial Manager: Pete Gaughan
Production Manager: Tim Tate
Vice President and Executive Group Publisher: Richard Swadley
Vice President and Publisher: Neil Edde
Media Project Manager 1: Laura Moss-Hollister
Media Associate Producer: Doug Kuhn
Media Quality Assurance: Josh Frank
Book Designer: Judy Fung
Compositor: Craig Woods, Happenstance Type-O-Rama
Proofreader: Nancy Bell
Indexer: Ted Laux
Project Coordinator, Cover: Lynsey Stanford
Cover Designer: Ryan Sneed

Copyright © 2011 by Wiley Publishing, Inc., Indianapolis, Indiana

Published simultaneously in Canada

ISBN: 978-0-470-62701-3
ISBN: 978-1-118-00790-7 (ebk)
ISBN: 978-1-118-00792-1 (ebk)
ISBN: 978-1-118-00791-4 (ebk)

Dear Reader,

Thank you for choosing *MCTS: Microsoft SharePoint 2010 Configuration Study Guide* (70-667). This book is part of a family of premium-quality Sybex books, all of which are written by outstanding authors who combine practical experience with a gift for teaching.

Sybex was founded in 1976. More than 30 years later, we're still committed to producing consistently exceptional books. With each of our titles, we're working hard to set a new standard for the industry. From the paper we print on, to the authors we work with, our goal is to bring you the best books available.

I hope you see all that reflected in these pages. I'd be very interested to hear your comments and get your feedback on how we're doing. Feel free to let me know what you think about this or any other Sybex book by sending me an email at `nedde@wiley.com`. If you think you've found a technical error in this book, please visit `http://sybex.custhelp.com`. Customer feedback is critical to our efforts at Sybex.

Best regards,

Neil Edde
Vice President and Publisher
Sybex, an Imprint of Wiley

To my wife Lin who is always gracious and shares me with my books and my computers.

Acknowledgments

I'd like to thank Jeff Kellum for again asking me to write a SharePoint book for Sybex. Kim Beaudet rode point on this project as developmental editor and made sure that all the pieces and players were put together correctly. Thank you for all your helpful guidance and reminders. Marilyn Miller-White was the technical editor for this book and was largely responsible for making sure I sounded intelligent and for confirming all the myriad details and intricacies in how SharePoint works. Kudos also go to Pete Gaughan, editorial manager; Connor O'Brien, editorial assistant; Jenni Housh, senior editorial assistant; and all the other fine folks at Sybex.

My greatest thanks go to my wife Lin, who spent many a night and weekend patiently watching me pound away at the keyboard as I produced this book. I also want to acknowledge my children, Michael, who continues to search for his dreams; David, his wife Kim, and their son (my grandson) Landon, who are building the next generation together; and Jamie, who has just finished one adventure and is about to launch into another. Finally, to my parents James and Barbara Pyles, who continue to be an inspiration to me on how to live life to its fullest. Blessings to all of you.

About the Author

James Pyles   A+, Network+, works as a consultant, author, editor, and technical writer. He has been involved in numerous Ethernet rollout projects, software and hardware installations and upgrades, and Windows and Unix operating system upgrades. He has provided support services for a city government IT department and a wireless network vendor, has supported a usability lab for Hewlett-Packard (HP), and has served as the technical writer for EmergeCore Networks, Aquent Studios, and iAnywhere/Sybase and as a developmental editor for Global Support Content Operations at Hewlett-Packard (HP).

His most recent book is *Using GIMP* (QUE, 2010). He also wrote *PC Technician Street Smarts 2nd Edition* (Sybex, 2009), completely updated for the 2009 version of the A+ exams; *MCTS: Microsoft Office SharePoint Server 2007 Configuration Study Guide: Exam 70-630* (Sybex, 2008); and *SharePoint 2007: The Definitive Guide* (O'Reilly, 2007). Additionally, he was the technical editor for *SharePoint for Project Management* (O'Reilly, 2008) and *Essential SharePoint 2007* (O'Reilly, 2008). James has been a regular contributor to *Linux Pro Magazine* and has occasionally written for *Ubuntu User Magazine*. He has bachelor's degrees in psychology and computer network support and a master's degree in counseling. James currently works at Keynetics Inc. in Boise, Idaho.

Contents at a Glance

Contents

Table of Exercises

Introduction

The Microsoft certification program contains three primary series: Technology, Professional, and Architect. The Technology Series certifications are intended to allow candidates to target specific technologies and are the basis for obtaining the Professional Series and Architect Series of certifications. The certifications contained within the Technology Series consist of one to three exams, focusing on a specific technology and do not include job-role skills. By contrast, the Professional Series of certifications focus on a job role and are not necessarily focused on a single technology but rather a comprehensive set of skills for performing the job role being tested. The Architect Series of certifications offered by Microsoft are premier certifications that consist of passing a review board of previously certified architects. To apply for the Architect Series of certifications, you must have a minimum of 10 years of industry experience.

When obtaining a Technology Series certification, you are recognized as a Microsoft Certified Technology Specialist (MCTS) on the specific technology or technologies on which you have been tested. The Professional Series certifications include Microsoft Certified IT Professional (MCITP) and Microsoft Certified Professional Developer (MCPD). Passing the review board for an Architect Series certification will allow you to become a Microsoft Certified Architect (MCA).

MCTS: Microsoft SharePoint 2010 Configuration Study Guide (70-667) will help you organize and focus your studies and your skill sets so that you will be completely prepared to pass the Microsoft SharePoint Server 2010, Configuring (70-667) certification exam.

The Microsoft Certified Professional Program

Since the beginning of its certification program, Microsoft has certified more than 2 million people. As the computer network industry continues to increase in both size and complexity, this number is sure to grow—and the need for *proven* ability will also increase. Certifications can help companies verify the skills of prospective employees and contractors.

Microsoft has developed its Microsoft Certified Professional (MCP) program to give you credentials that verify your ability to work with Microsoft products effectively and professionally. Several levels of certification are available based on specific suites of exams. Microsoft has recently created a new generation of certification programs:

Microsoft Technology Associate (MTA)   The MTA is Microsoft's new certification for those new to the field of IT. These exams focus on the fundamental skills and technologies an IT professional should be familiar with.

Microsoft Office Specialist (MOS)   The MOS is for power users who use Microsoft Office and Windows Vista.

Microsoft Certified Technology Specialist (MCTS)   The MCTS can be considered the entry-level certification for the new generation of Microsoft certifications. The MCTS certification program targets specific technologies instead of specific job roles. You must take and pass one to three exams.

Microsoft Certified IT Professional (MCITP)   The MCITP certification is a Professional Series certification that tests network and systems administrators on job roles, rather than only on a specific technology. The MCITP generally consists of one to three exams, in addition to obtaining an MCTS-level certification.

Microsoft Certified Professional Developer (MCPD)   The MCPD certification is a Professional Series certification for application developers. Similar to the MCITP, the MCPD is focused on a job role rather than on a single technology. The MCPD generally consists of one to three exams, in addition to obtaining an MCTS-level certification.

> In addition to the previously mentioned certifications, Microsoft offers two high-end credentials: Microsoft Certified Architect (MCA) and Microsoft Certified Master (MCM). Both are well respected but are also very difficult and expensive to obtain.

How Do You Become Certified on Microsoft SharePoint 2010?

In the past, students have been able to acquire detailed exam information—even most of the exam questions—from online "brain dumps" and third-party "cram" books or software products. For that matter, many candidates who were "good students" and able to pass tests by memorizing information from textbooks passed Microsoft certification exams while having little or no practical experience in managing Windows systems. They sadly gave birth to the phrase *paper MCSE*. Those days are gone forever.

Microsoft has taken strong steps to protect the security and integrity of its new certification tracks. Now prospective candidates must complete a course of study that develops detailed knowledge about a wide range of topics. It supplies them with the true skills needed, derived from working with the technology being tested. Although no test maps to a set of skills with 100 percent fidelity, Microsoft is working to make its exam content and format measure, as closely as computer-administered exams can, the true abilities of the people taking the exams.

To that end, the new generation of Microsoft certification programs is heavily weighted toward hands-on skills and experience. It is recommended that candidates have troubleshooting skills acquired through hands-on experience and working knowledge.

Fortunately, if you are willing to dedicate the time and effort to learn the Microsoft technologies you want to master, you can prepare yourself well for the exams by using the proper tools. By working through this book, you can successfully meet the exam requirements to pass the SharePoint configuration exam.

This book is part of a complete series of Microsoft certification study guides, published by Sybex, that together cover the new certifications, as well as the core MCSA and MCSE operating system requirements. Please visit the Sybex website at www.sybex.com for complete program and product details.

MCTS Exam Requirements

Candidates for MCTS certification on Microsoft SharePoint 2010 for configuring must pass just a single exam. Other MCTS certifications may require up to three exams. For a more detailed description of the Microsoft certification programs, including a list of all the exams, visit the Microsoft Learning website at www.microsoft.com/learning/mcpexams/default.mspx.

The Microsoft SharePoint 2010, Configuring Exam

The Microsoft SharePoint 2010, Configuring exam covers concepts and skills related to installing, configuring, and managing SharePoint server farms, site collections, and interoperations with other Microsoft technologies. It emphasizes the following elements of design and administration:

- Configuring Microsoft SharePoint Server 2010 Portal
- Managing search
- Configuring content management
- Configuring business forms
- Managing business intelligence
- Managing administration
- Deploying and upgrading Microsoft SharePoint Server 2010

This exam is quite specific regarding SharePoint Server 2010 requirements and operational settings, and it can be particular about how administrative and configuration tasks are performed within SharePoint. It also focuses on fundamental concepts of SharePoint's operation and its interoperability with other Microsoft Office suite products, particularly other Office 2010 applications as well as other external resources.

Microsoft provides exam objectives to give you a general overview of possible areas of coverage on the Microsoft exams. Keep in mind, however, that exam objectives are subject to change at any time without prior notice and at Microsoft's sole discretion. Please visit the Microsoft Learning website at www.microsoft.com/learning/default.mspx for the most current listing of exam objectives.

Types of Exam Questions

In an effort to both refine the testing process and protect the quality of its certifications, Microsoft has focused its current certification exams on real experience and hands-on proficiency. There is a greater emphasis on your past working environments and responsibilities and less emphasis on how well you can memorize. In fact, Microsoft says that certification candidates should have hands-on experience before attempting to pass any certification exams.

Microsoft continues to accomplish its goal of protecting the integrity of its exams by regularly adding and removing exam questions, limiting the number of questions that any individual sees in a beta exam, limiting the number of questions delivered to an individual by using adaptive testing, and adding new exam elements.

Exam questions may be in a variety of formats: depending on which exam you take, you'll see multiple-choice questions, select-and-place questions, and prioritize-a-list questions. Simulations and case study–based formats are included as well. You may also find yourself taking what's called an *adaptive format* exam. Let's take a look at the types of exam questions and examine the adaptive testing technique so you'll be prepared for all the possibilities.

Multiple-Choice Questions

Multiple-choice questions come in two main forms. One is a straightforward question followed by several possible answers, of which one or more is correct. The other type of multiple-choice question is more complex and based on a specific scenario. The scenario may focus on several areas or objectives.

Select-and-Place Questions

Select-and-place exam questions involve graphical elements that you must manipulate to successfully answer the question. For example, you might see a diagram of a computer network. A typical diagram will show computers and other components next to boxes that contain the text *Place here*. The labels for the boxes represent various computer roles on a network, such as a print server and a file server. Based on information given for each computer, you are asked to select each label and place it in the correct box. You need to place *all* the labels correctly. No credit is given for the question if you correctly label only some of the boxes.

In another select-and-place problem, you might be asked to put a series of steps in order by dragging items from boxes on the left to boxes on the right and placing them in the correct order. One other type requires that you drag an item from the left and place it under an item in a column on the right.

For more information on the various exam policies, go to www.microsoft .com/learning/en/us/certification/exam-policies.aspx.

Simulations

Simulations are the kinds of questions that most closely represent actual situations and test the skills you use while working with Microsoft software interfaces. These exam questions include a mock interface on which you are asked to perform certain actions according to a given scenario.

Because of the number of possible errors that can be made on simulations, be sure to consider the following recommendations from Microsoft:

- Do not change any simulation settings that don't pertain to the solution directly.
- When related information has not been provided, assume that the default settings are used.
- Make sure your entries are spelled correctly.
- Close all the simulation application windows after completing the set of tasks in the simulation.

The best way to prepare for simulation questions is to spend time working with the graphical interface of the product on which you will be tested.

Case Study–Based Questions

Case study–based questions first appeared in the MCSD program. These questions present a scenario with a range of requirements. Based on the information provided, you answer a series of multiple-choice and select-and-place questions. The interface for case study–based questions has a number of tabs, each of which contains information about the scenario. Currently, this type of question appears only in most of the Design exams.

 Microsoft will regularly add and remove questions from the exams. This is called *item seeding*. It is part of the effort to make it more difficult for individuals to merely memorize exam questions that were passed along by previous test-takers.

Tips for Taking the SharePoint 2010 Configuration Exam

Here are some general tips for achieving success on your certification exam:

- Arrive early at the exam center so that you can relax and review your study materials. During this final review, you can look over tables and lists of exam-related information.
- Read the questions carefully. Don't be tempted to jump to an early conclusion. Make sure you know *exactly* what the question is asking.
- Answer all questions. If you are unsure about a question, then mark the question for review, and return to the question at a later time.
- On simulations, do not change settings that are not directly related to the question. Also, assume default settings if the question does not specify or imply which settings are used.
- For questions you're not sure about, use a process of elimination to get rid of the obviously incorrect answers first. Often there are one or two you can dismiss immediately, assuming you know the subject for which you are being tested. This improves your odds of selecting the correct answer when you need to make an educated guess.

Exam Registration

You can take the Microsoft exams at any of more than 1,000 Authorized Prometric Testing Centers (APTCs). To locate a Prometric center near you, go to www.prometric.com. Outside the United States and Canada, contact your local Prometric.

Find out the number of the exam you want to take, and then register with the Prometric center nearest to you. At this point, you will be asked for advance payment for the exam. The exams are $125 each, and you must take them within one year of payment. You can schedule exams up to six weeks in advance or as late as one working day prior to the date of the exam. (The latter is generally but not universally true, so don't count on it.) You can cancel or reschedule your exam if you contact the center at least two working days prior to the exam. Same-day registration is available in some locations, subject to space availability. Where same-day registration is available, you must register a minimum of two hours before test time.

When you schedule the exam, you will be provided with instructions regarding appointment and cancellation procedures, ID requirements, and information about the testing center location. In addition, you will receive a registration and payment confirmation letter from Prometric.

Microsoft requires certification candidates to accept the terms of a nondisclosure agreement before taking certification exams.

Who Should Read This Book

I suppose it goes without saying that the primary audience of this book is anyone who intends on taking the Microsoft 70-667 certification exam: Microsoft SharePoint 2010, Configuration. Of course, this could include people from several different backgrounds and could include people who aren't actually planning on taking the test:

- People who are currently administering Microsoft Office SharePoint Server 2007 (MOSS 2007) for an organization that is planning or at least considering upgrading to Microsoft SharePoint Server 2010 should read this book, not only with the idea of becoming certified but also to learn about the many differences between the 2007 and 2010 versions of this application.

- People who are currently administering SharePoint Server 2010 but who either think they need to know more or want to solidify their qualifications in managing this technology by earning the 70-667 certification should read this book.

- People who are interested in information and content management, multiteam collaboration in an enterprise environment, and large-scale project organization and tracking managed using a multipurpose, web browser–based interface and think SharePoint may be the answer to their dreams or at least their questions should read this book.

Installing, configuring, and managing a SharePoint Server 2010 environment aren't easy tasks. In fact, despite that I have worked as an experienced SharePoint site administrator and I use words for a living, I have difficulty describing exactly what SharePoint Server

2010 is and what it does. I suppose that's because the range of activities and purposes served by SharePoint is really that vast and that varied. For that reason, if you are involved in administering SharePoint 2010, expect to be in the near future, or aspire to those roles, it's important to have resources that pull together all of the vital sources of information and organize them in a way that makes them accessible and easier to assimilate.

Although there are a number of fine books on the market on SharePoint Server 2010 administration and development, none specifically addresses SharePoint from the point of view of the 70-667 exam. That makes the focus of this book unique. If you plan to take this certification exam, no other book will present the required information to you in the way you need it mapped out. Other books might contain some or all of the required subject matter, but they will make you work quite a bit harder to cull the gems you're looking for as you're studying. Here, the gems are gathered together in one place, so all you have to do is open the book.

Like most people who work in a technical field, I tend to think and write in an organized and linear manner. Each chapter in this book builds on the last, so skipping around in the book won't be very helpful, at least not until you've gone through it at least once from cover to cover. Alternately, you can skip around from chapter to chapter and follow only the steps of the individual chapters.

What's in the Book?

What makes a Sybex study guide the book of choice for hundreds of thousands of MCPs? We take into account not only what you need to know to pass the exam but also what you need to know to take what you've learned and apply it in the real world. Each book contains the following:

Objective-by-Objective Coverage of the Topics You Need to Know   Each chapter lists the objectives covered in that chapter.

> The topics covered in this study guide map directly to Microsoft's official exam objectives. Each exam objective is covered completely.

Assessment Test   Directly following this introduction is an assessment test that you should take. It is designed to help you determine how much you already know about SharePoint Server 2010. Each question is tied to a topic discussed in the book. Using the results of the assessment test, you can figure out the areas where you need to focus your study. Of course, we do recommend you read the entire book.

Exam Essentials   To highlight what you learn, you'll find a list of exam essentials at the end of each chapter. The "Exam Essentials" section briefly highlights the topics that need your particular attention as you prepare for the exam.

Glossary   Throughout each chapter, you will be introduced to important terms and concepts that you will need to know for the exam. At the end of the book, a detailed glossary defines these terms, as well as other general terms you should know.

Review Questions, Complete with Detailed Explanations   Each chapter is followed by a set of review questions that test what you learned in the chapter. The questions are written with the exam in mind, meaning they are designed to have the same look and feel as what you'll see on the exam. Question types are multiple choice. You'll find other question types such as exhibits and select-and-place on the actual exam.

Hands-on Exercises   In each chapter, you'll find exercises designed to give you the important hands-on experience that is critical for your exam preparation. The exercises support the topics of the chapter, and they walk you through the steps necessary to perform a particular function.

Real-World Scenarios   Because reading a book isn't enough for you to learn how to apply these topics in your everyday duties, we have provided real-world scenarios in special sidebars. These explain when and why a particular solution would make sense in a working environment you'd actually encounter.

Interactive CD   Every Sybex study guide comes with a CD complete with additional questions, flashcards for use with an interactive device, a Windows simulation program, and the book in electronic format. Details are in the following section.

What's on the CD?

With this new member of our best-selling Study Guide series, we are including quite an array of training resources. The CD offers numerous simulations, bonus exams, and flashcards to help you study for the exam. We have also included the complete contents of the study guide in electronic form. The CD's resources are described here:

The Sybex E-book for *MCTS: Microsoft SharePoint 2010 Configuration Study Guide (70-667)*   Many people like the convenience of being able to carry their whole study guide on a CD. They also like being able to search the text via computer to find specific information quickly and easily. For these reasons, the entire contents of this study guide are supplied on the CD in PDF. We've also included Adobe Acrobat Reader, which provides the interface for the PDF contents as well as the search capabilities.

The Sybex Test Engine   This is a collection of multiple-choice questions that will help you prepare for your exam. There are four sets of questions:

- Two bonus exams designed to simulate the actual live exam.
- All the questions from the study guide, presented in a test engine for your review. You can review questions by chapter or by objective, or you can take a random test.
- The assessment test.

Sybex Flashcards   The flashcard-style of question offers an effective way to quickly and efficiently test your understanding of the fundamental concepts covered in the exam. The Sybex flashcards set consists of approximately 100 questions presented in a special engine developed specifically for this study guide series.

Contacts and Resources

To find out more about Microsoft Education and Certification materials and programs, to register with Prometric, or to obtain other useful certification information and additional study resources, check the following resources:

Microsoft Learning Home Page

www.microsoft.com/learning

This website provides information about the MCP program and exams. You can also order the latest Microsoft Roadmap to Education and Certification.

Microsoft TechNet Technical Information Network

www.microsoft.com/technet

800-344-2121

Use this website or phone number to contact support professionals and system administrators. Outside the United States and Canada, contact your local Microsoft subsidiary for information.

Prometric

www.prometric.com

800-755-3936

Contact Prometric to register to take an MCP exam at any of more than 800 Prometric Testing Centers around the world.

What Else You Will Need

You will need to practice using SharePoint Server 2010 for Internet Sites, Enterprise. Fortunately, you can download a trial version of this product that will allow you to use it free for 180 days. You will need to run SharePoint Server 2010 on either 64-bit Windows Server 2008 or 64-bit Windows Server 2008 R2 on 64-bit computer hardware. There are no versions of SharePoint 2010 that support 32-bit software or hardware. Although not absolutely necessary, it will be extremely helpful for you to have access to the Microsoft Office 2010 suite. Here is where you'll need to go to download the various software packages:

Windows Server 2008 R2 Trial Version

www.microsoft.com/windowsserver2008/en/us/trial-software.aspx

SharePoint Server 2010 Trial Version

http://technet.microsoft.com/en-us/evalcenter/ee388573.aspx

Microsoft Office 2010

http://office.microsoft.com/en-us/try/

Hardware and Software Requirements

You should verify that your computer meets the minimum requirements for installing the required software packages. Each download site contains the relevant information you'll need. In addition, Chapter 2, "Planning and Deploying a SharePoint 2010 Installation and Upgrade," contains detailed information about the hardware and software requirements, so it is highly recommended that you carefully review this entire chapter before installing the required software packages onto your computer.

The exercises in Chapter 2 will also guide you through the step-by-step process of installing SharePoint Server 2010 as a stand-alone server deployment. SharePoint can be deployed on a single server computer or on a server farm in a datacenter. Although the book's content includes material relevant to managing SharePoint in a server farm environment, it's unlikely you'll have a datacenter tucked away in a back closet of your house or apartment, so the practical focus of installing and setting up SharePoint addresses using a single computer.

This book was written using the trial versions of SharePoint Server 2010, Windows Server 2008 R2, and Office 2010 installed on a virtual machine in VMware Workstation 7 on a Windows 7 Professional 64-bit host computer. I also ran a virtual domain controller on Windows Server 2008 R2 and a virtual client Windows 7 machine.

The virtual machine was configured to use the following settings:

- Memory: 512 MB
- Hard disk: (SCSI 0:0) 40 GB (though I never used more than 7 GB of hard drive space)
- Virtual processors: 1
- Ethernet: Bridged
- USB controller: Present

As you can see, I set the resources to be rather modest, and during the writing of this book, I primarily had only the single virtual machine running. The virtual network was bridged to my home LAN so that SharePoint could have access to multiple virtual and actual host computers and to the Internet. The host Windows 7 Professional computer's resources at the time of this writing were as follows:

- Memory: 12 GB
- Two hard disks: (IDE) 75 GB for the OS and (IDE) 300 GB for the virtual environment and storage
- Processor: Dual-core Intel Xeon CPU 2.60 GHz

If you have the resources to afford a more powerful computer on which to run SharePoint 2010, I recommend it, particularly if you plan on also using a more extensive virtual network than the one I employed.

How to Contact the Author

You never write a book alone. Sure, I'm the only author of this text, but there is a team of people who don't have their names on the cover who worked hard to make sure the book in your hands is the best it possibly can be. Every editor involved has taken a great deal of time and energy and provided me with invaluable feedback about how I could make the book better. That said, the one resource I don't have access to while writing is the reader. I can know what you think only after the book is available on the bookstore shelves and online.

I'd still like to hear what you think (be nice), and I do read and respond to my emails. You can reach me by writing to james.pyles@gmail.com, and you can learn more about my work on my website at www.wiredwriter.net.

As I mentioned, the folks at Sybex work hard to keep you supplied with the latest tools and information you need for your work. Please check the website at www.sybex.com, where we'll post additional content and updates that supplement this book if the need arises. Enter MCTS: **Microsoft SharePoint 2010 Configuration Study Guide** in the Search box (or type the book's ISBN, which is **9780470627013**), and click Go to reach the book's updates page.

Remember, studying for this exam is something you want to do, and you are learning about a subject you are really interested in. With that in mind, don't make it all work. Have fun. Play with the technology. See how far you can take the exercises, modify them, try different combinations of settings, and figure out all the different ways that SharePoint works and what it does. Really get to know it inside and out as you are working through the chapters, and by the time you schedule and take the exam, you'll be ready. Good luck.

Assessment Test

1. You are a SharePoint administrator of a Microsoft Office SharePoint Server 2007 (MOSS 2007) environment, and you have been tasked by your CIO to investigate the feasibility of upgrading to SharePoint 2010. As part of your feasibility study, you are exploring new and upgraded features of the SharePoint platform. What do you discover? (Choose all that apply.)

   A. Remote BLOB Storage is used for server farms to provide high storage capacity by allowing BLOB customized pages stored on Windows Server 2008 and Windows Server 2008 R2 to be housed in a separate file system outside the Windows Server system.

   B. SharePoint Server 2010 comes equipped with a large number of diagnostic and performance monitoring tools, including Developer dashboard and Usage database.

   C. Windows PowerShell Administration v2.0 is currently available for use as the de facto command-line interface and scripting language in SharePoint Server 2010.

   D. List controls can be used to manage the number of queries sent to lists to improve performance, particularly lists containing a large number of items.

2. You are a SharePoint administrator of a Microsoft Office SharePoint Server 2007 (MOSS 2007) environment, and you have been tasked by your CIO to investigate the feasibility of upgrading to SharePoint 2010. As part of your feasibility study, you are exploring new and upgraded features of the SharePoint platform. What do you discover? (Choose all that apply.)

   A. Backup and restore functions in SharePoint Server 2010 have been completely transferred to Windows PowerShell to allow new granularity in the process.

   B. In Excel Services, the new unattended service account allows one-time access to Excel Services data to low-security users.

   C. Enterprise search now exclusively uses FAST Search to accelerate search functions in large, enterprise environments.

   D. Trusted locations are provided by default in SharePoint Server 2010.

3. Which of the following are valid service applications in SharePoint Server 2010? (Choose all that apply.)

   A. Access Services

   B. Business Community Services (BCS)

   C. Excel Services

   D. Visio Services

4. What are some of the factors that determine whether you deploy SharePoint Server 2010 on a single farm or on multiple farms? (Choose all that apply.)

   A. The requirement to use the Visual Upgrade feature

   B. The need for multiple dedicated services farms to satisfy use requirements

   C. Funding that is dedicated for special purposes requiring more than one farm

   D. Using multiple server farms to enhance performance

5.   If you plan to use the SharePoint Directory Management Services and Active Directory as part of an advanced incoming email feature setup, one required task is to create an organizational unit (OU) and delegate create, delete, and manage user accounts to Central Administration. Of the following options, which are generally true about this task? (Choose all that apply.)

   A.   You will need to work on a computer that is a domain controller.

   B.   You will need to start the task in the DNS Manager.

   C.   You can use Directory Management Services on either a server farm or a remote server farm.

   D.   You will finish the task in the Delegation of Control Wizard.

6.   You are the SharePoint administrator for your organization, and you are about to perform post-installation tasks for your server farm. You are describing how to set up usage data collection to your staff as part of that process. Of the following, what is true about configuring usage data collection? (Choose all that apply.)

   A.   You can configure usage data collection for a single event type using Windows PowerShell.

   B.   You can change the database used by usage data collection using Windows PowerShell.

   C.   You must be a member of the Farm Administrators group to configure usage data collection using Windows PowerShell.

   D.   You must be a member of the SQL Server Administrators group to configure usage data collection using Windows PowerShell.

7.   You are the SharePoint administrator for your organization, and you've been tasked with configuring your local SharePoint server farm environment to be able to consume application resources on other server farms within the organization managed by other administrators. To do this, you must perform various tasks to allow trust certificates to be exchanged between server farms. Of the following options, what is true about these tasks?

   A.   You can use either Central Administration or Windows PowerShell to perform the related tasks.

   B.   You can only use Central Administration to perform the related tasks.

   C.   You can only use Windows PowerShell to perform the related tasks.

   D.   You must perform separate tasks in both Central Administration and Windows PowerShell.

8.   There are a wide variety of tasks that you must perform as a SharePoint administrator, using Windows PowerShell when configuring service applications, yet for each of these PowerShell-related activities, you require the same set of credentials. Of the following, which are the required credentials? (Choose all that apply.)

   A.   You must be a member of the SharePoint_Shell_Access group.

   B.   You must be a member of the SharePoint Farm Administrators group.

   C.   You must be a member of the WSS_ADMIN_WPG local group on the computer containing SharePoint 2010.

   D.   You must be a member of the processadmin group for the SQL Server database containing the application service data.

9. You are a SharePoint administrator for your organization, and you are currently deploying enterprise search in SharePoint. You have created a search service application and have performed your first full crawl of the configured content sources, but the crawl hasn't functioned they way you had hoped. On the Search Administration page for the selected Search service application, you open the Administration Reports page and start reviewing the various documents present. On any specific document, what actions can you perform? (Choose all that apply.)

   A. You can filter the results by date range, with 12 hours being the default range.

   B. You can filter the results by application type.

   C. You can filter the results by search service application.

   D. You can filter the results by content source.

10. You are a SharePoint administrator for your organization, and you have recently deployed enterprise search in SharePoint. You have been tasked by the CIO with gathering statistics on websites searched by SharePoint users. You visit the Web Analytics page in Search Administration for the default Search service application. On this page, what reports can you view? (Choose all that apply.)

   A. Top Browsers

   B. Top Destinations

   C. Top Queries

   D. Top Visitors

11. You are a SharePoint administrator for your company, and you need to add a content database to a SQL Server instance in order to move a site collection that is running out of room on its current database to a new database. You know you have more than one option to use to create the new content database. Of the following, which are valid options? (Choose all that apply.)

   A. Central Administration

   B. Windows PowerShell

   C. SQL Server Management Studio

   D. The `Stsadm.exe` command-line tool

12. You are a SharePoint administrator for your company, and you need to add a content database to a SQL Server instance in order to move a site collection that is running out of room on its current database to a new database. You know you have more than one type of authentication method that can be configured when connecting to the SQL service when creating the database. Of the following, which are valid authentication options? (Choose all that apply.)

   A. Basic authentication

   B. SQL authentication

   C. Trusted authentication

   D. Windows authentication

13. You are a SharePoint administrator for your organization. You are discussing the procedures for creating and configuring a User Profile service application with your staff. You are presenting the general characteristics of the application. Of the following choices, which ones are personalization settings that can be managed in this application? (Choose all that apply.)

A. Audiences

B. Defining Managed Paths

C. My Site settings

D. Profile synchronization settings

14. You are a SharePoint administrator for your organization. You are discussing the procedures for creating and configuring a User Profile service application with your staff. You are discussing circumstances that may inhibit the creation and use of a User Profile service application. Of the following options, which must be present in order for you to create the application? (Choose all that apply.)

A. You must be running the Standard or Enterprise version of SharePoint Server 2010 in a full server farm.

B. At least one managed path must exist.

C. You must have an application pool that is used by My Sites.

D. You must be running an instance of Managed Metadata Services.

15. You are a SharePoint administrator for your organization. You have just upgraded your MOSS 2007 environment to SharePoint Server 2010. Now you need to upgrade the authentication systems on your web applications to claims-based authentication from the MOSS 2007 web application default authentication. What default authentication system does MOSS 2007 use?

A. Active Directory Federation Services

B. Forms-based

C. Secure Store Service

D. Windows Challenge/Response NTLM

16. You are a SharePoint administrator for your organization. You have just upgraded your MOSS 2007 environment to SharePoint Server 2010. Now you need to upgrade the authentication systems on your web applications to claims-based authentication from the MOSS 2007 web application default authentication. What is the procedure to perform this task?

A. Open Central Administration and in Quick Launch click Security. Under General Security, click Specify Authentication Providers. On the subsequent page, update the authentication type to the one you want in SharePoint 2010.

B. Open Windows PowerShell as an administrator, type in a script that will perform the authentication upgrade, and then press Enter.

C. You must perform the authentication upgrade in MOSS 2007 before upgrading to SharePoint by selecting Upgrade, Authentication Providers, and then Upgrade to SharePoint 2010 default authentication.

D. You must perform the authentication upgrade during the upgrade from MOSS 2007 to SharePoint 2010 by selecting the Upgrade Authentication For Web Applications option in the upgrade wizard.

17. You are a SharePoint administrator for your company, and you are preparing to deploy business intelligence (BI) in your environment. You and your staff are doing a high-level review of the components that contribute to BI. Of the following, which services are used to provide data to BI dashboards? (Choose all that apply.)

   A. Excel Services

   B. Managed Metadata Services

   C. PerformancePoint Services

   D. Visio Graphics Services

18. You are a SharePoint administrator for your company, and you are preparing to deploy business intelligence (BI) in your environment. You are reviewing the requirements for installing and managing PerformancePoint Services in SharePoint. Of the following, which are valid prerequisite steps? (Choose all that apply.)

   A. You will need to manually create the PerformancePoint Service application in Central Administration.

   B. Once the PerformancePoint Service is created, you must start the service.

   C. You must configure the unattended service account for PerformancePoint Services to allow access to Performance Point Services data sources.

   D. PerformancePoint Site Collection Features must be turned on.

19. You are a SharePoint administrator for your company, and you have just been tasked with configuring content deployment settings for your environment. You have already configured the content deployment settings as well as paths, jobs, and Quick Deploy. Now you are interested in configuring job history and reports. Of the following, what do you find is true about configuring and running content deployment job histories and reports? (Choose all that apply.)

   A. Every time a content deployment job runs, a report on the job status and details is generated and logged as a record for that job.

   B. To view the status of the deployment of specific content, you must specify the location of the content by URL.

   C. If a content deployment job has failed, you cannot open the Content Deployment Report page.

   D. To view a job history or job report for a content deployment job, you must select the desired job and click View History for that job in the job's menu.

20. You are a SharePoint administrator for your company, and you are in the process of enabling document converters on a web application in your environment. Document converters allow SharePoint users to convert one document format type to another either through a user interface or through an automated process such as a custom workflow. As you are going through the process of enabling document conversion, you are offered several conversion settings. Of the following, which are valid conversion settings? (Choose all that apply.)

   A. From InfoPath Form to Web Page

   B. From Word Document to Web Page

   C. From Word Document to Macros

   D. From XML to Web Page

21. You are a SharePoint administrator for your company, and you have been tasked with planning a sandbox solution for deployment. You are conducting a high-level review of SharePoint sandboxes, including the steps that must be performed by a farm administrator. Of the following, which steps are considered valid for preparing sandbox deployment? (Choose all that apply.)

    A. The farm administrator must enable and start the sandboxing service on each server that will run the sandbox solution.

    B. The farm administrator must activate and validate the sandbox solution.

    C. The farm administrator must apply a load-balancing scheme to all sandbox solutions if load balancing is a requirement.

    D. The farm administrator must set resource quotas that cannot be exceeded by all the combined site collections in the solution if resource quotas are a requirement.

22. You are a SharePoint administrator for your company, and you have been tasked with planning a sandbox solution for deployment. You are conducting a high-level review of SharePoint sandboxes, including sandbox isolation management and resources that an isolated sandbox environment is unable to access. Of the following, what are the resources an isolated sandbox cannot access? (Choose all that apply.)

    A. Cannot access resources on a different site collection within the sandbox

    B. Cannot access a database

    C. Cannot access the `manifest.xml` file

    D. Cannot access resources on the local server

23. You are a SharePoint administrator for your company, and you are planning the backup and recovery strategy for your server farm. You are developing your initial plan for the backup directory or folder where you will back up your server farm. What is the recommended procedure for backing up the farm to a folder?

    A. Back up the farm to a folder on the local computer.

    B. Back up the farm to a folder on the network.

    C. Back up the farm to a folder on the local computer and then transfer the backup to a remote location on the network.

    D. Back up the farm to a remote location on the network and then transfer the backup to a folder on the local computer.

24. You are a SharePoint administrator for your company, and you are planning the backup and recovery strategy for your server farm. You are developing your backup and recovery strategy. Backing up the entire farm regularly is a necessary task, but not all necessary elements are backed up during this process. Of the following, what is not backed up when you backup the farm? (Choose all that apply.)

    A. Business Data Connectivity service external content definitions

    B. Business Data Connectivity data sources

    C. Binary Large Object stores when using the FILESTREAM store provider

    D. Certificates required to establish trust relationships

25. You are a SharePoint administrator for your company, and you are currently managing the monitoring and analysis tools in SharePoint. You are currently configuring Diagnostic Logging using Windows PowerShell. Of the following, which PowerShell cmdlet should you use?

   A. `SPDiagLog`

   B. `SPDiagnosticLog`

   C. `SPLogLevel`

   D. `SPLogSet`

26. You are a SharePoint administrator for your company, and you are currently managing the monitoring and analysis tools in SharePoint. You are currently configuring Usage and Health Data Collection using Central Administration. Of the following, what is true about configuring this utility?

   A. You can configure this data collection tool to apply to a web application, a single server, a collection of servers, or the server farm.

   B. You can configure this data collection tool to apply to a single server, a collection of servers, or the server farm.

   C. You can configure this data collection tool to apply to a group of three servers or more including the entire server farm.

   D. You can configure this data collection tool to apply to the entire server farm only.

27. You are a SharePoint administrator for your organization, and you are in the process of optimizing SharePoint performance. You want to optimize BLOB cache settings by modifying a particular file for a web application. What is the name of this file?

   A. `blob.config`

   B. `blob.cache`

   C. `web.config`

   D. `web.cache`

28. You are a SharePoint administrator for your organization, and you are in the process of optimizing SharePoint performance. You want to optimize access to BLOB storage by configuring a disk-based BLOB cache. Of the following, what is the correct tool to use to accomplish this task?

   A. Central Administration

   B. The main page of the relevant site collection

   C. Internet Information Services (IIS) Manager

   D. Windows PowerShell

29. You are on the staff of a SharePoint administrator for your company, and you are learning Windows PowerShell basics as applied to the SharePoint environment. As part of your education, you have found out that there are three other main types of commands in PowerShell besides cmdlets. Of the following, what are those commands? (Choose three.)

    A. Applications

    B. Functions

    C. Scripts

    D. Variables

30. You are on the staff of a SharePoint administrator for your company, and you are learning Windows PowerShell basics as applied to the SharePoint environment. You are trying to learn cmdlet basics. At its most fundamental level, how is a cmdlet structured?

    A. A cmdlet is a verb-noun pair such as `Get-Fred` or `Set-Item`.

    B. A cmdlet is a noun-verb pair such as `Fred-Get` or `Item-Set`.

    C. A cmdlet is a verb/noun pair such as `Get/Fred` or `Set/Item`.

    D. A cmdlet is a noun/verb pair such as `Fred/Get` or `Item/Set`.

Answers to Assessment Test

1. B, C, D. For option A, Remote BLOB Storage is used for server farms to provide high storage capacity by allowing BLOBs from the all_docs table and customized pages in a database to be housed in a file system outside the SQL Server database, reducing the amount of storage required on the SQL Server itself. For more information, see Chapter 1, "What's New in Microsoft SharePoint 2010."

2. B, D. For option A, backup and restore can be performed either using the Central Administration website or using Windows PowerShell. For option C, FAST Search is an optional download, while enterprise search is available by default in SharePoint Server 2010. For more information, see Chapter 1, "What's New in Microsoft SharePoint 2010."

3. A, C, D. Business Community Services (BCS) is incorrect. The correct name is Business Connectivity Services (BCS). All other answers are valid services. For more information, see Chapter 2, "Planning and Deploying a SharePoint 2010 Installation and Upgrade."

4. B, C, D. Option A is bogus because the use of Visual Upgrade has nothing to do with server farm planning. All other options are correct. See Chapter 2, "Installing and Deploying SharePoint 2007," for more information.

5. A, C, D. You start the task in Active Directory Users and Computers, not the DNS Manager. See Chapter 3, "Configuring SharePoint Farm Environments," for more information.

6. A, B. Options C and D are bogus. See Chapter 3, "Configuring SharePoint Farm Environments," for more information.

7. C. The tasks related to importing and exporting trust certificates must be performed using Windows PowerShell. For more information, see Chapter 4, "Configuring Service Applications."

8. A, C. Only membership in the SharePoint_Shell_Access and the WSS_ADMIN_WPG local groups is required to perform the application service configuration tasks in Windows PowerShell. For more information, see Chapter 4, "Configuring Service Applications."

9. A, B, D. Since you are performing this action within a single search service application, you cannot filter the results based on other applications that exist outside of the one you are currently using. For more information, see Chapter 5, "Configuring Indexing and Search."

10. A, B, D. There is no Top Queries option, but you can choose Number Of Queries and view that report. See Chapter 5, "Configuring Indexing and Search," for more information.

11. A, B. You can either use Central Administration or use Windows PowerShell. Options C and D are not valid options. See Chapter 6, "Managing Operational Settings," for more information.

12. B, D. The only options available for you to select for authentication types are SQL authentication and Windows authentication. See Chapter 6, "Managing Operational Settings," for more information.

13. A, C, D. Defining managed paths is done in web application management, not in the User Profile service application. See Chapter 7, "Managing User Accounts and Roles," for more information.

14. A, C, D. Although you must be running either the Standard or Enterprise version of SharePoint Server 2010, it does not have to be running in a full server farm. This is a requirement only when you perform other tasks such as profile synchronization. See Chapter 7, "Managing User Accounts and Roles," for more information.

15. B. MOSS 2007 web applications were generally configured to use forms-based authentication or web SSO authentication. See Chapter 8, "Managing Authentication Providers," for more information.

16. B. You must use Windows PowerShell to run a specific script after MOSS 2007 has been upgraded to SharePoint Server 2010. No other option is available. See Chapter 8, "Managing Authentication Providers," for more information.

17. A, C, D. The services that primarily provide and manage BI information include Excel, PerformancePoint, and Visio. Managed Metadata Services is a hierarchical collection of managed terms that can be defined and then used as attributes for SharePoint items. See Chapter 9, "Managing Web Applications and Host Sites," for more information.

18. B, C, D. The PerformancePoint service application can be created in Central Administration, but you can also use the Farm Configuration Wizard to create the service right after your initial SharePoint deployment is finished. See Chapter 9, "Managing Web Applications and Host Sites," for more information.

19. A, B, D. If a content deployment job fails, you must click Failed in the Status column for the job to open the Content Deployment Report page. See Chapter 10, "Managing Site Collections," for more information.

20. A, B, D. Instead of From Word Document to Macros, the answer should read From Word Document with Macros to Web Page in order to be correct. See Chapter 10, "Managing Site Collections," for more information.

21. A, C, D. The site collection administrator can activate and validate the sandboxed solution as well as upload the solution to the site collection's solution gallery. See Chapter 11, "Deploying and Managing SharePoint Solutions," for more information.

22. A, B. The sandbox must be able to connect to the local server and access the `manifest.xml` file, which contains the configuration information defining the sandbox environment. For more information, see Chapter 11, "Deploying and Managing SharePoint Solutions."

23. C. The recommended procedure is to first back up the farm to a folder on the local machine and then transfer the backup to a remote location on the network. For more information, see Chapter 12, "Backing Up and Restoring SharePoint."

24. B, D. Although the SharePoint farm backup process backs up the Business Data Connectivity (BDC) service external content type definitions, it doesn't back up the actual data source. Backing up the farm does not back up any certificates used to create trust relationships. SharePoint backs up the remote Binary Large Object stores, also called BLOB stores, only if you use the FILESTREAM remote BLOB store provider to move data in remote BLOB stores. For more information, see Chapter 12, "Backing Up and Restoring SharePoint."

25. C. Use the `SPLogLevel` cmdlet and appropriate parameters to configure Diagnostic Logging in Windows PowerShell. The other cmdlets are bogus. For more information, see Chapter 13, "Monitoring the SharePoint Environment."

26. D. Any Usage and Health Data Collection tool settings you make are applied to the entire farm and cannot specify a smaller group of servers. For more information, see Chapter 13, "Monitoring the SharePoint Environment."

27. C. To configure the BLOB cache, you must locate and modify the `web.config` file in order to optimize access to BLOB storage for disk-based BLOB cache or a web application. For more information, see Chapter 14, "Optimizing SharePoint."

28. C. Use the Internet Information Services (IIS) Manager to locate and access the necessary file to specify a directory for the cache. For more information, see Chapter 14, "Optimizing SharePoint."

29. A, B, C. Valid PowerShell commands include applications, such as executables; functions, which are commands written in the PowerShell language; and scripts, which are text files with a `.ps1` extension containing PowerShell commands. Although variables can be part of a function or a script, they are not commands. For more information, see Chapter 15, "Working with Windows PowerShell."

30. A. A cmdlet is a verb-noun pair separated by a hyphen. In English, it might be expressed as `Get-Fred` or `Bring-Donuts`. For more information, see Chapter 15, "Working with Windows PowerShell."

Chapter

1

What's New in Microsoft SharePoint 2010

MICROSOFT EXAM OBJECTIVE COVERED IN THIS CHAPTER:

✓ **Installing and Configuring a SharePoint Environment**

 ▪ Deploy new installations and upgrades

If you picked up this book, it's because you're committed to using and administering Microsoft SharePoint Server in some capacity. Either you are a current Microsoft Office SharePoint Server 2007 (MOSS 2007) administrator who is anticipating upgrading to SharePoint Server 2010 or you are planning a first-time SharePoint deployment for your production environment. You may also be someone who has yet to experience SharePoint but is looking to expand your skill set. In any case, the information presented here will both prepare you for the 70-667 "TS: Microsoft SharePoint 2010, Configuring" certification exam and be invaluable in deploying and managing a SharePoint 2010 environment.

This book is written with the student in mind, but if you belong to any of the groups just mentioned, you qualify as a student—someone in a position to learn something new, whether for the purpose of sitting an exam or to hone your administrative skills in the production SharePoint arena. This book has been created from the point of view of a person building a personal lab or sandbox environment, but the content is equally applicable to the SharePoint administrator invested in rolling out SharePoint Server 2010 to production in the enterprise.

While subsequent chapters will address the specific information you'll need to know about how to upgrade MOSS 2007 to SharePoint Server 2010 and to deploy a first-time installation, you need to first take some time to understand just how different SharePoint Server 2010 is from MOSS 2007. It's not a matter of simply launching an upgrade executable and following a wizard. There's a whole new world of hardware and software requirements to learn and understand.

New Requirements Overview

Before launching into the specifics of the certification exam domains, it's important to take some time to get to know the basics of SharePoint Server 2010. Even if you're familiar with MOSS 2007, Microsoft's latest release of SharePoint has a lot of new features and contains perhaps a few surprises.

In a nutshell, these are the new requirements for SharePoint Server 2010:

- SharePoint Server 2010 is a 64-bit only application.

- SharePoint Server 2010 will be able to run only on 64-bit Windows Server 2008 or 64-bit Windows Server 2008 R2.

- SharePoint Server 2010 will be able to use only 64-bit SQL Server 2008 or 64-bit SQL Server 2005 for database services.

There are a number of other specifics, but before you continue, you must have access to both the required Windows Server and SQL Server versions, as well as a 64-bit hardware platform. If you are using 32-bit hardware in either your production or testing environment, you will not be able to install or upgrade to SharePoint Server 2010. Also, earlier versions of Windows Server and SQL Server will not be adequate.

At this point, you may be questioning the rationale of Microsoft in making decisions relative to a 64-bit platform. It's important both to understand why 32-bit hardware and server environments are no longer supported and to learn about other changes and compatibility issues.

If you currently administer MOSS 2007 in the enterprise, you likely already run 64-bit hardware and may even have upgraded to 64-bit Windows Server 2008 or Windows Server 2008 R2. If the advantages of running 64-bit aren't apparent to you (and especially if you're lamenting how moving from 32-bit is going to stretch your personal or professional budget), you'll need to learn more about why Microsoft moved in this direction.

> To find out the basics of x86 64-bit architecture, visit http://en.wikipedia .org/wiki/64-bit and http://en.wikipedia.org/wiki/X86-64.

The Advantages of 64-Bit Hardware

Comparing 64-bit hardware to 32-bit hardware is a little like comparing a mid-range sedan to a high-end sports car. Each has its purpose and does well in the area it's designed for, but the sports car will go a lot faster when asked.

Bus architecture supports more and wider registers and improves overall application performance speeds by reducing the need to write persistent data to memory.

The most memory a 32-bit system can support is 4 GB of RAM. A 64-bit system that is running a 64-bit edition of Windows Server can support up to 1024 GB of both physical and addressable memory. SharePoint is an application that's designed to grow with a company's needs. Its ability to use more memory means SharePoint can serve greater access and service requirements. 32-bit hardware supports up to 32 processors. That might seem like a lot, but in a truly demanding environment, particularly one where you anticipate needing to scale up based on business needs, the ability to expand to a maximum of 64 processors is a great advantage.

The Advantages of 64-Bit Server and Database Platforms

The aforementioned hardware advantages don't just apply to SharePoint Server 2010 as an application but to the Windows Server 2008 and SQL Server platforms in terms of speed, security, and scalability.

Even assuming a single physical server platform, Windows Server 2008 can take advantage of a lot more RAM and processing power than on a 32-bit machine, addressing up to 16 terabytes of virtual memory by using a flat addressing model. This gives SQL Server access to almost unlimited virtual memory, as well as physical memory. Database servers are extremely resource intensive, and any database administrator will immediately see the advantages.

Although the set of features available in 64-bit Windows Server 2008 is not appreciably different from its 32-bit counterpart, there are some important security considerations. 64-bit Windows Server 2008 offers greater buffer overflow protection because the first parameters of a procedure call are passed in registers. Since the correct values have to be assigned in the registers and both addresses and variables have to be aligned on the stack, the data buffer is less likely to become congested and thus present a security concern.

64-bit processors made by AMD and Intel include hardware support for data execution prevention (DEP) to prevent any malicious executables from running, even in the unlikely event of a buffer overflow. Also, Microsoft Patch Guard prevents any kernel mode drivers in third-party applications from extending or replacing kernel services in Windows Server 2008.

It's intuitively obvious that more processing power and more physical and virtual memory support equals "better," but in terms of scalability, having access to so much more memory than is supported on 32-bit platforms means that both Windows Server 2008 and SQL Server can load large amounts of working data entirely in memory. Users and administrators should notice no apparent performance lags as workload demands increase over time, even if the demands increase dramatically. This also results in decreasing the need for as many application servers, since larger loads can be handled by fewer servers.

Considerations of 32-Bit and 64-Bit

It's certainly possible to install some 64-bit applications on a 32-bit platform, but you won't see any of the advantages offered by the software. The software environment won't have the necessary hardware to execute all of its potential, much like putting high-test fuel in a 1970s vintage Volkswagen beetle. Performance may be improved somewhat, but you really need to join elements together that provide the most advantage, which means running 64-bit applications on 64-bit hardware.

64-bit Windows Server 2008 does include the *Windows on Windows 64-bit (WOW64)* translation layer, which emulates a 32-bit operating system, so running a mixed 32-bit and 64-bit environment is possible. Although this may seem like an advantage if you need to run a legacy application on a 64-bit platform, in fact this doesn't work with any of the 64-bit SharePoint applications and services. This means you cannot run a mixed 32-bit/64-bit environment, such as 64-bit SharePoint Server 2010 using 32-bit SQL Server 2005. The disadvantage from an up-front cost view is the requirement to upgrade all of your software and hardware platforms if you want to run SharePoint Server 2010.

Although this may seem terribly unfair of Microsoft, its analysis of SharePoint test data and feedback from customers running MOSS 2007 has indicated that the performance and scalability advantages far outweigh the initial cost of upgrading. Whether you agree with this decision or not, the reality of 64-bit is here, and it's here to stay.

Not all 64-bit processors are SharePoint Server 2010 friendly. The Intel Itanium 64-bit processor series uses a proprietary design that will not support any of the Microsoft SharePoint products and technologies. Before you choose to install or upgrade to SharePoint Server 2010, check the type of processors in your hardware.

Requirements by Environment

You have a general idea of the new requirements for SharePoint Server 2010; however, the specifics of those requirements vary depending on the type of installation you are planning.

Base Hardware Requirements

The following are the basic minimum hardware requirements for all installation and deployment types, regardless if deployed on a stand-alone physical server with an integrated database installation or on a per-server basis for each physical server in a server farm.

Hard Drive   80 GB of hard drive space for the base installation, plus additional hard drive space to support regular operational requirements. Microsoft recommends having twice as much hard drive space available as the amount of RAM for production environments.

Processor   64-bit processors in a quad-core, with 2.5 GHz per core.

RAM   A minimum of 4 GB of RAM per physical server for development or testing environments and 8 GB or more RAM for production per server.

Software Requirements

The following requirements apply to individual physical servers, regardless of whether they are stand-alone installations or individual servers deployed in a server farm. All the information presented represents the minimum requirements.

Database Server in a Farm

The following is the required software in a farm (chose one of the following):

- 64-bit Microsoft SQL Server 2005 with Service Pack 3 and with Cumulative Update 3 for SQL Server 2005 Service Pack 3
- 64-bit Microsoft SQL Server 2008 with Service Pack 1 and with Cumulative Update 2 installed with Cumulative Update 2 for SQL Server 2008 Service Pack 1

A Single Server with an Integrated Database

The following is the required software for an integrated database (choose one of the following):

- 64-bit Windows Server 2008 Standard with SP2
- 64-bit Windows Server 2008 R2 Standard

All of the following are required, regardless of the Windows Server 2008 type:

- Web Server (IIS) role
- Application Server role
- Microsoft .NET Framework version 3.5 SP1
- SQL Server 2008 Express with SP1
- Microsoft "Geneva" Framework
- Microsoft Sync Framework Runtime v1.0 (x64)
- Microsoft Filter Pack 2.0
- Microsoft Chart Controls for the Microsoft .NET Framework 3.5
- Windows PowerShell 2.0 CTP3
- SQL Server 2008 Native Client
- Microsoft SQL Server 2008 Analysis Services ADOMD.NET
- ADO.NET Data Services v1.5 CTP2

Also, the following list includes the optional software:

- 64-bit Microsoft SQL Server 2008 R2 if you want to work with PowerPivot workbooks
- Microsoft SQL Server 2008 R2 Reporting Services Add-in for SharePoint Technologies (SSRS) if you want to use Access Services in SharePoint Server 2010
- Microsoft Server Speech Platform if you want to have phonetic name matching function correctly in SharePoint Search 2010

Frontend Web Servers and Application Servers in a Farm

The following is the required software for frontend web servers and application servers in a farm (choose one of the following):

- 64-bit Windows Server 2008 Standard with SP2
- 64-bit Windows Server 2008 R2 Standard

All of the following are required, regardless of the Windows Server 2008 type:

- Web Server (IIS) role
- Application Server role
- Microsoft .NET Framework version 3.5 SP1
- Microsoft "Geneva" Framework

- Microsoft Sync Framework Runtime v1.0 (x64)
- Microsoft Filter Pack 2.0
- Microsoft Chart Controls for the Microsoft .NET Framework 3.5
- Windows PowerShell 2.0 CTP3
- SQL Server 2008 Native Client
- Microsoft SQL Server 2008 Analysis Services ADOMD.NET
- ADO.NET Data Services v1.5 CTP2

The following list includes the optional software:

- 64-bit Microsoft SQL Server 2008 R2 if you want to work with PowerPivot workbooks
- Microsoft SQL Server 2008 R2 Reporting Services Add-in for SharePoint Technologies (SSRS) if you want to use Access Services in SharePoint Server 2010
- Microsoft Server Speech Platform if you want to have phonetic name matching function correctly in SharePoint Search 2010

Client Computer Requirements

The following sections give the requirements that you may not have anticipated. Although the Microsoft Windows operating systems you would expect to be supported (Windows XP and newer) are indeed sufficient, the major issue is in web browser support. To take advantage of all of SharePoint Server 2010's authoring and publishing features, only certain web browsers are supported. Microsoft categorizes web browser functionality relative to SharePoint into two levels. We'll discuss them in the following sections.

Level I Web Browsers

Level 1 web browsers are browsers that can take advantage of advanced features offered by *ActiveX* controls and that can provide full functionality on all SharePoint sites, including the SharePoint Central Administration website.

The following list breaks down the various operating systems and browsers that support SharePoint:

- Windows XP
  - Internet Explorer 7
  - Internet Explorer 8 (32-bit)
  - Mozilla Firefox 3.5
- Windows Vista
  - Internet Explorer 7
  - Internet Explorer 8 (32-bit)
  - Mozilla Firefox 3.5

- Windows Server 2003 and 2008
  - Internet Explorer 7
  - Internet Explorer 8 (32-bit)
  - Mozilla Firefox 3.5
- Windows 7
  - Internet Explorer 8 (32-bit)
  - Mozilla Firefox 3.5
- Windows Server 2008 R2
  - Internet Explorer 8 (32-bit)
  - Mozilla Firefox 3.5

The following list includes the optional software:

- Microsoft Office 2010 client
- Microsoft Silverlight 3.0

Level II Web Browsers

Level II web browsers provide only basic functionality, allowing users to read and write in SharePoint sites and perform basic site administration. However, since ActiveX controls are not supported, users will not have access to full SharePoint 2010 functionality.

The following list is a breakdown of the various operating systems and browsers that support SharePoint:

- Apple Mac OS X Snow Leopard
  - Apple Safari 4.*x*
  - Mozilla Firefox 3.5
- Windows XP
  - Internet Explorer 7 (64-bit)
  - Internet Explorer 8 (64-bit)
- Windows Vista
  - Internet Explorer 7 (64-bit)
  - Internet Explorer 8 (64-bit)
- Windows Server 2003 and 2008
  - Internet Explorer 7 (64-bit)
  - Internet Explorer 8 (64-bit)
- Windows 7
  - Internet Explorer 8 (64-bit)
- Windows Server 2008 R2
  - Internet Explorer 8 (64-bit)

- UNIX/Linux 8.1
  - Mozilla Firefox 3.5

The following list includes the optional software:

- Microsoft Office 2010 client
- *Microsoft Silverlight 3.0*

For the non-Windows operating systems, Microsoft Office 2010 and Microsoft Silverlight won't be available. The previous list also assumes that the client computers will be running Microsoft Office 2007, although the official client compatibility information published by Microsoft doesn't explicitly state this.

In Exercise 1.1, I will show you how to determine your readiness to install SharePoint.

EXERCISE 1.1

Determine Your Readiness to Install SharePoint Server 2010 in a Single-Server Deployment

1. Open a web browser and go to http://technet.microsoft.com/en-us/library/cc262485.aspx.

2. Review the information on this page to determine whether your current hardware and software meets the minimum requirements for a SharePoint Server 2010 installation, as shown here.

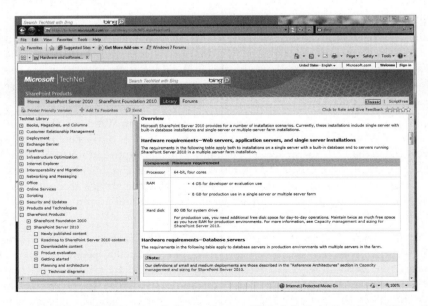

3. Locate and click the link Deploy A Single Server With A Built-in Database (SharePoint Server 2010).

4. Review the instructions for installing SharePoint Server 2010 as a single hardware server installation using a built-in database solution.

5. Save both links as favorites in your web browser and then close your web browser.

The information gathered in the previous exercise will help you determine your readiness for installing and working with SharePoint Server 2010 either in a home or small lab environment or in a sandbox testing environment at your business.

What's New and Different with SharePoint Server 2010?

Not everything that's new with SharePoint Server 2010 is completely new to SharePoint. There are features and services you know from MOSS 2007 that have taken on new functionality as well as features and utilities included that are completely new in SharePoint Server 2010. That means some parts of the interface and the backend configuration will seem familiar if you have administered prior SharePoint Server versions, while others will be strangers.

The following list shows you a number of the new features available for the first time in SharePoint Server 2010:

SharePoint Central Administration Website   This site is the interface for configuring the entire SharePoint Server 2010 environment. Administrators familiar with MOSS 2007 and prior SharePoint versions are familiar with this tool. For SharePoint 2010, it has been redesigned for greater ease of use, organizing common tasks and lists into functional areas, as you can see in Figure 1.1

Managed Accounts   This is actually a concept borrowed from Windows Server 2008 and is new in SharePoint Server 2010. Services or groups of services have accounts on a server platform, such as the SQL Server service account, which is required to deploy SharePoint on the server farm. To minimize the administrative cost of managing all the various service accounts, managed accounts let SharePoint take control of the service accounts and manage authentication, including sending notifications to the SharePoint administrator when the password for a managed service is about to expire.

Service Applications   These were referred to in MOSS 2007 as *shared services providers* (SSPs), were available only on SharePoint Server, and required a specific SSP setup. In SharePoint Server 2010, all services are installed by default and are available both on the server version and on Microsoft SharePoint Foundation 2010 (what was previously called Windows SharePoint Services or WSS). In MOSS 2007, when an SSP was associated with a web application, the web application carried the load for all the services contained within the SSP. Service applications in SharePoint 2010 can be individually selected, so a web application supports only the services it consumes. Additionally, you can publish a service application and share it across a single server farm or, for some services, across multiple server farms.

FIGURE 1.1   A SharePoint Central Administration website

Diagnostics, Monitoring, and Reporting   SharePoint Server 2010 comes equipped with a large number of diagnostic and performance monitoring tools, organized into different functional areas:

Developer Dashboard   This is designed to provide greater performance and tracing information that can be used to troubleshoot issues. The dashboard provides information about controls, queries, and execution time for the page-rendering process.

Unified Logging Service (ULS)   This is a troubleshooting tool that provides access to various log files and lets you filter your view to hone in on the data you specifically need.

Usage Database   This is part of the usage and health data collection system and provides information on SharePoint usage patterns.

SharePoint Maintenance Engine (SPME) Rules   This checks the administrative configuration, performance, security issues, and other areas, either periodically or on demand, and makes recommendations on how to solve potential issues. This was formerly known as the Best Practices Analyzer.

System Center Operations Manager (SCOM) Monitoring   This provides real-time alerts and troubleshooting of issues in SharePoint.

Out-of-Box Usage Reports   These are the default logging and reporting tools in SharePoint.

Remote BLOB Storage   Also called RBS, this is used for server farms to provide very high storage capacity by allowing BLOBs from the all_docs table and customized pages in the database to be housed in a file system outside the SQL Server database, thus reducing the amount of required storage on the SQL Server instance. Third-party RBS providers are required, and the RBS architecture is completely customizable, allowing specific RBS providers to offer targeted storage services.

Performance Controls   SharePoint Server 2010 has two specific methods of managing performance. Throttling allows the administrator to control the level of SharePoint operations during times of peak demand, and list controls limit the number of queries per list, managing performance relative to the number of queries in each list containing a large number of items.

Windows PowerShell **Administration**   This is both a new command-line interface and associated scripting language developed by Microsoft and originally released for Windows XP SP2 and Windows Server 2003. Version 2.0 has been released for Windows 7 and Windows Server 2008 R2 and is available for SharePoint Server 2010 administration. Although `Cmd.exe` and `Stsadm.exe`, which MOSS 2007 administrators are familiar with, have not been replaced for the sake of backward compatibility, PowerShell is considered the de facto command-line tool for SharePoint Server 2010. A unique feature in PowerShell is the cmdlet. A cmdlet (pronounced "command-let") either can be used as a single function or can be combined with other cmdlets to perform more complex actions and to automate administration. You can use the prebuilt cmdlets included with PowerShell by default or customize one or more cmdlets to suit specific needs. PowerShell, then, is not just a command shell but also a new scripting language.

Backup and Restore   This functionality has been updated and can now be performed using either the Central Administration website (Figure 1.2) or Windows PowerShell. New granularity has been built in, letting you back up and restore down to the site, subsite, and list levels.

Excel Services   There are a number of new features in Excel Services released in SharePoint Server 2010, such as the unattended service account, allowing low-security, one-time access to Excel Services data, multiuser collaboration that lets multiple SharePoint users edit an Excel document simultaneously, and the ability to completely deploy Excel Services from Windows PowerShell. Also, trusted locations are now provided by default.

Multi-Tendency   SharePoint Server 2010 now has the ability to isolate and separate information from different websites while at the same time sharing services and resources between the same sites. This is known as multi-tendency. Customers or users on a site are known as tenants, and although tenant data can be shared across multiple sites, data owned by the tenant can also be partitioned based on site subscriptions so that the data can be separated and grouped while other resources are freely shared.

FIGURE 1.2   A Backup and Restore page in Central Administration

 Real World Scenario

Determining a Need for Microsoft FAST Search Server

You are a Microsoft Office SharePoint Server 2007 administrator for an enterprise-level company. The CIO has tasked you with investigating the costs and benefits of upgrading to SharePoint Server 2010 as opposed to maintaining the current MOSS 2007 infrastructure.

One of the significant complaints you have heard from users of the current system is that enterprise search speed has become slower as the infrastructure has scaled up to accommodate business growth. As part of your upgrade investigation, you want to determine whether SharePoint Server 2010 will offer your organization a better-performing and richer-featured search experience.

You open a web browser on your computer, go to http://technet.microsoft.com, and locate the link to download Microsoft FAST Search Server 2010 for SharePoint. You may have to perform a search for *Microsoft FAST Search Server for SharePoint 2010*. On the download page, you review the information available to see whether the features offered represent a true enhancement of enterprise search. Find the system requirements data or link on the page. Determine whether any additional hardware and software is necessary to run Microsoft FAST Search Server besides what is required to operate a SharePoint Server 2010 environment.

Once you've completed your research, document your findings and then close your web browser.

SharePoint Enterprise Search   SharePoint search enables you to define a custom ranking model to use for search queries and uses Microsoft *Business Connectivity Services (BCS)* to crawl and index external data. End users will appreciate the new search capacities, especially connectors for Windows 7, which allows the same search of SharePoint sites to be conducted directly from Windows 7 and offers preview and drag-and-drop options. Search query suggestions are available both while the user is typing the query and after the query run.

Microsoft also offers the optional *FAST Search for SharePoint* to accelerate SharePoint search in enterprise environments and to provide enhanced features to search, such as previews of actual content in search results.

This list is hardly exhaustive but does give you an idea of what to expect when you start working with SharePoint Server 2010. The subsequent chapters of this book will provide both more detailed information regarding the topics presented here and a more complete presentation of everything contained, both new and updated, in SharePoint Server 2010.

In Exercise 1.2, you will explore the new SharePoint 2010 features.

EXERCISE 1.2

Explore Other New SharePoint Server 2010 Features

1.   Open a web browser; then go to `http://msdn.microsoft.com/en-us/library/ee557323(office.14).aspx` or search for *What's New In SharePoint Server 2010* at `http://msdn.microsoft.com`.

2.   When the web page loads, select one or more of the following links on this page and review the content:

- What's New: Business Connectivity Services (BCS)

- What's New: Enterprise Content Management (ECM)

- What's New: PerformancePoint Services

- What's New: Excel Services

- What's New: User Profiles and Social Data

- Word Automation Services Overview

3.   After reviewing the desired content, make these pages favorites in your web browser and then close your web browser.

As you can see, there is a lot more to learn about what's new in SharePoint Server 2010 than you might imagine. In many ways, Microsoft's current incarnation of SharePoint Server is more feature rich and more challenging to administer than any of its predecessors.

Another change you'll notice is that the Ribbon, introduced with Office 2007 and Windows Vista, is fully integrated into SharePoint Server 2010, as shown in Figure 1.2.

This makes it a natural fit with Office 2010. Word 2010 documents can be copied and pasted directly into a SharePoint 2010 site, and document formatting options within SharePoint are exactly the same as in Word.

FIGURE 1.3 Microsoft SharePoint Server 2010 Ribbon

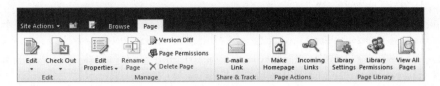

Blogs and wikis, as shown in Figure 1.3, were first made available in MOSS 2007 and have been improved. SharePoint Server 2010 also provides social networking capacities, adding social tagging and ratings to the interests and expertise listings in user profiles.

FIGURE 1.4 Default wiki page in SharePoint Server 2010

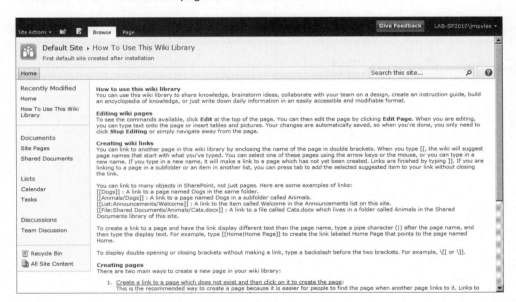

The InfoPath Forms Services, also introduced in MOSS 2007, has been enhanced so that building interactive forms and publishing them to the Web is much easier.

Representational State Transfer (REST) is a new architectural style for SharePoint that lets you create Excel spreadsheet or Visio diagram data, publish the data, and then update the original documents and have the web-published versions reflect the changes almost immediately. Access Services offers similar functionality, letting you quickly create, publish, and update a database application through a web browser.

Summary

In this chapter, you were introduced to SharePoint Server 2010, including many of its new features and upgrades from Microsoft Office SharePoint Server 2007 (MOSS 2007).

- The requirements of the hardware and software platform for SharePoint Server 2010 include 64-bit server hardware and 64-bit Windows Server 2008 Standard or 64-bit Windows Server 2008 Standard R2 and 64-bit SQL Server 2005 or 2008.

- The advantages of running SharePoint Server 2010 in a 64-bit environment include increased performance and scalability.

- A wider base of client computer operating systems and web browsers is supported by SharePoint Server 2010.

- SharePoint Server 2010 can use optional FAST Search for SharePoint to enhance performance and features on enterprise-level search.

- SharePoint Server 2010 can now be administered through Windows PowerShell 2.0 as a command-line interface and scripting language.

Exam Essential

Learning the Features Offered in SharePoint Server 2010   Learn about the new and upgraded features and capacities of SharePoint Server 2010 in preparation for installing a new system or upgrading an existing MOSS 2007 platform.

Review Questions

1. You are a SharePoint administrator of a Microsoft Office SharePoint Server 2007 environment, and you have been tasked by your CIO to investigate the viability of upgrading your production system to SharePoint Server 2010. Which of the following options are true? (Choose all that apply.)

   A. SharePoint Server 2010 is a 64-bit only application.

   B. SharePoint Server 2010 can run only on 64-bit Windows Server 2003, 64-bit Windows Server 2008, and 64-bit Windows Server 2008 R2.

   C. SharePoint Server 2010 can only use 64-bit SQL Server 2008 for database services.

   D. SharePoint Server 2010 deployed as a single server can use SQL Server 2008 Express Service Pack 1 as an integrated database.

2. You are the CIO for an enterprise-level company. You have been asked to prepare a report on the feasibility of upgrading your SharePoint system to 64-bit hardware and software by the CEO. As part of the task of preparing a report, you list the advantages of 64-bit hardware. Which of the following options do you include as advantages? (Choose all that apply.)

   A. 64-bit bus architecture supports more and wider registers, improving overall application performance speeds by reducing the need to write persistent data to memory.

   B. 32-bit systems can support only 8 GB of RAM, while 64-bit systems can support up to 512 GB of RAM.

   C. 32-bit systems support 32 processors in a hardware server, while 64-bit systems support up to 64 processors.

   D. The minimum amount of RAM required to install and work with SharePoint Server 2010 in a testing environment is 4 GB.

3. You are the CIO for an enterprise-level company. You have been asked to prepare a report on the feasibility of upgrading your SharePoint system to 64-bit hardware and software by the CEO. As part of the task of preparing a report, you describe how much virtual memory a 64-bit Windows Server 2008 machine can access. Which of the following is true?

   A. A 64-bit Windows Server 2008 machine can address up to 8 terabytes of virtual memory.

   B. A 64-bit Windows Server 2008 machine can address up to 16 terabytes of virtual memory.

   C. A 64-bit Windows Server 2008 machine can address up to 32 terabytes of virtual memory.

   D. A 64-bit Windows Server 2008 machine can address up to 64 terabytes of virtual memory.

4. You are a SharePoint administrator of a Microsoft Office SharePoint Server 2007 environment, and you have been tasked by your CIO to investigate the feasibility of upgrading to 64-bit SharePoint Server 2010. As part of your investigation, you look into the security advantages of upgrading to a 64-bit hardware and software platform. Which of the following do you report as advantages? (Choose all that apply.)

   A. Windows Server 2008 offers greater buffer overflow protection because the first parameters of a procedure call are passed in buffers.

   B. Windows Server 2008 offers greater buffer overflow protection because the first parameters of a procedure call are passed in registers.

   C. 64-bit processors include hardware support for data execution prevention (DEP) to prevent any malicious executables from running.

   D. Microsoft Patch Guard prevents any kernel mode drivers in Microsoft-only applications from extending or replacing kernel services in Windows Server 2008.

5. You are a SharePoint administrator of a Microsoft Office SharePoint Server 2007 environment, and you have been tasked by your CIO to investigate the feasibility of upgrading to SharePoint 2010. You discover that 64-bit Windows Server 2008 includes Windows and Windows 64-bit (WOW64) translation layer, which emulates a 32-bit operating system, allowing a mixed 32-bit/64-bit environment to coexist. One of your interns asks about the possibility of mixing 32-bit Windows Server 2008 machines with their 64-bit counterparts in a SharePoint Server 2010 upgrade. What is true about this suggestion?

   A. Although you cannot install SharePoint Server 2010 on a 32-bit Windows Server 2008 machine, you can use 32-bit SQL Server 2005 and 2008 for database services.

   B. Although you cannot install SharePoint Server 2010 on a 32-bit Windows Server 2008 machine, you can use 32-bit SQL Server 2008 for database services, but not 32-bit SQL Server 2005.

   C. You cannot install SharePoint Server 2010 on a 32-bit Windows Server 2008 machine, and you must use 64-bit SQL Server 2005 or 2008 for database services.

   D. You cannot install SharePoint Server 2010 on a 32-bit Windows Server 2008 machine, and you must use only 64-bit SQL Server 2008 for database services.

6. You are the CIO for an enterprise-level company. You have been asked to prepare a report on the feasibility of upgrading your SharePoint system to 64-bit hardware and software by the CEO. As part of the task of preparing a report, you run across information stating that not all 64-bit processors are compatible with SharePoint Server 2010. Of the following options, which processor type is to be avoided?

   A. 64-bit Intel Xeon processor w/2M

   B. AMD Athlon 64 3500 processor

   C. 64-bit Intel Itanium processor

   D. AMD Sempron 3000 64-bit processor

7. You are the CIO for an enterprise-level company. You have been asked to prepare a report on the feasibility of upgrading your SharePoint system to 64-bit hardware and software by the CEO. This includes the specific minimum hardware requirements for installing Share-Point Server 2010. You visit the related website at Microsoft and discover which of the following requirements? (Choose all that apply.)

   A. A production installation requires a minimum of 60 GB of hard drive spaces, plus additional space on the drive to support regular operational requirements.

   B. The minimum processor requirements are 64-bit processors in dual-core, with 2.5 GHz per core.

   C. A minimum of 4 GB of RAM per physical server for development or testing purposes.

   D. A minimum of 8 GB of RAM per production server.

8. You are a SharePoint administrator of a Microsoft Office SharePoint Server 2007 environment, and you have been tasked by your CIO to investigate the feasibility of upgrading to SharePoint 2010. You are currently looking into the required and optional software that must be installed on a single server with an integrated database for a SharePoint Server 2010 test deployment. Which of the following software packages must be installed on a Windows Server 2008 R2 machine in order to successfully install SharePoint Server 2010? (Choose all that apply.)

   A. Microsoft .NET Framework version 3.5 SP1

   B. Microsoft "Geneva" Framework

   C. Microsoft Chart Controls for the Microsoft .NET

   D. SharePoint Technologies (SSRS)

9. You are the DBA for your enterprise-level company, and you are meeting with the CIO and CEO to plan your company's efforts to upgrade to SharePoint Server 2010. You are tasked with inventorying the database servers in the server infrastructure and reporting on how many Microsoft SQL servers must be upgraded to support the proposed SharePoint deployment. Which of the following SQL Server versions will need to be upgraded? (Choose all that apply.)

   A. 32-bit Microsoft SQL Server 2000 with Service Pack 4

   B. 64-bit Microsoft SQL Server 2000 with Service Pack 4

   C. 64-bit Microsoft SQL Server 2005 with Service Pack 3

   D. 64-bit Microsoft SQL Server 2008 with Service Pack 1

10. You are a SharePoint administrator of a Microsoft Office SharePoint Server 2007 environment, and you have been tasked by your CIO to investigate the feasibility of upgrading to SharePoint 2010. You are currently looking into the required and optional software to be installed on Windows Server 2008 R2 in order to deploy SharePoint Server 2010 as a frontend web server or application server. Which of the following options are optional software for those server types? (Choose all that apply.)

   A. 64-bit Microsoft SQL Server 2008 R2 in order to work with PowerPivot workbooks

   B. Microsoft SQL Server 2008 R2 Reporting Services Add-in for SharePoint Technologies (SSRS)

   C. Microsoft Sync Framework Runtime v1.0 (x64)

   D. Microsoft Server Speech Platform

11. You are a SharePoint administrator of a Microsoft Office SharePoint Server 2007 environment, and you have been tasked by your CIO to investigate the feasibility of upgrading to SharePoint 2010. As part of your feasibility study, you must review the various desktops and web browsers available in corporate headquarters to determine which ones will be able to take full advantage of SharePoint Server 2010's advanced features offered through ActiveX controls. Which of the following desktop and web browser combinations will be able to use the advanced features? (Choose all that apply.)

   A. Windows XP with Internet Explorer 7

   B. Windows Vista with Internet Explorer 7

   C. Windows 7 with Firefox 3.5

   D. Windows 7 with Internet Explorer 8 (64-bit)

12. You are a SharePoint administrator of a Microsoft Office SharePoint Server 2007 environment, and you have been tasked by your CIO to investigate the feasibility of upgrading to SharePoint 2010. As part of your feasibility study, you must review the various desktops/servers and web browsers available in corporate headquarters to determine which ones will have access to only the basic functionality of SharePoint services due to a lack of ActiveX support. Which of the following desktop/web browser combinations have this limitation? (Choose all that apply.)

   A. Windows Server 2003 with Internet Explorer 7

   B. Apple Mac OS X with Apple Safari 4

   C. Windows Server 2008 R2 with Internet Explorer 8 (64-bit)

   D. Unix/Linux 8.1 with Mozilla Firefox 3.5

13. You are a SharePoint administrator of a Microsoft Office SharePoint Server 2007 environment, and you have been tasked by your CIO to investigate the feasibility of upgrading to SharePoint 2010. As part of your feasibility study, you must review new and upgraded features in SharePoint. Which of the following options are true? (Choose all that apply.)

   A. Shared services provider (SSPs) have been renamed to service applications in SharePoint Server 2010.

   B. Service applications are supported under SharePoint Server 2010 but not under Microsoft SharePoint Foundation 2010 (formerly known as Windows SharePoint Services or WSS).

   C. The SharePoint Central Administration website design remains unchanged between MOSS 2007 and SharePoint Server 2010.

   D. SharePoint Server 2010 Performance Controls includes throttling to allow the administrator to control SharePoint operations levels during peak demand periods.

14. You are a SharePoint administrator of a Microsoft Office SharePoint Server 2007 environment, and you have been tasked by your CIO to investigate the feasibility of upgrading to SharePoint 2010. As part of your feasibility study, you are exploring new and upgraded features of the SharePoint platform. Which of the following are true? (Choose all that apply.)

    A. Remote BLOB Storage is used for server farms to provide high storage capacity by allowing BLOBs to customized pages stored on Windows Server 2008 and Windows Server 2008 R2 to be housed in a separate file system outside the Windows Server system.

    B. SharePoint Server 2010 comes equipped with a large number of diagnostic and performance-monitoring tools, including the developer dashboard and usage database.

    C. Windows PowerShell Administration v2.0 is currently available for use as the de facto command-line interface and scripting language in SharePoint Server 2010.

    D. List controls can be used to manage the number of queries sent to lists to improve performance, particularly lists containing a large number of items.

15. You are a SharePoint administrator of a Microsoft Office SharePoint Server 2007 environment, and you have been tasked by your CIO to investigate the feasibility of upgrading to SharePoint 2010. As part of your feasibility study, you are exploring new and upgraded features of the SharePoint platform. Which of the following are true? (Choose all that apply.)

    A. Backup and restore functions in SharePoint Server 2010 have been completely transferred to Windows PowerShell to allow new granularity in the process.

    B. In Excel Services, the new unattended service account allows one-time access to Excel Services data to low-security users.

    C. Enterprise Search now exclusively uses FAST Search to accelerate search functions in large, enterprise environments.

    D. Trusted locations are provided by default in SharePoint Server 2010.

16. You are a SharePoint administrator of a Microsoft Office SharePoint Server 2007 environment, and you have been tasked by your CIO to investigate the feasibility of upgrading to SharePoint 2010. You are currently reviewing material regarding how Excel Services has changed. Which of the following options are true? (Choose all that apply.)

    A. Excel Services is a shared service that lets you load, calculate, and display Microsoft Excel workbooks on SharePoint Server 2010.

    B. The Excel Web Access web part is one of two primary interfaces for Excel Services added in SharePoint Server 2010.

    C. Excel Web Services for programmatic access was added in SharePoint Server 2010.

    D. SharePoint Server 2010 has enhanced Excel Services, so you can now edit and save a workbook programmatically.

17. You are a SharePoint administrator of a Microsoft Office SharePoint Server 2007 environment, and you have been tasked by your CIO to investigate the feasibility of upgrading to SharePoint 2010. You are currently reviewing material regarding Word Automation Services. Which of the following options are true? (Choose all that apply.)

   A. Word Automation Services is a shared service first introduced in MOSS 2007.

   B. Word Automation Services provides unattended, server-side conversion of documents into formats supported by Microsoft Word.

   C. Word Automation Services can now save documents in PDF format.

   D. Word Automation Services supports all automatic tasks that execute when a document opens, including recalculating all field types and XML mapping.

18. You are a SharePoint administrator of a Microsoft Office SharePoint Server 2007 environment, and you have been tasked by your CIO to investigate the feasibility of upgrading to SharePoint 2010. You are currently reviewing material regarding Business Connectivity Services (BCS). Which of the following options are true? (Choose all that apply.)

   A. Business Connectivity Services in SharePoint Server 2010 used to be called Business Data Catalog in MOSS 2007.

   B. Business Connectivity Services provides read/write access to external data from web services, databases, and other external systems from within SharePoint Server 2010.

   C. Business Connectivity Services provides read/write access to external data from within Microsoft Office 2007 and Microsoft Office 2010 applications.

   D. Business Connectivity Services provides read/write access to external data from within Microsoft Office 2010 applications only.

19. You are the CIO for an enterprise-level company. You have been asked to prepare a report on the new features in SharePoint Server 2010 as related to a possible plan to upgrade from MOSS 2007. Among the new features and services you've added to your report, which of the following statements have you discovered? (Choose all that apply.)

   A. The Ribbon, first introduced in Windows Vista and Microsoft Office 2007, has been fully integrated into SharePoint Server 2010.

   B. The content from Word 2010 documents can be directly copied and pasted into a SharePoint Server 2010 site.

   C. Document-formatting options in a SharePoint Server 2010 document are the same as those found in Word 2010.

   D. Microsoft FAST Search Server can be accessed directly from within a Microsoft Office 2010 application.

20. You are the CIO for an enterprise-level company. You have been asked to prepare a report on the new features in SharePoint Server 2010 as related to a possible plan to upgrade from MOSS 2007. Among the new features and services you've added to your report, which of the following statements have you discovered? (Choose all that apply.)

A. SharePoint Server 2010 social networking features let you add social tagging and ratings to the interests and expertise listings in user profiles.

B. SharePoint Server 2010 social networking features let you directly access third-party social networking sites and applications such as Facebook and Twitter. Note: This information was available to the reader who followed Exercise 1.2, visited `http://msdn.microsoft.com/en-us/library/ee557323(office.14).aspx`, and then clicked the link What's New: User Profiles and Social Data.

C. Representational State Transfer (REST) is a service in SharePoint Server 2010 that lets you create a spreadsheet or diagram and publish the data in SharePoint, and then when you update the original spreadsheet or diagram, the data is almost immediately updated in SharePoint.

D. SharePoint Enterprise Search uses connectors for Windows Vista and Windows 7 that let you conduct the same search of SharePoint sites from the desktop as you can from within SharePoint Server 2010.

Answers to Review Questions

1. **A, D.** In option B, Windows cannot use 64-bit Windows Server 2003, and in option C, Windows can also use 64-bit SQL Server 2005 for database services.

2. **A, C, D.** In option B, 32-bit systems can support only 4 GB of RAM, while 64-bit systems support up to 1024 GB of RAM.

3. **B.** A 64-bit Windows Server 2008 machine can use up to 1024 GB of physical memory and up to 16 terabytes of virtual memory.

4. **B, C.** Option A is in error because procedure calls are passed in registers, not buffers. Option D is incorrect, because Microsoft Patch Guard prevents any kernel mode drivers in third-party applications from extending or replacing kernel services, not Microsoft applications.

5. **C.** You must use 64-bit SQL Server 2005 or 2008 for database services. You cannot use any 32-bit server or database server platform. Both 64-bit SQL Server 2005 and 2008 are acceptable options.

6. **C.** The Intel Itanium 64-bit processor uses a proprietary design that will not support any of the Microsoft SharePoint products and technologies used by SharePoint Server 2010.

7. **C, D.** For option A, the minimum required hard drive space is 80 GB, not 60 GB. For option B, the minimum processor requirement is quad-core, not dual-core, though the other stated processor requirements in the answer are correct.

8. **A, B, C.** SharePoint Technologies (SSRS) is optional and needed only if you want to use Access Services in SharePoint Server 2010.

9. **A, B.** No 32-bit database server is supported by SharePoint Server 2010, and no version of Microsoft SQL Server 2000 is supported. The database servers listed in options C and D are both acceptable and will not need to be upgraded.

10. **A, B, D.** Each is an optional software package and not necessary to run SharePoint Server 2010 as a web server or application server. For option C, Microsoft Sync Framework Runtime v1.0 (x64) is a required package and must be installed for the aforementioned SharePoint server roles.

11. **A, B, C.** For option D, Windows 7 with Internet Explorer 8 (32-bit) will support advanced features, but IE 8 (64-bit) will not.

12. **B, C, D.** For option A, this server/web browser platform combination can take full advantage of ActiveX controls.

13. **A, D.** For option B, service applications are supported under both SharePoint Server 2010 and Microsoft SharePoint Foundation 2010. For option C, the SharePoint Central Administration website has been redesigned for greater ease of use, organizing common tasks and lists into functional areas.

14. B, C, D. For option A, Remote BLOB Storage is used for server farms to provide high storage capacity by allowing BLOBs from the all_docs table and customized pages in a database to be housed in a file system outside the SQL Server database, reducing the amount of storage required on the SQL Server itself.

15. B, D. For option A, backup and restore can be performed from either the Central Administration website or using Windows PowerShell. For option C, FAST Search is an optional download, while Enterprise Search is available by default in SharePoint Server 2010.

16. A, D. For options B and C, both Excel Services features were available in MOSS 2007. Note:This information was available to the reader who followed Exercise 1.2, visited `http://msdn.microsoft.com/en-us/library/ee557323(office.14).aspx`, and then clicked the link What's New: Excel Services.

17. B, C, D. For option A, Word Automation Services is a shared service new in SharePoint Server 2010. Note: This information was available to the reader who followed Exercise 1.2, visited `http://msdn.microsoft.com/en-us/library/ee557323(office.14).aspx`, and then clicked the link What's New: Word Automation Services Overview.

18. A, B, D. BCS does not allow access to external systems from within Microsoft Office 2007 applications. Note: This information was available to the reader who followed Exercise 1.2, visited `http://msdn.microsoft.com/en-us/library/ee557323(office.14).aspx`, and then clicked the link What's New: Business Connectivity Services (BCS).

19. A, B, C. Answers A, B, and C all describe SharePoint features that are new in SharePoint Server 2010. For option D, the answer is bogus.

20. A, C. For option B, SharePoint offers no such social networking capacity. For option D, the SharePoint Enterprise Search connector is available only for Windows 7, not for Windows Vista.

Planning and Deploying a SharePoint 2010 Installation and Upgrade

MICROSOFT EXAM OBJECTIVE COVERED IN THIS CHAPTER:

✓ **Installing and Configuring a SharePoint Environment**

- Deploy new installations and upgrades

Deploying SharePoint Server 2010 into your production environment can take several different paths depending on your current situation. If you administer a Microsoft Office SharePoint Server 2007 (MOSS 2007) infrastructure, you will be planning an upgrade strategy. If you are deploying SharePoint Server 2010 as a first-time installation, your planning process will be very different. You also need to consider the scope of the deployment. You may be installing SharePoint as a single-server solution with an integrated database or deploying SharePoint in a server farm with database services provided by SQL Server 2005 or 2008.

Regardless of your goals, you have to start with a plan. Particularly when studying for a certification exam, there is a tendency to want to immediately launch into installing the server and application software on a server or workstation machine and get down to business. This chapter will start by presenting how to plan for different SharePoint Server 2010 architectures and then proceed to the installation and deployment of both new and upgrade SharePoint environments.

Planning the SharePoint Server 2010 Environment

In Chapter 1, "What's New in Microsoft SharePoint 2010," you learned there's a great deal of preparation to be done, particularly in terms of your hardware and software platforms, prior to installing SharePoint Server 2010. You must make sure you have 64-bit hardware and that all your server and database software is 64-bit. However, even when you have met the basic requirements, you still need to plan for an installation or upgrade deployment based on your architecture and business requirements. Since your architecture design will follow your business needs as well as technical and structural requirements, planning must include both logical and topological components.

The 70-668 "PRO: SharePoint 2010, Administrator" certification exam tests specifically for capacity planning, performance tuning, and topology designing, which are skill sets not emphasized in the 70-667 "TS: Microsoft SharePoint 2010, Configuring" certification exam. However, some comprehension of deployment and upgrade planning is necessary to help you understand the principles behind the various deployment methods presented later in this chapter. The following planning information is not extensive and is presented only to lay the foundation for those deployment and upgrade scenarios.

Architecting SharePoint Components

Just as you'd expect an architect designing your home to be familiar with the tools required to plan for and build your house, you will need to learn the components contained within SharePoint that you can use to build your organization's SharePoint design architecture. You can arrange the various elements that make up your architecture in a variety of ways, depending on your isolation and sharing requirements. Isolation and sharing tend to be competing priorities, and to create a successful design that meets your needs, you need not only to understand what your goals are for each but also to examine your willingness to benefit from one element at the expense of the other. The following offers a high-level view of the logical SharePoint architectural components.

The Server Farm

At its most basic level, a server farm is a collection of physical server iron and logical servers grouped in a single location. The server farm is the top-level element in your design structure, and each server farm offers physical isolation of your resources from other server farms. SharePoint can be deployed in a single farm or across multiple server farms depending on your requirements. What determines whether you deploy on a single farm or in multiple farms depends on the following circumstances:

- Needing multiple dedicated services farms to accommodate heavier use of specific services
- Having separate operational divisions of responsibility in your organization requiring isolation of resources
- Funding that is dedicated for specific purposes requiring more than one farm
- Using separate datacenter locations
- Satisfying any industry or legal requirements for physical isolation between sites for your organization
- Using multiple server farms to enhance performance and scalability as well as licensing requirements and publishing environment goals

In general, if you plan on freely sharing multiple resources in your SharePoint environment, a single server farm is likely sufficient. If you require services and resources to be isolated for any of the reasons previously listed, you will likely require several server farms and probably one server farm per isolation requirement.

Of course, it is possible to satisfy at least some isolation requirements in a single server farm through the use of different *Internet Information Services (IIS)* application pools using different process identities, providing isolation for sites and service applications at the process level. However, in an enterprise-level environment with its needs operating and changing dynamically on many levels, planning for multiple server farms is the better option, assuming isolation is weighted more heavily than budget concerns.

Service Applications

In MOSS 2007, services were contained in shared services providers (SSPs). For SharePoint Server 2010, individual services are hosted in Microsoft SharePoint Foundation 2010, or what used to be called Windows SharePoint Services (WSS). This allows configuration of individual services, making management more flexible and letting third-parties create and provide customized services.

Service applications are associated with web applications, and specific services are typically deployed as needed in a particular farm. Only deployed services are referred to as service applications. This is a huge advantage in terms of conserving resources and optimizing performance. For instance, a specific web application can be configured to use only the services it needs rather than all the services available in a package.

The number of service applications that exist is vast, and, as previously mentioned, third-party vendors can create their own services for SharePoint Server 2010. A partial list of services includes the following:

- *Access Services*
- Business Connectivity Services (BCS)
- Excel Services
- *Managed Metadata Services (MMS)*
- Microsoft Office PerformancePoint Server 2007
- *Visio Services*

You can set up a single service application to be shared among multiple *web applications* or deploy multiple instances of the same service across a farm and, in some cases, across multiple farms. Also, there is no limitation regarding the number of services that can be deployed in any single farm.

A typical planning scenario requires that you either set up services to share across multiple web applications or isolate an individual service to one or a limited number of web applications.

Application Pools

As defined in Internet Information Services (IIS) 7.0, an *Application Pool* is a collection of one or more URLs that are serviced by one or a set of worker processes. You must select an existing Application Pool or create a new pool whenever you create a service or site collection in SharePoint Server 2010.

IIS application pools allow multiple SharePoint websites to run on a single server without the processes or code in one site interacting with any other sites. This is primarily a security benefit, since any outside intrusion on one site is isolated. Also, problematic or poor code running on one site is isolated so that other sites on the server are unaffected. For these reasons, you should plan to use dedicated application pools to isolate authenticated content and separate applications that contain password information.

Web Applications

A web application is any individual IIS website created to access and use SharePoint Server 2010 technologies and services, and each web application has its own domain name. Web applications in SharePoint Server 2010 use zones to contain and apply different access and policy rules for different sets of users. This is a particular advantage in managing large numbers of SharePoint users who need to access the same site but view and interact with different levels of content.

Planning for web applications should center on the need to either share or isolate specific web content. For instance, different content can be presented for authenticated vs. anonymous users, or information can be contained so that internal employees, customers, and partners all access different types of web content.

Policies for a web application let you set security and permissions at the level of the web application. You can set policies in Active Directory Domain Services users and user groups but not in SharePoint groups. Best practice suggests using these features to manage large numbers of users in user groups.

Zones

Zones are different logical paths expressed as URLs that allow access to the same web application. A web application can support up to five zones. The available zone names are Default, Extranet, Intranet, Internet, and Custom, and only one particular zone name can be used per web application. Zones using the same name across different web applications typically are available for the same user pool to control access for that group. For instance, your internal employees can use the Intranet zone to access all of the SharePoint sites configured to use that zone, giving that group the same sort of access to all relevant web applications. In effect, each zone is expressed as a separate website in IIS. Zones isolate users based on authentication type, network zone, and policy.

When planning for zone deployment, particular attention must be paid to the Default zone, since access to this zone may be gained by anyone who is able to use a link to this zone, such as a URL sent via an automated administrative email. The Default zone or any zone used for an outward-facing site must possess a high level of security.

Content Databases

A c*ontent database* is not the database server itself but the container for all the content for a single web application. That is, you have one content database for one web application; however, you can separate content for multiple websites into multiple content databases for a site collection. You can also use a single content database for multiple site collections, keeping in mind that the site collection or collections represent a single web app.

Isolation and sharing are expressed as the difference between one site collection using one database and numerous site collections sharing a database. The number of site collections using a database is also a scaling and performance issue. If you are deploying site collections with a high workload attached and greater expectancy for growth, make sure to use fewer site collections per database.

You can also plan your content database strategy by adding databases to site collections as they grow or associate specific site collections only with specific content databases. The latter approach lets you isolate a database serving particular site collections from all the other databases and thus isolate the content it contains.

Site Collections

A *site collection* is a grouping of SharePoint sites that all share the same administrative settings and all have the same owner. Each site collection has a top-level site and can contain multiple subsites.

Planning for sharing and isolation in a site collection deployment includes considerations for access to site content and navigation. For instance, you can set permissions on the top-level site to be either inherited or not inherited by subsites; however, permissions cannot be inherited between site collections nor can navigation be shared across collections.

Other planning issues before creating one or more site collections are developing a consistent URL scheme for the collections and determining how to use collections to contain or separate different organizational elements in your company.

The Host-Named Site Collections option lets you create multiple root-level site collections within a single web application. This site collection option can be created only using Windows PowerShell. Host-named site collections are available only through the Default zone. Host-named site collections allow SharePoint to use host header names rather than paths to determine which site collections and site collection content SharePoint users can access.

See Chapter 15, "Working with Windows PowerShell 2.0 Administration," for specific details on using this important tool in SharePoint.

A site collection comprises a hierarchical structure of subunits that can include different types subsites used for different purposes.

Sites   These are the individual site components within any given site collection and can be composed of lists, libraries, documents, or other web pages. All sites within a site collection share a common navigational structure. Also, all sites within a site collection are vulnerable to scripting exploits from other sites within the domain. Both navigation and exploit vulnerabilities as described are isolated within the site collection.

My Sites   These are specialized sites within SharePoint and are enabled by default as part of the User Profile service. They share the same properties and characteristics as any other site in a site collection.

Authentication

This is a particularly sensitive element in SharePoint Server 2010 in terms of planning. Once a user has authenticated into SharePoint, authorization determines which sites, site content, and other information the user can access. There are three methods of authentication available in SharePoint Server 2010:

- Standard Windows IIS authentication

- Claims-based authentication built on a collection of .NET Framework classes called Windows Identity Foundation, which allows a direct connection to your company's identity management system
- Forms-based authentication, which allows connections to more than one identity management system and does not use Active Directory

The chief planning consideration for authentication is the level of security required for a given web environment. There are three basic environments to consider:

- Internal Intranet
- External for Collaboration
- External for Anonymous Access

The recommended authentication method for Internal Intranet sites is Active Directory Domain Services (AD DS) if Active Directory is available. Authentication should be set up in a separate zone for external collaboration sites to allow access to the site by individual contributors only via a partner organization. By definition, anonymous access sites do not have authentication requirements, but you can use forms-based authentication if you want to have users register for tracking purposes.

An authentication scheme must be planned not only for SharePoint users but also for content crawling across web applications by the index component of the search server. Authentication methods for web applications are created when the application is created and the search crawler moves across a web application by zones, with the Default zone being first by default.

Planning considerations for crawler authentication of web application zones include the method of authentication for zones and the polling order set for the zones. If authentication for the crawler fails at a particular zone, the crawler stops and does not attempt to access other zones later in the polling order. You generally want to use the most stringent authentication for the Default zone, which the crawler will first encounter. Windows Challenge/ Response (NTLM) is the method of choice for the Default site, relative to planning authentication for crawling.

Continuity and Crisis Planning

The last major planning concern is to design your system for when something goes wrong. In other words, how are you going to continue doing business, at least as far as SharePoint is concerned, if an emergency or disaster occurs at the local, regional, or national level?

Although you may immediately consider events such as an earthquake, hurricane, or flood, the first continuity issue you should really think about is at the level of the user. Users can overwrite or accidentally delete key content that can have a detrimental effect on your company. Fortunately, SharePoint Server 2010 has a number of systems in place to respond to such events.

The *Records Center* site is specifically designed to act as a repository for all your company's critical legal and regulatory documents, preserving them so that, even if a user's local copy should be "misplaced," the content remains contained and available.

The Recycle Bin operates using a two-part process. Users with sufficient permissions can recover elements such as items, lists, and libraries using stage one, while site collection administrators can employ stage-two recovery to retrieve anything already deleted from the stage-one recycle bin.

Versioning is available to allow you to revert to an earlier version of a document should unwanted changes be saved or should the current version of the document become corrupt. Recovery of prior document versions can be performed by the document owners without administrator assistance, once versioning is enabled in SharePoint.

If the aforementioned methods do not suffice to recover lost elements or if a larger-scale crisis occurs, the backup and recovery system is available. The primary planning consideration is determining what components to protect using SharePoint backup, including the level of granularity for each component. This should help you determine also what type of backup tool to use, what backup method to employ, and how complete of a recovery process you want to implement.

The bottom line for backup and recovery is time and money. Setting up and implementing a system to back up and recover everything is a nice goal, but how long will the backup process take? Is every little bit of information contained in SharePoint truly something you couldn't live without or recover through some other process? How much is a particular piece of information worth to your business vs. the cost of implementing a plan to protect it?

 You can find a detailed presentation of backup and recovery issues in Chapter 12, "Backing Up and Restoring SharePoint."

Architecting SharePoint Topologies

Whether you are deploying SharePoint Server 2010 on a single server or throughout a server farm using a large array of hardware, SharePoint uses a traditional three-tier server role model for the provision of SharePoint in an environment. These three basic roles can be configured in a variety of topological designs, from small testing environments, small server farms, and medium architectures up to large farm deployments containing server roles in dedicated groups. To plan for your specific needs, you'll first need to understand the required server roles.

Server Roles

SharePoint's default required server roles are web server, application server, and database server. Depending on your requirements and the configuration of the server topology, all three roles can be contained on a single server computer, with two devices, or can be deployed across a series of servers, with one or more dedicated to a single role.

Web Servers

Web servers host websites, web pages, web services, and web parts, providing content to users via HTML documents, Cascading Style Sheets (CSS) documents, code such as

JavaScript, images, and other content. SharePoint is a web-based interface, and web services are required to allow access to applications and SharePoint services. The role does not have to be explicitly present in large, dedicated search farms, since web servers can connect to query servers directly from remote farms. However, in a small farm environment, the web server role is required and can be housed on a server computer also providing the query role.

The web server role by definition does not contain elements required for service applications, and no services besides web services run on the server computer.

Application Servers

Application software is installed on the computer hardware used to fulfill this role so that the services can be delivered to the SharePoint environment. Depending on the size of the environment and business requirements, the server computer can share this role with other roles, and more than one application can be installed on a single computer. Often in larger farms, a server computer will have several applications installed, which are usually grouped by similar usage and performance.

The *application server* role contains related roles and components based on the size of the farm on which they're deployed. Two basic deployments exist: services on a single farm deployment cannot be shared with other farms, and services on cross-farm deployments can be shared across multiple farms.

Single farm: client-related services provide the following:

- Excel Calculation Services
- Access Services
- *Word Services*
- Word Viewing
- PowerPoint
- Visio Graphics Services

Single farm: other, more generic deployments contain the following:

- Usage and Health Data Collection
- Performance Point
- State Service
- Master Data Service
- Microsoft SharePoint Foundation Subscription Settings

Cross-farm: search roles provide the following:

- Query services which include query components and index partitions
- Crawl services, which includes search administration elements and crawlers

Cross-farm: other, more generic services contain the following:

- Business Data Connectivity
- Managed Metadata
- *Secure Store Services*
- User Profile
- Web Analytics

In addition to the various components that run on the server for service applications, numerous necessary services run directly on the server, including but not limited to the following:

- Access Database Services
- Business Data Connectivity
- Excel Calculation Services
- Lotus Notes Connector
- Performance Point Service
- Search Query and Site Settings Service
- Secure Store Service
- SharePoint Server Search
- User Profile Service
- Word Automation Services

Database Servers

This role provides all database services for the SharePoint environment. In a small farm deployment, this role can be assigned to a computer server containing one or more of the other roles. In large, enterprise-server farm environments, server hardware is dedicated to the database role and grouped together.

- This role also contains related roles and components based on what specific task or tasks the database will be performing: Content database servers contain multiple content databases depending on the amount of information required for the SharePoint environment.
- Search databases contain multiple property and crawl databases as well as the search admin database.

Service databases: other services contain the following components:

- Business Data Connectivity
- Managed Metadata
- Service Store Service
- State Service
- Usage and Health Data Collection

- Windows SharePoint Services Subscription Settings
- User Profile databases:
    - Profile
    - Profile synchronization
    - Social tagging

Server Farm Topology Overview

Depending on your requirements, server farms have a number of different scaling profiles, and depending on the selected profiles, server roles are deployed in different manners. This can require as little as one server computer for a single-server farm limited deployment up to multiple server computers, each dedicated to providing a specific role and grouped by services, components, or usage similarities.

Limited-Server Farm Deployment

The single-server farm deployment is typically used for testing or training, and all server roles are installed on a single server machine. This deployment can support up to 100 users.

The two-server farm deployment installs the web and application server roles on one computer server, while database services are housed on a separate machine. This deployment can accommodate up to 10,000 users.

Small Farm Deployment

Small server farms are expressed in different designs based on the number of expected users, how the SharePoint environment will be required to scale over time, and the importance of search for your users.

Two-Tier Topology   A two-tier topology can service up to 10,000 to 20,000 users.

Web Server
Query Server

Web Server
Query Server
All Application
Roles Server

Database
Server

Three-Tier Topology   A three-tier topology requires a dedicated application server when moderate service usage is expected.

Web Query
Servers

Application
Server

Database
Server

Three-Tier Topology Optimized for Search   A three-tier topology optimized for search requires a dedicated search database server computer and a second database computer to fulfill all other database requirements. With this configuration, search is optimized for up to 10 million individual items.

Web Query
Servers

Application
Server

Database
Server

Database Server
for Search

Medium Farm Deployment

This is represented by only a single farm topological design that is optimized for search for up to 40 million individual items. Each of the services provided by the different server roles should be scaled based on utilization requirements, amount of content, and growth needs. If search volume is expected to exceed the recommended limits for this design, deploy a separate search farm to satisfy your requirements.

How many web servers you add to this deployment depends on the number of users served. A good rule of thumb, at least initially, is to deploy one web server for every 10,000 users you expect to access SharePoint. Then monitor usage over time, and adjust your web server design accordingly.

For the application server role, begin by deploying the role on a single server computer, except for search services, which should inhabit a separate, dedicated computer. Monitor the usage of specific services to determine how to scale out the application server deployment. Often Excel Services receives heavy usage, and you may need to expand your early application server deployment by adding additional hardware for this service.

Hardware for database services should be divided between search databases and all other database services within the farm, scaling for access and utilization.

Web Servers

Application Servers

Crawl and Query
Servers

All Other Application
Server Roles

Database Servers

Search Database
Servers

All Other Database
Servers

Large Farm Deployments

If you require a large farm design, it means your service utilization requirements, including search, are at the level of the enterprise organization. In this case, all services and databases should be grouped according to the similarity of characteristics and performance on dedicated server hardware. For instance, you can create a group of web servers to manage just incoming requests and a second group for administration and crawling.

Web Server Groups

Web Servers managing   Web Servers dedicated to
incoming requests   administration and crawling

Application Server Groups

Crawl Servers   Query Servers   Servers for all
other applications

Database Server Groups

Content Database   Search Database   All Other Database
Servers   Servers   Services Servers

Multiple Server Farm Topology Overview

So far, all the topology designs reviewed apply to individual server farms of various sizes; however, to accommodate enterprise-level business requirements, you will need to employ a multifarm deployment.

Only some services can be shared across farms, while others are limited for use within a single farm. All client-facing services are able to be shared only within a single farm environment.

Services that are contained within a single farm are as follows:

- Master Data Services
- Project

- State Service
- Performance Point
- Usage and Health Data Collection

These are the client-facing services:

- Access Service
- Excel Services
- PowerPoint
- Word Automation Services
- Word Viewing
- Visio Graphics Service

Services that can be shared across multiple farms are as follows:

- Business Data Connectivity
- Managed Metadata
- Search
- Secure Store Service
- User Profile
- Web Analytics

Multiple Server Farm Design

Deploying multiple server farms does not mean deploying multiple identical server farms. Each farm is constructed to fulfill a specific role within the organization. There is usually a farm that acts as the primary enterprise services farm and then separate farms that are specialized by department, service, or content. Also, not all farms contain all server roles. Some farms may contain only application servers and depend on other farms for database and web services. Other farms may contain two role types.

The types of multiple server farm designs and deployments are numerous and can be highly variable, given the large collection of possible requirements. The following examples are the most common topologies and will provide you with an idea of how a multiple server farm infrastructure is constructed and how the farms interact.

Company Collaboration Farm   This is usually the most varied of server farm environments, containing a mix of services that can be shared across farms and those contained within individual farms. The farm can, but doesn't have to, possess the database server role and can delegate database services to a different farm. This farm generally contains web and application servers and must include all client-facing services. Application servers are pooled into different groups depending on function. For instance, you can have one application pool that contains just client-facing services and another for services used for websites such as team sites.

Enterprise Services Farm   This farm usually contains only application pools providing services that can be shared across all server farms used by your organization.

Published Content Farm   This farm contains no services but rather offers all published web content. Any services required by this farm are provided by one or more separate farms.

Specialized Department Farm   If you have one or more departments or teams within your company requiring access and utilization restrictions that are significantly high, you can deploy a specialized farm to offer the services specifically needed by this department. This also has security benefits, isolating the department's content from other farms and thus other parts of the organization, letting the department have direct control over managing its own metadata.

Other Multifarm Designs   As previously mentioned, a multiple farm environment doesn't have to be organized in the fashion just presented. For instance, if search is a priority for your enterprise, you can create a server farm dedicated just to search and another farm to provide all other SharePoint services. You can also create a primary corporate collaboration farm, as previously mentioned, and then create separate farms to service each of the departments within the company. You can even deploy multiple farms in a nonenterprise SharePoint environment by designing farms exclusively for each of your company's departments without any other farm specialization.

To review a list of technical diagrams outlining SharePoint Server 2010 deployments, go to http://technet.microsoft.com/en-us/library/ cc263199%28office.14%29.aspx.

SharePoint Server 2010: Deploying and Upgrading

In general, if you plan to utilize SharePoint Server 2010 in your business infrastructure, either you will be deploying it as a new installation or you will be upgrading from a previous version of SharePoint. Upgrade planning and procedures will be specific to a currently existing Microsoft Office SharePoint Server 2007 deployment. Planning and deploying a clean install of SharePoint Server 2010 will be presented first. The upgrade planning activities, including additional topological information, will be subsequently presented in the "Upgrading to SharePoint Server 2010" section later in this chapter.

Deploying SharePoint Server 2010

For you to administer SharePoint Server 2010, you must be able to demonstrate the ability to deploy SharePoint across a number of installation and configuration scenarios. For the purpose of following the exercises presented in this chapter and in the rest of the book, the primary focus will be on deploying SharePoint on a single-server machine with a built-in database. This will be the deployment version you will likely use to study for the exam and was the scenario used in writing this book.

See the introduction of this book for information on the hardware and software configuration used in the process of writing this book.

However, you must also be proficient in deploying SharePoint Server 2010 in environments where database services are provided by a Microsoft SQL Server instance and in multiple-machine architectures.

SharePoint Server 2010 Licensing

There are two licensed versions of SharePoint Server 2010 available for download and deployment:

SharePoint Server 2010 (Enterprise Client Access License Features)   This licensing option is used primarily for organizations needing to create either customer-facing Internet site or internal extranet sites and needing to have access to the complete set of enterprise features and capacities of SharePoint.

SharePoint Server 2010 for Internet Sites, Enterprise   This licensing option is used primarily for organizations needing to create public-facing Internet sites or basic internal extranet sites and needing access only to SharePoint's standard collaboration features.

This book was written using SharePoint Server 2010 (Enterprise Client Access License features) in order to have access to all the features available and in order to present as much detail about the various deployment and usage options in SharePoint as possible.

Deploying SharePoint on a Single Server with a Built-in Database

This installation and initial configuration process is a multistep process but is the fastest way to deploy SharePoint Server 2010, since you are working with a single-server deployment that does not require a separate database server setup. This deployment is primarily used to evaluate SharePoint and test its new and updated features and capacities. This configuration was also the setup used to write this book and is ideal for the student preparing for the 70-667 certification exam.

Required tasks performed by this installation include the following:

- *Microsoft SQL Server 2008 Express* is installed.

- The SharePoint Products And Technologies Configuration Wizard creates the configuration database and content database for SharePoint sites.

- The *SharePoint Products and Technologies Configuration Wizard* installs the *SharePoint Central Administration website*.

The following exercises map to the requirements for installing and performing the initial configuration tasks for SharePoint Server 2010 on a single server with a built-in database.

You must have downloaded the file for the SharePoint 2010 Internet Sites executable onto the device, virtual or actual, where you plan to install SharePoint. You must also have access to the product key and be an administrator on the local server.

In Exercise 2.1, you will install the prerequisite software on a server prior to installing SharePoint.

EXERCISE 2.1

Installing SharePoint Server 2010 Prerequisites

1. On the server, navigate to the location of the OfficeServer.exe file and launch the executable.

2. When the User Account Control dialog box appears, click Yes.

3. When the Microsoft SharePoint Server 2010 splash screen appears, under Install, click Install Software Prerequisites.

4. When the Welcome To The Microsoft SharePoint Products And Technologies 2010 Preparation Tool launches, click Next, as shown here.

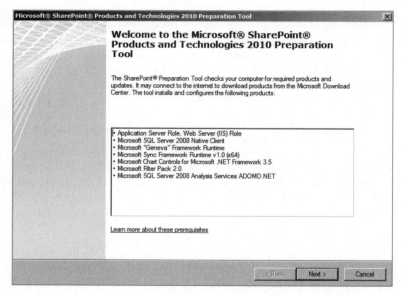

5. When the License Terms For Software Products dialog box appears, click the I Accept The Terms Of The License Agreement(s) check box, and then click Next to begin installing the prerequisite packages.

6. When the Installation Complete dialog box appears, click Finish.

You will be returned to the SharePoint Server 2010 splash screen and are ready to immediately install SharePoint Server 2010. You must have the product key for your version of SharePoint Server 2010 available at this time.

Exercise 2.2 shows you how to perform a SharePoint Server 2010 single-server installation from the point of running the Setup.exe file.

EXERCISE 2.2

Installing SharePoint Server 2010 on a Single Server with a Built-in Database

1. On the SharePoint Server 2010 splash screen, under Install, click Install SharePoint Server.

2. In the Enter Your Product Key dialog box, enter your product key in the available field and, when the key is confirmed, click Continue.

3. When the Read The Microsoft Office License Terms dialog box appears, review the terms of the licensing agreement, select the I Accept The Terms Of This License Agreement check box, and then click Continue.

4. When the Choose The Installation You Want dialog box appears, click Standalone, as shown here, to begin the installation process. This can take some time.

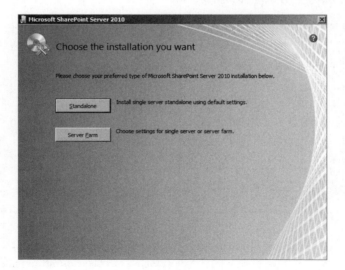

5. After the installation is complete, when the Run Configuration Wizard dialog box appears, make sure the Run The SharePoint Products And Technologies Configuration Wizard Now check box is selected; then click Close.

6. When the Welcome To SharePoint Products dialog box opens, click Next.

EXERCISE 2.2 *(continued)*

7. When the SharePoint Products Configuration Wizard dialog box notifies you that some services may have to be restarted or reset, click Yes to launch the wizard. This process can take some time.

8. When the Configuration Successful page appears, click Finish.

If the SharePoint Products configuration fails, you can review the PSC-Diagnostics log files. A link to the files is available on the Configuration Failed page, as shown here or you can locate it at %COMMONPROGRAMFILES%\ Microsoft Shared\Web Server Extensions\14\LOGS. Click Finish to close the Configuration Failed page.

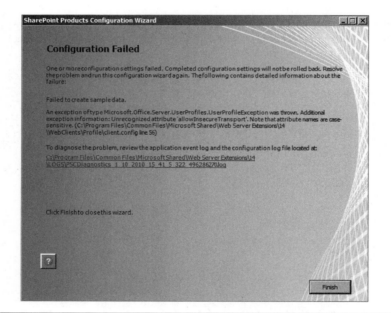

If the configuration fails, after closing the Configuration Failed page on the SharePoint Server 2010 splash screen, under Install, click Install SharePoint Server. When prompted to choose Repair or Remove, select Repair and attempt to fix the configuration installation. If successful, the Completed Successfully page will appear after the repair operation is complete. Click Close to finish the installation process.

Once you have successfully installed SharePoint Server 2010 and completed the SharePoint Products Configuration Wizard (`Psconfig.exe`), there are some post-installation tasks to perform such as creating the first site collection.

In Exercise 2.3, you will create the first site collection after SharePoint Server 2010 is installed.

Creating the First Site Collection in SharePoint Server 2010

1. At the keyboard of the server where SharePoint Server 2010 has been installed, click Start and then click SharePoint 2010 Central Administration.

2. When the User Account Control dialog box appears, click Yes.

3. When prompted by the Windows Security dialog box, enter the username and password you configured as the administrator of the server, select the Remember My Credentials check box, and then click OK.

4. When the Central Administration page appears, under Application Management, click Create Site Collections, as shown here.

5. When the Create Site Collection page appears, select the desired web application and then, under Title and Description, give your new site collection a name and optional description in the available fields.

6. Under Web Site Address, use the drop-down menu and select /sites/. Then, in the field just to the right, give your new site collection URL a unique suffix such as **default**.

7. Under Template Selection, select one of the site template tabs and then select a site template, as shown here.

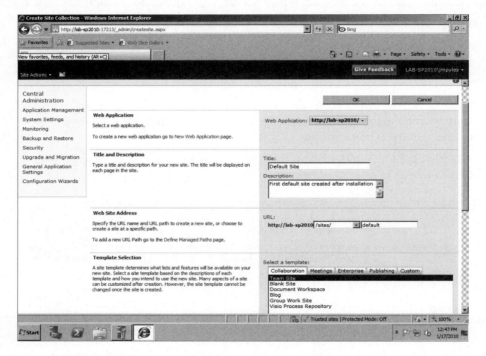

8. Under the Primary Site Collection Administrator section, enter the name of an administrator on the server, which should be your own name, and then click Check Names.

9. If you created another administrator user on the server, enter that name in the field under Secondary Site Collection Administrator and then click Check Names.

10. Under Quota Template, accept the default setting of No Quota and then click OK to finish.

It may take a few minutes for the site collection to be created. Once finished, a confirmation page will appear stating that the new top-level site was successfully created. You can either click the link to open the new top-level site in a new browser window or click OK to return to the Central Administration page.

When you open the new top-level site, you will be asked to authenticate again. Afterward, the site opens, as shown in Figure 2.1.

In this example, the site template used was the Team Site template on the Collaboration tab. You can choose to use any site template you desire for the top-level site.

FIGURE 2.1 The new, default top-level site home page

In the previous example, you used the default web application. There are actually two web applications installed by default: SharePoint – 80 and SharePoint Central Administration v4. The SharePoint – 80 web application is the only one available in which to begin to create site collections, and it uses port 80 by default. For a number of reasons, including security, you may want to create additional web applications for your site collections.

A web application is an Internet Information Services (IIS) website that is a logical container for your site collections. Creating one or more web applications is a prerequisite to creating site collections, and each application is represented by a separate IIS website defined by a shared or unique application pool. When you create a web application, you should give it a unique domain name for easy identification and to inhibit cross-site scripting attacks.

To create a web application, besides requiring access to SharePoint Central Administration, you must be a member of the Farm Administrators SharePoint group, and if you are using SQL Server for database services, you will also need to be a member of the SQL Server fixed server roles dbcreator and sysadmin.

You can use a number of methods to create a new web application. In Exercise 2.4, I'll show you the most basic method of creating a new web application.

EXERCISE 2.4

Creating a Web Application in a Single-Server Deployment

1. At the keyboard of the server where SharePoint Server 2010 has been installed, click Start and then click SharePoint 2010 Central Administration.

2. When the User Account Control dialog box appears, click Yes.

3. When prompted by the Windows Security dialog box, enter the username and password you configured as the administrator of the server, select the Remember My Credentials check box, and then click OK.

4. When the Central Administration page appears, under Application Management, click Manage Web Applications.

5. On the Web Application Management page, click New on the Ribbon.

6. When the Create New Web Application page appears, under Authentication, click Classic Mode Authentication.

7. Under IIS Web Site, select of the two following options to set up the new web application:

   ▪ Click Use An Existing Web Site and then select the website on which to install your new web application.

   ▪ Click Create A New IIS Web Site and then type the name of the website in the Name box.

8. In the Port field, either accept the port number if using an existing website or accept the suggested number populating the field if you are creating a new website.

9. In the Host Header field, enter an optional URL for the web application.

10. In the Path field, if using an existing website, accept the path for that site; if you're using a new website, accept the suggested path.

11. Under Security Configuration, in Authentication Provider, select either Negotiate (Kerberos) or NTLM.

12. In Anonymous, click Yes to allow anonymous access or No to prohibit it.

13. In Secure Sockets Layer (SSL), click Yes to enable SSL, which requires that you request and install an SSL certificate, or click No to not enable SSL.

14. Under Public URL, enter the domain name for the web application.

15. Under Application Pool, perform one of the following actions:

    ▪ Click Use Existing Application Pool and then select the application pool you want to use from the drop-down menu.

    ▪ Click Create A New Application Pool and then either enter the name of the new application pool or accept the default name.

16. Under Select A Security Account For This Application Pool, perform one of the following actions:

   - Click Predefined to use a predefined security account, and then select the security account from the drop-down menu.

   - Click Configurable to specify a new security account to be used for an existing application pool.

17. Under Database Name And Authentication, perform the following actions:

   - In Database Server, either accept the default database server name/instance or enter your preference here using the format <SERVERNAME\instance>.

   - In Database Name, either accept the default database or enter your preference here.

   - In Database Authentication, select either Windows Authentication (Recommended) or SQL Authentication. If you choose the latter option, you must enter the name of the account you want the web application to use to authenticate to the SQL Server database in the Account field; then enter the password in the Password field.

18. If desired, use the optional Failover Database Server field to enter the name of a specific failover database that you want to associate with a content database.

19. Under Service Application Connections, select either Default or Custom in the drop-down menu to choose which service application connections will be available to the web application.

20. Under Customer Experience Improvement Program, click either Yes or No, and then click OK to create the new web application.

See Chapter 4, "Configuring Service Applications," for more information regarding service application settings.

Deploy a Single Server with SQL Server

Contrary to what you may think, a server farm can be as small as one or two physical machines, at least in the beginning. A farm can consist of a single SharePoint server and a single SQL database server. The significant difference in the setup is not just selecting Server Farm instead of Standalone, but also running the Farm Configuration Wizard after you've completed the installation and after running the SharePoint Products And Technologies Configuration Wizard.

A critical prerequisite is that you must be able to provide credentials for several different account types to deploy a server farm. Those accounts are as follows:

SQL Server Service Account   Used to run SQL server.

Setup User Account   Used to run both Setup and the SharePoint Products And Technologies Configuration Wizard.

Server Farm Account or Database Access Account   Used to configure and manage the farm, to act as the application pool identity in Central Administration, and to run the SharePoint Foundation Workflow Timer service.

You must have SQL Server 2005 or SQL Server 2008 already installed and ready to act as the database for SharePoint before you proceed.

See Chapter 7, "Managing User Accounts and Roles," for more information on administrative and service accounts.

Installing Software Prerequisites

Install the software prerequisites on the designated server hardware running Windows Server 2008 or Windows Server 2008 R2 just as you did in Exercise 2.1. The task is identical.

Installing SharePoint Server 2010 as a Single Server in a Server Farm

The installation process begins exactly as it did in Exercise 2.2, steps 1 through 3. When the Choose The Installation You Want page appears, perform the following steps:

1. Click the Server Farm button.

2. On the Server Type tab, click Complete.

3. Click Install Now. The installation process begins, which can take some time.

4. After the installation is complete, when the Run Configuration Wizard dialog box appears, make sure the Run The SharePoint Products And Technologies Configuration Wizard Now check box is selected, and then click Close.

5. When the Welcome To SharePoint Products dialog box opens, click Next.

6. When the SharePoint Products Configuration Wizard dialog box notifies you that some services may have to be restarted or reset, click Yes to launch the wizard.

7. When the Connect To A Server Farm page appears, click Create A New Server Farm and then click Next.

8. When the Specify Configuration Database Settings page appears, enter the name of the computer running SQL Server in the Database Server field.

9. Either use the default or enter the name of your configuration database in the Database Name field.

10. Enter the username of the server farm account in the Username field in the format DOMAIN\username.

11. Enter the user password in the Password field; then click Next.

12. When the Specify Farm Security page appears, enter a strong passphrase of eight characters composed of uppercase characters, lowercase characters, numerals, and special (nonalphanumeric) characters; then click Next.

13. When the Configure SharePoint Central Administration Web Application page appears, either select the Specify Port Number check box and enter the specific port number you want Central Administration to use or clear the aforementioned check box and accept the default.

14. Select either NTLM or Negotiate (Kerberos) for authentication; then click Next.

15. When the Completing The SharePoint Products And Technologies Configuration Wizard page appears, review your selections; if satisfied, click Next. The process may take some time.

16. When the Configuration Successful page appears, click Finish.

If the SharePoint Products configuration fails, you can review the PSCDiagnostics log files. A link to the files is available on the Configuration Failed page, or you can locate it at %COMMONPROGRAMFILES%\Microsoft Shared\ Web Server Extensions\14\LOGS. Click Finish to close the Configuration Failed page.

If you are prompted for a username and password again, you will need to add the Central Administration website to the list of trusted sites in your Internet Explorer browser and configure the authentication settings. You may also want to disable Enhanced Security in Internet Explorer. If you are using a proxy server, you may receive an error message indicating that you need to configure the proxy server settings to bypass the proxy server.

On the SharePoint server farm page, you can run the wizard to configure the farm or perform the task manually. See the next section, "Multiple Servers for a Three-Tier Farm," for more.

See Chapter 3, "Configuring SharePoint Farm Environments," for full details on configuring the server farm, including adding web servers to the farm, configuring diagnostic logging, and more.

Multiple Servers for a Three-Tier Farm

A two-tier server farm is composed of one or more servers offering web and application services on the first tier and one or more servers offering database services on the database tier. A three-tier farm creates individual levels for web and application servers.

Web Query
Servers

Application
Server

Database   Database Server
Server   for Search

Before proceeding, you will need to make sure that all your Windows Server 2008, Windows Server 2008 R2, SQL Server 2005, and SQL Server 2008 machines are fully patched and updated. You also need to run the Microsoft SharePoint 2010 Products Preparation tool on each of the Windows Server 2008 and 2008 R2 machines to verify that they are fully compatible with SharePoint.

You must have SQL Server 2005 or SQL Server 2008 already installed and ready to act as the database for SharePoint before you proceed. In addition, SQL Server 2005 must have local and remote connections enabled and configured to use the TCP/IP protocol, and SQL Server 2008 must have the TCP/IP protocol enabled for the network configuration.

In general, it's recommended that you run the preparation tool on all machines first, then install the software prerequisites on all machines, then install SharePoint Server 2010 on the machines, then run the SharePoint Products And Technologies Configuration Wizard, and then create the server farm. SharePoint is usually installed on web servers before application servers.

Installing SharePoint Server 2010 on Server Farm Servers

After you install the software prerequisites on all servers, you can perform the SharePoint server farm installation on each server, as described in the earlier "Installing SharePoint Server 2010 as a Single Server in a Server Farm" section. After the installation, do not immediately run the SharePoint Products And Technologies Configuration Wizard.

Creating and Configuring the Server Farm

These are the typical steps to installing SharePoint in a server farm environment. This list presents the information at a high level:

1. Select which server will host the SharePoint Central Administration website and run the SharePoint Products And Technologies Configuration Wizard on that machine before you run the wizard on the other servers.

2. When you run the wizard on all the servers that will be part of the server farm, you follow the same steps you described previously in this chapter in the "Installing Share-Point Server 2010 as a Single Server in a Server Farm" section.

3. After the wizard has finished, the Central Administration site will open in a separate browser window. On the Help Make SharePoint Better page, you can either choose to participate or choose not to participate; then click OK.

4. At this point, on the SharePoint farm page, you can choose to run the wizard and configure the server farm automatically; to choose to take more control of the configuration process, click Cancel and configure the farm manually.

 See Chapter 3 for full details on configuring the server farm, including adding web servers to the farm, configuring diagnostic logging, and more.

Installing Language Packs

Internationalization is often a key factor in any large organization's business strategy. Whether you are offering your products to a multinational audience or are working with global partners, it's important to be able to present your web content in more than one language. Regardless of whether you're installing SharePoint Server 2010 as your first SharePoint deployment or upgrading from a prior version of SharePoint, if you need to interact with site users who speak and read more than just a single language, the ability to install language packs for SharePoint Server 2010 is important.

Language packs are additional site templates that contain languages besides the default English and can be installed on web servers that will be accessed from worldwide locations. When a site or site collection is created with one of these templates, all the content within the site is presented in the language for which the template was created. You can only create new sites and site collections with such templates. A template in another language cannot be applied to an already created "English-only" site with the expectation that the content will be rewritten in another language.

SharePoint Server 2010 comes in different language versions including English, French, and Spanish. If, for instance, you install the French version of SharePoint and later need to deploy additional sites in English, you will need to install the English language pack on the web server that will be accessed by your English-speaking audience. To create a site or site collection in a language other than the default, you must install that language pack before creating those sites.

NOTE Sites and site collections created with a language pack with a specific language ID will contain column heads, toolbars, and navigation links that are all consistent with that language. However, some content such as dialog boxes, error messages, and notifications will not be presented in that language, since those features are dependent on technologies outside the language packs. For instance, Microsoft .NET Framework, Microsoft Windows Workflow Foundation, and Microsoft ASP.NET are localized only for a limited number of languages.

Acquiring Language Packs

Individual language packs support only a single language per language pack, so you only need to download the files for the languages you want to support. If you plan to use more than one language pack, avoid overwriting a prior download with a subsequent language pack by selecting different directories for each download. You can download language packs from here:

```
www.microsoft.com/downloads/details.aspx?FamilyId=a0c7c05d-8fca-4391-bc70-
b62c9af91123&displaylang=en
```

Preparing a Web Server for Language Pack Installation

A web server requires that you have installed the additional language files needed, have installed SharePoint Server 2010, and run the SharePoint Products And Technologies Configuration Wizard before you install the language packs. Installing additional language files on Windows Server 2008 is a straightforward task. You must be an administrator on the local machine.

1. Sitting at the server keyboard, click Start ➢ Control Panel; then click Region And Language.

2. In the Regional And Language Options dialog box, select the Keyboards And Languages tab, and under Display Language, click Install/Uninstall languages.

3. In the Install Or Uninstall Languages dialog box, click Install Display Languages.

4. On the Select The Languages To Install page, select the desired languages from the list; alternatively, click the Browse button to navigate to the location of the required .cab files and select them. Then click Next.

5. Accept the stated terms and then click Next.

6. Click Install.

Once the required files have been installed, you can proceed to the next part of the process, installing the language pack.

Installing a Language Pack

Installing a language pack is relatively simple. Go to the download page, select the necessary language pack, and then download it to the desired directory on a SharePoint web server. Launch the executable and follow the steps in the installation wizard.

The critical part of the process is to run the SharePoint Products And Technologies Configuration Wizard after you've installed the language pack. Failure to do so will mean that the language pack will not be installed properly. To run the SharePoint Products And Technologies Configuration Wizard again, do the following:

1. On the server, click Start ➢ SharePoint 2010 Products Configuration Wizard.

2. Click Next on the Welcome To SharePoint Products page.

3. When the alert dialog box appears, click Yes.

4. When the Modify Server Farm Settings page appears, click Do Not Disconnect From This Server Farm; then click Next.

5. Should the Modify SharePoint Central Administration Web Application Settings page appear, accept the defaults and click Next.

6. On the Completing the SharePoint Products And Technologies Configuration Wizard page, click Next.

7. On the Configuration Successful page, click Finish.

Final Deployment Tasks

During the initial deployment of SharePoint, you may have encountered some issues or errors in your Internet Explorer web browser associated with security. The following can be used in response if these circumstances arise.

Adding Central Administration Web Site to Trusted Sites

After running the SharePoint Products And Technologies Configuration Wizard, if you are prompted to authenticate again to access Central Administration, you will likely need to add that site to Internet Explorer's list of trusted sites.

1. On the Internet Explorer toolbar, click Tools and then click Internet Options.

2. In the Internet Options dialog box, select the Security tab.

3. On the Security tab, under Select A Zone To View Or Change Security Settings, select Trusted Sites, and then click Sites.

4. Clear the Require Verification (Https:) For All Sites In This Zone check box, enter the URL of the Central Administration site in the Add This Website To The Zone field, and then click Add.

5. Click Close in the Trusted Sites dialog box and then click OK in the Internet Options dialog box.

Disabling Internet Explorer Enhanced Security Settings

If you still have difficulty getting Internet Explorer to correctly load the Central Administration site or any other site you deem both safe and necessary in SharePoint, you can perform the following steps to disable IE's enhanced security:

1. Click Start ➢ All Programs ➢ Administrative Tools ➢ Server Manager.

2. In the Server Manager dialog box, select the root of Server Manager.

3. Under Security Information, click Configure IE ESC.

4. When the Internet Explorer Enhanced Security Configuration dialog box opens, under Administrators, click Off to disable the enhanced security settings, as shown in Figure 2.2; then click OK.

FIGURE 2.2   Internet Explorer Enhanced Security Configuration dialog box

5. Close the Server Manager dialog box.

Configuring Proxy Server Settings to Bypass the Proxy Server for Local Addresses

If you are using a proxy server and you see a proxy server error message when you attempt to access the Central Administration site or another site you deem safe and necessary in SharePoint, perform the following steps to set the proxy server settings to bypass local addresses:

1. On the Internet Explorer toolbar, click Tools and then click Internet Options.

2. In the Internet Options dialog box, select the Connections tab.

3. On the Connections tab under Local Area Network (LAN) settings, click LAN Settings.

4. In the Local Area Network (LAN) Settings dialog box under Automatic Configuration, clear the Automatically Detect Settings check box.

5. Under Proxy Server, select the Use A Proxy Server For Your LAN check box.

6. In the available fields, enter the address and port for the proxy server.

7. Select the Bypass Proxy Server For Local Addresses check box.

8. Click OK in the Local Area Network (LAN) Settings dialog box.

9. Click OK in the Internet Options dialog box.

Post-installation Configuration

A number of post-installation configuration settings are required, including configuring incoming and outgoing email alerts, configuring search, and setting up optional mobile account notification.

See Chapter 4 for information on configuring incoming email, outgoing email, and mobile account alerts as post-installation tasks. See Chapter 5, "Configuring Indexing and Search," for information on configuring search settings as a post-installation task.

Upgrading to SharePoint Server 2010

Upgrading from Microsoft Office SharePoint Server 2007 to SharePoint Server 2010 involves many unique challenges, not the least of which is upgrading all your hardware to 64-bit platforms. Also, all of your Windows Server and SQL Server machines have to conform to the requirements necessary to run SharePoint Server 2010.

See Chapter 1 for all the hardware, server, and application requirements for running a SharePoint Server 2010 environment. The basic requirements for a new installation are the same as for an upgrade.

What Is *Visual Upgrade*?

They say you should never judge a book by its cover, but the "look and feel" is very important in UI design. When Microsoft introduced the Ribbon to the Windows Vista and Microsoft Office 2007 interfaces, there was a great outcry among users because the location and function of all the controls and features they were used to using dramatically changed. Sometimes people don't like change.

The Visual Upgrade feature allows the server administrator or owner of a particular site collection to determine the appearance of a site collection or collections post-upgrade. Although the default look and feel is MOSS 2007, the administrator performing the upgrade can change the appearance of all site collections to SharePoint Server 2010, and the change will be accomplished during the upgrade. The administrator can also let site owners make that decision. For instance, using an in-place upgrade, after a site is upgraded, a site owner can use the preview option to view the site collection appearance. At that point, the site owner can either accept the visual upgrade or revert to the MOSS 2007 if desired.

Planning and Preparing for Upgrade

There are a wide variety of factors to consider well before initiating the upgrade. Unlike creating a SharePoint Server 2010 environment from scratch, you need to take what you have already built under MOSS 2007 and preserve as much of the infrastructure and content as possible, taking down as little of your production environment for as brief amount of time as possible.

To be sure you are as prepared as possible, consider the following practices for upgrading.

Review Supported Upgrade Paths

You may well expect that with the right preparation, you can upgrade your MOSS 2007 environment to SharePoint Server 2010, which is basically true, but there are a number of deployment considerations that can get in the way. For instance, you must deploy to the same type of topology you are starting with. Also, some SharePoint editions do not have a direct upgrade path to SharePoint Server 2010.

UPGRADE TOPOLOGIES PATHS

The specific topology you are starting with will determine your upgrade options:

MOSS 2007 Stand-Alone Server with SQL Server 2005 Express Edition   This topology can be upgraded only to a SharePoint Server 2010 stand-alone server with Microsoft SQL Server 2008 Express. It cannot be upgraded to any farm topology.

MOSS 2007 Single Server with SQL Server   This topology can be upgraded to a SharePoint Server 2010 single server with SQL Server but not to a stand-alone server with SQL Server 2008 Express.

Any Size MOSS 2007 Farm Topology   This can be upgraded to any size SharePoint Server 2010 farm topology but not to any stand-alone deployment.

UPGRADE PRODUCTS PATHS

Standard editions can be upgraded only to Standard editions, and Enterprise editions can be upgraded only to Enterprise editions, which means you cannot upgrade MOSS 2007 Standard edition to SharePoint Server 2010 Enterprise edition. That said, you can upgrade SharePoint Server 2010 Standard to SharePoint Server 2010 Enterprise.

A number of cross-product upgrades are supported:

- You can upgrade SharePoint Foundation 2010, Microsoft Office Forms Server 2007, and Microsoft Office PerformancePoint Server 2007 to SharePoint Server 2010.

- Microsoft Search Server 2007 can be upgraded to either SharePoint Server 2010 or Microsoft Search Server 2010.

- Microsoft Office Project Server 2007 with Windows SharePoint Services 3.0 with SP2 or Office SharePoint Server 2007 with SP2 can be upgraded to SharePoint Server 2010 Enterprise edition plus Microsoft Project 2010.

SharePoint Server 2010 Upgrading Practices

In addition to reviewing the hardware, server, database, and application requirements as already recommended, you must take care to address the following issues:

- Make sure MOSS 2007 on all servers has Service Pack 2 or newer applied.

- Correct any issues with any applications that may not be working or not working well, and uninstall any software that is no longer being used. Any problems you leave behind could cause the upgrade to fail.

- Upgrade all your server hardware to 64-bit, upgrade server software to Windows Server 2008 Service Pack 1 (SP1) and Cumulative Update 2 or Windows Server 2008 R2, and upgrade database software to SQL Server 2005 SP3 and Cumulative Update 3 or SQL Server 2008.

- Do not add any server hardware after beginning the upgrade process.
- Run the pre-upgrade checker to verify and correct any outstanding issues.
- Perform a full backup of your current SharePoint environment prior to the upgrade.

SharePoint Server 2010 Approaches

Depending on various factors, you will need to choose a specific method or approach to performing the upgrade once you have met all the prerequisites. Once you've selected an approach, you should perform a trial upgrade on a single server to determine any special issues you may face. This will allow you to correct the problem before the full-scale upgrade, or if it cannot be easily corrected, you can develop a plan for anticipating the problem and use a workaround.

Four common upgrade methods are available:

In-Place Upgrade　This upgrade method allows you to install SharePoint Server 2010 on the same hardware that you have MOSS 2007 installed, also upgrading all of your content and configuration settings in the server farm. This has the benefit of letting you perform the upgrade in one stroke as well as preserving all or almost all of your data and setup. The dark side of this method is that in order to perform the upgrade in a single action, you need to take your server farm offline completely during the upgrade process, meaning that SharePoint will not be available at all. This is the quickest of the upgrade paths.

Database Attach Upgrade　This method allows you to upgrade the content of your server farm when you move from MOSS 2007 to SharePoint Server 2010 without upgrading the configuration settings. This approach is most often used when you want to upgrade your hardware or modify your server farm topology at the same time. The process requires that you first configure a new server or server farm using SharePoint Server 2010.

The chief advantage is that you can upgrade numerous content databases at the same time, making the overall upgrade faster. You can even combine multiple farms into a single farm while upgrading. The chief disadvantage is that no server or farm settings are upgraded in the process. You are required to manually transfer the settings from the MOSS 2007 environment to the SharePoint Server 2010 environment.

Hybrid Approach 1: Read-Only Databases　The chief feature of this upgrade approach is setting your databases to read-only, which allows content to be read during the upgrade. This means your existing server farm remains up and running, minimizing the downtime from the SharePoint user point of view. This method lets you upgrade multiple databases simultaneously as well as upgrade hardware.

As with the database attach upgrade method, the server and farm settings are not upgraded and must be manually configured. This goes for any specialized settings you may have made in MOSS 2007.

Hybrid Approach 2: Detach Databases　This approach somewhat combines the advantages of the first two methods, letting you perform an in-place upgrade for the content and settings while detaching and upgrading your databases in a parallel process. This preserves not only your data and farm settings but also any customizations you may have made. You can also upgrade numerous content databases simultaneously, speeding up the upgrade process.

There are few disadvantages to the approach, except that, like all the methods already mentioned except for the in-place upgrade method, you will need to plan for the amount of time it takes to transmit databases over your network and be able to directly access all of your database servers.

Perform the Pre-upgrade Checks

The SharePoint Server 2010 pre-upgrade checker is an `Stsadm.exe` command-line operation that you run on your MOSS 2007 platform to discover any potential issues that might prevent or inhibit the upgrade to SharePoint Server 2010. You must have Service Pack 2 installed for this option to be available.

 To acquire the Cumulative Update packages for SharePoint Server 2007, go to http://beta.blogs.msdn.com/opal/archive/2009/10/28/october-2009-cumulative-update-packages-for-sharepoint-server-2007-and-windows-sharepoint-services-3-0-are-published.aspx.

The pre-upgrade checker, once run, produces a report on the following:

- A list of all servers and farm elements and an upgrade readiness report for all servers
- A list of alternate access mapping URLs used in the farm
- A list of all installed site definitions, site templates, features, and language packs installed in the server farm
- A list of all customizations not supported by the upgrade
- A list of any database or site orphaned objects in the farm, such as lists, list items, and websites
- A list of any missing or invalid configuration settings
- An upgrade readiness report on all databases

If, after viewing the reports, you determine that you need to postpone the upgrade until any deficits have been corrected, you can remedy the outstanding issues and then run the pre-upgrade checker again to verify that everything has been corrected.

To run the pre-upgrade checker, you must be a member of the local Administrators group on the server running MOSS 2007. Perform the following actions to proceed:

1. Click Start, right-click Command Prompt, and then select Run As Administrator.

2. When prompted by the security dialog box, click Yes.

3. When the command prompt window opens, navigate to the following directory:

   `%COMMONPROGRAMFILES%\Microsoft Shared\Web Server Extensions\12\bin`

4. At the command prompt, type **STSADM.EXE -o preupgradecheck**; then press Enter.

The pre-upgrade checker runs on the local server and examines your server farm settings. Once finished, the report will open in your web browser. You can also view the report here:

```
%COMMONPROGRAMFILES%\Microsoft Shared\Web Server Extensions\12\LOGS
```

 See Chapter 15, "Working with Windows PowerShell 2.0 Administration," for more information about performing upgrade operations from the command line.

Performing an In-Place Upgrade to SharePoint Server 2010

Before initiating the upgrade, back up your entire MOSS 2007 server farm including all of your SQL server databases. Practice restoring the server farm and databases, making sure the backup and restore process is successful before you begin the upgrade.

There are four general steps in performing this method of upgrade from MOSS 2007 to SharePoint Server 2010:

1. Install SharePoint Server 2010 on all the servers in your server farm.
2. Install any required language packs on your servers.
3. Run the SharePoint Products And Technologies Configuration Wizard on the front end web server that contains the Central Administration website.
4. Run the configuration wizard on all the other frontend web servers and application servers in the farm.

 To determine which server is running SharePoint Central Administration, open the Servers In Farm page at http://server_name: adminport/_admin/ farmservers.aspx, and note which server or servers have Central Administration services running. If you are running multiple server farms, each with a Central Administration website, select a farm in which to perform the first upgrade, follow the procedure cited earlier, and then repeat the process on the other server farms.

Running the Prerequisite Installer

Prior to running the SharePoint Server 2010 setup, you must run the prerequisite installer on each MOSS 2007 web server in order to be able to install the software needed to support SharePoint Server 2010.

1. Insert the SharePoint 2010 product disc into the optical drive of the server machine.
2. Open the installation folder on the disc, and run PrerequisiteInstaller.exe.
3. When the SharePoint Products And Technologies 2010 Preparations utility opens, click Next.

4. When the Licensing Terms page appears, accept the licensing agreement by selecting the available check box; then click Next.

5. After the required software is installed, on the next page that appears, click Next.

6. When the Installation Complete page appears, review the list of prerequisites installed; then click Finish.

Running SharePoint Server 2010 Setup

After you have completed installing the prerequisite software, you must run `Setup.exe` on all of your MOSS 2007 web servers. The setup process is virtually identical to how a fresh install is conducted.

1. Run `Setup.exe`.

2. Enter the product key on the available page when prompted; then click Continue.

3. Review the license agreement, accept it by selecting the available check box, and then click Continue.

4. When the Upgrade Earlier Versions page appears, click Install Now.

5. After the installation is complete, on the completion page, clear the Run The Share-Point Products And Technologies Configuration Wizard Now check box, and then click Close.

After you have run the installation on all your web servers, you can proceed with running the SharePoint Products And Technologies Configuration Wizard on each of your web servers starting with the server containing the Central Administration page.

 If you are upgrading a single server, you can proceed immediately from running the prerequisite installer to `Setup.exe` to the Products And Technologies Configuration Wizard without interruption.

Running the SharePoint Products and Technologies Configuration Wizard for Upgrade

To start the configuration wizard, click Start ➢ Administrative Tools ➢ SharePoint Products And Technologies Configuration Wizard. Then proceed through the wizard in the same manner as when you run it during a fresh install, until the Visual Upgrade page appears.

1. On the Visual Upgrade page, select one of the following options:

   - Select change existing sharepoint sites to use the new user experience. administrators control the user experience for end users and then select either of the following:

     - Preserve customized pages but update template and application pages to use the new UI.

- Reset all customized pages to their original templates. This option will delete modifications from customized pages and cannot be undone. Preserve the look and feel of existing sharepoint sites, and allow end users to update their sites' user experience.

2. When the Completing the SharePoint Products And Technologies Configuration Wizard page appears, verify the settings; then click Next.

3. A message appears notifying you that if you have a server farm with multiple servers, you must run Setup on each server before continuing. If you have already run Setup on your other servers or if this is the only server in your farm, click OK to continue the wizard.

4. When the configuration is successful, the Upgrade In Progress page appears. Review the settings on the page; then click Finish.

5. When the Upgrade Status page opens, if prompted, enter your username and password so that the upgrade can continue.

Performing Post-upgrade Application Service Tasks for an In-Place Upgrade

Once you have completed the in-place upgrade process, there are some additional tasks to perform, since SharePoint Server 2010 has a number of new services that didn't exist under MOSS 2007. The most straightforward way to enable the service applications to host any new services in the current server farm is to use the Farm Configuration Wizard in Central Administration under Upgrade And Migration.

See Chapter 4 for more information about creating and configuring service applications tasks after an in-place upgrade.

Upgrading the Taxonomy Data for Profile Services for an In-Place Upgrade

Taxonomy data is used to classify data so it can be standardized, shared, and used on multiple systems. Under MOSS 2007, taxonomy data is stored in the shared services provider (SSP) database as part of the Profile Services data. In SharePoint Server 2010, this data must be moved to the managed metadata database. You are required to create a service application for the Managed Metadata service before you can move and upgrade the data.

See Chapter 4 for more information about creating and configuring service applications.

After that is accomplished, use Windows PowerShell to reconnect the data to the Managed Metadata and User Profile service applications. You must be a member of the SharePoint_Shell_Access role on the configuration database and a member of the WSS_ADMIN_WPG local group on the computer where SharePoint 2010 is installed.

1. Click Start and then click Microsoft SharePoint 2010 Products.

2. Click SharePoint 2010 Management Shell.

3. At the command prompt, type **Move-SPProfileManagedMetadataProperty -ProfileServiceApplicationProxy <SPServiceApplicationProxyPipeBind> -Identity <string>**; then press Enter.

Performing a Database Attach Upgrade to SharePoint Server 2010

As you previously read, the database attach upgrade method allows you to upgrade only the content in your SharePoint environment from MOSS 2007 to SharePoint Server 2010 without upgrading your configuration settings. This approach lets you change server hardware or your server farm topology as part of the upgrade.

Before beginning the upgrade from MOSS 2007 to SharePoint Server 2010, you must create a new server farm environment. The first part of creating the new environment involves installing SharePoint 2010 using the steps you reviewed in the earlier "Multiple Servers for a Three-Tier Farm" section. If necessary, revisit that part of this chapter before proceeding.

Next, you must create a new web application for each one that existed in the old SharePoint environment.

Then manually re-create each server farm configuration setting including the following:

- Outgoing email server
- All server farm–level security and permission settings
- All services settings including search settings
- Included paths
- Quota templates

Manually transfer all of your customization settings to the new farm environment including the following:

- Custom site definitions
- Custom style sheets
- Custom web parts
- Custom web services
- Custom features and solutions
- All administrator-approved form templates and data connection files
- Language packs

To export form templates and data connection files using the command line, type **Stsadm .exe -o exportipfsadminobjects -filename <path to export CAB>**; then press Enter.

To import the files into the new environment using Windows PowerShell, type **Import-SPIPAdministrationFiles**; then press Enter.

When you perform a database attach upgrade, you are essentially backing up your databases from the old MOSS 2007 server farm and restoring them in the new SharePoint Server 2010 server farm. This is what allows you to change your server hardware at the same time as you upgrade SharePoint. During the restore, the upgrade process runs, upgrading the entire database.

As previously mentioned, you must first verify that all your software and hardware meet the required specifications for your desired SharePoint Server 2010 environment, including SQL Server. You must also belong to the db_owner fixed database role and the db_backup-operator fixed database role on the database servers and belong to the dbcreator fixed server role and the db_owner fixed database role in the server farm to which the database will be attached. Additionally, you must be a member of the local Administrators group on all the servers you will be using for the upgrade.

There are two basic steps to performing the upgrade:

- Backing up the MOSS 2007 databases using SQL Server tools
- Restoring the database backup to the new farm

There is a third, optional task where you can set the MOSS 2007 version of the databases to read-only before backing them up. You would do this if you wanted to perform a hybrid upgrade method. If you choose this option, users on MOSS 2007 can continue to read SharePoint content but will not be able to make any changes.

Backing Up the Database

This procedure must be performed physically at the machine or machines hosting the SQL Server database for MOSS 2007.

The steps presented here can be performed on both SQL Server 2005 and SQL Server 2008. The procedure is somewhat different if you need to perform a backup on SQL Server 2000.

1. At the keyboard of the database server machine, click Start ➤ All Programs, Microsoft SQL Server 2005 or Microsoft Server 2008, and then click SQL Server Management Studio.

2. In the Connect To Server box, input the relevant connection information; then click Connect.

3. After the connection is made to the desired instance of the database engine, in Object Explorer, expand the server tree by expanding the name of the server.

4. Expand Databases, right-click the desired database, click Tasks, and then click Back Up.

5. When the Back Up Database dialog box opens, under Source, in the Database box, verify that the name of the desired database appears.

6. In the Backup type box, select Full.

7. Under Backup Component, select Database.

8. Under Backup Set, in the Name field, either accept the default or enter a name for the backup set.

9. Under Destination, select either Disk or Tape. Then specify the destination path or, to create a different destination, click Add.

10. To begin the backup, click OK.

Restoring the Database on SQL Server 2005 and 2008 Enterprise Editions

Although the backup process is identical for both SQL Server 2005 and SQL Server 2008, the restore process is slightly different. The following instructions can be used on both editions of the SQL database server:

1. In SQL Server Management Studio, right-click Databases and then click Restore Database.

2. When the Restore Database dialog box appears, on the General page, in the To database field, type the name of the database you are restoring.

3. In the To A Point Of Time field, accept the default entry, which is Most Recent Possible.

4. Click From Device and then click Browse to select the location of the backup file.

5. In the Specify Backup dialog box, under Backup Media, select File.

6. Under Backup location, click Add.

7. In the Locate Backup File dialog box, select the desired file you want to restore and then click OK.

8. In Select The Backup Sets To Restore, select the Restore check box next to the most recent full backup.

9. In the Restore Database dialog box, on the Options page, under Restore options, select the Overwrite The Existing Database check box; then click OK to start the restore.

Verifying the Presence of Custom Components for the Database

Once the database has been restored, you must connect the database to web applications. Before you can approach this task, you must first verify that you have all the custom components that are required. You can do this with Windows PowerShell.

On the SQL Server instance, open Windows PowerShell. At the command prompt, run the cmdlet:

```
Test-SPContentDatabase -Name <database name> -WebApplication <URL>
[-ServerInstance <ServerInstanceName>] [-DatabaseCredentials <Domain\username>]
```

The root site for the web application must be included in the first content database that you add when you add the content databases. This means that you must review the root of the web application from the original server farm to make sure of the location of the first site collection. Then, after adding the database to the root site, you can add the other content databases for the web application. The process of adding databases automatically creates any required site collections.

WARNING   Do not create any site collections before you restore all the content databases.

Adding a Content Database to a Web Application

Once you have verified that you possess all the required customizations, you can proceed to add a content database to a web application using the Stsadm.exe command-line and the addcontentdb operation.

On the command line, run the type the following command and parameters; then press Enter:

```
stsadm -o addcontentdb -url <URL> -databasename <database name>
[-forcedeleteupgradelock] [-preserveolduserexperience true/false ]
[-databaseserver <server name>] [-databaseuser <user name>]
[-databasepassword <password>] [-sitewarning <site warning count>]
[-sitemax <site max count>]
[-assignnewdatabaseid] [-clearchangelog]
```

NOTE   For more information on addcontentdb, go to http://technet.microsoft .com/en-us/library/cc263422.aspx.

Post-upgrade Tasks for a Database Attach Upgrade

The next step is to upgrade the taxonomy data for profile services. This task is identical to the one you reviewed earlier in this chapter in the section "Upgrading the Taxonomy Data for Profile Services for an In-Place Upgrade."

NOTE   You will also need to configure the Secure Store Service for Excel Services. See the details regarding this task in Chapter 4.

Updating InfoPath Form Template Links

During the database attach upgrade process, all InfoPath form templates were exported from the old environment and imported into the new environment. Now that the upgrade is complete, you still need to update the links to point to the correct URLs for the form templates. You do this using Windows PowerShell. To complete this task, you must be a member of the SharePoint_Shell_Access role on the configuration database and a member of the WSS_ADMIN_WPG local group on the computer where SharePoint 2010 Products is installed.

1. Click Start ➢ Administrative Tools.

2. In Administrative Tools, click SharePoint 2010 Management Shell.

3. When Windows PowerShell opens, at the prompt, type the following:

```
Update-SPInfoPathAdminFileURL -find <old URL to replace> -replace <new URL>
```

4. Press Enter.

After completing this process, move to the "Final Upgrade Tasks" section of this chapter.

Final Upgrade Tasks

Even under the best of circumstances, you'll still want to review the records on the upgrade to determine whether there were any problems. Of course, if errors occurred, you'll want to view the logs and diagnose the issues so that you can correct them.

Verifying the Upgrade Status

As you've already experienced, the upgrade process, regardless of procedure, consists of several distinct processes, any of which could experience difficulties. You may not want to wait until the upgrade is complete to discover any issues that may have occurred. There are a number of different tasks you can engage in to verify whether your upgrade is progressing well and has completed successfully.

Reviewing the log and error files can be performed during portions of the overall upgrade process and after the upgrade is complete. For instance, once `Setup.exe` has run, the SharePoint Products And Technologies Configuration Wizard has completed, and the Central Administration website opens, then the content upgrade commences, and you can review the setup and configuration log files and error files. To view the log files, you will need to be a local Administrator on the server.

 To find out how to enable Windows Installer logging, go to http://support .microsoft.com/kb/223300.

To review the `Setup.exe` log files, use Windows Explorer, navigate to %USERTEMP% or %WINDIR%\Users\user account\AppData\Local\Temp, and then locate the `SharePoint Server SetupYYYYMMDDHHMMSSSSS.log` file, where YYYYMMDD is the date and HHMMSSSSS is the time. Hours are formatted on a 24-hour clock and include minutes, seconds, and milliseconds.

To review the SharePoint Products And Technologies Configuration Wizard log file, navigate to this location using Windows Explorer:

```
COMMONPROGRAMFILES%\Microsoft Shared\Web server extensions\14\LOGS
```

Look for `PSCDiagnostics_MM_DD_YYYY_HH_MM_SS_SSS_randomnumber.log` where MM_DD_YY is the date and HH_MM_SS_SSS is the time. Hours are also formatted on a 24-hour clock using the same pattern as the `Setup.exe` log files.

To review the upgrade log file and error log file once the upgrade has completed, navigate to here:

```
%COMMONPROGRAMFILES%\Microsoft Shared\Web server extensions\14\LOGS
```

To locate the upgrade log, look for `Upgrade-YYYYMMDD-HHMMSS-SSS.log`. To locate the error log file, look for `Upgrade-YYYYMMDD-HHMMSS-SSS.err`.

These files will open in any text editor such as Notepad. If all has gone well, you should see a message in the upgrade log file that states "Upgrade session finished successfully!" If this message is missing, use the Find function to search for *ERROR* to locate entries related to component and database connection failures. Search for *WARNING* to find issues related to missing components or features. You may also have to use a log parser to run queries against the log files. Once you find and resolve any issues, you can restart the upgrade.

In addition to reviewing the log files, you can also verify the upgrade by using the Central Administration website to view the version number on the Servers In Farm page. You must be a member of the Farm Administrators group to perform this task. In Central Administration, under the System Settings section, click Manage Servers In This Farm. Under Farm Information, next to Configuration Database Version, make sure the number starts with 14.

You can also check the upgrade status from the Central Administration home page under Upgrade And Migration by clicking Check Upgrade Status. You can view the upgrade status from the command line by opening a command line window and navigating directories to this location:

`%COMMONPROGRAMFILES%\Microsoft Shared\Web Server Extensions\14\bin`

Then enter **Stsadm -o localupgradestatus** and press Enter. The `localupgradestatus` operation does not take any parameters. This operation is effective only on the local server and cannot check on other servers in the farm. You will be notified if any server components still need to be upgraded.

Reviewing Upgraded Sites

Once the upgrade has completed, you will want to view your upgraded sites to verify that they appear as expected. If you used Visual Upgrade, you can use this feature to preview the sites directly. You can also check the Site Settings page by using the URL `http:// siteurl/_layouts/settings.aspx`, where `siteurl` is the URL specific to the desired site. If using the Site Settings page isn't effective, go back to your log files to see whether the problem is listed.

To be complete, test all of your web parts by building a web parts page that uses all of your customized web parts. Determine whether any of them seem broken. Also test to see whether the styles and appearance of your web pages are as expected. Often if there is a problem, the most likely solution is to correct a broken link to one or more items. Be especially diligent in checking any special customizations, and verify that all permissions work for all of your groups.

Restarting the Upgrade

If you encountered problems with the initial upgrade anywhere along the line and then corrected them, you'll need to restart the upgrade to finish the job. For instance, if during an in-place upgrade should the server restart or the upgrade should otherwise fail, you'll need to restart the upgrade at the part of the process where the SharePoint Products And Technologies Configuration Wizard (`Psconfig.exe`) runs.

For a database attach upgrade, any sites that cannot be upgraded will be skipped in the upgrade process; after the outstanding issues have been fixed, you can restart the upgrade for just the skipped sites by using Windows PowerShell.

RESTARTING THE SERVER FARM UPGRADE FROM THE COMMAND LINE

You must be a member of the local Administrators group on the server to perform the following steps:

1. Open a command-line window.

2. Navigate to this directory:

   `%COMMONPROGRAMFILES%\Microsoft shared\Web server extensions\14\Bin\`

3. At the prompt, type the following:

   `psconfig -cmd upgrade -inplace v2v -passphrase <passphrase> -wait`

   where `passphrase` is the string you originally configured for server farm security; then press Enter.

Any sites that were skipped during the in-place or database attach upgrade will now be upgraded.

RESTARTING THE UPGRADE FOR A DATABASE USING WINDOWS POWERSHELL

To perform this task, you must be a member of the SharePoint_Shell_Access role on the configuration database and a member of WSS_ADMIN_WPG local group on the server machine hosting SharePoint 2010.

1. Click Start ➢ SharePoint 2010 Products Configuration Wizard.

2. Click SharePoint 2010 Management Shell.

3. At the Windows PowerShell prompt, type **upgrade-spcontentdatabase -id <GUID>**, where GUID is the globally unique identifier for the database; then press Enter.

   The upgrade for the database will commence.

If you do not know the GUID for the content database, at the PowerShell command prompt, type **Get-SPContentDatabase -Identity <content_database_name>**, where content_database_name is the name of the database; then press Enter.

This completes the majority of tasks associated with a fresh install of SharePoint Server 2010 and the two major upgrade paths from MOSS 2007 to SharePoint Server 2010. There are still a number of configuration duties to be performed to get your SharePoint environment up and running effectively.

Summary

In this chapter, you received an extensive summary of how to install SharePoint Server 2010 as well as how to upgrade from MOSS 2007 to SharePoint Server 2010.

- Planning a hardware, software, and topology environment for a fresh installation of SharePoint Server 2010
- Planning various approaches for upgrading MOSS 2007 to SharePoint Server 2010
- Performing a fresh installation of SharePoint Server 2010 on a single server with built-in database
- Exploring other SharePoint Server 2010 installation scenarios
- Reviewing the different approaches to upgrading MOSS 2007 to SharePoint Server 2010
- Examining and performing post-installation and post-upgrade tasks

Exam Essentials

Planning the SharePoint Server 2010 Environment   Understand how to architect the components in SharePoint including the server farm, service applications, applications pools, and so on. Also demonstrate the ability to architect SharePoint topologies in relation to server roles and server farm design.

Deploying and Upgrading SharePoint Server 2010   Display your knowledge in deploying SharePoint Server 2010 in the areas of licensing, installation prerequisites, and installation and deployment types and methods through post-installation tasks.

Review Questions

1. What are some of the factors that determine whether you deploy SharePoint Server 2010 on a single farm or on multiple farms? (Choose all that apply.)

   A. The requirement to use the Visual Upgrade feature

   B. The need for multiple dedicated server farms to satisfy use requirements

   C. Funding that is dedicated for special purposes requiring more than one farm

   D. Using multiple server farms to enhance performance

2. Which of the following are valid service applications in SharePoint Server 2010? (Choose all that apply.)

   A. Access Services

   B. Business Community Services (BCS)

   C. Excel Services

   D. Visio Services

3. What is true about application pools in SharePoint Server 2010? (Choose all that apply.)

   A. Application pools are defined by Internet Information Services (IIS) 6.0.

   B. An application pool is a collection of one or more URLs serviced by one or a set of worker processes.

   C. IIS application pools allow multiple SharePoint websites to run on a single server without processes in one site interacting with any of the other sites.

   D. Dedicated application pools increase security for authenticated content.

4. What is true for web applications in SharePoint Server 2010? (Choose all that apply.)

   A. A web application is any individual IIS website created to access and use SharePoint Server 2010.

   B. A web application is any individual IIS site collection created to access and use SharePoint Server 2010.

   C. Each web application has its own individual domain name.

   D. Each web application shares a domain name path.

5. Zones are different logical paths expressed as URLs that allow access to the same web application. Which of the available zones requires the greatest security?

   A. Default

   B. Extranet

   C. Intranet

   D. Internet

   E. Custom

6. In your continuity and crisis planning, in protecting data from errors made by SharePoint users, which of the following are considered to be the most appropriate safeguards? (Choose all that apply.)

A. The Records Center is a specifically designed repository that protects all legal and regulatory documents.

B. The Recycle Bin uses a two-part process that allows recovery of deleted data.

C. Versioning allows a document to be reverted to an earlier version should the current version become damaged or corrupted.

D. All documents must be fully backed up every night to be protected from user errors or damage.

7. In architecting SharePoint topologies, if you are deploying a single farm, which services can you expect to be available just on your individual farm? (Choose all that apply.)

A. Business Data Connectivity

B. Excel Calculation Services

C. Query Services

D. Word Services

8. The database server role provides all database services for SharePoint. This role must contain several required components. Which components would you expect to find? (Choose all that apply.)

A. Business Data Connectivity

B. Service Store Service

C. State Service

D. Word Automation Services

9. A limited server farm deployment is typically used to test a new SharePoint deployment or for training purposes. This deployment can support about 100 users and employs a single hardware server. You can also deploy SharePoint on a small farm deployment, the next step up from limited server farm deployment, and use two physical servers, one for web and application server roles and the other for the database. How many users can you expect to support in a small farm deployment?

A. 500

B. 1,000

C. 10,000

D. 20,000

10. In planning for a multiple-server farm design, what is true about such designs? (Choose all that apply.)

   A. Not all farms in a multifarm design must have the same topology.

   B. All farms in a multifarm design must use the same topology.

   C. A farm in a multifarm design can rely on web servers on other farms and does not have to contain web servers of its own.

   D. The enterprise services farm topology is the default topology for a multiserver farm design.

11. Deploying SharePoint Server 2010 on a single server with a built-in database is often used for testing SharePoint or for training. For this installation type, which of the following are required tasks? (Choose all that apply.)

   A. Microsoft SQL Server 2005 Express must be installed.

   B. Microsoft SQL Server 2008 Express must be installed.

   C. The SharePoint Products And Technologies Wizard must create the SharePoint Central Administration website.

   D. The SharePoint Products And Technologies Wizard must create all the site collections for SharePoint.

12. For the SharePoint Server 2010 on a single server with a built-in database installation, you typically run the SharePoint Products And Technologies Wizard immediately after you finish running `Setup.exe`. If the configuration wizard should fail, what are your options? (Choose all that apply.)

   A. On the Configuration Failed page, click the available link to locate the PSCDiagnostics log files in order to determine the problem.

   B. Navigate to `%COMMONPROGRAMFILES%\Microsoft Shared\Web Server Extensions\14\LOGS` to locate the log files and attempt to determine the problem.

   C. On the Configuration Failed page, under Repair Or Remove, select Repair.

   D. On the SharePoint Server 2010 splash screen, under Install, click Install SharePoint Server. When prompted to choose Repair or Remove, select Repair.

13. One of the post-installation tasks for a single-server installation with a built-in database is to create at least one web application. If you choose not to create a web application, what are your options for deploying a site collection?

   A. You will be unable to create a site collection until you create the first web application.

   B. The only web application created by default once SharePoint is installed is SharePoint Central Administration v4, and you can only create additional site collections using this web app.

   C. The SharePoint – 80 and SharePoint Central Administration v4 web applications are created by default, but you can only use SharePoint – 80 to create site collections.

   D. The SharePoint – 80 and SharePoint Central Administration v4 web applications are created by default, and you can use both web apps to create site collections.

14. You are a SharePoint Server 2010 administrator, and you have installed language packs for French, German, and Spanish so that you can create site collections using those languages for your company's European customers. You have just deployed a partner site collection in French and have received feedback that some of the site content is still in English. Of the following, what could be the cause?

    A. After installing the language pack, you forgot to rerun the SharePoint Products And Technologies Wizard, resulting in some corruption in the site collection's content when it was created.

    B. One of the other SharePoint administrators in your organization manually translated some of the content into English by mistake.

    C. Some content in language packs for site collections is created in English by default, so this is no error.

    D. Some content, such as error messages and dialog boxes, depend on technologies outside the language pack and may appear in English.

15. You are a SharePoint 2010 administrator, and you have just finished installing SharePoint Server 2010 as a single-server deployment. You have opened the Central Administration website but have experienced some errors. What are the likely errors and their solutions? (Choose all that apply.)

    A. Internet Explorer 8 security may be interfering with Central Administration being opened correctly; you can add the Central Administration site to the Trusted Sites list in IE8.

    B. The default Internet Explorer enhanced security settings on your server may be interfering with Central Administration being opened correctly; you can disable those settings for the Administrator account in Administrative Tools using the Server Manager page.

    C. The Internet Explorer 8 default accessibility settings may not be correctly set; you can go into Internet Options to permit greater accessibility by using the Advanced tab.

    D. If you are using a proxy server, Internet Explorer 8 may be blocking access to the proxy server; you can set IE8 to bypass the proxy server for local addresses.

16. You are the SharePoint administrator for your company, and you are in the process of upgrading your MOSS 2007 environment to SharePoint Server 2010. You are using Share-Point Visual Upgrade and giving the site administrators for the SharePoint site collections access to this tool. Of the following, what do you expect the site administrators to do with Visual Upgrade?

    A. The site administrators can use the Visual Upgrade UI to perform upgrades to their site collections using a graphical tool to drag and drop sites into new topologies.

    B. The site administrators can preview what their site collections will look like using Visual Upgrade and decide whether they want the sites to use the old MOSS 2007 look or the new SharePoint Server 2010 look.

    C. The site administrators can use Visual Upgrade to preview site collection organization, navigational links, and application pool connections.

    D. Site administrators do not have sufficient access permissions to use Visual Upgrade, which can be operated only by the SharePoint administrator group.

17. You are the SharePoint administrator for your company, and you've been tasked with developing a plan to upgrade your current MOSS 2007 deployment to SharePoint Server 2010. You currently administer your MOSS 2007 server farm with separate tiers for web servers, application servers, and database servers. Your environment uses the Office SharePoint Server 2007 Enterprise edition. Of the following, which are valid upgrade paths to SharePoint Server 2010? (Choose all that apply.)

    A. You can upgrade to a SharePoint Server 2010 single-server deployment using SQL Server 2005.

    B. You can upgrade to a SharePoint Server 2010 server farm deployment using the same topology of separate tiers for each of the three server roles.

    C. You can upgrade to a SharePoint Server 2010 server farm deployment with a two-tier topology, with web and application server roles on one tier and database servers on a separate tier.

    D. You can upgrade to any SharePoint Server 2010 Standard edition single or server farm deployment.

18. You are the SharePoint administrator for your organization. You have been tasked with upgrading your MOSS 2007 server farm to SharePoint Server 2010. You require an upgrade procedure that upgrades both your content databases and configuration settings at the same time. You have been assured by your CIO that you can take SharePoint offline for an extensive period of time, and you are required to perform little or no manual configuration of the system during the upgrade. Which is the most viable upgrade path for you to take given these parameters?

    A. In-place upgrade

    B. Database attach upgrade

    C. Hybrid approach 1: read-only databases

    D. Hybrid approach 2: detach databases

19. You are the SharePoint administrator for your organization, and you are going to perform an in-place upgrade of your MOSS 2007 environment to SharePoint Server 2010. You have run `Setup.exe` on all your web servers and are about to run the SharePoint Products And Technologies Configuration Wizard. Are there any conditions regarding which server the wizard must be run on first?

    A. You must run the wizard first on the web server hosting the Central Administration website.

    B. You must run the wizard first on the web server that experiences the greatest use by SharePoint users.

    C. You must run the wizard first on the web server that experiences the least use by SharePoint users.

    D. There is no preference.

20. You are the SharePoint administrator for your organization, and you have just upgraded your MOSS 2007 platform to SharePoint Server 2010. Now you must manage SharePoint's taxonomy data. Taxonomy data is used to classify data so it can be standardized, shared, and used on multiple systems. The upgrade process from MOSS 2007 to SharePoint Server 2010 requires that you move this data from the shared services provider (SSP) database to the managed metadata database. How can you accomplish this task?

A. On the command line, use `Stsadm.exe` and the required parameters to initiate the move.

B. Use the appropriate commands and parameters in Windows PowerShell to initiate the move.

C. Use the Central Administration server farm management tools to initiate the move.

D. Rerun the SharePoint Products And Technologies Configuration wizard to initiate the move.

Answers to Review Questions

1. **B, C, D.** Option A is bogus, because the use of Visual Upgrade has nothing to do with server farm planning. All other options are correct.

2. **A, C, D.** Business Community Services (BCS) is incorrect. The correct name is Business Connectivity Services (BCS). All other options are valid services.

3. **B, C, D.** For option A, application pools are defined by IIS 7.0, not 6.0. All other options are correct.

4. **A, C.** Options B and D are bogus. All other options are correct.

5. **A.** The Default zone, or any customer-facing zone, requires the greatest attention since access to this zone may be gained by anyone who can use a link to the zone.

6. **A, B, C.** Although you want to create and use a sufficient backup and recovery strategy, conducting a full backup of all documentation on a daily basis is not good resource management, especially to protect each individual document contained in SharePoint. Backup is the last possible resort for protecting a document from loss.

7. **B, D.** Only Excel Calculation Services and Word Services are confined to a single server farm. Business Data Connectivity and Query Services are available across multiple farms.

8. **A, B, C.** You would typically find Word Automation Services on an application server role but not commonly on a database server role.

9. **C.** A two-tier small farm deployment involving two physical server machines can support up to 10,000 users.

10. **A, C.** Not all farms in a multiserver farm design must be the same, and in fact an individual farm doesn't have to contain any web servers and can rely on web servers contained in a separate farm. There is no particular default topology for a multifarm design.

11. **B, C.** The built-in database for this installation is always Microsoft SQL Server 2008 Express. Microsoft SQL Server 2005 Express is bogus. Although the SharePoint Products And Technologies Wizard creates the configuration and content databases for SharePoint as well as the Central Administration website, it does not actually create the site collections.

12. **A, B, D.** You can either click the link on the Configuration Failed page or manually navigate to the location of the log files to determine what went wrong. You can also return to the SharePoint Server 2010 splash screen to initiate a repair, but you cannot initiate a repair directly from the Configuration Failed page.

13. **C.** Although both the SharePoint – 80 and SharePoint Central Administration v4 web applications are created by default, the Central Administration v4 web application is for the exclusive use of the Central Administration website. To create site collections for all other purposes, you must use the SharePoint – 80 web application, unless you choose to create additional web applications.

14. D. Assuming the default language for your SharePoint Server 2010 deployment is English, you can use one or more language packs to create site collections from templates that render the content in another language. However, some features, such as notifications, dialog boxes, and error messages, depend on other technologies like Microsoft .NET Framework, Microsoft Windows Workflow Foundation, and Microsoft ASP.NET and therefore may not be localized for the desired language. Not running the configuration wizard after installing the language pack would not have resulted in a working site collection at all, so option A is incorrect. Options B and C are bogus.

15. A, B, D. Option C is bogus. All other options are valid.

16. B. Visual Upgrade is a tool that lets you preview and determine how site collections will appear after the upgrade. All the other options are bogus.

17. B, C. You can upgrade any size MOSS 2007 server farm to any size SharePoint Server 2010 server farm but cannot upgrade from a server farm topology to any form of single-server deployment. Also, an Enterprise edition of SharePoint cannot upgrade to a Standard version, and vice versa.

18. D. Although the in-place upgrade may seem a logical choice, it is the quickest upgrade path, and part of the parameters for the upgrade is that time is not an issue. The detach databases combines the advantages of all the other methods, but it does take longer than the in-place upgrade.

19. A. The SharePoint Products And Technologies Configuration Wizard must first be run on the web server hosting Central Administration, since the Central Administration site is the interface providing administration tools for managing the rest of the farm. Afterward, you can run the wizard on your other web servers in any order. The other options are bogus.

20. B. To initiate the move, you need to open Windows PowerShell and execute the command **Move-SPProfileManagedMetadataProperty -ProfileServiceApplicationProxy <SPServiceApplicationProxyPipeBind> -Identity <string>**. All other options are bogus.

Chapter

3

Configuring SharePoint Farm Environments

MICROSOFT EXAM OBJECTIVE COVERED IN THIS CHAPTER:

✓ **Installing and Configuring a SharePoint Environment**

  ▪ Configure SharePoint Farms

  ▪ Deploy and Manage SharePoint Solutions

Once you have installed your SharePoint Server 2010 environment or upgraded from Microsoft Office SharePoint Server (MOSS) 2007, you will need to perform a number of additional tasks to enable SharePoint to provide the desired services to your company's internal and external users, customers, and partners. Although you may be eager to configure SharePoint's service applications and get the ball rolling, so to speak, there's still plenty of work that needs to be done on the server farm first.

This chapter focuses on configuring several required and optional settings, including incoming and outgoing emails, diagnostic logging, and Remote Blob Storage.

Server Farm Configuration Overview

After you have successfully installed SharePoint Server 2010 on the hardware in your server farm and completed the post-installation tasks, it's time to set up the server farm for production operations. There's still plenty of work to be done before your users can enjoy all the advantages of the new SharePoint deployment. Here's a rundown of what you need to do:

- Configure *usage and health data collection.*
- Configure *diagnostic logging.*
- Configure incoming and outgoing email integration.
- Configure a mobile account.
- Install and configure Remote BLOB Storage.

The data collection and logging configuration tools are important for any troubleshooting and fine-tuning tasks, and SharePoint alerts require that incoming and outgoing email be set up. Alerts can also optionally be sent via Short Message Service, so mobile users can be served as well. Although some of this work is optional, performing all of these tasks will give you the maximum value from all the services provided by SharePoint Server 2010.

Usage and Health Data Collection Configuration

Up to this point in the installation and deployment of your SharePoint environment, ideally all has gone well, but you can't depend on everything being picture-perfect forever. Any responsible administrator of any system will have an eye on a number of system logs to monitor both the usage patterns in the system and the day-to-day "health" of the environment. SharePoint is no different in this respect than other technical platforms, and there are a number of tasks you must perform before these logging features become available.

 Some of the exercises you are about to engage in require the use of Windows PowerShell. Although PowerShell is not included as part of a specific domain for the certification exam, understanding how to use PowerShell in SharePoint is very important, and the exam assumes you will have this skill set. It's also important to keep in mind that some configuration activities can be performed both in Central Administration and with PowerShell, while others can be accomplished only in Central Administration or only in PowerShell.

In Exercise 3.1, you'll see how to use the Central Administration website to configure both usage and health data collection. This is an activity that affects the entire server farm and cannot be set for an individual server. You must be a member of the Farm Administrators group to successfully perform this task.

Keep in mind that logging requires resources from the system, and you may notice an impact on performance and disk usage. Only select logging for those events for which you require regular reports. If you need to log a specific event, enable logging for the event only for the required duration, and then disable logging for that event when the duration has elapsed.

Usage data collection settings are also applied to all events. You cannot set event collection settings for individual event types from Central Administration, only with Windows PowerShell. Also, although you can configure usage using Windows PowerShell, you cannot configure just health data collection settings with this method.

EXERCISE 3.1

Configuring Usage and Health Data Collection in Central Administration

1. Navigate to the Central Administration home page, and then click Monitoring.

2. On the Monitoring page under Reporting, click Configure Usage And Health Data Collection.

    You may see a message at the top of the page stating "Warning: this page is not encrypted for secure communication. User names, passwords, and any other information will be sent in clear text. For more information, contact your administrator." This can appear if SSL encryption is not enabled.

3. When the Configure Usage And Health Data Collection page appears, under Usage Data Collection, select the Enable Usage Data Collection check box to enable usage data collection.

4. Under Event Selection, select the check boxes for the events you want to log in the Events To Log List.

EXERCISE 3.1 *(continued)*

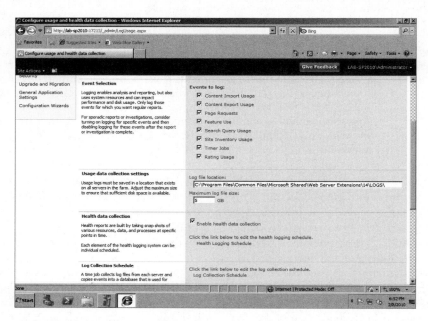

5. Under Usage Data Collection Settings, in the Log File Location field, type the path of the folder you want usage and health information to be written to or accept the default path, keeping in mind that the path must exist on all servers in the server farm.

6. In the Maximum Log File Size field, enter a value between 1 and 20 for the maximum disk space for the logs in gigabytes.

7. Under Health Data Collection, select the Enable Health Data Collection check box.

8. Click Health Logging Schedule and select the desired the timer jobs to set the schedule for when the jobs will run.

9. Under Logging Database Server section, select either Windows Authentication or SQL Authentication.

10. Click OK when you're done.

You can set up usage data collection using PowerShell. Exercise 3.2 describes the process. You must be a member of the SharePoint_Shell_Access role on the configuration database and a member of WSS_ADMIN_WPG local group on the server computer containing SharePoint 2010 to successfully complete this task.

EXERCISE 3.2

Configuring Usage a Data Collection Using Windows PowerShell

1. Click Start ➢ All Programs.

2. Click Microsoft SharePoint 2010 Products.

3. Click SharePoint 2010 Management Shell.

4. When Windows PowerShell opens, at the command prompt, type the following; then press Enter:

    ```
    Set-SPUsageService [-LoggingEnabled {1 | 0}[AU: You should mention 1 and 0 are
    choices: enabled is 1 not enabled(false) is 0--MW]] [-UsageLogLocation <Path>]
    [-UsageLogMaxSpaceGB <1-20> [-Verbose]
    ```

    -LoggingEnabled enables usage data logging, and the UsageLogMaxSpaceGB parameter lets you specify the maximum amount of drive space used for logging. You must also specify a path for UsageLogLocation that exists on all farm servers.

In Exercise 3.1, you learned that enabling usage and health data collection in Central Administration allowed you to perform logging for the entire server farm and for as many events as you selected. You typically perform this action when you want to acquire ongoing reports on the same event types.

Exercise 3.3 will show you how to use Windows PowerShell to set up usage data collection for a single, specific event. This action can be performed using Windows PowerShell only, and you can only configure the DaysRetained setting. You must belong to the same groups as defined in Exercise 3.2.

EXERCISE 3.3

Configuring Usage Data Collection for a Single Event Type Using Windows PowerShell

1. Click Start ➢ All Programs.

2. Click Microsoft SharePoint 2010 Products.

3. Click SharePoint 2010 Management Shell.

4. When Windows PowerShell opens, at the command prompt, type the following; then press Enter:

    ```
    Set-SPUsageDefinition -Identity <GUID> [-Enable] [-DaysRetained <1-30>]
    [-Verbose]
    ```

Enter the Enabled parameter in order to enable usage logging for this usage definition. You use the DaysRetained switch to specify how long you want the usage data to be retained in the log before it's deleted, using a range of 1 to 30 days. Also, to view the progress of the command execution, use the Verbose parameter.

You have the ability to log usage data in a different database, but only by using Windows PowerShell. Exercise 3.4 shows you how. You must be a member of the same groups as in Exercises 3.2 and 3.3.

EXERCISE 3.4

Configuring Usage Data Logging in a Different Database Using Windows PowerShell

1. Click Start ➢ All Programs.

2. Click Microsoft SharePoint 2010 Products.

3. Click SharePoint 2010 Management Shell.

4. When Windows PowerShell opens, at the command prompt, type the following; then press Enter:

   ```
   Set-SPUsageApplication -DatabaseServer <Database server name> -DatabaseName
   <Database name> [-DatabaseUsername <User name>] [-DatabasePassword <Password>]
   [-Verbose]
   ```

You must use both the DatabaseUsername and DatabasePassword parameters if you are logged into the server with an account that's different from the database owner. The Verbose parameter lets you view the progress of the command's execution. Also, you must specify the value for the DatabaseServer parameter, even if the new database is on the same database server as the old database.

If you do not have reports from usage and health logging configured to be sent to you via email, you will still see alerts appear across the top of the Central Administration main page. To review the reports, click the available link and then click the link for the specific report to review the information, as shown in Figure 3.1.

Diagnostic Logging Configuration

Another very important task to accomplish once you've deployed a new install or an upgrade is to configure the diagnostic log settings in SharePoint Server 2010. This is another log that "takes the pulse" of SharePoint relative to specific events, letting you detect and ideally prevent potential problems. Diagnostic logging has a set of default behaviors that you may want to change, including changing the location where log files are written to, limiting the amount of disk space used for logging, backing up log files, and so on.

This section will show you how to set up diagnostic logging to meet your technical requirements using both Central Administration and Windows PowerShell.

Exercise 3.5 shows you the step-by-step process of configuring diagnostic logging using the Central Administration website. You must be a member of the Farm Administrators SharePoint group in order to perform this task.

FIGURE 3.1   Web Analytics Edit Dialog Box

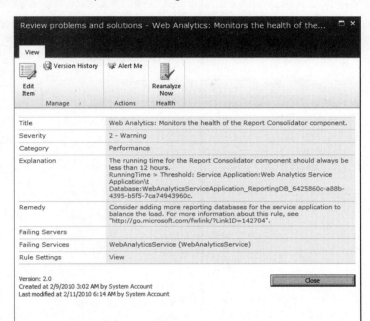

After clicking OK, if you receive an error message like the one in Figure 3.2, review the message, click the Go Back To Site link to return to the Central Administration main page, and correct the error. You can also click the Troubleshoot Issues With Microsoft SharePoint Foundation link to try to solve the problem with the Central Administration help pages.

If you're successful, you will be taken to the Central Administration Monitoring page.

There's actually a little bit more to the process than the steps previously outlined suggest. If you have created a collection of configuration settings that aren't optimal, you can reset diagnostic logging back to the default settings by selecting the All Categories box, selecting Reset to default in the Least Critical Event To Report To The Event Log list, and then selecting Reset to default in the Critical Event To Report To The Trace Log list.

EXERCISE 3.5

Configuring Diagnostic Logging Using Central Administration

1. On the Central Administration page, click Monitoring.

2. On the Monitoring page under Reporting, click Configure Diagnostic Logging.

3. On the Diagnostic logging page, under Event Throttling, you can select the All Categories check box to enable event throttling for all events, or you can expand each event and granularly configure throttling to meet your specific requirements.

4. Use the Least Critical Event To Report To The Event Log menu to select one of the following:

    ▪ None

    ▪ Critical

    ▪ Error

    ▪ Warning

    ▪ Information

    ▪ Verbose

5. Use the Least Critical Event To Report To The Trace Log menu to select one of the following:

    ▪ None

    ▪ Unexpected

    ▪ Monitorable

    ▪ High

    ▪ Medium

    ▪ Verbose

EXERCISE 3.5 *(continued)*

6. Under Event Log Flood Protection, verify that the Enable Event Log Flood Protection check box is selected.

7. Under Trace Log, either accept the default path for the location where the trace log will be written or specify a path. The location must exist on all servers in the farm.

8. In the Number Of Days To Store The Log Files field, accept the default value of 14 or specify a value.

9. If you want to limit the amount of disk space used by the trace log, select the Restrict Trace Log Disk Space Usage check box and then either accept the default value in GB or specify your own value.

10. When you're done, click OK.

FIGURE 3.2   Diagnostic Logging Configuration Error Message

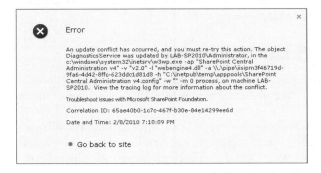

Exercise 3.6 will show you how to perform the same task from Windows PowerShell.

EXERCISE 3.6

Configuring Diagnostic Logging Using Windows PowerShell

1. Open Windows PowerShell.

2. At the prompt, type the following; then press Enter:

```
Set-SPLogLevel -TraceSeverity {None | Unexpected | Monitorable | Medium | High
| Verbose} -EventSeverity {None | Information | Warning | Error | Critical |
Verbose} [-Identity <Category name...>]  -Verbose
```

The Identity parameter is used to specify one or more categories that you want to change, such as Data Layer. If you do not specify the Identity parameter, all categories will be modified.

To view the current diagnostic logging settings, at the command prompt, type `Get-SPLogLevel`; then press Enter. The result is shown in Figure 3.3.

FIGURE 3.3   Diagnostic Logging Settings in the Management Shell

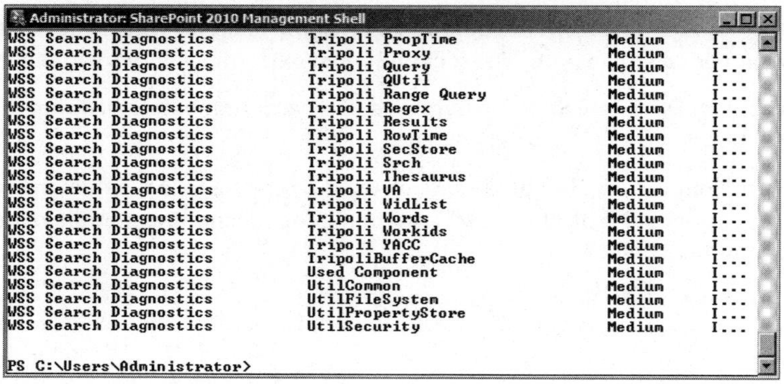

You can also set all the categories back to their defaults in PowerShell by typing `Clear-SPLogLevel` and then pressing Enter.

Configuring Email Integration

Although setting up email integration is considered optional, it's one of the more important actions you can make in SharePoint Server 2010 once you've finished your installation or upgrade.

There is a great deal of information you can input to SharePoint from email, including posting to the discussion board in SharePoint. You can also archive email conversations in SharePoint and show your Outlook calendar meetings in a SharePoint site calendar. Of course, you must have configured *incoming email integration* first.

Configuring *outgoing email integration* lets SharePoint communicate with users and admins in SharePoint so that automatic alerts are sent by the system. Each SharePoint user must specifically request what alerts they want to receive. You must configure the outgoing email feature before users have access to this functionality.

Configuring Incoming Email

I wish I could say this is quick and easy, but even if I did, it wouldn't be true. Here's a basic overview of what is required:

- At least one server in the server farm must be running the SMTP service and must be using a valid SMTP server address.

- Each frontend web server must be running both the SMTP service and the Windows SharePoint Services Web Application service.

- The following must be members of the Administrators group on the local computer containing the email drop folder:
  - The application pool identity account for Central Administration
  - The logon account for the Windows SharePoint Services Timer service
  - The application pool identity accounts for your web applications

If you choose not to run the SMTP service on one of the servers in your farm, you must have access to and know the name of another server running the SMTP service.

It's generally considered preferable to have the SMTP service installed on one of your own servers, since it gives you greater control over the availability of incoming email. You also do not have to configure permissions to an SMTP server outside your server farm in order to use the email drop folder option.

A number of the activities involved in configuring incoming emails are also required for configuring outgoing emails, so once you have incoming email integration set up, configuring outgoing email integration doesn't require many separate steps.

Installing the SMTP Service

For incoming email integration, the first required step is to install the SMTP service on all frontend web servers in your server farm that you want to be able to use incoming emails. This is an activity you do outside of SharePoint and by using the Windows Server 2008 or Windows Server 2008 R2 Server Manager in Administrative Tools. To perform this task, you must be an administrator on each of the local web servers. Exercise 3.7 will show you the details.

EXERCISE 3.7

Installing the SMTP Service

1. Click Start ➢ All Programs ➢ Administrative Tools.

2. In the list that appears, click Server Manager.

3. When Server Manager opens, click Features in the left pane.

4. In the Server Manager main pane, in Features Summary, click the Add Features link on the right.

5. When the Add Features Wizard launches, select the SMTP Server check box in the Features list.

6. When the Add Role Services And Features Required For SMTP Server dialog box appears, click Add Required Role Services and then click Next.

EXERCISE 3.7 *(continued)*

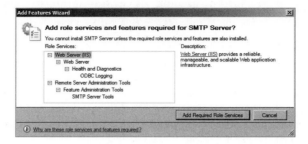

7. When the Introduction to Web Server (IIS) screen appears, click Next.

8. When the Select Roles Services For IIS screen appears, click Next.

9. When the Confirm Installation Selections screen appears, click Install.

10. When the Installation Results screen appears, click Close.

11. Close the Server Manager.

Configuring the SMTP Service

Now that the *SMTP service* and all of its required components are installed, you next need to configure the service to receive emails from the mail server for the domain. You can either receive mail from all servers except those you put on an exclude list or refuse mail from all servers except for those you put on an accept list. You must be a member of the Administrators group on the local server to perform the following task. Exercise 3.8 will walk you through the process of configuring the SMTP service.

IIS 6.0 is required for SMTP, even though IIS 7.5 is available with Windows Server 2008 R2. IIS 6.0 Management Tools are specifically required in order to configure SMTP on this server platform.

EXERCISE 3.8

Configuring the SMTP Service

1. Click Start ➢ All Programs ➢ Administrative Tools.

2. In the list that appears, click Internet Information Services (IIS) 6.0 Manager.

3. In the Internet Information Services (IIS) 6.0 Manager window, in the left pane, expand the name of the server on which you want to configure SMTP services.

4. Right-click the desired SMTP virtual server (there will likely be only one) and then click Start. If the Start option isn't available, the SMTP virtual server is already started.

5. Right-click the virtual server again and click Properties.

EXERCISE 3.8 *(continued)*

6. When the Properties dialog box appears, click the Access tab; under Access Control, click Authentication.

7. In the Authentication dialog box, verify that the Anonymous Access check box is selected and then click OK.

8. On the Access tab under Relay Restrictions, click Relay.

9. In the Relay Restrictions dialog box, do one of the following:

   - Click the All Except List Below radio button to accept mail from all servers.

   - Click ONLY THE LIST BELOW to accept mail from just servers on an accept list and click ADD. Then in the Computer dialog box, select Single Computer and add the IP address of the desired mail server. Select Group Of Computers and add the sub-net address and subnet mask; alternatively, select Domain and enter the domain name, as shown in here. Finally, click OK.

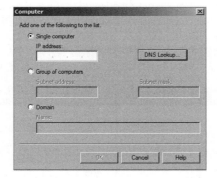

10. Click Start ➢ All Programs ➢ Administrative Tools ➢ Services.

11. In the Services list in the main pane, right-click Simple Mail Transfer Protocol (SMTP) and then select Properties.

12. In the Simple Mail Transfer Protocol (SMTP) dialog box, on the General tab, open the Startup Type menu and select Automatic.

13. Click OK and then close the Services window.

 When configuring relay restrictions, if you choose to deny all mail server connections, specifying an accept list, and you choose to restrict access by domain name, you will receive a warning dialog box stating that perform-ing this action requires a DNS reverse lookup on each connection, which will dramatically impact server performance.

Configuring Basic Incoming Email Services

Although there are a number of advanced tasks to perform depending on your specific circumstances and requirements, Exercise 3.9 is all you have to do to finish setting up basic incoming email services. When you complete this task, your users will be able to send emails directly to SharePoint lists and libraries. To successfully perform this task, you must be an administrator on the server that is running SharePoint Central Administration.

EXERCISE 3.9

Configuring Basic Incoming Email Services

1. On the Central Administration website, click System Settings.

2. On the System Settings page, under E-Mail And Text Messages (SMS), click Configure Incoming E-mail Settings.

3. On the Configure Incoming E-Mail Settings page, under Enable Incoming E-mail, select the Yes radio button and select Automatic under Settings Mode.

4. Under Incoming E-Mail Server Display Address, in the E-mail Server Display Address field, enter the display name for the email server, such as **mail.test.com**.

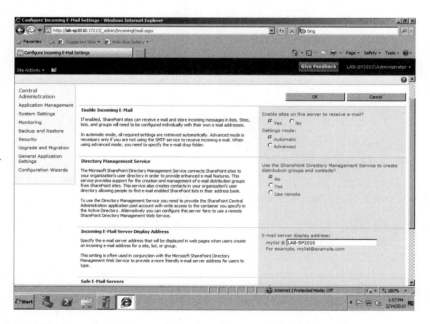

5. Accept the default settings on the rest of the page and then click OK.

To use the Directory Management Service, you must either run Active Directory in your environment or configure the server farm to access and use a remote SharePoint Directory Management web service.

If you are using a single computer with built-in database deployment for SharePoint Server 2010, these are all of the activities you have to perform to enable incoming email. There are more advanced scenarios available for a variety of production environments, as you're about to discover.

Advanced Configuration of Incoming Email

Although the previous exercises in this chapter have shown you how to enable the basic incoming email feature, you can use a number of methods to enhance incoming email functionality. Some of these methods require that you run SharePoint Server 2010 in an Active Directory domain. This will allow SharePoint's Directory Management Service to use the contact addresses created for document libraries to automatically be sent to Active Directory Users And Computers in the organizational unit (OU) for SharePoint.

Using the SharePoint Directory Management Service also lets your users create distribution lists directly in a SharePoint site. This requires additional administrative overhead since the Directory Management Service will be communicating with Active Directory Domain Services (ADDS), but on the other hand, you won't have to manually add each new contact address with Active Directory available.

For the following advanced tasks, you will need to be running Active Directory Domain Services in your network, and SharePoint Server 2010 will need to be joined to the domain.

Adding a DNS Host (A) Resource Record

If you are running your own Microsoft Exchange Server and routing email within your organization, you are required to create a host (A) resource record in DNS Manager. This will associate the DNS domain names of any hosts in your network to their IP addresses. In any reasonably sized production environment, the IT department likely has already performed this task, but if not, here is how you can accomplish it. You must be a member of the Administrators group on the local computer to complete these steps.

1. On the domain controller, click Start ➢ All Programs ➢ Administrative Tools ➢ DNS.

2. In DNS Manager, select the forward lookup zone for the domain containing the subdomain for SharePoint Server 2010.

3. Right-click the zone, and then click New Host (A or AAAA).

4. In the New Host dialog box, in the Name field, type the host or subdomain name for SharePoint Server 2010.

5. Type the FQDN for the server running SharePoint in the Fully Qualified Domain Name (FQDN) field in the format **subdomain.domain.com**.

6. Type the IP address to which the FQDN is to resolve in the IP Address field.

7. When the confirmation message box appears, click OK.

8. In the New Host dialog box, click Done.

    The new A resource record will now appear in the DNS Manager.

Creating a Local Domain

When you created the A resource record for the SharePoint subdomain, if the domains listed under the SMTP server in IIS don't match the FQDN you entered for the email server, you'll need to create a local domain. The following steps show you how:

1. Click Start ➢ All Programs ➢ Administrative Tools, and in the list that appears, click Internet Information Services (IIS) 6.0 Manager.

2. In the IIS Manager, expand the SMTP server in the left pane.

3. Right-click domains; on the Action menu, click New and then click Domain.

4. When the New SMTP Domain Wizard launches, select Alias and then click Next.

5. Under Domain Name, type the address of the mail that is to be received by the domain in the Name field, which must be the same address as the one you specified in step 5 of the "Adding a DNS Host (A) Resource Record" section.

6. Click Finish.

7. When the confirmation message appears, click OK.

    Restart the SMTP service to allow any email messages in the Queue folder to move on to the email Drop folder, which will then be sent on by the Windows SharePoint Services Timer server to the list or library to which they've been addressed.

Creating an Organizational Unit in Active Directory and Delegate Authority

If you are going to use SharePoint Directory Management Services, you will need to first create an OU in Active Directory. You'll need to be on the Windows Server 2008 computer that is a domain controller.

You can use Directory Management Services on either your server farm or your remote server farm. You must configure the application pool identity account in Central Administration to have the Create, Delete, And Manage User Accounts user access to the container you point to in Active Directory. An Active Directory administrator must configure the OU and assign the same access type to the container.

1. Click Start ➢ All Programs ➢ Administrative Tools; in the list that appears, click Active Directory Users And Computers.

2. In Active Directory Users And Computers, in the left pane, right-click the second-level domain containing your server farm, click New, and then click Organizational Unit.

3. Give the OU a name and then click OK.

4. Right-click the OU and then click Delegate Control.

5. When the Delegation Of Control Wizard launches, click Next.

6. On the Users And Groups page, click Add and then type the name of the application pool identity account used by SharePoint Central Administration.

7. In the Select Users, Computers, And Groups dialog box, click OK.

8. On the Users Or Groups page of the wizard, click Next.

9. On the Tasks To Delegate page of the wizard, select the Create, Delete, And Manage User Accounts check box; then click Next.

10. When you are on the last page of the wizard, click Finish.

Delegating Create and Delete All Child Objects and Adding Delete Subtree Permissions

If you intend on creating and deleting child objects along with user accounts, you'll have to also delegate Create All Child Objects And Delete All Child Objects control of the OU to the application pool identity account.

This is a separate procedure but works pretty much the same as delegating the right to the application pool identity account. You right-click the OU and use the Delegate Control Wizard again, this time using the Create A Custom Task To Delegate option on the Delegate page of the wizard. From there, you just select This Folder, Existing Objects In This Folder, And Creation Of New Objects In This Folder. Click Next and then Create All Child Objects And Delete All Child Objects; then finish the wizard.

However, if you do choose to delegate the Create All Child Objects And Delete All Child Objects control of the OU to the application pool identity account, you may run into a new problem. Although delegating control to the application pool identity for Central Administration lets administrators enable email for a SharePoint list, email for a list or document library cannot be disabled again. If you, as the administrator, attempt to do so, Central Administration tries to delete email contracts from the entire OU rather than from the list.

You'll need to add the Delete Subtree permission for the application pool identity for Central Administration to get around this problem. Go back into Active Directory Users And Computers on the domain controller.

1. In Active Directory Users And Computers, click the View menu and then click Advanced Features.

2. Right-click the OU and then click Properties.

3. In the Properties dialog box, select the Security tab and then click Advanced.

4. Under Permission Entries, double-click the application pool identity account for Central Administration.

5. Under Permissions, select Allow for Delete Subtree.

6. Click OK three times to close the dialog boxes for Permissions and Properties and to close Active Directory Users And Computers.

7. Restart Internet Information Services for your server farm.

There are a number of other advanced tasks, such as adding an SMTP connector in Microsoft Exchange Server 2007, but these tasks are outside the scope of a SharePoint Server 2010 administrator and are best handled by a specialist in that area. This technically is also true of the Active Directory–related exercises you just reviewed, but it's helpful to be able to operate somewhat outside of your specific field from time to time.

Configuring Outgoing Email

Many of the exercises required to set up the outgoing email feature in SharePoint you've already completed, if you configured incoming email. These tasks include installing and configuring the SMTP service, installing IIS 6.0 Management Tools, and setting SMTP to start automatically. If you haven't performed these tasks on your system, please see the instructions in Exercises 3.7 and 3.8.

You can configure outgoing email for the entire server farm and for a specific web application. Alerts from the entire farm can serve all of your SharePoint users, and if you choose to configure outgoing alerts on a web application basis, you can divide users into groups so that only the required group will receive alerts from a specific application.

Both tasks can be performed either using Central Administration or using the command-line.

Setting up the outgoing email feature allows SharePoint to notify you and your users of specific events, letting you track changes and updates in various site collections. Exercise 3.10 will show you the details. You must be a member of the Farm Administrators group on the server running Central Administration to successfully complete this exercise.

EXERCISE 3.10

Configuring Outgoing Email in Central Administration

1. Navigate to Central Administration; on the main page, click System Settings.

2. On the System Settings page, under E-mail And Text Messages (SMS), click Configure Outgoing E-mail Settings.

3. On the Outgoing E-mail Settings page, under Mail Settings, type the SMTP server name for outgoing email in the Outbound SMTP Server field in the format **mail.test.com**.

4. Type the display email address in the From Address field.

5. Type the email address users will send replies to in the Reply-To Address field.

6. In the Character Set list, select the character set that most closely fits your language.

EXERCISE 3.10 *(continued)*

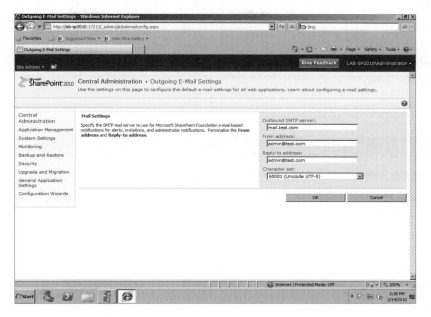

7. When you are finished, click OK.

You can perform the same task using the `Stsadm.exe` command-line tool. Microsoft doesn't specifically require that you use Windows PowerShell. Exercise 3.11 outlines the steps. You must have the same level of access as you did for Exercise 3.10. You must be on the server computer that contains SharePoint.

EXERCISE 3.11

Configuring Outgoing Email Using the Stsadm.exe Command-Line Tool

1. Open the command-line utility and navigate to %COMMONPROGRAMFILES%\Microsoft shared\Web server extensions\14\Bin.

2. At the command prompt, type the following; then press Enter:

stsadm –o email –outsmtpserver <SMTP server name> –fromaddress <valid e-mail address> –replytoaddress <valid e-mail address> –codepage <valid code page>

An example of the input string is **stsadm -o email -outsmtpserver mail.test.com -fromaddress person@test.com -replytoaddress person@test.com -codepage 50500**.

Although you can configure outgoing email for the entire server farm, you can also do so on the level of a specific web application. Exercise 3.12 shows you how. Before beginning this exercise, you will need to configure basic outgoing email as described in either Exercise 3.10 or 3.11. You must be a member of the Farm Administrators group on the server computer containing Central Administration.

EXERCISE 3.12

Configuring Outgoing Email for a Web Application in Central Administration

1. Navigate to Central Administration; under Application Management, click Manage Web Applications.

2. On the Web Applications Management page, select the desired web application. Open the General Settings drop-down menu on the Ribbon and then click Outgoing E-Mail.

3. When the Web Application Outgoing E-Mail Settings box appears, type the email address you want email recipients to see in the From Address field.

4. Type the email address you want recipients to reply to in the Reply-To Address field.

5. In the Character Set list, select the character set that best matches your language.

6. Click OK.

To perform the same task using the Stsadm.exe command-line utility, follow the steps in Exercise 3.13.

EXERCISE 3.13

Configuring Outgoing Email for a Web Application Using the Stsadm.exe Command-Line Tool

1. Open the command-line utility and navigate to %COMMONPROGRAMFILES%\Microsoft shared\Web server extensions\14\Bin.

2. At the command prompt, type the following; then press Enter:

```
stsadm -o email -outsmtpserver <SMTP server name> -fromaddress <valid email
address> -replytoaddress <valid email address> -codepage <valid code page>
-url <url name>
```

An example of the input string is **stsadm -o email -outsmtpserver mail.test.com -fromaddress person@test.com -replytoaddress person@test.com -codepage 50500 -url http://server_urlname.**

Configuring Mobile Accounts for SharePoint

When you configured SharePoint for outgoing emails, you gave SharePoint the ability to notify users of changes to libraries and lists at the requests of those users. New in SharePoint Server 2010 is the ability to send the same alerts to a user's mobile device using the *Short Message Service (SMS)*. Setting up alerts to be sent to mobile devices lets your workforce receive information and react quickly to changes in SharePoint.

You can configure these alerts to be sent either from the entire server farm or from a selected web application. Alerts from the entire farm can serve all your SharePoint users, and if you choose to configure outgoing alerts on a web application basis, you can divide users into groups so that only the required group will receive alerts from a specific application.

Mobile alerts are usually sent from a company intranet to onsite users. If a mobile user is away from the company site, users may not receive the alerts.

Many but not all of the tasks for creating a mobile account, retrieving mobile account information, and deleting a mobile account can be performed in both Central Administration and with Windows PowerShell.

Creating and Configuring Mobile Accounts

Creating a mobile account can be accomplished either using Central Administration or using a Windows PowerShell cmdlet. Exercise 3.14 shows you how to do it in Central Administration. You must be a member of the Farm Administrators group on the computer server containing Central Administration.

EXERCISE 3.14

Creating a Mobile Account for the Server Farm in Central Administration

1. Navigate to Central Administration and click System Settings.

2. On the System Settings page, under Email And Text Messages (SMS), click Configure Mobile Account.

3. On the Mobile Account page, under Text Message (SMS) Service Settings, click the Microsoft Office Online link.

4. When the Find An Office 2010 Mobile Service Provider page appears, use the Choose Your Wireless Service Provider's Country/Region list to select the required country or region.

EXERCISE 3.14 *(continued)*

5. In the Choose Your Current Wireless Service Provider list, select the required wireless service provider.

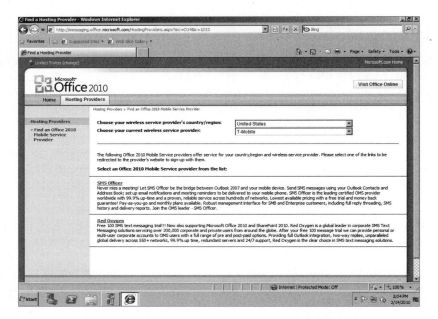

6. When you are taken to the provider's website, apply for the SMS service.

7. After you receive the required information from the service provider, return to the Central Administration Mobile Accounts Settings page.

8. Type the URL of the SMS service in the URL Of The Text Message (SMS) Service field beginning with **https://**.

9. Type the username and password you received from the SMS service provider in the User Name and Password fields available.

10. Click Test Service to verify that the connection and authentication information is correct.

11. When finished, click OK.

You can perform the same task using Windows PowerShell cmdlets. Exercise 3.15 goes through the steps. In addition to being an administrator on the local server containing Central Administration and being a member of the Farm Administrators group, you must be a member of the SharePoint_Shell_access role on the configuration database and a member of the WSS_ADMIN_WPG local group on the computer where SharePoint 2010 Products is installed.

EXERCISE 3.15

Creating a Mobile Account for the Server Farm Using Windows PowerShell

1. Click Start ➤ Microsoft SharePoint 2010 Products and then click SharePoint 2010 Management Shell.

2. At the command prompt, type the following; then press Enter:

```
set-spmobilemessagingaccount -identity sms -webapplication <http://
centraladministrationurl> -serviceurl <https://serviceproviderurl> -userID
<username> -password <userpassword>
```

An example of the required code is **set-spmobilemessagingaccount -identity sms -webapplication http://centralserver:8080 -serviceurl https://www.provider.com/omsservice.asmx -userID person@test.com -password abc1234**.

After you create the mobile account, you must perform some configuration tasks if you want the mobile account to receive notices from a web application. You can also edit a mobile account using these steps. Exercise 3.16 provides the instructions. You must be a member of the Farm Administrators group on the computer containing Central Administration to successfully complete this exercise.

EXERCISE 3.16

Using Central Administration to Configure a Mobile Account to Receive Notices from a Web Application

1. Navigate to Central Administration; under Application Management, click Manage Web Applications.

2. On the Web Applications page, open the General Settings menu on the Ribbon and then click Mobile Account.

3. In the Web Application Text Message (SMS) Service Settings box, click the Microsoft Office Online link.

4. When the Find An Office 2010 Mobile Service Provider page offers you the Choose Your Wireless Service Provider's Country/Region list, select the required country or region.

5. Select the desired wireless service provider in the Choose Your Current Wireless Service Provider list.

6. On the service provider's web page, acquire the necessary information; then return to the Central Administration Mobile Accounts Settings page and enter the data.

7. Type the SMS service provider's URL in the URL Of The Text Message (SMS) Service field, starting with **https://**.

8. Enter the user's credentials in the User Name and Password fields.

9. Verify that the connection and authentication information is correct by clicking Test Service.

10. When finished, click OK.

As you can see, the process is substantially similar to creating a mobile account to receive messages from the server farm, except that the steps were performed for the specific web application. The same task can be done using Windows PowerShell cmdlets, and the task is virtually identical to the one you performed in Exercise 3.15. The only difference is that for -webapplication, instead of entering the URL for Central Administration, you enter the URL for the web application.

You can retrieve mobile account information for both a server farm and a web application using Windows PowerShell using the command get-spmobilemessagingaccount -webapplication. To retrieve information from the server farm, after -webapplication, enter the URL of Central Administration. To retrieve information from a web application, after -webapplication, enter the URL of the web application.

Deleting a Mobile Account

Deleting a mobile account configured to receive notices from either the server farm or a web application pretty much involves the same set of steps, and both actions are performed in Central Administration. To delete a mobile account from a server farm, follow these steps:

1. On the Central Administration main page, click System Settings.

2. On the System Settings page, under E-mail And Text Messages (SMS), click Configure Mobile Account.

3. On the Mobile Account Settings page, clear all the check boxes present and then click OK.

To delete a mobile account from a web application, follow these steps:

1. In Central Administration, under Application Management, click Manage Web Applications.

2. Open the General Settings menu on the Ribbon and then click Mobile Account.

3. On the Web application Text Message (SMS) Service Settings page, clear all the check boxes and then click OK.

Installing and Configuring Remote BLOB Storage

I'm sure you realize that nothing is perfect. That includes Microsoft SQL Server, and even if you believe it's the best database server in the world, it can still get overloaded and crowded with data. It also doesn't deal as well with unstructured binary files as it does with structured data, and a lot of data is unstructured in binary large object (BLOB) files. If only there were some way of using an external data store to contain those binary data files for SharePoint. Now there is.

Installing and configuring Remote BLOB Storage (RBS) lets you store your BLOB data with an EBS provider so that both your structured and unstructured data is being placed in, housed in, and retrieved from the optimal storage types for those data forms.

This doesn't mean that you absolutely must use RBS, and you certainly can store your unstructured data files in SQL, but it's not the best solution available, particularly if data access and retrieval is important, and it almost always is. Although setting up RBS may be more work, it often is worth the effort. If you choose to employ the RBS option, you face three basic tasks:

1. Enabling the FILESTREAM and provisioning the RBS data store
2. Installing the RBS
3. Enabling and testing the RBS

RBS is a library application programming interface (API). It's integrated as an add-on feature for both Microsoft SQL Server 2008 and Microsoft SQL Server 2008 Express and is designed to move BLOB data stored on database servers to what is called *commodity storage solutions* or *third-party RBS storage*. RBS comes with the RBS FILESTREAM provider, which uses the RBS APIs to store BLOBs.

This work is done on Microsoft SQL Server, and as a SharePoint administrator, you may not have a hand in performing the following tasks. However, since this feature is tied directly to SharePoint Server 2010, the information is presented, and in a small enough company or in a large company with limited IT resources, you may need to have these skills.

The following tasks require that you belong to the Administrators group for all the web servers and application servers in the server farm. You must also belong to the dbcreator and securityadmin fixed server roles on the computer running SQL Server 2008 or SQL Server 2008 Express.

Enabling the FILESTREAM and Provisioning the RBS Data Store

The first task you must perform is to enable *FILESTREAM* on the SQL Server instance:

1. On the computer running SQL Server, click Start ➤ All Programs; in the list that appears, click Microsoft SQL Server 2008.
2. In the list that appears, click Configuration Tools and then click SQL Server Configuration Manager.
3. In the SQL Server Configuration Manager, locate the desired SQL Server, right-click it, and then click Properties.

4. In the SQL Server Properties dialog box, click the FILESTREAM tab and then select the Enable FILESTREAM For Transact-SQL Access check box.

5. Click Enable FILESTREAM for file I/O streaming access and then enter the name of the Windows share in the Windows Share Name field if you want to read and write FILESTREAM data from Windows.

6. Select Allow Remote Clients To Have Streaming Access To FILESTREAM Data if remote clients are required to access FILESTREAM data on the share.

7. Click Apply.

8. Click Start ➢ All Programs ➢ Microsoft SQL Server and then select SQL Server Management Studio.

9. In SQL Server Management Studio, click New Query to open the Query Editor.

10. In the Query Editor, enter the following and then click Execute:

```
EXEC sp_configure filestream_access_level, 2
RECONFIGURE[
```

Now that FILESTREAM is enabled, you need to provision the BLOB store in SQL Server:

1. On the SQL Server instance, open the SQL Server Management Studio as shown in step 8 of the previous task and then expand Databases.

2. Select the content database for which you want to create the BLOB store and then click New Query.

3. In the Query pane, enter and execute each of the following SQL queries in the sequence you see here. You must replace [WSS_Content] with the actual content database name and replace c:\BLOBStore with the volume/directory where you want the BLOB store created.

WARNING You can provision a BLOB store only once, so it's important that you are exact in your execution the first time. If you try to provision the same BLOB store more than once, you will receive an error message. You will have better success if you create the BLOB store on a volume dedicated for the task and not containing an operating system, applications, paging files, log files, or other file types.

```
use [WSS_Content]
if not exists (select * from sys.symmetric_keys where name = N'##MS_
DatabaseMasterKey##')create master key encryption by password = N'Admin Key
Password !2#4'


use [WSS_Content]
if not exists (select groupname from sysfilegroups where groupname=N'RBSFiles
treamProvider')alter database [WSS_Content]
 add filegroup RBSFilestreamProvider contains filestream
```

```
use [WSS_Content]

alter database [WSS_Content] add file (name = RBSFilestreamFile, filename =
'c:\Blobstore') to filegroup RBSFilestreamProvider
```

> You can also copy this code online at http://technet.microsoft.com/
> en-us/library/ee748631(office.14).aspx and then paste it in the
> Query pane.

Installing the RBS

Now that you've enabled FILESTREAM and provisioned the BLOB store on the SQL
server, you must install RBS on all the web servers and application servers in your
SharePoint server farm as well as your database server.

Installing RBS on the Database Server and First Web Server

1. Select a web server in your farm, open a web browser, navigate to http://go.microsoft
   .com/fwlink/?LinkID=165839&clcid=0x409, and then download the RBS_X64.msi file.

> Do not install RBS by running RBS_X64.msi and then launching the Install
> SQL Remote BLOB Storage Wizard because the wizard imposes specific
> default values that will not work well with SharePoint Server 2010.

2. On the server, click Start and in the text field type **command prompt**.
3. In the list of results, right-click Command Prompt, click Run As Administrator, and
   then click Yes in the dialog box that appears.
4. Enter the following at the command prompt and then press Enter, using the name
   of the required database instead of WSS_Content and using the SQL Server instance
   name instead of DBInstanceName, doing so once only.
   ```
   msiexec /qn /lvx* rbs_install_log.txt /i RBS_X64.msi
   TRUSTSERVERCERTIFICATE=true
   FILEGROUP=PRIMARY DBNAME="WSS_Content"
   DBINSTANCE="DBInstanceName"
   FILESTREAMFILEGROUP=RBSFilestreamProvider
   FILESTREAMSTORENAME=FilestreamProvider_1
   ```

> You can also copy this code online at http://technet.microsoft.com/
> en-us/library/ee748631(office.14).aspx.

Once you've performed those steps, it should take about one minute for the action
to execute.

Installing RBS on All Web Servers and Application Servers

The process of installing RBS on all the remaining servers in your server farm is almost identical. At each server, you must download the RBS_X64.msi file and then run a specific command at the command line as administrator. Only the code string is different, and you want go to the URL cited in the previous note to download that string, replacing WSS_Content with the database name and replacing DBInstanceName with the name of the SQL Server instance.

```
msiexec /qn /lvx* rbs_install_log.txt /i RBS_X64.msi
DBNAME="WSS_Content"
DBINSTANCE="DBInstanceName" ADDLOCAL="Client,Docs,Maintainer,ServerScript,
FilestreamClient,FilestreamServer"
```

You must perform this task on all your web and application servers.

To confirm the installation on each server, you must go to the same location as the RBS_X64.msi file and locate the rbs_install_log.txt log file, which is created in the same directory. Open the file with a text editor, and within the last 20 lines of the log file, locate the entry "Product: SQL Remote Blob Storage – Installation completed successfully."

On the computer running SQL Server 2008, verify that the RBS tables were created in the content database. The table names should all be preceded with *mssqlrbs*.

Enabling and Testing RBS

After performing multiple, repetitive tasks on all the servers in your server farm, you must enable and test RBS on only one web server with RBS installed. It doesn't matter which web server you select.

Enabling RBS on a Web Server

On a web server, open Windows PowerShell. At the command prompt enter the following and press Enter, replacing http://sitename with the URL to the web application connected to the content database:

```
$cdb = Get-SPContentDatabase -WebApplication http://sitename
$rbss = $cdb.RemoteBlobStorageSettings
$rbss.Installed()
$rbss.Enable()
$rbss.SetActiveProviderName($rbss.GetProviderNames()[0])
$rbss
```

Testing the RBS Store

These steps are performed on the SQL Server computer:

1. Click Start ➢ All Programs ➢ Microsoft SQL Server 2008 and then click SQL Server Management Studio.
2. In the Management Studio, expand Databases.

3. Select the content database on which you enabled RBS and then click New Query.

4. Navigate to the RBS data store directory.

5. Navigate to the file list and open the most recently modified folder, besides $FSLOG.

6. Within the selected folder, open the most recently modified file, which should be the file you just uploaded.

That concludes the primary post-installation or upgrade server farm tasks. Next, you'll proceed to configuring service applications and host sites.

Summary

In this chapter, you saw the various post-installation or post-upgrade tasks that are performed on the SharePoint Server 2010 server farm.

- Enabling and configuring usage and health data collection

- Enabling and configuring diagnostic logging

- Configuring incoming email to allow SharePoint users to send information to lists and libraries directly from Outlook

- Configuring outgoing email to let users and administrators receive alerts when anything changes in the SharePoint environment

- Configuring mobile accounts to receive alerts from the server farm or from specific web applications

- Installing and configuring Remote BLOB Storage (RBS) to allow database servers to offload unstructured data to third-party data stores

Exam Essentials

Understanding the Various Post-installation or Post-upgrade Tasks That Must Be Performed in the SharePoint Server 2010 Server Farm   Review and perform all of the mandatory and some or all of the optional tasks in the server farm after installing SharePoint Server 2010 or performing an upgrade from MOSS 2007.

Configuring Both Server Farm–Level and Web Application–Level Tasks after Installation or Upgrade   Perform the mandatory and optional post-installation or post-upgrade tasks in SharePoint Server 2010 that offer the same or similar services from either the server farm level or the web application level.

Review Questions

1. You are a SharePoint Server 2010 administrator for your organization, and you've recently completed installing your SharePoint platform. Now you are in the process of performing post-installation tasks on the server farm. You want to set up usage and health data collection and are determining the different methods of performing these tasks. Of the following, which are appropriate methods of setting up usage and health data collection? (Choose all that apply.)

   A. Set up usage and health data collection for the server farm using Central Administration.

   B. Set up usage and health data collection using Windows PowerShell.

   C. Set up usage data collection in Central Administration and health data collection using Windows PowerShell.

   D. Set up usage data collection in Windows PowerShell and health data collection using Central Administration.

2. You are a SharePoint Server 2010 administrator for your organization, and you've recently completed installing your SharePoint platform. Now you are in the process of performing post-installation tasks on the server farm. You start to set up diagnostic logging using Central Administration. You are in the process of configuring how long the system will store diagnostic log files. Of the following options, which one is the most correct?

   A. Choose the default of 7 days.

   B. Choose the default of 14 days.

   C. Override the default of 10 days and choose 21 days.

   D. Override the default of 21 days and choose 10 days.

3. You are a SharePoint Server 2010 administrator for your organization, and you've recently completed installing your SharePoint platform. Now you are in the process of performing post-installation tasks on the server farm. You are in the process of setting up diagnostic logging in Central Administration, but because of a lack of familiarity in using the tool, you have made configuration settings for event throttling that do not fit your technical plan for the deployment. How can you reset the configuration to the default values in Central Administration so you can begin again?

   A. You can select the All Categories check box for event throttling and then select the Reset To Default option in the menus for both Least Critical Event To Report To The Event Log and Least Critical Event To Report To The Trace Log.

   B. You can select the All Categories check box for event throttling and then select the Reset To Defaults check box that appears beneath it.

   C. You can select the All Categories check box for event throttling and then select the Reset To Default check boxes under both the Least Critical Event To Report To The Event Log and Least Critical Event To Report To The Trace Log lists.

   D. At the bottom of the Configure Diagnostic Logging page, you must click the Reset To Defaults button, close the Configure Diagnostic Logging page, and then reopen the page to reset the settings to their default values.

4. You are a SharePoint Server 2010 administrator for your organization, and you've recently completed installing your SharePoint platform. Now you are in the process of performing post-installation tasks on the server farm. You have already set up diagnostic logging in Central Administration. One of your staff would like to review the diagnostic log settings using Windows PowerShell. What procedure do you tell her to use?

   A. You tell her to open Windows PowerShell on the server housing Central Administration, type **View-SPLogLevel** at the prompt, and then press Enter.

   B. You tell her to open Windows PowerShell on the server housing Central Administration, type **Clear-SPLogLevel** at the prompt, and then press Enter.

   C. You tell her to open Windows PowerShell on the server housing Central Administration, type **Get-SPLogLevel** at the prompt, and then press Enter.

   D. Diagnostic log settings can be viewed only from Central Administration, so you tell her to navigate to the Configure Diagnostic Logging page in Central Administration to view the settings.

5. You are a SharePoint Server 2010 administrator for your company, and you have recently deployed SharePoint for your organization. You are in the process of performing post-installation tasks on the server farm. You want to configure incoming email integration so your users can add content to SharePoint using their Outlook email clients. Of the following, which are required prerequisites before setting up incoming email? (Choose all that apply.)

   A. At least one server in the server farm must be running the SMTP service and the Windows SharePoint Services Web Application service.

   B. Each frontend web server must be running the SMTP service and the Windows SharePoint Services Web Application service.

   C. If you choose not to run the SMTP service on one of the farm servers, you must have access to and know the name of another server running the SMTP service.

   D. The application pool identity account in Central Administration must be a member of the Administrators group on the local computer containing the email drop folder.

6. You are a SharePoint Server 2010 administrator for your company, and you have recently deployed SharePoint for your organization. You are in the process of performing post-installation tasks on the server farm. You want to configure incoming email integration. What is the first step you must take for this task?

   A. You must install the SMTP service on all frontend web servers in your server farm that you want to be able to use incoming emails.

   B. You must install the SMTP service on all frontend web servers in your server farm, regardless of whether they will be using incoming emails.

   C. You must install the SMTP service on all application servers in your server farm that you want to be able to use incoming emails.

   D. You must install the SMTP service on all application servers in your server farm, regardless of whether they will be using incoming emails.

7. You are a SharePoint Server 2010 administrator for your company, and you have recently deployed SharePoint for your organization. You are in the process of performing post-installation tasks on the server farm. You want to configure incoming email integration. You are at the step in the process where you must install the SMTP service on one of your servers. Of the following options, which one is the correct procedure?

    A. Navigate to Central Administration; under E-Mail And Text Messages (SMS), click Enable Incoming Emails.

    B. Navigate to Central Administration. Under System Settings, click Enable Incoming Emails. Then, on the Incoming Emails page, select the Enable SMTP Service check box.

    C. On the desired server in Administrative Tools, click Server Manager. In the Server Manager, select the SMTP Server check box.

    D. On the desired server in Administrative Tools, click Server Manager, click Add Features, and select the SMTP Server check box when the wizard launches.

8. You are a SharePoint Server 2010 administrator for your company, and you have recently deployed SharePoint for your organization. You are in the process of performing post-installation tasks on the server farm. You want to configure incoming email integration. You are at the step in the process where you must install the SMTP service on one of your servers. During the installation process, what required component is also set up?

    A. Dynamic Host Configuration Protocol (DHCP)

    B. Domain Name System (DNS)

    C. Internet Information Services (IIS)

    D. Transmission Control Protocol (TCP)

9. You are a SharePoint Server 2010 administrator for your company, and you have recently deployed SharePoint for your organization. You are in the process of performing post-installation tasks on the server farm. You want to configure incoming email integration. You are at the step in the process where you must configure the SMTP service on one of your servers. In what manager must you perform the configuration?

    A. The SMTP Manager

    B. The IIS Manager

    C. The SQL Manager

    D. The IP Manager

10. You are the SharePoint Server 2010 administrator for your organization. You have installed SharePoint as a single server with a built-in database in order to do sandbox testing prior to a full-scale production deployment. You are currently configuring basic incoming email services. Of the following, which options are required for just a basic configuration? (Choose all that apply.)

    A. In Central Administration, you must configure the name of the email server in E-Mail And Text Messages (SMS).

    B. In Central Administration, you must enable incoming emails to be automatic in E-Mail And Text Messages (SMS).

    C. In the DNS Manager, you must add a DNS host (A) resource record.

    D. In the Internet Information Services (IIS) 6.0 Manager, you must create a local domain.

11. You are the SharePoint Server 2010 administrator for your organization, and you have recently completed installing SharePoint as a production deployment. You are in the process of performing post-installation tasks for the server farm and are configuring the outgoing email feature. Of the following, which are required prerequisites to enable outgoing email? (Choose all that apply).

   A. At least one server in the server farm must be running the SMTP service and the Windows SharePoint Services Web Application service.

   B. Each frontend web server must be running the SMTP service and the Windows SharePoint Services Web Application service.

   C. If you choose not to run the SMTP service on one of the farm servers, you must have access to and know the name of another server running the SMTP service.

   D. The application pool identity account of Central Administration must be a member of the Administrators group on the local computer containing the email drop folder.

12. You are the SharePoint Server 2010 administrator for your organization, and you have recently completed installing SharePoint as a production deployment. You are in the process of performing post-installation tasks for the server farm and are configuring the outgoing email feature. Of the following options, which are true for the outgoing email feature? (Choose all that apply.)

   A. You can configure outgoing email for the server farm in Central Administration.

   B. You can configure outgoing email for an individual web application in Central Administration.

   C. You can configure outgoing email for the server farm using the `Stsadm.exe` command-line.

   D. You can configure outgoing email for an individual web application using the `Stsadm.exe` command-line tool.

13. You are the SharePoint Server 2010 administrator for your organization, and you have recently completed installing SharePoint as a production deployment. You are in the process of performing post-installation tasks for the server farm and have configured the outgoing email feature. You also want to set up mobile accounts for SharePoint so SharePoint users can receive notices from SharePoint in their mobile devices. Of the following options, which ones are true about configuring mobile accounts? (Choose all that apply.)

   A. Configuring mobile accounts in SharePoint is a required server farm task.

   B. You can use Windows PowerShell to configure SharePoint to send notices to mobile accounts from a web application.

   C. You can use Windows PowerShell to configure SharePoint to send notices to mobile accounts from the server farm.

   D. You can use Windows PowerShell to retrieve mobile account information from the server farm and a web application.

14. You are the SharePoint Server 2010 administrator for your organization, and you are conducting post-installation tasks for the server farm. You want to enable Remote BLOB Storage (RBS) so you can store unstructured data on a third-party platform, rather than your SQL Server instance. Of the following, which options are generally true of installing and setting up RBS? (Choose all that apply.)

   A. You must enable FILESTREAM on SQL Server.

   B. You must provision the BLOB store in Central Administration.

   C. You must install RBS on your web servers and your application servers.

   D. You can enable RBS on a web server from Windows PowerShell.

15. You are the SharePoint Server 2010 administrator for your organization, and you are conducting post-installation tasks for the server farm. You have just enabled Remote BLOB Storage (RBS), and now you want to test the RBS store. Select the correct method for performing the test.

   A. On the SQL Server computer in SQL Server Management Studio, right-click Databases and then click test RBS.

   B. On the SQL Server computer in SQL Server Management Studio, expand Databases, right-click RGB, and then click Test.

   C. On the SQL Server computer in SQL Server Management Studio, expand Databases, select the desired content database, click New Query, and in the RBS data store directory look for the most recently modified folder.

   D. On the SQL Server computer in SQL Server Management Studio, right-click Databases, select the desired content database and right-click it, click Properties, select the RBS Data Store tab, and look for the most recently modified item in the list that appears.

16. You are the SharePoint Server 2010 administrator for your organization, and you are conducting post-installation tasks for the server farm. You want to enable Remote BLOB Storage (RBS). You are discussing this new SharePoint feature with your staff members, who are unfamiliar with RBS. Of the following, what information is true about RBS? (Choose all that apply.)

   A. RBS is a library API.

   B. RBS is an SDK.

   C. RBS is an integrated add-on service for Microsoft SQL Server 2008.

   D. RBS is an optional plug-in for Microsoft SQL Server 2008 Express.

17. You are the SharePoint Server 2010 administrator for your organization, and you are conducting post-installation tasks for the server farm. You want to enable Remote BLOB Storage (RBS) and understand that your first task is to enable FILESTREAM. Of the following, which options are true about this task? (Choose all that apply.)

    A. To enable FILESTREAM in SQL Server, the first thing you do is open SQL Server Configuration Manager.

    B. To enable FILESTREAM in SQL Server, the first thing you do is open SQL Server Management Studio.

    C. To enable FILESTREAM in SQL Server, the last thing you do is open SQL Server Configuration Manager and run a query.

    D. To enable FILESTREAM in SQL Server, the last thing you do is open SQL Server Management Studio and run a query.

18. One of the advanced tasks for configuring incoming email is creating a local domain if, when you created an A resource record for DNS, the domain for the SMTP server in IIS didn't match the FQDN entered for the mail server. Of the following, which options are true about the task of creating a local domain? (Choose all that apply.)

    A. You must create a local domain in the Internet Information Services (IIS) 6.0 Manager.

    B. Once you have finished creating the local domain, you must restart the SMTP service.

    C. You must create the local domain in the Simple Mail Transport Protocol (SMTP) Manager.

    D. Once you have finished creating the local domain, you must restart the IIS service.

19. If you plan to use the SharePoint Directory Management Services and Active Directory as part of an advanced incoming email feature setup, one required task is to create an organizational unit (OU) and delegate Create, Delete, And Manage User Accounts to Central Administration. Of the following, which options are generally true about this task? (Choose all that apply.)

    A. You will need to work on a computer that is a domain controller.

    B. You will need to start the task in the DNS Manager.

    C. You can use Directory Management Services on either a server farm or a remote server farm.

    D. You will finish the task in the Delegation Of Control Wizard.

20. You are the SharePoint Administrator for your organization, and you are about to perform post-installation tasks for your server farm. You are describing how to set up usage data collection to your staff as part of that process. Of the following, which options are true about configuring usage data collection? (Choose all that apply.)

    A. You can configure usage data collection for a single event type using Windows PowerShell.

    B. You can change the database used by usage data collection using Windows PowerShell.

    C. You must be a member of the Farm Administrators group to configure usage data collection using Windows PowerShell.

    D. You must be a member of the SQL Server Administrators group to configure usage data collection using Windows PowerShell.

Answers to Review Questions

1. **A, B, D.** Although you can set up usage data collection independently in Windows Power-Shell, you can't set up health data collection independently in PowerShell. All other options are correct.

2. **B.** Option B is the most correct answer because the default value is 14 days. All the other options provide bogus information.

3. **A.** Option A is the correct procedure. All other options are bogus.

4. **C.** Option A is not a valid command, and using option B will reset the diagnostic log setting to their defaults. Option D is bogus.

5. **B, C, D.** Option A would have been correct if it had said that at least one server in the farm must be running the SMTP service and must be using a valid SMTP server address.

6. **A.** The SMTP service needs to be installed on web servers in the farm only if you want those servers to use the incoming email service, not on all servers. Options C and D are bogus.

7. **D.** You cannot perform this task from Central Administration, since you must install the SMTP service on each of the server computers on which you want to run the service. Option C is a bogus method.

8. **C.** During the Add Features Wizard when you're installing SMTP, the IIS tools component is also included. All the other options are bogus.

9. **B.** On the servers for which you've installed the SMTP service, you must configure the service in the Internet Information Services (IIS) 6.0 Manager. All other options are bogus.

10. **A, B.** You would perform the tasks described in options C and D for advanced incoming email configuration. For the basic configuration, they are not necessary.

11. **B, C, D.** Enabling outgoing emails has the same prerequisites as enabling incoming emails as far as the SMTP service goes.

12. **A, B, C, D.** All options are true. Windows PowerShell is not required to perform the command-line configuration of the outgoing email feature.

13. **B, C, D.** Configuring mobile accounts in SharePoint is an optional task. All other options are correct.

14. **A, C, D.** You must provision the BLOB store on the SQL Server instance and not from Central Administration in SharePoint. All other options are correct.

15. **C.** All of the options besides C are bogus.

16. **A, C.** RBS is a library API and is an integrated add-on feature for both Microsoft SQL Server 2008 and Microsoft SQL Server 2008 Express. It is not an optional plug-in.

17. A, D. You begin to enable FILESTREAM in SQL Server using SQL Server Configuration Manager and finish the job by running a query in SQL Server Management Studio.

18. A, B. The options for C and D are bogus.

19. A, C, D. You start the task in Active Directory Users And Computers, not the DNS Manager.

20. A, B. While you can configure usage data collection for a single even and change the database used for data collection using Windows PowerShell, the required permissions do not include being a member of the Farm Administrators group or the SQL Server Administration group.

Chapter

4

Configuring Service Applications

MICROSOFT EXAM OBJECTIVE COVERED IN THIS CHAPTER:

✓ **Maintaining a SharePoint Environment**

  ▪ Configure Service Applications

We live in a world driven by information, and that, in part, is why you are reading this book and pursuing a certification in information technology. Yet we also are in a world where that information is supposed to provide some sort of service—and so it is with the technology of SharePoint.

SharePoint is designed to provide specific services to its users, and in SharePoint Server 2010, you can select just those services your users, partners, and customers require. This chapter focuses on configuring resources that can be shared across sites within your server farm or even across multiple farms.

There are really two large and related portions to this chapter. The first part addresses the post-installation or post-upgrade tasks associated with service application configuration and services. This is much like laying the foundation so you have a platform on which to build. The other part is the actual services application management, which includes both configuring service applications and creating and configuring individual application services.

Service Applications Configuration Overview

Just when you think you've gotten past configuring your server farm, you are still faced with the Farm Configuration Wizard. This is a quick and straightforward way to deploy services on your server farm. You'll take a brief look at this wizard before proceeding to the next steps in service configuration.

Service applications and web applications are associated by *service application connections*. Services on a server are stopped, started, and managed individually. Central Administration and Windows PowerShell are both used to manage services and to create service application connections between a service application and a web application. You will also need to configure the *Security Token Service (STS)* to respond to requests for security tokens.

 The configuration of individual services such as Access Services and Excel Services will be covered in the second half of this chapter.

Server Farm Configuration Wizard

The quickest and easiest way to enable all of your major services in the SharePoint server farm is to use the SharePoint Farm Configuration Wizard. This simple and powerful tool lets you deploy major services such as Excel Services and Visio Graphics Services to the entire farm. Exercise 4.1 will show you how it works.

EXERCISE 4.1

Using the Farm Configuration Wizard

1. Navigate to Central Administration. In the Quick Launch menu on the left, click Configuration Wizards.

2. On Configuration Wizards page, click Launch The Farm Configuration Wizard.

3. On the Configure Your SharePoint Farm page, select Walk Me Through The Settings Using This Wizard; then click Next.

4. Under Service Account, select either Use Existing Managed Account or Create New Managed Account. Then enter a username and password of an account with farm administrator permissions in the available fields.

5. Use the available check boxes to select the desired services; then click Next. Many of the services may already be selected and unavailable to be deselected.

6. When the Create Site Collection page appears, you can click Skip and create the first site collection later, or you can create the first site collection during the wizard.

7. To create the first site collection, give the site collection a name in the Title field.

8. Add an optional description in the Description field.

9. Under Web Site Address, append the URL with a descriptive name for the site collection URL in the URL field.

10. Under Template Selection, choose the desired template tab, choose the desired template, and then click OK.

11. When you get to the last page of the wizard showing you a list of services running on the site collection, click Finish.

The Farm Configuration Wizard is used to add services only. Once the services are added, you cannot run the wizard again to remove services. If you run the wizard and see that services are selected and grayed out, it means the services have already been configured for the farm, either because you set them up in a prior run of the wizard or because you configured the services through some other means. If you need to remove services, you can do so manually.

Service Applications and Services

Managing the individual services running on each server in your farm and creating and managing service applications to be used as resources by SharePoint web applications go hand in hand. This section of the chapter walks you through the process of starting and configuring services and then moves on to managing service applications and beyond.

Initial Configuration of Services

The tasks related to managing the services running on servers in the farm range from starting or stopping a specific service to configuring global services. Exercise 4.2 illustrates how to stop and start a service using Central Administration. You must be a member of the Farm Administrators group to successfully perform this task.

EXERCISE 4.2

Stopping and Starting a Service in Central Administration

1. Navigate to Central Administration. On the main page, click System Settings.

2. On the System Settings page, click Manage Services On Server under Servers.

3. To select the server for which you want to configure services, click Change Server in the Server menu and then select the desired server's name.

4. Open the View list and either select Configurable to view just configurable services or select All to view all services, as shown here.

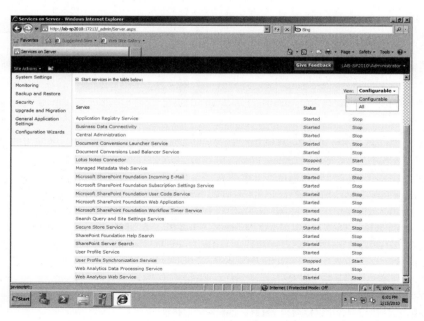

5. In the Action column, click Start or Stop, depending on what you want to do with the desired service or services.

6. If a confirmation dialog box appears, click OK.

You can perform the same actions from Windows PowerShell. Exercise 4.3 takes you through the steps. You will need to know the GUID of the service you want to manage. You will also need to be a member of the SharePoint_Shell_Access role on the configuration database and a member of the WSS_ADMIN_WPG local group on the computer containing SharePoint 2010 to successfully accomplish this task.

EXERCISE 4.3

Starting and Stopping a Service in Windows PowerShell

1. Click Start ➢ All Programs ➢ Microsoft SharePoint 2010 Products; then click Share-Point Management Shell.

2. At the command prompt, type the following and afterward press Enter:

    ```
    Start-SPServiceInstance -Identity <GUID of the service >
    ```

    This starts the service.

3. Click Start ➢ All Programs ➢ Microsoft SharePoint 2010 Products; then click Share-Point Management Shell.

4. At the command prompt, type the following and afterward press Enter:

    ```
    Stop-SPServiceInstance -Identity <GUID of the service>
    ```

    This ends the service.

When you build a web application for a single purpose, you can probably hard-code everything, since your application will be accessed for only one reason. However, most of the applications in SharePoint are going to be accessed from multiple websites for multiple reasons, so the settings for these applications must be more accessible so they'll apply to all sites contained within a web application.

Some of the services running on your server farm machines have global settings that require more complex management procedures. The following series of exercises will show you how this is done under the hood, using the general task of configuring global workflow settings as an example.

Configuring Global Workflow Settings Example

Workflows in SharePoint are a series of associated tasks that produce a single outcome by automating the progress of an item or document through a sequence of checks or actions related to a business goal. For example, a documenter or other content contributor may submit a deliverable for review and approval. The reviewers, such as development and technical editors, each will have an approve or reject option, so each person controls a portion of the workflow.

Each approver can receive the content from the contributor and either approve it, sending it to the next step in the workflow, or reject it, sending it back to the contributor with suggestions for changes, which the contributor must make before resubmitting the content. At the end of the process, the contributor and the reviewers may have interacted with several revisions of the content before it completed the workflow process and was given final approval.

Workflow settings can be applied globally to all websites contained within a web application. The subsequent exercises will illustrate how to configure global application settings for workflow.

Exercise 4.4 shows you how to either enable or disable declarative workflows in SharePoint using Central Administration. This feature lets you determine whether you want users to be able to deploy declarative workflows. This means users who possess the Design permission level on a site can create and deploy their own workflows using the Workflow Editor in Microsoft SharePoint Designer 2010 or in a third-party application. You must be a member of the Farm Administrators group to successfully complete this exercise.

EXERCISE 4.4

Enabling or Disabling Declarative Workflows

1. On the Central Administration main page, click Application Management in the Quick Launch menu on the left.

2. On the Application Management page, click Manage Web Applications under Web Applications.

3. On the Web Applications Management page, select the web application you want to manage.

4. On the Ribbon in the Manage group, open the General Settings menu and select Workflow.

5. In the Workflow Settings dialog box, under User-Defined Workflows, either click Yes to enable declarative workflows for all sites in the application or click No to disable declarative workflows in the web application, as shown here.

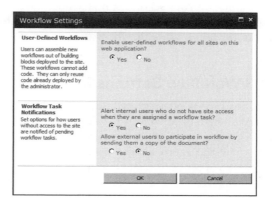

6. Click OK to close the dialog box.

Usually, only authenticated SharePoint users will receive email messages in response to workflow tasks, but you can configure workflow global settings to allow unauthenticated users to also be notified. This can be used with contributors who are external partners or customers. Exercise 4.5 provides the instructions for how to allow internal users without site access to participate in workflows. These are SharePoint users who do not have specific access to the site in which you want them to participate in workflows. You must be a member of the Farm Administrators group to successfully complete this task.

EXERCISE 4.5

Enabling Nonauthenticated Users to Participate in Workflows

1. From the Central Administration main page, click Application Management in the Quick Launch menu on the left.

2. On the Application Management page, click Manage Web Applications under Web Applications.

3. On the Web Applications Management page, select the web application you want to manage.

4. On the Ribbon in the Manage group, open the General Settings menu and select Workflow.

5. In the Workflow Settings dialog box, under Workflow Task Notifications, click Yes for the Alert Internal Users Who Do Not Have Site Access When They Are Assigned A Workflow Task? option.

6. Click OK to close the dialog box.

Each external user who you intend to access this option must also be granted minimally the Contribute permission level to the task list used by the required workflow. The setup is almost identical to what you performed in Exercise 4.5. Follow all the steps described in Exercise 4.5, but at step 5, click Yes for the Alert Internal Users Who Do Not Have Site Access When They Are Assigned A Workflow Task? option. Then complete the action described in step 6.

As previously mentioned, this is just an example of configuring global settings for an application. There are many other global setting tasks that can be accomplished in SharePoint; the following are some examples:

- Managing connections in directory services
- Managing enterprise application definitions
- Managing site directory links

Configuring specific services will be presented later in this chapter, and non-application-driven global setting configurations will be described in subsequent chapters.

Configuring the Security Token Service

The STS is a specialized web service that responds to requests for security tokens and provides identity management for web applications that use a security token service.

A security token consists of a collection of identity claims, such as a username, role, or anonymous identifier, and a security token can be issued in a variety of formats, such as Security Assertion Markup Language (SAML). Tokens must be protected with an X.509 certificate to ensure the integrity of the token's contents in transit and to validate trusted issuers.

All the Windows PowerShell code samples in this and subsequent chapters are generic and contain only example code, including the values contained between <>. Please see Chapter 15, "Working with Windows PowerShell 2.0 Administration," for details regarding how to enter production values and use "real-world" code.

An Identity Provider-STS (IP-STS) is a web service that handles requests for trusted identity claims. An IP-STS accesses an identity store, such as a database, to store and manage identities. Clients who want to create and manage identities can use the IP-STS, as can Relying Party STS (RP-STS) applications that need to validate any identities offered them by the clients.

For more information on IP-STS and RP-STS, go to http://msdn .microsoft.com/en-us/library/ee748489.aspx.

A number of tasks are associated with configuring the STS for use by web applications in SharePoint. The following example will show you how to configure a SharePoint claims-based web application. This task is performed using Windows PowerShell, so you'll need to log in to SharePoint with an account belonging to the SharePoint_Shell_Access role on the configuration database and also as a member of the WSS_ADMIN_WPG local group on the computer containing SharePoint 2010. All the code in the following exercise is example code and not meant to be run "as is" in production.

The tasks performed in this section assume that the SharePoint server farm is part of an Active Directory domain.

Configuring a SharePoint Claims-Based Web Application Using Windows PowerShell

1. Open Windows PowerShell, and at the prompt, type the following to create an X509Certificate2 object.

```
$cert = New-Object
System.Security.Cryptography.X509Certificates.X509Certificate2("path to
cert file")
```

2. Type the following example to create a claim type mapping to use in your trusted authentication provider:

```
New-SPClaimTypeMapping "http://schemas.xmlsoap.org/ws/2005/05/identity/
claims/emailaddress"
-IncomingClaimTypeDisplayName "EmailAddress" -SameAsIncoming
```

3. Type the following to create a trusted login provider, first creating the value for the realm parameter:

```
$realm = "urn:" + $env:ComputerName + ":domain-int"
```

4. Type the following to create a value for the `signinurl` parameter, pointing to the Security Token Service web application:

```
$signinurl = "https://nicstu-test-2/FederationPassive/"
```

5. Type the following to create a trusted login provider, using the same `IdentifierClaim` value as in the claim mapping:

```
$map1.InputClaimType.
$ap = New-SPTrustedIdentityTokenIssuer -Name
"WIF" -Description "Windows  Identity Foundation" -Realm

$realm -ImportTrustCertificate $cert
-ClaimsMappings $map1[,$map2..] -SignInUrl

$signinurl -IdentifierClaim $map1.InputClaimType
```

6. Type the following to create a web application, first creating a value for the application pool account for the current user, which must be a managed account:

```
$account = "DOMAIN\" + $env:UserName
```

 To create a managed account, use New-SPManagedAccount.

7. Type the following to create a value for the web application URL:

```
$wa = New-SPWebApplication -name "Claims WIF"
-SecureSocketsLayer -ApplicationPool "SharePoint SSL"
```

```
-ApplicationPoolAccount $account -Url $webappurl -Port 443
-AuthenticationProvider $ap
```

8. Type the following to create a claim object:

```
$claim = New-SPClaimsPrincipal
-TrustedIdentityTokenIssuerr $ap -Identity
$env:UserName
```

9. Type the following to create a site:

```
$site = New-SPSite $webappurl -OwnerAlias
$claim.ToEncodedString() -template "STS#0"
```

Editing Bindings and Configuring the Web.config File

Once you create the SharePoint claims-based web application as shown in the previous example, edit bindings and configure the Web.config file. You will need to be in Windows PowerShell or on the Stsadm.exe command line.

1. At the command prompt, type **INETMGR** and press Enter. When INETMGR appears in the list, double-click to open the Internet Information Services (IIS) Manager, as shown in Figure 4.1.

FIGURE 4.1   Internet Information Services (IIS) Manager

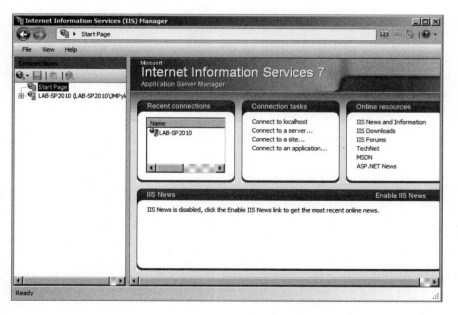

2. Right-click Claims Web Application in the left pane and select Edit Bindings.

3. Select https; then click Edit.

4. Under SSL Certificate, select any of the listed certificates.

5. In the left pane, right-click /_trust/ and then select Explore.

6. Open the `Web.config` file with a text editor.

7. Locate the `<AudienceUri>` area in the file and type **`https://webappname/`**, where **webappname** is the URL of the desired web application.

8. Save and close the `Web.config` file.

Configuring a Web Application to Use STS

Once you have edited the bindings and configured `Web.config` file, configure a Security Token Service web application.

1. On a domain controller, open the Active Directory Federation Services (AD FS) 2.0 Management Console.

2. In the left pane, expand Policy and select Relying Parties.

3. In the main pane, click Add Relying Party.

4. When the Active Directory Federation Services (AD FS) 2.0 Configuration Wizard launches, click Next.

5. Select Enter Relying Party Configuration Manually; then click Next.

6. Verify that Active Directory Federation Services (AD FS) 2.9 Server profile is selected, and then click Next.

7. Accept the default of not using an encryption certificate; then click Next.

8. Type the name of the desired web application's URL, append /_trust in the available field, such as `https://webapplication/_trust/`, and then click Next.

9. Type an identifier, click Add, and then click Next.

10. On the Summary page, click Next and then click Close.

11. When the Rules Editor Management Console opens, expand New Rule in the left pane and select Predefined Rule.

12. Select Create Claims From LDAP Attribute Store.

13. In the main pane, open the Attribute Store drop-down list and select Enterprise Active Directory User Account Store.

14. Under LDAP Attribute, select sAMAccountName.

15. Under Outgoing Claim Type, select E-Mail Address.

16. In the left pane, click Save and then close the console.

Service Application Management

Once you have performed the initial post-installation configuration tasks for service administration, it's time to set up the service applications and put them to work. SharePoint provides a large number of services to web applications and to the site collections and sites accessed by SharePoint users. When setting up service application resources in SharePoint, there are two general and very important components:

- The general configuration of service applications
- Setting up specific service application

Managing Service Applications

Managing service applications involves making connections between the service application and the web application, publishing service applications so that they can be consumed by other farms, connecting to service applications on remote farms, and performing other global activities. This section will take you through all the areas involved in enabling service application access for targeted users.

Connecting and Disconnecting Service Applications to Web Applications

It certainly makes sense that once you've enabled service applications in SharePoint, you'd want to connect them to the various web applications containing site collections and individual sites so that your users and customers can access all the collaboration services available.

As described earlier in this chapter, when you create a service application, a service application connection is also created. This connection, also called an application proxy, associates the service application to the web application using membership in the service application connection group, or the application proxy group.

When you create a new service application connection in Central Administration, it's automatically added to the server farm's Default group of service application connections, but this behavior can be circumvented. If you create the new service application in Windows PowerShell, the connection is not automatically added to the Default service group. If you so choose, you can add it to the Default group by using the -default parameter.

Exercise 4.6 will start you off with adding a service application group using Central Administration. You must be a member of the SharePoint Farm Administrators group to successfully complete this task.

EXERCISE 4.6

Adding a Service Application Connection Using Central Administration

1. From the Central Administration main page, click Application Management.

2. On the Application Management page, click Configure Service Application Associations under Service Applications.

3. On the Service Application Associations page, if necessary, use the View drop-down menu to select Web Applications.

4. In the list of web applications, in the Application Proxy Group column, click the name of the service application connection group you want to add or edit (Default may be the only option).

5. When the Configure Service Application Associations box appears, to add the service connection to the group, select the check box next to the desired service application, as shown here.

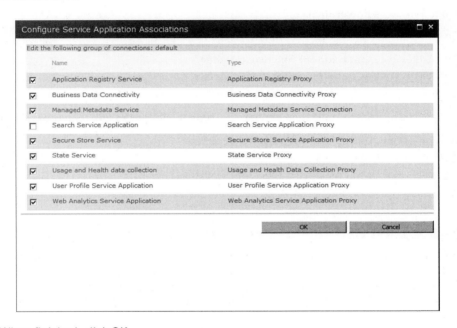

6. When finished, click OK.

To edit the page by adding or removing connections, access the Configure Service Application Associations box again and select or deselect the desired check boxes next to the service application names.

 You can also manage custom but not default service applications connection from Application Management in Central Administration by clicking Manage Web Applications, selecting a web application, and then clicking Service Connection on the Web Applications tab on the Ribbon. Use the menu on the box that appears to select Custom and then select or deselect the desired check boxes.

You can also use Windows PowerShell to add and remove service application connections. Exercise 4.7 provides the instructions. The code included in the following activity is example code and not meant to be run "as is" in a production environment. To successfully accomplish this task, you must be a member of the SharePoint_Shell_Access role on the configuration database and a member of the WSS_ADMIN_WPG local group on the computer containing SharePoint 2010.

EXERCISE 4.7

Adding and Removing a Service Application Connection Using Windows PowerShell

1. Open Windows PowerShell.

2. To add a service application connection, type the following and then press Enter:

    ```
    Add-SPServiceApplicationProxyGroupMember
    [-Identity <the service application proxy group>]
    [-Member <members to add to the service application proxy group>]
    ```

3. To remove a service application connection, type the following and then press Enter:

    ```
    Remove-SPServiceApplicationProxyGroupMember
    [-Identity <SPServiceApplicationProxyGroupPipeBind>]
    [-Member <SPServiceApplicationProxyPipeBind[]>]
    ```

Allowing Trust Certificates to Be Exchanged between Farms

Up until this point, you have probably been thinking about configuring services on your server farm so they can be consumed by web applications and users with access to the farm; however, Chapter 2, "Planning and Deploying a SharePoint 2010 Installation and Upgrade," outlined how to design a SharePoint deployment using a number of different multifarm topologies.

To allow cross-server farm access to resources, the SharePoint administrator must take a number of actions, such as exporting and copying certificates and establishing trust on both the consuming and publishing farms.

The administrator of the farm consuming the resource must provide two trust certificates to the farm publishing the resource: a root certificate and an STS certificate. The administrator of the publishing farm must provide a root certificate to the consuming farm. The following sections outline how to accomplish the required tasks.

All of the tasks in this section are performed using Windows PowerShell. Exercise 4.8 will show you how to exchange trust certificates between the publishing and consuming farms. This task must be performed in the consuming farm, and you must be a member of the SharePoint_Shell_Access role on the configuration database and a member of the WSS_ADMIN_WPG local group on the computer containing SharePoint 2010.

EXERCISE 4.8

Exporting Certificates Using Windows PowerShell

1. Open Windows PowerShell.

2. To export the root certificate from the consuming farm, type each of the following commands at the prompt and then press Enter after each command, replacing <C:\ConsumingFarmRoot.cer> with the path of the root certificate:

```
$rootCert = (Get-SPCertificateAuthority).RootCertificate
```

```
$rootCert.Export("Cert") | Set-Content <C:\ConsumingFarmRoot.cer>
-Encoding byte
```

3. To export the STS certificate from the consuming farm, type the following commands and then press Enter after each command, replacing <C:\ConsumingFarmSTS.cer> with the path of the STS certificate:

```
$stsCert = (Get-SPSecurityTokenServiceConfig).LocalLoginProvider
.SigningCertificate
```

```
$stsCert.Export("Cert") | Set-Content <C:\ConsumingFarmSTS.cer>
-Encoding byte
```

4. To export the root certificate from the publishing farm, on a server running Share-Point in the publishing farm, type the following commands and then press Enter after each command, replacing <C:\PublishingFarmRoot.cer> with the path of the root certificate:

```
$rootCert = (Get-SPCertificateAuthority).RootCertificate
```

```
$rootCert.Export("Cert") | Set-Content <C:\PublishingFarmRoot.cer>
-Encoding byte
```

The final task in this section, copying the certificates, is quite simple. Copy the root certificate and the STS certificate from the server in the consuming farm to the server in the publishing farm. Copy the root certificate from the server in the publishing farm to the server in the consuming farm.

Your next step is to establish trust on the consuming farm by importing the root certificate that you just copied from the publishing farm and then to create a trusted root authority using Windows PowerShell. Exercise 4.9 shows you how.

Each trusted root authority must have a unique name.

Importing the Root Certificate and Creating a Trusted Root Authority on the Consuming Farm

1. Open Windows PowerShell.

2. On a server in the consuming farm, type the following commands at the command prompt and then press Enter, replacing <C:\PublishingFarmRoot.cer> with the path of the root certificate that you copied to the consuming farm from the publishing farm and replacing <PublishingFarm> with a unique name that identifies the publishing farm:

   ```
   $trustCert = Get-PfxCertificate    <C:\PublishingFarmRoot.cer>

   New-SPTrustedRootAuthority <PublishingFarm> -    Certificate $trustCert
   ```

Establishing trust on the publishing farm requires that you not only import the root certificate and create a trusted root authority but also import the STS certificate and create a trusted service token issuer. Exercise 4.10 outlines the details.

Importing the Root and STS Certificates and Creating a Trusted Authority and Token Issuer

1. Open Windows PowerShell.

2. To import the root certificate and create a trusted root authority, on a server in the publishing farm, type the following commands at the prompt and then press Enter after each command, replacing <C:\ConsumingFarmRoot.cer> with the name and location of the root certificate that you copied to the publishing farm from the consuming farm and replacing <ConsumingFarm> with a unique name that identifies the consuming farm:

   ```
   $trustCert = Get-PfxCertificate <C:\ConsumingFarmRoot.cer>

   New-SPTrustedRootAuthority <ConsumingFarm> -Certificate $trustCert
   ```

3. To import the STS certificate and create a trusted service token issuer, type the following commands at the prompt and then press Enter after each command, replacing <C:\ConsumingFarmSTS.cer> with the path of the STS certificate that you copied to the publishing farm from the consuming farm and replacing <ConsumingFarm> with a unique name that identifies the consuming farm:

   ```
   $stsCert = Get-PfxCertificate <c:\ConsumingFarmSTS.cer>

   New-SPTrustedServiceTokenIssuer <ConsumingFarm> -Certificate $stsCert
   ```

NOTE Each trusted root authority must have a unique name, and each trusted service token issuer must have a unique name.

Publishing Service Applications

As you may recall from Chapter 2, some service applications can be published across farms and made available over remote connections:

- Business Data Connectivity
- Managed Metadata
- People
- Search
- Secure Store
- Web Analytics

Publishing these service applications across farms first requires that you establish a trust between the publishing and consuming farms, as you did in the previous section of this chapter.

Publishing cross-farm service applications lets you offer a single service to numerous farms so that you can optimize your resources and avoid redundant service publication. You can also provide enterprise-wide services without having to deploy a dedicated enterprise services farm.

You have the option of publishing a cross-farm service application using either Central Administration or Windows PowerShell. Exercise 4.11 shows you how to use Central Administration to accomplish the task. You must be a member of the SharePoint Farm Administrators group to complete the exercise successfully.

NOTE When you click a service, you are clicking the service name the way you click a hyperlink. When you click a row, you click next to the link to select the row but not actually open the service.

EXERCISE 4.11

Publishing a Service Application Using Central Administration

1. On the Central Administration main page, click Application Management. On the Application Management page, click Manage Service Applications under Service Applications.

2. Click the row for the service application you want to publish to select it. On the Ribbon, click Publish, as shown here.

EXERCISE 4.11 *(continued)*

3. When the Publish Service Application box appears, use the Connection Type drop-down menu to select the desired connection type, as shown here.

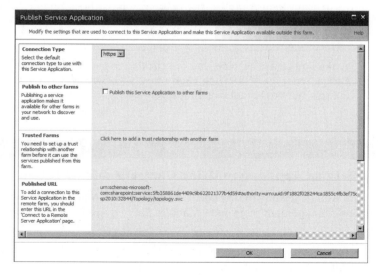

4. Select the Publish This Service Applications To Other Farms check box.

EXERCISE 4.11 *(continued)*

5. Under Published URL, copy the URL string to a text editor so that the string can be provided to the remote farms so they can connect to your published service application.

   Copy this information down and save it. You'll need it for Exercise 4.13.

6. Under Description Text, you can provide an optional description of the link in the Description field for the administrators of remote farms connecting to the service application.

7. In the Information URL field, you can provide a "human-friendly" URL that will be displayed to the administrators of remote farms connecting to the service application.

8. When you are done, click OK.

You can perform the same task using Windows PowerShell. Exercise 4.12 will show you how. You must be a member of the SharePoint_Shell_Access role on the configuration database and a member of the WSS_ADMIN_WPG local group on the computer containing SharePoint 2010.

EXERCISE 4.12

Publishing a Service Application Using Windows PowerShell

1. Open Windows PowerShell.

2. At the command prompt, type the following command and then press Enter, making note of the output so you can provide the information to the administrators of connecting remote farms:

   `Publish-SPServiceApplication -Identity  <GUID of the service application>`

3. At the prompt, type the following and press Enter to provide other farms with the data required for them to consume your published service application:

   `Get-SPTopologyServiceApplication`

Save the output from the `Get-SPTopologyServiceApplication` command. You'll need it for Exercise 4.14.

Connecting to a Service Application on a Remote Farm

Once a service application is published, it can be used by a remote farm as a resource when connecting to that resource on the source farm. Now that there is a service application available for cross-farm consumption, you can go through the process of making the connection to that application.

Performing connection tasks is very similar to performing the publishing tasks. You can use either Central Administration or Windows PowerShell. Exercise 4.13 will show you how to use Central Administration to connect to a service application on a remote farm. You must be a member of the SharePoint Farm Administrators group to successfully complete this exercise.

EXERCISE 4.13

Connecting to a Remote Service Application Using Central Administration

1. On the Central Administration main page, click Application Management. Then on the Application Management page, click Manage Service Applications under Service Applications.

2. On the Ribbon, open the Connect drop-down menu and select the desired service application.

3. When the Connect To A Remote Service Application field appears, paste or type the URL you gathered in step 5 of Exercise 4.11 in the field; then click OK.

4. In the new Connect To A Remote Service Application dialog box, click the row containing the name of the desired service application, select the check box to add the service application to the farm's default list of service application selections, and then click OK.

5. When prompted, either accept the default entry or type a new name for the connection in the Connection Name field; then click OK.

6. Click OK again to finish the process.

7. To associate the new service application with a local web application, see Exercise 4.6 or 4.7.

You can also accomplish this task using Windows PowerShell. Exercise 4.14 will show you the steps. You must be a member of the SharePoint_Shell_Access role on the configuration database and a member of the WSS_ADMIN_WPG local group on the computer containing SharePoint 2010.

EXERCISE 4.14

Connecting to a Remote Service Application Using Windows PowerShell

1. Open Windows PowerShell.

EXERCISE 4.14 *(continued)*

2. At the command prompt, type the following command and then press Enter, replacing `<Publishing farm topology service URL>` with the output of the `Get-SPTopologyServiceApplication` command you ran in step 4 of Exercise 4.12:

    `Receive-SPSharedServiceApplicationInfo -FarmUrl <Publishing farm topology service URL>`

3. At the prompt, type the following command and then press Enter:

    `New-SP*ServiceApplicationProxy cmdlet -Name <Unique name for the service application proxy> -Url <URL of the published service application>`

4. To associate the new service application with a local web application, see Exercise 4.6 or 4.7.

 Real World Scenario

Working with Another Administrator to Share Resources

Although you may get the idea from the textbook scenarios that you'll be the only Share-Point administrator in your company, in fact there will be an entire collection of technical staff members who are all working together to integrate each of their areas into the overall purpose and goal of the business. When you create a resource, such as a Secure Store Service service application in your server farm, administrators of other server farms will want to have access to the resource so they don't have to duplicate the effort.

Remember, part of the planning process you go through before you install and deploy SharePoint is defining which server farms will contain which specific resources and defining how those resources will be shared among other server farms for the organization. You may have immediate control and responsibility over your individual farm environment, but you must plan and manage as part of a much larger team.

Also, as part of that team, you can benefit from the work of the other SharePoint administrators, accessing their resources remotely so the users connecting to web applications on your farm can be more productive.

Deleting a Service Application

As with the other related exercises, you can also delete a service application using either Central Administration or Windows PowerShell. The tasks are substantially similar to creating a service application, and you may have even noticed the option to do so on the Service Application page in Central Administration.

This is how you delete a service application in Central Administration:

1. Navigate to Central Administration, click Application Management, and then click Manage Service Applications.

2. On the page that appears, click the row containing the service application you want to delete and then click Delete in the Ribbon.

3. When the confirmation box appears, select the check box next to Delete Data Associated With Service Applications to remove the service application database.

4. When you're finished, click OK to complete the action.

If you wanted to delete the service application but retain the database, in step 3 do not select the check box.

To perform the same task in Windows PowerShell, do the following:

1. In Windows PowerShell at the prompt, type the following and then press Enter to retrieve the service application you want to delete:

```
$spapp = Get-SPServiceApplication -Name "<Service application display name>"
```

2. To delete the selected service application but retain the associated database, type the following at the prompt and then press Enter:

```
Remove-SPServiceApplication $spapp
```

3. To delete both the selected service application and the database, type the following at the prompt and press Enter:

```
Remove-SPServiceApplication $spapp -RemoveData
```

You will receive a confirmation message to which you type **Y** and then press Enter. Another message will appear letting you know the operation is being performed.

Configuring Individual Service Applications

The content in this part of the chapter is probably what you think about when you consider configuring services in SharePoint. It's certainly the content that the end users, partners, and customers you support think about. The services that the user sees in SharePoint are the tools that they use: Access Services, Excel Services, Visio Services, and the like.

The following sections contain the exercises necessary to create, configure, and use these services. This is the point in SharePoint where your work as an administrator directly touches the people who depend on you and upon SharePoint to make sure their jobs get done.

Managing Access Services

Access Services is new in SharePoint Server 2010 and allows people to host Access databases directly within SharePoint. You can create, edit, and update linked Access 2010 databases and then view them directly in SharePoint. Once an Access database is linked to SharePoint, any changes you make to the database are almost instantly reflected in what you see in SharePoint.

Exercise 4.15 gives you the opportunity to configure Access Services in SharePoint using Central Administration. This is the only step in allowing your users to take advantage of this new SharePoint feature; however, subsequent exercises will show you how to modify the default configuration settings to more closely fit your organization's business needs. You must be a site administrator for the Access Services service application and have the Designer permissions to successfully complete this exercise.

EXERCISE 4.15

Configuring Access Services in Central Administration

1. On the Central Administration main page, click Manage Service Applications under Application Management.

2. In the list on the Manage Service Applications page, select the desired Access service you want to configure.

3. On the Access Services Settings page, under Lists and Queries, enter a value from 1 to 255 for Maximum Columns Per Query, with 32 being the default value.

4. Set the Maximum Rows Per Query setting to a value between 1 and 200000, with 50000 being the default.

5. Set the Maximum Sources Per Query setting to a value between 1 and 20, with 8 being the default.

6. Set the Maximum Calculated Columns Per Query setting to a value between 0 to 32, with 10 being the default.

7. Set the Maximum Order By Clauses Per Query setting to a value between 1 and 8, with 4 being the default.

8. Set Allow Outer Joins by selecting or clearing the check box Outer Joins Allowed, with inner joins always being allowed.

9. Set Allow Non Remote-able Queries by selecting or clearing the Remote-able Queries Allowed check box.

10. Set Maximum Records Per Table to any positive integer, with 500000 being the default and –1 indicating that there is no limit.

11. Under Application Objects, set Maximum Application Log Size to any positive integer, with the default being 3000 and –1 indicating that there is no limit.

12. Under Session Management, set Maximum Request Duration in seconds to a value between 1 and 2007360 (24 days), with a default value of 30 and with –1 meaning there is no limit.

13. Set Maximum Sessions Per User to any positive integer, with a default of 10 and with –1 meaning there is no limit.

14. Set Maximum Sessions Per Anonymous User to any positive integer, with a default of 25 and with –1 meaning there is no limit.

15. Set Cache Timeout to a value in seconds between 1 and 2007360 (24 days), with a default of 300 and with –1 meaning there is no limit.

16. Set Maximum Session Memory to a value in megabytes between 0 (disable) and 4095, with a default of 64.

17. Under Memory Utilization, set Maximum Private Bytes (In MB) to any positive integer, with a default of –1 indicating the use of 50 percent of the physical memory on the computer.

18. Under Templates, set Maximum Template Size (In MB) to any positive integer, with a default of 30 and with –1 indicating there is no limit.

19. When you are done, click OK.

You may have to create an Access Services application before you can configure it in your SharePoint deployment. Exercise 4.16 will show you how to create and delete such an application in Central Administration. You must be an administrator of the Access Services service application to successfully perform this task.

EXERCISE 4.16

Adding and Deleting an Access Service Application

1. From the Central Administration main page, click Manage Service Applications under Application Management.

2. On the Ribbon, open the New menu and select Access Services.

3. When the Create page opens, give the new service application a name in the Service Application Name field.

4. In the Database Name field, either accept the default database or enter a new database server and name.

5. Choose an existing application pool or create a new one.

6. Choose whether to create an Access Services application proxy.

7. When finished, click OK.

8. When you want to delete an Access Services service application, in Central Administration, under Application Management, click Manage Service Applications.

9. On the Manage Service Applications page, select the Access Services service application you want to delete.

10. On the Ribbon, click Delete.

11. When the confirmation dialog box appears, click OK.

Once you have enabled Access Services, you can use these services in a variety of ways. Each of the following methods presented requires that you have Designer permissions. Five web database templates are provided for Access Services users, and sites can be created from these templates, just like using any other site template in SharePoint.

- Assets Web Database
- Charitable Contributions Web Database
- Contacts Web Database
- Issues Web Database
- Projects Web Database

Using a Web Template to Create an Access Services Website

The following procedure uses Central Administration as a starting point.

1. On the Central Administration main page, click Site Actions; then click New Site.

2. On the New SharePoint site page, give the new site a name in the Title field and an optional description in the Description field.

3. In the URL name field, append a descriptive name to the URL for the new site.

4. Under Template Selection, select the Web Databases tab.

5. In the Select A Template area, select the desired template.

6. Under Permissions, choose either to use the same permissions as the parent site or to use unique permissions.

7. Under Navigation, choose whether to display the site on the top link bar of the parent site.

8. Under Navigation Inheritance, choose whether to use the top link bar from the parent site.

9. Click Create.

Make note of the URL for the Access Services website. You'll need the URL for the next task.

Uploading an Offline Access Template to SharePoint

There are also methods of uploading and modifying templates from Microsoft Access 2010 to SharePoint.

1. Open Microsoft Access 2010 and then open the desired template.

2. If necessary, make modifications to the template and then save the template locally in Access.

3. Select the Access Office button, point to Share, and then click Publish To Access Services, as shown in Figure 4.2.

FIGURE 4.2   Access Services and SharePoint

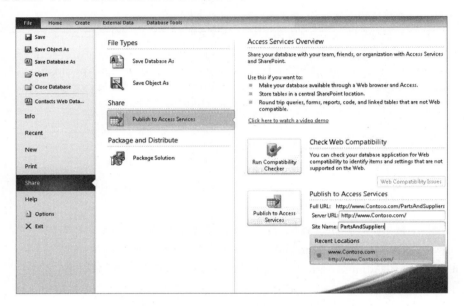

4. Choose Save As and then click the Address bar.

5. Type the URL of your Access Services site.

6. Give the file a name and then click Save.

Managing Excel Services

If you're familiar with MOSS 2007, you know how versatile and useful Excel Services are in allowing users to view and share Excel workbooks in SharePoint. In SharePoint Server 2010, this service application also enables data-connected Excel Services workbooks and worksheets to be refreshed and updated from a variety of data sources.

Enabling and configuring Excel Services is substantially similar to when you enabled Access Services in Exercise 4.15. In Exercise 4.17, you'll perform the steps yourself.

EXERCISE 4.17

Configuring Excel Services in Central Administration

1. On the Central Administration main page, click Manage Service Applications under Application Management.

2. On the Service Applications page, click Excel Services.

3. On the Manage Excel Services page, click Global Settings.

4. For the File Access method under Security, select one of the following:

- Select Impersonation to enable Excel Calculation Services (ECS) to authorize users who attempt to access workbooks stored in HTTP and UNC locations.

- Select Process Account if you have ECS application servers opening workbooks in HTTP and UNC locations. Under Connection Encryption, select either Not Required or Required.

- Under Allow Cross Domain Access, select Allow Cross Domain Access to display files from one HTTP domain to another.

5. Under Load Balancing and then under Load BalancingScheme, select one of the following:

- Select Workbook URL to specify which ECS process opens a workbook and to ensure requests from a specific workbook are always sent to the same ECS server.

- Select Round-Robin With Health Check to determine which ECS process is used to open a workbook.

- Select Local if the ECS process available is local to the server computer where the workbook is located.

6. Under Session Management, type the maximum number of sessions with Excel Services that an individual user is allowed per ECS application server in the Maximum Sessions Per User field, where –1 indicates no limit and 25 is the default value.

7. In the Maximum Private Bytes field under Memory Utilization, type the value in megabytes for the maximum amount that an ECS process can use, where –1 indicates a value equaling 50 percent of the physical memory on the server machine.

8. In the Maximum Size Of Workbook Cache field, type the value in megabytes that you want allocated to workbooks being used by Excel Services.

9. Select the Caching Enabled check box to allow caching of objects not being used in any sessions.

10. Under External Data and under Unattended Service Account, type the target application ID from the Secure Store Service in the Application ID field.

11. When you are finished, click OK.

Step 10 in Exercise 4.17 addresses the unattended service account, which is an account ECS can impersonate when making a data connection using a non–Windows Secure Store

Service authentication or a None authentication method. If you require such connections and you do not configure this feature, the authentication will fail.

Once Excel Services is enabled, you can extend the ECS capacities from Central Administration in a number of ways to add and modify user-defined functions (UDFs).

To configure UDF support, you must enable UDFs on all trusted file locations containing workbooks that need to access UDFs, and you must register UDF assemblies on the Excel Services user-defined function assembly list. You must be a local administrator on the server machine containing the Central Administration site. With those permissions, you can also delegate Excel Services administrator permissions without granting access to manage other Central Administration services or features.

Exercise 4.18 will show you how to enable UDFs on trusted file locations using Central Administration.

EXERCISE 4.18

Enabling User-Defined Functions for Trusted Site Locations Using Central Administration

1. On the Central Administration main page, click Manage Service Applications under Application Management.

2. On the Manage Service Applications page, click the Excel Services Web Service Application.

3. On the Manage Excel Services page, click Trusted File Locations.

4. On the Trusted File Locations page, click the trusted file on which you want to enable user-defined functions.

5. On the Edit Trusted File Location page, select the User-Defined Functions Allowed check box under User-Defined Functions.

Once you've enabled user-defined functions, you can manage, add, edit, and delete a user-defined function assembly. Exercise 4.19 takes you through this set of processes.

EXERCISE 4.19

Managing Excel Services User-Defined Function Assemblies

1. On the Central Administration main page, click Manage Service Applications under Application Management.

2. On the Manage Service Applications page, click the Excel Services Web Service Application.

3. On the Manage Excel Services page, click User Defined Function Assemblies.

4. On the Excel Services User Defined Functions page, click Add User-Defined Function Assembly.

EXERCISE 4.19 *(continued)*

5. On the Add User-Defined Function Assembly page, under Assembly, type the path of the assembly containing the user-defined functions in the Assembly field.

6. Under Assembly Location, select either Global Assembly Cache to indicate a global location where signed assemblies are deployed or File Path to indicate a local or network share.

7. Under Enable Assembly, select the Assembly Enabled check box to let ECS call the assembly and then type an optional description in the Description field.

8. Click OK to add the assembly.

9. To edit the assembly, on the Excel Services User Defined Functions page, click the UDF assembly you want to edit, click the arrow that appears, and then click Edit.

10. To delete the assembly, click the UDF assembly you want to delete on the Excel Services User Defined Functions page, click the arrow that appears, and then click Delete.

11. When the confirmation box appears, click OK.

Managing PerformancePoint Services

PerformancePoint Server 2007, once a separate Microsoft product, has been merged into SharePoint Server 2010 and is now called *PerformancePoint Services* for SharePoint. This consolidates the dashboard, scorecard, and analytical features of PerformancePoint directly into SharePoint, expanding SharePoint's business intelligence abilities by tying PerformancePoint capacities to SharePoint's Excel Services and other *business intelligence* (BI) tools.

Although you can enable and configure PerformancePoint Services using the Farm Configuration Wizard, if you are running SharePoint as a single-server deployment with Microsoft SQL Server, you can instead set up PerformancePoint manually.

 If you have performed a clean installation of Microsoft SharePoint Server 2010 on a single server with a built-in database, PerformancePoint Services is configured for you. That means, in the test setup for this book, you don't need to take any further action to enable and configure PerformancePoint Services.

If you choose to configure PerformancePoint Services manually, the general list of required activities includes the following:

- Creating one or more web applications in SharePoint

- Creating one or more service applications in SharePoint

- Enabling PerformancePoint site and site collection features

PerformancePoint Services data source connections are located in document libraries, while the data content, such as KPIs and scorecards, is located in lists. Each library and list containing SharePoint Services data and data source connections must be set up as a trusted source. You can mark either all of your lists and libraries as trusted or only those that contain PerformancePoint services data and data connections.

Once PerformancePoint Services is up and running, you can launch PerformancePoint Dashboard Designer from a site or site collection and start creating dashboards, KPIs, and scorecards, as well as publishing those items that already exist. The PerformancePoint Dashboard Designer is typically launched from the Business Intelligence Center, but you can set it up to be launched from other sites.

The first step in manually configuring PerformancePoint Services is to create a web application. In Chapter 2, see Exercise 2.4 for basic instructions on creating a web application. Also see Chapter 9, "Managing Web Applications and Host Sites."

The easiest way to create a PerformancePoint Services site is to select the Business Intelligence Center template while going through the Farm Configuration Wizard; however, you can also add PerformancePoint Services content to any existing site manually. Exercise 4.20 shows you how this is done.

EXERCISE 4.20

Enabling PerformancePoint Services for a Site Manually

1. On the parent site for the site collection where you want to enable PerformancePoint Services, click Site Actions and then click Site Settings.

2. On the Site Settings page, select Site Collection Features under Site Collection Administration.

3. On the Features page, click Activate next to SharePoint Server Publishing Infrastructure in the list of features that appears.

4. After the Active Status button appears, navigate to the site for which you want to enable PerformancePoint Services as a site feature.

5. Click Site Actions and then click Site Settings.

6. On the Site Settings page, click Manage Site Features under Site Actions.

7. In the list of features that appears, click Activate next to PerformancePoint Services Site features and wait until the Active status button appears.

The PerformancePoint Site Template option will appear as a site template under the Enterprise tab once you have enabled PerformancePoint Services as a site collection feature.

Once you have enabled SharePoint Publishing Infrastructure and PerformancePoint Services for site collections and sites, to continue to manually configure PerformancePoint Services, you must create a service application. You have performed very similar tasks earlier in this chapter, and the steps are virtually the same for creating a service application for PerformancePoint Services as it is for Access Services.

See Exercise 4.16 for a walk-through, and substitute PerformancePoint Services for Access Services in the instructions.

After either selecting an existing application pool or creating a new one, you can choose the optional step of selecting Register A New Managed Account. If you do so, you will need to create a new managed account and use it as the application pool identity by running the following Windows PowerShell script:

```
PS> $w = Get-SPWebApplication -identity <your web application>
PS> $w.GrantAccessToProcessIdentity("<insert service account>")
```

This is required to allow access to the associated content database. This will grant db_owner access to SharePoint Foundation content databases, but PerformancePoint Services will not function if you do not do so. Remember, this script must be run only if you select the optional Register A New Managed Account option before creating the service application.

 You may have to start the PerformancePoint Services service on the server computer. To review the steps for doing so, see Exercise 4.2 or Exercise 4.3.

The next step in the manual configuration process is to configure the Secure Store Service and proxy, which are required in order to store the unattended service account's password for the PerformancePoint Services service application. The unattended service account is a shared domain account used to access the PerformancePoint Services data sources. See the section "Configuring the Secure Store Service" later in this chapter.

Now you need to verify that the service application connection, the PerformancePoint Services service application, and the Secure Store Service are all associated with the web application.

To do this in Central Administration, click Manage Web Applications under Application Management. Then on the Web Applications tab, click Service Connections. You should see the default group of service applications, but if you didn't choose Make This Application Service The Default when you created the PerformancePoint Services service application, it won't appear in this list. Use the drop-down menu and switch from Default to Custom if you don't see the PerformancePoint Services service application in the default list.

Once you have PerformancePoint Services up and running, quite a lot of options are available to you. However, you must remember that PerformancePoint was once a separate server product. You may have content on PerformancePoint Server 2007 that you want to import into SharePoint. The following will walk you through the steps of how this is done. To actually perform this task, you will need to have a separate PerformancePoint Server 2007 product running and a SQL Server that contains valid content.

Importing Data from PerformancePoint Server 2007 into SharePoint

To import data, follow these steps:

1. In SharePoint, go to the main page of Central Administration.

2. Under Application Management, click Manage Service Applications.

3. Select the PerformancePoint Service application from the list on the page that appears.

4. On the Ribbon, click Manage to open the PerformancePoint Services settings page.

5. When the page appears, click Import PerformancePoint Server 2007 Content.

6. When the import wizard launches, click Next.

7. Type the name and instance of the SQL Server instance used for PerformancePoint Server 2007 content in the available field.

8. Select the authentication method, enter a valid username and password, and then click Next.

9. Select the database you want to import, such as the default name PPSMonitoring, and then click Next.

10. Select a site collection, site, and list where you want to import the Dashboard items and then click Next.

11. In the site collection you selected in the previous step, select a site and document library where you want to import your data sources and then click Next.

12. Review your settings on the page that appears; if you are satisfied, click Import.

13. After the import completes, on the results page, look for any errors indicating items that didn't import.

14. Click View List or View Library to review the data that was successfully imported, if desired.

15. When finished, click Done to close the wizard.

Configuring the Secure Store Service

The *Secure Store Service* is used by SharePoint Server 2010 to allow designers to create target applications that map user and group credentials to the credentials of external data sources. This lets external content types in the *Business Data Connectivity* (BDC) service read, write, create, and edit content stored in the external data sources. You also read in the previous section of this chapter that you must enable the Secure Store Service in order to be able to use PerformancePoint Services.

This section will present you with the necessary steps to enable the Secure Store Service application in SharePoint. The first task is to provide a passphrase that will be used to generate a key used to encrypt and decrypt the credentials stored in the Secure Store Service database. You must be a Service Application Administrator for the desired instance of the Secure Store Service.

> The passphrase must contain at least eight characters, which can be uppercase, lowercase, numerals, and the following special characters:
>
> ! " # $ % & ' ( ) * + , - . / : ; < = > ? @ [\ ] ^ _ ` { | } ~

Initializing an Instance of a Secure Store Service Application

To initialize an instance of a secure store service application, follow these steps:

1. Select the desired instance of a Secure Store Service application and then click the Edit tab.
2. Under Key Management, click Generate New Key.
3. On the Generate New Key page, type the passphrase in the Pass Phrase field. Then type the same passphrase again in the Confirm Pass Phrase field.
4. Click OK to generate the key.

> The passphrase isn't stored, so you should write it down and keep it in a safe place.

The steps in the previous task also show how to generate a new encryption key should you desire. You can also force the Secure Store Service database to be reencrypted using the new key.

You may have to refresh the encryption key if you add a new application server, restore a previously backed up Secure Store Service database, or receive an "Unable to get master key error" message. The following steps show you this procedure. You will need to belong to the Service Application Administrator group for the instance of the Secure Store Service.

Refreshing a Secure Store Service Application Encryption Key

To refresh a secure store service application encryption key, follow these steps:

1. Select the desired instance of a Secure Store Service application and then click the Edit tab.
2. Under Key Management, click Refresh Key.
3. In the Pass Phrase field, type the passphrase you initially used to generate the encryption key and then click OK.

At this point, you are ready to create a target application so that you can map user, group, or claim credentials to a set of credentials on an external data source. After you create the target application, associate it with the external content type or application model so you can gain access to the external data source. You will need to be a Service Application Administrator for the instance of the Secure Store Service.

Creating a Target Application

To create the target application, follow these steps:

1. Select the desired instance of a Secure Store Service application; then click the Edit tab.

2. Under Manage Target Applications, click New.

3. Type a text string in the Target Application ID field that will be used by the Secure Store Service application as a unique identifier for the target application.

4. In the Display Name field, type the text string you want to use to display the identifier.

5. In the Contact Email field, type the email address of the primary contact person for this application.

6. If you desire, in the Target Application Page URL, enter the URL of a custom web page so users can add their credentials for the destination data source and then select one of the following:

   - Use Provided Page if you want users to add their credentials automatically when accessing the page.

   - Use Custom Page if you want users to provide their credentials manually when accessing the page.

   - Use None to not provide a sign-up page, which requires the Secure Store Service administrator to add individual credentials.

7. In the Target Application Type field, type either **Group** for group credentials or **Individual** for individual credentials to be mapped to the external data source.

8. Select the Windows check box if the credentials on the external data source are Windows credentials.

9. Click Next.

10. In the Specify the credential fields for your Secure Store Target Application, enter the required information in the available fields to provide credentials to the external data source, such as username and password.

11. To create an additional field on this page for credentials, click Add Field and then use one of the following field types:

    - Generic for values that do not apply to any other field types

    - User Name for usernames

    - Password for passwords

    - PIN for personal identification numbers

    - Windows User Name for a username on a Windows account

    - Windows Password for the password on a user's Windows account

12. When you are done, click Next.

13. On the Specify The Membership Settings page, list all the users you want to be able to manage the target application settings in the Target Application Administrators field.

14. If the target application type is a group, list the required user groups in the Members field.

15. When you are done, click OK.

Managing Visio Services

Like Access Services and Excel Services, the *Visio Graphics Service* lets users view and share Visio diagrams in SharePoint. When you data-connect a Visio diagram in SharePoint, the diagram refreshes in SharePoint whenever it is modified at the source.

The following group of exercises demonstrates how to enable Visio services in SharePoint if you have not already enabled them using the Farm Configuration Wizard.

Creating and deleting the Visio Graphics Service in Central Administration is virtually identical to performing the same tasks for other services such as Access Services and Excel Services; however, you can also create and delete the service using Windows PowerShell. You must be a member of the SharePoint_Shell_Access role on the configuration database and a member of the WSS_ADMIN_WPG local group on the computer containing SharePoint 2010 Products.

Creating and Deleting the Visio Services Service Application Using Windows PowerShell

Follow these steps:

1. Open Windows PowerShell. At the prompt, type the following and press Enter:

   ```
   New-SPVisioServiceApplication <ServiceAppName>
   -serviceapplicationpool <AppPoolName> -AddToDefaultGroup
   ```

   You must substitute the correct values for the service application name and the application pool name where indicated.

2. To delete the service application, type the following at the prompt and then press Enter:

   ```
   Remove-SPServiceApplication <ServiceAppName>
   ```

   You must substitute the correct value for the service application name where indicated.

 You can also view a list of all Visio Services service applications via Windows PowerShell using the command Get-SPVisioServiceApplication.

Creating and Deleting a Visio Graphics Services Service Applications Proxy Using Windows PowerShell

Creating and deleting a Visio Graphics Services service applications proxy can also be done using Windows PowerShell. A service applications proxy allows other farms to access and use the service application remotely.

1. To create the Visio Graphics Services service application proxy, at the Windows PowerShell prompt type the following and then press Enter, using the correct service application name:

   ```
   New-SPVisioServiceApplicationProxy <ServiceAppName>
   ```

2. To delete the service application proxy, type the following and press Enter, using the correct proxy ID:

```
Remove-SPServiceApplicationProxy <ProxyID>
```

You can also view a list of all Visio Graphics Service service applications via Windows PowerShell using the command `Get-SPVisioServiceApplicationProxy`.

Earlier in the chapter, you learned about global settings for service applications. You can set global settings for Visio Graphics Services in the same way you did for Excel Services in Exercise 4.17.

Configuring Global Settings for the Visio Graphics Service

From Central Administration, once you click Manage Service Applications under Application Management and then click the Visio Graphics Services service application you want to configure, perform the following steps:

1. Set the Maximum Diagram Size value in megabytes that can be rendered, setting smaller sizes for servers under heavy loads in order to manage performance speeds.

2. Set the Minimum Cache Age value in minutes that a diagram remains cached in memory, with smaller values allowing for more frequent data refresh operations.

3. Set the Maximum Cache Age value in minutes, after which time the diagrams will be cleared.

4. Set the Maximum Recalc value in seconds before refresh operations time out.

5. Set External Data when using external data sources and when you require the Secure Store Services to be operational and configured to provide credentials to the correct external source.

6. When you are finished, click OK.

Generally, the smaller the values you configure for cache age, the more CPU and memory performance you're asking out of your server.

Configuring Global Settings for Visio Graphics Service with Windows PowerShell

You can perform the same action using Windows PowerShell, which requires that you belong to the SharePoint_Shell_Access role on the configuration database and that you're a member of the WSS_ADMIN_WPG local group on the computer that contains SharePoint 2010. Open Windows PowerShell, and at the prompt follow these steps:

1. To manage the performance parameters in the service application, type the following and then press Enter, typing in the actual values for minutes, size in megabytes, seconds, minutes, and Visio service application you see represented in the code:

```
Set-SPVisioPerformance -MaxDiagramCacheAge <Minutes>
-MaxDiagramSize <SizeMB> -MaxRecalcDuration <Seconds>
-MinDiagramCacheAge <Minutes> VisioServiceApplication <VisioServiceApp>
```

2. To manage the data configuration parameters in the service application, type the following and then press Enter, typing the actual values for VisioServiceApp and ApplicationID you see represented in the code:

```
Set-SPVisioExternalData
-VisioServiceApplication <VisioServiceApp>
-UnattendedServiceAccountApplicationID <ApplicationID>
```

Trusted data providers are external databases used by Excel Services and Visio Graphics Services that are specifically trusted by these services when processing information. You can create a trusted data provider for Visio Graphics Services in either Central Administration or Windows PowerShell.

Creating a Trusted Data Provider for Visio Graphics Services in Central Administration

To create a trusted data provider for the Visio Graphics Service in Central Administration, follow these steps:

1. On the Central Administration main page, click Manage Service Applications under Application Management.

2. Click the Visio Graphics Service service application where you want to create a trusted data provider.

3. Click Trusted Data Providers.

4. Click Add A New Trusted Data Provider.

5. Enter the provider ID in the Trusted Data Provider ID field.

6. Enter the provider type in the Trusted Data Provider Type field.

7. Enter a description of the trusted data provider in the Trusted Data Provider Type Description field.

8. When you are finished, click OK.

If you want to edit a trusted data provider, follow the steps listed previously and in step 4 click Edit Trusted Data Provider. Edit the information and then click OK. To delete a trusted data provider, click Delete Trusted Data Provider in step 4.

Managing a Trusted Data Provider for Visio Graphics Services Using Windows PowerShell

You can manage Visio Graphics Services the same way using Windows PowerShell:

1. To create a trusted data provider for the Visio Graphics Service, type the following at the Windows PowerShell prompt and then press Enter, providing the proper parameters:

```
New-SPVisioSafeDataProvider -DataProviderId <ProviderID> -DataProviderType
<Int32> VisioServiceApplication <VisioServiceApp>
```

2. To edit a trusted data provider, type the following at the prompt and then press Enter, providing the proper parameters:

```
Set-SPVisioSafeDataProvider -DataProviderId <ProviderID> -DataProviderType
<Int32> -Description <String>
-VisioServiceApplication <VisioServiceApp>
```

3. To delete a trusted data provider, type the following at the prompt and then press Enter, providing the proper parameters:

```
Remove-SPVisioSafeDataProvider -DataProviderId <ProviderID> -DataProviderType
<Int32> -VisioServiceApplication <VisioServiceApp>
```

Although this chapter has certainly covered a representative sample of the individual service applications that can be configured in SharePoint, it by no means is exhaustive. Chapter 5, "Configuring Indexing and Search," will address the configuration of search services, and Chapter 6, "Managing Operational Settings," shows how to create and set up others, such as InfoPath Forms Services and User Profile Services configuration.

Summary

In this chapter, you received a summary on creating and configuring SharePoint Server 2010 service applications.

- Using the Farm Configuration Wizard to set up your service applications in a single process
- Managing services on servers in the farm
- Performing the initial configuration tasks for services in SharePoint, including global settings

- Creating and managing individual service applications and service application proxies
- Connecting to service applications on a remote farm
- The introduction of individual service applications such as Access Services, Excel Services, and Visio Graphics Services

Exam Essentials

Understanding the Various Tasks Required to Set Up Services and Service Applications   Set up the general environment supporting the creation and configuration of services and service applications in SharePoint, including the ability to access service applications on remote server farms.

Configuring Service Applications and Service Application Proxies for Individual Services   Perform the mandatory and optional tasks to enable SharePoint users to take advantage of the many services available.

Review Questions

1. You are a SharePoint administrator for your organization. You are ready to deploy service applications to SharePoint so your users can access the many advantages SharePoint offers. Of the following options, which is the most straightforward method of service application deployment?

   A. In Central Administration, click Manage Services On A Server under System Settings and then configure services applications for the server farm.

   B. In Central Administration, click Manage Service Applications under Application Management. Then click New, select each service application in turn, and configure the service.

   C. In Central Administration, click Manage Services On A Server Farm under System Settings and then launch the Farm Configuration Wizard.

   D. In Central Administration, click Configuration Wizards in the Quick Launch menu and then click Launch The Farm Configuration Wizard.

2. You are the SharePoint administrator for your organization, and you are in the process of setting up your server farm for service applications. You are performing the initial tasks for services configuration and need to start and stop various services on your server farm servers besides using the SharePoint Farm Configuration Wizard. Of the following options, which is the most correct procedure for managing services on multiple servers?

   A. At the desired server, click Start ➢ All Programs ➢ Administrative Tools, click Services, and then click the service you want to start or stop.

   B. At the desired server, click Start ➢ Control Panel ➢ Administrative Tools, click Services, and then click the service you want to start or stop.

   C. At the Central Administration main page, click System Settings, click Manage Services On The Server Farm, and then click the service you want to start or stop.

   D. At the Central Administration main page, click System Settings, click Manage Services On Server, click Change Server, select the desired server's name, and then select the service you want to start or stop.

3. Once you create a service application, it must be connected to a web application to be accessible by users on the sites in site collections that are dependent on the web application. As the SharePoint administrator for your company, what should you do to connect a service application to the desired web application?

   A. You can use either Central Administration or Windows PowerShell.

   B. You can use Central Administration only.

   C. You can use Windows PowerShell only.

   D. You must perform separate tasks in both Central Administration and Windows PowerShell.

4. You are the SharePoint administrator for your organization, and you've been tasked with configuring your local SharePoint server farm environment to be able to consume application resources on other server farms within the organization managed by other administrators. To do this, you must perform various tasks to allow trust certificates to be exchanged between server farms. Of the following options, what is true about these tasks?

   A. You can use either Central Administration or Windows PowerShell to perform the related tasks.

   B. You can only use Central Administration to perform the related tasks.

   C. You can only use Windows PowerShell to perform the related tasks.

   D. You must perform separate tasks in both Central Administration and Windows PowerShell.

5. You must perform a wide variety of tasks as a SharePoint administrator using Windows PowerShell when configuring service applications, yet for each of these PowerShell-related activities, you require the same set of credentials. Of the following, which are the required credentials? (Choose all that apply.)

   A. You must be a member of the SharePoint_Shell_Access group.

   B. You must be a member of the SharePoint Farm Administrators group.

   C. You must be a member of the WSS_ADMIN_WPG local group on the computer containing SharePoint 2010 Products.

   D. You must be a member of the processadmin group for the SQL database containing the application service data.

6. You are a SharePoint administrator for your organization, and you are in the process of publishing certain services for consumption by other server farms in the SharePoint environment. During the publication process, you must acquire a specific piece of information to give to the administrator of the server farm that will be consuming your published service. Of the following options, which are true about what you must provide? (Choose all that apply.)

   A. When you publish the service application in Central Administration, you must acquire the URL to the published service.

   B. When you publish the service application in Central Administration, you must acquire the FQDN to the published service.

   C. When you publish the service application using Windows PowerShell, you must acquire the URL to the published service using the `Get-SPTopologyServiceApplication` command.

   D. When you publish the service application using Windows PowerShell, you must acquire the FQDN to the published service using the `Get-SPTopologyServiceApplication` command.

7. You are a SharePoint administrator for your organization, and you are in the process of connecting to another server farm in your SharePoint environment in order to access a published application service. You are using Central Administration to perform this task. You have been given the appropriate information by the administrator of the publishing server farm to connect to the application and have input that data in the Connect To A Remote Service Application field. You complete the process and click OK on the Connect To A Remote Service Application page, but no one using the default site collection can access the new resource. Of the following options, what could be wrong? (Choose all that apply).

   A. You could have entered the incorrect string in the Connect To A Remote Service Application field.

   B. You could have entered the incorrect name in the Connection Name field on the Connect To A Remote Service Application page.

   C. You could still need to associate the new service application with the required local web application.

   D. The users of the default site collection in the web application may not be using the correct permissions to access the resource.

8. You are a SharePoint administrator for your organization, and you are in the process of connecting to another server farm in your SharePoint environment in order to access a published application service. You are using Windows PowerShell to perform this task. You have the correct string information to enter in order to connect to the remote resource. There are two commands you must issue at the command prompt in order to successfully accomplish this task. When do you enter the string provided by the remote server farm administrator?

   A. You enter the string in the first command.

   B. You enter the string in the second command.

   C. You enter the string in both the first and second commands.

   D. You do not enter the string. The string is required only when you make this connection from Central Administration.

9. You are a SharePoint adminstrator for your organization, and you are in the process of deleting an application service that is no longer required. You are using Central Administration to accomplish the task. You want to delete the service but retain the database related to the service for further use. On the Manage Service Applications page, what must you do to successfully complete the job?

   A. Select the application service you want to delete, clear the Connect To Database check box next to the service name and click Delete in the Ribbon. When the confirmation box appears, click OK.

   B. Select the application service you want to delete and click Delete in the Ribbon. When the confirmation box appears, do not select the Delete Data Associated With Service Applications check box. Then click OK.

   C. Select the application service you want to delete and click Delete in the Ribbon. When the confirmation box appears, select the Do Not Delete Data Associated With Service Applications check box and then click OK.

   D. Whenever you delete an application service, the database is automatically deleted. There is no option to retain it.

10. You are a SharePoint administrator for your organization, and you are preparing a presentation to the board of directors on the advantages of SharePoint Server 2010. One of the points you want to cover is how Access Services allows you to create SharePoint sites using web database templates. Of the following, which Access-based website templates are available by default? (Choose all that apply.)

A. Charitable Contributions Web Database

B. Contacts Web Database

C. Issues Web Database

D. Organizational Web Database

11. You are a SharePoint administrator for your organization, and you have recently enabled the Access Service application service. You have been tasked with creating a new website based on a specific web database template. You are on the New SharePoint Site page and ready to select a template. Under Template Selection, which tab must you choose to see the template selections?

A. None. The web database templates appear on the tab open by default.

B. The Web Database tab.

C. The Web Database Template tab.

D. The Enterprise tab.

12. You are a SharePoint administrator for your organization, and you're configuring Excel Services in Central Administration. You want to enable the unattended service account so that Excel Services can access a non-Windows information sources. What other service must you enable in SharePoint to allow the unattended service account to access external data?

A. The Secure Store Service

B. The Security Token Service

C. The Single Sign-on Service

D. The User Defined Functions Service

13. PerformancePoint Server 2007 functionality has been fully integrated into SharePoint Server 2010 and no longer exists as a separate Microsoft product. You are a SharePoint administrator for your organization. Another member of the IT department is responsible for retiring your company's PerformancePoint Server 2007 deployment, and you are tasked with importing the information contained on that server into SharePoint. What other server information is required by the Import PerformancePoint Server 2007 Content Wizard in Central Administration?

A. The wizard requires the URL of the Windows Server 2003 machine hosting PerformancePoint Server 2007.

B. The wizard requires the URL of the SQL Server instance containing the database for PerformancePoint Server 2007.

C. The wizard requires the name and instance of the SQL Server instance used for PerformancePoint Server 2007.

D. The wizard requires the hostname or IP address of the Windows Server 2003 machine hosting PerformancePoint Server 2007.

14. You are a SharePoint administrator for your organization, and you are running a test deployment of SharePoint Server 2010 as a single-server installation with a built-in database. You want to explore the option of configuring PerformancePoint Services in Central Administration, but when you attempt to create the PerformancePoint Services service application, you find that the required option does not exist. What is the most likely cause of this problem?

   A. You must create a web application for PerformancePoint Services before the option to create a PerformancePoint Services service application becomes available.

   B. You can only enable and configure PerformancePoint Services in SharePoint Server 2010 by using the Farm Configuration Wizard.

   C. You must import PerformancePoint Server 2007 data into SharePoint before the PerformancePoint Services service application options becomes available.

   D. On a single-server installation with a built-in database, PerformancePoint Services is automatically configured.

15. You are a SharePoint administrator for your organization. You have enabled the PerformancePoint Services service application, created a web application, created the site collection and sites in the application, and enabled PerformancePoint features for the site collection and in the relevant sites. You are discussing PerformancePoint with a new IT staff person, and she asks how PerformancePoint information is stored in SharePoint. Of the following, which are the correct answers? (Choose two.)

   A. PerformancePoint Services data source connections are located in document libraries.

   B. PerformancePoint Services data source connections are located in lists.

   C. PerformancePoint Services data content is located in document libraries.

   D. PerformancePoint Services data content is located in lists.

16. You are a SharePoint administrator for your organization. You have enabled the PerformancePoint Services service application, and created a web application, and created the site collection and sites within the web application. You now want to enable PerformancePoint Services in the site collection and for sites in the collection. Which specific features must be enabled? (Choose two.)

   A. You must activate SharePoint Publishing Infrastructure for the site collection.

   B. You must activate PerformancePoint Services Site features for specific sites.

   C. You must activate PerformancePoint Services Publishing for the site collection.

   D. You must activate PerformancePoint Services Infrastructure features for specific sites.

17. You are a SharePoint administrator for your organization, and you want to enable the Secure Store Service application to allow designers to create target applications that map credentials to external data sources. In the process of creating an encryption key for the Secure Store Service, you enter a passphrase as required. Later, you realize you've forgotten the passphrase you used. Where can you find the passphrase stored so you can recover it?

A. The passphrase is stored in the application log on the server used to generate the encryption key.

B. The passphrase is stored in the log generated by the Secure Store Service when it was initialized.

C. The passphrase is stored in the registry on the computer used to generate the encryption key.

D. The passphrase is not stored.

18. You are a SharePoint administrator for your organization. You have initialized an instance of the Secure Store Service application and generated an encryption key. You are briefing your staff on this process and are describing the circumstances when the encryption key may need to be refreshed. Of the following options, which are valid circumstances? (Choose all that apply.)

A. When you add a new application server

B. When you add a new web server

C. When you restore a previously backed up Secure Store Service database.

D. When you receive an "Unable to get master key error" message

19. You are a SharePoint administrator for your organization, and you are configuring the Visio Graphics Services service application in Central Administration. A number of settings require you input values for the cache age. The SharePoint users who make extensive use of Visio ask that you maximize the amount of time a diagram remains in the cache before it is cleared to get the most out of the service. What potential problems could this cause? (Choose all that apply.)

A. It could result in a potential performance slowdown because of greater CPU use on the server.

B. It could result in a potential performance slowdown because of greater memory use on the server.

C. It could result in a potential performance slowdown because of greater network activity between user locations and the server.

D. There are no issues related to maximizing the amount of time a diagram remains in the cache.

20. You are a SharePoint administrator for your organization, and you are discussing services application administration in SharePoint Server 2010 with your staff. Currently, you are discussing the steps for configuring Visio Graphics Services in SharePoint. One person asks whether there is any significant difference in configuring Visio Graphics Services and Access or Excel Services in Central Administration. What is the answer you most likely will provide?

A. Visio Graphics Service must be configured in Windows PowerShell.

B. Visio Graphics Service must be configured by running the Farm Configuration Wizard.

C. Visio Graphics Service requires that a trusted data provider be created at the same time the Visio Service is configured.

D. There is no significant difference.

Answers to Review Questions

1. D. Options A, B, and C are bogus. Option D is the quickest and most straightforward method of configuring service applications in the SharePoint server farm.

2. D. Using Central Administration, you can select the desired server and manage the services running on that server.

3. A. You can perform the task in either Central Administration or Windows PowerShell. The other options are bogus.

4. C. The tasks related to importing and exporting trust certificates must be performed using Windows PowerShell.

5. A, C. Only membership in the SharePoint_Shell_Access and WSS_ADMIN_WPG local groups is required to perform the application service configuration tasks in Windows PowerShell.

6. A,C. Regardless of whether you use Central Administration or Windows PowerShell, you must acquire and save the URL to the published service. The administrator for the SharePoint Server farm wanting to consume the published service will require the URL to point to the service application they want to use.

7. A, C. You must enter the URL to the remote resource correctly in order to make the connection. You must also associate the application service to your local web application that contains the site collection needing the resource before it can be accessed.

8. A. You enter the text string containing the URL to the remote resource at the first command, as in **Receive-SPSharedServiceApplicationInfo -FarmUrl <Publishing farm topology service URL>**.

9. B. Only option B describes the correct procedure. The other options are bogus.

10. A, B, C. The options are Assets Web Database, Charitable Contributions Web Database, Contacts Web Database, Issues Web Database, and Projects Web Database.

11. B. Only option B is correct. All of the other options are bogus.

12. A. The Security Token Service (STS) is a specialized web service that responds to requests for security tokens but is not specifically involved in the functioning of the unattended service account. The Single Sign-on Service stores and maps credentials to allow portal site-based applications to retrieve data from third-party applications but is not relevant to the unattended service account. User-defined functions (UDFs) can be enabled to extend the functionality of Excel Services but are used only once Excel Services is configured and operating.

13. C. To import the required data, you must input the name and instance of the SQL Server used for the PerformancePoint Server 2007 content. All other options are bogus.

14. D. If you performed a clean installation of SharePoint Server 2010 on a single-server installation with a built-in database, PerformancePoint Services is automatically created and configured, and there are no further configuration tasks available.

15. A, D. The data source connections are stored in document libraries while the data content, such as KPIs and scorecards, are stored in lists.

16. A, B. Only options A and B are the correct answers. Options C and D are bogus.

17. D. The passphrase is not stored, so it is recommended that you write it down at the time you are initializing an instance of the Secure Store Service application.

18. A, C, D. You will not likely have to refresh the encryption key when you add a new web server to the server farm. All other options are valid circumstances that may require a refresh of the key.

19. D. Keeping the diagram in cache for the maximum amount of time requires little out of the server, but the more frequently a diagram is refreshed, the more performance is required from the server's CPU and memory.

20. D. Although the Visio Graphics Service can be configured by using Windows PowerShell or by running the Farm Configuration Wizard, they are not absolutely required. You only need to create a trusted data provider for Visio Graphics Service if you intend to use an external database for the service.

Chapter 5

Configuring Indexing and Search

MICROSOFT EXAM OBJECTIVES COVERED IN THIS CHAPTER:

✓ **Maintaining a SharePoint Environment**

- ▪ Configure Service Applications
- ▪ Configure Indexing and Search

✓ **Managing a SharePoint Environment**

- ▪ Manage Operational Settings

Search is a SharePoint service that has needed improvement for some time, and in SharePoint Server 2010 it has certainly gotten the required attention. Not only has enterprise search been improved in the basic version, but FAST Search for SharePoint has been added to the mix to satisfy more sophisticated requirements.

Both basic enterprise search and FAST Search for SharePoint bring a richer search experience to the user by offering more flexible navigation and refinement of related searches. Query completion, spell checking, and wildcard use have also been added or improved for SharePoint Server 2010. Features for determining the relevance of social data such as tagging and usage or clicks are new as well.

Enterprise search recognizes that a lot of significant information lives outside of SharePoint, so expanded and improved connectors to index websites, file servers, Exchange, Lotus Notes, and many others have been added. Business Connectivity Services (BCS) now makes it easier to index arbitrary sources of data such as custom databases, and you can create a search connection without coding using SharePoint Designer. Compared to its predecessors, search in SharePoint Server 2010 is a whole new world.

We'll cover the basic enterprise search features and tasks first, and then we'll cover managing search farm topology using FAST Search for SharePoint.

Enterprise Search Overview

There's a lot that's new for SharePoint enterprise search, from the point of view of both the end user and the SharePoint administrator. As a SharePoint administrator, you'll be interested in all the new features. Not only will you need to be able to install, configure, and manage search in SharePoint, but you'll have to do so with an eye on the needs of your consumers.

SharePoint Search for Users

From a user's perspective, there are only two aspects to search that matter: the search query and the results.

Understanding Search Queries for Users

Anyone who uses web search in any capacity knows that the quality of the answers you get back depends on how well you ask the question. That said, an end user shouldn't have to worry about how well they craft a query in a search engine, and it's up to the designers of search to make the process as easy and transparent as possible. Here's what enterprise search in SharePoint currently offers:

- SharePoint Server 2010 search now supports the Boolean operators AND, OR, and NOT in search strings both for free-text queries and for property queries. For example, you can now type (**"SharePoint Search" OR "Bing Search") AND (title:"Keyword Syntax" OR title:"Query Syntax"**).

- SharePoint search queries now support using the asterisk (*) as a wildcard at the end of a text string for both search keywords and document properties. For example, typing **micro*** will return documents containing words such as *Microsoft* and *microchip*. Typing **author:ja*** will return documents containing *James* and *Japanese*. If type **micro* author:ja***, you will find documents containing both *Microsoft* and *James Pyles*.

- Search query suggestion offers tips to the user as they are typing their query in the search field in the Search Center, and these suggestions are based on past queries from other users.

- The Search Center also offers suggestions after the search results have been returned to help users refine their search further, such as "Did you mean...?"

- After completing a search in SharePoint, users can create a connector for the same search in Windows 7 so that the same search from Windows 7 will find relevant documents from the most recent SharePoint sites search crawl.

Understanding Search Results for Users

Perhaps you only get as much out of search as you put into it, but then again, SharePoint has added some improvements so that the user doesn't have to work so hard to get meaningful information from a search result:

- SharePoint Server 2010 search offers improved search results for people, particularly in locating specific names and expertise.

- When users search for themselves as a way to test the people search process, SharePoint recognizes this as "self-search" and returns all the related metadata, including the number of times the user's My Site profile was viewed and the search strings that were used to locate the user's name.

- Search also has improved results for queries on nickname and phonetic name searches, such as the results for *James* and *Jim* as well as *Lynn* and *Lin*.

- Search relevance improvements allow a higher ranking to be assigned documents that have been accessed more often from a search results page.

- SharePoint now can add relevance based on inferred metadata so that, after a crawl, document metadata can include the content of the document to assist when explicit metadata is missing or incorrect.

SharePoint Search for Administrators

Although it's important for you to understand the benefits of enterprise search for the end user, the real news is what SharePoint Server 2010 enterprise search has to offer you in terms of the UI, new features, and new functionality:

- The Farm Configuration Wizard automates a variety of deployment functions after the SharePoint installation or upgrade, including creating the fully functional search system on the server, creating the search topology that supports an index for up to 100 million crawled documents, and creating a Search Center that users can access to issue queries.

  The Search Center is created automatically only if you select the Search Center option during the wizard process.

- The improved UI for Central Administration collects the different farm-wide search tasks in a single location on the General Application Settings page, as shown in Figure 5.1.

- Search administration is now an independent service rather than being bundled with other services in a shared services provider (SSP) as you may have experienced in Microsoft Office SharePoint Server 2007 (MOSS 2007); thus, you can now create search service applications that operate independently of one another.

FIGURE 5.1   General Application Settings page in Central Administration

- Search crawl components can now be configured to increase crawl frequency and volume, increase performance by distributing the crawl load, and provide redundancy should a search server fail.

- Search query component performance is improved by allowing an increase in the number of queries search can manage at any one time, by reducing the amount of time it takes to return search results, and by provisioning failover capacity for query components.

- You can now tune search operations while users continue to access search.

- Search operations can be monitored by SharePoint health and performance monitoring, and customized reports can assist in analyzing search system operations.

- SharePoint search can now search for external content outside SharePoint sites by crawling and federating, such as crawling file shares and Lotus Notes, as well as using federation for access to search results gathered by other crawlers or search engines.

- Administrative tasks for search can now be automated using Windows PowerShell scripts.

Managing Enterprise Search from General Application Settings

When you run the Farm Configuration Wizard, you can select the Search Service Application option to enable search in SharePoint. Once search is enabled, in Central Administration, you can configure a number of features in search by accessing the General Application Settings page. The following activities illustrate how to work with basic search in SharePoint. There are two general features you will work with in this section: farm-wide search administration and *crawler impact rules*.

Administering Farm-wide Search

As you read previously, all the configuration settings for search have been gathered together in a single area of Central Administration. The following tasks will show you the most common ways to administer search. Exercise 5.1 shows you how to enable a proxy server for search.

EXERCISE 5.1

Configuring a Search Proxy Server

1. Navigate to Central Administration and click General Application Settings.

2. On the General Application Settings page, click Farm-Wide Search Administration under Search.

3. On the Farm-Wide Search Administration page, to configure a proxy server, click None to the right of the Proxy Server row.

4. When the Search Proxy Setting dialog box appears, select Use The Proxy Server Specified under Proxy Server Settings.

5. In the Address field, enter the URL of the proxy server.

6. In the Port field, enter the port number used by the proxy server.

7. If you so desire, select the Bypass Proxy Server For Local (Intranet) Addresses check box if you want to enable that function.

8. If you don't want to use a proxy server for some web addresses you administer, enter the beginning of their addresses in the Do Not Use Proxy Server For Addresses Beginning With field, separating them with semicolons.

9. Select the Use These Proxy Settings For Access To Federated Sites if you want to enable that function.

10. When finished, click OK.

The connection timeout setting for search and the request for acknowledgment time are both set for 60 seconds. Exercise 5.2 will show you how to change the default settings.

Configuring the Search Timeout Settings

1. Navigate to Central Administration and click General Application Settings.

2. On the General Application Settings page, click Farm-Wide Search Administration under Search.

3. On the Farm-Wide Search Administration page, click the 60, 60 link at the right of the Time-Out (Seconds) row.

4. When the Search Time-Out Setting dialog box appears, change the default value of 60 in the Connection Time (In Seconds) field to the desired value.

5. Change the default value of 60 in the Request Acknowledgement Time (In Seconds) field to the desired value.

6. Click OK.

Normally, search will not automatically trust that sites are legitimate, particularly if the certificate name does not exactly match. Exercise 5.3 shows you how to override this behavior.

EXERCISE 5.3

Modifying the Search SSL Settings

1. Navigate to Central Administration and click General Application Settings.

2. On the General Application Settings page, click Farm-Wide Search Administration under Search.

3. On the Farm-Wide Search Administration page, at the right of the Ignore SSL Warnings row, click No.

4. In the Search SSL Setting dialog box, to allow search to ignore SSL warnings, select the Ignore SSL Certificate Name Warnings check box and then click OK.

Administering Crawling Features

You can perform a large number of tasks to administer enterprise search features in SharePoint, and Exercise 5.4 will show you how to review and manage general elements in search configuration.

There are other ways to perform some of these tasks by accessing links found on the Search Administration page under Search Server Application that will be covered in subsequent exercises.

Before continuing to administer search, you want make sure the search service application is connected to the desired web application. Exercise 5.5 will illustrate how this is done.

EXERCISE 5.4

Reviewing and Managing the Search Administration Page

1. Navigate to Central Administration and click General Application Settings.

2. On the General Application Settings page under Search, click Farm-Wide Search Administration.

3. On the Farm-Wide Search Administration page, click the desired application under Search Service Applications (there is only one by default).

4. On the Search Administration page for the selected application, review the information available under System Status, such as the crawl status, background activity, and recent crawl rate, as shown here.

EXERCISE 5.4 *(continued)*

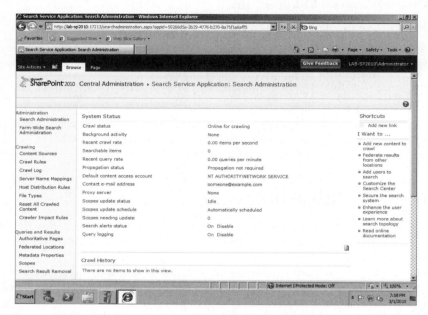

5. To change the default content access account, click the account name. When the Default Content Access Account dialog box appears, enter the desired content name that has read access to the content being crawled, enter and confirm the password for the account, and then click OK.

6. To change the contact email address, click the default email address. In the Search Email Setting box, enter the new contact email address and then click OK.

7. If you want to configure a proxy server, click the None link next to Proxy Server. In the Search Proxy Setting box, configure the proxy server settings (see Exercise 5.1 for details).

8. To change the Scopes update schedule, click the link for the schedule. In the Specify Update Schedule box, select either On Demand Updates Only or Automatically Scheduled Update and then click OK.

9. To enable or disable search alerts status, click the link next to the heading.

10. To enable or disable query logging, click the link next to the heading.

11. Under Crawl History, review the items in the view.

12. Under Search Topology, review the items available (see the "Managing the Enterprise Search Topology" section later in this chapter for details).

13. When finished on this page, navigate back to the Central Administration main page.

EXERCISE 5.5

Connecting the Search Service Application to a Web Application

1. In Central Administration, click Application Management.

2. On the Application Management page, click Configure Service Application Associations under Service Applications.

3. On the Service Applications Associations page, click the link in the Application Proxy Group area for the desired web application, which is usually called Default.

4. On the Configure Service Application Associations page, select the Search Services Application check box, making sure it is the only selected search service application proxy, and then click OK.

This allows the service to connect to the web application containing the sites to be crawled.

Both Search Service Application and FAST Query SSA cannot be set as the search service application proxy at the same time. You'll learn more about the FAST Search service later in this chapter.

The next step is creating a content source to be crawled. Exercise 5.6 will show you how to do this in Central Administration. This task can be done both for the standard SharePoint search application or for FAST search, which you'll learn about later in the chapter.

EXERCISE 5.6

Creating a Content Source

1. In Central Administration, click Application Management and then click Manage Service Applications.

2. On the Manage Service Applications page, select the desired search service application.

3. In the left menu under Crawling, click Content Sources. On the Manage Content Sources page, select New Content Source.

4. On the next page, under Name, give the content source a name in the available field.

5. Under Content Source Type, select the desired content type from the available radio buttons:

   - SharePoint Sites
   - Web Sites
   - File Shares
   - Exchange Public Folders

EXERCISE 5.6 *(continued)*

- Line Of Business Data

- Custom Repository

6. Under Start Addresses, enter the URLs from which search should begin the crawl in the Type Start Addresses Below (One Per Line) field, as shown here.

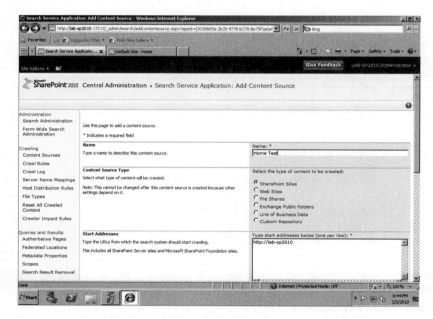

7. Under Crawl Settings, select either Crawl Everything Under The Hostname For Each Start Address or Only Crawl The Site Collection Of Each Start Address.

8. Under Crawl Schedules, use the Full Crawl menu to select None or the default value; or, click Create Schedule and in the Manage Schedules box select the days and times when you want to start for Full Crawls.

9. Use the Incremental Crawl menu to select None or the default value; or, click Create Schedule and in the Manage Schedules box select the days and times when you want to start for Incremental Crawls.

10. Under Content Source Priority, either accept Normal as the default crawl priority or select High Priority.

11. To start a crawl immediately, select Start Full Crawl Of The Content Source.

12. When you are finished, click OK.

When you are selecting the content source type, you can crawl only one type of content for a content source. This means you can add URLs for multiple SharePoint sites, or you can add URLs for multiple file shares, but you cannot add URLs for both SharePoint sites and file shares in a single content source.

A number of other routine search administration tasks are performed on the Search Administration page of the desired search service application by accessing links on the left-side menu of the page.

Crawl rules allow you to include or exclude specific paths in a URL from being crawled as well as specifying authentication accounts. Rules are applied in the order in which they are written during a content crawl. You must conduct a full crawl of the content source for the new rule to be implemented. Exercise 5.7 will show you how to configure a crawl rule.

Begin this and the following exercises on the Search Administration page of the default search service application.

EXERCISE 5.7

Creating a Crawl Rule

1. On the Search Administration page of the default search service application, click Crawl Rules under Crawling at the left of the page.

2. On the Manage Crawl Rules page, click New Crawl Rule.

3. On the Add Crawl Rule page, under Path, enter the hostname or hostnames of the sites on which you want the rule to apply, specifying the sites on the URLs to be affected by the rule and using this format: http://hostname/*; http://*.*; ://hostname/.

4. After selecting the path, note the two empty check boxes and either accept the default and make no selection or select the check box Follow Regular Expression Syntax, Match Case, Or Both.

5. Under Crawl Configuration, decide to include or exclude all items in the path you used in the previous set.

6. If you chose to exclude all items, you can choose to select Exclude Complex URLs, such as those containing question marks.

7. If you chose to include all times, you can also use one or more of the available check boxes or none of them:

   - Follow Links On The URL Without Crawling The URL Itself

   - Crawl Complex URLs Such As Those Containing Question Marks

   - Crawl SharePoint Content As Http Pages

EXERCISE 5.7 *(continued)*

8. If you chose to include all items in the path, you can also choose the method of authorization under Specify Authorization to access the sites in question, as you can see here.

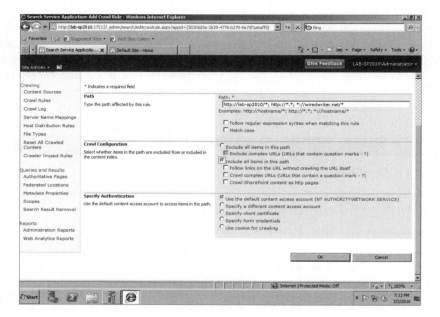

9. When you are done, click OK.

10. When the rule is configured, you can enter the URL in the test field on the Manage Crawl Rules page and then click the Test button to verify the rule matches the URL.

Content crawls will impact websites and the servers hosting them. You can set up crawler impact rules to minimize that impact if you think they are required. Exercise 5.8 shows you this simple process.

EXERCISE 5.8

Creating a Crawler Impact Rule

1. On the Search Administration page of the default search service application, click Crawler Impact Rules under Crawling at the left of the page.

2. On the Crawler Impact Rules page, in the Site column, click to the right of the desired site to open the menu and then click Edit.

3. On the Edit Crawler Impact Rule page, under Site, enter the site's name without entering the protocol (that is, `http://`) such as **Testsite.aspx**.

4. Under Request Frequency, either select Request Up To The Specified Number Of Documents At A Time radio and then enter a number in the Simultaneous Requests field or select Request One Document At A Time And Wait The Specified Time and then enter a value in seconds in the available field.

5. To create the rule, click OK.

6. If there is more than one rule configured, in the Order column on the Crawler Impact Rules page, use the menus to select which rule will be evaluated first, second, and so on.

Other Crawling Rules

There are a number of other links under Crawling, but most of the tasks performed on those pages are relatively straightforward. Here's a summary:

Crawl Log   Click this link to see the log files for crawls for each content source. Columns on the page show the number of successes, warnings, errors, top-level errors, and deletes. Click the number in the desired row and column to see the details for that value. For instance, Figure 5.2 shows you the details of a crawl error.

FIGURE 5.2   Crawl log error detail

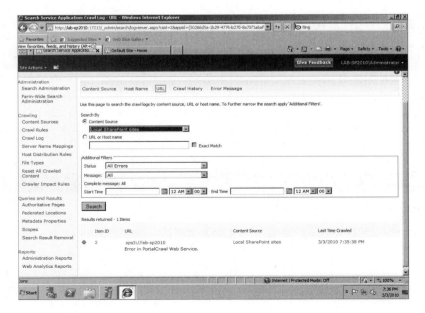

On this page, you can search crawl logs by content source or URL and further refine your search by status, message, and start and end times. The error message is displayed at the bottom of this page. Click to the right of the URL of the content source in the error message, and choose to open the item in a new window, re-crawl the item, or remove it from the index.

Server Name Mappings   When you click this link, if no mappings exist, you can create one by clicking New Mapping. On the Add Server Name Mapping page, you can indicate the address of the content to be crawled and then specify an address that will be shown in the search results to make the address more recognizable or more "human readable."

Host Distribution Rules   You cannot configure these rules for a single SharePoint Server instance with a built-in database deployment. To configure the host distribution rules, you must be using a deployment with more than one crawl database available. See the "Adding and Removing a Host Distribution Rule" section later in this chapter for more details.

File Types   When you click this link, you are taken to a page with a list of all the content file types that are included in a content search by default. Such filename extensions include .aspx, .docx, .html, .php, and so on. To add a new file extension type, click the New File Type link, and on the Add File Type page, enter the file extension in the available field and then click OK. On the Manage File Types page, click to the right of a file extension name to open the menu and select Delete if you want to remove the file type from the page. This will mean that file type will not be included during content crawls.

Reset All Crawled Content   Click this link to erase the content index. If you do this, no search results will be available until you run another crawl. If you do not want to receive an email alert regarding this action, verify that the Deactivate Search Alerts During Reset check box is selected. Click Reset Now to perform the action.

Administering Query and Result Features

The Search Administration page for any search service application also contains a Queries And Results section with links to various features that can be configured. This section will show what each feature does and how to use it.

Exercise 5.9 tells you how to set up authoritative pages. *Authoritative web pages* are those pages you determine link to the most relevant information, and search uses these pages to determine the search rank of every page in the index. You use the Authoritative Pages utility to organize most authoritative to nonauthoritative sites.

EXERCISE 5.9

Configuring Authoritative Web Pages

1.   On the Search Administration page of the default search service application, click Authoritative Pages under Queries And Results on the left of the page.

2. On the Specify Authoritative Pages page, in the Most Authoritative Pages field under Authoritative Web Pages, enter the URLs of the most important URLs by content relevancy, entering one URL per line.

3. If necessary, in the Second-Level Authoritative Pages field, enter the URLs of pages that have a lesser relevancy than most authoritative.

4. In the Third-Level Authoritative Pages field, enter the URLs of pages that have a lesser relevancy than the second-level pages.

5. Under Non-authoritative Sites, in the Sites To Demote field, enter the URLS of those sites and pages that you want to have content marked as least relevant.

6. To make sure ranking recalculation will occur when you click OK, select the Refresh Now check box or clear the check box to have the ranking calculated at a later time.

7. When you're ready, click OK.

Federated locations are a way for you to expand the field of SharePoint search. Search federation lets your users not only search content in the search index on the server but search many other locations as well. Adding federated locations lets queries be sent to remote search engines and feeds such as www.bing.com as well as databases and other external content sources. Users can take advantage of this by adding and setting up either Federated Search Results web parts or Top Federated Results web parts on desired web part pages to display specified search results. Results will also be displayed on the default search results page.

You can either import a federated search connector or add a location manually. Exercise 5.10 will start you off by showing you how to import a search connection.

Importing Federated Locations Search Connectors

1. On the Search Administration page of the default search service application, click Federated Locations under Queries and Results on the left of the page.

2. On the Manage Federated Locations page, click Online Gallery to find a new location for downloading and importing.

3. When the Enterprise Search From Microsoft page opens in a separate browser tab or window, click Federated Search Connectors in the left menu.

4. In the Download Sample Connectors menu on the right of the page, expand the category of your choice and click the desired connector, as shown here.

EXERCISE 5.10 *(continued)*

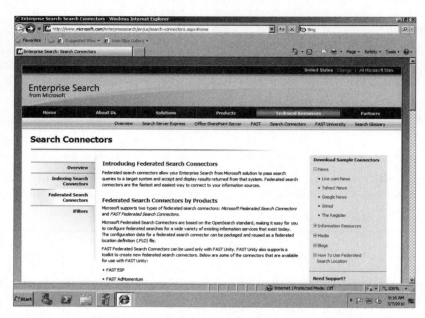

5. When the File Download dialog box appears, click Save, navigate to the location of the server where you want to save the file, and click Save, closing the dialog box after the file is downloaded, if necessary.

6. Unless you plan to download more FLD files, close the Enterprise Search From Microsoft web page.

7. On the Manage Federated Locations page, click Import Location.

8. On the Import Federated Location page, under Location Definition File, click Browse and navigate to the location where you saved the FLD file.

9. In the Choose File To Upload dialog box, select the FLD file and then click Open.

10. When the path to the FLD file populates the FLD file, click OK.

11. On the page showing the success message, you can either click Edit Location to modify the settings for the location or click Done if you're finished.

12. If you click Edit location, on the Edit Federated Location page, you can choose to modify items such as the display name, the description, the trigger that determines how the user's query matches the location, the location information, and so on. When you're done here, click OK to complete the import and return to the Manage Federated Locations page.

In step 11, if you had clicked Done, the file import would have been immediately completed. You only need to edit the location if you want to change the default configuration. Exercise 5.11 shows you how to add a location manually.

Manually Configuring Federated Locations Search Connectors

1. On the Search Administration page of the default search service application, click Federated Locations under Queries and Results on the left of the page.

2. On the Manage Federated Locations page, click New Location.

3. On the Add Federated Location page, you must create all the information that is normally added when you import a federated location.

4. Under General Information, add the required items Location Name, Display Name, and Description in the available fields.

5. Under Author, add an optional author for the location, which can be a person or an organization.

6. Under version, add a version number, which is typically 1.0.0.0 for the first version of a location connector.

7. Under Trigger, either accept the option Always: Query Should Always Match or select Prefix: Query Must Begin With A Specified Prefix. Then enter the prefix in the Add Prefix field or select Pattern: Query Must Match A Specified Pattern. Then add the pattern, which can be a regular expression in the Add Pattern field.

8. Under Location Information, select a Location Type such as Search Index On This Server (the default), FAST Index, or OpenSearch 1.0/1.1.

9. In the Query Template field, open the editor and add a template for passing queries to the location type's URL, which specifies not only the location but also the specific data to be queried. For example, type **{searchTerms} scope:Targeted_Best_Bets**.

10. Open the More Results editor and add an optional URL for a web page that offers additional search results for the query. For example, type **http://server/SearchCenter/ Pages/Results.aspx?k={searchTerms}**.

11. Under Display Information, either accept the default format for Federated Search Results, Display Metadata or clear the User Default Formatting check box and manually configure the formatting in the XSL, Properties, and Sample Data editors, as shown here.

EXERCISE 5.11 *(continued)*

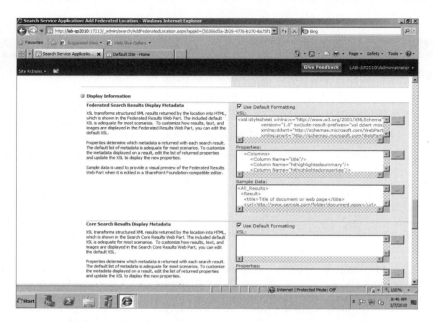

12. For Core Search Results Display Metadata, either accept the default formatting or clear the Use Default Formatting check box and manually configure the formatting in the XSL, Properties, and Sample Data editors.

13. For Top Federated Results Display Metadata, either accept the default formatting or clear the Use Default Formatting check box and manually configure the formatting in the XSL, Properties, and Sample Data editors.

14. Under Restrictions and Credentials, either select No Restrictions if anyone can access and use the location or select Use restriction of only site administrators from specific URLs can use the location and then use the Allowed Sites editor to add a list of URL domains separated by semicolons such as `http://firstsite;http://secondsite`, and so on.

15. Under Specify Credentials, depending on the federated location, you may have no selections with the Default authentication text being displayed, or you may have authentication selections under categories such as Common or User, with some authentication types being basic authentication, digest authentication, Kerberos, or similar items.

16. When you are finished, click OK to add the federated location.

> Federated search is the simultaneous search of multiple databases or web resources used primarily for automated web-based library and information retrieval systems. Core search is the traditional search method used by Google and others, in which only sources that have been directly indexed by the search engine's crawler can be searched, accessed, and retrieved.

As you can see, importing a location is much faster, is more efficient, and has much less likelihood of introducing errors into the federated location configuration. Once you have the federated locations imported and configured, you will still need to specify the location in the properties of any federated location web parts you choose to add to specific sites.

Metadata property mappings are used to map properties taken from crawled documents and managed properties that users employ in their search queries. For instance, various document types will have different names for the crawled property that identifies the document's authors. You can map these various crawled properties to a single managed property *author* so that when a user searches for a document's author, typing **author** will pull results from the different mapped crawled properties. The process of adding and editing a metadata property mapping is virtually the same. Exercise 5.12 takes you through the steps.

EXERCISE 5.12

Editing a Metadata Property Mapping

1. On the Search Administration page of the default search service application, click Metadata Properties under Queries And Results on the left of the page.

2. On the Metadata Property Mappings page, under the Property Name column, click to the right of the desired property name to open the menu and then click Edit/Map Property.

3. On the Edit Managed Property page, under Name, type or edit the property name and description in the available fields and either select or clear the Has Multiple Values check box.

4. Under Mappings To Crawled Properties, you can select either Include Values From All Crawled Properties or Include Values From A Single Crawled Property Base On The Order Specified.

5. In the Crawled Properties Mapped To This Managed Properties field, you can select any of the crawled properties present and then use the Move Up and Move Down buttons to change the list order, or you can use the Remove Mapping button to remove the crawled property from the list.

6. Use the Add Mapping button to open the Crawled Property select box, select the desired category and crawled property name, and then click OK to add the new crawled property.

EXERCISE 5.12 *(continued)*

7. Under Use In Scopes, select or clear the Allow This Property To Be Used In Scopes check box depending on your requirements.

8. Under Optimize Manage Property Storage, you can select or clear the Reduce Storage Requirements For Text Properties check box or Add Managed Property To Custom Results check box depending on your requirements.

9. When finished adding or editing the managed property mapping, click OK.

Mapped properties are categorized by managed and crawled properties. On the Metadata Properties Mappings page, click Categories; on the Categories page, click to the right of a category name to open the menu and then click Edit Category. You'll be able to edit the category name and the bulk crawled property settings.

On the Metadata Property Mappings page, under the Total column, you can click any of the crawled property names to open them for editing and then add or edit managed properties to be mapped to the crawled property.

You can set one or more scopes for search that refine searches on specific locations or content, limiting the field of the search, which saves time and resources. *Scopes* can be used in addition to location and property rules to provide users with more accurate results. For instance, creating a scope for a particular site in SharePoint limits the search to that site and its subsites, offering more results from the desired content providers. The default All Sites scope, on the other hand, applies no focus for searches of all the SharePoint site collections.

There are two basic tasks related to scopes. The first is to add or edit a scope, and the second is to add or edit rules within the scope. Exercise 5.13 teaches you how to add or edit a scope.

EXERCISE 5.13

Adding a Search Scope

1. On the Search Administration page of the default search service application, click Scopes under Queries and Results on the left of the page.

2. On the View Scopes page, click New Scope.

3. On the Create Scope page, give the scope a name in the Title field and a description in the Description field.

4. Under Target Results Page, select either Use The Default Search Results Page or Specify A Different Page For Searching This Scope and then enter the desired URL on the Target Results page such as `testing.aspx`.

5. Click OK when finished.

You can also edit an existing scope on the View Scopes page by clicking to the right of the scope name to open the menu, selecting Edit Properties And Rules, and then clicking Change Scope Settings.

In addition to creating a scope from scratch, you can open the menu to the right of an existing rule and select the Copy option. Once you've created a copy of the scope, you can give it a different name and edit the properties and rules for the scope as you require.

Once a scope has been created, you can add one or more rules to the scope to define its behavior. Exercise 5.14 shows you how this is done.

EXERCISE 5.14

Adding a Search Scope Rule

1. On the Search Administration page of the default search service application, click Scopes under Queries and Results on the left of the page.

2. On the View Scopes page, click to right of the name of the scope you created in the previous exercise. In the list that appears, click Edit Properties And Rules.

3. On the Scope Properties And Rules page, click New Rule under Rules.

4. On the Add Scope Rule page, select the type of rule you want to define under Scope Rule Type such as Web Addresses, Property Query, Content Source, or All Content.

5. Depending on what option you selected in the previous step, you will have to add different information types, such as by selecting Web Address and adding the URL or the path to the resource or by selecting Property Query and then adding an Add property restriction using the available menu and field, such as **Author = James Pyles**.

6. Under Behavior, select Include, Require, or Exclude to determine what action is applied to the web address, property, or content source rule.

7. When you are done, click OK.

You can also edit existing rules in a similar fashion.

The final option under Queries And Results on the search service application's Search Administration page is Search Result Removal. This page contains a simple field where you can enter the URLs to sites you want to remove from any search results returned in SharePoint. Adding a URL to this field will also automatically create a crawl rule that will exclude the specified URL from any future crawls. Just add the desired URL to the field and then click Remove Now.

Administering Reporting Features

On the search service application's Search Administration page, the final category in the menu on the left is Reports. By default, two report types are displayed: *Administration Reports* and *Web Analytics Reports*.

Administration Reports

When you click Administration Reports, you can view the different default report types to determine the health and functioning of the search service. The default folder is the Search Administration Reports folder. Clicking that link takes you to a list of the available reports for search:

CrawlRatePerContentSource   This is the graphic view of recent crawl activity aggregated by content course.

CrawlRatePerType   This offers you a graphic view of recent crawl activity by items and actions for specific URLs.

QueryLatency   This is the graphic view of recent query activity displaying latency from the major segments of the query pipeline, as well as the query averages per minute.

QueryLatencyTrend   This is the graphic view of recent query activity as trending.

SharepointBackendQueryLatency   This is the graphic view of recent query activity with latency details for the index and property database portion of the query pipeline as well as query averages per minute.

There is also another folder on that page called Advanced Reports, which contains the following:

CrawlProcessingPerActivity   This is the graphic view of where crawl processing happens in the pipeline.

CrawlProcessingPerComponent   This is the graphic view of where crawl processing happens in the pipeline per minute.

CrawlQueue   This is the graphic view of the state of the crawl queue.

You can click to the right of any of these reports to view or modify the report properties or permissions, as shown in Figure 5.3.

NOTE   There could also be an Alter Me option presented.

Click the name of a report to open it, such as Crawl Rate Per Content Source. On this page, you can see the report of crawl rate activity for the past 12 hours by default. You can filter the results by application type, individual content sources, and the date and time range; then click Apply Filters on the right side of the page to view your selections, as shown in Figure 5.4.

On the All Documents page for search administration reports, you can also click to the left of a particular report and select a check box in order to activate the Library Tools ribbon and perform various actions, as shown in Figure 5.5. You can select either the Documents or Library tab under Library Tools to access different features.

FIGURE 5.3   Menu for viewing or editing report properties and permissions

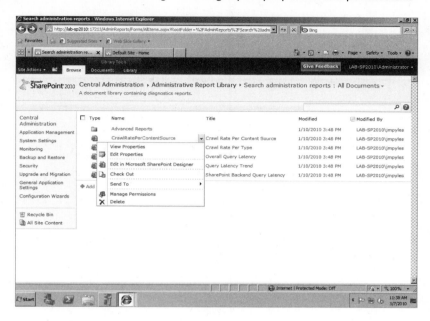

FIGURE 5.4   Crawl Rate Per Content Source report

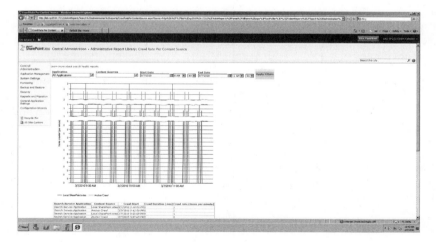

FIGURE 5.5 Library Tools options

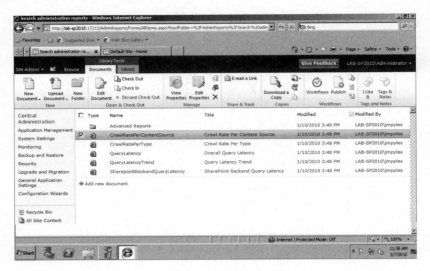

 Real World Scenario

Researching Errors in SharePoint Search Services

You are a SharePoint administrator for the Acme Development Company. Over the past 30 days, you and your staff have installed and configured SharePoint Server 2010 as a fresh install and deployed it across your organization's enterprise environment.

You come to work on Monday morning and learn your department has been getting calls from some users stating that the search function doesn't seem to be working. You review the crawl logs, and they show no new crawled documents. You start investigating and see in the event log Event ID: 92 with a description stating that a crawl component for a particular search application could not communicate with the query server.

You go to Microsoft's TechNet site and run a search on the error message. When the search results are displayed, you select the most likely result and discover the relevant information about the error, including potential solutions here:

    http://technet.microsoft.com/en-us/library/ee513077(office.14).aspx

After reviewing the information and continuing your investigation, you discover that the search service credentials were not up-to-date. You solve the problem by rebooting the servers that are experiencing this difficulty.

Web Analytics Reports

Along with reports on search features, you can view reports on usage data for the different SharePoint sites and site collections on the Search Administration page by clicking Web Analytics Reports under Reports. On the Web Analytics Reports page, click the desired web application; then on the Summary page, click the name of the desired report. The following reports are available:

- Summary
- Number of Page Views
- Number of Daily Unique Visitors
- Number of Referrers
- Top Pages
- Top Visitors
- Top Referrers
- Top Destinations
- Top Browsers
- Number of Queries
- Number of Collections
- Top Site Collection Templates
- Customized Reports

 If you have only recently enabled analytics, you may not see any data displayed because insufficient time has passed for data to be collected.

You can filter these reports by date range and export them to spreadsheet format.

Managing the Enterprise Search Topology

Enterprise search in SharePoint Server 2010 consists of a number of topological components that provide the different elements required for search to operate correctly. The following information and steps will illustrate how you configure search indexing, crawling, and other functions.

Administering an Index Partition and Query Components

In the world of SharePoint Server 2010 search, index partitions are groups of query components, each used to contain a subset of the full-text index and return search results to the submitter of the search query. Each of these index partitions is associated with a specific property database that contains the metadata associated with a specific set of crawled content. You can construct the topology for search by creating query components on selected servers in your server farm.

On a single-server installation with a built-in database, the SharePoint Search topology cannot be changed. You will not be able to perform this exercise on the SharePoint Server 2010 installation configured for this book.

Adding an Index Partition to a Search Service Application

You can add an *index partition* to a search service application and place query components on different farm servers to distribute the load of query services. The following steps take you through the process. The first query component is created automatically when a new index partition is created.

1. In Central Administration, click Manage Service Applications under Application Management.

2. On the Service Applications page, click the link for the search server application on which you want to add an index partition.

3. On the Search Administration page, click the Modify button under Search Application Topology.

4. When the Add Query Component dialog box appears in the Server list, click the farm server on which you want to add the first query component for the new index partition.

5. In the Associated Property Database list, click the name of the property database for which you want to associate the new index partition.

6. In the Location Of Index field, enter an optional location on the server for storing the index files after they're received from the crawl components, or accept the default location.

7. Under Failover-Only Query Component, leave the Set This Query Component As Failover-Only check box empty since you are creating a new index partition.

8. When you are done, click OK.

9. On the Manage Search Topology page, click Apply Topology Changes to start the SharePoint timer jobs that will add the new index partition and the first query component to the server you selected.

Removing an Index Partition to a Search Service Application

Not only can you add an index partition, but you can remove it as well. The following steps take you through the process of removing an index partition from a search service application. This task also cannot be performed on a SharePoint Server 2010 single-server installation with a built-in database.

1. In Central Administration, click Manage Service Applications under Application Management.

2. On the Service Applications page, click the link for the search server application on which you want to remove an index partition.

3. On the Search Administration page, click the Modify button under Search Application Topology.

4. On the Manage Search Topology page, click the query component in the index partition you want to remove and then click Delete.

5. In the dialog box that appears, click OK to confirm your decision.

6. On the Manage Search Topology page, click Apply Topology Changes to start the SharePoint timer jobs that will remove the index partition and the query components from the server.

If you choose to delete all the query components from an index partition, you will also remove the index partition from the farm. All the data from the partition will automatically be copied and distributed to the remaining partitions. If there is only one index partition for a search service application, you will be unable to remove it.

Adding a Query Component to an Index Partition

As you learned earlier, a query component is a container for a particular subset of the full-text index and is used to return search results to the query submitter. A query component is part of an index partition and is also associated with a specific property database containing the metadata associated with a set of crawled content. Just as you can add or remove an index partition to a search service application, you can also add and remove a query component to an index partition. The next task will show you how. As with the tasks involving adding and removing an index partition, adding and removing a query component cannot be performed on a SharePoint Server 2010 single-server installation with a built-in database.

1. In Central Administration, click Manage Service Applications under Application Management.

2. On the Service Applications page, click the link for the search server application on which you want to remove an index partition.

3. On the Search Administration page, click the Modify button under Search Application Topology.

4. On the Manage Search Topology page, click a query component in the index partition you want to modify and then click Add Mirror.

5. In the Location Of Index field, you can add an optional location on the server to use for storing index files after receiving them from crawl components, or you can use the default location.

6. Under Failover-Only Query Component, select the Set This Query Component As Failover-Only check box only if you want the query component to receive queries in the event of the primary query component failing in this index partition. Otherwise, do not select the check box.

7. Click OK when you are finished.

8. On the Manage Search Topology page, click Apply Topology Changes to start the SharePoint timer job that will add the new mirror query component for the index partition you selected.

Removing a query component from an index partition is very much like removing an index partition from a search service application, except after you click the Modify button in step 3, click the query component on the Manage Search Topology page you want to remove and then click Delete. After that, click OK. On the Manage Search Topology page, click Apply Topology Changes.

 WARNING Remember, if you remove all the query components from an index partition, you remove the index partition, and all the data will be copied to other partitions. You cannot remove the last index partition.

Administrating Crawl Databases and Components

Crawl databases are used by a specific search service application to store information about the location of content sources as well as crawl schedules and other crawl operation–related data. As you previously read, you can distribute the database load by adding crawl databases on different servers running SQL Server. Crawl databases are associated with crawl components, and you can dedicate a component to a specific host by creating host distribution rules.

Adding and Removing a Crawl Database

The following steps will show you how to add or remove a crawl database to a search service application. You will be unable to perform this task on a single SharePoint Server deployment with a built-in database.

1. In Central Administration, click Manage Service Applications under Application Management.

2. On the Service Applications page, click the link for the search server application on which you want to remove an index partition.

3. On the Search Administration page, click the Modify button under Search Application Topology.

4. On the Manage Search Topology page, click New and then click Crawl Database.

5. When the Add Crawl Database dialog box appears, under Add Crawl Database, point to the database server on which you want to add the crawl database and enter the database name and the database authentication credentials or accept the default values in these areas.

6. If you so desire, enter the information for a failover database server in the Failover Database Server field, but you must have SQL Server database mirroring enabled to select this option.

7. Under Dedicated Database, if you so desire, select the Dedicate This Crawl Store To Hosts As Specified In Host Distribution Rules check box.

8. Once you have finished, click OK.

9. On the Manage Search Topology page, click Apply Topology Changes to start the SharePoint timer job that will add the new crawl database to the SQL Server computer.

10. To delete the crawl database, follow steps 1 through 3. Then after clicking the Modify button, click the desired crawl database on the Manage Search Topology page and then click Delete.

11. When the verification box appears, click OK.

12. On the Manage Search Topology page, click Apply Topology Changes to start the SharePoint timer job that will delete the new crawl database from the SQL Server computer.

Before you can delete a crawl database, you must first disconnect any associations between the crawl components and the crawl database, either by assigning the components to a different crawl database or by removing the crawl components. If you do not do so, the Delete button will not appear as expected in step 10 of the previous task.

A crawl component is the portion of a crawl database that processes the crawls of content sources, propagates the resulting index files to query components, and adds the data about the location and crawl schedule to the associated crawl database.

Adding and Removing a Crawl Component to a Crawl Database

As you learned in the previous task, you can add or remove a crawl component from a crawl database associated with a search service application. The following steps outline how to do so. Like all other search topology tasks, you will not be able to complete these steps if you are using a single SharePoint server with a built-in database deployment.

1. In Central Administration, click Manage Service Applications under Application Management.

2. On the Service Applications page, click the link for the search server application on which you want to remove an index partition.

3. On the Search Administration page, click the Modify button under Search Application Topology.

4. On the Manage Search Topology page, click New and then click Crawl Component.

5. When the Add Crawl Component dialog box appears, use the Server list to select the farm server on which you want to add the crawl component.

6. Use the Associated Crawl Database list to select the crawl database you want to associate with the new crawl component.

7. If you so desire, you can use the Temporary Location Of Index field to enter the location of the server you want to use for creating index files before propagating them to the query components, or you can accept the default location.

8. When you are finished, click OK.

9. On the Manage Search Topology page, click Apply Topology Changes to start the SharePoint timer job that will add the new crawl component to the specified server.

10. To remove the component, follow steps 1 through 3. After clicking the Modify button, select the crawl component on the Manage Search Topology page that you want to remove. Then click Delete.

11. When the confirmation box appears, click OK to add the crawl component to the removal job queue.

12. On the Manage Search Topology page, click Apply Topology Changes to start the SharePoint timer job that will delete the crawl component from the server.

Administering Property Databases and Host Distribution Rules

In addition to crawl databases, SharePoint search also uses *property databases*, which contain metadata associated with crawled content. These property databases can be added to and removed from SQL Server database servers in the server farm in much the same way as crawl databases. Since this is a search topology task, it cannot be performed on a single SharePoint Server deployment with a built-in database.

Adding and Removing a Property Database

The steps for adding the property database are almost identical to adding and removing a crawl database. Follow steps 1 through 3 in the "Adding and Removing a Crawl Database" section; but after clicking the Modify button, click New on the Manage Search Topology page and then click Property Database. Then, when the Add Property Database dialog box appears, either accept the defaults or add your own information for the database server name, database name, and authentication credentials. You can also choose to specify a failover database server if you want, but you must have SQL Server database mirroring enabled to do so. After that, follow the final steps of clicking OK and then Apply Topology Changes to start the SharePoint timer job.

The process of removing the property database is identical to that of removing a crawl database, including the requirement that you must remove any associations with query components before the property database can be successfully deleted.

Adding and Removing a Host Distribution Rule

The final task in managing search topologies is adding and removing a host distribution rule. Host distribution rules are used to associate a server computer with a specific crawl database. The default distribution rule is to load balance hosts across crawl databases based on the availability of space; however, you can choose to override this behavior and connect a host to a specific crawl database. This is sometimes done based on availability and performance requirements. There must be more than one crawl database available in the search service application to add a host distribution rule.

1. In Central Administration, click Manage Service Applications under Application Management.

2. On the Service Applications page, click the search service application on which you want to add the host distribution rule.

3. On the Search Administration page, click Host Distribution Rules in the left navigation bar.

4. On the Host Distribution Rules page, click Add Distribution Rule.

5. On the Add Host Rule page, enter the name of the desired host in the Hostname field.

6. Use the Distribution Configuration list to select the crawl database you want to be involved in the crawling action on the selected host.

7. Click OK to add the new job to the queue.

8. On the Host Distribution Rules page, click Apply Changes.

9. Click OK to apply the rule.

To remove a rule, follow steps 1 through 3. Then on the Host Distribution Rules page, hover your cursor over the host distribution rule you want to remove, click the down arrow that becomes available, and then click Delete. In the confirmation box, click OK to add the job to the queue. Click Apply Changes and then click OK.

Managing FAST Search for SharePoint

The "FAST" part of FAST Search for Microsoft was originally a recursive acronym: Fast Search and Transfer ASA. FAST is actually FAST Enterprise Search Platform (ESP), a service-oriented architecture development platform that offers a foundation on which to build an application noted for efficient indexing of searchable content across an enterprise-level data space.

Although SharePoint Server 2010's out-of-the-box search solution is quite capable of servicing the enterprise, FAST Search Server 2010 for SharePoint is an add-on based on FAST Search that is integrated into SharePoint, combining the best of SharePoint and FAST. FAST brings SharePoint search to a whole new level, representing a superset to the off-the-rack SharePoint search tool.

As an administrator, you now have two search options to choose from within SharePoint. Here's what you need to know about FAST.

Installation and Configuration of FAST Search Server 2010 for SharePoint

FAST Search Server isn't installed on any of the servers that contain SharePoint Server 2010, so you cannot use the same physical computer containing SharePoint for the FAST Search Server. Although adding and configuring FAST Search Server as a backend for SharePoint is part of the material you are responsible for in the 70-668 "PRO: SharePoint 2010, Administrator" exam, the actual installation and post-installation configuration of FAST Search Server itself probably is not. Nevertheless, this information will be presented in summary here as background.

FAST Search Servers

There are two separate FAST Search Server products that can be downloaded and installed:

- Microsoft FAST Search Server 2010 for SharePoint Internet Sites:

  http://www.microsoft.com/downloads/details.aspx?familyid=AA37E8B0-C4D6-4452-A476-B81EE0BFBDA5&displaylang=en

- Microsoft FAST Search Server 2010 for SharePoint:

  http://www.microsoft.com/downloads/details.aspx?familyid=BCC37C48-11FB-40A2-8CFB-743DE20260F6&displaylang=en

Also, just as you must purchase SharePoint under a licensing agreement, FAST Search Server is a separate server product and is purchased independently of SharePoint.

Installation Requirements

A necessary prerequisite for installing FAST Search Server 2010 for SharePoint is to first install SharePoint and SQL Server. SharePoint must be installed with the Farm install option, and the Complete (Advanced Installation) option must be selected. Further, if you want to enable the document preview option so you can preview Word and PowerPoint documents in search results before opening them, you must install Microsoft Office Web Applications before running the SharePoint product configuration wizard.

You can only install FAST Search Server on Windows Server 2008 SP2 x64 or Windows Server 2008 R2 x64. You can use any version including Standard, Enterprise, and Datacenter. You cannot run any other server roles on the computer besides FAST Search Server.

 To avoid query timeout errors for the period of time around midnight on daylight saving time (DST) dates, it's recommended that you turn off the automatic DST adjustment on the computer or computers running FAST Search Server.

Deployment Scenarios

FAST Search Server 2010 for SharePoint can be deployed either as a stand-alone installation or in a multiple-server deployment. Usually you install FAST as stand-alone either to test or evaluate the search server or for a very small production environment.

The multiple-server deployment is more typical for a production environment. One server is deployed as the admin server and is responsible for providing administrative services. Other FAST servers are deployed as nonadmin servers that provide search, indexing, and document processing. You can install any number of nonadmin servers to scale out the deployment.

Installation Procedures

The full installation process for FAST Search Server involves three parts:

- Running the Prerequisite Installer
- Installing FAST Search Server 2010 for SharePoint
- Running the post-installation configuration

> This is not a comprehensive guide to installing and configuring FAST Search Server 2010 for SharePoint. To find detailed information, visit http://technet.microsoft.com/en-us/enterprisesearch/ee441234.aspx.

Running the Prerequisite Installer

You must be a member of the local Administrators group on the server you are performing this task.

1. Download the Prerequisite Installer file `prerequisiteinstaller.exe` and launch the file.
2. On the welcome page, click Next.
3. During the prerequisite software installation, you may have to restart the computer.
4. On the Prerequisite Installer Installation Complete screen, click Finish.

You may have to install the following after the Prerequisite Installer finishes:

- For Windows Server 2008 with SP2, FIX, a hotfix that provides a method to support the token authentication without transport security or message encryption in WCF, is available for the .NET Framework 3.5 SP1 (`http://go.microsoft.com/fwlink/?LinkID=160770`).
- For Windows Server 2008 R2, FIX, a hotfix that provides a method to support the token authentication without transport security or message encryption in WCF, is available for the .NET Framework 3.5 SP1 (`http://go.microsoft.com/fwlink/?LinkID=166231`).

Installing FAST Search Server 2010 for SharePoint

To install FAST Search Server 2010 for SharePoint, follow these steps:

1. This installation process must be run on every server computer on which you want to operate FAST Search Server. You must be the local administrator on those computers.
2. Download the installation file for FAST Search Server, launch it, and then allow the installation process to progress to completion.
3. After the installation is complete, go to `c:\FASTsearch`, which is the default location for FAST Search Server, and manually create the directories:
   - `data`
   - `data\data_security`

- `data\data_security\admin`
- `data\data_security\worker`

4. Perform an antivirus scan on the directory containing FAST Search Server.

Performing Post-Installation Configuration

Once FAST Search Server is installed, there are three post-installation configuration scenarios:

- Configuring a stand-alone server deployment
- Configuring an admin server in a multiple-server deployment
- Configuring a nonadmin server in a multiple-server deployment

All three post-installation configuration scenarios are managed by a post-installation configuration script located in `c:\FastSearch\installer\scripts`.

Configuring a Stand-Alone Server Deployment

To configure a stand-alone server deployment, follow these steps:

1. On the computer with FAST Search Server installed, click Start, right-click Windows PowerShell, and select Run As Administrator.

2. Navigate to `C:\FASTSearch`, type the following, and then press Enter in order to enable scripts to run:

```
Set-ExecutionPolicy RemoteSigned
```

3. If prompted, press Y for Yes.

4. Navigate to `C:\FastSearch\installer\scripts`.

5. Type the following and then press Enter, replacing the sample values with their real counterparts:

```
.\psconfig.ps1 -action i -roleName single -userName domain\user
-localMachineName fully_qualified_local_server_name
-databaseConnectionString database_connection_string
-databaseName database_name
```

6. When prompted, enter a password for the FAST Search Server user and a certificate password.

7. Add yourself or the appropriate user or group to the local FASTSearchAdministrators group that was created when you ran the `psconfig` command.

8. Restart the server.

9. When the server has restarted, open Windows PowerShell again, navigate to `C:\FASTSearch`, type the following, and press Enter in order to verify that all modules are running:

```
nctrl status.
```

Because this is a stand-alone FAST Search Server installation, your next step is to add FAST Search Server 2010 for SharePoint as a backend for Microsoft SharePoint Server.

Configuring a FAST Search Server as an Admin Server for a Multiple-Server Environment

To configure a multiple-server deployment of FAST Search Server, your first task is to configure the admin server to run administrative services; then you add one or more nonadmin servers, which will connect to the admin server. Prior to setting up the admin server, you must configure a deployment file, which is usually an XML file that specifies how components and services are distributed in the multiple-server environment.

The specifics of the file are beyond the scope of this chapter, so an example will not be provided.

1.   Follow steps 1 through 4 from the "Configuring a Stand-Alone Server Deployment" section; on the next step, enter the following code at the prompt and then press Enter.

```
.\psconfig.ps1 -action i -roleName admin
-userName domain\user - localMachineName fully_qualified_local_server_name
-databaseConnectionString database_connection_string
-databaseName database_name
-deploymentFile deployment_file_name
```

2.   Follow the rest of the steps from the "Configuring a Stand-Alone Server Deployment" section.

Configuring a FAST Search Server as a Non-admin Server for a Multiple-Server Environment

This task is almost the same as the last two except that you must ensure the admin server is running first. Then follow these steps:

1.   At the same step as the previous two tasks, enter the following code at the command prompt and then press Enter.

```
.\psconfig.ps1 -action i -roleName nonadmin
-userName domain\user
-localMachineName fully_qualified_local_server_name -adminMachineName
fully_qualified_local_server_name
```

2.   Perform all the rest of the steps required for the previous two exercises.

Now that your FAST Search Server environment is installed and configured, it's time to add FAST Search Server as a backend for SharePoint Server 2010.

Adding FAST Search Server 2010 as a Backend for SharePoint

You can expect to be responsible for the following content on the 70-668 "PRO: SharePoint 2010, Administrator" exam. There are a number of tasks required to set up FAST Search Server as a backend resource for SharePoint, both in SharePoint's Central Administration and in FAST Search Server. This section will exclusively address the tasks that can be performed on SharePoint:

- Creating and configuring the content search service application for FAST Search Server
- Creating and configuring the query search service application for FAST Search Server
- Enabling queries from SharePoint to FAST Search Server

Each of these general tasks has one or more exercises associated with it.

Creating and Configuring the Content Search Service Application for FAST Search Server

To crawl content that will be indexed in FAST Search Server, you must create and configure the content search service application, which is used to crawl and send content to FAST for use by SharePoint. Exercise 5.15 will show you the process.

EXERCISE 5.15

Configuring a Content Search Service Application

1. In Central Administration, click Application Management and then click Manage Service Applications.

2. On the Manage Service Applications page, click New and select Search Service Application.

3. When the Create New Search Service Application page appears, in the service application name field under Name, give the application a name.

4. Under FAST Service Application, select the FAST Search Connector radio button.

5. Under Search Service Account, either select an account from the drop-down list or click Register New Managed Account to create a new account.

6. Under Application Pool For Search Admin Web Service, either select Use Existing Application Pool to accept the default or click Create New Application Pool and then enter a name in the Application Pool Name field.

7. For a security account, either accept the default by clicking PREDEFINED or select CONFIGURABLE and then select or create a managed account.

8. Under Base Port, enter the desired port number or accept the default.

9.   Under Content Distributors, in the available field, enter the location or locations of content distributors using the format FQDN:port, separated by semicolons.

10. Under Content Collection Name, enter a name for the content collection containing the content to be crawled such as **sp**.

11. When finished, click OK.

There are a number of other tasks that can be performed, but they are common to both the standard SharePoint search option and FAST Search, and they include creating a content source, resetting the content index, limiting content to be crawled, and changing crawler impact rules.

Creating and Configuring a Query Search Service Application

The query search service application provides the query results from crawled content, and the creation and configuration process is almost the same as Exercise 5.15. Follow steps 1 through 3 to get to the Create New Search Service Application page. The actions you take for steps 4 through 8 are the same except on step 4 you choose FAST Search Query rather than FAST Search Connector. After setting the Base Port, perform the steps in Exercise 5.16.

Configuring a Query Search Service Application

1.   Under Query Service Location, enter one or more locations of the query service in the format protocol://FQDN:port, such as **http://BackEndSearch:13098**.

2.   Under Administration Service Location, enter the location of the administration service in the format protocol://FQDN:port, such as **Net.tch://BackEndSearch:12043**.

3.   Under Resource Store Location, enter the location of the resource store in the format protocol://FQDN:port, such as **Net.tch://BackEndSearch:12011**.

4.   Under Account For Administration Service, enter the account name.

5.   When you are done, click OK.

The query service application you just added to the service application list must now be connected to the desired web application or applications. See Exercise 5.5 for details.

Enabling Queries from SharePoint to FAST Search Server

The final set of tasks involved in configuring FAST as the backend search server for SharePoint is to enable communications channels for the HTTP and HTTPS protocols.

This must be done using Windows PowerShell on the SharePoint server containing Central Administration.

The task for enabling the HTTP and HTTPS protocols is essentially the same. You must create a SharePoint Server STS certificate on the SharePoint Server computer containing Central Administration and then transfer that certificate to all the FAST Search Server query servers (if you have only one query server, only that server requires the certificate).

On the SharePoint Server with Central Administration, open Windows PowerShell and select Run As Administrator. To generate the STS certificate enabling queries over HTTP, run the following at the command prompt, replacing the example values with the true values for the FAST Search Server:

```
$currentdir = pwd
$sharepointSTSCertFilename = Join-Path
-Path $currentdir -ChildPath 'MOSS_STS.cer'
$fastsearchqrserver = 'fs14qrserver.mydomain.com'
$fastSSAName = 'FASTSearchServiceApplication'
$stsCert = (Get-SPSecurityTokenService).LocalLoginProvider.SigningCertificate
$stsCert.Export("cert") | Set-Content
-encoding byte $sharepointSTSCertFilename
$queryServiceLocationValue = "http://" + $fastsearchqrserver + ":13287"
Set-SPEnterpriseSearchExtendedQueryProperty
-SearchApplication $fastSSAName
-Identity "FASTSearchQueryServiceLocation" -Value $queryServiceLocationValue
Set-SPEnterpriseSearchExtendedQueryProperty
-SearchApplication $fastSSAName
-Identity " FASTSearchQueryServiceWinAuth" -Value "false"
Get-SPEnterpriseSearchExtendedQueryProperty -SearchApplication $fastSSAName
IISReset
```

The certificate for HTTP will be created in the directory where the command was run. You will need to copy the file to a location that is accessible to the FAST Search Server, and from there, the administrator for FAST Search Server will need to perform the import procedure.

To generate the STS certificate enabling queries over HTTPS, run the following at the command prompt, replacing the example values with the true values for the FAST Search Server:

```
$currentdir = pwd
$sharepointSTSCertFilename = Join-Path
-Path $currentdir -ChildPath 'MOSS_STS.cer'
$fastsearchqrserver = 'fs14qrserver.mydomain.com'
$fastSSAName = 'FASTSearchServiceApplication'
$sharepointServicesCertFilename = Join-Path
-Path $currentdir -ChildPath 'MOSS_SERVICES.pfx'
$sharepointServicesCertPassphrase =
```

```
$host.ui.PromptForCredential("Need Credentials",

"Please enter a passphrase for the SharePoint Services Cert", "CERT_
PASSPHRASE", "")

$tempStringValue = [System.Runtime.InteropServices.Marshal]::SecureStringToBSTR(
$sha repointServicesCertPassphrase.Password)

$plainTextPassPhrase = [System.Runtime.InteropServices.Marshal]::PtrToStringAuto
($tempSt ringValue)

$stsCert = (Get-SPSecurityTokenService).LocalLoginProvider.SigningCertificate

$stsCert.Export("cert") | Set-Content

-encoding byte $sharepointSTSCertFilename

$sharePointCertStore = new-object System.Security.Cryptography.X509Certificates
.X509Store('SharePoi nt',

[System.Security.Cryptography.X509Certificates.StoreLocation]::LocalMachine)

$sharePointCertStore.Open([System.Security.Cryptography.X509Certificates.
OpenFlags]::ReadOnly)

$servicesCert = $sharePointCertStore.Certificates.Find([System.Security
.Cryptography.X509Certificates.X509FindType]::FindBySubjectName,'SharePoint
Services', $false)

$servicesCert.Export("pfx", $plainTextPassPhrase) | Set-Content

-encoding byte $sharepointServicesCertFilename

$servicesCert2 = new-object System.Security.Cryptography.X509Certificates
.X509Certificate2

$servicesCert2.Import($sharepointServicesCertFilename, $plainTextPassPhrase,
[System.Security.Cryptography.X509Certificates.X509KeyStorageFlag
s]::DefaultKeySet)

$trustedPeopleCertStore =

new-object System.Security.Cryptography.X509Certificates.X509Store
('TrustedP eople', [System.Security.Cryptography.X509Certificates
.StoreLocation]::Lo calMachine)

$trustedPeopleCertStore.Open([System.Security.Cryptography.X509Certificates
.OpenFlags]::ReadWrite)

$trustedPeopleCertStore.Add($servicesCert2)

$trustedPeopleCertStore.Close()

$queryServiceLocationValue =

"https://" + $fastsearchqrserver + ":13286"

Set-SPEnterpriseSearchExtendedQueryProperty

-SearchApplication $fastSSAName -Identity "FASTSearchQueryServiceLocation"

-Value $queryServiceLocationValue

Set-SPEnterpriseSearchExtendedQueryProperty

-SearchApplication $fastSSAName -Identity "FASTSearchQueryServiceWinAuth"

-Value false

Get-SPEnterpriseSearchExtendedQueryProperty

-SearchApplication $fastSSAName

IISReset
```

Two files will be created in the directory where you run this command: the STS certificate and the MOSS_SERVICES.pfx file. Copy them both to a location where they can be accessed by the FAST Search Server. From there, the administrator for the FAST Search Server will need to perform the import procedure.

From the SharePoint Administrator's point of view, FAST Search Server is now set up as a backend for SharePoint Server 2010.

At this point, the SharePoint Server 2010 major features have been configured and available. Of course, there's plenty to manage and maintain in the day-to-day operations of SharePoint, which is how you'll spend much of your time.

Summary

In this chapter, you learned a great deal about setting up enterprise search and FAST Search Server for SharePoint.

- Understanding the new features in SharePoint enterprise search for users
- Learning the wide variety of crawl features to be managed for enterprise search
- Configuring the query and result features for search
- Reviewing the health and functionality reports for search
- Managing the enterprise-search topology in the server farm
- Adding FAST Search Server as a backend for SharePoint

Exam Essentials

Understanding the Various Tasks Associated with Administering Farm-wide Search Demonstrate the ability to manage all of the required tasks to enable and refine search services for SharePoint, including crawl, query, and report-related utilities.

Understanding the Activities to Be Performed to Manage the Enterprise-Search Topology Perform the mandatory activities to enable and manage crawl databases and database components on the SQL servers in the server farm.

Understanding What Has to Be Done to Add FAST Search Server as a Backend for SharePoint Enable the connection between SharePoint and FAST Search Server to allow for a more enhanced search service for SharePoint users.

Review Questions

1. You are a SharePoint administrator for your company. You have recently deployed SharePoint Server 2010 in your organization and are in the process of configuring enterprise search. You receive a message from one of the people in the Research department who uses search extensively and is asking what has improved in SharePoint search. Of the following, what are correct answers for SharePoint's search features and capacities? (Choose all that apply.)

    A. SharePoint 2010 search now supports Boolean operators.

    B. SharePoint 2010 search now supports the use of a wildcard character.

    C. SharePoint 2010 search now provides a search center on all sites by default.

    D. After completing a search in SharePoint, a user can create a connector for the same search in Windows 7.

2. You are a SharePoint administrator for your company. You have recently deployed Share-Point Server 2010 in your organization and are in the process of configuring enterprise search. You receive a message from one of the people in the Research department who uses search extensively and is asking specifically about what has improved in search results. Of the following, what are correct answers for SharePoint's search features and capacities? (Choose all that apply.)

    A. SharePoint relevance improvements allow a higher ranking to be assigned to documents that users have tagged as being important.

    B. SharePoint recognizes "self-search" when a user searches for their own name and returns all related metadata, including the number of times the user's My Site has been viewed.

    C. Search offers improved results on queries for nicknames and phonetic names such as James and Jim.

    D. Document information returned by a search can now include content of a document to assist when metadata is missing or incorrect.

3. You are a SharePoint administrator for your organization. You and your staff are about to deploy SharePoint Server 2010 in the work environment, and you are currently planning how to deploy search. You have come to the conclusion that deploying search using the Farm Configuration Wizard would be the quickest and most effective method. Of the following, what reasons for this do you give your staff? (Choose all that apply.)

    A. The Farm Configuration Wizard automates the creation of search scopes, crawl impact rules, and federated locations.

    B. The Farm Configuration Wizard creates the search topology.

    C. The Farm Configuration Wizard supports a search index for up to 100 million crawled documents.

    D. The Farm Configuration Wizard creates a Search Center by default for users to access and from which they can issue queries.

4. You are a SharePoint administrator for your organization. You and your staff are about to deploy SharePoint Server 2010 in the work environment, and you are currently planning how to deploy search. You are reviewing some of the features and capacities of search. Of the following, which options are true about SharePoint 2010 search? (Choose all that apply.)

   A. Federated location allows search to crawl external sources such as Lotus Notes and Google News.

   B. Administrative tasks for search can now be automated using Windows PowerShell scripts.

   C. You can now tune search operations while users continue to access search.

   D. You can monitor search health by adding a health and performance monitoring web part to a web part page.

5. You are a SharePoint administrator for your organization, and you are currently deploying enterprise search in SharePoint. You have created a search service application and are currently creating a content source to be crawled. During the process, you are offered a list of options for content types. Of the following, which are valid content types? (Choose all that apply.)

   A. Line-of-business data

   B. Lotus Notes public folders

   C. SharePoint sites

   D. Websites

6. You are a SharePoint administrator for your organization, and you are currently deploying enterprise search in SharePoint. You have created a search service application and are currently creating a crawl rule. A new member of your staff who is not familiar with SharePoint or how enterprise search functions asks about the purpose of a crawl rule. Of the following, what are valid answers? (Choose all that apply.)

   A. Crawl rules let you include specific paths in a URL to be crawled.

   B. Crawl rules let you exclude specific paths in a URL from being crawled.

   C. Crawl rules must be listed in the order they are to be applied during the crawl.

   D. You can initiate a crawl rule during either a full crawl or an incremental crawl.

7. You are a SharePoint administrator for your organization, and you are currently deploying enterprise search in SharePoint. You have created a search service application and have performed your first full crawl of the configured content sources, but the crawl hasn't functioned the way you had hoped. You consult the crawl log for one of the content sources to see whether you can find the problem. On the selected page, what columns do you expect to see? (Choose all that apply.)

   A. Errors

   B. Warnings

   C. Failures

   D. Successes

8. You are a SharePoint administrator for your organization, and you are currently deploying enterprise search in SharePoint. A new member of your staff who is not familiar with SharePoint or how enterprise search functions asks about the various file types that search crawls by default. In Central Administration, you navigate to a search service application and to the File Types page. Of the following, what file types on this page are crawled by default? (Choose all that apply.)

A. ASPX

B. DOCX

C. ODT

D. PHP

9. You are a SharePoint administrator for your organization, and you are currently deploying enterprise search in SharePoint. A new member of your staff who is not familiar with SharePoint or how enterprise search functions asks about federated locations. Of the following, what do you say is true about federated locations? (Choose all that apply.)

A. Federated locations are used to crawl external content sources such as Google News.

B. You can import FLD files for a specific federated location search connection.

C. You can manually create a federated location search connection.

D. You can use Windows PowerShell to either import or create a federated location search connection.

10. You are a SharePoint administrator for your organization, and you are currently deploying enterprise search in SharePoint. A new member of your staff who is not familiar with SharePoint or how enterprise search functions asks about why you are mapping managed metadata properties. Of the following, what is the most valid answer?

A. Since different content sources may use different names for a specific metadata property such as Author, you must map the SharePoint Managed metadata property to those different names used by different content sources so that a search for a SharePoint metadata property will return data from the mapped sources.

B. Since SharePoint can use different specific metadata property names depending on the site or site collection, you must map the different SharePoint metadata properties to those metadata properties used by various content sources so that searches from different sites and site collections will return data from all the mapped sources.

C. Although SharePoint uses a set of standardized managed metadata property names, those names are proprietary Microsoft names and do not comply to the standards used on the Web. You must create mapping so that search queries using the proprietary metadata names will return data from the mapped sources.

D. Usually, various content sources will use metadata property names that are not human readable, so you must map those content names to human-readable SharePoint managed property names.

11. You are a SharePoint administrator for your organization, and you are currently deploying enterprise search in SharePoint. A new member of your staff who is not familiar with Share-Point or how enterprise search functions asks about the advantage of configuring search scopes. Of the following, which are valid answers you can give? (Choose all that apply.)

   A. Search scopes limit the field of a search in order to conserve resources.

   B. Search scopes limit the field of a search in order to produce more accurate results.

   C. Search scopes limit the field of a search in order to prohibit search results from inappropriate or adult-related sites.

   D. Search scopes limit the field of a search in order to return a single content type and restrict all other types.

12. You are a SharePoint administrator for your organization, and you are currently deploying enterprise search in SharePoint. You have created a search service application and have performed your first full crawl of the configured content sources, but the crawl hasn't functioned they way you had hoped. On the Search Administration page for the selected Search Service Application, you open the Administration Reports page and start reviewing the various documents present. On any specific document, what actions can you perform? (Choose all that apply.)

   A. You can filter the results by date range, with 12 hours being the default range.

   B. You can filter the results by application type.

   C. You can filter the results by search service application.

   D. You can filter the results by content source.

13. You are a SharePoint administrator for your organization, and you have recently deployed enterprise search in SharePoint. You have been tasked by the CIO with gathering statistics on websites searched by SharePoint users. You visit the Web Analytics page in Search Administration for the default search service application. On this page, what reports can you view? (Choose all that apply.)

   A. Top Browsers

   B. Top Destinations

   C. Top Queries

   D. Top Visitors

14. You are a SharePoint administrator for your organization, and you have recently performed a single server with built-in database SharePoint installation to test SharePoint Server 2010 prior to making a recommendation for an enterprise-wide installation. You have just deployed search in your test environment, and you want to add an index partition to your default search service application. You find that you are unable to accomplish this task. What is the most likely cause of the problem?

    A. You have attempted to accomplish this task in Central Administration, but it can only be done using Windows PowerShell.

    B. This task can only be accomplished in a server farm environment using one or more separate SQL servers.

    C. You have failed to create one or more content sources prior to configuring the index partition.

    D. You are not logged into SharePoint as the local server administrator.

15. You are a SharePoint administrator for your company, and you have recently deployed a SharePoint Server 2010 server farm. You have configured enterprise search and have set up and tested a crawl database for the default search service application. You've finished testing the crawl database and want to delete it, since you're planning on deploying crawl databases for production in the next few days. You've selected the test database on the Manage Search Topology page but cannot find the Delete button to remove the database. What could be the problem? (Choose all that apply.)

    A. You must first disconnect any associations between the crawl components and the crawl database by any appropriate means.

    B. You must first assign the crawl components to a different crawl database.

    C. You must first remove the crawl components before deleting the crawl database.

    D. You must first delete all of the content from the crawl database.

16. You are a SharePoint administrator for your organization, and you've been tasked by your CIO to implement FAST Search Server 2010 for SharePoint. Another administrator has been tasked with specifically managing the installation and deployment of FAST Search Server, and you must perform the work within SharePoint to add FAST as a backend service for SharePoint. You are consulting with the FAST Search Server admin, and she is discussing the general requirements for installing and deploying FAST. Of the following, which does she say are valid steps in this process? (Choose all that apply.)

    A. Running the Prerequisite Installer

    B. Installing FAST Search Server 2010 for SharePoint

    C. Running the FAST Search Server Products and Tools Wizard

    D. Running the Post-Installation Configuration

17. You are a SharePoint administrator for your organization, and you've been tasked by your CIO to implement FAST Search Server 2010 for SharePoint. Another administrator has been tasked with specifically managing the installation and deployment of FAST Search Server, and you must perform the work within SharePoint to add FAST as a backend service for SharePoint. You are consulting with the FAST Search Server admin, and she is discussing the general process of post-installation configuration. Of the following, which does she say are valid configuration options? (Choose all that apply.)

   A. Configuring a stand-alone server deployment

   B. Configuring an admin server in a multiple-server deployment

   C. Configuring a member server in a multiple-server deployment

   D. Configuring a nonadmin server in a multiple-server deployment

18. You are a SharePoint administrator for your organization, and you want to set up FAST Search Server 2010 as a backend for SharePoint. The FAST Search Server admin has finished deploying the server set up on his end. What is the first thing you need to in SharePoint?

   A. You need to create a new search service application that points to the FAST search connector.

   B. You need to edit the default search service application so that it points to the FAST search connector.

   C. You need to create a new search service application that points to the FAST search connector and then delete the default search service application.

   D. You need to point the default search service application to SharePoint Search and create a new search service application pointing to the FAST search connector.

19. You are a SharePoint administrator for your organization, and you want to set up FAST Search Server 2010 as a backend for SharePoint. You have almost completed the configuration process but need to enable queries from SharePoint to the FAST Search Server. Of the following, which are the valid communication protocols you can configure? (Choose all that apply.)

   A. FTP

   B. HTTP

   C. HTTPS

   D. ASPX

20. You are a SharePoint administrator for your organization, and you want to set up FAST Search Server 2010 as a backend for SharePoint. You have almost completed the configuration process but need to enable queries from SharePoint to the FAST Search Server. By what process do you enable the communication channels?

   A. You must use Central Administration.

   B. You must use Windows PowerShell.

   C. You can use either Central Administration or Windows PowerShell.

   D. You must use a combination of Central Administration and Windows PowerShell.

Answers to Review Questions

1. A, B, D. Although you can add search web parts to any web part page on a site, the Search Center remains a specialized site in SharePoint and is not added to any other site template.

2. B, C, D. Higher rankings are assigned to documents that have been accessed more frequently in search but not by any sort of manual tagging process.

3. B, C. Although the Farm Configuration Wizard does a lot of the heavy lifting for post-installation configuration, including deploying search, it cannot automate the creation of specific search scopes, crawl impact rules, and federated locations. Also, the Search Center is created by the Farm Configuration Wizard only if you select the Search Center option while running the wizard. This is not a default process.

4. A, B, C. Although you can view customized reports on search in a search service application, you cannot view this data in a web part on a web part page.

5. A, C, D. Although you can select Exchange Public Folders as a content type when creating a content type to be crawled, Lotus Notes Public Folders is not a valid option. You can also choose File Shares and Custom Repository.

6. A, B, C. You must conduct a full crawl of the content source for a new rule to be implemented. This cannot be done during an incremental crawl.

7. A, B, D. Columns on the crawl log page are Successes, Warnings, Errors, Top Level Errors, and Deletes.

8. A, B, D. Open Document Template (ODT) is typically used by OpenOffice.org and is not a file type crawled by default.

9. A, B, C. To download and import an FLD file from an Internet source, you cannot use Windows PowerShell.

10. A. All of the other options are bogus.

11. A, B. Options C and D are bogus.

12. A, B, D. Since you are performing this action within a single search service application, you cannot filter the results based on other applications that exist outside of the one you are currently using.

13. A, B, D. There is no Top Queries option, but you can choose Number Of Queries and view that report.

14. B. Adding an index partition and then placing query components on different farm servers is done to distribute the load of query services and requires a server farm environment with one or more SQL servers. The task cannot be performed on a single-server deployment with built-in database. You do not need to use Windows PowerShell to accomplish this task, and the task isn't dependent on having a content source created. Although not being logged in with the proper credentials could be a problem, option B is the most likely issue, given the stated deployment.

15. A, B, C. Before you can delete a crawl database, you must disconnect any associations between the crawl components and the crawl database, either by assigning the crawl components to a different crawl database or by removing the crawl components. In this case, options A, B, and C are correct. Answer D is bogus.

16. A, B, D. Option C is bogus. All other answers are valid parts of the process.

17. A, B, D. The Member Server deployment is bogus. All other answers are valid options, depending on the desired topology.

18. A. You cannot use both the basic "out-of-the-box" SharePoint enterprise search and FAST search in the same deployment, so you need to create a new search service application pointing to the FAST search connector. You do not need to delete the default search service application, and editing the default search service application to point to the FAST search connector is not an option.

19. B, C. You must configure HTTP and HTTP communication channels between SharePoint and FAST Search Server, making the STS certificate for HTTP available to the FAST server and making the STS certificate and the MOSS_SERVICES.pfx file for HTTPS available to the FAST server.

20. B. On the SharePoint Server 2010 computer containing Central Administration, you must open Windows PowerShell, run as administrator, and run different scripts depending on the type of communications protocol you are enabling.

Chapter

6

Managing Operational Settings

MICROSOFT EXAM OBJECTIVES COVERED IN THIS CHAPTER:

✓ **Maintaining a SharePoint Environment**

■ Configure Service Applications

✓ **Managing a SharePoint Environment**

■ Manage Operational Settings

In general, managing SharePoint operational settings includes the collective tasks required to maintain the SharePoint server and server farm environment as well as site, site collection, and solution administration. Since this area is vast, it is addressed in a number of chapters in this book, starting with this one. In this chapter, you will learn how to manage metadata operations, database management, and reporting services as they pertain to SharePoint, and you'll learn how to maintain the Business Connectivity Services (BCS).

Managing Metadata

The short definition of *metadata* is that it's "data about data." That doesn't seem terribly illuminating, though. In slightly more detail, metadata is information about the data to which it refers and is used by disciplines such as information management, information science, and information technology to organize content. In an old-fashioned library, it's what the Dewey decimal system used to be (somewhat) to the books in the library.

The advantage of using metadata for data management is that a single metadata system can organize and track not only a wide variety of content but also a wide variety of content containers including books, CDs, database tables, DVDs, graphics, web pages, and so on.

Specifically applied to SharePoint, managed metadata is a hierarchical collection of managed items that lets you define data and then structure that information within SharePoint information containers, such as libraries and lists.

Administering Managed Metadata Operations

As you've discovered by now, everything users consume in SharePoint is provided as a service. For users to be able to consume a service, it first has to be created and then made available, both within and across site collections and web applications. Beyond that, service connectors must be established to the applications and then term stores have to be added for tagging and tag clouds.

A *term store repository* in SharePoint lets you centralize vocabulary management across multiple site collections.

Administering a Managed Metadata Service Application

The first step in administering managed metadata is to create the managed metadata service application. Exercise 6.1 will show you how to do this. To successfully complete this task, you must be an administrator on the machine containing the SharePoint Central Administration site.

EXERCISE 6.1

Creating a Managed Metadata Service Application

1. Navigate to Central Administration and click Manage Service Applications under Application Management.

2. On the Manage Service Applications page, click the Service Applications tab, which may be already selected.

3. On the Ribbon, click New and then click Managed Metadata Service.

4. On the Create A New Managed Metadata Service page, type a name for the service in the Name field.

5. In the Database Server field, type the name of the database server that is hosting the term store or accept the default setting.

6. In the Database Name field, type the name of the database that you want to host the term store.

   When SharePoint is installed, the managed metadata service and a database for that service, using the same name, are created. You may have to add yourself as an administrator of that database if you want to use it. If you want to use a different database on a separate SQL Server database server computer, you may have to run SQL Server Management Studio to get the name of the database.

7. Select the authentication type to connect to the SQL Server instance, such as Windows authentication or SQL authentication. If you choose SQL authentication, type the account name in the Account field and then type the account's password in the Password field.

8. If you choose to use SQL server failover, type the name of the database server to be used for failover in the Failover Database Server field; otherwise, leave the field empty.

9. Under Application Pool, select either Use Existing Application Pool and then select a pool from the drop-down list or select Create New Application Pool and then select an account under which to run the pool.

EXERCISE 6.1 *(continued)*

If you want to run the new pool under an existing account, select Predefined and then select the account from the drop-down list. To use a managed account, select Configurable and then either select an account from the drop-down list or click Register New Manage Account and create a new managed account. However, it is optimal to create application pools only for customizations and to consolidate the rest. See Chapter 14, "Optimizing SharePoint," for more details.

10. If you optionally want the managed metadata service to access a content type library in addition to a term store, type the URL to the site collection containing the content type library in the Content Type Hub field.

11. If you plan on having another web application import content types shared with this service and you want to record any errors associated with this process, select Report Syndication Import Errors From Site Collections Using This Service Application.

12. To create a connection to this service automatically when a new web application is added to the farm, select Add This Service Application To The Farm's Default List.

13. When you're finished, click OK.

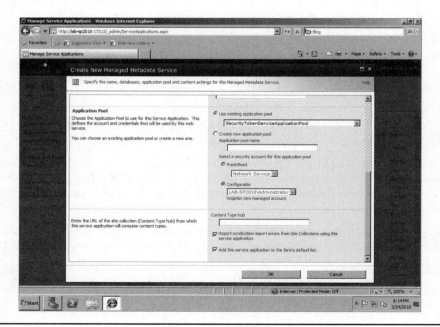

A content type library, mentioned in the prior exercise in step 10, contains a reusable collection of metadata used by SharePoint lists or document libraries. Using content types lets you manage the settings for categories of information from a centralized point.

Editing or updating an existing managed metadata service application is a substantially similar task to creating one, with the differences outlined in Exercise 6.2.

EXERCISE 6.2

Editing a Managed Metadata Service Application

1. Navigate to Central Administration, and click Manage Service Applications under Application Management.

2. On the Manage Service Applications page, select the row for the service you want to update by clicking in a column for the row other than on the service name.

3. On the Ribbon, click Properties.

   Clicking the service name in step 2 will open the Term Store Management Tool.

At this point, edit any of the information or properties you created starting in step 4 of Exercise 6.1 and then click OK when you're finished.

The service becomes available in the web application where the service was created, but you must publish the service if you want to share it with other web applications. Exercise 6.3 shows you the procedure.

EXERCISE 6.3

Publishing a Managed Metadata Service Application

1. Navigate to Central Administration, and click Manage Service Applications under Application Management.

2. On the Manage Service Applications page, click the Service Applications tab, if it hasn't already been selected.

3. Select the row of the service you want to publish, but do not click the service name.

4. On the Ribbon, click Publish.

5. When the Publish Service Application screen opens, use the drop-down menu under Connection Type to select a connection type such as HTTP or HTTPS.

6. Under Publish To Other Farms, select the Publish This Service Application To Other Farms check box to make the service available to other server farms.

EXERCISE 6.3 *(continued)*

7. Under Trusted Farms, click the Click Here To Add A Trust Relationship With Another Farm link, and when the Trusts screen opens, select a farm in the list, click the New button, and use the Establish Farm Trust screen to create a name for the trust. Then add a root certificate for the Trust relationship and provide an STS certificate for the Trust relationship.

8. Under Published URL, make a note of the URL to the service so you can provide it to administrators who want to make a connection to the service.

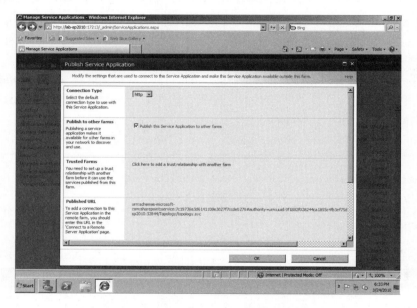

9. Type a description of the published service in the Description field.

10. If you have created a web page with information about this service, type the URL of the web page in the Help URL field.

11. When you're finished, click OK.

Typing a description in step 9 and creating a help web page for the published service as in step 10 are optional steps, but that information may be helpful to other SharePoint administrators who want to connect to the service you created.

Deleting a service is fairly simple. For instance, follow steps 1 through 3 in Exercise 6.3 and on the Ribbon click Delete. Click OK; when prompted, click OK again. Do not click Delete Data Associated With The Service Application because this option yields no result. Once you delete the service, you cannot recover it, and any web application that has a connection to the deleted service will be unable to use the connection.

Administering Managed Metadata Service Connections

In the previous section of this chapter, you learned how to create a managed metadata service application and particularly how to publish it so that other server farms can consume the resource. Now you'll learn the tasks associated with creating a connection to the resource.

> This entire process is very similar to publishing and creating connections to just about any other service, as you saw in Chapter 4, "Configuring Service Applications."

Exercise 6.4 will show you how to create a connection to an already published managed metadata service connection from a separate server farm. You will need the URL to the published service on the farm where it resides in order to successfully complete this task.

EXERCISE 6.4

Creating a Connection to a Managed Metadata Service Application

1. Navigate to Central Administration, and click Manage Service Applications under Application Management.

2. On the Manage Service Applications page, click the Service Applications tab, if it's not already selected.

3. On the Ribbon, click Connect and then in the menu click Managed Metadata Service Connection.

EXERCISE 6.4 *(continued)*

4. On the Connect To A Remote Service Application page, type the URL to the managed metadata service in the Farm Or Service Application address field, and then click OK.

5. Select the service application you want to connect to by clicking its name in the appropriate row.

6. If you want to have your connection provide the service to all web applications in your server farm, select Make This Connection To Be The Default For All Sites On My Farm and then click OK.

7. If you desire, type a descriptive name for the connection in the Connection Name field and then click OK.

8. When you are notified that the connection has been created, click OK.

Ironically, creating the connection doesn't define all of the behaviors between the connection and the service. To accomplish this, you must update the connection after you create it. Exercise 6.5 shows you the process.

EXERCISE 6.5

Updating a Managed Metadata Service Connection

1. Navigate to Central Administration, and click Manage Service Applications under Application Management.

2. On the Manage Service Applications page, click the service connection row of the service you want to publish, but do not click the service name.

3. On the Ribbon, click Properties.

4. If you desire, select the This Service Application Is The Default Storage Location For Keywords check box to store new enterprise keywords in the term store associated with the connection.

   Only one connection can be the default location for keyword storage.

5. If you want to make the content types associated with the managed metadata service accessible to users of the sites in the web application, select Consumes Content Types from the Content Type Gallery At <URL> field.

   This option is available only if the service provides access to a content type library.

6. If you want to update existing instances of changed content types in subsites and libraries, select Push-Down Content Type Publishing Updates From The Content Type Gallery To Sub-Sites And Lists Using The Content Type.

7. When finished, click OK.

Deleting a connection is very much like deleting a service. On the Manage Service Applications page, you click to the right of the connection, not on the connection's name. Then on the Ribbon, click Delete. Clicking Delete Data Associated With The Service Application Connections will have no impact. Click OK when you're done.

Managing Term Store Administrators

A *term store* is a container for terms, which are words or phrases that are associated with a particular item in SharePoint. Terms can be collected in sets of related terms, and term sets can then be collected into groups. You can create *managed terms*, or terms you can predefine, and then organize them into a hierarchy. These terms are then selected by users in a column in a document library.

You can also use managed keywords, which are words and phrases you add to SharePoint items, tagging them in whatever manner you choose, to develop an appropriate *folksonomy*.

You can learn about folksonomies at http://en.wikipedia.org/wiki/Folksonomy.

Users can then tag items using whatever keywords they believe fit the items. Unlike managed terms, keywords are not usually organized into hierarchies, and usually, as an administrator, you have to add a Keyword column. However, some content types in SharePoint use a Keyword column by default.

Although all this may seem rather conceptual, the practical use for managed metadata allows departments and divisions to develop different metadata services with different scopes. For instance, each department can have its own local metadata service for site collections in a web application, another metadata service can be shared among all the departments in a single division that use multiple web applications within a server farm, and a third global metadata service is used for the entire enterprise-level organization across all server farms.

Using the Term Store Management Tool

Once the managed data services and service connection are available, you can use the Term Store Management Tool to create metadata terms for the SharePoint enterprise environment. This tool is a centralized database that allows term sets to be shared across the SharePoint farm. The following set of steps shows you the basics of how to use this tool.

If you cannot access this page or cannot add a term, you may have to add yourself as a term store administrator. See Exercise 6.7 for details.

1. On the main page in Central Administration, click Manage Service Applications under Application Management.

2. On the Manage Service Applications page, click the desired managed metadata service.

3. When the Term Store Management Tool page opens, select the desired language under Taxonomy Term Store on the left and then expand Managed Metadata Service.

4. Expand System and then click Keywords.

5. On the page that appears, to add an Enterprise Keywords column, select the Enterprise Keywords check box under Add Enterprise Keywords.

6. Under Metadata Publishing, to allow the Managed Metadata and Enterprise Keywords columns to be shared as social tags on My Sites, select the Save Metadata On This List As Social Tags check box.

7. Click OK.

You can also create terms for a document library in a site collection. Exercise 6.6 shows you how to create a Managed Metadata column in a library, such as a document library, which will then allow you to create terms that you can assign to documents in the library. In this example, you'll need to have a document library available and navigate to the library in order to get started.

EXERCISE 6.6

Creating Metadata Terms for a Library

1. Navigate to the desired document library.

2. On the Library Tools menu, click the Library tab. Then on the Ribbon, click Create Column.

3. When the Create Column window opens, type the name you want the column to have in the Column name field.

4. Under The Type Of Information In This Column Is, select Managed Metadata.

5. Select Customize Your Term Set and give the term set a descriptive name in the Description field.

6. Under Additional Column Settings, if you want to add more conditions for the column settings, add a description of those conditions in the Description field. Then select either Yes or No for Require That This Column Contains Information and for Enforce Unique Values. Finally, select or deselect the Add To Default View check box.

EXERCISE 6.6 *(continued)*

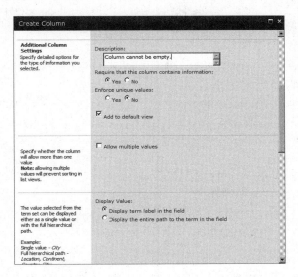

7. Select Use A Managed Term Set, type one or more terms in the Find Term Sets That Include The Following Terms field separated by semicolons, and click the Find button, which looks like a pair of binoculars, to locate the desired terms.

8. When the desired term set appears that contains the desired list of values to display for the column you are creating, click the term to select the first level of the hierarchy you want to show in the column.

9. If you are using an open term set, you can select Yes under Allow 'Fill In' Choices if you want to enable this feature.

10. If desired, type or browse for a default value for the column in the Default Value field.

11. Click OK to create the column.

  The metadata terms you create are stored in the library in the terms store. You can find the metadata terms in the term store by using the Term Store Management Tool.

Once a term store exists, you can add an administrator to the store and, if necessary, later remove the administrator. Exercise 6.7 shows you how to add a term store administrator.

EXERCISE 6.7

Adding a Term Store Administrator

1. On the Central Administration home page, click Manage Service Applications under Application Management.

2. On the Manage Service Applications page, click the Service Applications tab, if it isn't already selected.

3. Select the Managed Metadata service you want and then click Manage in the Ribbon.

4. When the Term Store Management Tool opens, in the Properties pane, either type the name of the user in the Term Store Administrators field or use the address book to add a user.

5. When you are finished, click Save.

If you later need to remove an administrator, repeat the process and select the name you want to remove in the Term Store Administrators field and delete the name. Click Save to make the process final.

Term store administrators possess a variety of abilities over the term store, including being able to create and delete term groups; assign or remove users from the group manager role; assign or remove users from the contributor role; import a term set; create, edit, or remove term sets; and edit the working languages for a term store.

Managing Database Operations for SharePoint

Database operations for SharePoint can include a wide variety of tasks, perhaps more database and database server–related tasks than you might consider for a SharePoint administrator. However, all of the content consumed in SharePoint is stored in databases, and to ensure the smooth operation of your environment, you must be able to manage and monitor the databases you rely upon.

Administering Database Operations

Although this might sound like you are being turned into a database administrator (DBA) instead of a SharePoint administrator, you aren't actually responsible for managing all database operations. You do have a responsibility to manage those aspects of the database that have a direct impact on SharePoint operations, including monitoring the health of the database. You also need to be able to add database content, move site collections from one database to another, and, if necessary, manage a server farm using a read-only content database.

Adding a Content Database

It's not beyond your purview as a SharePoint administrator to add content to a database and then attach it to a web application. The basics of performing this task using Central Administration are illustrated in Exercise 6.8. You must know the name of the database server on the farm for which you want to connect. You must also be the administrator on the local computer containing Central Administration and belong to the dbcreator fixed server role on the database server.

EXERCISE 6.8

Adding a Content Database Using Central Administration

1. Navigate to Central Administration and click Application Management.

2. Under Databases, click Manage Content Databases.

3. On the Manage Content Databases page, click Add A Content Database.

4. When the Add Content Database page appears, use the Web Application menu to select the desired web application for the new database.

5. Type the name of the database server you want to host the new database in the Database Server field.

6. Type the name of the database you want to use in the Content Database field.

7. Under Database Authentication, select either Windows Authentication or SQL Authentication. If you choose the latter, use the Account And Password field to enter the necessary credentials.

8. If you want to use a failover server, specify the server in the Failover Database Server field.

9. Specify the total number of top-level sites that can be created using the database as well as the number of sites that, when crossed, will trigger a warning message.

EXERCISE 6.8 *(continued)*

10. When finished, click OK.

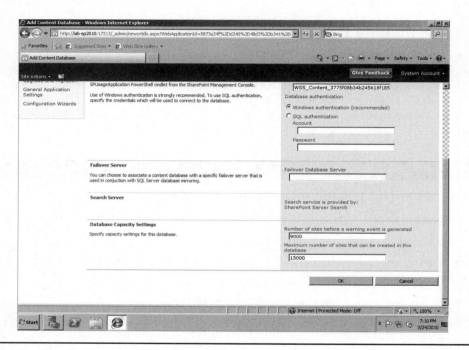

You can perform the same task using Windows PowerShell. To do so, you must be a member of the SharePoint_Shell_Access role on the configuration database and a member of the WSS_ADMIN_WPG local group on the computer where SharePoint 2010 Products is installed.

Open Windows PowerShell, type the following command, and then press Enter, replacing -Name with the name of the content database you want to create, and replacing -WebApplication with the name of the specific web application to which you want to connect the database.

```
New-SPContentDatabase -Name <String> -WebApplication <SPWebApplicationPipeBind>
```

Typically, the web application is enclosed in quotes, such as "SharePoint - 80", but you can also specify it by its URL or URL: port number, such as http://test or http:/test:12345. A typical example is as follows:

```
New-SPContentDatabase -Name "SPContentDB" -WebApplication "SPWebApp1"
```

Moving Site Collections between Databases

One error message that will likely send a cold chill down the spine of a neophyte SharePoint administrator is the announcement that a database has insufficient space because of the size of a site collection. Your SharePoint environment isn't expected to be static, and if your company is growing, so are your site collections.

> When you create a site collection, you should set site quotas and email alerts to notify you when site space limitations are in danger of being exceeded.

Although you shouldn't have to move a site collection from a cramped to a roomier database very often, you will find yourself performing this task from time to time. Interestingly enough, you may also encounter the opposite, when one or more site collections doesn't grow to the expected size. In that case, you have the option to move multiple site collections to a single content database.

You typically perform these tasks using Windows PowerShell, but it's also possible using SharePoint's backup and restore features.

> See Chapter 12, "Backing Up and Restoring SharePoint," for more information on this procedure.

A number of prerequisites must be satisfied before you can perform such a move. You must be a member of the db_owner fixed database role and the SharePoint_Shell_Access role in the SQL Server source content database, administration content database, destination content database, and configuration database. You must also belong to the WSS_ADMIN_WPG group on the local computer.

You must have already created the content database to which you want to move the site collection, and the source and destination databases must reside on the same instance of SQL Server. Also, the source and destination content databases must be attached to the same web application.

> If you haven't added the destination content database yet, see Exercise 6.8 for details.

Even when all those conditions have been met, it's always a good idea to determine the size of the site collection before moving it from one content database to another. The free space available in the content database should be three times the amount of space required by the site collection.

You can perform this task only using Windows PowerShell. Open PowerShell; at the prompt, type the following; and then press Enter, replacing `http://ServerName/Sites/SiteName` with the name of the site collection:

```
$used = (Get-SPSiteAdministration -Identity <http://ServerName/Sites/SiteName>)
.DiskUsed
```

The `$used` variable contains the amount of disk space being used by the site collection.

The Windows PowerShell command `Move-SPSite` is used to move a single site collection from one content database to another. To move numerous site collections, you must use the `Get-SPSite` and `Move-SPSite` commands.

To move a single site collection from one database to another, type the following command at the PowerShell prompt and then press Enter, replacing `http://ServerName/Sites/SiteName` with the name of the site collection and replacing `<DestinationContentDb>` with the name of the destination database:

```
Move-SPSite <http://ServerName/Sites/SiteName> -DestinationDatabase
<DestinationContentDb>
```

To move multiple site collections from one content database to another, type the following command at the PowerShell prompt and then press Enter, replacing `<SourceContentDb>` with the name of the source content database and replacing `<DestinationContentDb>` with the name of the destination content database:

```
Get-SPSite -ContentDatabase <SourceContentDb> | Move-SPSite -DestinationDatabase
<DestinationContentDb>
```

In moving multiple site collections from one database to another, you are moving the entire contents from one database to another, rather than selecting specific site collections to move.

Running a Server Farm on a Read-Only Database

You may decide to conduct server farm operations against a read-only content database for a number of reasons. You can perform this action as part of an upgrade or disaster recovery procedure. This allows users to continue to access SharePoint during the maintenance or emergency condition. Users will not be able to write and save changes to the SharePoint content database during this time.

If a SharePoint user tries to execute an action requiring writing to the content database, the user will discover that the task is unavailable either because it has been disabled in the UI or because the user no longer has permissions to execute the action. Occasionally, a write task will appear to be available but will return an error when the user tries to complete the write task.

It's important to understand that only the SharePoint server farm content databases are in a read-only state. The Central Administration content database, configuration database, and search database all continue to operate as read/write.

Other content databases can be set to read-only using the SQL Server Management Studio tool. To do so, perform these steps:

1. Open the SQL Server Management Studio utility on your computer and connect to the desired database server.

2. Right-click the desired content database and then click Properties.

3. Select the Options page and scroll to the State section of the Other options list.

4. In the Database Read-Only row, click the arrow next to False, select True, and then click OK.

When you set a content database to read-only, all of the connections to the database are stopped except for the connection used to set the read-only flag. When the read-only flag is removed, the other connections are restored.

Prior to setting a content database to read-only, you should make sure which site collection will be affected. You must use Windows PowerShell to find out which content database is associated with which site collection. As with other similar tasks, you must be a member of the SharePoint_Shell_Access role on the configuration database and a member of the WSS_ADMIN_WPG local group on the computer where SharePoint 2010 Products is installed.

At the PowerShell command prompt, type the following command and then press Enter, replacing <Site URL> with the URL of the site collection you want to determine is or is not associated with the content database. The command will return the name of the content database associated with the site.

```
Get-SPContentDatabase -Site <Site URL>
```

To set the desired content database to a read-only state, you will need access to SQL Server Management Studio and belong to the db_owner fixed database role for the required database. Exercise 6.9 shows you the steps.

EXERCISE 6.9

Setting a Content Database to Read-Only

1. Open SQL Server Management Studio, right-click the content database on which you want to set as read-only, and then click Properties.

2. Select the Options page and, in the Other options list, scroll to the State section.

3. In the Database Read-Only row, select the arrow next to False and set it to True.

4. When you are finished, click OK.

Repeat these steps on all the content databases you want to set as read-only.

SQL Server Reporting Services (SSRS)

Microsoft SQL Server 2008 Reporting Services (SSRS) is a server-based reporting system designed to offer a complete set of reporting functions for numerous data source types. SSRS allows the SQL Server administrator to manage a suite of utilities that can be used to create, manage, and return reports within the Microsoft Visual Studio environment. As a SharePoint administrator, you won't be responsible for having a comprehensive knowledge of SSRS, but you will need to understand how to integrate this tool within SharePoint and use it to monitor the health of the databases relative to your content.

SQL Server 2008 Reporting Services SharePoint Integration

SRSS SharePoint Services integrated mode allows SRSS reports to be viewed directly from a SharePoint site. SharePoint treats SQL Server SRSS reports, report models, and shared data sources the same way as any other content that is accessed via the SharePoint interface. Using SRSS SharePoint integrated mode, you can check reports in and out, configure alerts to notify you when report content changes, and even workflow report in the reporting environment.

SQL Server 2008 SharePoint integrated mode is available only for SQL Server 2008 R2. The SQL Server 2008 R2 CTP Reporting Services Add-in for Microsoft SharePoint Technologies 2010 must be installed on a computer running SharePoint Server 2010. Once the add-in is installed and the servers are configured to use integration, you can publish SQL Reporting Services content to a SharePoint library and manage reports as you would any other document managed in SharePoint.

Supported operating systems are as follows:

- Windows Server 2008 R2

- Windows 7

- Windows Vista

- Windows XP Service Pack 3

The add-in requires about 25 MB of hard drive space. To find the download, go to www.microsoft.com/downloads/ and search for *SQL Server 2008 R2 CTP Reporting Services Add-in for Microsoft SharePoint Technologies 2010* on the download site. In the search results, select the link that specifies the reporting services add-in for SharePoint Server 2010.

On the download page, read all the information and then download the add-in to the desired server.

The following steps assume you have not yet downloaded the add-in package to the required SharePoint Server computers. You must install the add-in package on all the front-end web servers in your server farm. The recommended procedure is to use the Installation Wizard to install the add-in on the first frontend web server and then subsequently use the files-only method to install the add-in on all the other web servers. Only after the add-in has been installed on all the web servers in the farm can you use Central Administration to configure the report server integration.

Preparing to Install the Reporting Services Add-in

To get started, follow these steps:

1. Log in to the SharePoint Server containing Central Administration with an account that has farm administrator permissions.

2. In addition to SharePoint Server being active, verify that SQL Server 2008 is online and acting as the report server.

3. Go to the download page at Microsoft.com and navigate to the location of the add-in download.

4. Select the desired language on the download page so that the Report Viewer web part will be available in that language.

5. Start the download of the rsSharepoint.msi file.

6. Once the download is complete, copy the rsSharepoint.msi file to all the frontend web servers on the server farm.

After the files have been downloaded and copied to the required web servers in the server farm, you can install the add-in on the first web server using the Installation Wizard. Remember that the service cannot be configured until after all the files are installed on the frontend web servers.

Installing the Reporting Services Add-in Using the Installation Wizard

To install the add-in, follow these steps:

1. On the first frontend web server, log in and navigate to the location of the rsSharePoint.msi file.

2. Double-click the rsSharePoint.msi file to launch the Installation Wizard.

3. When the wizard launches, navigate through the welcome page, the license agreement page, and the registration information page, performing the required actions on each page.

4. Click Install to run Setup.

5. After Setup has run, go to Central Administration and click Application Management to see that Reporting Services has been added as a new section and that links are available to be used to configure integration settings.

Now that the add-in has been installed on the first frontend web server using the Installation Wizard, you can proceed with installing the add-in on the remaining web servers in the farm using the files-only method. You can start the installation on one web server; once it begins to run, you can move to the next server and start a separate installation process, and so on.

This method uses the Installation Wizard to copy the application files to the computer. After the files have been copied, run the following actions to complete the installation.

You can also use the files-only mode installation method if you encounter errors performing the installation using the regular Setup.

Installing the Reporting Services Add-in Using Files-Only Mode

1. Run rsSharePoint.msi SKIPCA=1.

2. Open a command-line utility and navigate to the location of the rsCustomAction.exe file.

 Setup should have copied the file to the path \Documents and Settings\<your name>\LOCALS~1\Temp.

3. At the command prompt, type the following and then press Enter. This process may take several minutes and will restart the W3SVC.

    rsCustomAction.exe /i

4. After Setup is finished, go to Central Administration, click Application Management, and verify that Reporting Services has been created.

Now that the add-in has been installed on all the required web servers, you must activate and configure Reporting Services in Central Administration.

 One of the requirements you may not have responsibility for is the creation of a report center connected to a report server database on SQL Server 2008 to act as the target report server for SharePoint. This setup usually falls to the SQL Server administrator in your organization, but if this requirement is not met, you will not be able to use the SQL Server 2008 R2 CTP Reporting Services Add-in for Microsoft SharePoint Technologies 2010.

Activating Reporting Services in Central Administration

To activate Reporting Services, follow these steps:

1. In Central Administration, click Site Actions and then click Site Settings.

2. On the Site Settings page, click Site Collection Features under Site Collection Administration.

3. On the Features page, find Report Server Integration Feature and next to it click the Activate button.

Now that the feature has been activated, you can configure the add-in.

Configuring the Reporting Services Add-in in Central Administration

To configure Reporting Services, follow these steps:

1. In Central Administration, click Application Management.

2. On the Application Management page, click the Manage Integration Settings link under Reporting Services.

3. On the Manage Integration Settings page, enter the URL to the SQL Server 2008 report server in the Report Server Web Service URL field.

If you were not provided the URL to the report server, you can acquire it by using the Reporting Services Configuration tool to connect to the report server; then click Web Service URL and copy the URL displayed into the Report Server Web Service URL field referenced in the previous step.

4. Under Authentication Mode, select either Windows Authentication or Trusted Authentication and then click OK.

5. Under Reporting Services, click Grant Database Access and, if necessary, specify the name of the report server.

6. Specify whether the instance is the default or a named instance and then click OK.

7. When the Enter Credentials dialog box opens, enter the username and password used to connect to the report server in order to retrieve service account information.

8. Under Reporting Services, click Set Server Defaults.

9. For Report History Default, set the value for the number of copies of report history to retain site-wide.

10. For Report Processing Timeout, set the value for the number of seconds that must elapse before report processing times out.

11. For Report Processing Log, determine whether the report server should generate logs and, if so, set a value in days for how long the logs are to be retained.

12. For Enable Windows Integrated Security, determine whether a connection to the report data source can be made using the Windows security token of the user requesting the report.

13. For Enable Ad Hoc Reporting, set this option to let users perform ad hoc queries from the Report Builder report. Deselect it if you do not want the report server to create click-through reports for the reports that use a report model as a data source.

14. When you're finished, click OK.

Now you should be able to see and manage report server items directly from inside a SharePoint site. When the Reporting Services add-in was installed, the Custom Reporting Services application pages were added to a SharePoint web application. Pages should now be available that let you set data source properties, report history, report processing options, schedules, subscriptions, and so on.

Viewing Report Server Items

Report server items are located in libraries or in folders in a library. For a given site, open the default document library and look for items with an .rdl file extension. Once you locate the reporting services item or items in the library, perform the following actions:

1. Select the desired item.

2. Click to the right of the item to click the down-arrow and open the menu for the item.

3. Choose the desired action in the menu, such as View Properties or Edit Properties.

Using the Report Viewer Web Part

You can use the *Report Viewer web part* on a SharePoint site to view report server data. This is a custom web part that is installed on SharePoint when the Reporting Services Add-in is installed. The web part lets you view, navigate, print, and export reports for the report server running in SharePoint integrated mode. The web part reads report definition files with the .rdl file extension but cannot read any other report formats.

You can add the Report Viewer Web Page part to a web part page in the same manner as you add other web parts. When you click Site Actions, Edit Page, and then Add A Web Part, all under All Web Parts in Miscellaneous, select SQL Server Reporting Services Report Viewer.

You can then use the web part to open reports stored in a library, library folder, report history, or link from a Library web part to a Report Viewer web part. You also can only view a single report in a Report Viewer web part. If you need to view multiple reports, you'll need to either create a dashboard with this capacity or add multiple Report Viewer web parts to a web parts page, with each web part displaying data from a different report.

Managing Business Data Connectivity

Microsoft Business Connectivity Services is a collection of features and services used to connect SharePoint solutions to external data sources and to define external content types based on external data. These external content types can be presented and interacted with in SharePoint lists and web parts as well as in Microsoft Office 2010 applications such as Outlook and SharePoint Workspace 2010.

BCS can connect to data sources such as SQL Server databases, SAP applications, and web services. BCS lets you design and build solutions that can extend SharePoint's collaboration abilities to information sources well outside SharePoint's traditional grasp. For instance, BCS can allow you to combine various services and features from external data sources and Office 2010 client applications within SharePoint to provide solutions targeting highly specific requirements.

Performing Administrative Tasks in Business Data Connectivity

You can perform a number of administrative tasks for BDC in Central Administration. The first one is assigning an administrator for a particular instance of the BDC service application. Exercise 6.9 will show you how. To complete this task, you must be a member of the Farm Administrators group. Once you assign an administrator for the instance of this service application, that person will be able to perform the same task and assign other administrators.

EXERCISE 6.9

Assigning an Administrator to an instance of the Business Data Connectivity Service

1. Navigate to Central Administration and click Manage Service Applications under Application Management.

2. On the Service Applications tab, click the desired instance of Business Data Connectivity.

3. On the Business Data Connectivity page, click the Edit tab.

4. Under Permissions, click Set Metadata Store Administrators.

5. On the Set Metadata Store Permissions page under Permissions, type the name for the user or account you want to make and administrator and then click Add.

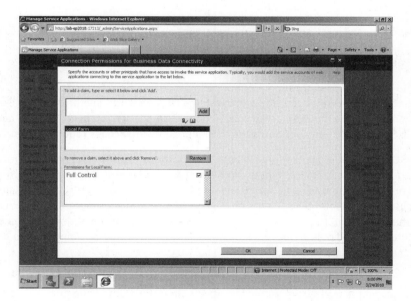

6. You can assign one or a combination of the permissions Edit, Execute, Selectable In Clients, and Set Permissions.

7. If you desire, click Propagate Permissions To All Sub-items if you want the permissions you're assigning to apply to all items nested in the BDC service application.

The permissions you had the option of setting in the previous exercise are defined as follows:

▪   Edit allows editing of external systems, BDC models, and external content types.

▪   Execute allows executing operations, such as create, read, update, delete, or query, on external content types.

- Selectable In Clients allows creating external lists on external content types.
- Set Permissions allows setting permissions on external content types, external systems, and BDC models.

 Real World Scenario

Learning More about Business Data Connectivity Authentication

You are a SharePoint administrator for your company and have recently deployed a SharePoint Server 2010 server farm for one of your organization's major divisions. You have been tasked with creating a series of connections to external data sources required by the management team and are currently reviewing the documentation regarding authentication and authorization to several databases on a SQL Server in a separate division of your organization.

You know you must create an identity in SharePoint and on the SQL Server that has the required permissions and access to data on external data sources as well as the ability to retrieve that data for use in SharePoint.

You want to configure pass-through authentication for users from SharePoint to SQL Server databases for ease of use. You work with the DBA who administers the SQL Server instance containing the required databases, and the DBA assists you in creating an account on the SQL Server and then configures the authentication and access requirements.

Once the SQL data source is configured with the appropriate authentication, you must configure permissions in SharePoint using Central Administration. You give an Active Directory group, on the Business Data Connectivity permissions page, the permissions Edit, Execute, and Selectable In Clients permissions. The management team, which will be using this group and requires access to this external data source, must have the ability to update, edit, and delete objects such as BDC models as well as being able to create lists on the external data source.

Once you've completed this task, you assist the members of the management team with accessing the data directly from within the team's SharePoint site collection.

Managing External Systems

An external system is a source of information completely outside SharePoint, such as a relational database or a web service, that is accessed by users or services within a SharePoint solution. One or more instances of an external system can be set up to an external data source and must include the connection and authentication information for the external system.

Once you assign an administrator or administrators to the desired instances of the BDC service, you or a BDC administrator can perform a number of other tasks. One major class of tasks is managing external systems. Remember, for a BDC administrator to perform such tasks, you must have given them the correct permissions for such tasks, as previously stated.

Exercise 6.10 gets you started with setting permissions on an external system. When you perform this task, you determine who can perform edit and execute operations in the system or on external content types stored on the system. You can also decide who can create external lists and who else can set permissions on the system. You must be a member of the Farm Administrators group or the assigned administrator for this instance of the BDC service application to perform this task.

EXERCISE 6.10

Setting Permissions on an External System

1. Navigate to Central Administration and click Manage Service Applications under Application Management.

2. On the Service Applications tab, click the desired instance of Business Data Connectivity.

3. On the Business Data Connectivity page, click Edit.

4. Under View, click Application Models.

5. Click the check box for the external system on which you want to set permissions.

6. In the Permissions group, click Set.

7. In the available fields, type the user accounts, groups, or claims for which you want to add permissions and then click Add.

8. Set one or a combination of the permissions Edit, Execute, Selectable In Clients, or Set Permissions.

9. If you desire, click Propagate Permissions To All Sub-items.

As you can see, Exercise 6.10 was substantially similar to Exercise 6.9. The permission types granted are the same as you previously assigned a BDC service application instance administrator.

In the desired BDC instance, on the Edit tab as you saw in the previous exercise in step 3, you have access to a wide variety of actions. For instance, if you want to view all external systems, in the View group, click External Systems. Once you've done that, you can click View External Content Types to see the content types available for a particular external system. Under the View group, when you click External Systems, you can also click next to a particular system, click the arrow to make the menu appear for that external system, and then click Delete to remove it.

In addition to setting permission on an external system, you can configure some of the settings of that system from Central Administration. Exercise 6.11 takes you through the process.

By default, the only external system you can configure is a web service.

EXERCISE 6.11

Configuring an External System

1. Navigate to Central Administration and click Manage Service Applications under Application Management.

2. On the Service Applications tab, click the desired instance of Business Data Connectivity.

3. On the Business Data Connectivity page, click Edit.

4. In the View group, click External Systems.

5. Click the arrow next to the desired external system and, in the menu that appears, click Settings.

6. You can view or edit the settings.

   Depending on the nature of the service running on the external system, the configuration options will vary quite a bit.

7. When finished, click OK.

If, for instance, you are configuring a web service, the following settings are available:

- WSDL URL is the full web address of the Web Service Description Language or .wsdl file of the service.

- Under WSDL Authentication Mode, you can configure the default method incoming credentials are passed through the service:

  - PassThrough uses the credentials of the logged in user for authentication to the service.

  - RevertToSelf uses the application pool account under which BCS is running for authentication to the service.

  - Credentials uses basic or digest authentication rather than Windows authentication and uses the Secure Store service to map the user's credentials to the specific individual or group credentials required by the service.

  - WindowsCredentials is used for Windows authentication and uses the Secure Store service to map the user's credentials to the specific individual or group credentials required by the service.

- WSDL SSO ApplicationId is used if you selected Credentials or WindowsCredentials under WSDL Authentication Mode and is the target application identifier for the service, which is configured in the Secure Store service.

You can also configure multiple instances of an external system. Multiple external system instances allow solution designers to set different security settings on external data connections in order to support multiple methods of connecting to the same external system. You can access these instances on any external system by following steps 1 through 4 from Exercise 6.11 and then performing the steps in Exercise 6.12.

EXERCISE 6.12

Configuring an Instance of an External System

1. Double-click the desired external system to view its instances.

2. Click the arrow next to the desired instance and, in the menu, click Settings.

3. View or edit the settings for the available service.

4. If you are using integrated security, in the Integrated Security field, type the string **SSPI**, and the BDC service will use the user's Windows credentials to connect to the external system; otherwise, leave the field blank.

5. The Connection Pooling field is selected if the BDC service has ownership of connections to external systems in a pool as an optimization.

6. When you're finished, click OK.

By default, the only instances of an external system you can configure are databases and web services. For both, you can configure Authentication Mode, just as you saw previously after Exercise. 6.11. For web services, you can also configure Web Service URL and SSO ApplicationId as previously shown. In addition, you can configure Web Service Proxy Timeout in milliseconds, which is the amount of time the service will wait before ending a request to a web service for external data.

For databases, you can configure Access Provider, which is the type of database; Data Source, which is the name of the database server; Initial Catalog, which is the name of the database; and Integrated Security and Connection Pooling, as previously mentioned.

Managing BDC Models

Part of managing BDC is managing BDC models. BDC models are XML files that contain collections of descriptions of one or more external content types. They also contain information about related external data systems and environmental properties. The models contain metadata that defines the fields of the data in each external content type, as well as the operations that are supported on the external data system.

The BDC service application supports the various operations used to import and export BDC models, as well as setting permissions for the models and viewing the external content types they contain. You can perform the same functions on resource file, which contain the localized names and properties for one or more of the external content types.

The primary reason for importing a BDC model is to add the model and the content containing external content types and external systems into the metadata catalog in SharePoint. Exercise 6.13 will show you how this is done. To begin, you must navigate to Central Administration and, just as you've done in previous exercises, click Manage Service Applications under Application Management, access the desired BDC instance, and then click the Edit tab. To perform this task, you must belong to the Farm Administrators group or be an administrator of the service application.

EXERCISE 6.13

Importing a BDC Model or Resource File

1. Under BDC models, click Import.

2. On the Import BDC Model page, type the full path to the model file in the DBC Model File field, or click Browse and navigate to the location of the model file or resource file.

3. In the File Type field, type either **Model** or **Resource** to identify the file type.

4. If you are importing a resource file, continue with the following steps; otherwise, you have completed the task.

5. Under Advanced Settings, to continue to import a resource file, click Localized Names to import the localized names for the external content types in a specific locale.

6. Click Properties to import properties for external content types.

7. Click Permissions to import permissions for external content types.

8. Use the Use Setting field to type a unique name for a set of environment settings if you plan to save the group of imported resource settings in a file that you can later export for that environment.

For imported resource files, imported localized names are merged with the existing localized names in the BDC service database. Imported properties are merged with the existing property descriptions in the BDC service database. Imported permissions are stored with the existing permissions data in the BDC service application. If an entry for an existing external content type is present in the access control list (ACL), the import operation will overwrite the existing permissions. This could lock out any users who access the content type currently stored in the service application by writing the permissions of a different user to the ACL.

What you can import you can also export. The operation to export a BDC model or resource file is almost the same as the import operation. On the Business Data Connectivity Service page, click the Edit tab to get started. Exercise 6.14 describes the rest.

EXERCISE 6.14

Exporting a BDC Model or Resource File

1. Under View, click BDC Models.

2. On the Business Data Connectivity Models page, select the model or resource file you want to export.

3. Under BDC models, click Export.

4. On the Export page, type either **BDC Model** or **Resource** in the File Type field.

5. If you are exporting a resource file, continue with the following steps; otherwise, proceed to the final step in the task.

6. Under Advanced Settings, to export a resource file, click Localized Names to export localized names for external content types in a specific locale.

7. Click Properties to export properties for external content types.

8. Click Permissions to export permissions for external content types.

9. Click Proxies to export an implementation-specific proxy used to connect to an external system.

10. Use the Use Setting field to type the unique name of the file containing environmental settings to export if you saved a set of resources in the file to be exported for a specific environment.

11. When finished, click Export.

When you click Export, the network location interface on your computer will appear, allowing you to navigate to a location to which you can save the BDC model or resource file.

You also have the ability to set permissions on a BDC model. Follow the steps in Exercise 6.15 to learn the process.

EXERCISE 6.15

Setting Permissions on a BDC Model

1. Under View, click BDC Models.

2. On the Business Data Connectivity Models page, select the check boxes for each of the BDC models on which you want to set permissions.

3. Under Permissions, click Set.

4. In the available field, type the user accounts, groups, or claims for which you want to give permissions and then click Add.

5. To set the permissions, click Edit if you want to allow the designated accounts to edit the BDC model.

6. Click Set Permissions if you want to allow the designated accounts to set permissions on the BDC model.

7. If you want to propagate these permissions to nested items in the model, click Propagate Permissions To All Sub-items.

You've already seen how to view all the BDC models by clicking the Edit tab and then, under View, clicking BDC models. You can also view a model's external content types by clicking the arrow next to a particular model and, in the menu that appears, clicking View External Content Types.

To delete a BDC model, you also click BDC Models under View and then on the Models page select the model you want to delete. Next, click Delete under BDC Models and then, when you are prompted, click OK.

Managing External Content Types

An external content type is an XML file that is used to define objects such as Contact, Customer, or Order and is used in a business application. The definition includes fields of data contained in the object; operations used to create read, update, or delete the object; any actions users can perform on the object; and any information used to support connecting to the external data source for the object's data.

An external content type is also used to define data stored on supported external systems such as a SQL Server database, some other relational database, a SharePoint site, a web service, or other data container.

You can add an external content type to a BDC service application in several ways:

- Create a new external content type with SharePoint Designer 2010.
- Create a new external content type with an external content type designer in Visual Studio 2010.
- Import an application model containing one or more external content types into the BDC service application.

Although you, as a SharePoint administrator, are not expected to create external content types, once they are imported, you will be asked to perform any number of tasks related to these content types.

Exercise 6.16 will show you how to set permissions on an external content type. You will need to belong to the Farm Administrators group or be an administrator on the selected instance for the BDC service application to perform this task. This task begins in the same location as all the other related BDC exercises.

EXERCISE 6.16

Setting Permissions on an External Content Type

1. Click the Edit tab and click External Content Types under View.

2. Select the check boxes for each of the external content types on which you want to set permissions.

3. Under Permissions, click Set.

4. In the available field, enter the user accounts, groups, or claims for which you want to grant permissions and then click Add.

5. To set permissions, click Edit to allow the selected accounts to edit the external content types.

6. Click Execute to allow the selected accounts to execute create, read, update, delete, and query operations.

7. Click Selectable In Clients to allow the selected accounts to create external lists of any of the external content types.

8. Click Set Permissions if you want to allow the selected accounts to set permissions on the external content types.

9. Click Propagate Permissions To All Sub-items to allow the permissions to propagate to items nested under the external content types.

As you can see, the steps are very much like the previous exercise where you set permissions on a BDC model. Although you can set permissions to allow designated accounts to perform a default set of actions, you can also add a customized action to an external content type. The action can be a program or a web page that is accessible via URL.

Once the action is associated with the content type, you can pass parameters to the action based on the contents of one or more customized fields in the content type. When you set the action, it will not become available in any previously existing external lists for the content type; however, it will become available for external lists created after you create the action.

To successfully perform this exercise, you must possess the same permissions as you did for the previous task. Exercise 6.17 will take you through the steps.

EXERCISE 6.17

Adding an Action to an External Content Type

1. Click the Edit tab, and click External Content Types under View.

2. Select the external content type on which you want to add the action.

3. Click the arrow near the content type to show the menu and then click Add Action.

4. On the Add Action page, type the name of the action, which can be any text string, in the Action Name field.

5. Type the complete URL of the command in the Navigate To The URL field.

The command can include any parameters and placeholders for the parameters. The parameters will be populated with the contents of one or more of the fields in the external content type. Placeholders should be numbered with integers starting with zero and progressing, as in 0, 1, 2, 3, and so on, and contained in curly brackets, as in {0}. An example of a URL providing the parameters p0, p1, and p2 is http://www.wiredwriter .com/test.aspx?p0={0}&p1={1}&p2={2}. Remember that not all commands will provide numeric parameters.

1. If you want to include parameter placeholders in the URL, for each desired parameter starting with {0}, click Add Parameter in the Parameter Property field. In the list that appears, click the field containing the contents you want to pass for that parameter; repeat for each parameter you want to include.

2. If you want to associate an icon with the custom action, click Standard Icon under Icon to select an icon from the list. Or, in The Image At This URL, type the complete URL to an image you want to use for the icon.

3. Click Default Action if you want this to be a default action.

4. When you are done, click OK to add the action.

Profile pages are used to display information for an item in an external content type. You can specify such a page for an instance of a BDC service application. They are stored in a site in the server farm that hosts the BDC service, and you can choose where the profile page will be hosted.

After clicking the Edit tab, click Host under Profile Pages. Then on the Entity Profile Host page, type the URL of the site where profile pages are created and stored, which must be in the same server farm as where the BDC service application instance exists. Any user who creates or updates profile pages must have read/write permissions on the site, while users who will only view the profile pages need read-only permissions only. If you create a new site for this purpose in a new web application, associate the web application with the desired instance of the BDC service application.

You can also create or update a profile page for an external content type. Exercise 6.18 shows you step-by-step.

EXERCISE 6.18

Creating or Editing a Profile Page for an External Content Type

1. Click the Edit tab and click External Content Types under View.

2. On the View External Content Types page, select the desired content type.

3. Click next to the content type to make the arrow appear and then, in the menu, click Create/Upgrade Profile Page.

4. On the Create/Upgrade Profile Pages page, to create a new version of the profile page, overwriting the current page, select the Allow Overwriting Of Existing Profile Pages check box.

5. To create a new profile page without overwriting the existing pages, clear the Allow Overwriting Of Existing Profile Pages check box.

6. When you're done, click OK.

You can create or update profile pages for multiple external content types by clicking the Edit tab and clicking Create/Upgrade under Profile Pages.

To delete an external content type, after clicking the Edit tab, under View, click External Content Types. On the page that appears, select the content type you want to delete. Click next to the content type, and when the arrow appears, click the arrow and then click Delete in the menu.

Summary

In this chapter, you learned a about a number of aspects of SharePoint operations.

- Managing metadata service applications, connections, and term stores
- Administering database operations, such as adding content to a database, moving site collections between databases, and using an read-only database
- Using SQL Server Reporting Services by integrating it into SharePoint and viewing reporting from SharePoint using web parts
- Performing Business Data Connectivity administration such as managing external systems, BDC models, and external content types

Exam Essentials

Learning the Administrative Tasks Associated with Metadata Service Applications
Demonstrate the ability to manage all the required tasks related to creating and maintaining a metadata service application and application connections and publishing the application.

Managing Database Operations Related to SharePoint Perform all the tasks necessary to manage information in content databases that SharePoint depends upon, move data from one database to another, and read SQL Server reports regarding such content from within SharePoint.

Performing Business Data Connectivity Administration Demonstrate all the behaviors related to effective creation and management of Business Data Connectivity services, including administering permissions on service applications and connections, importing and exporting BDC model and resource files, and managing external content types.

Review Questions

1. You are a SharePoint administrator for your company, and you've been tasked by the CIO with providing specific external data sources required by the management team relating to strategic planning for the next fiscal year. This is the first step in creating a managed metadata service application that will be used by the management team to access the external data. In Central Administration, you begin the process of creating the service application and input the name of the SQL server containing the desired database. Next, you need the name of the database but don't have it readily available. Of the following options, which one will most likely provide the name of the database residing on the SQL server?

    A. Run the SharePoint 2010 Products Configuration Wizard to acquire the name of the database.

    B. Run Windows PowerShell in administrator mode to query SQL Server for the database name.

    C. Run the SQL Server Management Studio tool to get the name of the database.

    D. Leave a voice mail for the DBA responsible for SQL Server asking her for the name of the database.

2. You are a SharePoint administrator for your company, and you've been tasked by the CIO with providing specific external data sources required by the management team relating to strategic planning for the next fiscal year. This is the first step in creating a managed metadata service application that will be used by the management team to access the external data. In Central Administration, you begin the process of creating the service application, and now you must select an authentication method. Of the following, which are valid authentication types to use with SQL Server in this situation? (Choose two.)

    A. Basic authentication

    B. SQL authentication

    C. Trusted authentication

    D. Windows authentication

3. You are a SharePoint administrator for your company, and you've been tasked by the CIO with providing specific external data sources required by the management teams of several key divisions of the company relating to strategic planning for the next fiscal year. You have created the managed metadata service application, but now you must publish it so that teams using other SharePoint server farms can access the application. You are currently publishing the application and are configuring the connection type. Of the following, which are valid default connection types available when publishing the metadata service application? (Choose all that apply.)

    A. FTP

    B. HTTP

    C. HTTPS

    D. TCP

4. You are a SharePoint administrator for your company, and you've been tasked by the CIO with providing specific external data sources required by the management teams of several key divisions of the company relating to strategic planning for the next fiscal year. You have created the managed metadata service application, but now you must publish it so that teams using other SharePoint server farms can access the application. You have published the application and performed all the other required tasks, but the administrator of the other SharePoint server farms cannot create a connection to your application. You suspect the problem occurred when you published the application. Of the following, what are the most likely causes of this problem? (Choose all that apply.)

    A. You selected a connection type other than HTTP or HTTPS.

    B. You failed to create a description for the published service and without it the other server farm administrators cannot locate the published service.

    C. You failed to select the Publish This Service Application To Other Farms check box on the Publish Service Application page.

    D. You failed to create a trust relationship with the other farms using the Establish Farm Trust page during the publication process.

5. You are a SharePoint administrator for your company, and you've been tasked by the CIO with providing specific external data sources required by the management teams of several key divisions of the company relating to strategic planning for the next fiscal year. You have created a managed metadata service connection to a metadata service application that's been published on another server farm. You want to define additional behaviors of the connection and now are in the process of updating the connection. Management teams are accessing the external data in a variety of sites and site collections using lists and libraries, among other interfaces. How can you make sure that updated content will be able to be accessed throughout these venues? (Choose all that apply.)

    A. On the Managed Metadata Service Connection page, click the Refresh button in the Ribbon to update all the libraries and lists in all of the site collections using the service.

    B. On the Managed Metadata Service Connection page, select Consumes Content Types From The Content Type Gallery At and then enter the URL of the content gallery.

    C. On the Managed Metadata Service Connection page, select Push-Down Content Type Publishing Updates From The Content Type Gallery To Sub-sites and list using the content type.

    D. On the Managed Metadata Service Connection page, select Update in the Ribbon, and then select Update All Content Types in the menu that appears.

6. You are a SharePoint administrator for your company, and you've been tasked by the CIO with providing specific external data sources required by the management teams of several key divisions of the company relating to strategic planning for the next fiscal year. You have created a term store to be used as a container for various terms associated with data items to team members accessing the external data service you created. You want to hand off responsibility of the term store to a member of your staff, and to do that, you need to create your staff member as a term store administrator. Of the following options, where will you most likely be able to perform this task?

   A. In Central Administration by selecting the Business Data Connectivity instance and then, on the Ribbon, clicking Manage to open the Term Store Management Tool

   B. In Central Administration by selecting the Business Data Connectivity instance and then, on the Ribbon, clicking Properties to open the Term Store Management Tool

   C. In Central Administration by selecting the Business Data Connectivity instance and then, on the Ribbon, clicking Administrators to open the Term Store Management Tool

   D. In Central Administration by selecting the Business Data Connectivity instance and then, on the Ribbon, clicking New, and then selecting Term Store Management to open the Term Store Management Tool

7. You are a SharePoint administrator for your company, and you need to add a content database to a SQL Server instance in order to move a site collection that is running out of room on its current database to a new database. You know you have more than one option to use to create the new content database. Of the following, which are valid options? (Choose all that apply.)

   A. Central Administration

   B. Windows PowerShell

   C. SQL Server Management Studio

   D. The Stsadm command-line tool

8. You are a SharePoint administrator for your company, and you need to add a content database to a SQL Server instance in order to move a site collection that is running out of room on its current database to a new database. You know more than one type of authentication method can be configured when connecting to the SQL service when create the database. Of the following, which are valid authentication options? (Choose all that apply.)

   A. Basic authentication

   B. SQL authentication

   C. Trusted authentication

   D. Windows authentication

9. You are a SharePoint administrator for your company. You have recently received an alert in SharePoint stating that a site collection is running out of room on its current database. You create a larger database on the SQL Server instance and prepare to move the site collection from the smaller database to the larger one. Of the following options, which can you use to move the site collection? (Choose all that apply.)

    A. Central Administration Application Management

    B. Central Administration Backup and Restore

    C. Central Administration System Settings

    D. Windows PowerShell

10. You are a SharePoint administrator for your company, and you are preparing an upgrade operation for SharePoint. To that end, you must set the content database to read-only. You inform all your SharePoint users when the operation will occur, the duration of the operation, and what to expect. Then you and your staff prepare for the upgrade. In setting the content database to read-only, what method must you use?

    A. Central Administration

    B. Windows PowerShell

    C. SQL Server Management Studio

    D. The `Stsadm.exe` command-line tool

11. You are a SharePoint administrator for your company, and you are preparing an upgrade operation for SharePoint. To that end, you must set the database to read-only. You are briefing your staff on the operation and describing which databases will be set to read-only. Of the following, which databases will be set to read-only? (Choose all that apply.)

    A. The Central Administration content database

    B. The SharePoint server farm content database

    C. The Configuration database

    D. The Search database

12. You are the SharePoint administrator for your company, and as part of configuring the health and monitoring system in SharePoint, you are performing actions that will enable SQL Server Reporting Services (SRSS) integration. There are a number of tasks that must be performed, and the first one is preparing SharePoint for the integration. Of the following, which are valid steps in the preparation? (Choose all that apply.)

    A. From Central Administration, accessing the SQL Server instance that will act as the report server

    B. On the Reporting Services add-in download page, selecting the desired language for the download

    C. Once the Reporting Services add-in package has been downloaded, copying it to all application servers in your server farm

    D. Setting the reporting server database to read-only while the Reporting Services add-in is being installed

13. You are the SharePoint administrator for your company, and as part of configuring the health and monitoring system in SharePoint, you are performing actions that will enable SQL Server Reporting Services (SRSS) integration. You must install the SRSS add-in package on all web servers in the server farm. Choosing the first web server, what is the method you should use?

   A. The Installation Wizard.

   B. Files-Only Mode.

   C. Either the Installation Wizard or Files-Only Mode.

   D. The add-in must be installed on all web servers using Windows PowerShell.

14. You are the SharePoint administrator for your company, and as part of configuring the health and monitoring system in SharePoint, you are performing actions that will enable SQL Server Reporting Services (SRSS) integration. You have installed the SRSS add-in package on all web servers in the server farm. As a result, what has changed in Central Administration?

   A. Under Application Management, Reporting Services has been added.

   B. Under Monitoring, Reporting Services has been added.

   C. Under System Settings, Reporting Services has been added.

   D. Nothing has changed in Central Administration.

15. You are the SharePoint administrator for your company, and as part of configuring the health and monitoring system in SharePoint, you have enabled SQL Server Reporting Services (SSRS) in SharePoint. As part of installing the SRSS add-in, the Report Viewer web part was added. You are assisting a SharePoint website administrator in using the web part on his team's web part page. Of the following, what report types can the Report Viewer web part read? (Choose all that apply.)

   A. Administrative Reports

   B. Diagnostic Logs

   C. Health Reports

   D. SRSS Reports

16. You are a SharePoint administrator for your organization. You have been tasked with configuring Business Data Connectivity (BDC) services to enable connections to external data sources such as SQL servers, SAP applications, web services, and other sources. You want to assign a member of your staff to have administrator access to the BDC service. What are the permission types you can assign her? (Choose all that apply.)

   A. Edit

   B. Execute

   C. Select

   D. Set Permissions

17. You have been assigned to be an administrator of an instance of the Business Data Connectivity service by a SharePoint administrator in your organization. You have been tasked with managing external systems associated with the BDC service including setting permissions on an external system, which you have been assigned rights to do. Of the following, which are valid permission options you can set to an external system? (Choose all that apply.)

    A. Edit

    B. Execute

    C. Selectable In clients

    D. Set Permissions

18. You have been assigned to be an administrator of an instance of the Business Data Connectivity service by a SharePoint administrator in your organization. You have been tasked with managing external systems associated with the BDC service. You are currently configuring an external system to use a service. Of the following, which is the only service an external system can be configured to use by default?

    A. Application service

    B. Database service

    C. User Profile service

    D. Web service

19. You have been assigned to be an administrator of an instance of the Business Data Connectivity service by a SharePoint administrator in your organization. You have been tasked with managing external systems associated with the BDC service. You are currently configuring an external system to use a service, and you are about to choose a WSDL Authentication Mode. You want to choose the mode that uses the application pool account under which Business Connectivity Services is running. Of the following, which is the correct mode?

    A. PassThrough

    B. RevertToSelf

    C. Credentials

    D. WindowsCredentials

20. You are a SharePoint administrator for your organization, and you are configuring BDC services in the server farm. You want to import a BDC model that contains a collection of descriptions for an external content type. You are aware that you can also use the import process for resource files, but you're not sure if the import process is identical to the process for importing a BDC model. You investigate, and find which of the following are true? (Choose all that apply.)

    A. You can select to import either a BDC model or a resource file in one action, but you can't import both at the same time.

    B. Resource files import properties for external content types, and BDC models don't.

    C. Resource files import permissions for external data types, and BDC models don't.

    D. There is no difference in the process of importing a BDC model or a resource file.

Answers to Review Questions

1. C. Although you could just ask the DBA responsible for the SQL Server instance in question the name of the database, using SQL Server Management Studio will most likely provide you with the information you need.

2. B, D. SQL authentication and Windows authentication are the only two options available when creating a managed metadata service application in Central Administration.

3. B, C. The only options available on the Publish Service Application screen in the drop-down menu are HTTP and HTTPS. The other options are bogus.

4. C, D. Option A cannot be the answer, since you can only select HTTP or HTTPS as connection types. Failing to create a description couldn't be the problem, since, although the description text provides a friendlier description of the service, it's not required to successfully publish the application service.

5. B, C. If the service allows access to a content type library, choosing the action described in option B provides the URL to the content type library, and option C allows the data from the content type library to be pushed down to all subsites, lists, and libraries. Options A and D are bogus.

6. A. Only the option described in A opens the Term Store Management Tool so you can create a term store administrator.

7. A, B. You can either use Central Administration or use Windows PowerShell. Options C and D are not valid options.

8. B, D. The only options available for you to select for authentication types are SQL authentication and Windows authentication.

9. B, D. The primary method of moving a site collection from one database to another is with Windows PowerShell, although you can also use Backup and Restore in Central Administration. No other Central Administration tool will accomplish this task.

10. C. While you can use Windows PowerShell to determine which site collection uses a given content database, you must use SQL Server Management Studio to set the database to a read-only state.

11. B. Only the SharePoint server farm content database will have the read-only flag set. All other databases will continue to be completely available.

12. A, B. You must be able to connect to the report server from SharePoint, and choosing a language on the download site makes sure that the Report Viewer web part, which will be installed with the add-in, will be available in that language. You do not need to set the report server database to read-only, and you must copy the add-in package to all web servers in the farm, not all application servers.

13. A. It is recommended that you install the add-in package on the first web server using the Installation Wizard and use the Files-Only Mode for all other web servers.

14. A. The Reporting Services area has been created under Application Management and contains a number of links that allows you to administer SRSS services.

15. D. The SQL Server Reporting Services Report Viewer, otherwise called the Report Viewer web part, can only read SRSS reports that use the `.rdl` extension. It can interpret no other file or report type.

16. A, B, D. Option C would have been correct if it had been Selectable In Clients.

17. A, B, C, D. You are allowed to set the same permissions on an external system that can be assigned to you as an administrator of a BDC service.

18. D. You can only configure an external system to use a web service by default.

19. B. PassThrough uses the credentials of the logged in use, Credentials uses either basic or digest authentication, and WindowsCredentials uses Windows authentication and utilizes the Secure Store Service to map a user's credentials to the credentials required by the service.

20. A, B, C. Although you can import both a BDC model and a resource file, during the import operation you must choose one or the other. Resource files import localized names, properties, and permissions to external content types, but BDC models don't.

Chapter

7

Managing User Accounts and Roles

MICROSOFT EXAM OBJECTIVE COVERED IN THIS CHAPTER:

✓ **Maintaining a SharePoint Environment**

- ▪ Configure Service Applications
- ▪ Manage Accounts and User Roles

For all its technological and collaborative advantages, SharePoint wouldn't be much good to anyone unless people were able to access and use it. For that to happen, you must have the ability to create and manage users and roles on SharePoint. Beyond that, user accounts are considered a resource in SharePoint, and you must have the ability to manage people not only as system users but as system resources. Users and organizations have profiles and profile properties that can be managed, and users can belong to groups you can configure to be targeted audiences for specific content. Like any other aspect of SharePoint, the job starts with configuring user profiles as a service.

Managing the User Profile Service

The *User Profile service* is another shared service in SharePoint Server 2010. This service lets you create and manage SharePoint user profiles, and these profiles can be accessed from sites, site collections, and server farms. As a SharePoint farm administrator, you can manage user profiles yourself or delegate this task to the service application administrator.

Administering the User Profile Service Application

Service applications in SharePoint 2010 provide a central location from which to manage all of the different features and actions associated with the service. The *User Profile service application* offers you a central place from which to specifically manage personalization settings. These settings include the following:

- Audiences
- My Site settings
- Organization browsing and management settings
- Profile synchronization settings
- User profile properties

This section in the chapter teaches you the process of creating and configuring the User Profile service application. Before you can continue with this part of the chapter, you must meet the following requirements:

- The version of SharePoint Server 2010 you are using must be either Standard or Enterprise.
- You must have configured at least one site collection that uses the My Site Host template.

- You must have an application pool that can be used by My Sites.
- You must be running an instance of the Managed Metadata Services.
- At least one managed path must exist.

See Chapter 6, "Managing Operational Settings," for information on Managed Metadata Services and Chapter 10, "Managing Site Collection," for more on site collections and My Sites.

Creating the User Profile Service Application

The first step in administering user profiles is to create a User Profile service application. This can be done either in Central Administration or with Windows PowerShell. Exercise 7.1 will show you how to accomplish the task in Central Administration. You must be a member of the Farm Administrators group to successfully complete the exercise.

EXERCISE 7.1

Creating a User Profile Service Application in Central Administration

1. Navigate to Central Administration and click Manage Service Applications under Application Management.

2. On the Manage Service Applications page, select the Service Applications tab, if it isn't already selected, to activate the Ribbon.

3. Click Create on the Ribbon, click New, and then click User Profile Service Application, as shown here.

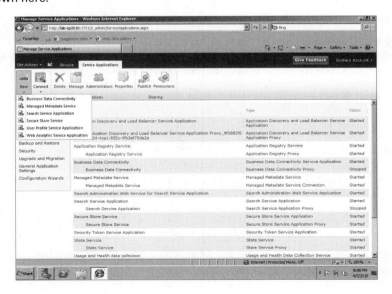

4. When the Create New User Profile Service Application box opens, type a unique name for the User Profile service application under Name.

5. Under Application Pool, select Use Existing Application Pool to choose an existing pool under which you'll consolidate most of your services or select Create A New Application Pool to create a new pool to be used mainly for customizations.

6. For Select A Security Account For This Application Pool, select Predefined to choose an existing predefined security account or select Configurable to select an existing managed account.

7. Under Profile Database, type the name of the database server where the profile database will be located in the Database Server field.

8. In the Database Name field, type the name of the database.

9. Select either Windows Authentication (Recommended) or SQL Authentication and, if you choose the latter, enter the username and password for the SQL Server authentication method.

10. If you want to use SQL Server database mirroring, type the name of the database server to be used in the Failover Database Server field and then select an authentication method as you did for the database server.

11. Under Synchronization Database, to use a synchronization database, type the name of the server in the Database Server field and then name the synchronization database in the Database Name field.

12. Select either Windows Authentication (Recommended) or SQL Authentication and, if you choose the latter, enter the username and password for SQL Server.

13. If you want to use SQL Server database mirroring for the synchronization server, type the name of the database server to be used in the Failover Database Server field and then select an authentication method as you did for the database server.

14. Under Social Tagging, enter the name of the database server and database as well as the authentication method, just as you did for the failover database server and the synchronization database server.

15. If you want to use SQL Server database mirroring for the social tagging database server, type the name of the database server to be used in the Failover Database Server field and then select an authentication method as you did for the database server.

16. Under Profile Synchronization Instance, select a machine in the server farm on which you want to run the Profile Synchronization service.

17. Under My Site Host URL, type the URL of the site collection where the My Site host has been created.

EXERCISE 7.1 *(continued)*

18. Under My Site Managed path, type the managed path where individual My Site websites are to be created.

19. Under Site Naming Format, select a format for naming personal sites such as User Name (Do Not Resolve Conflicts), User Name (Resolve Conflicts By Using domain_ username), or Domain And User Name (Will Not Have Conflicts).

20. Under Default Proxy Group, choose whether you want to make the proxy of the User Profile service as part of the default proxy group.

You can enable self-service site creation in a web application hosting My Site websites to allow users the ability to create their own My Site websites. Users must possess the Create Personal Site permission, which is enabled by default for all authenticated users. Learn more about turning the self-service site creation feature on or off in Chapter 10, "Managing Site Collections."

As previously mentioned, the identical task can be performed using Windows PowerShell. Relative to the number of steps involved, it appears that it is much easier, or at least much faster, to create a User Profile service application using PowerShell than Central Administration, but you must have a fair degree of comfort working with the command-line interface to do so.

Exercise 7.2 shows you how this is accomplished. To successfully complete this task, you must be a member of the SharePoint_Shell_Access role on the configuration database and a member of the WSS_ADMIN_WPG local group on the computer where SharePoint 2010 is present.

EXERCISE 7.2

Creating a User Profile Service Application Using Windows PowerShell

1. Run Windows PowerShell as an administrator.

2. At the command prompt, type the following (all on one line, even though we had to break the code to fit here in the book) and then press Enter, inserting the actual names for the User Profile application and application pool for the sample values in the code.

```
$app_UPA = New-SPProfileServiceApplication -Name UPA -PartitionMode
  -ApplicationPool $appPool
```

One of the prerequisites for creating a User Profile service application is that at least one managed path must be present. Exercise 7.3 takes you through the steps of defining a managed path using Central Administration. You must be a member of the Farm Administrators group to successfully complete this exercise.

EXERCISE 7.3

Defining a Managed Path

1. Navigate to Central Administration and click Application Management.

2. On the Application Management page, click Manage Web Applications under Web Applications.

3. On the Manage Web Applications page, select the desired web application and then, on the Ribbon, click Managed Paths.

4. When the Define Managed Paths box appears, under Add A New Path, type the path within the URL namespace in the Path field, as shown here.

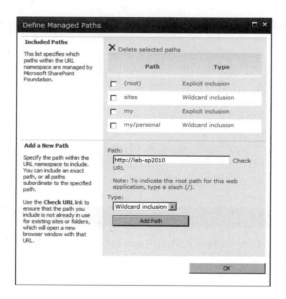

5. Click Check URL to verify that the URL functions and that the site indicated in the Path Field opens in a separate browser window.

6. In the type list, select Wildcard Inclusion to include all paths that are subordinate to the specified path or select Explicit Inclusion to include the site indicated by the specified path and not include subordinate sites.

7. To delete a specific path or paths, under Included Paths, select the check boxes for the undesired paths and then click Delete Selected Paths.

8. When you are finished, click OK.

Once you've created a User Profile service application, you may want to edit its settings. Exercise 7.4 shows you how this is done. You must be a member of the Farm Administrators group to successfully complete this exercise.

EXERCISE 7.4

Editing a User Profile Service Application

1. Navigate to Central Administration and click Manage Service Applications under Application Management.

2. On the Manage Service Applications page, click User Profile Service Application in the Type column to select it.

3. On the Ribbon, click Operations and then click Properties.

4. When the Edit User Profile Service Application box opens, edit the desired properties present.

5. When you are done, click OK.

The process of deleting a User Profile service application is almost the same as editing said service application. Once you've selected User Profile Service Application in the Type column and then clicked Operations, click Delete in the menu that appears. Then, in the Delete Service Application box, verify you've selected the correct service application and then select Delete Data Associated With The Service Applications. Click OK when you're finished.

Delegating Authority of a User Profile Service Application

Once you have created and configured a User Profile service application, you can assign managerial authority over the service application to another user, easing the administrative burden on you. This task can be performed either using Central Administration or using Windows PowerShell.

Exercise 7.5 will illustrate the Central Administration method. You must be a member of the Farm Administrators group to successfully complete this exercise.

EXERCISE 7.5

Assigning an Administrator to a User Profile Service Application in Central Administration

1. Navigate to Central Administration and click Manage Service Applications under Application Management.

2. On the Manage Service Applications page, select the desired User Profile service application.

3. On the Ribbon, click Administrators.

4. When the Administrators For User Profile Service Application box opens, type the user or group account in the available field and then click Add, as shown here.

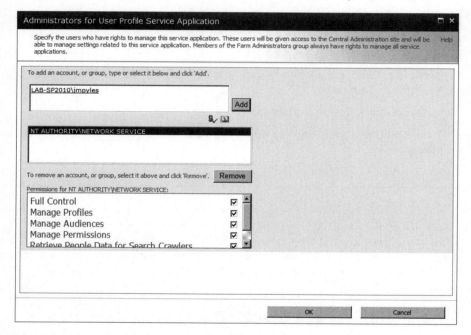

5. For Permissions For Administrator, select Full Control.

6. Click OK when you are finished.

The same task can be performed using Windows PowerShell, and Exercise 7.6 explains the procedure. You need to be a member of the SharePoint_Shell_Access role on the configuration database and a member of the WSS_ADMIN_WPG local group on the computer where SharePoint 2010 is present to successfully complete this exercise.

EXERCISE 7.6

Assigning an Administrator to a User Profile Service Application Using Windows PowerShell

1. Run Windows PowerShell as an administrator.

2. Type the following lines of code at the command prompt, minus the comments (//), each on a separate line, and then click Enter:

```
// // Display a list of all service applications and their GUIDs
Get-SPServiceApplication
// Create a variable that contains the guid for the User Profile service for
// which you want to delegate Full Control
$serviceapp = Get-SPServiceApplication <guid>
// Create a variable that contains the list of administrators
// for the service application
$security = Get-SPServiceApplicationSecurity $serviceapp -Admin
// Create a variable that contains the claims principal for a user account
$principalUser1 = New-SPClaimsPrincipal -Identity "domain\user" -IdentityType
WindowsSamAccountName
// Give Full Control permissions to the claims principal you just created
Grant-SPObjectSecurity $security -Principal $principalUser1 -Rights "Full Control"
// Apply the changes to the User Profile service application
Set-SPServiceApplicationSecurity $serviceapp -objectSecurity $security -Admin
```

You must change some of the values in the lines of sample code presented in the previous exercise. For <guid>, type the GUID for the User Profile service for which you want to delegate full control to the new administrator. For <domain\user>, type the domain\username pair for the user being assigned to administer the User Profile service.

 To find the GUID for the User Profile service or other services running in SharePoint, open Windows PowerShell, type **Get-SPServiceApplication** at the prompt, and then press Enter. When the output of the command is returned, locate the User Profile service in the DisplayName column and then the GUID for the service in the Id column. The GUID for the User Profile service will look something like 89b203c8-5baa-4f24-8de8-992739e710ad.

There will come a time when you'll need to remove an administrator of a User Profile service application, such as when the user changes job duties or leaves the company. You can also perform this task on the Manage Service Application page under Application Management in Central Administration. Just select the User Profile service application, click Operations on the Ribbon, and then click Administrators. On the Administrators For User Profile Service Application page, select the desired user or group account, click Remove, and then click OK.

The same task can be performed in Windows PowerShell. Open Windows PowerShell as an administrator, type the following, minus the comments (//), and then press Enter:

```
// Get a list of all service applications and their GUIDs
Get-SPServiceApplication
// Create a variable that contains the guid of the User Profile service
// application
// for which you want to remove an administrator
$serviceapp = Get-SPServiceApplication <guid>
// Create a variable that contains the list of administrators for the
// User Profile service application
$security = Get-SPServiceApplicationSecurity $serviceapp -Admin
// Remove the user from the list of service application administrators
Revoke-SPObjectSecurity $security -Principal <user name>
-Rights "Full Control"
// Apply the changes to the User Profile service application
Set-SPServiceApplicationSecurity $serviceapp
-objectSecurity $security -Admin
```

For <guid>, enter the GUID of the User Profile service for which you want to remove the administrator. For <user name>, substitute the username of the administrator.

Delegating Authority over User Profile Service Features

In addition to assigning administrative authority over a User Profile service application, SharePoint administrators with farm administrator rights can assign authority over selected features of the User Profile service application to specific users. For instance, you could assign a particular user Manage Audiences rights in a User Profile service application but give them no authority over any other features. This person would be known as a *feature administrator*. The ability to create one or more feature administrators is helpful when you want to delegate some authority over a User Profile service application but retain authority over other, more key features.

You can delegate authority over any of the following tasks to a feature administrator:

- Manage Audiences
- Manage Permissions
- Manage Profiles
- Manage Social Data
- Retrieve People Data For Search Crawlers

You can perform this task using either Central Administration or Windows PowerShell; however, the use of the different interfaces isn't interchangeable. You usually perform the task in Central Administration if you are running SharePoint as a stand-alone deployment. You are more likely to use Windows PowerShell to perform this task in an enterprise-level environment where you want to automate the process.

Exercise 7.7 will show you how to create a feature administrator using Central Administration. To successfully complete this exercise, you must belong to the Farm Administrators group, or you must have been delegated permission to administer the User Profile service application.

Delegating Administration of User Profile Service Features Using Central Administration

1. Navigate to Central Administration and click Manage Service Applications under Application Management.

2. In the list of service application that appears, click User Profile Service Application.

3. On the Ribbon, click Operations and then click Administrators.

4. When the Administrators For User Profile Service Application box opens, type the name of the user or group account you want to delegate to in the available field and then click Add.

5. Under Permissions For Administrator, select the feature or features you want to delegate to the designated user.

6. Click OK.

As was previously mentioned, the steps performed in Exercise 7.7 are usually done in a stand-alone SharePoint deployment. In an enterprise-level server farm environment, you are more likely to perform this task using Windows PowerShell.

Open Windows PowerShell as an administrator and run the following commands, typing them one line at a time, minus the comments (//), and then press Enter:

```
// Display a list of all service applications and their GUIDs
Get-SPServiceApplication
// Create a variable that contains the guid for the User
// Profile service for which you want to delegate Full Control
$serviceapp = Get-SPServiceApplication <guid>
// Create a variable that contains the list of administrators
// for the service application
$security = Get-SPServiceApplicationSecurity $serviceapp -Admin
// Create a variable that contains the claims principal for a user account
$principalUser1 = New-SPClaimsPrincipal -Identity "domain\user"
-IdentityType WindowsSamAccountName
// Give "Manage Social Data" permissions to the claims
// principal you just created
Grant-SPObjectSecurity $security -Principal $principalUser1
```

```
-Rights "Manage Social Data"
// Apply the changes to the User Profile service application
Set-SPServiceApplicationSecurity $serviceapp -objectSecurity $security -Admin
```

For <guid>, enter the GUID of the User Profile service for which you want to delegate feature authority. For <domain/user>, enter the domain-username pair for the user to whom you want to delegate authority. In the previous sample code, the feature being delegated is the Manage Social Data permission. If you want to delegate authority over a different feature, substitute the name of that feature in the relevant sections of the code.

User and Organization Profile Management

The User Profile service application comes with a default set of user profile properties. In addition to the defaults, you can add, edit, and delete customized user profile properties in the service application. This allows you to track specific data by associating specific properties of users with important business processes.

In addition to managing user profiles, you can also administer organizational profiles including components such as organization profile properties and organization subtypes. This section of the chapter will show you the various related tasks.

Administering Custom User Profile Properties

The first step in administering a customized user profile property is to create one. Exercise 7.8 will show you how. To successfully complete the task, you must belong to the Farm Administrators group or be a service application administrator for the User Profile service application. This task is related to the creation and management of My Sites. See Chapter 10 for more on My Site administration.

EXERCISE 7.8

Creating a Custom User Profile Property

1. Navigate to Central Administration and click Manage Service Applications under Application Management.

2. On the Manage Service Applications page, select the desired User Profile service application in the Type column.

3. On the Manage Profile Service page, click Manage User Properties under People.

4. On the Manage User Properties page, click New Property.

5. On the Add User Profile Property page, under Property Settings, type the name of the new user property to be used by the service application in the Name field such as **AuthorProperty**.

6. Type the name of the custom property as you want it displayed to users in the Display Name field such as **Author Property**.

EXERCISE 7.8 *(continued)*

7. Use the Type drop-down menu to select the data type for the property such as String.

8. Type the maximum number of characters you want to allow for values for this property in the Length field such as **255**.

9. Click Configure A Term Set to be used for this property and then select a term set from the drop-down menu to associate the profile property with a managed term set.

10. Under Sub-type To Profile, select Default User Profile Subtype to associate a default user profile subtype to use with the user profile property.

11. Under User Description, type the data or instructions you want to impart to users about this user profile property in the Description field such as a brief description of the characteristics of author users in SharePoint.

12. Under Policy Settings, select the policy setting such as Required, Optional, or Disabled and the default privacy setting you want to give to this property such as Only Me, My Manager, My Workgroup, My Colleagues, or Everyone. If desired, select User Can Override to enable the user to override this setting.

13. Under Edit Settings, select whether users can edit the values of the property.

14. Under Display Settings, determine whether or how the property will be seen by users.

15. Under Search Settings, select Alias, Indexed, or both to determine the kinds of searches you want associated with the user profile.

16. Under Property Mapping For Synchronization, click Remove to delete or change an existing mapping, if desired.

17. Under Add new Mapping, specify the source data connection, attribute, and synchronization direction for the mapping and then click Add.

18. When you are finished, click OK.

If you select String (Multi Value) in the Type menu in step 7, the property will be permanently set as a multivalued property and you will not be able to change it after you click OK. The only way to edit this value is to delete the property and add it again as a new single-value property.

For the Display Name settings and the User Description settings, if you use multiple languages in your SharePoint sites, you can provide different display names for each language by clicking Edit Languages. When the dialog box opens, click Add Language, select the desired language from the menu, and then type the display name.

Compared to creating a custom user profile property, editing the property is a relatively simple task. Exercise 7.9 shows you how. You require the same permissions to edit a property as you do to create one.

EXERCISE 7.9

Editing a Custom User Profile Property

1.   Navigate to Central Administration and click Manage Service Applications under Application Management.

2.   On the Manage Service Applications page, select the desired User Profile service application in the Type column.

3.   In the Manage Profile Service box, click Manage User Properties under People.

4.   On the page that appears, in the Property Name column, select the desired user profile property and then click Edit.

5.   On the Edit User Profile Property page, edit the desired elements and then click OK.

To delete a custom user property profile, follow the steps in Exercise 7.9 up through step 4. Then in the Property Name column, select the desired user profile property, and then click Delete. When the verification dialog box appears, click OK.

Administering the Organization Profile Property

Like the default user profile properties, the default organization profile properties can be augmented by adding customized profile properties. This is done for the same reason: to associate such properties with key information for tracking purposes. Organization profile components available to be managed include the following:

- Delegation for organizations
- Organization profile properties
- Organization properties
- Organization subtypes

This will enable you to track specific data regarding particular profiles that isn't available with the default properties such as team or division projects. For instance, if you create a custom property for a key business project assigned to a given team in the organization, you can track the organization activity around that project.

As with customized user profile properties, the first step in managing a customized organization profile property is to create one. Exercise 7.10 starts you off. To successfully complete the task, you must belong to the Farm Administrators group or you must be a service application administrator for the User Profile service application. This task is related to the creation and management of My Sites. See Chapter 10 for more on My Site administration.

EXERCISE 7.10

Creating a Custom Organization Profile Property

1. Navigate to Central Administration and click Manage Service Applications under Application Management.

2. On the Manage Service Applications page, click the desired User Profile service application.

3. On the User Profile Service Application page, click Manage Organization Properties under Organizations.

4. On the View Organization Profile Properties page, click New Property.

5. On the Add Organization Profile Property page, under Property Settings, type the name of the customized profile property to be used by the User Profile service application in the Name field.

6. In the Display Name field, type the name for the customized property you want to be displayed to users.

7. Open the Type drop-down list and select a data type for the property.

8. Type the maximum number of characters allowed for values of the property in the Length field.

9. Under Sub-type Of Profile, select Default Organization Profile Subtype to associate the organization profile property with the default organization profile subtype.

10. Under User Description, type the information or instructions about the property you want users to see in the Description field.

11. Under Property Settings, select the policy setting and default privacy setting you want for the property.

12. Under Edit Settings, choose whether users will be able to change the values of the property.

13. Under Display Settings, choose if or how the property will be viewed by users.

14. Under Search Settings, select Alias, Indexed, or both, depending on the type of searches you want associated with this profile property.

15. Under Add New Mapping, specify the source data connection, attribute, and synchronization direction for the mapping; then click Add.

16. When you are finished, click OK.

The process is very similar to Exercise 7.8, including the notes regarding the multivalue selection for Type and the multiple language options for Display Name and User Description. See Exercise 7.8 for more details.

The processes for editing and deleting a custom organization profile property are virtually the same as for performing the same actions on a custom user profile property. Exercise 7.9 and the paragraph after it describe the details of editing and deleting a property.

Basically, you navigate back to the Manage Service Applications page and select the User Profile service application. From there, on the page that appears, click Organizations as you did before and then Manage Organization Properties. In the Property Name column, click the name of the desired customized property and click either Edit or Delete, depending on your purpose.

You can delegate the authority to manage both user profile properties and organization profile properties. The steps are almost identical to those in Exercise 7.7. You perform exactly the same set of steps up to step 5 and then, under Permissions for Administrator, click Manage Profiles. Then click OK.

As in the task for delegating authority over user profile properties, you typically use Central Administration to perform this task in a stand-alone SharePoint deployment. For enterprise-level server farm environments, you should use Windows PowerShell.

To delegate administrative authority over user and organization profile properties, open Windows PowerShell as an administrator, type the following commands, and then press Enter:

```
$security = Get-SPProfileServiceApplicationSecurity $serviceApp -Admin
Grant-SPObjectSecurity $security $principal "Manage Profiles"
Set-SPProfileServiceApplicationSecurity $serviceApp -Admin $security
```

The sample code retrieves the SPObjectSecurity object that maps to the administrator access control list (ACL) on the User Profile service application. The new user is added to the ACL and assigned administrator rights for the Manage Profiles feature in the User Profile service.

Managing Profile Synchronization

While you've been exploring user and organizational profiles that are specific to SharePoint thus far, in fact, there is more than one location profile information can be stored. User and group profiles stored in SharePoint's profile store can be synchronized with profile data stored in both directory services and business systems throughout the enterprise. To perform the following tasks related to *profile synchronization*, you must have been assigned administrator rights tothe User Profile service. You must also possess at least Replicate Directory Changes permissions on Active Directory Domain Services (AD DS) if this is the directory service to be used.

One or more directory services must be available on the same network where you are running SharePoint Server 2010 in order for you to perform profile synchronization tasks. Directory services that can be synchronized with SharePoint include the following:

- Active Directory Domain Services (AD DS)
- Business Data Connectivity Services
- Novell eDirectory version 8.7.3 (LDAP)

- SunOne version 5.2 (LDAP)
- IBM Trivoli 6.2 (LDAP)

> You must use either a Standard or Enterprise version of SharePoint Server 2010 and run in a server farm. You cannot perform profile synchronization using a stand-alone installation of SharePoint with a built-in database, as is the test environment configured for this book.

Additional requirements are as follows:

- An instance of the User Profile service application must exist and be started.
- If you are using SQL Server 2008, it specifically must be with Service Pack 1 (SP1) with Cumulative Update 2 (CU2).
- If you are using Windows Server 2008 R2, hotfix KB976462 must be installed.

> As of this writing, you can find the hotfix at http://go.microsoft.com/ fwlink/?LinkID=166231.

Profile synchronization can be set to occur when profile data has changed either in SharePoint or in the directory service. You determine how and when the import and export processes occur when you configure profile synchronization. By default, no user profile property is set to export.

Some user profile properties in SharePoint are automatically mapped to their counterparts in the external directory service by default, including first name and last name. If you set synchronization to occur on a recurring schedule, the synchronization is incremental. This means the only information that is synchronized is data that has changed since the last scheduled synchronization. You can also use either a nonrecurring full synchronization or a nonrecurring incremental synchronization.

The tasks for profile configuring and starting profile synchronization must be performed in the order they are presented here.

The first task to perform is starting the User Profile Synchronization service, which is not started by default.

> You can start and stop the profile synchronization service in the same way that you do any other service. For details, see Exercise 4.2 or Exercise 4.3 in Chapter 4, "Configuring Service Applications."

To successfully perform this task, you must be a member of the Farm Administrators group on the computer containing Central Administration and the local administrator on the computer where the User Profile Synchronization service is deployed, which should be the same computer. The Farm Administrators account must also be a service administrator for the User Profile service you are configuring.

When you start the User Profile Synchronization service, you are asked to associate the service with the desired User Profile service application. Use the Select The User Profile Service Application drop-down menu to make your selection and then click OK. You must then wait 5–10 minutes before performing the following steps.

Starting the User Profile Synchronization Service

On the computer containing Central Administration and the User Profile Synchronization service, select Start ➢ Control Panel ➢ Administrative Tools ➢ Services.

1. Verify that the Forefront Identity Manager Synchronization service and the Forefront Identity Manager service are running, as in Figure 7.1, and if not, start the services.

FIGURE 7.1   User Profile Synchronization service

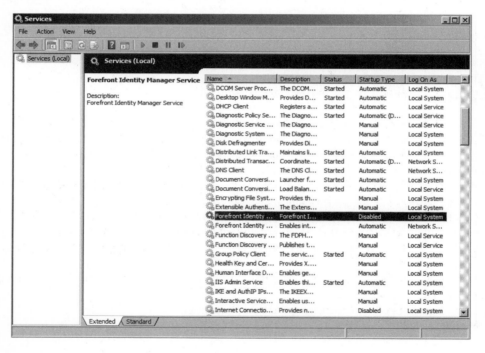

2. Navigate to %Programfiles%\Microsoft Office Servers \14.0\Synchronization Service\MaData and verify that ILMMA and MOSS-<User Profile Service application name> are present (the folders will be empty).

3. Restart the IIS service using IISReset by opening a command-line window, typing iisreset/noforce computername, and then pressing Enter, replacing computername with the name of the computer on which you are starting the User Profile Synchronization service.

Creating a Profile Synchronization Connection

Once the service has started, your next task is to create a new Profile Synchronization connection. To do this, you must know which directory service containers you want to synchronize with SharePoint. It is also important to create only one Profile Synchronization connection per directory service forest. If you are synchronizing with AD DS, you must have a minimum of Replicate Directory Changes permissions in AD DS. If you plan to export properties such as profile pictures to AD DS, you will also need AD DS Create All Child Objects permissions.

1. In Central Administration, click Manage Service Applications under Application Management.

2. On the Manage Service Applications page, click the name of the desired User Profile service application.

3. On the User Profile Service Application page, click Configure Synchronization Connections under Synchronization.

4. On the Synchronizations Connections page, click Create New Connection.

5. On the Add New Synchronization Connection page, type the name of the new synchronization connection in the Connection Name field.

6. Use the Type list to select the desired directory service.

7. If you select Business Data Connectivity, you must type the name for the connection in the Name box, select a Business Data Connectivity Application from the Business Data Connectivity Entity box, select either the 1:1 mapping or the 1:many mapping, and then click OK; otherwise, skip this step, and proceed with the subsequent steps.

8. Under Connection Settings, type the name of the directory service forest you want to connect to, type the account credentials for the directory service and the desired port, and then either select Auto Discover Domain Controller or type the name of the domain controller in the Domain Controller Name field.

9. Select the Use SSL-Secured Connection check box if you want to use a Secure Sockets Layer connection to connect to the directory service.

10. Under Containers, click Populate Containers and then select the desired containers for which you want to create connections; otherwise, click Select All to make connections for all containers.

11. When finished, click OK.

Editing Profile Synchronization Connection Filters

Once at least one Profile Synchronization connection has been made, you can edit the connection filters. To begin, follow steps 1 through 3 of the previous task to get to the Synchronization Connections page. Then perform the following. You'll need the same permissions as you did in the previous task.

1. On the Synchronization Connections page, click the connection you want to edit and then select Edit Connection Filters.

2. On the Edit Connection Filters page, under Exclusion Filters For Users, select the user property for which you want to apply a synchronization filter in the attributes list.

3. Select All Apply (AND) if you want all filters applied or select Apply Any (OR) if you want only one filter condition to be met.

4. Configure the specific filter parameters you want and then click Add.

5. Under Exclusion Filters For Groups, select the desired group property from the attributes list and then select either All Apply (AND) or Apply Any (OR).

6. Select and configure the desired filter parameters and then click Add.

7. When you are finished, click OK.

In steps 3 and 5, you can select from a number of different attributes, each of which requires a different set of steps to configure.

Mapping User Profile Properties

To set up user profile mapping, you need to possess the same permissions as in the previous tasks. In Central Administration, you must navigate to the Manage Service Applications page as you did previously, click the desired User Profile service application, and then, under People, click Manage User Properties. Then perform the following steps:

1. On the Manage User Properties page, right-click the desired user property and then select Edit from the menu that appears.

2. On the Edit User Profile Property page, under Add New Mapping, select the desired Profile Synchronization connection from the Source Data Connection list.

3. Select the desired directory service attribute from the Attribute list.

4. Select Import if you want to import the property value from the directory service into SharePoint, or select Export if you want to export the property value from SharePoint to the directory service.

5. When you've made your selection, click Add.

6. When you have finished, click OK.

If you want to synchronize user profile pictures between SharePoint, AD DS, and Outlook 2010 using the Outlook social connector, set the Data Source Connection for the Picture Property Mapping to Export.

Once the mappings are set up, your next step is to configure the profile synchronization settings. You must possess the same permissions as in the other task and verify that you have Full Control permissions as a service administrator for the User Profile service you are configuring. You must also be a system administrator on SQL Server. Navigate to the Manage Profile Service page in Central Administration and under Synchronization, click Configure Synchronization Settings; then perform the following steps.

1. On the Configure Synchronization Settings page, under Synchronization Entities, select Users And Groups to synchronize both types of information or select only Users to synchronize just user information.

2. Under Synchronize BDC Connections, clear the Include Existing BDC Connections For Synchronization check box if you want to exclude any data imports from the Business Data Connectivity service.

3. Under External Identity Manager, select Use SharePoint Profile Synchronization to use SharePoint's synchronization engine or select Enable External Identity Manager if you want to use an external synchronization application such as Microsoft Identity Lifecycle Manager 2007.

4. When you are finished, click OK.

When setting up synchronization settings, you should run a full synchronization for just users and then run an incremental synchronization of both users and groups. Also, if you choose to use an external synchronization engine, you will disable all the profile synchronization options in SharePoint.

Configuring a Nonrecurring Profile Synchronization

Once the configuration of profile synchronization is complete, you are able to set up non-recurring or recurring profile synchronization. You must possess the same permissions as you needed to create a profile synchronization connection.

1. In Central Administration, click Manage Service Applications under Application Management.

2. On the Manage Service Applications page, click the desired User Profile service application.

3. On the User Profile Service Application page, click Start Profile Synchronization under Synchronization.

4. On the Start Profile Synchronization page, select either Start Incremental Synchronization or Start Full Synchronization and then click OK, as shown in Figure 7.2.

When using AD DS, you must run full synchronization first and then again when any new profile property mapping is created. Once the synchronization is completed, you will be able to search for a known profile or accounts beginning with a known domain name from within the Manage User Profiles page.

Configuring a Recurring Profile Synchronization

To set up recurring profile synchronization, follow steps 1 through 3 in the prior section to get to the User Profile Service Application page, and click Configure Synchronization Timer Job under Synchronization. Then on the Edit Timer Job page under Recurring Schedule, use the radio buttons and menus to set the frequency and start times of the Profile Synchronization job, as shown in Figure 7.3. When finished, click OK.

Daily is the recommended scheduling frequency.

Managing User and Group Social Features

By default, any authenticated user can create a personalized My Site in SharePoint and then configure the personal and *social features* in their My Site. You can modify how a

SharePoint user utilizes the social features within their My Site, including altering their permissions, activating or deactivating social tags, and so on. This section of the chapter will address how you can perform such tasks.

FIGURE 7.2   The Start Profile Synchronization page

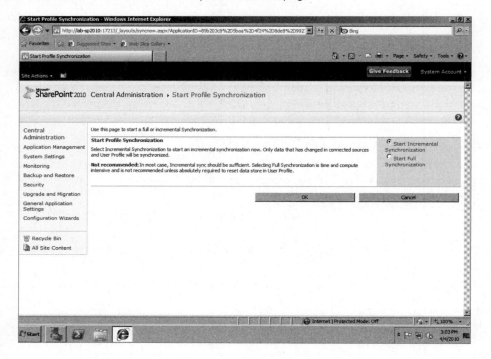

   See Chapter 10 for more on My Sites.

The three general features you can enable for users and groups in the User Profile service are Use Personal Features, Create Personal Site, and Use Social Features. Use Personal Features includes the ability to use My Colleagues, My Links, My Personalization links, and user profile properties within a My Site. The Create Personal Site feature allows users to create a My Site website, and Use Social Features includes using social tags, Note Board, and ratings.

The following set of tasks shows you how to change user access to these features. An instance of the User Profile service application must be active in SharePoint to complete these tasks as well as an instance of the Managed Metadata Service. You must also be a member of the Farm Administrators group or have been delegated permission to administer the User Profile service application. The first task is to enable users and groups to use personal and social features. Exercise 7.11 gets you started.

FIGURE 7.3   Setting the recurring schedule for profile synchronization

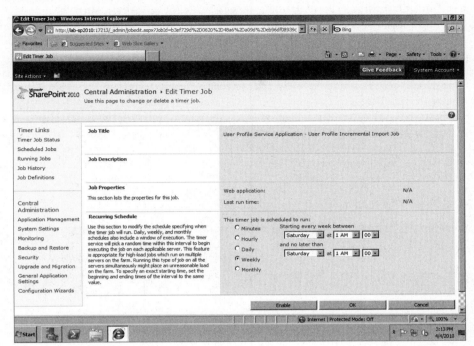

Enabling Users or Groups to Use Personal and Social Features

1. In Central Administration, click Manage Service Applications under Application Management.

2. On the Manage Service Applications page, click the desired User Profile service application to open it.

3. Under People, click Manage User Permissions.

4. When the Permissions For User Profile Service Application box opens, type or select the desired user or group account, and then click Add.

5. Under Permissions For, check the feature or features you want to allow the selected account or accounts to access, and then click OK.

In SharePoint Server 2010, users have the option of marking documents and items in document libraries and lists with social tags and referencing note board by default. For instance, on the Ribbon of a document library, the selections I Like It and Tags & Notes are available. You, as a SharePoint administrator, have the ability to deactivate these features, but you cannot enable or disable social tags and note boards on the level of the individual web application in a server farm. Any changes you make will be server farm wide. Also, any user data associated with these features may be lost.

Activating and deactivating these features is usually done in Central Administration for a stand-alone SharePoint deployment and performed using Windows PowerShell in an enterprise environment.

Since these social features are activated by default, to deactivate them in Central Administration, click Manage Farm Features under System Settings. On the Manage Farm Features page, click the Deactivate button next to Social Tags and Note Board Ribbon Controls, as shown in Figure 7.4. If you have previously deactivated this option, click the Activate button.

FIGURE 7.4   The Manage Farm Features page

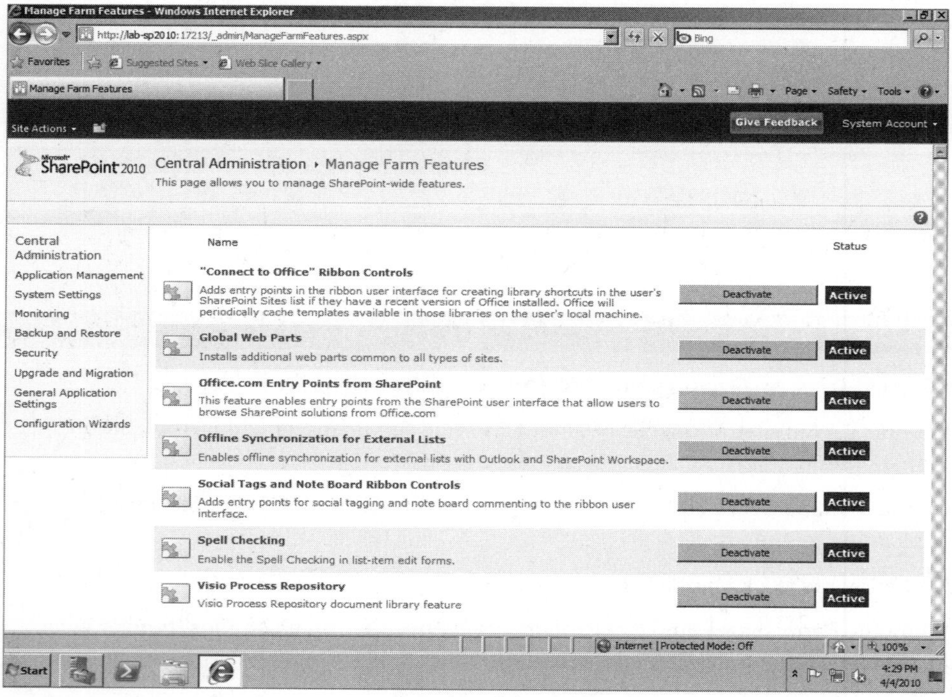

To deactivate or activate the social features in the server farm using Windows PowerShell, you must be a member of the SharePoint_Shell_Access group on the configuration database and a member of the WSS_ADMIN_WPG local group on the computer where SharePoint 2010 is present.

To deactivate the social features in the farm, open Windows PowerShell as an administrator, type the following at the prompt, and press Enter:

```
Get-SPFeature -Farm
Disable-SPFeature -Identity "SocialRibbonControl"
```

To enable these social features, perform the same task using the following code:

```
Get-SPFeature -Farm
Enable-SPFeature -Identity "SocialRibbonControl"
```

While the previous set of steps enables and disables social tags and note board for the entire farm, you can also prevent specific users or groups from accessing these features but allow the features to remain available to everyone else. Of course, you will need to be running an instance of the User Profile service application and have social tags and note boards enabled. Also, an instance of the Managed Metadata Service must exist and be active. Exercise 7.12 takes you through the process.

EXERCISE 7.12

Disabling Social Tags and Note Boards for a User or Group

1. In Central Administration, click Manage Service Applications under Application Management.

2. On the Manage Service Applications page, click the desired User Profile service application.

3. On the User Profile Service Application page, click Manage User Permissions under People.

4. In the Permissions For User Profile Service Application box, type or select the user or group account you do not want to have access to social features, and then click Add.

5. Under Permissions for, clear the Use Social Features check box and then click OK.

The ability to administer the User Profile service application not only lets you manage the service related to notes and tags but also lets you manage notes and tags specific to an individual. You can, for instance, remove all tags created by a certain person or delete one individual tag. As with the other tasks in this section of the chapter, you must have an instance of the User Profile service application running in SharePoint to proceed with the subsequent exercises.

Exercise 7.13 will show you how to remove all tags or notes associated with a specific SharePoint user or for a URL. This is a common task to perform when an employee has left the company. Keep in mind that removing social tags doesn't remove any of the related terms in the term store. If you need to remove the related terms, you'll need to use the Term Store Manager.

See Chapter 6, "Managing Operational Settings," for more information about the term store and the Managed Metadata service application.

To successfully perform this exercise, you must have rights to create My Site websites and either be a member of the Farm Administrators group or be a service application administrator. You may also need to have My Sites websites available in your SharePoint deployment.

EXERCISE 7.13

Deleting All Tags and Notes for a User or URL

1. In Central Administration, click Manage Service Applications under Application Management.

2. On the Manage Service Applications page, click the desired User Profile service application.

3. On the Manage Profile Service page, under My Site Settings, click Manage Social Tags And Notes.

4. On the Manage Social Tags And Notes page, use the Type list to select the social item you want to delete.

5. Type either the username in the User field or the first part of the URL in the URL field, and then click Find.

6. Select the specific social items you want to remove and then click Delete.

You can also delete all notes and tags for a user or URL for a particular date range. To do so, follow steps 1 through 5 in the previous exercise, then enter a start and end date in the Date Range fields, and finally click Find. Select the social items you want to remove and then click Delete. The items for the user or URL within the selected date range will be removed.

You can even use the same process to remove a specific tag or note. Follow steps 1 through 5 in Exercise 7.13, type a text string for the tag or note you want to remove in the Tag/Note Contains fields, and then click Find. When the search results are returned, select the social items you want to remove, and then click Delete.

Managing Audiences

An *audience* is a grouping of users defined by their membership in a Microsoft Exchange distribution list (DL), by a SharePoint group, or by rules configured by a SharePoint administrator. The rules applied to an audience can be based on user profile data or membership in an identity management system, such as Active Directory Domain Services (AD DS) or Business Connectivity Services (BCS). Audiences and their definitions are contained in the User Profile service application and allow organizations to target content to specific users or groups of users. This allows you, the SharePoint administrator, to specify data deployment to a specific group or groups only and not to all authenticated SharePoint users.

Put another way, an audience, as part of a User Profile service application, lets you target content to specific users based on a quality existing in the user's profile such as job title, task, or team. An audience can be defined by one or any combination of items such as any custom or default properties in the user profiles, location in the structure of the organization, any distribution list membership, or membership in a Windows security group or SharePoint group.

In SharePoint Server 2010, information targeting can be defined down to the list item level. Before being able to target an audience, the audience must be compiled to identify its membership using data crawling in the identity management system. This process cannot run during user profile synchronization, and audiences are not used in place of configuring permissions for SharePoint users and groups. An audience is used to allow administrators and managers to aim specific information to specific groups of users. For instance, you may want to provide data on the latest sales figures in a web part for the sales team but not have other teams or groups of SharePoint users see the same data. Being part of an audience does not allow members of the audience access to data on a permissions level but rather allows managers the ability to determine which users are part of a specific audience for which you want to aim particular information.

The first task to perform is to add an audience. When you add an audience, you are creating a group of members for which you want to target specific information. When you add an audience, you also add an audience rule by default, as well as creating an owner for the audience. You'll learn how to add more audience rules later, but Exercise 7.14 will show you how to add your first audience. You won't be able to view the audience members until you compile the audience, which you will also do in a later task.

To successfully complete this task, you must be a member of the Farm Administrators group, a service application administrator for the User Profile service application containing the audience, or an administrator for the Audience feature in the User Profile service application containing the audience.

EXERCISE 7.14

Adding an Audience

1. In Central Administration, click Manage Service Applications under Application Management.

2. On the Manage Service Applications page, click the desired User Profile service application.

3. On the Manage Profile Service page, click Manage Audiences under People.

4. On the View Audiences page, click New Audience.

5. On the Create Audience page, under Properties, type the name for the new audience in the Name field such as **Sales Team**.

6. Type a detailed description of the audience in the Description field such as **Magic Product Sales Group in Idaho**.

EXERCISE 7.14 *(continued)*

7. Type the name of the user account you want to own the audience in the Owner field, such as **JMPyles**, and then click Check Names.

8. Select Satisfy All Of The Rules or Satisfy Any Of The Rules to determine the members of the audience and then click OK.

9. On the Add Audience Rule page, to add a rule based on a user, follow steps 10 through 12. To add a rule based on a user profile property, follow steps 13 through 15.

10. Under Operand, to add a rule based on the user, select User or select Property to add a rule based on a property of the audience.

11. Select Reports Under to create a rule based on your organization's hierarchy or select Member Of to create a rule based on a group or distribution list.

12. To test the rule, type or select the username in the Value field, selecting a person who manages the user you want in your audience to test the Reports Under rule and selecting the group or distribution you want to include to test the Member Of rule.

13. To add a rule based on a user profile property, select Property under Operand and then select a specific property from the available list such as PositionState.

14. Use the Operator list to select an operator for the property such as * or +.

15. In the Value field, type the value you want to use to evaluate the property against the rule such as **ID**.

16. When you are done, click OK.

To add a rule that contains more complex logic, you must use the Share-Point Server 2010 object model. To find out more about this object model, visit http://msdn.microsoft.com/library/microsoft.office.server .audience.audience%28office.14%29.aspx.

Once you have at least one audience created, you can edit the properties of the audience. Exercise 7.15 will get you started. To begin, follow steps 1 through 3 to get to the People section of the Manage Profile Service page.

EXERCISE 7.15

Editing an Audience

1. Under People, click Manage Audiences.

2. On the View Audiences page, click next to the name of the audience, such as Sales Group, you want to edit to make the arrow appear and then click Edit.

EXERCISE 7.15 *(continued)*

3. On the Edit Audience page, under Properties, change the name or description of the audience if you desire, such as changing the description to the **Magic Product Sales Group in California**.

4. In the Owner field, change the name of the owner to a different name than the current owner, such as **LJPyles**, and then click Check Names.

5. For Value, change the text from ID to CA.

6. When you are finished, click OK.

 Real World Scenario

Planning Audience and Audience Rule Organization

You are a SharePoint administrator for your organization, and you have been tasked with creating a number of audiences for the purpose of targeting relevant information based on user profile data. You have divisions in five major U.S. cities, and the CIO wants authenticated SharePoint users in each city to receive information based on their locale. In addition, at each location, you are to create different audiences for managers, sales and marketing, and new employees so that relevant data can be routed appropriately.

You are considering the basis for creating audiences, such as user profile data, Active Directory service group membership, and Microsoft Exchange distribution lists. You are also reviewing the types of audience rules that can be created by default in SharePoint and whether the "off-the-shelf" rules will be sufficient.

You decide to consult with one of the SharePoint developers, and she suggests using the Microsoft Office Server Audience class to create audience rules that are more complex and that may offer more flexibility when creating audiences. You both review the information on this topic at msdn.microsoft.com and develop a plan you can present to the CIO.

You can delete an audience using many of the same steps as in Exercise 7.15. Just navigate to the People section on the Manage Profile Service page and click Manage Audiences. On the View Audiences page, click near the audience you want to delete so the arrow appears and then click Delete.

Once you have created an audience with its one default rule, you can add more rules, edit rules, and delete rules for the audience. As you saw in Exercise 7.14, each audience rule consists of an operand, an operator, and a value. The operand is used to identify the user or property you want to include in the query for the rule. The operator determines whether users being compared to the value are included or excluded by the rule. The value is the point of comparison used by the query.

When you create multiple rules for an audience, you must apply one of the two available sets of logic: satisfy all of the rules or satisfy any of the rules. In the former selection, users must match all of the rules for the audience in order to be members of the audience. In the latter selection, users can match any one of the existing rules to be considered audience members.

Adding or editing an audience rule is substantially similar to the activities in which you engaged in Exercises 7.14 and 7.15. To delete a rule, select the rule on the View Audience Properties page; then, on the bottom of the Edit Audience Rule page, click Delete and then click OK to confirm your action.

So far, all the tasks you've performed are well and good, but as you recall, an audience cannot be used until it's compiled. Once you have created an audience and added the necessary rules, the next step is to compile it. Exercise 7.17 guides you through this process. The compiling task is very straightforward.

EXERCISE 7.17

Compiling an Audience

1. In Central Administration, click Manage Service Applications under Application Management.

2. On the Manage Service Applications page, click the User Profile service application.

3. On the Manage Profile Service page, click Compile Audiences under People.

Although that was a very simple task, you may not want to have to manually compile your audiences all of the time. Fortunately, you can schedule the compilation process to occur at regular intervals. Exercise 7.18 shows you step-by-step.

EXERCISE 7.18

Scheduling an Audience to Be Compiled

1. In Central Administration, click Manage Service Applications under Application Management.

2. On the Manage Service Applications page, click the User Profile service application.

3. On the Manage Profile Service page, click Schedule Audience Compilation under People.

4. On the Specify Compilation Schedule page, select the Enable Scheduling check box.

5. Select the start time using the Start At list.

6. Schedule the frequency of the compiling process by choosing Daily, Weekly, or Monthly.

7. When you are finished, click OK.

The audience will be compiled automatically based on the schedule you have created.

Finding just a few audiences may not be much of a chore, but if you create a large number of audiences, locating a specific one may not be easy if you are searching manually. You can use the search feature to locate any particular audience. Just navigate to the Manage Profile Service page and click Manage Audiences under People. On the View Audiences page, type the first few letters of the name of the audience in the Find Audiences That Start With field, and then click Find. The desired audience will appear in the search results.

Summary

In this chapter, you learned a about a variety of user and organizational profile management responsibilities carried by the SharePoint administrator, including the following:

- Creating and editing the User Profile service application
- Creating and editing User Profile service features
- Managing user and organizational profiles
- Configuring profile properties and managing profile synchronization
- Creating, compiling, and managing audiences and administrating audience rules

Exam Essentials

Understanding the Administrative Tasks Associated with the User Profile Service Application   Show the ability to create an instance of the User Profile service application, edit the service application, and delegate authority to manage the application to others.

Managing User and Organization Profiles and Properties   Demonstrate how to create and manage profiles for user and organization groups, as well as configure and manage the properties for those profiles, which includes profile synchronization.

Creating, Compiling, and Managing Targeted Audiences   Indicate competence in the tasks related to the creation and configuration of targeted audience groups, including creating a group, adding and editing audience rules, and compiling an audience.

Review Questions

1. You are a SharePoint administrator for your organization. You are discussing the procedures for creating and configuring a User Profile service application with your staff. You are presenting the general characteristics of the application. Of the following choices, which ones are personalization settings that can be managed in this application? (Choose all that apply.)

    A. Audiences

    B. Defining Managed Paths

    C. My Site settings

    D. Profile synchronization settings

2. You are a SharePoint administrator for your organization. You are discussing the procedures for creating and configuring a User Profile service application with your staff. You are discussing circumstances that may inhibit the creation and use of a User Profile service application. Of the following options, which must be present in order for you to create the application? (Choose all that apply.)

    A. You must be running the Standard or Enterprise version of SharePoint Server 2010 in a full server farm.

    B. At least one managed path must exist.

    C. You must have an application pool that is used by My Sites.

    D. You must be running an instance of Managed Metadata Services.

3. You are a SharePoint administrator for your organization. You are discussing the procedures for creating and configuring a User Profile service application with your staff. Of the following processes regarding the creation of this application, which one is the most true?

    A. You should use Central Administration when creating the application for a stand-alone deployment and use Windows PowerShell for creating it in the enterprise.

    B. You should use Central Administration when creating the application for the enterprise and use Windows PowerShell for creating it in a stand-alone deployment.

    C. You can use either Central Administration or Windows PowerShell regardless of deployment.

    D. You can use only Central Administration.

4. You are a SharePoint administrator for your organization, and you have created a User Profile service application. You want to delegate authority to manage the application to a member of your staff and need to verify what role the staff person must possess to make this possible. Of the following, what role or group at a minimum must the person belong to in order for you to delegate this authority?

    A. The person must be a member of the Farm Administrators group.

    B. The person must be a member of the SharePoint_Shell_Access role.

    C. The person must be an local administrator on the server containing Central Administration.

    D. The person must be a SharePoint authenticated user.

5. You are a SharePoint administrator for your organization, and you have created a User Profile service application. You want to delegate authority to manage the application to a member of your staff, but you want to limit the specific features the person can administer. Of the following, what options can you select? (Choose all that apply.)

A. You can delegate the ability to Manage Audiences.

B. You can delegate the ability to Manage Permissions.

C. You can delegate the ability to Retrieve People Data For Search Crawlers.

D. You must delegate the ability to manage all features in the application.

6. You are a SharePoint administrator for your organization, and you have created a User Profile service application. You want to delegate authority to manage the application to a member of your staff. You are reviewing the various procedures for delegating authority over a User Profile service application. Of the following, which one is true about how to delegate authority to the application?

A. You should use Central Administration when delegating this authority in a stand-alone deployment and use Windows PowerShell for delegating it in the enterprise.

B. You should use Central Administration when delegating this authority for the enterprise and use Windows PowerShell for delegating it in a stand-alone deployment.

C. You can use either Central Administration or Windows PowerShell regardless of deployment.

D. You can use only Central Administration.

7. You are a SharePoint administrator for your organization, and you have created a User Profile service application. The User Profile service application comes with a default set of user profile properties, but you also need to create a series of custom user profile properties to track various business processes. You want to make these properties available to different language groups. What does your research tell you about this?

A. You can set the user description in different languages when you are configuring the display name settings.

B. You can set the custom property in specific languages when you click New Property on the Manage User Property page.

C. You can set the customization to display in more than one language when you are adding a new mapping.

D. You can only set the customized profile property to display in the default language used in your SharePoint deployment.

8. You are a SharePoint administrator for your organization, and you have created a User Profile service application. The User Profile service application comes with a default set of organization profile properties. Of the following, which components in an organization profile can be managed? (Choose all that apply.)

A. Delegation for organizations

B. Organization paths

C. Organization profile properties

D. Organization properties

9. You are a SharePoint administrator for your organization, and you have created a User Profile service application. The User Profile service application comes with a default set of user and organization profile properties. In addition, you need to create some customized user and organization profile properties. In the process of creating the search settings for both, what are the differences in setting options?

   A. You can set either Alias or Indexed search options for custom user profile properties but only Alias for custom organization profile properties.

   B. You can set either Alias or Indexed search options for custom organization profile properties but only Indexed for custom user profile properties.

   C. Custom user profile properties can only use the Alias search option, and Custom organization properties can only use the indexed search option.

   D. There is no difference. The search settings for either profile property are identical.

10. You are a SharePoint administrator for your organization, and you have created a User Profile service application. You want to be able to access, use, and synchronize user and group profiles from a number of different sources in the SharePoint environment. You are developing a plan with your staff and discussing what directory services types can be synchronized with the SharePoint profile store. Of the following, what are correct choices? (Choose all that apply.)

   A. Active Directory Domain Services (AD DS)

   B. Business Data Connectivity Services

   C. SunOne version 5.2 (LDAP)

   D. Windows NT Server 4.0 Directory Services

11. You are a SharePoint administrator for your organization, and you have created a User Profile service application. You want to be able to access, use, and synchronize user and group profiles from a number of different sources in the SharePoint environment. You are developing a plan with your staff and discussing any specific requirements that may have previously been overlooked. Of the following, what requirements are valid? (Choose all that apply.)

   A. You must use either a Standard or Enterprise version of SharePoint Server 2010 and run in a server farm.

   B. If you are using SQL Server 2008, it specifically must be with Service Pack 1 (SP1) with Cumulative Update 2 (CU2).

   C. The Forefront Identity Manager Synchronization Service must be stopped.

   D. The Forefront Identity Manager Service must be running.

12. You are a SharePoint administrator for your organization, and you have created a User Profile service application. You want to be able to access, use, and synchronize user and group profiles from a number of different sources in the SharePoint environment. You are developing a plan with your staff and discussing automation of the synchronization process. Of synchronizations that can be automated, what are the valid options? (Choose all that apply.)

   A. Full

   B. Differential

   C. Incremental

   D. Mirror

13. You are a SharePoint administrator for your organization, and you have created a User Profile service application. You want to be able to access, use, and synchronize user and group profiles from a number of different sources in the SharePoint environment. You are developing a plan with your staff and discussing automation of the synchronization process. By default, the User Profile Synchronization service is not started. You want to be able to delegate the responsibility of starting the service. What permissions must the person have to be able to perform this task? (Choose all that apply.)

   A. The person must be a member of the Farm Administrators group on the computer containing Central Administration.

   B. The person must be the local administrator on the computer where the User Profile Synchronization service is present.

   C. The person must be a service administrator for the User Profile service being configured.

   D. The person must be a member of the Forefront Identity Manager Service's administration group.

14. You are a SharePoint administrator for your organization, and you have created a User Profile service application. You want to be able to access, use, and synchronize user and group profiles from a number of different sources in the SharePoint environment. You are developing a plan with your staff and discussing automation of the synchronization process. After starting the User Profile Synchronization Service, what is the next necessary task?

   A. Creating a Profile Synchronization connection

   B. Creating Profile Synchronization connection filters

   C. Configuring a nonrecurring profile synchronization

   D. Mapping user profile properties

15. You are a SharePoint administrator for your organization, and you have created a User Profile service application. You want to be able to access, use, and synchronize user and group profiles from a number of different sources in the SharePoint environment. You have performed all the other necessary steps and are now ready to configure profile synchronization. Of the following, what permissions must you possess to successfully complete this task in Central Administration? (Choose all that apply.)

   A. You must have Full Control permissions as a Service Administrator for the User Profile service.

   B. You must be a system administrator on SQL Server.

   C. You must be a member of the SharePoint_Shell_Access role.

   D. You must be a member of the Farm Administrators group.

16. You are a SharePoint administrator for your organization, and you have created a User Profile service application. You want to be able to access, use, and synchronize user and group profiles from a number of different sources in the SharePoint environment. You have performed all the other necessary steps and are now ready to configure profile synchronization. When using AD DS, you must run full synchronization. What other event will require a full synchronization under this condition?

A. When any new profile mapping is created.

B. When changing permissions for a person, you are delegating to manage profile synchronization.

C. When synchronizing to Business Data Connectivity Services.

D. When synchronizing to SunOne version 5.2 (LDAP).

17. You are a SharePoint administrator for your organization, and you have created a User Profile service application. You want to be able to access, use, and synchronize user and group profiles from a number of different sources in the SharePoint environment. You want to configure recurring profile synchronization. What option on the User Profile Service Application page lets you do this?

A. The Activate Configure Synchronization option

B. The Activate Recurring Synchronization option

C. The Configure Synchronization Timer Job option

D. The Recurring Synchronization Timer Job option

18. The Create Personal Site feature allows users to create a My Site website and Social Features including using social tags, Note Board, and ratings. As a SharePoint administrator, you have the ability to modify how a SharePoint user utilizes social features within their My Site website. You are discussing the corporate plan for how authenticated users will use these social features with your staff. In your review, what do you determine is true in this area? (Choose all that apply.)

A. Users can access I Like It and Tags and Notes selections in both libraries and lists.

B. As an administrator, you can disable social features at the farm, site collection, and site levels.

C. As an administrator, you can delete all tags and notes for a specific user.

D. By default, all authenticated users can create a personalized My Site website.

19. You are a SharePoint administrator for your organization, and you are developing a plan with your staff to create audiences so that specific content can be targeted to defined groups. An audience is a grouping of users defined by their membership in certain groups or containers. Of the following, what can be used to define an audience? (Choose all that apply.)

A. A Business Data Catalog group

B. A Microsoft Exchange distribution list

C. A SharePoint group

D. Rules configured by a SharePoint administrator

20. You are a SharePoint administrator for your organization, and you are developing a plan with your staff to create audiences so that specific content can be targeted to defined groups. An audience is a grouping of users defined by their membership in certain groups or containers. After creating an audience, defining rules, and making sure the audience has an owner, what must you do before the audience can be used?

A. Compile the audience.

B. Distribute the audience.

C. Configure the audience.

D. Publish the audience.

Answers to Review Questions

1. A, C, D. Defining managed paths is done in web application management, not in the User Profile service application.

2. B, C, D. Although you must be running either the Standard or Enterprise version of Share-Point Server 2010, it does not have to be running in a full server farm. This is a requirement only when you perform other tasks such as profile synchronization.

3. C. Although there are some creation processes that typically use Central Administration for one deployment type and Windows PowerShell for another, the creation of a User Profile service application isn't one of them.

4. D. You can assign this responsibility to any SharePoint authenticated user, although it is likely you will choose someone with the necessary technical background as well.

5. A, B, C. You can delegate one or more specific features without delegating total control of the application to another user.

6. A. Use Central Administration to perform this task in a stand-alone deployment and Windows PowerShell in an enterprise environment.

7. A. For the Display Name settings and the User Description settings, you can use multiple languages in your SharePoint sites and provide different display names for each language by clicking Edit Languages. When the dialog box opens, click Add Language, select the desired language from the menu, and then type the display name.

8. A, C, D. Option B is incorrect, but in addition to the other choices, you can also administer organization subtypes.

9. D. You can set either Alias, Indexed, or both for custom user profile properties and custom organization profile properties.

10. A, B, C. Windows NT Server 4.0 Directory Services is not supported, but in addition to the other correct selections, Novell eDirectory version 8.7.3 (LDAP) and IBM Trivoli 6.2 (LDAP) are.

11. A, B, D. Both the Forefront Identity Manager Synchronization Service and the Forefront Identity Manager Service must be running.

12. A, C. You can only set automated synchronizations to full or incremental. The other options do not exist.

13. A, B, C. Option D is bogus, but all other permissions listed are required to perform start the User Profile Synchronization service.

14. A. You must create a profile synchronization connection after starting the User Profile Synchronization service but before performing any other task.

15. A, B, D. Option C is not required to perform this task in Central Administration.

16. A. When using AD DS, you must run full synchronization first and then again when any new profile property mapping is created.

17. C. Only C is the correct option. All the other selections are bogus.

18. A, C, D. A SharePoint administrator can only disable social features at the farm level.

19. B, C, D. All groups listed are valid options except the Business Data Catalog group, which is bogus.

20. A. Audience members don't become available until the audience is compiled. The other options are bogus.

Chapter

8

Managing Authentication Providers and Permissions

MICROSOFT EXAM OBJECTIVE COVERED IN THIS CHAPTER:

✓ **Maintaining a SharePoint Environment**

- Manage Authentication Providers

- Manage Accounts and User Roles

In any networked environment, ideally you have access to only the information and services your credentials allow you to access. This is true for both people and other services and systems. The gatekeepers to every site and service in SharePoint are the authentication systems you configure, and from the point of view of the casual observer, their numbers are vast. Beyond that, you have the responsibility of making SharePoint user permissions and roles work with authentication providers, including the task of configuring custom permissions. You also need to recognize when an access issue is authentication based. Each of these areas is covered in this chapter.

Managing Authentication Methods

This section is the primary focus of the chapter. As mentioned in the introduction, as a SharePoint administrator, you are responsible for understanding and configuring a variety of authentication methods, including the following:

- Kerberos
- Claims-based authentication
- Forms-based authentication
- Windows Challenge/Response NTLM
- Secure Store Service (SSS)
- Active Directory Federation Services (ADFS)

The Secure Store Service was described in detail in Chapter 4, "Configuring Service Applications," but the other authentication methods will be presented, including the specific tasks required to install and configure the services.

Configuring authentication methods is performed after the installation and initial configuration of SharePoint. When you are ready to create sites and site collections, you must configure authentication at the level of the web application where the site collections will live. Authentication methods typically used are Kerberos and claims-based authentication but can include many others.

NTLM is the default authentication protocol for most SharePoint environments, but sometimes administrators change back and forth between Kerberos and NTLM. Of course, Active Directory Federation Service (AD FS) extends single sign-on security and functionality beyond what can exist within a single security boundary.

Chapter 3, "Configuring SharePoint Farm Environments," showed you how to create a web application and configure services for the application. See Chapter 9, "Managing Web Applications and Host Sites," and Chapter 10, "Managing Site Collections," for more information related to configuring a web application and site collection security.

Administering Kerberos

Kerberos is an industry-standard authentication method that is implemented in Active Directory Domain Services (AD DS). If you plan on using Kerberos authentication on your server farm, you must install and configure several applications on the computers in your farm. The goals of these tasks are to allow communication between SharePoint and the SQL Server database, allow access to the Central Administration web application, and allow access to other web applications including the portal site and My Site web applications.

Configuring Kerberos will require that SharePoint 2010 be installed on Windows Server 2008 or Windows Server 2008 R2 and that all of your Active Directory domain controllers be running Windows Server 2008 or Windows Server 2008 R2. Make sure all your server computers are fully updated before proceeding.

SharePoint Server 2010 Search cannot crawl SharePoint Server 2010 web applications that are configured to use Kerberos authentication if the web applications are hosted on IIS virtual servers that are bound to nonde-fault ports. You must use TCP port 80 and Secure Sockets Layer (SSL) port 443. If you want to use nondefault ports and have SharePoint Server 2010 Search be able to successfully complete crawls, you must use either Basic authentication or NTLM authentication.

Another Kerberos requirement is the ability to create service principal names (SPNs) in AD DS, which requires that you have domain administrative-level access. The SPNs must include the port numbers if you plan on using nondefault ports.

The server farm topology typical for Kerberos authentication includes separate computers acting as frontend web servers, application servers, and SQL Server instances. One application server must also be running Search Query and another usually runs Search Indexing. The database server should be SQL Server 2008 with the SQL Server service running as account mydomain\sqlsvc and the default instance of SQL Server listening on TCP port 1433.

Configuring Kerberos for SQL Communication

A number of Kerberos-related tasks must be performed on Windows Server 2008 to enable SQL Server communication before installing SharePoint Server 2010 on any of the server computers in the farm.

The first required task involved in configuring Kerberos for any service installed on a computer running Windows Server 2008 is creating an SPN for the domain account being used to run the service on the host computer. An SPN comprises the following components:

- A service name such as HTTP
- A hostname, which can be real or virtual
- A port number

As previously mentioned, the default instance of SQL server running on the server computer listens on port 1433 for requests. If the service name was HTTP and the default instance of SQL Server was named sqlsvr, the SPN would look like HTTP/sqlsvr:1433.

The SPNs are created on the instance of the SQL Server instance on the Windows Server 2008 machine hosting SQL for the server farm. To set an SPN for an Active Directory domain account, you can either use setspn.exe, which is part of the Resource Kit tools for Windows Server 2008, or use the adsiedit.msc utility for the Active Directory domain controller.

Creating an SPN for the SQL Server Service Account

The following example shows you how to use the adsiedit.msc method. You will need to have a domain controller running in your networked environment and require domain administrative permissions on the controller.

1. Log in to the Active Directory domain controller.

2. In the Run field, type **ADSIEDIT.MSC,** and press Enter.

3. In the Actions pane on the right, click More Actions and then click Connect To.

4. When the Connection Settings dialog box appears, either accept the default name in the Name field or type in the desired name.

5. Under Connection point, select the Select A Well Known Naming Context option and then use the drop-down menu to select the desired option.

6. Select the desired options and click OK (you should only have to perform steps 3 through 6 once).

7. In the Management Console dialog box, expand the Domain Container folder.

8. Expand the folder containing user accounts, such as CN-Users.

9. Locate the container for the SQL Server Service account, such as CN=sqlsvr.

10. Right-click the account name and then click Properties.

11. Scroll down the properties list, select serverPrincipleName, and click Edit.

12. In the Value To Add field in the Multi-Valued String Editor dialog box, type the name of the SPN such as **HTTP/sqlsvr:1433** and then click Add.

13. Click OK to close the Multi-Valued String Editor and then click OK to close the Properties dialog box.

Once you have installed SharePoint Server 2010 on the server farm, you want to test your ability to use Kerberos authentication to connect SharePoint to SQL. You can do this by installing SQL Client Tools on one of your SharePoint servers and using the utility to confirm your ability to connect to SQL.

Confirming Kerberos Authentication to the SQL Host

To perform the following, go to www.microsoft.com/downloads and then search for *Microsoft SQL Server Management Studio Express*. Follow the instructions for downloading and installing the utility on one of your SharePoint server machines.

Once you have the utility installed, run Management Studio. When the Connect To Server dialog box appears, type the name of the SQL Server host computer in the available field and then click Connect.

To confirm that Kerberos was used to authenticate the connection, on the SQL Server host computer, run the Event Viewer and review the Security event log. If Kerberos authentication was successfully used, you'll see a Success Audit record for a Logon/Logoff category event. For Logon Process, you should see Kerberos listed. Also, Logon Type should be 3, and Source Network Address should list the IP address of the SharePoint computer you used to make the connection.

For more information on verifying authentication and how to check the Event Viewer, see the "Errors" section later in this chapter.

Deploying the Server Farm for Kerberos Authentication

Chapter 3 described the various server farm topologies that can be used depending on your business and technical goals for a SharePoint Server 2010 server farm. Deploying the farm for Kerberos authentication is typically performed in a specific order. Once you have installed SharePoint on all the servers in the farm, have run the SharePoint Configuration Wizard, and have joined all of the servers to the farm, you would configure services and applications in the following manner:

1. Configure services on the farm servers starting with the SharePoint Foundation 2010 Search service, then the SharePoint Server 2010 Search Indexing service, and finally the SharePoint Server 2010 Search Query service.

2. Create the web application that will be used for the portal site and the My Site using Kerberos authentication.

3. Create a site collection using the Collaboration Portal template in the portal site web application.

Although the process of creating a web application was covered in Chapter 4, additional exercises will be presented here to highlight the order of creating said web apps specific to Kerberos authentication. Exercise 8.1 will show you the process of creating the web application for the portal site.

EXERCISE 8.1

Creating the Portal Site Web Application with Kerberos Authentication

1. Navigate to Central Administration and click Manage Web Applications under Application Management.

2. On the Web Applications Management page, on the Web Applications tab, click New on the Ribbon.

3. In the Create A New Web Application box, under Authentication, accept the default selection of Classic Mode Authentication.

4. Under IIS Web Site, select Create A New IIS Web Site, if it is not already selected.

5. Give the portal site a name in the Name field and a description in the Description field.

6. In the Port field, type **80**.

7. In the Host Header field, type a URL such as `mainportal.domainname.local`. For Path, accept the default.

8. Under Security Configuration, select Negotiate (Kerberos) and accept the rest of the default settings.

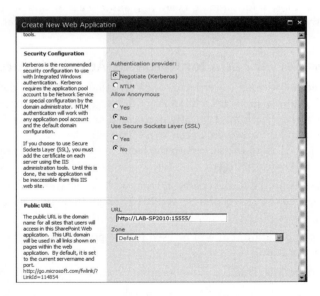

9. Under Public URL, accept the URL selection and select the Default zone.

10. Select Create New Application Pool.

11. Accept the default name in the Application Pool Name field or create a new name.

12. Select Configurable.

13. Select Register New Managed Account; then in the box that appears, enter the administrator user you want to manage the web application in the format *domain/ username* and click OK.

14. Accept the rest of the defaults.

15. When you are done, click OK.

Create the My Site Web Application

The process of creating a My Site web application using Kerberos is just about the same as doing so for a portal site. You still use port 80, but you give the site a unique name and a description such as My Sites. You still create the application in the Default zone and create a new application pool, naming it something like MySitePool. Other than that, use the same steps as you did in Exercise 8.1.

After creating web applications that are configured to use Kerberos authentication, it's time to create site collections within the applications. Chapter 10 will provide the details about the mechanics of creating and maintaining sites and site collections, but Exercise 8.2 will show you, in brief, the next step, which is specifically creating a collaboration portal site on the portal web application. This is the collaboration gateway into SharePoint.

Creating the Enterprise Wiki Using the Collaboration Portal Template

1. Navigate to Central Administration, and on the Application Management page, under Site Collections, click Create Site Collection.

2. On the Create Site Collection page, select the web application you created for the portal site that you configured to use Kerberos authentication. See Exercise 8.1 for the name of that application.

3. Give the new site collection a name and description in the available field and give the site collection URL a path.

4. Under Template Selection and under Select A Template, click the Publishing tab and then select the Collaboration Portal template.

5. Under Primary Site Collection Administrator, type the domain and name of the user you want in this role, such as **domain\admin**.

6. Under Secondary Site Collection Administrator, specify the SharePoint user you want in this role.

7. When you are ready, click OK.

8. Verify that the portal site collection was successfully created.

You can create other site collections on the web applications you set up to use Kerberos authentication. The next step, and it's an important one, is to make sure Kerberos authentication is actually working. To perform the Exercise 8.3, you must log into a server running SharePoint but not a frontend web server configured for network load balancing (NLB).

EXERCISE 8.3

Verifying Successful Kerberos Authentication

1. Log in to the required server in the domain as the administrator for the web application hosting the desired site collection (such as domain\admin).

2. Launch Internet Explorer. Attempt to follow the URL for the portal site collection and verify that the home page for the portal site loads in the browser.

3. Close the browser and log out of the server.

4. Log in to one of the load-balanced frontend web servers.

5. Run the Event Viewer by clicking Start ➢ Event Viewer or Start ➢ Control Panel ➢ Administrative Tools ➢ Event Viewer.

6. Expand Windows Logs, open the Security log, and verify a Success Audit record (when you open the item, you may have to click the Details tab to get a human-friendly view of the data).

7. Verify that the username is that of the administrator you used to access the portal site, that Kerberos authentication was used, that the login type was 3 (for network login), and that the IP address was that of the server computer you used to access the portal site collection.

Now that you've verified that people can authenticate using Kerberos, you still need to make sure Search Indexing is working correctly. Before you can do this, Search must complete a full crawl of the Kerberos-authenticated site collection.

Once the full crawl is completed, open a web browser and go to the portal site collection main page. Type a valid keyword in the search field and start the search. If you receive search results, indexing is working correctly. If not, review the following:

- Verify that you are using a valid keyword.

- Verify that the Search service is running on the Search and Search Indexing and Search Query servers.

- Verify that there are no issues with search propagation from Search Indexing server to the Search Query server.

- Verify that the crawl ran successfully.

If the crawl failed with one or more access denied errors, Kerberos authentication may have failed, or the crawl account does not have the proper access.

See Chapter 5, "Configuring Indexing and Search," for more information on search and search indexing.

Administering Claims-Based Authentication

Claims-based authentication isn't cast from the traditional mold of authentication and authorization you are probably used to employing. Instead, it uses an identity system that allows users to present claims that include information about who the user is and what systems and content they can access. Claims-based authentication has been available for SharePoint since 2007 and is the authentication system of choice for SharePoint.

The claims-based authentication system has the benefit of working with any corporate identity system, including Active Directory, LDAP, application-specific databases, and user-centric identity models such as LiveID and OpenID. The "claims" users make to the system can include their age and group membership and are then validated against a trusted source, granting the user access to SharePoint and other systems integrated into the SharePoint environment.

The prerequisites to configuring a claims-based web application in SharePoint are that SharePoint must be installed and then the configuration wizard must be run. You must then either run the farm configuration wizard or, in the case of individual SharePoint deployments, configure your SharePoint platform. You must configure the first web application and use the Farm Administrators account for the application pool account. Finally, you must configure the first SharePoint site collection.

Exercise 8.4 shows you how to easily set up a web application for claims-based authentication.

EXERCISE 8.4

Creating the Portal Site Web Application with Claims-Based Authentication

1. Navigate to Central Administration and click Manage Web Applications under Application Management.

2. On the Manage Web Applications page, click New on the ribbon.

3. On the Create a New Web Application page, select Claims Based Authentication under Authentication.

4. Create the other values for the new web application as you did in Exercise 8.1, giving the host header and path unique values but maintaining the rest of the selections.

5. Click OK and then verify that the new web application has been created.

The only difference between this task and Exercise 8.1 is that you selected Claims Based Authentication instead of Classic Mode Authentication. After you create the web application, create the first site collection in the new web application, which should be your portal site. See Exercise 8.2 for the specific steps required to complete this operation.

Although authentication systems in general assume that the person gaining access must have some special right to services and data, just like on most websites on the Internet, you may want to allow unrestricted access to part of your web infrastructure. To that end, you can configure anonymous claims-based authentication. You will need to use an account that has site collection administrator rights to complete Exercise 8.5.

EXERCISE 8.5

Configuring Anonymous Access for a Claims-Based Web Application

1. Navigate to Central Administration, and click Security in Quick Launch.

2. On the Security page, click Specify Authentication Providers under General Security.

3. On the Authentication Providers page, use the Web Application menu to select the web application you created for claims-based authentication.

4. Click the zone for the web application.

5. On the Edit Authentication page, select the Enable Anonymous Access check box under Anonymous Access.

6. Click Save.

7. Navigate to the main page for the portal site collection on the relevant web application.

8. Click Site Actions and then select Site Permissions.

9. On the Site Permissions page, click Anonymous Access on the Ribbon.

10. Select either Entire Web Site or Lists And Libraries, depending on the scope of access you want to grant anonymous users, as shown here.

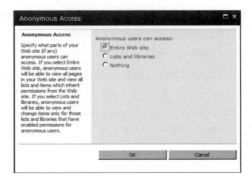

11. Click OK.

You can use this basic set of steps to edit the authentication for any web application and the site collections it contains, not just those web applications created for claims-based authentication.

Converting Forms-Based Authentication to Claims-Based Authentication

Up until this point in the chapter, you may not have given much thought to whether your SharePoint deployment was an upgrade from Microsoft Office SharePoint Server (MOSS) 2007 or a fresh install, but the next exercise is focused on the upgrade scenario.

MOSS 2007 web applications were generally configured to use *forms-based authentication* or web SSO authentication. If you have upgraded your MOSS 2007 server farm to SharePoint Server 2010, you can convert the authentication type from forms-based to claims-based, but not during the conversion process itself. If you do not perform this action, you won't be able to use the web applications created under MOSS 2007 in your SharePoint 2010 environment. Once you perform the authentication conversion, you'll be ready to migrate users and permissions to SharePoint 2010.

The first part of the process involves using Windows PowerShell to convert the existing web applications, post-upgrade, to claims-based authentication. To successfully perform this action, you must be a member of the SharePoint_Shell_Access group on the configuration databases and a member of the WSS_ADMIN_WPG local group on the computer containing SharePoint 2010.

Open Windows PowerShell as an administrator, run the following code, and then press Enter, substituting the example name for the server with the actual server name:

```
$w = Get-SPWebApplication "http://<server>/"
$w.UseClaimsAuthentication = "True";
$w.Update()
$w.ProvisionGlobally()
```

You still have to make changes in the authentication type using Windows PowerShell, and you still need to make additional configuration changes using Central Administration. Exercise 8.6 describes how to configure a web application originally set to use forms-based authentication to use claims-based authentication required by an LDAP provider. You must be a site collection administrator to successfully complete this task.

EXERCISE 8.6

Configuring a Forms-Based Web Application to Use an LDAP Provider

1. Navigate to Central Administration and click Manage Web Applications under Application Management.

2. On the Manage Web Applications page, click New on the Ribbon.

3. Under Authentication, select Claims Based Authentication.

EXERCISE 8.6 *(continued)*

4. Under Authentication Type, select Enable ASP.NET Membership and Role Provider.

5. Type the membership provider name and the role manager name in the available fields such as **membership** and **rolemanager**.

6. When you are done, click OK to create the Web application.

You can perform the same task by running Windows PowerShell as an administrator, typing the following code at the command prompt, and then pressing Enter:

```
$ap = New-SPAuthenticationProvider -Name "ClaimsForms" -ASPNETMembershipProvider
"membership"
-ASPNETRoleProviderName "rolemanager"
$wa = New-SPWebApplication -Name "Claims Windows Web App" -ApplicationPool
"Claims App Pool"
-ApplicationPoolAccount "internal\appool"
  -Url http://servername -Port 80
-AuthenticationProvider $ap
```

You will need to replace the example values with the actual names in your production system.

Now that you have created the web application, you must perform several tasks to modify Web.config files for the Central Administration web application, the Security Token Service web application, and the forms-based authentication claims-based web application. Each of those tasks is performed in Windows PowerShell run as administrator.

Configuring the Central Administration Web.config File

To configure the Central Administration Web.config file, follow these steps:

1. For the server computer where Central Administration is installed, click Start ➢ Run.

2. In the Run field, type **INETMGR** and press Enter to launch the IIS Manager.

3. In the IIS Manager, navigate to the SharePoint Central Administration site, right-click, and then click Explore.

4. Navigate to and then open the Web.config file.

5. In the Web.config file, locate the section <Configuration> <system.web>.

6. Add the following code to this section of the Web.config file and then save your changes:

```
<membership defaultProvider="AspNetSqlMembershipProvider">
      <providers>
        <add name="membership"
            type="Microsoft.Office.Server.Security.
LdapMembershipProvider, Microsoft.Office.Server, Version=14.0.0.0,
```

```
Culture=neutral, PublicKeyToken=71e9bce111e9429c"
            server="yourserver.com"
            port="389"
            useSSL="false"
            userDNAttribute="distinguishedName"
            userNameAttribute="sAMAccountName"
            userContainer="OU=UserAccounts,DC=internal
,DC=yourcompany,DC= distinguishedName
(of your userContainer)"
            userObjectClass="person"
            userFilter="(ObjectClass=person)"
            scope="Subtree"
            otherRequiredUserAttributes="sn,givenname,cn" />
    </providers>
  </membership>
  <roleManager enabled="true" defaultProvider=
"AspNetWindowsTokenRoleProvider" >
      <providers>
        <add name="roleManager"
            type="Microsoft.Office.Server.Security.
LdapRoleProvider, Microsoft.Office.Server,
Version=14.0.0.0, Culture=neutral,
PublicKeyToken=71e9bce111e9429c"
            server="yourserver.com"
            port="389"
            useSSL="false"
            groupContainer="DC=internal,DC=yourcompany,
DC= distinguishedName (of your groupContainer)"
            groupNameAttribute="cn"
            groupNameAlternateSearchAttribute="samAccountName"
            groupMemberAttribute="member"
            userNameAttribute="sAMAccountName"
            dnAttribute="distinguishedName"
            groupFilter="((ObjectClass=group)"
            userFilter="((ObjectClass=person)"
            scope="Subtree" />
      </providers>
  </roleManager>
```

7. Close the Web.config file for the Central Administration site, but leave the IIS Manager open.

Configuring the Security Token Service Web.config File

The next step is to configure the Security Token Service `Web.config` file. To do so, follow the next set of steps:

1. With the IIS Manager still open, navigate to the SharePoint web services site.

2. Navigate to the SecurityTokenServiceApplication subsite, right-click, and then click Explore.

3. Open the `Web.config` file and locate `<Configuration>` `<system.web>`.

4. In this section, add the following code and then save your changes:

```
<membership>
     <providers>
       <add name="membership"
        type="Microsoft.Office.Server.Security
.LdapMembershipProvider, Microsoft.Office.Server, Version=14.0.0.0,
Culture=neutral, PublicKeyToken=71e9bce111e9429c"
            server="yourserver.com"
            port="389"
            useSSL="false"
            userDNAttribute="distinguishedName"
            userNameAttribute="sAMAccountName"
            userContainer="OU=UserAccounts,DC=internal
DC=yourcompany,DC=com"
            userObjectClass="person"
            userFilter="(&amp;(ObjectClass=person))"
            scope="Subtree"
            otherRequiredUserAttributes="sn,givenname,cn" />
     </providers>
   </membership>
   <roleManager enabled="true" >
     <providers>
       <add name="rolemanager"
            type="Microsoft.Office.Server.Security.
LdapRoleProvider, Microsoft.Office.Server, Version=14.0.0.0,
Culture=neutral, PublicKeyToken=71e9bce111e9429c"
            server="yourserver.com"
            port="389"
            useSSL="false"
            groupContainer="DC=internal,DC=yourcompany,DC=com"
            groupNameAttribute="cn"
```

```
            groupNameAlternateSearchAttribute="samAccountName"
            groupMemberAttribute="member"
            userNameAttribute="sAMAccountName"
            dnAttribute="distinguishedName"
            groupFilter="(&amp;(ObjectClass=group))"
            userFilter="(&amp;(ObjectClass=person))"
            scope="Subtree" />
      </providers>
    </roleManager>
```

5. After saving the `Web.config` file, close it, but leave the IIS Manager open.

Configuring the Forms-Based Authentication Claims-Based Web Application Web.config File

Now you need to perform a similar action on the forms-based authentication claims-based web application `Web.config` file:

1. With the IIS Manager open, navigate to the claims forms site.

2. Right-click Claims Forms and select Explore.

3. Open the `Web.config` file.

4. Find the `<configuration>` `<system.web>` section and then find the `<membership defaultProvider="1">` section.

5. Add the following code, and then save your changes:

```
<add name="membership"
            type="Microsoft.Office.Server.Security.
LdapMembershipProvider, Microsoft.Office.Server, Version=14.0.0.0,
Culture=neutral, PublicKeyToken=71e9bce111e9429c"
            server="yourserver.com"
            port="389"
            useSSL="false"
            userDNAttribute="distinguishedName"
            userNameAttribute="sAMAccountName"
            userContainer="OU=UserAccounts,
DC=internal, DC=yourcompany,DC=com"
            userObjectClass="person"
            userFilter="(&amp;(ObjectClass=person))"
            scope="Subtree"
            otherRequiredUserAttributes="sn,givenname,cn" />
```

6. Find the `<roleManager defaultProvider="c" enabled="true" cacheRolesInCookie="false">` section, add the following code, and then save your changes:

```
<add name="roleManager"
             type="Microsoft.Office.Server.Security.
LdapRoleProvider, Microsoft.Office.Server, Version=14.0.0.0,
Culture=neutral, PublicKeyToken=71e9bce111e9429c"
             server="yourserver.com"
             port="389"
             useSSL="false"
             groupContainer="DC=internal,DC=yourcompany,
DC=com"

             groupNameAttribute="cn"
             groupNameAlternateSearchAttribute="samAccountName"
             groupMemberAttribute="member"
             userNameAttribute="sAMAccountName"
             dnAttribute="distinguishedName"
             groupFilter="(&amp;(ObjectClass=group))"
             userFilter="(&amp;(ObjectClass=person))"
             scope="Subtree" />
```

7. After you have saved your changes, close the Web.config file, and then close the IIS Manager.

Now use Windows PowerShell to create an SPClaimsPrincipal and a site collection. Open Windows PowerShell as an administrator. At the command prompt, type the following code and then press Enter, substituting the example values for the actual production values:

```
$cp = New-SPClaimsPrincipal -Identity "membership:SiteOwner"
-IdentityType FormsUser
$sp = New-SPSite http://servername:port -OwnerAlias $cp.Encode()
-Template "STS#0"
```

Migrating Users and Permissions from MOSS 2007 to SharePoint Server 2010

The last task in this process is migrating users and permissions from MOSS 2007 to SharePoint 2010.

Open Windows PowerShell as an administrator, type the following code at the command prompt, and then press Enter, changing the example values to the production values:

```
$w = Get-SPWebApplication "http://<server>/"
$w.MigrateUsers(True)
```

Configuring Kerberos Authentication for Claims to Windows Token Service

This section of the chapter assumes you are working in an Active Directory domain environment and will need to add one or more *service principal name (SPN)* entries to Active Directory. You will need to make sure you do not create any SPN entries that are duplicates in the system and that none of your added entries are currently being used by other accounts or services. To check, after you create the necessary SPN entries, check the System log on your domain controllers and look for event ID 11 entries. See the "Errors" section later in this chapter for details.

Although not required, the following set of exercises assumes you are running separate frontend web servers, application servers, and SQL Server servers, as well as at least one external data source. The first task will be for you to set up constrained delegation for the shared service application pool account. You will need to have administrative rights to the domain controllers in your Active Directory domain system.

You must have at least one SPN registered for the account you plan to use in the following exercise. For more information, review "Creating an SPN for the SQL Server Service Account" from earlier in this chapter.

Configuring Constrained Delegation for the Shared Service Application Pool Account

You can create an SPN on the domain controller at the command line by running the SETSPN.EXE tool, as well as using the method illustrated earlier in this chapter. At the command prompt, type the following code and then press Enter, substituting the example values for your production values:

```
setspn -A http/uniquespn1
domainname\useraccount
```

1. Log in to your domain controller, click Start ➢ Administrative Tools ➢ Active Directory Users And Computers.
2. Expand the Domain node and then select Users.
3. Right-click the application pool identity user account and then select Properties.
4. On the Delegation tab, make sure the Trust This User For Delegation To Specified Services Only option is selected.
5. Click use any authentication protocol.
6. Click Add and then click Users or Computers.
7. Type the domain name and user account that is running the service you want to have accept Kerberos credentials, such as domainname\useraccount, and then click OK.

8. After the available services values for the selected account appear, select MSSQLSvc for the external data source and then click OK.

9. Click OK again to close the Properties dialog box.

Configuring Constrained Delegation for the Claims to Windows Token Service Account

This task is virtually identical to the previous exercise except, in step 3, right-click the application pool identity account for the Windows Server 2008 machine acting in the Application Server role in the server farm (and not the identity user account). Follow all the other steps in the same way.

 By default, the claims to the Windows token service runs under the Local System account on the application server.

Configuring the Claims to Windows Token Service on the Application Server

Your final task is to grant WSS_SPG group permissions to convert claims to Windows identity on the application server. To do so, search for and locate the `wtshost.exe` file on the application server and locate the `<allowedCallers>` element under the `<windowsTokenService>` section. Then add `<add value="WSS_WPG" />`. The entry will look something like the following example:

```xml
<?xml version="1.0"?>
<configuration>
  <configSections>
    <section name="windowsTokenService" type="yourcompany.IdentityModel.
WindowsTokenService
.Configuration.WindowsTokenServiceSection, yourcompany.IdentityModel.
WindowsTokenService,
Version=1.0.0.0, Culture=neutral,
PublicKeyToken=31bf3856ad364e35"/>
  </configSections>
  <windowsTokenService>
    <allowedCallers>
      <clear/>
      <add value="WSS_WPG" />
    </allowedCallers>
  </windowsTokenService>
</configuration>
```

Open a command-line window, type the following code at the command prompt, and then press Enter to start the claims to Windows token service:

```
net start c2wts
sc config c2wts start= auto
```

Administering Active Directory Federation Services

Active Directory Federation Service (AD FS) allows Federated Identity and Access Management by providing secure sharing of digital identity and entitlements rights across security and enterprise boundaries. AD FS extends the ability to use single sign-on (SSO) functionality available within a single security or enterprise boundary to applications facing the Internet, as well as to customers, partners, and suppliers, offering a streamlined user experience along with accessing the web-based applications of an organization.

The AD FS service provides extensible, reliable, scalable, and secure identity federation and supports SAML token types as well as other client authentication methods such as Kerberos, X.500, and username/password methods. It is also able to use multiple identity store types, such as Active Directory Domain Services (AD DS) and Active Directory Lightweight Directory Services (AD LDS).

The SAML authentication method is typically used in enterprise federation systems, but before you can use a SAML security token for a SharePoint Server 2010 claims-based web application, you must configure AD FS.

Adding AD FS as a Federated Identity Provider in SharePoint 2010

SharePoint Server 2010 brings a completely new method of handling user identities based on Windows Identity Foundation to the table. This is an exciting authentication option that can allow secure, seamless authentication and connectivity from SharePoint to many popular third-party platforms, including Facebook, Google, Twitter, and Yahoo!, as well as other SharePoint server farms and various line-of-business applications. However, before you can enjoy all of these benefits, you first have to add AD FS to SharePoint. The result is that, instead of users connecting to SharePoint directly and authenticating via Active Directory, upon connecting to SharePoint, users will be redirected to an AD FS–hosted web page where they will authenticate using Windows authentication.

Chapter 4's "Configuring the Security Token Service (STS)" section describes all the necessary steps to add AD FS as a Federated Identity Provider using Windows PowerShell. The following information adds some details regarding performing part of the same process using Central Administration and Windows PowerShell.

The following exercises can be performed on a SharePoint 2010 single-server deployment with an onboard database or running against a SQL Server database server. The first step in the process is to create a claims-based web application. You should already be familiar with the process of creating a new web application. On the Create A New Web Application page, under Authentication, select Claims Based Authentication, and under IIS Web Site, create a new IIS web site, use Port 80, add a new Host Header such as ADFSTest.com, and add a path if necessary, as shown in Figure 8.1.

FIGURE 8.1   Create New Web Application dialog box

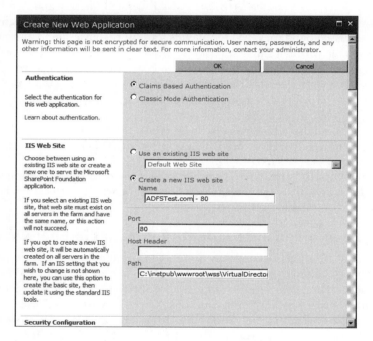

After you create the web application, create your first site collection. See Exercise 8.2 for the specific steps. Since claims-based authentication is SharePoint's default authentication method, you shouldn't notice anything different or unusual about your new site collection.

As noted in Chapter 4, SharePoint Foundation ships with a fully functional Security Token Service (STS), so when you first installed SharePoint Server 2010, the STS became fully functional and was already able to use the local Active Directory instance to authenticate users and offer SharePoint a ready-made description of each identity as a series of claims. Since this means the STS is an Identity Provider (IP-STS), you don't really have to do anything more to take advantage of SharePoint's built-in STS and use it as an identity provider. You can, however, set up the SharePoint STS to trust a different IP-STS, which will make it a relying party (RP-STS), thus extending Share-Point to use external systems as identity providers.

You will need to have a domain controller active to provide an AD DS environment and then a server set to the Active Directory Federation Services (AD FS) role after the server has been joined to the domain. AD FS installs into the Default website in IIS and also creates a self-signed certificate for the default site. The task of setting up a domain controller for these roles is beyond the scope of this text. For details, see TechNet's AD DS Installation and Removal Step-by-Step Guide for Windows Server 2008 and Windows Server 2008 R2 at http://technet.microsoft.com/en-us/library/cc755258(WS.10).aspx.

Once AD FS is installed and configured, it will create a separate instance of SQL Server 2008 Express edition to store its configuration information. The configuration of AF DS should include validating the certificate being used by the Default website and exporting the certificate. The certificate file is needed to add AD FS as a Federated Identity Provider in SharePoint. This is done on the server containing SharePoint Server 2010 Central Administration.

On the required server machine, open Windows PowerShell as an administrator, type or paste the following script at the command prompt, and then press Enter. You need to replace the example values with the production values, including the actual name of the certificate file that was exported from AF DS.

```
$cert = New-Object System.Security.Cryptography.X509Certificates.
X509Certificate2
("c:\[YOUR_STS_SIGNING_CERT].cer")
$map1 = New-SPClaimTypeMapping "http://schemas.xmlsoap.org/ws/2005/05/
identity/claims/emailaddress"
-IncomingClaimTypeDisplayName "EmailAddress"
-SameAsIncoming
$realm = "urn:" + $env:ComputerName + ":adfs"
$signinurl = "https://[YOUR_SERVER_NAME]/adfs/ls/"
$ap = New-SPTrustedIdentityTokenIssuer -Name "ADFS20Server" -Description "ADFS
2.0 Federated Server" -Realm $realm
-ImportTrustCertificate $cert -ClaimsMappings $map1
-SignInUrl $signinurl -IdentifierClaim $map1.InputClaimType
```

Adding the AD FS Identity Provider in Central Administration

Once you've completed running the script, perform the following actions to add the Federated Identity Provider in Central Administration:

1. In Central Administration, click Manage Web Applications under Application Management.
2. On the Web Applications Management page, on the Web Applications tab, click the desired web application to select it.
3. On the Ribbon, click the Authentication Providers button.

4. In the Edit Authentication window that appears, under Identity Providers, select the Federated Identity Provider option and the ADFS20Server option, as shown in Figure 8.2.

FIGURE 8.2 Edit Authentication dialog box

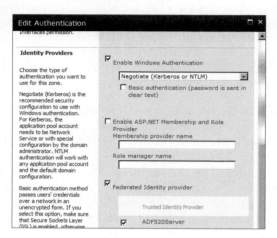

5. You can either select or remove the selection for Enable Windows Authentication or allow it to remain.

6. When you're done, click OK.

Unlike MOSS 2007, SharePoint Server 2010 can use multiple authentication providers for a web application. If you want to create a web application that will use only AF DS, you should either clear the Windows Authentication option if necessary or create another web application that uses only AF DS.

Previously in this chapter, in the "Configuring Kerberos Authentication for Claims to Windows Token Service" section, you read about the SAML authentication method. In Chapter 4's "Configuring the Security Token Service (STS)" section, under SAML authentication and IP-STS Identity Providers, you learned a number of tasks related to configuring the STS Service for use by web applications in SharePoint including configuring SharePoint claims-based Web application. The exercises in that section of Chapter 4 will complete the process of adding a Federated Identity Provider.

Configuring Authentication Using a SAML Security Token

You are a SharePoint administrator for your organization, and you have been tasked with creating a Security Token Service in SharePoint 2010. Although SharePoint ships with a fully functional STS that acts as an identity provider (IP-STS), you must set up a SharePoint STS to trust a different IP-STS and act as a relying party (RP-STS). This requires a number of additional steps be performed on your part.

You have configured an STS (IP-STS) web application using Windows PowerShell. Now you need to configure a relying party STS (RP-STS) web application. Your SharePoint deployment exists in an environment, and AD FS is active and available.

You review the steps for completing the task at `http://technet.microsoft.com/en-us/library/ff607753%28office.14%29.aspx` and then proceed with opening the AD FS Management Console and configuring the relying party. After you have accomplished this task, you continue with establishing a trust relationship with the IP-STS, exporting the trusted IP-STS certificate, defining a unique identifier for claims mapping, creating a new authentication provider, and lastly creating the web application you need to configure to use SAML.

Managing Custom Permissions

Although both SharePoint and Active Directory come with a default set of user and administrative roles, each with their own sets of access permissions, you can also set up customized permissions within SharePoint. Before you pursue this option, review the standard permissions that exist for SharePoint by default.

The following permissions and their access parameters are for users relative to site collections created with the Team Site template:

Limited Access

- Browse User Information
- Use Client Integration Features Open

Read

- View Items
- Open Items
- View Versions
- Create Alerts
- View Application Pages
- Use Self-Service Site Creation
- View Pages
- Browse User Information
- Use Remote Interfaces
- Use Client Integrations Features
- Open

Contribute

- Read permissions, Plus:
- Manage Unsafe Content

Design

- Approve permissions, Plus:
- Manage Lists
- Add and Customize Pages
- Apply Themes and Borders
- Apply Style Sheets

Full Control

- All Permissions

The following permissions and their access parameters are for users relative to site collections created with all other site collection templates:

Read Restricted

- View Items
- Open Items
- View Pages
- Open

View Only

- Limited Access permissions, plus:
  - View Items
  - View Versions
  - Create Alerts
  - Create Mobile Alerts
  - View Application Pages

Approve

- Contribute permissions, plus:
  - Override Checkout
  - Approve Items

Manage Hierarchy

- Design permissions minus Approve Item permissions, plus:
  - Manage Permissions

- View Usage Data
- Create Subsites
- Manage Web Site
- Manage Alerts

Configuring Custom SharePoint Permissions

The default permission levels may not give you the type or amount of control over user access to site content, sites, or site collections; however, you can also configure custom permission levels to suit your needs. To perform the following tasks, you must be a member of the Administrators group for the site collection, must be a member of the Owners group for the site, or must have Manage Permissions privileges. Exercise 8.7 gets you started by showing you how to customize an existing permission level.

EXERCISE 8.7

Customizing an Existing Permission Level

1. On the desired site, click Site Actions and then click Site Settings.

2. On the Site Settings page for the desired site, click Site Permissions under User And Permissions.

3. On the Permission Tools/Edit tab of the Ribbon, click Permission Levels.

4. In the list of permissions levels that appears, click the name of the permission level you want to customize.

5. In the next list, clear or select the desired check boxes to add or remove permissions from the permissions level.

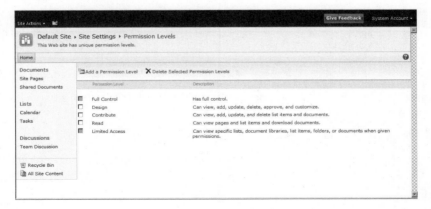

6. Click Submit.

You also have the ability to take a single permission level, copy it, and then adjust the permissions of that level to create a new, customized permission that you can then assign to users and groups. Exercise 8.8 illustrates how to copy a specific permission level and use it to create a new, customized level.

EXERCISE 8.8

Copying and Customizing an Existing Permission Level

1. On the desired site, click Site Actions and then click Site Settings.

2. On the Site Settings page for the desired site, click Site Permissions under User And Permissions.

3. On the Permission Tools/Edit tab of the Ribbon, click Permission Levels.

4. In the list of permissions levels that appears, click the name of the permission level you want to copy.

5. When the permissions level page opens, scroll to the bottom of the page and click the Copy Permission Level button.

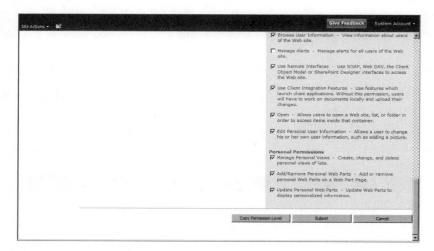

6. On the Copy Permission Level page, give the copied permission level a name in the Name field.

7. Give the copied permission level a description in the Description field.

8. Click or deselect the check boxes on this page to add or remove permissions as desired.

9. Click Create.

Finally, when neither editing an existing permission nor copying and editing a permission level won't do, you can always create a completely new permission level from scratch. Exercise 8.9 shows you how.

EXERCISE 8.9

Creating a New Permission Level

1. On the desired site, click Site Actions and then click Site Settings.

2. On the Site Settings page for the desired site, click Site Permissions under User And Permissions.

3. Under the Permission Tools/Edit tab of the Ribbon, click Permission Levels.

4. On the toolbar above the permissions list, click Add A Permission Level.

5. When the Add A Permission Level page appears, as shown here, give the new permission level a name and description in the available fields.

6. Under Permissions, either select the Select All check box to select all available permissions or select only the check boxes for the permissions you want to add to the new, customized permissions level.

7. When ready, click Create.

Errors

This isn't the most pleasant subject to consider when configuring authentication and permissions, but you certainly must be prepared for the possibility that something could go wrong. If and when it does, it will be very helpful to know what to do about it.

Although every possible error type isn't listed here, a few of the more common errors related to the topics presented should help you understand what an error message or symptom means and some of the possible solutions.

Errors on Multiple Systems

Although all the errors listed here are related to SharePoint, authentication, and permissions, not all of them occur on the same system. You will need to know not only how to understand and manage errors but also where to look for error messages. The following list includes errors found on domain controllers, on SQL Server instances, and within a web browser.

Remember, this list is hardly comprehensive. It's just to give you an idea of what you may encounter and where to start looking. You'll need to expand this skill set to be truly effective as a systems troubleshooter.

Error Message: Event ID 11 in the Domain Controller System Log

Event   The event type will always be Error, and the event source can be either KDC or Kerberos. The event description will be either that multiple accounts with a machine name or domain name exist or that the Kerberos client received an error from a specific server stating the password used to encrypt a Kerberos service ticket is different from on the target server, usually because of identically named machine accounts existing within the domain.

Cause   The event ID 11 error is caused when two or more computers have the same service principal name registered and the Key Distribution Center (KDC) receives a ticket request that then discovers that the SPN exists more than one time when checked on the global catalog (GC) for domain forestwide verification.

Solution   The solution is to find the computers containing the duplicate SPNs and then either delete the computer from the domain, unjoin and then rejoin the computer in the domain, or use the ADSIEdit utility (`asdiedit.msc`) to correct the duplicate SPN.

Error Message: 401.1 Is Displayed When You Browse to a Website That's Using Integrated Authentication and Is Hosted on IIS 5.1 or Newer

Event   The error message can look like HTTP 401.1, Unauthorized: Logon Failed. You receive the error only when you try to browse to the website using a web browser directly from the server on which the site is hosted. Visiting the site from a remote, client computer will let you log on to the site normally.

The Security event log on the host server registers the event type as Failure Audit, the event source as Security, and the event category as Logon/Logoff. One of the more telling symptoms is that strange characters can be displayed in the event message itself, such as for Logon Process, rather than the expected text or number values.

Cause   This is usually caused when you install a service pack on the affected machine that includes a loopback check security feature designed to help stop reflection attacks on the computer. This feature will cause authentication to fail if the fully qualified domain name (FQDN) or custom host header is different from the name of the local computer.

Solution   The most common workaround for this issue involves editing a registry key.

Disable Loopback Check

1. On the affected computer, click Start ➤ Run. In the Run box, type **regedit** and then click OK.

2. In the Registry Editor, navigate to the registry key HKEY_LOCAL_MACHINE\ SYSTEM\CurrentControlSet\Control\Lsa.

3. Right-click Lsa, select New, and then click DWORD Value.

4. Type DisableLoopbackCheck and then click Modify.

5. In the Value data field, type **1**, and then click OK.

6. Close the Registry Editor and restart the computer.

Error Message: Event 3351 SQL Server Database Login Failed

Event   This error is usually associated with a particular SharePoint service that is unable to log in and access content for SharePoint websites stored in the SQL Server 2008 database. In the event log, event ID 3351, "SQL database login failed will appear."

Cause   The name or password for the SharePoint service account either was invalid before the service attempted to log on to the SQL Server or became invalid during the session.

Solution   To resolve the issue, you must run the following procedure logged in as a member of the Farm Administrators group in SharePoint.

Assigning the Database Access Account

1. In Central Administration, click Security in Quick Launch. On the Security page, under General Security, click Configure Service Accounts.

2. On the Configure Service Accounts page, under Credential Management, use the top drop-down menu to select the desired web application pool for the web application.

3. In the Select An Account For This Component drop-down list, click the domain account you want to associate with the web Application Pool or click Register a New Managed Account to associate a new domain account with the application pool.

4. When you've finished making your selections, click OK.

5. To verify that the account you selected has the correct permissions on the SQL Server, contact the DBA and have them verify the permissions using SQL Server Management Studio. Once permissions have been verified, open Windows Power-Shell as an administrator, enter the following code, and then press Enter:

```
Get-SPSite | Format-Table -Property ID,WebApplication,ContentDatabase
```

The list produced will display the websites for each web application and the list of sites that use the available database.

Error Message: Event ID 3353 Backup Failed Due to Insufficient Permissions

Event   A SharePoint Server 2010 backup fails. When you check the event log, you find the message "Event ID: 3353 Description: Unable to write to the backup folder."

Cause   This is most likely caused by the SQL Server service account or the SharePoint Timer Service account not having Full Control permissions to the backup folder. If some-one performed the backup procedure from Windows PowerShell, the user didn't have Full Control permissions to the backup folder.

Solution   In addition to assigning the previously mentioned accounts Full Control permissions and NTFS permissions to the backup folder, make sure anyone required to perform a backup or restore using Windows PowerShell also has those permissions. If the backup folder is a network share, make sure the relevant services and users have access to both the share and the folder. If backup and restore operations are being performed between two SharePoint server farms, verify that both farms have the aforementioned permissions.

Error Message: Event 6395 Insufficient Permissions to Write to the Configuration Data Cache

Event   A timer job used to automate writing data in the configuration database in SQL Server 2008 to the local SharePoint filesystem cache failed. You check the event log and find the message "Event ID: 6395 Insufficient permissions to write to the configuration data cache."

Cause   The configuration cache directory security settings were updated in a farm-wide procedure, but that procedure does not update configuration objects locally. The required local groups were unable to access the configuration data cache in response to the timer job and perform the write procedure.

Solution   Access and verify that the WSS_ADMIN_WPG and WSS_RESTRICTED_WPG local groups have updated permissions to write to the %systemdrive%\Users\All Users\ Microsoft\SharePoint\Config directory. To perform this task, you must have Modify permission to the relevant directory.

Error Message: Event 6590 Application Pool Account Must Be Registered as Kerberos

Event   You discover that the application pool used for IIS services to add users to Active Directory has insufficient permissions to complete the task. You check the event log and discover the message "Event ID: 6590 Description: The application pool account has insufficient permissions to add user accounts to Active Directory."

Cause

- There are several reasons why this error might occur.
- If you are using Kerberos for authentication, the web application pool account is not registered as a security provider name.
- If you are using forms-based authentication or web single sign-on (SSO), the authentication provider could not be loaded because a membership provider name wasn't specified.
- The web application pool was changed, but the changes weren't saved because it wasn't restarted.

Solution   There are multiple methods you can use to apply the correct solution to this error.

Determine Which Authentication Type the Site Is Using

1. Go to Central Administration and click Security in Quick Launch.
2. On the Security page under General Security, click Specify Authentication Providers.
3. On the Authentication Providers page, click the Web Application menu if necessary, click Change Web Application, and then select the desired option.
4. Click the zone for the application and review the authentication settings on the Edit Authentication page.
5. Make any necessary changes and then click Save.

Registering the Application Pool Account as an SPN   If this seems the likely cause of the error, you will need to make sure the service account used by the application pool is the registered SPN for all domains listed with the web applications. See the section "Creating an SPN for the SQL Server Service Account" under "Configuring Kerberos for SQL Communication" in this chapter for details.

Specifying Membership Provider Name and a Role Manager

1. In Central Administration, click Security in Quick Launch.
2. On the Security page, click Specify Authentication Providers under General Security.
3. On the Specify Authentication Providers page, select the desired web application and then select the zone for the application.
4. On the Edit Authentication page, under Authentication Type, select either Forms or Web Single Sign On and then click Save.
5. Return to the same page and, under Membership Provider Name, type the name in the Membership Provider Name field.

6. Under Role Manager Name, type the desired name in the Role Manager Name field.

7. Click Save.

Editing Authentication Settings for a Zone

1. Perform steps 1 through 3 from the previous solution to get to the Edit Authentication page.

2. Under Authentication Type, select the desired authentication option.

3. Under IIS Authentication Settings, select the desired setting.

4. Click Save.

There are a wide variety of error messages that can be located on the platforms mentioned. This section contains only a small sample. Both TechNet and `http://support.microsoft.com` are excellent resources for learning more.

Summary

In this chapter, you learned about the different authentication types you can configure in SharePoint, as well as the default user permissions, customizing user permissions, and some of the more common error messages. Details include the following:

- Administering Kerberos in an AD DS environment
- Administering claims-based authentication
- Configuring Active Directory Federation Services (AD FS)
- Setting up custom user permissions
- Interpreting error messages on different platforms related to SharePoint

Exam Essentials

Managing Authentication Methods   Understand the dynamics of administering Kerberos in an Active Directory domain, as well as managing claims-based and forms-based authentication and setting up Active Directory Federation Services.

Managing Custom Permissions   Comprehend the standard SharePoint user permissions as well as how to use these permissions to create customized versions, either by copying a permission level or by creating one from scratch.

Reviewing Error Messages   Know where to look for error messages when something goes wrong with authentication and permissions, how to interpret errors, and what steps to take to correct them.

Review Questions

1. You are a SharePoint administrator for your organization, and you're planning to configure Kerberos authentication for web applications in your server farm. To make sure you are fully prepared, you do some research on all the requirements and drawbacks regarding Kerberos authentication in SharePoint. Of the following information, what did you discover is true about Kerberos authentication and SharePoint search? (Choose all that apply.)

    A.   SharePoint Search cannot crawl web applications using Kerberos authentication if the web applications are in IIS virtual servers using TCP port 80.

    B.   SharePoint Search cannot crawl web applications using Kerberos authentication if the web applications are using Secure Sockets Layer (SSL).

    C.   If you want to use nondefault ports and have SharePoint Search crawls be successful on your web applications, you must use either Basic or NTLM authentication.

    D.   If you want to use Secure Sockets Layer (SSL) on SharePoint web applications and have SharePoint successfully crawl those applications, you must use port 443 for SSL.

2. You are a SharePoint administrator for your organization, and you're planning to configure Kerberos authentication for web applications in your server farm. To make sure you are fully prepared, you do some research on all the requirements and drawbacks regarding Kerberos authentication in SharePoint. You discover you must create service principal names (SPNs) for the different services running in an Active Directory Domain Services (AD DS) environment. Of the following, what did you discover is true about this process? (Choose all that apply.)

    A.   If you are using nonstandard ports, the port number must be part of the SPN.

    B.   You must have domain administrative rights to the domain to create an SPN in AD DS.

    C.   The real hostname must be included in the SPN but not the virtual hostname.

    D.   You can use either `setspn.exe` on Windows Server 2008 or `adsiedit.msc` on the Active Directory domain controller to set an SPN for an Active Directory domain account.

3. You are a SharePoint administrator for your organization. You have successfully created an SPN for the SQL Server service account. Now you want to test your ability to use Kerberos authentication to connect SharePoint to SQL. You install and use the Microsoft SQL Server Management Studio Express utility on one of your computers and use it to connect to the SQL host computer. Of the following, what else must you do to confirm that the connection was successful?

    A. On the SharePoint Server machine you used to make the connection, use the Event Viewer to verify that a success audit is present listing Kerberos as the authentication type and listing the IP address of the SQL Server computer with which you made the connection listed as the destination network address.

    B. On the SQL Server machine to which you made the connection, use the Event Viewer to verify that a success audit is present listing Kerberos as the authentication type and listing the IP address of the SharePoint machine you used to make the connection as the source network address.

    C. On the SharePoint machine in SQL Server Management Studio Express, in the navigation pane on the left, expand Events and then expand Audits, and verify that a security audit is present with Kerberos listed as the authentication type and the IP address of the SQL server machine listed as the destination network address.

    D. Once you type the name of the SQL host computer in the available field in the SQL Server Management Studio Express tool and press Connect, you will automatically receive a success message if the connection was completed. Otherwise, you will receive a failure notice.

4. You are a SharePoint administrator for your organization, and you are creating a web application for a portal site that will use Kerberos authentication. As you go through the creation process, which step or steps are absolutely required to make sure Kerberos will be used for authentication? (Choose all that apply.)

    A. You must select Classic Mode Authentication.

    B. You must select Claims based Authentication.

    C. You must select Negotiate (Kerberos).

    D. You must select Default as the zone.

5. You are a SharePoint administrator for your organization, and you have created both a web application and a portal site collection that use Kerberos for authentication. You want to test that Kerberos is being used successfully to connect to the site collection. Of the following, what are the correct procedures? (Choose all that apply.)

    A. Log in to the SharePoint server hosting the web application, open a web browser, and attempt to connect to the site collection.

    B. Log in to the SharePoint server hosting the web application, open Event Viewer, and verify the success audit in the Security log.

    C. Log in to a remote machine, open a command-line window, and attempt to ping the SharePoint server hosting the web application.

    D. Log in to a remote machine, open a command-line window, and attempt to ping the domain name of the site collection.

6. You are a SharePoint administrator for your company. You have configured a web application to use Kerberos authentication. To verify that Search Indexing is working correctly, you initiate a full crawl of the application. Once the crawl is complete, you open a web browser on the main page of the portal site collection in the web application, type a keyword in the search field, and attempt a search. You don't receive any search results. What could be the problem? (Choose all that apply.)

A. The search service may not be running on the Search and Indexing server.

B. The search service may not be running on the Search Query server.

C. The search service may not be running on the frontend web server.

D. The full crawl may not have run successfully.

7. You are a SharePoint administrator for your organization, and you are investigating the possibility of using claims-based authentication on some of the web applications in Share-Point. You understand that claims-based authentication uses an identity system that allows users to present claims about who they are, using information such as group membership or age. As you discuss the benefits of this authentication method with your staff, what are some of the obvious advantages and disadvantages? (Choose all that apply.)

A. This method can work with Active Directory.

B. This method cannot work with LiveID and OpenID.

C. This method can work with LDAP.

D. This method cannot work with anonymous logins.

8. You are a SharePoint administrator for your organization. You have just upgraded your MOSS 2007 environment to SharePoint Server 2010. Now you need to upgrade the authentication systems on your web applications to claims-based authentication from the MOSS 2007 web application default authentication. What default authentication system does MOSS 2007 use?

A. Active Directory Federation Services

B. Forms-based

C. Secure Store Service

D. Windows Challenge/Response NTLM

9. You are a SharePoint administrator for your organization. You have just upgraded your MOSS 2007 environment to SharePoint Server 2010. Now you need to upgrade the authentication systems on your web applications to claims-based authentication from the MOSS 2007 web application default authentication. What is the procedure to perform this task?

A. Open Central Administration and click Security in Quick Launch. Under General Security, click Specify Authentication Providers. On the subsequent page, update the authentication type to the one you want in SharePoint 2010.

B. Open Windows PowerShell as an administrator, type in a script that will perform the authentication upgrade, and then press Enter.

C. You must perform the authentication upgrade in MOSS 2007 before upgrading to SharePoint, by selecting Upgrade, Authentication Providers, and then Upgrade to SharePoint 2010 default authentication.

D. You must perform the authentication upgrade during the upgrade from MOSS 2007 to SharePoint 2010 by selected the Upgrade Authentication For Web Applications option in the upgrade wizard.

10. You are a SharePoint administrator in your organization. You have been tasked with configuring a web application using forms-based authentication to connect to LDAP. What are the essential steps in this process to successfully complete this task?

A. In Central Administration, on the web page for the web application, you must select Claims Based Authentication.

B. In Central Administration, on the web page for the web application, you must select Enable LDAP Membership And Role Provider.

C. In Central Administration, on the web page for the web application, you must select Enable ASP.NET Membership And Role Provider.

D. You can only perform this task using Windows PowerShell.

11. You are a SharePoint administrator in your organization. You have been tasked with configuring a web application using forms-based authentication to connect to LDAP. You have successfully modified the web application, and now you must configure several files called `Web.config` using INETMGR. For which services must you configure these files? (Choose all that apply.)

A. Central Administration

B. Security Token Service

C. Forms-based Authentication Service

D. Claims-based Authentication Service

12. You are a SharePoint administrator in your organization. You have been tasked with configuring a web application using forms-based authentication to connect to LDAP. You have successfully modified the web application and modified several `Web.config` files for the required services. What is the last task you must complete?

A. Migrating users and groups from MOSS 2007 to SharePoint 2010

B. Migrating users and permissions from MOSS 2007 to SharePoint 2010

C. Migrating lists and libraries from MOSS 2007 to SharePoint 2010

D. You have successfully completed all required tasks.

13. You are a SharePoint administrator for your organization, and you've been tasked with configuring Kerberos authentication for Claims claims to Windows Token Service. As you research this task, you discover a number of requirements and caveats. Of the following, what is true about this task? (Choose all that apply.)

   A. You must have at least one SPN registered for the account you plan to use for this task.

   B. You must create SPNs using the `setspn.exe` tool on the command-line.

   C. You must avoid creating any SPN entries that are duplicates in the system.

   D. You must run separate frontend web servers, applications servers, and SQL Server instances to be successful in this task.

14. You are a SharePoint administrator for your organization, and you've been tasked with configuring Kerberos authentication for Claims claims to Windows token service. As you research this task, you discover that you must edit the `wtshost.exe` file when you configure the claims to the Windows token service on an application server. In what format is this file written?

   A. ASP

   B. PHP

   C. TXT

   D. XML

15. You are a SharePoint administrator for your organization, and you've been tasked with adding Active Directory Federated Services (AD FS) as a federated identity provider in SharePoint 2010. Although the required tasks can all be performed in Windows PowerShell, you discover that you can also perform certain tasks in Central Administration. With AD FS installed in SharePoint, what are some of the steps in adding AD FS as an identity provider in Central Administration? (Choose all that apply.)

   A. You must be on the Web Applications Management page.

   B. You must be on the Service Applications Management page.

   C. You can click Authentication Provider on the Ribbon.

   D. You can click Authentication Providers on the toolbar below the Ribbon.

16. You are a SharePoint administrator for your organization. You are reviewing the standard SharePoint permission levels for users and discover that you need to create a set of modified permission levels to exercise greater control over user access to resources, based on your company's security policy. You assign the task of creating the modified permission levels to one of your staff and instruct her as to the different methods that can be used. Of the following, which are valid methods of creating customized permission levels? (Choose all that apply.)

   A. You can customize an existing permission level.

   B. You can copy an existing permission level, customize it, and save it with a new name.

   C. You can import an already customized permission level from another SharePoint deployment.

   D. You can create a new permission level from scratch and customize it.

17. You are a SharePoint administrator for your organization. One of the services in SharePoint is unable to connect to and access information stored in a SQL Server database. The event ID is 3351, which you know means that the name or password the service is using to access the SQL Server instance is invalid. Of the following options, what can you do to correct this situation?

   A. Get the DBA in charge of the SQL Server instance to provide you with valid credentials so you can add them to the service in SharePoint.

   B. In Central Administration under Security on the Configure Service Accounts page, create an account that will have correct permissions to access the SQL Server instance.

   C. In Central Administration on the Manage Service Applications page, create an account that will have the correct permissions to access the SQL server.

   D. Get the DBA in charge of the SQL server to export valid credentials to the necessary service in SharePoint so the service will have appropriate access.

18. You are a SharePoint administrator for your organization. You discover that the application pool used for IIS services to add users to Active Directory has insufficient permissions to complete the task. You check the event log and verify that the event ID is 6590. What is the likely cause and solution?

   A. The application pool is using the wrong authentication type, and you must specify the correct authentication provider in the web application.

   B. The service account used by the application pool is not a registered SPN for all domains listed with the web applications. You will need to register the application pool account as an SPN.

   C. The membership provider name and role manager for the service account used by the application pool have not been specified, and you need to go into Central Administration and specify them on the Edit Authentication page.

   D. Any of the causes and solutions could be valid for this particular event.

19. You are a SharePoint administrator for your organization, and you are informed that the error log on the domain controller indicates that SharePoint services running in the domain are using duplicate SPN entries for web applications using Kerberos authentication. The DC administrator informs you there are several solutions to this problem. Of the following, what are valid solutions? (Choose all that apply.)

   A. Use the ADSIEdit utility to correct the duplicate SPNs.

   B. Use Windows PowerShell to locate and delete the duplicate SPNs.

   C. Find the computers containing the duplicate SPNs and delete the computers from the domain.

   D. Find the computers containing the duplicate SPNs and unjoin them from; then rejoin them to the domain.

20. You are a SharePoint administrator for your organization. You've recently created a new site collection in a web application, and you are checking the site collection using a web browser on the server computer hosting the collection. Instead of accessing the site collection main page, though, you receive an "HTTP 401.1 Unauthorized Logon Failed" message when you try to sign on to the site. What makes the error more mysterious is that users at client computers are able to easily reach and log on to the site collection. After you research this issue, what is the likely cause of the problem?

A. You are using Internet Explorer 6.0 on the server machine, and you need to upgrade to the current version.

B. You are not running the latest service pack on the server computer and need to update to the current version.

C. You recently installed a service pack on the server computer that included a loopback check security feature responsible for the problem.

D. The registry key HKEY_LOCAL_MACHINE\SYSTEM\CurrentControlSet\Control\ Lsa on the server computer has become corrupted, and you need to restore the key using the most recent backup.

Answers to Review Questions

1. B, C. IIS virtual servers must use standard TCP port 80 for websites and standard port 443 for SSL if you are using Kerberos and want search crawls to be successful. Nonstandard port numbers won't work for search crawls if you are using Kerberos.

2. A, B, D. You can use either the real or virtual hostname in the SPN.

3. B. You must look for the success audit in the Event Viewer on the SQL host machine to verify that Kerberos was used to make the connection. All of the other options are bogus.

4. C. You can use either Classic Mode or Claims Based and select whatever zone you desire, but you must select Negotiate (Kerberos).

5. A, B. To verify that you are connecting to the site collection via Kerberos, you must first attempt to visit the site collection using a web browser and then check for a "Success Audit" message confirming that you connected from the IP address of the machine you used using Kerberos. Pinging the host machine or domain name will confirm only that you have a network connection, not that Kerberos authentication is working.

6. A, B, D. The search service isn't required to be running on the frontend web server. All other options are potential reasons for the search results failure.

7. A, C. Claims-based authentication can also work with LiveID and OpenID, and you can configure anonymous logins to work with this method.

8. B. MOSS 2007 web applications were generally configured to use forms-based authentication or web SSO authentication.

9. B. You must use Windows PowerShell to run a specific script after MOSS 2007 has been upgraded to SharePoint Server 2010. No other option is available.

10. A, C. Option B is bogus, and you can perform this task either in Central Administration or using Windows PowerShell.

11. A, B. Although the first two options are correct, the third service containing the `Web.config` file is forms-based authentication claims-based web application.

12. B. You must migrate all users and permissions from MOSS 2007 to SharePoint Server 2010. All other options are bogus.

13. A, C. You can use either the `setspn.exe` tool or the `adsiedit.msc` utility to create an SPN. Although it's recommended to run separate web servers, application servers, and database servers, it's not an actual requirement.

14. D. The `wtshost.exe` file on the application server is written in XML.

15. A, C. To add the AD FS Identity Provider in Central Administration, you navigate to the Web Applications Management page, select the desired web application, click Authentication Providers on the Ribbon to open the Edit Authentication window, and select the Federated Identity Provider options.

16. A, B, D. Option C is bogus. All other options are valid methods of creating a customized permission level.

17. B. The correct procedure is to assign a database access account to the service in SharePoint Central Administration.

18. A, B, C. There are multiple possible causes and solutions for this error including those listed in options A, B, and C.

19. A, C, D. You cannot use Windows PowerShell to provide a solution to this problem. All other options are valid solutions.

20. C. The loopback check security feature included in the Service Pack caused authentication to fail from the web browser on the server computer, because either the fully qualified domain name (FQDN) or the custom host header is different from the local server computer name. The workaround solution is to disable loopback check by editing the HKEY_LOCAL_MACHINE\SYSTEM\CurrentControlSet\Control\Lsa registry key.

Chapter

9

Managing Web Applications and Host Sites

MICROSOFT EXAM OBJECTIVE COVERED IN THIS CHAPTER:

✓ **Deploying and Managing Applications**

   ▪ Managing Web Applications

The concept of Business Intelligence (BI) is difficult to describe because it isn't composed of a single component. In general, BI is a collection of all the computer-related applications and techniques used to locate, mine, and analyze business data regarding sales revenue by product or department or as associated with income vs. cost. Applied to SharePoint, this is a collection of applications and tools that provide these data-mining features, and that is why this topic is contained in a chapter on managing web applications. While Chapter 4, "Configuring Service Applications," introduced SharePoint application configuration, this chapter will dig deeper into the use of the BI applications and describe how you can use them for specific jobs. The applications featured include PerformancePoint, Visio, and Excel.

Managing Business Intelligence

I'm sure you're sick of hearing how we're living in the Information Age. We've been living in the Information Age since anywhere between the 1970s and 1990s depending on what set of inventions and innovations put us at "critical mass."

Business decisions, like most other critical decisions, thrive on information. However, that information must be of the right type, on relevant topics, organized correctly, and delivered to the appropriate audience at just the right time. It sounds like quite a lot to orchestrate. BI is the art and science of supporting better and timelier business decisions based on giving the right people and groups the right information, organized for quick assimilation, right when they need it.

As far as SharePoint goes, Microsoft Business Intelligence is the suite of applications and services used to locate, observe, analyze, and plan business decisions. Tools typically used within the SharePoint environment include scorecards, dashboards, and management reporting and analytics. The tools for BI are built using applications and utilities you probably use all of the time and are quite familiar with, including Excel, PerformancePoint, and Visio. BI on SharePoint Server 2010 also uses Report Builder and Reporting Services, and SQL Server brings Reporting Services, Integration Services, and Analysis Services into the mix.

This chapter will focus on Excel, PerformancePoint, and Visio as the workhorses of BI.

All the information related to Visio Graphics Services can be found in the "Managing Visio Services" section of Chapter 4 and will not be presented in this chapter.

BI is heavily related to SharePoint and has been ever since MOSS 2007, but it isn't always easily defined. BI is those processes and utilities that allow you to display and organize business-critical data to corporate managers, decision makers, and any other key individuals or groups within the company. Tools can include charts, spreadsheets, dashboard, or other organized UIs.

A number of tools and features in SharePoint either individually or in combination with several utilities allow you to configure and display BI information. In the following sections, you will learn how to perform numerous BI-related tasks using three essential services:

- PerformancePoint Services
- Visio Graphics Services
- Excel Services

Administering PerformancePoint

PerformancePoint Services within SharePoint Server 2010 is a performance management service used to monitor and analyze business activities using a variety of tools including dashboards, scorecards, and key performance indicators (KPIs). This service comes out of a stand-alone solution called Microsoft Office PerformancePoint Server 2007 but is now integrated in SharePoint Server 2010 Enterprise version. Although PerformancePoint is currently under the SharePoint umbrella, so to speak, it retains the features contained in the previous server version as well as offers additional features.

 See "Managing PerformancePoint Services" in Chapter 4 for more information on PerformancePoint Services.

Configuring PerformancePoint Services

Enabling and configuring PerformancePoint Services in SharePoint 2010 requires that you perform a series of prerequisite steps. In all likelihood, you've already performed at least some of them.

- You must have at least one web application in which you want to create a site collection.

- To be able to open the PerformancePoint Dashboard Designer from a site other than the Business Intelligence Center, you will need to enable the PerformancePoint Services site feature on the desired site.

- When you ran the Farm Configuration Wizard to create service applications and proxies, the PerformancePoint service application was also created. If you did not, you will need to create the PerformancePoint service application to provide a resource that can be shared across sites in a server farm.

- Once the PerformancePoint service application is created, you must start the service.

- PerformancePoint Services and the Secure Store Service must be associated with the same web application.

NOTE The Secure Store Service application and proxy must be created and running in order for the PerformancePoint service to store the unattended service account password, which is a shared domain account that's used to allow access to PerformancePoint Services data sources. See "Configuring the Secure Store Service" in Chapter 4 for details.

- The unattended service account must be configured for PerformancePoint Services to connect to data sources.

- The most typical site collection scenario relative to PerformancePoint is to create a site below the top-level site of a site collection using the Business Intelligence Center site template. The template provides a PerformancePoint Services site by default that allows you to use all of the various PerformancePoint objects, including dashboards.

You should have one or more web applications created in your SharePoint deployment by this point if you've been following the tutorials in this book in a linear fashion. If not or if you need more assistance in this area, see Chapter 4.

If you ran the Farm Configuration Wizard after installing SharePoint, you had the option to select PerformancePoint Services as one of the services you wanted to run in the farm. If you didn't make that selection, you can run the wizard again and choose PerformancePoint Services. If you don't want to run the wizard, you can create a PerformancePoint Services service application, either in Central Administration or using Windows PowerShell. Exercise 9.1 shows you the Central Administration method. This exercise provides an abridged set of instructions for creating a service application. If you need more details, see Chapter 4.

EXERCISE 9.1

Creating a PerformancePoint Services Service Application in Central Administration

1. Navigate to Central Administration and click Manage Service Applications under Application Management.

2. On the Manage Service Applications page, click New on the Ribbon and then select PerformancePoint Services.

3. When the Create a PerformancePoint Services Service Application box appears, type a name for the new service application in the available field.

4. Either choose an existing application pool or create a new pool.

5. Accept the default managed account that's available and then click Create.

If in step 5 you had chose Register A New Managed Account And Use It As The Application Pool Identity, you would need to run the following Windows PowerShell script, which grants you access to the associated database. This will grant you db_owner access to the SharePoint Foundation content databases. If you register a new managed account but do not run the script, PerformancePoint Services will fail to work.

```
PS> $w = Get-SPWebApplication -identity <your web application>
PS> $w.GrantAccessToProcessIdentity("<insert service account>")
```

Substitute your production values for the sample values in the code just presented.

You can also create a PerformancePoint Services service application using Windows PowerShell. Open and run Windows PowerShell as an administrator, type the following code, and then press Enter, substituting your production values for the sample values:

```
New-SPPerformancePointServiceApplication
-Name  <PPS ServiceApp Name> -applicationpool <App Pool Name>
```

Type the following code and press Enter again, also substituting production values for sample values:

```
New-SPPerformancePointServiceApplicationProxy
-ServiceApplication <PPS ServiceApp Name> -Name  <PPS Service AppProxy> -Default
```

Once the PerformancePoint service is created, you must start it. For assistance with this task, see Exercise 4.2 in Chapter 4.

The Secure Store Service application and proxy must be created and running in order for the PerformancePoint service to store the *unattended service account* password, which is a shared domain account that's used to allow access to PerformancePoint Services data sources. See "Configuring the Secure Store Service" in Chapter 4 for details.

PerformancePoint Services and the Secure Store Service must be associated with the same web application. To check to see whether this is the case, perform the following steps:

1. In Central Administration, click Manage Web Applications under Application Management.

2. On the Manage Web Applications page, click Service Connections on the Web Applications tab.

3. When the Service Application Associations page appears, you will see either the default group or the custom group containing the service applications associated with the web application.

If one or both services aren't associated with the web application, add the service applications using the procedures outlined in Exercise 4.6 or Exercise 4.7 in Chapter 4.

The final part of the process of configuring PerformancePoint Services in SharePoint is to set up the unattended service account. The unattended service account is a shared domain account used to allow access to PerformancePoint Services data sources. PerformancePoint Services uses the Secure Store Service to store the unattended service password. Before performing the steps in the following exercise, verify that the Secure Store Service is running. Exercise 9.2 takes you through the steps. The username you plan to use as the unattended account must have a local logon to the frontend web server machines to have access to the PerformancePoint Dashboard Designer.

EXERCISE 9.2

Configuring the Unattended ServiceAccount for PerformancePoint Services

1. Navigate to Central Administration and click Manage Service Applications under Application Management.

2. Under Manage Service Applications, click PerformancePoint Service Application.

3. On the PerformancePoint Service Application page, click Manage on the Ribbon.

4. Click the PerformancePoint Service Settings link; the PerformancePoint Service Application Settings page appears.

5. Under Unattended Service Account, enter the username and password for the user account to be used for querying data sources.

6. Verify that the Secure Store Service name and unattended service account name appears.

WARNING   If you receive an error message, the Secure Store Service key may not have been generated correctly or the key was not refreshed after a new key was created. See "Refreshing a Secure Store Service Application Encryption Key" in Chapter 4 for more information.

The first part of the process is activating the SharePoint Publishing Infrastructure. Exercise 9.3 illustrates this procedure.

EXERCISE 9.3

Activating the SharePoint Publishing Infrastructure

1. Navigate to the parent site for which you want to enable the PerformancePoint site feature.

2. Click Site Actions, and then click Site Settings, and in the list that appears, click Site Collections Administration.

3. On the Site Collections Administration page, click Site Collection Features.

4. On the Site Collection Features page, locate SharePoint Publishing Infrastructure and click Activate next to it.

5. After the Active blue status button appears, leave the page.

Once you've activated the SharePoint Publishing Infrastructure, you can enable the PerformancePoint Services site feature for the site. Exercise 9.4 shows you how this is done.

EXERCISE 9.4

Enabling the PerformancePoint Service Site Feature

1. Navigate to the parent site for which you want to enable the PerformancePoint site feature.

2. Click Site Actions and click Site Settings in the list that appears.

3. On the Site Settings page, click Manage Site Features under Site Actions.

4. On the Manage Site Features page, locate PerformancePoint Services Site features in the list and click Activate next to it.

5. When the Active blue status button appears, you can leave the page.

You are now able to create a Business Intelligence Center site and a PerformancePoint site in which to access the Dashboard Designer and begin creating a dashboard.

At this point, you should have a site collection created in SharePoint and available for your BI activities. If you need more information about creating and managing a site collection, see Chapter 10, "Managing Site Collections." Exercise 9.5 will walk you through the steps of creating a site in a site collection using the Business Intelligence Center site template. This will cause a PerformancePoint Services site to become available. You'll start at the top-level page of the desired site collection.

If you did not perform any of the previous PerformancePoint Services–related exercises, the Business Intelligence Center site template will not be available.

EXERCISE 9.5

Creating a Business Intelligence Center Site with a Template

1. On the top-level page of the site collection, click Site Actions and then click New Site.

2. On the Create page under Filter By, make sure the Enterprise tab is selected.

3. Click the Business Intelligence Center template in the main pane.

4. Type a title and URL for the site in the available fields.

5. If you desire, click More Options and then, on the New SharePoint Site page, configure information in the title and address fields, set the URL for the site, configure permissions to be either unique or use the same permissions as the parent site, and configure navigation, as shown here.

6. Click Create.

The Business Intelligence Center will be created and appear as in Figure 9.1.

FIGURE 9.1   Business Intelligence Center

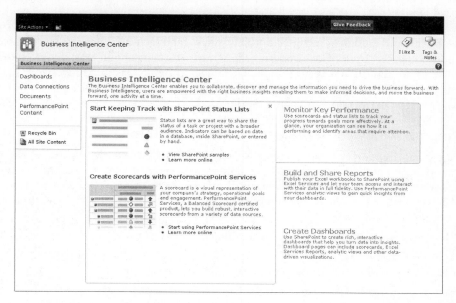

You are now able to manage PerformancePoint Services including working with dash-boards, scorecards, and other PerformancePoint objects directly from the PerformancePoint Services site. If, however, you need to work with PerformancePoint Services from a different site, you will need to enable the PerformancePoint Services site feature for that location.

Creating Data Connections for PerformancePoint Services

PerformancePoint Services uses a trusted data connection library in SharePoint Server 2010 to store data sources for the PerformancePoint Dashboard Designer. The trusted data connection library is a document library that has been determined to be secure and safe and provides restrictions over the data files in the library. By default, this library is created when PerformancePoint Services is provisioned.

You can configure the security settings for the data sources and have users connect using the following:

- Unattended service account

- Unattended user account and add authenticated user in connection (Analysis Services only)

- Per-user identity (requires Kerberos protocol)

For more information on Kerberos authentication, see Chapter 8, "Managing Authentication Providers."

SharePoint administrators can manage data connections on a server by creating more than one data connection library. When a user updates a data source connection in a document library, the data is shared and updated when a workspace file is opened in the Dashboard Designer.

Data source connections are created in the PerformancePoint Dashboard Designer. To open the Dashboard Designer, navigate to the Business Intelligence Center site you created earlier in this chapter. Under Create Scorecards With PerformancePoint Services, click the Start Using PerformancePoint Services link. Then, click the Run Dashboard Designer button. Once Dashboard Designer is installed, you are ready to develop PerformancePoint dashboards and to perform the following set of tasks.

Creating an Analysis Services Data Connection

The first data connection type you'll create is for an Analysis Services data source. You can create this data source in the Dashboard Designer by entering the name of the Analysis Services server, by entering the database and cube name, or by using a connection string and the cube name. The authentication method for the web application and site collection should already be configured.

1. In the Dashboard Designer on the Create tab, click Data Source.

2. When the Select A Data Source Template box opens, in the Category pane, click Multidimensional, click Analysis Services, and then click OK.

3. Type the name for the data source in the left navigation pane.

4. Under Data Source Settings, select the authentication method for the data source.

5. Use the Formatting Dimension drop-down menu to select the desired dimension formatting required for the report.

6. Use the Cache Lifetime field, type the refresh rate (in minutes) for the cache.

7. In the center pane, click the Editor tab.

8. Under Connection Settings, select either Use Standard Connection or Use The Following Connection:

   - If you choose Use Standard Connection, type the full path for the server to which you want to connect, select the database name in the Database box, and optionally type the name of the role, such as **administrator** or **database**, in the Roles field.

   - If you choose Use The Following Connection, type the connection string to the server to which you want to connect, including the cube name, and use the Cube drop-down menu to select the specific cube you want to use as the data source in the database.

9. Click Test Connection to verify that the connection works.

To use PowerPivot as a data source in PerformancePoint Services, you must apply the hotfix associated with the Microsoft Knowledge Base article at http://support.microsoft.com/kb/975954.

Creating a PowerPivot Data Connection

PerformancePoint Services can use PowerPivot models as a data source, using the data to construct interactive dashboards featuring PerformancePoint Services objects such as KPIs, analytic charts, scorecards, and so on. You must have PowerPivot for SharePoint 2010 installed and enabled to take advantage of this data source. You must also have ADOMD 10 installed on the server on which you are creating the dashboard. Otherwise, you will not have access to the PowerPivot workbook as a data source. The Unattended Service Account and Add Authenticated User Name In Connection String authentication option is unavailable when you use PowerPivot as a data source.

1. In the Dashboard Designer on the Create tab, click Data Source, as shown in Figure 9.2.

FIGURE 9.2 The Create tab in the Dashboard Designer

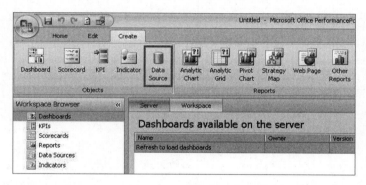

2. When the Select A Data Source Template box opens in the Category pane, click Multidimensional, as shown in Figure 9.3. Then click Analysis Services and OK.

FIGURE 9.3 Selecting a data source template

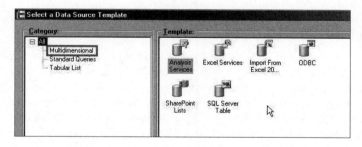

3. Type a name for the data source in the left navigation pane.

4. In the center pane, click the Editor tab and select Use the Following Connection under Connection Setting.

5. Type the connection string to the PowerPivot data source using the format `PROVIDER=MSOLAP;DATA SOURCE=http://testing/Documents/PowerPivot_Example.xlsx`, substituting your production values for these sample values.

6. Select the cube from the drop-down menu; always use the cube name Sandbox for a PowerPivot model.

7. Under Data Source Settings, select the desired authentication method.

8. Select the desired dimension in the Formatting Dimension list.

9. Type the refresh rate (in minutes) in Cache Lifetime.

10. Click Test Connection.

Creating a SharePoint List Data Connection

So far, you've used data sources that are external to SharePoint, but you can also use a SharePoint list as a data source. One of the limitations is that SharePoint list data can be read only using PerformancePoint Services. If you want to edit the list data, you must do this directly from within SharePoint. Authentication types are limited to the unattended service account or per-user identity (which requires Kerberos). Otherwise, the process of creating the data connection is nearly the same as the other data source types.

1. In the Dashboard Designer on the Create tab, click Data Source.

2. When the Select A Data Source Template box opens, in the Category pane, click Tabular List and then click SharePoint list.

3. Type the name of your data source in the left navigation pane.

4. In the center pane, click the Editor tab, and under Data Source Settings, select the desired authentication method.

5. Type the refresh rate (in minutes) in Cache Lifetime.

6. Use the List drop-down menu to select the desired SharePoint list from the collection.

7. Click Test Data Source to confirm the connection.

Creating an Excel Services Data Source Connection

List data isn't the only type of SharePoint information that can be accessed by PerformancePoint. Data contained in Excel files can be used as a data source connection if the files have been published to Excel Services on a SharePoint site. Unlike list data, however, it's possible to modify the parameter values from within PerformancePoint Services, rather than having to perform the task only within Excel Services.

A limitation to using Excel Services data as a data source connection is that only the unattended service account and per-user identity can be used to authenticate. Also, you cannot use Excel Services as a data source when the site or library containing the workbook allows anonymous access.

1. In the Dashboard Designer on the Create tab, click Data Source.

2. When the Select A Data Source Template box opens, in the Category pane, click Tabular List and then click Excel Services.

3. Click OK.

4. Type the name of the data source in the left navigation pane.

5. In the center pane, click the Editor tab and select the desired authentication method under Data Source Settings.

6. Type the refresh rate (in minutes) in Refresh Interval.

7. Under Connection Settings, type the URL to the SharePoint site in the available field.

8. Use the Document Library drop-down menu to select the document library in SharePoint where the Excel workbook is located.

9. Use the Excel Workbook drop-down menu to select the desired workbook.

10. Use the Item Name drop-down menu to select either Named Range or Table.

11. Click Test Data Source to confirm that the connection works.

If you are connecting to an Office Excel 2007 workbook, you must type the item name in step 10 because it will not appear in the drop-down menu.

Importing an Excel Workbook into PerformancePoint Services

In addition to using Excel data in Excel Services for a data source connection, you can also import information from an Excel workbook directly into PerformancePoint. This process creates an internal copy of the Excel file in PerformancePoint, and all imported information can then be modified on the Edit tab in the Dashboard Designer. The internal copy of the Excel file is completely disconnected from the original file.

1. In the Dashboard Designer on the Create tab, click Data Source.

2. When the Select A Data Source Template box opens, in the Category pane, click Tabular List and then click Import From Excel Workbook.

3. Click OK.

4. Type the name of the data source in the left navigation pane.

5. In the center pane, click Import.

Creating a SQL Server Table Data Source Connection

You can use SQL Server data as a data source connection, but only table or view data can be accessed, and this data cannot be modified from within the Dashboard Designer. Authentication methods that can be used are the unattended service account and per-user identity.

1. In the Dashboard Designer on the Create tab, click Data Source.

2. When the Select A Data Source Template box opens, in the Category pane, click Tabular List, click SQL Server Table, and then click OK.

3. Type the name for the data source in the left navigation pane.

4. In the center pane, click the Editor tab, and select the authentication method for the data source under Data Source Settings.

5. Use the Refresh Interval field, type the duration rate (in minutes) for the cache.

6. Under Connection Settings, select either Use Standard Connection or Use The Following Connection.

   - If you choose Use Standard Connection, type the full path for the server to which you want to connect and select the database name in the Database box.

   - If you choose Use The Following Connection, type the connection string to the server to which you want to connect and use the Table drop-down menu to select the specific table you want to use as the data source in the data base.

7. Click Test Data Source to verify that the connection works.

Deploying PerformancePoint Objects

Once you have PerformancePoint configured, the next step is creating the actual PerformancePoint objects, such as dashboards, charts, grids, maps, and so on. This section of the chapter will show you the related tasks. Since these are tasks you would typically perform when managing sites and site collections, see Chapter 10 for more information.

Deploying a PerformancePoint Dashboard

As you might guess from its name, the PerformancePoint Dashboard Designer creates the various items used in PerformancePoint dashboards, such as filters, reports, and scorecards. When you create these items, they are saved in a SharePoint list, so you can reuse the items and share them with other dashboard authors. Once you have assembled all your items into a dashboard, deploy it to a document library in SharePoint that you've created specifically for PerformancePoint dashboards.

To successfully perform the following task, you must possess at least design permission at the top-level SharePoint site containing the subsite or folder in which your dashboard content is contained.

1. Navigate to the Business Intelligence site and then to the PerformancePoint Services site.

2. Launch Dashboard Designer.

3. In the Workspace Browser pane, click PerformancePoint Content.

4. In the Ribbon, click the Home tab and then click Refresh.

5. In the center pane of the workspace, double-click the dashboard you want to publish, and wait for the pane to refresh and display the list of dashboard items that dashboard authors have saved to SharePoint.

6. If you desire, click the Editor tab to verify that each dashboard page contains all the items you want to include in your dashboard.

7. Add or change any items in the dashboard if you want; then, in the Workspace Browser, right-click the dashboard and click Save.

8. Right-click the Dashboard again and then click Deploy To SharePoint.

9. When deploying a dashboard for the first time to SharePoint, the Deploy To box opens and lets you select the desired dashboards library, lets you specify the page template for the dashboard using the Master Page list, and may offer the Include Page List For Navigation check box if the dashboard is larger than one page.

10. When you are finished with these selections, click OK.

11. In the Deploy To SharePoint Site box that opens, review the information available and test the dashboard items. Also make a note of the URL of the dashboard, which you can send to interested parties via email when you are ready to share the dashboard.

Although the task of deploying a dashboard was presented first, it's really the last step in the process. You will need to add or create a number of items that can then be included in a dashboard. The following tasks show you how to create analytic reports, which are dynamic visuals representing data. Examples are bar charts, line charts, pie charts, and tables or grids. These items pull information from SQL Server 2008 Analysis Services or SQL Server 2005 Analysis Services.

Creating an Analytic Chart or Grid

The first part of the task is to make sure your data source is available. After that, you create and configure the chart for the dashboard. The task assumes you have already navigated to the PerformancePoint Services site under the Business Intelligence site.

1. In the Dashboard Designer, click the Home tab and then click Refresh.

2. In the Workspace Browser, click Data Connections.

3. In the center pane of the workspace, review the list of data sources on the Server and Workspace tabs and verify the desired data sources are present.

4. In the Workspace Browser, click PerformancePoint Content.

5. On the Ribbon, click the Create tab.

6. On the Ribbon, under Reports, click Analytic Chart or Analytic Grid, depending on your requirements (for this exercise, choose Analytic Chart). See Figure 9.4.

FIGURE 9.4   Creating an analytic chart or grid on the Create tab in the Dashboard Designer

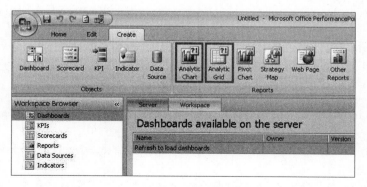

7. When the Create An Analytic Chart Report Wizard launches, select the desired SQL Server Analysis Services data source for Select A Data Source.

8. Click Finish.

9. When the analytic report opens in the center pane of the workspace, click the Properties tab.

10. Type the name you want to use for the report in the Name field.

11. If you desire, specify a location for the report by clicking the Display Folder button and then selecting or creating a folder.

12. In the Workspace Browser, right-click the report and then click Save.

Configuring a Report to Display Data Using the Design Tab

Now that the basic structure of the report has been constructed, you must still configure it to display data. You can choose between the Details and Query tabs when performing this function.

To use the Details option, in the Dashboard Designer, click the Design tab, and drag items from the Details pane into the preview window of the report. Continue this process until the preview appears as you desire.

To use the Query option, click the Query tab and then either specify or edit the custom Multidimensional Expressions (MDX) query used to display data. One problem with using the Query option is that dashboard users might be unable to drill up or down in the data. For this reason, the Design option is recommended. Use the Query option if you are familiar with MDX.

1. In the Dashboard Designer, in the center pane, click the Design tab.

2. In the Details pane, expand Measures, Dimensions, or Named Sets to show the desired list of items.

3. Depending on the specific option you expanded in the previous step, drag an item into Series (or Rows), Bottom Axis (or Columns), or Background, but make sure you put at least one item in each Series (or Rows) and Bottom Axis (or Columns) section so that data will be displayed in the report.

4. For Dimension Members, accept the default selection of All. Or, right-click a dimension and then click Select Members.

5. If you use the Select Members option, when the Select Members dialog box opens, expand the desired list of members in the dimension hierarchy, select the desired items to be displayed in the report, and then click OK.

6. To add more items, in the Details pane, expand Measures, Dimensions, or Named Sets; drag items into the available sections; and then configure the dimension members as you desire.

7. On the Ribbon's Edit tab, use the View group to specify the view type and settings for the report.

8. In the Workspace Browser, right-click the report and then click Save.

Configuring a Report to Display Data Using the Query Tab

To configure a report to show data using the Query option, select the Query tab rather than the Design tab in the Dashboard Designer. In the MDX pane, specify the desired query for the report. The following is an example that shows sales information for various products and sales territories. Depending on your requirements, you would replace the sample data with your production information.

```
SELECT
HIERARCHIZE( { [Product].[Product].[Product Category Name].&[8], [Product].
[Product].[Product Category Name].&[7], [Product].[Product].[Product Category
Name].&[6], [Product].[Product].[Product Category Name].&[5], [Product].
[Product].[Product Category Name].&[4], [Product].[Product].[Product Category
Name].&[3], [Product].[Product].[Product Category Name].&[2], [Product].
[Product].[Product Category Name].&[1] } )
ON COLUMNS,
HIERARCHIZE( { [Sales Territory].[Territory Hierarchy].[Sales Territory
Group].&[North America], [Sales Territory].[Territory Hierarchy].[Sales
Territory Group].&[Europe], [Sales Territory].[Territory Hierarchy].[Sales
Territory Group].&[Asia] } )
ON ROWS
FROM [Sales]
WHERE ( [Measures].[Sales Amount] )
```

Follow these steps to finish the task:

1. To preview the chart or grid, click the Design tab in the center pane.

2. On the Ribbon's Edit tab, use the View group to specify the type and settings for the report.

3. In the Workspace Browser, right-click the report and then click Save.

Once you've created and configured your chart or grid, you can edit it by going back into the Dashboard Designer and, in the center pane, clicking either the Design or Query tab, depending on the method you used to configure the report. Then modify the settings and selections you originally configured. Once you're done, in the Workspace Browser, right-click the report and then click Save.

Another PerformancePoint object is a strategy map. A strategy map is an item you use in a dashboard that uses a scorecard as a data source and uses a Visio diagram as its visual display structure. The process of creating and configuring a strategy map requires that you connect individual shapes in a Visio diagram to KPIs in a scorecard. You indicate performance for shapes in the map as being on or off target by color.

Before proceeding with this task, you must have Microsoft Office Visio installed on the same machine as the Dashboard Designer. The 64-bit version of the Dashboard Designer is compatible only with the 64-bit version of Visio 2010. The 32-bit version of the Dashboard Designer is compatible with the 32-bit versions of either Visio 2007 or Visio 2010.

Before you can successfully complete this task, it is desirable for you to have a Visio 2007 or Visio 2010 diagram available that is not made up of complex shapes. You must also have a scorecard available that you previously created in the Dashboard Designer.

Although it's desirable for you to have created a Visio diagram before beginning construction on the strategy map, you can create the Visio diagram during the creation of the strategy map by importing stencils into the Dashboard Designer.

Creating a Strategy Map

A strategy map report displays a number of difference performance measures for an organization using Office Visio 2007 diagram shapes to illustrate relationships between objectives and KPIs. Performance for each objective and KPI is shown by the use of color in the diagram.

1. Open the Dashboard Designer and, in the Workspace Browser pane, right-click Reports and then click New Report.

2. In the Select A Report Template box in the Template pane, select Strategy Map (see Figure 9.5).

3. When the Create A Strategy Map Report Wizard launches, select a scorecard in the Select A Scorecard window of the wizard and then click Finish.

4. When the strategy map opens in the center pane of the workspace, click the Properties tab.

5. Type the name of the report in the Name field.

FIGURE 9.5   The Select A Report Template box

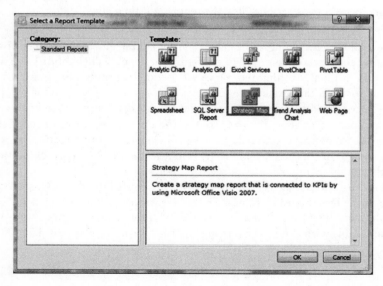

6. Click the Display Folder button to select or create a folder for the location of the report.

7. In the Workspace Browser, right-click the strategy map and then click Save.

8. Click the Edit tab and then click Edit Strategy Map.

9. When the Strategy Map Editor opens, click Import Visio File if you have a preexisting diagram available. If not, click Stencil, browse to the location of the Visio stencils, and then click Open to use the stencil shapes to create the diagram in the Strategy Map Editor.

10. Click a shape in the Visio diagram and then click Connect Shape.

11. When the Connect Shape dialog box opens, click the cell you want to connect to the selected Visio shape and click a cell in the Target column if you want the shape to automatically update, indicating that performance is on or off target.

12. Click Connect.

13. If you want to replace the text in the shape with text used in the scorecard KPI, select the Show KPI Name In Shape Text check box.

14. Continue to add and edit shapes, connect them with cells in the scorecard until you have all of the elements set up as you want, and then click Close in the Connect Shape dialog box.

15. In the Strategy Map Editor dialog box, click Apply.

16. In the Workspace Browser, right-click the strategy map and then click Save.

To edit the strategy map, in the Dashboard Designer, open the strategy map, click the Edit tab on the Ribbon, and then click Edit Strategy Map. Then modify the information you previously configured such as changing shape connections to scorecard cells, changing diagrams, or disconnecting shapes. You can make all shapes fit on a single Visio page by clicking Resize To Fit, and you can make all shapes fit on one printed page by clicking Fit For Print. When you're done, in the Workspace Browser, right-click the strategy map and then click Save.

Configuring Zones in a Dashboard Template

As you recall from the "Deploying a PerformancePoint Dashboard" section, you create a dashboard in the Dashboard Designer by selecting a specific template. Each of the available templates contains one or more dashboard zones in a specific configuration. If the default zones in a template aren't sufficient for your needs, you can add, remove, or change the sizes of zones in the template, as well as add more pages. One caveat is to not add too many zones to a page, because the zones will appear overly small and difficult to use.

1. In the Dashboard Designer, in the Workspace Browser pane, click PerformancePoint Content.

2. On the Ribbon's Editor tab, select the desired dashboard template.

3. Right-click Dashboard Content in order to add or edit zones in the template as follows:

    - Click Add Left to add a zone to the left of the pointer.
    - Click Add Right to add a zone to the right of the pointer.

- Click Add Above to add a zone above the pointer.
- Click Add Below to add a zone below the pointer.
- Click Split Zone to divide the zone nearest the pointer into two zones.
- Click Delete Zone to remove the zone nearest the pointer.

4. To change the size of one or more zones in the template, right-click the desired zone in the Dashboard Content section and then click Zone Settings (or right-click the header of the zone if the zone contains an item).

5. In the Zone Settings dialog box, specify the desired height and width of the zone on the Size tab.

6. On the Orientation tab, select Horizontal, Vertical, or Stacked to arrange items in the zone in rows, in columns, or by layers.

7. Click OK to save and close the Zone Settings dialog box.

8. In the Workspace Browser, right-click the report and then click Save.

 Real World Scenario

Setting Up PerformancePoint Services

You are a SharePoint administrator for the Acme Development Company. You have been tasked with creating a test BI environment for the management team to demonstrate SharePoint's ROI in the area of monitoring and presenting business data for company sales revenue by product and department.

You are provided with several data sources to use and a list of how the information is to be displayed in a dashboard using KPIs, scorecards, strategy maps, and charts.

With the required information available, you begin by creating a PerformancePoint service application in SharePoint's Central Administration and configuring an unattended service account. You then create a web application specifically for the BI task and associate the service application with the web application. Then you create a site collection in the new web application and enable the site collection for SharePoint Publishing Infrastructure as well as the PerformancePoint Services site feature. Now you're able to create a site within the site collection using the Business Intelligence Center site template.

Using the information provided to you by the management team, you create a number of data source connections on the Business Intelligence Center site using the Dashboard Designer, and then in Dashboard Designer, you create the specific PerformancePoint objects. Finally, you deploy the requested PerformancePoint dashboard and notify the management team so they can review the results.

Administering Excel Services

Excel Services in SharePoint Server 2010 is a shared service used to publish Excel 2010 workbooks so that they are available throughout your organization and as part of your company's BI solution. Published Excel workbooks can then be managed and secured based on your company's business requirements.

Excel Services comprises three elements: Excel Calculation Services (ECS), Excel Web Access (EWA), and Excel Web Services (EWS), which together interact with SharePoint and Excel Services to form a key component of business intelligence in SharePoint.

In Excel Services, trusted file locations are SharePoint sites, UNC paths, or websites you allow a server running Excel Calculation Services to access Excel workbooks for the purpose of display and manipulation within SharePoint. This allows you to access workbooks from a wide variety of sources and add their unique data to BI functionality and at the same time control which sources are used to ensure SharePoint security.

Trusted data providers are a database type combined with a protocol, such as SQL Server and ODBC DSN that you allow Excel Calculation Services to access to acquire information for your BI solution in SharePoint. Excel Calculation Services will not access data that does not have its source as a trusted data provider. Although Excel Calculation Services contains default entries for common data providers, you can add more data providers you deem safe for your SharePoint environment.

Trusted data connection libraries for Excel Services are SharePoint document libraries containing Office data connection files (identified with an .odc extension), which are used to provide central management of connections to external data sources. Excel Calculation Services can be set up to require .odc files for all data connections, allowing you to control which external data sources can be used rather than allowing Excel Calculation Services to use embedded connections to external data sources.

As you saw in the previous section of this chapter, Excel Services is a significant source of information for business intelligence, particularly relevant to PerformancePoint Services. Although you can find some information on managing Excel Services in Chapter 4, the data here will provide more detail on this classic service in SharePoint.

Managing Excel Services Custom Application

In general, the main focus of Excel Services in SharePoint is to extend the abilities of Excel Calculation Services and Excel workbooks in SharePoint. As a SharePoint administrator, user-defined functions (UDFs) are the primary methods you will work with to customize applications and workbooks in Excel Services.

You will need to configure Excel Services to support UDFs, enable UDFs on trusted file locations, and register UDF assemblies on the Excel Services user-defined function assembly list. These tasks are performed in Central Administration.

Other methods to extend Excel Services are ECMAScript (the JavaScript object model) and the REST API, both of which are beyond the scope of tasks performed by a SharePoint administrator.

Exercise 9.7 gets you started by showing you how to enable user-defined functions on trusted file locations.

EXERCISE 9.7

Enabling User-Defined Functions on a Trusted File Location

1. Navigate to Central Administration and click Manage Service Applications under Application Management.

2. On the Manage Service Applications page, click the desired Excel Services web service application.

3. On the Manage Excel Services page, click Trusted File Locations.

4. On the Trusted File Locations page, click the trusted file for which you want to enable user-defined functions.

5. On the Edit Trusted File Location page, select the User-defined Functions Allowed check box under User-Defined Functions.

6. Click OK.

The next task involves managing Excel Services user-defined function assemblies and includes adding, editing, and deleting a user-defined function assembly. Exercise 9.8 walks you through the steps.

As a SharePoint administrator, you are unlikely to be expected to have an intimate knowledge of Excel Services user-defined functions. The development and comprehension of them are more in the purview of SharePoint developers. Go to msdn.microsoft.com and search for *Excel Services User-Defined Functions* for more detailed information.

EXERCISE 9.8

Managing Excel Services User-Defined Function Assemblies

1. Navigate to Central Administration and click Manage Service Applications under Application Management.

2. On the Manage Service Applications page, click the desired Excel Services web service application.

3. On the Manage Excel Services page, click User Defined Function Assemblies.

4. On the Excel Services User Defined Functions page, click Add User-Defined Function Assembly.

5. On the Add User-Defined Function Assembly page, under Assembly, type the name of the assembly or the full path of an assembly that contains the user-defined functions in the Assembly field.

6. For User Assembly location, select either Global Assembly Cache, which is a global location from where signed assemblies can be deployed and run with full trust, or File Path, which is the local or network file location.

7. Under Enable Assembly, select the Assembly Enabled check box to allow Excel Calculation Services to call the assembly.

8. Type a description in the Description field and then click OK.

To edit a user-defined function assembly, on the Excel Services User Defined Functions page, click next to the desired user-defined function assembly to make the arrow available. Then in the list that appears, click Edit.

To delete a user-defined function assembly, on the Excel Services User Defined Functions page, click next to the desired user-defined function assembly to make the arrow available; in the list that appears, click Delete. When prompted, click OK.

Managing Excel Services Connections

SharePoint's Excel Services has the ability to connect to external data sources and refresh the available data. To connect to external data sources, Excel Services uses trusted data connection libraries. These are lists in SharePoint that contain the data connection files designed to work with external data connections and enable Excel Services and Excel clients to make such connections.

Both trusted data connection libraries and trusted data providers must be configured in SharePoint before Excel Services can access these sources.

Exercise 9.9 covers the actions required to manage trusted data connection libraries, including adding, configuring, and deleting a trusted data connection library. You must be a member of the Farm Administrators group to successfully perform these tasks.

Managing Excel Services Trusted Data Connection Libraries

1. Navigate to Central Administration and click Manage Service Applications under Application Management.

2. On the Manage Service Applications page, click the desired Excel Services application.

EXERCISE 9.9 *(continued)*

3. On the Manage Excel Services page, click Trusted Data Connection Libraries.

4. On the Excel Services Application Trusted Data Connection Libraries page, click Add Trusted Data Connection Library.

5. On the Excel Services Application Add Trusted Data Connection Library page, under Location, type the URL of the trusted data connection library in the Address field.

6. Type a description for the trusted data connection library in the Description field.

7. Click OK.

To edit the trusted data connection library, on the Excel Services Application Trusted Data Connection Libraries page, click next to the desired data connection library to cause the arrow to appear and then click Edit. To delete the trusted data connection library, perform the same action, but click Delete. When prompted, click OK.

Trusted data providers are the data providers used by Excel Calculation Services to access information, and they consist of two parts: a database type and a protocol for accessing the data. Excel Calculation Services does not access a data source that is not a trusted data provider.

Exercise 9.10 shows you how to manage Excel Services trusted data providers, including adding, editing, and deleting a trusted data provider. You must belong to the Farm Administrators group to successfully complete the following tasks.

EXERCISE 9.10

Managing Excel Services Trusted Data Providers

1. Navigate to Central Administration and click Manage Service Applications under Application Management.

2. On the Manage Service Applications page, click the desired Excel Services application.

3. On the Manage Excel Services page, click Trusted Data Providers.

4. On the Excel Services Application Trusted Data Providers page, click Add Trusted Data Provider.

5. On the Excel Services Application Add Trusted Data Provider page, type the provider ID in the Provider ID field under Provider, such as the type of SQL Server.

6. Under Provider Type, select OLE DB to access data using Object Linking and Embedding (OLE), ODBC to access data using Open Database Connectivity (ODBC), or ODBC DSN to access data using Open Database Connectivity with Data Source Name (ODBC DSN).

7. Give the trusted data provider a description in the Description field.

8. Click OK.

To edit a trusted data provider, on the Excel Services Application Trusted Data Providers page, click next to the desired data provider to make the arrow appear and then click Edit. To delete a trusted data provider, perform the same action, except select Delete. When prompted, click OK.

Managing Excel Services Trusted Locations

When you install SharePoint Server 2010 and run the Microsoft SharePoint 2010 Product Wizard, a default trusted file location is created for Excel Services. This trusted location site trusts the entire SharePoint server farm and enables any file to be loaded from the farm or stand-alone deployment on Excel Services. Although this makes it easier for administrators to perform the initial configuration, you can also define other trusted file locations in order to expand Excel workbook abilities and to augment security.

Trusted file locations can be SharePoint sites, UNC paths, or HTTP websites from which a server running Excel Calculation Services has permissions to access workbooks. Exercise 9.11 shows you how to manage an Excel Services trusted file location, including adding and configuring the location. You must belong to the Farm Administrators group to complete the following tasks.

EXERCISE 9.11

Managing Excel Services Trusted Locations

1. Navigate to Central Administration and click Manage Service Applications under Application Management.

2. On the Manage Service Applications page, click the available link for Excel Services Application, which should be the default service.

3. On the Manage Excel Services Application page, click Trusted File Locations.

4. On the Excel Services Application Trusted File Locations page, click Add Trusted File Location.

5. On the Excel Services Application Add Trusted File Location page, under Location, type the URL or UNC path of the SharePoint document library you want to add as a trusted file location.

6. Under Location Type, select the location type in the menu such as Microsoft SharePoint Foundation, UNC, or HTTP.

7. Under Trust Children, select Children Trusted if you want to trust all child libraries under the trusted location library.

8. Give the location a description in the Description field.

9. Under Session Management, type the value in seconds that an Excel Calculation Services session will stay open before shutting down in the Session Timeout field, with the default value being 450 seconds.

10. Type the value in seconds an Excel Web Access session stays open before it shuts down in the Short Session Timeout field, with the default value being 450 seconds.

11. In the New Workbook Session Timeout field, type the value in seconds that an Excel Calculation services session for a new workbook stays open before shutting down, with the default value being 1800 seconds.

12. In the Maximum Request Duration field, type the value in seconds for the maximum amount of time a single request is in session, with the default value being 300 seconds.

13. In the Maximum Chart Reader Duration field, type the value in seconds for the maximum amount of time spent rendering a single chart, with the default values being three seconds.

14. In the Maximum Workbook Size field, under Workbook Properties, type the value in megabytes for the maximum size of a workbook Excel Calculation Services can open, with the default value being 10 MB.

15. In the Maximum Chart of Image Size field, type the value in megabytes for the maximum size of a chart or image that Excel Calculation Services can open, with the default value being 1 MB.

16. Under Calculation Behavior, type the value in seconds that a computed value for a volatile function is cached for automatic recalculations in the Volatile Function Cache Lifetime field, with the default value being 300 seconds.

17. For Workbook Calculation Mode, select File to perform calculations for a specific file, Manual to have recalculation occur only upon a manual Calculate request, Automatic if you want any value change to autotrigger a recalculation, or Automatic Except Data Tables if you want any change in value to autotrigger a recalculation of all other values dependent on the changed value.

18. Under External Data, select None for Allow External Data to access no external data connections, Trusted Data Connection Libraries Only, or Trusted Data Connection Libraries And Embedded.

19. For Warn On Refresh, select the Refresh Warning Enabled check box if you want to be notified before refreshing external data for files for the location.

20. For Display Granular External Data Errors, select the Granular External Data Errors check box if you want to see specific error messages when external data failures occur for files at the location.

21. For Stop When Refresh on Open Fails, select the Stopping Open enabled check box if you do not want to see a file at the trusted location when refresh fails.

22. For External Data Cache Lifetime, select Automatic Refresh (Periodic/On-Open) and type a value in seconds to determine the maximum time the system can use external data query results before refresh, with the default value being 300 seconds. Or select Manual Refresh and type **-1** to prevent a data refresh after the first data query or allow the default value of 300 seconds to remain.

23. Type the value for the maximum number of queries that can run in a single session in the Maximum Concurrent Queries Per Session field, with the default value being five queries.

24. For Allow External Data Using REST, select the Data Refresh From REST Enabled check box to allow all requests from the REST API to refresh external data connections.

25. Under User-Defined Functions, for Allow User-Defined Functions, select User-Defined Functions Allowed to allow this feature to be available for Excel Calculation Services for workbooks from this location.

26. Click OK.

Once you've completed this rather lengthy exercise, if you want to go back in and edit your settings, on the Excel Services Application File Locations page, click next to the desired trusted file location to make the arrow appear and then click Edit. To delete the trusted file location, perform the same action, but select Delete. When prompted, click OK.

Configuring a Secure Store for Excel Services

As you may recall from the "Configuring the Secure Store Service" section of Chapter 4, the Secure Store Service replaced the single sign-on (SSO) feature you may have known in Microsoft Office SharePoint Server (MOSS) 2007. Excel Services supports the Secure Store Service and can use it to store credentials for a database, using the credentials to authenticate to data sources.

The general set of steps you need to perform in order to configure a Secure Store Service for Excel Services are as follows:

1. Creating the shared Secure Store Service

2. Generating a key

3. Adding an application ID

4. Setting credentials to be associated with the application ID

The tasks of creating a Secure Store Service and generating a key are covered in the "Configuring the Secure Store Service" section of Chapter 4. You need to add an application ID to map the credentials of a user, group, or claim to a set of credentials on the external data source Excel Services wants to use.

This process is performed at the same time you are creating the Secure Store Service and generating the new key. Exercise 9.12 will show you how to add an application ID to Excel Services and set permissions in the Secure Store Service application. You must belong to the Farm Administrators group to successfully accomplish this task.

EXERCISE 9.12

Adding an Application ID and Setting Permissions

1. Navigate to Central Administration and click Manage Service Applications under Application Management.

2. On the Manage Service Applications page, select the desired instance of an Excel Services application and then click Global Settings.

3. On the Excel Services Application Settings page, under the External Data section, type the application ID used to reference the unattended service account credentials you want to use in the Application ID field.

4. Verify that the Excel Services process identity has permission to access the application ID.

5. Click OK.

6. On the Manage Service Applications page, select the desired Secure Store Service instance and then click the Edit tab.

7. On the Secure Store Service page, select the check box next to the Excel Services Target application ID you just created.

8. On the Ribbon, click the Set Credentials button.

9. Type the username and password for the credentials you want to have stored, and you may also have to type the username of the credential owner if this is an individual application ID.

10. Click OK.

Summary

In this chapter, you learned not only the basics of BI in SharePoint but also the different components making up BI, including the following:

- Understand the basic concept of business intelligence and its role in the SharePoint Server 2010 platform.

- Demonstrate the ability to install and configure PerformancePoint Services, enabling the creation of the Business Intelligence Center and the PerformancePoint Services site.

- Comprehend the actions required to create data connections for PerformancePoint services using the Dashboard Designer in the PerformancePoint Services site.

- Show how to create different PerformancePoint objects using the Dashboard Designer and how to deploy a dashboard.

- Illustrate managing Excel Services including custom applications, creating Excel Services connections, managing trusted locations, and configuring a Secure Store.

Exam Essentials

Understanding the Various Tasks Associated with PerformancePoint Services   Understand the numerous elements associated with PerformancePoint Services as it uses data sources including Excel and Visio to provide business intelligence information using dashboards, scorecards, and KPIs.

Understanding the Activities Related to Administering Excel Services   Comprehend the various functions in administering Excel Services, but as a stand-alone service and as a data source for business intelligence in SharePoint.

Review Questions

1. You are a SharePoint administrator for your company, and you are preparing to deploy business intelligence (BI) in your environment. You and your staff are doing a high-level review of the components that contribute to BI. Of the following, which services are used to provide data to BI dashboards? (Choose all that apply.)

   A. Excel Services

   B. Managed Metadata Services

   C. PerformancePoint Services

   D. Visio Graphics Services

2. You are a SharePoint administrator for your company, and you are preparing to deploy business intelligence (BI) in your environment. You are reviewing the requirements for installing and managing PerformancePoint Services in SharePoint. Of the following, which are valid prerequisite steps? (Choose all that apply.)

   A. You will need to manually create the PerformancePoint Services application in Central Administration.

   B. Once the PerformancePoint Services service is created, you must start it.

   C. You must configure the unattended service account service for PerformancePoint Services to allow access to PerformancePoint Services data sources.

   D. PerformancePoint Site Collection Features must be turned on.

3. You are a SharePoint administrator, and you are setting up PerformancePoint Services in SharePoint to deploy your business intelligence solution. You know you must have both PerformancePoint and the Secure Store Service associated with the same web application. What are some of the steps you must take to verify this is the case? (Choose all that apply.)

   A. In Central Administration, you must go into Application Management and then into Manage Web Applications.

   B. On the Service Application Associations page, you can see the service associations either under the default group or in the custom group.

   C. In Central Administration, you must go into Application Management and then into Manage Service Applications.

   D. You can optionally check the associations using Windows PowerShell.

4. You are a SharePoint administrator, and you are setting up PerformancePoint Services in SharePoint to deploy your business intelligence solution. You are in the process of configuring a trusted data connection library to store data resources for the PerformancePoint Dashboard Designer. What are the valid security settings you can use for data sources? (Choose all that apply.)

   A. Anonymous user account

   B. Per-user identity (requires Kerberos protocol)

   C. Unattended service account

   D. Unattended user account and add authenticated user in connection (Analysis Services only)

5. You are a SharePoint administrator, and you are setting up PerformancePoint Services in SharePoint to deploy your business intelligence solution. You are in the process of configuring a trusted data connection library to store data resources for the PerformancePoint Dashboard Designer. Of the following, what is most true about creating data source connections?

   A. Data source connections are created in the Dashboard Designer.

   B. Data source connections are created in Central Administration under Manage Web Applications.

   C. Data source connections are created in Central Administration under Manage Service Applications.

   D. Data source connections are created using Windows PowerShell.

6. You are a SharePoint administrator, and you are setting up PerformancePoint Services in SharePoint to deploy your business intelligence solution. You are in the process of creating the Business Intelligence Center site, so you can begin using the Dashboard Designer, but when you look for the Business Intelligence Center site on the appropriate page, it doesn't appear. Of the following, what could be the problem? (Choose all that apply.)

   A. You didn't activate the SharePoint Publishing Infrastructure.

   B. You didn't enable the PerformancePoint Services site feature.

   C. You didn't create the PerformancePoint Services site.

   D. You didn't run the PerformancePoint Dashboard Designer creator.

7. You are a SharePoint administrator, and you are setting up PerformancePoint Services in SharePoint to deploy your business intelligence solution. You are in the process of configuring a trusted data connection library to store data resources for the PerformancePoint Dashboard Designer. Of the following, what are valid data source connections? (Choose all that apply.)

   A. Analysis Services

   B. PowerPivot

   C. SharePoint Libraries

   D. SharePoint Lists

8. You are a SharePoint administrator, and you are setting up PerformancePoint Services in SharePoint to deploy your business intelligence solution. You are in the process of configuring a trusted data connection library to store data resources for the PerformancePoint Dashboard Designer. You are considering importing an Excel workbook into PerformancePoint as opposed to creating an Excel Service data source connection. If you do so, what would be true about the imported workbook data?

   A. The process creates an internal copy of the Excel file in PerformancePoint.

   B. You can set a refresh rate in minutes for the workbook in the Dashboard Designer.

   C. All information imported from the Excel workbook can be modified directly in the Dashboard Designer.

   D. Every time the original Excel workbook is modified, the imported copy is automatically modified.

9. You are a SharePoint administrator, and you have set up PerformancePoint Services in SharePoint in order to deploy your business intelligence solution. You are now ready to create a dashboard and deploy it. Of the following, what are valid PerformancePoint dashboard objects you can configure and add to a dashboard? (Choose all that apply.)

A. Analytic charts

B. Analytic grids

C. Reporting zones

D. Strategy maps

10. You are a SharePoint administrator, and you have set up PerformancePoint Services in SharePoint in order to deploy your business intelligence solution. You are now ready to create a dashboard and deploy it. You are in the process of creating a strategy map. Of the following, which is the data source for this dashboard object?

A. Access

B. Excel

C. SQL Server

D. Visio

11. You are a SharePoint administrator, and you have set up PerformancePoint Services in SharePoint in order to deploy your business intelligence solution. You are now ready to create a dashboard and deploy it. You want to modify the configuration of the dashboard and change the size and location of zones to display data in a manner you can control. Of the following, what options do you have? (Choose all that apply.)

A. You can change the location of zones in a dashboard.

B. You can delete zones in a dashboard.

C. You can split a single zone into two zones in a dashboard.

D. You can stack zones as 3D objects in a dashboard.

12. You are a SharePoint administrator for your company, and you are configuring Excel Services as part of your overall business intelligence (BI) solution. You are performing a high-level review of Excel Services as related to BI with your staff. Of the following, which is the primary method you will work with to customize applications and workbooks in Excel Services?

A. ECMAScript (the JavaScript object model)

B. REST API

C. Trusted file locations

D. User-defined functions (UDFs)

13. You are a SharePoint administrator for your company, and you are configuring Excel Services as part of your overall business intelligence (BI) solution. You know that Excel Services can connect to external data sources and refresh the available data. What prerequisite tasks must be performed before connecting to these sources? (Choose all that apply.)

A. Trusted data connection libraries must be configured.

B. Trusted data connection lists must be configured.

C. Trusted data providers must be configured.

D. Trusted data stacks must be configured.

14. You are a SharePoint administrator for your company, and you are configuring Excel Services as part of your overall business intelligence (BI) solution. You are currently adding a trusted data provider for Excel Services in Central Administration. You must select a provider type for SQL Server. Of the following, which are valid options? (Choose all that apply.)

A. OLE DB

B. OLE DB DSN

C. ODBC

D. ODBC DSN

15. You are a SharePoint administrator for your company, and you are configuring Excel Services as part of your overall business intelligence (BI) solution. You know that a trusted location must be created for Excel Services for files can be loaded from the SharePoint server farm. What is the default process for creating the first trusted file location for Excel Services?

A. Running the SharePoint 2010 Product Wizard creates the default trusted location.

B. Running the Server Farm Configuration Wizard creates the default trusted location.

C. You must manually create the default trusted location in Central Administration.

D. You must manually create the default trusted location using Windows PowerShell.

16. You are a SharePoint administrator for your company, and you are configuring Excel Services as part of your overall business intelligence (BI) solution. You are in the process of creating a trusted file location for Excel Services, and you are setting a location type for a file location. Of the following, which are valid file location options? (Choose all that apply.)

A. HTTP

B. Microsoft SharePoint Foundation

C. UNC

D. WWW

17. You are a SharePoint administrator for your company, and you are configuring Excel Services as part of your overall business intelligence (BI) solution. You are currently configuring the Secure Store Service for Excel Services to store credentials for a database using the credentials to authenticate to data sources. There are a general set of steps you must follow to accomplish this task. Of the following, which are valid steps? (Choose all that apply.)

A. Generating a key

B. Adding an application ID

C. Setting the key to associate with the application ID

D. Setting credentials to be associated with the application ID

18. You are a SharePoint administrator for your company, and you are configuring Excel Services as part of your overall business intelligence (BI) solution. You are currently configuring the Secure Store Service for Excel Services to store credentials for a database using the credentials to authenticate to data sources. You need to add an application ID to map credentials to the credentials of the external data source required by Excel Services. Of the following, which sort of credentials are considered valid? (Choose all that apply.)

A. Anonymous

B. Claim

C. Group

D. User

19. You are a SharePoint administrator for your company, and you are configuring Excel Services as part of your overall business intelligence (BI) solution. You are in the process of performing a high-level review of the Secure Store Service as it relates to the business intelligence solution in SharePoint. Of the following, why must the Secure Store Service application and proxy be created and running?

A. To store the unattended service account password for the PerformancePoint service

B. To store the unattended service account password for the PerformancePoint web application

C. To store the unattended service account password for the PerformancePoint Dashboard Designer

D. To store the unattended service account password for the single sign-on service

20. You are a SharePoint administrator for your company, and you are currently going through a high-level review of the PerformancePoint service with your staff, as it relates to the Microsoft SharePoint Business Intelligence solution. PerformancePoint Services in SharePoint originated in Microsoft Office PerformancePoint Server 2007. Of the following, which version of SharePoint includes PerformancePoint Services?

A. SharePoint Server 2010 Enterprise version

B. SharePoint Server 2010 Internet version

C. SharePoint Server 2010 Intranet version

D. SharePoint Server 2010 Web version

Answers to Review Questions

1. **A, C, D.** The services that primarily provide and manage BI information include Excel, PerformancePoint, and Visio. Managed Metadata Services is a hierarchical collection of managed terms that can be defined and then used as attributes for SharePoint items.

2. **B, C, D.** The PerformancePoint Services service application can be created in Central Administration, but you can also use the Farm Configuration Wizard to create the service right after your initial SharePoint deployment is finished.

3. **A, B.** You must check on the Manage Web Applications page rather than the Manage Service Applications page. There is no option to check these associations using Windows PowerShell.

4. **B, C, D.** Option A is bogus. The other options are correct.

5. **A.** Data source connections are created only in the Dashboard Designer. The other options are bogus.

6. **A, B.** You need to activate the SharePoint Publishing Infrastructure in the parent site for the site collection in which you want to create the Business Intelligence Center site and enable the PerformancePoint Services site feature. If you fail to take these actions, other templates will be available, but the Business Intelligence Center site template will be absent. The other options are bogus.

7. **A, B, D.** Although you can use SharePoint Lists as a data source connection for PerformancePoint, you cannot use SharePoint Libraries.

8. **A, C.** The imported workbook is completely disconnected from the original, so any changes to the original will not be reflected in the imported copy. Although you can set a refresh rate for an Excel Service data source connection, you cannot do the same with an imported workbook.

9. **A, B, D.** Although you can configure the location and size of zones in a dashboard, there is no such object as a Reporting zone.

10. **D.** The strategy map connects dashboard items to shapes in a Visio diagram.

11. **A, B, C.** Although you can stack by layers in a dashboard, they do not manifest as 3D objects.

12. **D.** Although you can also extend Excel Services using ECMAScript and REST API, the primary method is user-defined functions (UDFs). You can enable UDFs on a trusted file location, but it's not a method of extending Excel Services as such.

13. **A, C.** Both trusted data connection libraries and trusted data providers must be configured in SharePoint before Excel Services can access external data sources. The other options are bogus.

14. A, C, D. OLE DB DSN is a bogus option. The other options are valid.

15. A. When you install SharePoint Server 2010 and run the Microsoft SharePoint 2010 Product wizard, a default trusted file location is created for Excel Services. The other options are bogus.

16. A, B, C. You can select a SharePoint site, a UNC path, or a web location (HTTP). WWW is not a valid option.

17. A, B, D. After creating the shared Secure Store Service, the general steps include generating a key, adding an application ID, and setting credentials to be associated with the application ID. Associating the key with the application ID is a bogus step.

18. B, C, D. You cannot map anonymous credentials to a set of credentials on an external data source.

19. A. The PerformancePoint service needs the Secure Store Service to store unattended service account password to allow access to the PerformancePoint Services data sources.

20. A. PerformancePoint Services is integrated in SharePoint Server 2010 Enterprise version. All other options are bogus.

Chapter
10

Managing Site Collections

MICROSOFT EXAM OBJECTIVE COVERED IN THIS CHAPTER:

✓ **Deploying and Managing Applications**

- Managing Site Collections

In the previous chapters of this book, you learned how to manage and maintain a wide variety of SharePoint features that are required to provide an optimal SharePoint user experience but that SharePoint users are almost completely unaware of. This chapter focuses on all the elements related to SharePoint sites and site collections, which are the heart of the user's interface with SharePoint. In addition to site collection creation and management, this chapter will delve into web content management and conversion.

Site Collections Administration

You may already understand what a site collection is, either because of prior SharePoint experience or because the concept seems rather intuitive. Basically, a site collection is a hierarchical tree structure of websites consisting of a single top-level site with a number of subsites beneath it on the tree. Any subsite can also have numerous subsites on lower hierarchical levels.

Although previous chapters have shown you site and site collection creation as part of managing other features, this section will focus on how to create, manage, and delete site collections. Other activities include how to manage storage limits, lock sites, and delete unused websites.

Managing Site Collections

A site collection is a group of sites, including a top-level site and all subsites that have the same site owner and share the same administrative settings, and the sites may have the same permissions and navigation. When you first create a site collection, you are actually creating just the top-level site. You then must create the number and type of subsites in the desired structure.

All site collections you create must exist within a web application. You can either create a site collection in an existing web application or create a web application specifically for the site collection.

 See Chapter 4, "Configuring Service Applications," and Chapter 9, "Managing Web Applications and Business Intelligence," for more information.

Before going into site collection creation, start by viewing existing site collections within a web application. Exercise 10.1 will show you this process in Central Administration. You must be a member of the Farm Administrators group to successfully perform this task.

EXERCISE 10.1

**Viewing Site Collections in a Web Application
Using Central Administration**

1. Navigate to the Central Administration page and then click Application Management.

2. On the Application Management page, click View All Site Collections under Site Collections.

3. Use the Web Application drop-down menu and select Change Web Application.

4. Select the web application for which you want to view site collections.

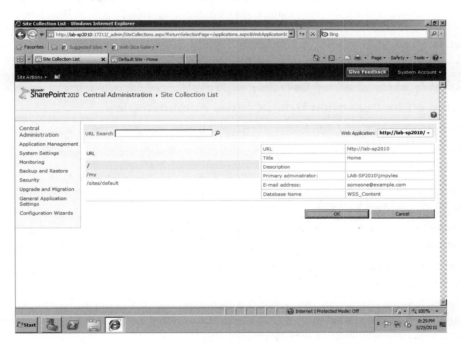

5. When the list of site collections appears, click the desired site collection in the URL column if you want to view the details of the collection.

6. When you are finished, click OK.

The strategy for how to organize web applications and site collections usually follows intent and function. If you have created a web application for a specific project or purpose, create only the site collection you require to fulfill that purpose using that web application. However, if you have a more involved set of tasks or projects to accomplish, create a web application and then whatever number and type of site collections within that web application you require.

Site collections are created using site templates, which allow the site to be created with a structure and set of tools that match a particular job. The default site templates include collaboration, meetings, enterprise, publishing, and custom. Within each general category, one or more specific templates exist to accommodate to your needs.

A number of preconditions must be met before you create a site collection. The first one is obvious: have a web application available in which to create the site collection. The other preconditions depend on your requirements.

If you plan to define values for the amount of data to be stored in your site collection and want to receive email alerts regarding changes in storage site, you'll need to have a quota template available. You will need a custom-managed wildcard path if you want to create the site collection anywhere besides in the root (/) directory or /sites/ directory.

You can create a site collection using either Central Administration or Windows PowerShell. Exercise 10.2 shows you the Central Administration method. You must be a member of the Farm Administrators group to successfully complete this task.

EXERCISE 10.2

Creating a Site Collection Using Central Administration

1. Navigate to the Central Administration page and then click Application Management.

2. On the Application Management page, click Create Site Collections under Site Collections.

3. On the Create Site Collection page, select the web application under Web Application in which you want to create the site collection.

4. Under Title And Description, give the new site collection a name and description in the available fields.

5. Under Web Site Address, type a URL for your site collection, either under the root (/) or under /sites/.

6. Under Template Selection, in the Select A Template Area, select the desired tab and then select the desired template, or select the Custom tab to create an empty site on which you will later apply a template.

7. Under Primary Site Collection Administrator, type the name of the desired user in the available field in the format domain\username and then check the name.

8. Under Secondary Site Collection Administrator, type the name of the desired user in the available field in the format domain\username, and then check the name.

9. If you want to use a quota to manage storage size for the site collection, under Quota Template, select the desired template from the Select A Quota Template list.

10. When you are finished, click OK.

    For step 5 in the previous task, if you select a wildcard inclusion path, you must type the site's name to use in the site collection's URL.

When a site collection is created, to indicate the location of the site, you can use an explicitly named path such as http://sharepoint/sites/ groupsite. The "wildcard" path sites indicates that any child URLs of http://sharepoint/sites/, for example, are site collections. A wildcard inclusion path means that all paths are subordinate to the specified path. This is opposed to an explicit inclusion path, which includes only the site that is indicated by the specified path.

To create a site collection using Windows PowerShell, you must be a member of the SharePoint_Shell_Access role in the configuration database and be a member of the WSS_ADMIN_WPG local group on the computer where SharePoint 2010 exists.

Open Windows PowerShell as an administrator, type the following string at the prompt, and then press Enter; make sure to replace the sample values with your production values:

```
Get-SPWebTemplate
$template = Get-SPWebTemplate "STS#0"
// This is for a team site template
New-SPSite -Url "<URL for the new site collection>" -OwnerAlias "<domain\
user>" -Template $template
```

A practical example to create a document workspace is as follows:

```
Get-SPWebTemplate
$template = Get-SPWebTemplate "STS#@"
New-SPSite -Url "http://sharepoint/sites/documentsite" -OwnerAlias
"sharepoint\jmpyles" -Template $template
```

SharePoint site collections represent dynamic environments, capable of being customized in a wide variety of ways, but the SharePoint platform changes also with the creation and deletion of site collections. Once a site collection has outlived its usefulness, you can remove it from SharePoint using either Central Administration or Windows PowerShell. Exercise 10.3 provides the specific instructions. You must be a member of the Farm Administrators group to perform this task.

EXERCISE 10.3

Deleting a Site Collection Using Central Administration

1. Navigate to the Central Administration page and then click Application Management.

2. On the Application Management page, click Delete A Site Collection under Site Collections.

3. On the Delete Site Collection page, click the down arrow for the Site Collection drop-down menu and then select Change Site Collection.

EXERCISE 10.3 *(continued)*

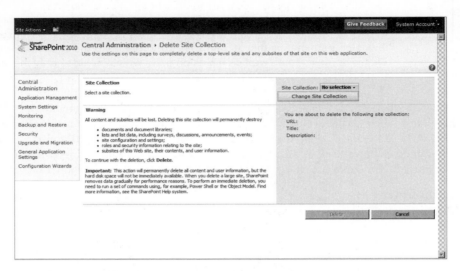

4. When the Select Site Collection screen appears, click the down arrow for the Web Application drop-down menu and then click Change Web Application.

5. When the Select Web Application screen appears, select the name of the web application containing the site collection you want to delete.

6. On the Select Site Collection screen, select the relative URL for the site collection you want to delete and then click OK.

7. Review the Warning section, verify that the information is correct, and then, on the Delete Site Collection screen, click Delete.

The most common cmdlet in Windows PowerShell with which to delete a site collection is Remove-SPSite. Use the -GradualDelete parameter to delete the site collection gradually, thus reducing the load on the SharePoint system during the deletion process.

To delete a site collection using Windows PowerShell, you must be a member of the SharePoint_Shell_Access role in the configuration database and be a member of the WSS_ADMIN_WPG local group on the computer where SharePoint 2010 exists.

Open Windows PowerShell as an administrator, type the following string at the prompt, and then press Enter; make sure to replace the sample values for your production values:

```
Remove-SPSite -Identity "<URL>" -GradualDelete
```

A portal site is the gateway into your site collection system in SharePoint. There can be different portal sites for different purposes, and you can have a main portal site for all the site collections that fall under your administration. You can have various site collections and web applications connected to your main portal site to facilitate navigation across your environment. After you accomplish this, a link will be added to the breadcrumb trail in the upper-left of the current site collection.

The portal site must exist, and you must have the URL to this site. Exercise 10.4 will illustrate the required steps. You must be the site collection administrator to successfully perform this exercise. You must perform this task on the website you want to connect to the portal site, not on the portal site itself.

EXERCISE 10.4

Configuring a Connection to a Portal Site

1. On the site where you want to set up the connection to the portal site, click Site Actions and then click Site Settings.

2. On the Site Settings page, under Site Collection Administration, click Portal Site Connection.

3. On the Portal Site Connection page, select Connect To Portal Site.

4. Type the URL to the portal site in the Portal Web Address field.

5. In the Portal Name field, type the name of the portal site.

6. Click OK.

Once you have created a site collection, such as a repository or a records center, you may want to create a connection that will let you send documents to that location. A connection is a path that specifies the web application containing site collections from which you want to send documents and specifies the destination repository or records center at which the documents will arrive. The most common reason you will create such a connection is as a conduit to an archive or information management center.

Exercise 10.5 will show you how to create a connection. You will already need to have the appropriate site collection created as the destination, and you will need the URL of the destination available. You must also be a member of the Farm Administrators group.

EXERCISE 10.5

Creating a Documents Repository Connection

1. Navigate to the Central Administration page and then click General Application Settings.

2. On the General Application Settings page, click Configure Send To Connections.

3. On the Configure Send To Connections page, select the web application under Web Application that contains the site collections from which documents will be sent.

4. In the Send To Connections list, select New Connection.

EXERCISE 10.5 *(continued)*

5. In the Display Name field, type the name of the connection. This is what users will see as an option to use when sending documents.

6. In the Send To URL field, type the URL of the destination site connection, which you acquired before beginning this task.

7. If you desire, select Click Here To Test to verify the URL.

8. If you want the connection in a list that users see when they click Send To, select Allow Manual Submission from the Send To menu.

9. In the Send To action list, select Copy if you want users to send a copy of the original document to the destination. Click Move if you want users to delete the document at the source and move the document to the destination. Click Move And Leave A Link if you want users to delete the document at the source, move it to the destination, but leave a link to the document at the source.

10. When the Explanation dialog box appears, type the information you want added to the audit log when a user sends a document using the connection.

11. Click Add Connection and then click OK.

Once you create a connection, you can edit it as shown in Exercise 10.6. The same permissions are needed as those for creating the connection.

EXERCISE 10.6

Editing a Documents Repository Connection

1. Navigate to the Central Administration page and then click General Application Settings.

2. On the General Application Settings page, click Configure Send To Connections.

3. On the Configure Send To Connections page, select the desired web application in the Web Application field.

4. In the Send To Connections list, select the desired connection.

5. Edit any of the connection settings; when you're done, click Update Connection.

6. Click OK.

To delete a connection, after you select the desired connection in the Send To Connections list, click Remove Connection, and then click OK.

Managing Site Collection Quotas and Locks

In Exercise 10.2, one of the final steps is to select a *quota template* for the site collection if you want to manage its storage size. The quota template contains the storage limit values that determine how much data can be stored in a site collection. You can save a set of quota configurations as a template and then use that template to create multiple site collections you want to possess the same storage limitations.

You can modify the storage values of a template, but those modifications don't affect any site collections that were previously made with the quota template. You would have to go back into each site collection configuration and edit the storage size quota manually.

When you create a site collection with a storage quota template, the storage limitations are applied to the top-level site and all the subsites in the collection. The storage limit includes all data contained in the different versions of the site collection, if versioning is enabled, and for even the contents in the recycling bin.

When a site collection configured with a storage limit approaches or reaches that limit, the system sends an email message containing a notice to the site collection administrator (if the site collection administrator's email address was included when the quote template was created). The site collection administrator can delete surplus content to resolve the issue or contact the farm administrator and request the storage limit be increased. The farm administrator can either apply a new quota template to the site collection to increase the storage limit or manually increase the site collection's limits.

This section of the chapter will show you different techniques related to these circumstances. Exercise 10.7 will show you how to change the settings in an existing quota template. You must be a member of the Farm Administrators group to perform this task.

EXERCISE 10.7

Creating and Changing Quota Template Settings

1. Navigate to the Central Administration page and then click Application Management.

2. On the Applications Management page, click Specify Quota Templates under Site Collections.

3. On the Quota Templates page, select the template under Template Name you want to change in the Template To Modify list.

EXERCISE 10.7 *(continued)*

4. Under Storage Limit Values, to create a storage limit, verify that the Limit Site Storage To A Maximum Of check box is selected, and then type the storage limit in megabytes in the available field.

5. To have an email sent to the site collection administrator when the storage threshold is reached, select the Send Warning E-mail When Site Storage Reaches check box, and then type the threshold value in megabytes in the available field.

6. Click OK.

You can set a lesser value in step 5 than you did in step 4 so that the email is sent prior to the actual limit being reached, rather than when it's nearly reached.

After you have created a site collection and applied a quota template, you may find it necessary to change the data storage limitation for the site collection. You can do this by manually changing the quota template to be used by the site collection. Exercise 10.8 outlines the procedure. You must be a member of the Farm Administrators group to perform this task.

You can also change the quota size for an individual site collection directly. As previously mentioned, if you change the values for a particular quota template, any site collections made with that template before the change will be unaffected. Exercise 10.9 will show you how to change the storage limits for a site collection using Central Administration. You need to be a member of Farm Administrators group to successfully perform this task.

EXERCISE 10.8

Changing the Quote Template for a Site Collection

1. Navigate to the Central Administration page and then click Application Management.

2. On the Applications Management page, under Site Collections, click Configure Quotas And Locks.

3. On the Site Collection Quotas And Locks page, under Site Collection, use the Site Collection list to specify the desired site collection.

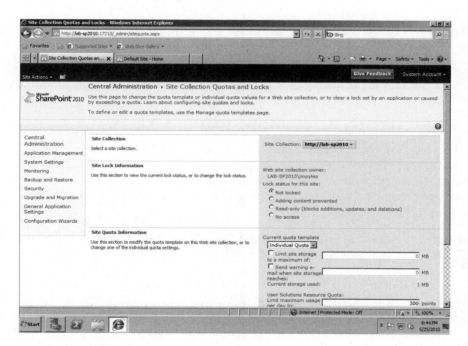

4. Under Site Quota Information, expand Current Quota Template, and select the new quota template to apply.

5. Click OK.

EXERCISE 10.9

Changing the Storage Limits for a Site Collection

1. Navigate to the Central Administration page and then click Application Management.

2. On the Applications Management page, under Site Collections, click Configure Quotas And Locks.

EXERCISE 10.9 *(continued)*

3. When the Site Collection Quotas And Locks page opens, under Site Collection, select the desired site collection in the Site Collection list.

4. Under Site Quota Information, verify that the Limit Site Storage To A Maximum check box is selected and type the desired value in megabytes in the available field.

5. To have an email warning sent to the site collection administrator when the storage limit has been nearly reached, select the Send Warning E-mail When Site Storage Reaches check box and type the desired value in megabytes in the available field.

6. Click OK.

You can perform the same task as in Exercise 10.9. Open Windows PowerShell as an administrator, type the following code at the prompt, and then press Enter, substituting your development values for the sample values:

```
Set-SPSite -Identity "<Site>" -MaxSize <Limit>
```

You've seen how to apply and modify a site collection quota template, but not how to create one. The next series of exercises will address this issue. To approach these tasks, you must be running either the standard or enterprise version of SharePoint 2010, you must have outgoing email configured, and the Disk Quota Warning timer job must be running.

See Chapter 3, "Configuring SharePoint Farm Environments," for more on configuring outgoing email.

Remember that quota templates apply to the total collection of information on a site collection, including the top-level site and all subsites. Quota templates can also be applied to a site collection containing a sandboxed solution, which is a restricted execution environment used to test how programs access and interact with specific resources. A sandboxed solution is contained and cannot affect the larger server farm environment.

See Chapter 11, "Deploying and Managing SharePoint Solutions," for more about sandbox environments.

Exercise 10.10 will show you step-by-step how to create a data storage quota template to be used in the creation of site collections. You will need to be a member of the Farm Administrators group to perform this task.

For sandboxed solutions, a point is a measure of resource usage relative to CPU cycles, RAM, page faults, or other consumed resources.

EXERCISE 10.10

Creating a New Site Quota Template

1. Navigate to the Central Administration page and then click Application Management.

2. On the Applications Management page, under Site Collections, click Specify Quota Templates.

3. On the Quota Templates page, under Template Name, click Create A New Quota Template.

4. In the New Template Name field, type the name of the template.

5. To base your new template on an existing quota template, expand the Template To Start From list and click the desired template.

6. Under Storage Limit Values, select the Limit Site Storage To A Maximum check box and then type the storage limit in megabytes in the available field.

7. To have the site collection administrator receive an email when the storage limit is close to being reached, select the Send Warning E-mail When Site Collection Storage Reaches check box and type a value in megabytes lower but close to the value you typed in the previous step in the available field.

8. To set limits on sandbox environments, under the Sandboxed Solutions With Code Limits section, type the daily usage points in the Limit Maximum Usage Per Day To field.

9. Type the daily usage warning limit in points in the Send Warning E-mail When Usage Per Day Reaches field.

10. Click OK.

To edit an existing quota template, follow the steps listed in Exercise 10.7. To delete a quota template, on the Specify Quota Templates page under Template Name, expand the Template To Modify list, select the desired template, and at the bottom of the page click Delete and then OK. Deleting a quota template will not affect any site collections previously made with the template.

If necessary, you can apply a *lock* to a site collection to prevent users from accessing the site collection. You can do this if the site collection has exceeded its storage limit and you want to prevent any additional data from being added. The lock can be removed once the data storage issue has been resolved.

You can apply a lock either using Central Administration or using Windows PowerShell. Exercise 10.11 shows you the procedure with Central Administration. You need to be a member of the Farm Administrators group to successfully complete this task.

EXERCISE 10.11

Creating a Site Collection Lock

1. Navigate to the Central Administration page and then click Application Management.

2. On the Applications Management page, under Site Collections, click Configure Quotas And Locks.

3. On the Site Collection Quotas And Locks page, select the desired site collection in the Site Collection list under Site Collection.

4. Under Site Lock Information, make one of the following selections:

    ▪ Select Not Locked to unlock a previously locked site collection.

    ▪ Select Adding Content Prevented to stop users from adding new data to the site collection, which allows users to still update and delete content.

    ▪ Select Read-Only (blocks additions, updates, and deletions) to completely stop users from affecting any data on the site collection.

    ▪ Select No Access to prevent users from having any access to the site collection whatsoever and have them receive an access-denied message when they attempt access.

5. Click OK.

If you select either Read-Only (blocks additions, updates, and deletions) or No Access, type a reason for this action in the Additional Lock Information field.

To perform the same task using Windows PowerShell, open Windows PowerShell as an administrator, type the following string at the command prompt, and then press Enter, substituting the sample values with your production values. For <state>, enter Unlock, NoAdditions, ReadOnly, or NoAccess depending on your requirements.

```
Set-SPSite -Identity "<SiteCollection>" -LockState "<State>"
```

General Site Management

As you know, a single site collection can contain any different sites and site types that have specific site administration requirements. In a large SharePoint server farm environment, there are bound to be a number of site collections that go unused and require attention.

My Site sites for SharePoint users need to be created and maintained, multi-tendency sites are created for atypical administrative and tenant purposes, and social communication sites such as wikis must be attended. This section of the chapter will focus on site-related content and exercises.

Even an unused website collection consumes SharePoint resources. Of course, you should have a procedure for determining when it's time to delete a site collection so you don't remove a resource that's just temporarily inactive but will be used in the future. Individual sites in a collection can be created and deleted by the site administrator, but you as the SharePoint administrator will have the overall responsibility for creating and deleting site collections.

If you determine that it's appropriate to delete a site collection and if you haven't been able to confirm this with the administrator who has been using the collection, you should back up the site collection prior to deleting it in the unlikely event that the collection was expected to remain in existence.

 See Chapter 12, "Backing Up and Restoring SharePoint," for more information.

Site collections can be set to be automatically deleted after they have remained unused for a certain period of time. The default time period for disuse is 90 days after site creation. You can set the automated deletion system to notify site collection owners that the site collection will be deleted anywhere from a minimum of 30 days to a maximum of 365 days. During this time period, you should be aware that the site is going to be deleted and make sure regular email notices are being sent to the primary and secondary (if in existence) site collection administrators.

Once the automation system deletes a site collection, it is gone forever, including all subsites and any and all data contained in the document libraries and lists.

Exercise 10.12 will show you the site collection deletion process. You must be a member of the Farm Administrators group to perform this task.

EXERCISE 10.12

Configuring Automated Site Collection Deletion

1. Navigate to the Central Administration page and then click Application Management.

2. On the Application Management page, under Site Collections, click Confirm Site Use And Deletion.

3. On the Site Use Confirmation And Deletion page, under Web Application, change the web application to the one containing the desired site collection.

4. Under Confirmation And Automatic Deletion Settings, select the Send E-mail Notification To Owners Of Unused Site Collection check box.

5. In the available field, type the number of days after site creation or after the last site usage is confirmed that you want email notifications to start being sent to the site collection owner and then specify whether the notices should be sent daily, weekly, or monthly.

6. To have the site automatically deleted if not confirmed, select the Automatically Delete The Site Collection If Use Is Not Confirmed check box and then type the number of notifications you want sent to the site collection owner prior to the site collection being deleted, with the default value being 28.

7. Click OK.

My Site Management

My Site websites are the personal sites provided to each SharePoint user, allowing them to construct and customize their own website environment. These sites are specifically oriented toward social networking and include a My Networks page for managing each person's colleagues, interests, and newsfeed settings. The My Content page lets users manage their own documents and photos, and the My Profile page provides an interface in which users can maintain social tags and notes.

A SharePoint administrator must create the User Profile service application and a designated administrator for the User Profile service application. The SharePoint administrator or a User Profile service application–designated administrator can then create the My Site websites, the Trusted My Site host locations, personalization site links, and links to Microsoft Office 2010 client applications.

  See Chapter 4 for more details on these tasks.

The tasks presented in this section address how to set up, configure, and delete My Sites. Exercise 10.13 gets you started with setting up My Sites websites. You should already have created the User Profile service and the My Site host location in the desired web application.

You must be a member of the Farm Administrators group or a service application administrator for the User Profile service application to be able to perform this task.

EXERCISE 10.13

Setting Up My Sites

1. On the Central Administration home page, click Manage Service Applications under Application Management.

2. On the Manage Service Applications page, click the name of the desired User Profile service.

3. On the Manage Profile Service page, under My Site Settings, click Setup My Sites.

4. On the My Site Settings page, under Preferred Search Settings, type the URL of the Search Center users will use in the Preferred Search Center field, such as http://mysitename/SearchCenter/pages/.

5. Select a search scope for finding people and documents.

6. Under My Site Host, enter the URL for the dedicated site collection hosting personal sites in the My Site Host Location, such as http://main_portal_site/, or accept the default URL.

7. Under Personal Site Location, enter the URL of the location where you want to create the personal sites such as http://main_portal_site/location/personal_sites/.

EXERCISE 10.13 *(continued)*

---

8. Under Site Naming Format, select the format you want to use to name new personal sites.

9. Under Language Options, select Allow Users To Choose The Language Of Their Personal Site if you want users to be able to determine in what language their My Site content will be displayed.

10. Under Read Permission Level, type the accounts for which you want to grant Read permissions for the personal site.

11. Under My Site E-Mail notifications, type the sender's name for all My Site email notifications in the Sender's Name field.

12. Click OK.

In step 6, if you change the default My Site host location, you will create a link to a new My Site host location, but you will not provision the My Site host at the new location. Changing the default settings for Personal Site Location and Site Naming Format will not affect any existing personal sites. Also, to make sure that any email notifications sent from My Sites aren't treated as junk mail by your Microsoft Exchange Server, add the IP address to the server hosting the My Site websites to the Save list in Exchange.

You can add links to trusted My Site host locations when you want to give your users access to My Site websites on more than one User Profile service application. You typically perform this task when you want to target specific users or groups based on particular organizational or business requirements. This task can be performed by the SharePoint administrator who is a member of the Farm Administrators group or by User Profile service application administrators. Exercise 10.14 will show you how to add a trusted My Site host location.

EXERCISE 10.14

Adding a Trusted My Site Host Location

1. On the Central Administration home page, click Manage Service Applications under Application Management.

2. On the Manage Service Applications page, on the Service Applications tab, select the desired User Profile Service.

3. On the Ribbon, click Manage.

EXERCISE 10.14 *(continued)*

4. On the Manage Profile Service page, under My Site Settings, click Configure Trusted Host Locations, as shown here.

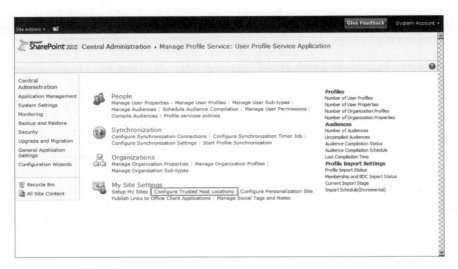

5. On the Trusted My Site Host Locations page, click New Link.

6. On the Add Trusted Host Location page, type the URL of the trusted personal site location in the URL field.

7. Type a description for the location in the Description field.

8. If you desire, type the usernames or group names for desired targeted audiences in the Target Audience field and then verify the names.

9. Click OK.

To delete a trusted host location, follow steps 1 through 4 in the previous exercise; then on the Trusted My Site Host Locations page, select the check box next to the trusted host location you want to delete and click Delete Link.

There is a great deal of interoperability between Office 2010 clients and SharePoint 2010. One item in the vast list of connections between the two Microsoft products is the ability to save an Office 2010 document to your My Site website in SharePoint. Once you have completed Exercise 10.15, when a SharePoint user chooses Save As to save an Office document, they will have the option to go into the Favorite Links area of the Save As dialog box and select their SharePoint My Site as a location to which to save the document. To successfully complete this task, you must be an administrator on the local server computer hosting the SharePoint Central Administration website.

EXERCISE 10.15

Adding a Link to Office 2010 Client Applications

1. On the Central Administration home page, click Manage Service Applications under Application Management.

2. On the Manage Service Applications page, click in the Type column next to the desired User Profile Service to select it.

3. On the Ribbon, click Manage.

4. On the Manage Profile Service page, click Publish Links To Office Client Applications under My Site Settings.

5. On the Published Links To Office Client Applications page, click New Link.

6. On the Add Published Link page, type the URL to the location where users will be able to publish their links in the URL field.

7. Type a description of the link in the Description field, which will appear in the Favorite Links area when a user employs Save As to save a document.

8. Select the target location the link represents, such as a document library.

9. To use the targeted audiences feature, type the user or group you want to add in the Target Audiences field; then verify the name, using semicolons to separate names if you type in more than one name.

10. Click OK.

To delete a link, follow steps 1 through 4 in the previous exercise; next, on the Published Linked To Office Client Applications page, select the check box next to the link you want to delete and then click Delete Link.

Multi-tenancy Sites Management

Multi-tenancy isn't one of the more intuitive SharePoint concepts to grasp. It refers to the ability to partition data of shared services or software in order to meet the needs of multiple tenants, as opposed to setting up separate hardware platforms or running multiple instances of the service. In other words, the service or application lives in more than one hosted environment. The individual site collections or customers consuming resources are called *tenants*.

Administrators belonging to the Farm Administrators group can host multiple tenants on the same server farm so they can centrally manage the deployment of services and features. A separate administrator role called the *tenant administrator* can then manage how these delegated features and services are made available for consumption by customer site collections.

Looking at it another way, a tenant or customer with a name of "number one" exists on Site Collection 1 on web application Alpha, while a tenant with a name of "number two" exists on Site Collection 2 on web application Beta. Services "owned" by the farm administrator can be leased to tenant administrators for use by customer sites. The farm administrator provides a Tenant Administration site within SharePoint for tenant administrators to use to manage leased resources for site collections. Site owners and administrators work with the tenant administrator to access and consume these resources.

Actually, each tenant administration site is deployed as its own site collection. Web applications that are providing hosting services would keep track of the tenants and isolate any one tenant's data from the rest of the tenants. A service, such as search, could be provided to both "number one" and "number two," but each customer would be unaware that the other was consuming the same resource from the same application. Further, "number one," when using the search service, would only be able to access content within their own site collection and would not be able to access the "number two" site collection data, even though, in essence, they are using the same service.

Each customer or site collection belongs to a particular site group. A site can belong to only one site group at a time, and a site cannot join a site group containing sites existing on a different web application. On the other hand, a site group can span more than one content database. Site group administration is managed only by Windows PowerShell, even though tenant management occurs within a web page GUI.

Although multiple site groups can consume the same resource at the web application level, the resource is partitioned, with each site group accessing only its own partition, which is how individual customer data is kept isolated.

Configuring Multi-tenancy Using Windows PowerShell

To configure multi-tenancy, you must open Windows PowerShell as an administrator and go through the following steps. Remember that all the values provided here are sample values. You must insert your production values in order for the scripts to be effective in your environment.

 A subscription is a GUID that is used to identify subscription members and any data associated with the subscriber. You determine which site collections belong to which tenancy using the membership identity found in the subscription.

1. To create a subscription and assign sites to it, type the following at the prompt and then press Enter:

   ```
   $sub = new-spsitesubscription
   ```

   The $sub object is a variable that contains the new spsitesubscription.

2. To pull the site collection or set of site collections you want to join to the site group, type the following at the prompt and then press Enter:

   ```
    get-spsite
   $site = get-spsite | where {$_.url -eq "http://test"}
   ```

The $site object is a variable that contains a site collection.

3. To add the site collection $site to the newly created site subscription $sub and then check to make sure it has been added correctly, type the following lines of code at the prompt, pressing Enter after each line:

```
set-spsite -identity $site -sitesubscription $sub
get-spsitesubscription
```

4. To create a Subscription Settings service application and proxy, you must first start the WSS Subscription Settings service and then actually create the service application and proxy. Type each line of the following code at the prompt and press Enter after each line:

```
$appPool  = New-SPIISWebServiceApplicationPool -Name SettingsServiceApppool
-Account domain\use
$sa = new-spsubscriptionsettingsserviceapplication
-Name SubscriptionSettingsServiceApplication -Databasename
SubscriptionSettingsServiceApplicationDB -applicationpool $appPool
$sap = new-SPSubscriptionSettingsSericeApplicationProxy -ServiceApplication
$sa
```

5. To create a tenant admin site for a site group, type each line of the following code at the prompt and press Enter after each line:

```
$sub = get-spsitesubscription -identity "http://server"
$tasite = new-spsite -url "http://test/sites/tenantadminsite1" -template
"tenantadminsite#0" -ownername domain\username -sitesubscription $sub
```

The task of creating a subscription and assigning sites assumes that the search service application has already been provisioned using Windows PowerShell. The list of subsequent steps shows you that procedure.

Configuring a Search Service Application for Hosted Sites

In Chapter 5, "Configuring Indexing and Search," you configured search as a set of post-installation tasks; however, in the current context, you may need to configure a search service application for hosted sites. You can perform this task using Windows PowerShell only. The following uses sample code in the PowerShell script. You will need to replace the same code with your production values.

1. Open Windows PowerShell as an administrator.

2. To create an application pool, type the following at the prompt and then press Enter, replacing the sample code with your production code:

```
$app = new-spserviceapplicationpool -name contososearch-apppool -account
domain\user
```

3. To create a search service application, type the following at the prompt and then press Enter, replacing the sample code with your production code and adding the -partitioned parameter after the -name parameter if you plan on having the application consumed in the hosted environment.

```
$searchapp = new-spenterprisesearchserviceapplication -name
ContosoSearchServiceApplication -applicationpool $app
```

4. To create a search service application proxy, type the following code at the prompt and then press Enter, replacing the sample code with your production code and adding the -partitioned parameter after the -name parameter if you plan on having the application consumed in the hosted environment:

```
$proxy = new-spenterprisesearchserviceapplicationproxy -name
Contososearchserviceapplicationproxy -Uri $searchapp.uri.absoluteURI
```

5. To provision the search administration component, type the following code at the prompt and then press Enter, replacing the sample code with your production code:

```
set-spenterprisesearchadministrationcomponent -searchapplication
$searchapp  -searchserviceinstance $si
```

6. To create a crawl topology, type the following at the prompt and then press Enter, replacing the sample code with your production code:

```
$ct = $searchapp | new-spenterprisesearchcrawltopology
```

7. To create a new crawl store, type the following code at the prompt and then press Enter, replacing the sample code with your production code:

```
$csid = $SearchApp.CrawlStores | select id
$CrawlStore = $SearchApp.CrawlStores.item($csid.id)
```

8. To create a new crawl component for the crawl topology, type the following at the prompt and press Enter, replacing the sample code with your production code:

```
$hname = hostname
new-spenterprisesearchcrawlcomponent -crawltopology $ct -crawldatabase
$Crawlstore -searchserviceinstance $hname
```

9. To set the new crawl topology as active, type the following code at the prompt and then press Enter, replacing the sample code with your production code:

```
$ct | set-spenterprisesearchcrawltopology -active
```

10. To create a new query topology, type the following at the prompt and then press Enter, replacing the sample code with your production code:

```
$qt = $searchapp | new-spenterprisesearchquerytopology -partitions 1
```

11. To create a variable for the query partition, type the following code at the prompt and then press Enter, replacing the sample code with your production code:

```
$p1 = ($qt | get-spenterprisesearchindexpartition)
```

12. To create a new query component, type the following at the prompt and then press Enter, replacing the sample code with your production code:

```
new-spenterprisesearchquerycomponent -indexpartition $p1 -querytopology $qt
-searchserviceinstance $si
```

13. To create a variable for the property store DB, type the following at the prompt and then press Enter, replacing the sample code with your production code:

```
$PSID = $SearchApp.PropertyStores | Select id
$PropDB = $SearchApp.PropertyStores.Item($PSID.id)
```

14. To set the query partition to use the property store DB, type the following at the prompt and then press Enter, replacing the sample code with your production code:

```
$p1 | set-spenterprisesearchindexpartition -PropertyDatabase $PropDB
```

15. To activate the query topology, type the following at the prompt and then press Enter, replacing the sample code with your production code:

```
$qt | Set-SPEnterpriseSearchQueryTopology -Active
```

You can verify that the search service application proxy is online by typing `$proxy.status` at the prompt and then pressing Enter after step 4. It should be online by default. To verify that the local search service instance has been started, type the following at the prompt and then press Enter:

```
$si = get-spenterprisesearchserviceinstance -local
$si.status
```

Creating and Activating Features and Hosting

Now that you have a feature installed in the farm and the search service application configured for a hosted environment, the feature is available to all sites in the farm and can now be activated, letting you manage the feature pages. This allows you to offer only the features available to a given site group through Windows PowerShell commands. The following set of steps is the end of the process of configuring multi-tenancy. Open Windows PowerShell as an administrator, and begin the following steps:

1. To create a feature set, type the following at the prompt and then press Enter, replacing the sample code with your production code:

```
$fs =New-SPFeatureSet
```

2. To add features to a feature set, type the following at the prompt and then press Enter, replacing the sample code with your production code:

```
$farm = Get-SPFarm
$feature1 =$farm.FeatureDefinitions | where{$_.ID -eq "02464c6a-9d07-4f30-ba04-e9035cf54392"}
Add-SPFeatureSetMember -Identity $fs -FeatureDefinition $feature1
```

3. To add a feature set to a subscription, type the following at the prompt and then press Enter, replacing the sample code with your production code:

```
Set-SPSiteSubscriptionConfig -Identity $sub -FeatureSet $fs
```

Administering the SharePoint Wiki

Although Wikipedia is probably the world's most famous wiki, wiki sites are ubiquitous on the Web and within the realm of business as a means to publish, contain, and organize information in an enterprise environment. A wiki allows collaboration and coauthoring of content in a single location and allows for the discussion and management of such data relative to team- and group-level projects. There are two methods of creating an *enterprise wiki* in SharePoint: using Central Administration and Windows PowerShell. Exercise 10.16 will show you the Central Administration procedure. You must be a member of the Farm Administrators group to successfully complete the task.

EXERCISE 10.16

Creating a Wiki Using Central Administration

1. On the Central Administration home page, click Create Site Collection under Application Management.

2. On the Create A Site Collection page, under Web Application use the drop-down list to select the web application where you want to create the wiki site.

3. Give the new wiki site a name in the Title field and a description in the Description field.

4. Under Web Site Address, select root (/) to create an enterprise wiki or /sites/ to create the wiki at a specific path and then add a site name after /sites/.

5. Under Template Selection, click the Publishing tab and then click Enterprise Wiki.

6. Under Primary Site Collection Administrator, type the name of the user you want to make the primary administrator for the wiki and then check the name.

7. Under Secondary Site Collection Administrator, type the name of the user you want to make the secondary administrator for the wiki, and then check the name.

8. If you want to use quotas to manage storage for the wiki site, click the desired template in the Select A Quota Template list under Quota Template.

10. Click OK.

Instead of creating the wiki as a site collection, you can also create it as a subsite to another site. On the site's main page, under Site Actions, click New Site and proceed to create the wiki site using the appropriate template and steps.

Creating a Wiki Using Windows PowerShell

As previously mentioned, you can also perform the same task using Windows PowerShell. The minimum permission requirement is to belong to the Add-SPShellAdmin group, which lets you add a user to the SharePoint_Shell_Access role for a specified database.

1. Open Windows PowerShell as an administrator.

2. To display all site templates, type the following at the prompt and then press Enter:

```
Get-SPWebTemplate
```

3. To create a variable containing the name of the enterprise wiki template, type the following at the prompt and then press Enter, replacing the sample code with your production code:

```
$wikitemp = Get-SPWebTemplate "ENTERWIKI#0"
```

4. To create the enterprise wiki site, type the following command at the prompt and then press Enter, replacing the sample code with your production code:

```
New-SPSite http://wikisite.com/CWiki -OwnerAlias <domain\user> -Template
$wikitempl
```

Web Content Management

Managing information in SharePoint can be considered one of its main functions, but this section of the chapter focuses on issues ranging from file types to web and other content management. Admittedly, this is something of a "catchall" section, but the ability of SharePoint to manage data and data types is vast, and documenting those capacities can cover a great deal of territory.

Managing File Types

Depending on your frame of reference, you may be used to dealing with file types such as DOCX, XLS, HTML, XML, and so on. In fact, SharePoint is capable of uploading, downloading, and managing a large number of file types within its framework including ADE, ASA, ASP, DLL, HTR, VBS, and so forth.

For security purposes, you may want to block specific file types from being saved or retrieved by any web application on a SharePoint server. Exercise 10.17 will show you the process. You must be a member of the Farm Administrators group for the web application to complete this task.

EXERCISE 10.17

Blocking File Types

1. On the Central Administration home page, click Security.

2. On the Security page, click Define Blocked File Types under General Security.

3. On the Blocked File Types page, click the Web Application list to select the desired web application, as shown here.

5. To block a specific file type, scroll to the bottom of the Type Each File Extension On A Separate Line text box, type the file extension you want to block, and then click OK.

6. To stop blocking a file type, select the file type from the available list, press the Delete key on your keyboard, and then click OK.

Administering Content Deployment

Content deployment is the process of moving content from one site collection to another, usually across two or more server farms. The most common purpose for content deployment is to move content from an authoring environment to a production environment. The authoring environment is kept separate from what your consumers experience so that information is not prematurely released or released in an erroneous form.

This section of the chapter shows you how to configure content deployment settings, how to manage deployment paths and jobs, how to manage quick deployment, and how to view content deployment jobs reports.

Content Deployment Setting Management

Content deployment settings must be configured for both the source and destination site collections. Another way of looking at it is that a site collection must be set up for both incoming and outgoing content deployment jobs. This is performed on the Central Administration site for the source and destination site collections in the relevant server farms. Once done, you can use the Content Deployment Settings page to accept or reject incoming content jobs for your entire server farm. You can also delegate the responsibility for receiving incoming jobs and sending outgoing jobs to specific servers in the farm.

There are three typical roles for farms in terms of content deployment:

- Authoring farm: This is the source of the content to be exported and must be configured for outgoing (export) settings.

- Staging farm: This is a management area for incoming and outgoing content and must be configured for incoming (import) and outgoing (export) settings.

- Production farm: This is the destination for content and must be configured for incoming (import) settings.

Any particular piece of content travels in only one direction, from source to destination. A staging area can exist if you have numerous authoring and production platforms so that all content passes through a single launching environment, but once content is deployed from an authoring site, it does not return.

Exercise 10.18 will show you how to configure content deployment settings. You will need to be a member of the Farm Administrators group to perform the following exercises. Before you begin, be aware that both the export server and the import server must host an instance of the Central Administration website.

EXERCISE 10.18

Configuring Content Deployment Settings

1. On the Central Administration home page, click General Application Settings.

2. On the General Application Settings page, click Configure Content Deployment under Content Deployment, as shown here.

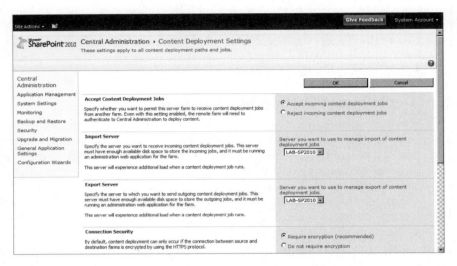

3. On the Content Deployment Settings page, under Accept Content Deployment Jobs, to configure the web application for importing content, select Accept Incoming Content Deployment Jobs, which is the typical setting for a production environment.

4. To configure the web application for exporting content, select Reject Incoming Content Deployment Jobs, which is the typical setting for an authoring environment.

5. To select a server in your farm to receive incoming content, under Import Server, use the Server You Want To Use To Manage Import Content Deployment Jobs menu to select the desired server, which is the typical setting for a production environment.

6. To select a server in your farm to send deployment jobs, under Export Server, use the Server You Want To Use To Manage Export Of Content Deployment Jobs menu to select the desired server, which is the typical setting for an authoring environment.

7. Under Connection Security, if you require HTTPS for security reasons, select Require Encryption (Recommended), which also requires that you specify a destination Central Administration website that begins with https:// for the content deployment path. If you do not require encryption and want to use HTTP, select Do Not Require Encryption.

8. Under Temporary Files, type the path to the temporary file that both import and/or export servers will use for storage of temporary files, which typically is on the local system drive.

9. Under Reporting, in the Number Of Reports To Retain For Each Job field, type the number of reports you want to keep for each deployment job originating at your farm.

10. Click OK.

Content Deployment Paths and Job Management

The next step in the process of administering content deployment is to create a path between the source and destination site collections. The connection is used to publish content from the source to destination. These site collections can be in the same server farm or in two different server farms.

To create a destination site collection for content deployment, you must select the Select Template Later option when you create the site. This is not the same thing as using the Blank Site template. Another option is to use Windows PowerShell and create the destination site collection using New-SPSite.

A content deployment job is used to schedule the actual moving of content across the content deployment path from source to destination. You can customize the scheduling and frequency of content deployment to meet your publishing requirements. Once the content is deployed, it should not be changed on the destination site. This may cause content deployment jobs to fail. Content must be changed or added at the source site.

A content deployment job can be set up to copy the entire contents of the source site collection or only a subset of sites within the collection. You can also choose to deploy only new, changed, or deleted content or to deploy all content. You can use Quick Deploy to deploy content outside the usual schedule.

The initial required tasks are to create a new content deployment path and a new content deployment job. Exercise 10.19 covers the steps for creating a deployment path. A prerequisite for this task is that Central Administration on the destination server must have been configured to accept incoming content deployment jobs. You must also be a member of the Farm Administrators group on the Central Administration server.

Creating a New Content Deployment Path

1. On the Central Administration home page, click General Application Settings, and then under Content Deployment, click Configure Content Deployment Paths And Jobs.

2. On the Manage Content Deployment Paths And Jobs page, click New Path.

3. On the Create Content Deployment Path page, type the name for the new path in the Type The Name Of This Path Field, as shown here.

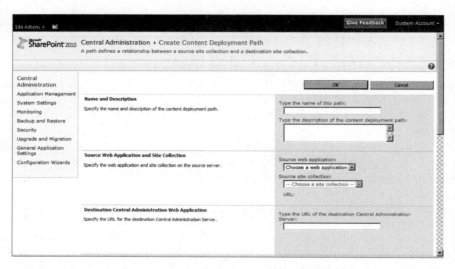

4. Type a description for the path in the Type A Description Of The Content Deployment Path field.

5. Under Source Web Application And Site Collection, use the Source Web Application menu to select the desired web application.

6. Use the Source Site Collection menu to select the desired source site collection.

7. After the source location is displayed in URL, under Destination Central Administration Web Application, type the URL of the destination Central Administration server in the Type The URL Of The Destination Central Administration Server field, using either http:// or https:// depending on which option you selected in Exercise 10.18.

8. Under Authentication Information, select either Use Integrated Windows Authentication to encrypt credentials sent from the source to destination or Use Basic Authentication for no encryption of credentials.

9. Type the username and password for the account to be used to connect to the destination server and then click Connect.

10. Verify that the Connection Succeeded message appears and that the list of relevant destination web applications and site collections appears in the Destination Web Application and site collection section; then select the desired destination web application.

11. Select the desired site collection in the Destination Site Collection list.

12. Under User Names, if you want the usernames associated with the content to be included when the path issued, select the Deploy User Names check box.

13. Under Security Information, in the Security Information In The Content Deployment list, select All, which is the default, to deploy all security information associated with the content when it is deployed, select Role Definitions Only to send only role definitions when content is deployed, or select None to send no security information during deployment.

14. Click OK.

If you want to deploy content to another site collection within the same web application, you must make sure that the source and destination site collections are in separate content databases.

You can perform the identical task using Windows PowerShell. Open PowerShell as an administrator, type the following code at the prompt, and then press Enter after each line in the command, replacing the sample code with your production code:

```
$credentials=Get-Credential
New-SPContentDeploymentPath -Name <Name of the new deployment path>
-SourceSPWebApplication <GUID, URL or a valid SPWebApplication object
of the source Web application> -SourceSPSite <GUID, URL or a valid
SPSite object of the source site> -DestinationCentralAdministrationURL
<URL of the Central Administration Web site on the destination server>
-DestinationSPWebApplication <GUID, URL or a valid SPWebApplication object
of the destination Web application> -DestinationSPSite <GUID, URL or a valid
SPSite object of the destination site> -PathAccount $credentials
```

Creating a new content deployment job lets you schedule the job to run on a certain frequency, from one time only to once every 15 minutes. You can also run a job manually. A job schedule can be created using either Central Administration or Windows PowerShell. Exercise 10.20 will show you the Central Administration method. You must be a member of the Farm Administrators group on the server running Central Administration to successfully complete this task.

EXERCISE 10.20

Creating a New Content Deployment Job

1. On the Central Administration home page, click General Application Settings, and then click Configure Content Deployment Paths And Jobs.

2. On the Manage Content Deployment Paths And Jobs page, click New Job.

EXERCISE 10.20 *(continued)*

3. On the Create Content Deployment Job page, use the Name and Description fields to give the new job a name and description.

4. Under Path, use the Select A Content Deployment Path menu to select the desired deployment path.

5. Under SQL Snapshots, select either Do Not Use SQL Snapshots or Automatically Create And Manage Snapshots For Content Deployment.

 This option is available only if Microsoft SQL Server 2008 Enterprise edition is available and being used.

6. Under Scope, either select Entire Site Collection to deploy the content of the whole site collection or select Specific Sites Within The Collection and then click Select Sites to specify which sites in the collection should be used for the deployment.

7. Under Frequency, to specify a schedule, select the Run This Job On The Following Schedule check box, and then select the desired frequency.

8. Under Notification, to receive an email notification when the job succeeds, select the Send E-mail When The Content Deployment Job Succeeds check box.

9. To receive an email notification if a job fails, select the Send E-mail If The Content Deployment Job Fails check box.

10. In the Type E-mail Addresses field, type the email address or addresses to which you want the notifications sent.

11. Click OK.

The Specific Sites With The Collection option in step 6 creates a scoped content deployment job that assumes all content in the site hierarchy above the specified scope has previously been deployed to the destination site collection. Do not select this option for a content deployment job if you have not already deployed the content above the specified level in the content hierarchy.

You can perform the same task using Windows PowerShell. Open PowerShell as an administrator, type the following code, and then press Enter, replacing the sample code with your production code:

```
New-SPContentDeploymentJob -Name   <Name of the new deployment job>
-SPContentDeploymentPath   <GUID, name or a valid SPContentDeploymentPath
object of the path to be used by the job>
```

Manually Running a Content Deployment Job

To manually run a job, navigate to the Manage Content Deployment Paths And Jobs page, and on the menu for the desired job, click Run Now. You will see the status for the job displayed in the Status column.

To manually run a job using Windows PowerShell, open PowerShell as an administrator, type the following code, and then press Enter, replacing the sample code with your production code:

```
Start-SPContentDeploymentJob -Identity   <GUID, name or a valid
SPContentDeploymentJob object of the job to be started>
```

Editing a Content Deployment Path

To edit a content deployment path in Central Administration, navigate to the Manage Content Deployment Paths And Jobs page and, on the menu for the path, click Edit. Edit the desired information and then click OK.

To perform the same task using Windows PowerShell, open PowerShell as an administrator, type the following code at the prompt, and then press Enter, replacing the sample code for your production code:

```
Set-SPContentDeploymentPath -Identity   <GUID, name or a valid
SPContentDeploymentPath object of the path to be changed>
```

Disabling or Deleting a Content Deployment Path

To perform this task, navigate to the Manage Content Deployment Paths And Jobs page and click the menu for the desired path. To delete the path, click Delete; when prompted, click OK. To disable the path, click Disable in the menu.

To delete a content deployment path using Windows PowerShell, open PowerShell as an administrator, type the following code at the prompt, and then press Enter, replacing the sample code with your production code:

```
Remove-SPContentDeploymentPath -Identity   <GUID, name or a valid
SPContentDeploymentPath object of the path to be deleted>
```

Once you disable or delete a path, all the deployment jobs associated with that path will also be deleted.

Editing a Content Deployment Job

This is practically the same task as editing a path. Navigate to the Manage Content Deployment Paths And Jobs page. On the menu for the desired job, click Edit and then edit the job schedule.

To do the same thing using Windows PowerShell, open PowerShell as an administrator, type the following code at the prompt, and then press Enter, replacing the sample code with your production code:

```
Set-SPContentDeploymentJob -Identity   <GUID, name or a valid
SPContentDeploymentJob object of the job to be changed>
```

Testing, Canceling, and Deleting a Content Deployment Job

You may want to test a scheduled job to verify that it works. To do so in Central Administration, navigate to the Manage Content Deployment Paths And Jobs page. On the menu for the desired job, click Test Job and then review the job's status in the Status column. There is no Windows PowerShell equivalent for the Central Administration task.

Canceling a job is also another task that can be performed only in Central Administration. On the Manage Content Deployment Paths And Jobs page, click Cancel on the menu for the job and then verify that the job was canceled in the Status column.

You can delete a job using the same menu for the job as you used to test and cancel a job but by selecting Delete. In Windows PowerShell, to delete a job, open PowerShell as an administrator, type the following code, and then press Enter, replacing the sample code with your production code:

```
Remove-SPContentDeploymentJob -Identity   <GUID, name or a valid
SPContentDeploymentJob object of the job to be deleted>
```

Quick Deploy Job Management

As previously mentioned, users can employ the Quick Deploy job to rapidly deploy web page content without going through the usual job scheduling process. You, as the administrator, must enable the Publishing feature at the site collection level to make this process available to users, and users must be members of the Quick Deploy user group to access the feature.

Like any other job, a Quick Deploy job requires a content deployment path. Although a Quick Deploy job is automatically created when you create a new content deployment path, the job itself isn't active until you, or anyone in the Farm Administrators group, enables Quick Deploy jobs for the path. Afterward, you can change the settings for Quick Deploy jobs, adjusting the schedule and notification parameters. Quick Deploy jobs aren't typically manual. By default, Quick Deploy jobs run every 15 minutes after the user clicks the Quick Deploy button on the Publish tab for the web page. Only the farm administrator can manually run a Quick Deploy job using the Manage Content Deployment Paths And Jobs page in Central Administration. Quick Deploy job content can also be deployed along with a regularly scheduled job deployment.

As an administrator, you won't be running any deployment jobs as part of your regular duties, but you may be asked to modify or manually deploy such a job. Exercise 10.21 shows you how to modify Quick Deploy job settings. To perform this task, you must be a member of the Farm Administrators group and a member of the Site Collection Administrators group on the source site collection.

EXERCISE 10.21

Modifying Quick Deploy Job Settings

1. On the Central Administration home page, click General Application Settings and then click Configure Content Deployment Paths And Jobs.

2. On the Manage Content Deployment Paths And Jobs page, click Quick Deploy Settings on the menu for the path you want to edit.

3. On the Quick Deploy Jobs settings page, select the Allow Quick Deploy Jobs Along This Path check box under Allow Quick Deploy Jobs.

4. Under SQL Snapshots, select either Do Not Use SQL Snapshots or Automatically Create And Manage Snapshots For Content Deployment.

5. Under Quick Deploy Schedule, select the desired frequency for how often to run Quick Deploy jobs.

6. Under Users, click Specify Quick Deploy Users to add the users who require the ability to run such jobs.

7. Under Notification, select the Send E-mail When The Content Deployment Job Succeeds check box and/or the Send E-mail If The Content Deployment Job Fails check box depending on the notifications you want sent.

8. Enter one or more email addresses in the Type E-mail Addresses field to specify who will receive the email notifications.

To manually start a Quick Deploy job, in Central Administration under General Application Settings, click Configure Content Deployment Paths And Jobs. Then, on the resulting page, on the menu for the desired Quick Deploy job, click Run Now. You can then view the job's status in the Status column.

You can test a Quick Deploy job by clicking Test Job in the same menu, and you can cancel a job by clicking Cancel in the menu.

Viewing Content Deployment Jobs and Reports

Every time a content deployment job runs, a report on the job status and details is generated and logged as a record for that job. The record contains information such as the name, description, and path for the job, as well as the status of the run; errors and warnings; source and destination URLs; start, end, and deployment times; and compressed content size. As an administrator, you can check deployment of any specific content, see the current content deployment job report, and review the content deployment job history or report. Exercise 10.22 will show you how to check the record for the deployment of specific content. You must be a member of the Farm Administrators group to successfully complete this task.

Viewing Deployment of Specific Content

1. On the Central Administration home page, click General Application Settings.

2. On the General Application Settings page, click Check Deployment Of Specific Content under Content Deployment.

3. On the Content Deployment Object Status page, type the URL of the specific content for which you want to view in the URL field.

4. Click Check Status.

5. The requested information appears in the Source Object Details And Destination Object Details areas of the page.

Viewing the current content deployment job report is almost the same task but not quite. Exercise 10.23 shows you the steps. You must be a member of the Farm Administrators group to complete this exercise.

Viewing the Current Content Deployment Job Report

1. On the Central Administration main page, click General Application Settings and then click Configure Content Deployment Paths And Jobs.

2. On the Manage Content Deployment Paths And Jobs page, for the list of jobs in the Status column, click the item for the job you want to view the report.

3. If only Failed is present in the column, click Failed.

4. When the Content Deployment Report page opens, review the information presented.

Exercise 10.24 shows you how to view the job history and job report for content deployment. You require the same qualifications as the previous two exercises.

Viewing the Job History and Job Report for Content Deployment

1. To view a job history or job report for a content deployment job, navigate to the Manage Content Deployment Paths And Jobs page; in the list of jobs, click the desired job to open the menu.

2. In the menu for the desired job, click View History to open the Job History page.

3. On the Job History page, if you want to review a report for a specific job, on the Job History list in the Status column, click the desired item for the job run, and then review the data on the Content Deployment Report page.

4. If you want to review the job history to view a different report, click View Job History under Quick Links.

Managing Web Content

In addition to web page content management, SharePoint provides a number of tools to manage all the stored content and documents managed by SharePoint users. This section of the chapter discusses managing document conversions and variations.

Sometimes how a document is formatted isn't suitable for a desired use. SharePoint supports installing *document converters* that let users migrate documents from one format to another, either through a UI or through an automated process such as a custom workflow, while preserving the source content. The Document Conversion Launcher service in SharePoint balances the load of server requests for conversions by using scheduling. You must configure and start the Document Conversion Load Balancer service before you can configure the Document Conversions Launcher service.

The first task is to enable the Document Conversion Launcher or Load Balancer service. Exercise 10.25 shows you how this is done in Central Administration. You must be a member of the Farm Administrators group to successfully complete these instructions.

EXERCISE 10.25

Enabling the Document Conversion Launcher or Load Balancer Services

1. On the Central Administration main page, click Manage Services On Server under Systems Settings.

2. On the Services On Server page, for either Document Conversion Launcher Service or Document Conversion Load Balancer Service, click Start in the Action column.

3. When you click Start For The Document Conversion Load Balancer Service and the service is started, click the service name to open it.

4. When you click Start for the Document Conversion Launcher Service and the service is started, click the service name to open it.

5. On the Launcher Service Settings page, under Select Server, either accept the server selection or click Change Server on the server menu; then, on the Select Server page, click the name of the desired server, as shown here.

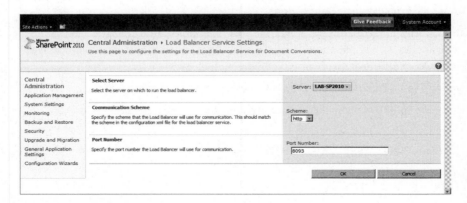

EXERCISE 10.25 *(continued)*

6. Under Load Balancer, select the load balancer server you want to use with the launcher.

7. Under Port Number, type the port number you want the launcher to use, making sure it's a port number not used by any other service on the server and is open in your firewall.

8. Click OK to start the launcher service.

You can use the procedure in Exercise 10.25 to start the Document Conversion Launcher service and the Load Balancer Service in two separate actions. Once both services are started, you can modify the settings associated with each of them.

To modify the settings for the Document Conversion Launcher Service, in Central Administration under System Settings, click Manage Services On Server and then, on the Services On Server page, click Document Conversion Launcher Service. Then adjust the desired settings under Select Server, Load Balancer, and Port Number as you did previously and click OK.

To modify the settings for the Document Load Balancer Service, navigate to the Services On Server page again and click Document Conversion Load Balancer Service. Then select the desired server; under Communication Scheme, select the communications scheme for the load balancer such as HTTP. Then type in the port number and click OK to finish.

Once the appropriate services have been started and configured, you need to enable and configure document converters for a web application, enabling the document converters to be used by all site collections contained within the web application. Exercise 10.26 tells you how to accomplish this task. You must be a member of the Farm Administrators group.

EXERCISE 10.26

Enabling Document Converters on a Web Application

1. On the Central Administration main page, click General Application Settings.

2. On the General Applications Settings page, click Configure Document Conversions under External Service Connections.

3. On the Configure Document Conversion page, under Web Application, either accept the selected web application or, on the Web Application menu, click Change Web Application and click the desired web application to select it.

4. Under Enable Document Conversion, click Yes to enable this feature.

5. Under Load Balancer Server, select the desired server in the Load Balancer server menu.

6. Under Conversion Schedule, click Minutes, Hourly, or Daily to configure the frequency at which conversion occurs.

EXERCISE 10.26 *(continued)*

7. Under Converter Settings, select one of the following depending on your requirements:

   - Customize "From InfoPath Form to Web Page" (XML into HTML)

   - Customize "From Word Document to Web Page" (DOCX into HTML)

   - Customize "From Word Document with Macros to Web Page" (DOCM into HTML)

   - Customize "From XML to Web Page" (XML into HTML)

8. When the Document Converter Settings page appears, under Converter Settings, perform any of the following actions:

   - Clear the Make This Document Converter Available For All Document Libraries On The Server check box to disable this service, or leave it selected by default.

   - Type the desired value in the Time-Out Length (Seconds) field to set the amount of time until a document conversion times out, or leave the default value of 300.

   - Type the desired value in the Maximum Retries field to set the number of times the conversion retires after time out, or accept the default value of 3.

   - Type the desired value in the Maximum File Size (in KB) field to set the max size of a file the converter will attempt to manage or leave the field blank.

9. Click OK.

10. Click OK on the Configure Document Conversion page.

Now that you've set up document conversion, you can also enable and configure the variations feature for web content management, which makes content available to specific audiences on different sites by copying content from a source variation site to one or more target variation sites. You often do this when users require content to be delivered in a specific language. If people who need content in Spanish, for example, go to the root site written in English, they are redirected to a target variation site where the content is presented to them in the required language.

You can use the variationsfixuptool operation to analyze, report, and fix potential problems in the variation feature and to investigate and report how many variation jobs are running for a specific site collection. You must belong to the local Administrators group on the server.

1. On the server machine hosting SharePoint 2010, open a command-line window and navigate to the directory %COMMONPROGRAMFILES%\Microsoft shared\Web server extensions\14\Bin.

2. Type the following command at the prompt and then press Enter, replacing the sample values with your production values:

   ```
   stsadm -o variationsfixuptool -url  <source variation site URL>
   ```
   Available switches to use with this command include **-recurse**, **-label**, **-fix**, **-scan**, **-spawn**, and **-showrunningjobs**.

🌐 **Real World Scenario**

Managing Site Collections for Content Deployment

You are a SharePoint administrator for the Acme Development Company. You have been tasked with enabling site collections on a web application with web content deployment and variations management for the publishing department.

You previously created a web application for this department and deployed a site collection for their use, setting up their site collection to have a portal site as a gateway. You also created a documents repository connection for the publishing department so that contributors on other site collections can send their documents to the publishing department's site collection. When creating the connection, you specified the web application from which documents are sent and the web application containing the repository used by the publishing department.

The publishing department has requested that you do not limit the amount of content that can be stored in their site collection by setting quotas and locks.

Now you go on to configure content deployment settings in Central Administration. Since the publishing department site collection will be both receiving content from outside sources and deploying that content to the appropriate destinations, you configure content deployment for both import and export functions. You also enable content conversion so the publishing department can manage web content pages and so that they can convert web documents to different formats.

Summary

In this chapter, you learned the essential requirements for site collection administration, including the following:

- Creating, modifying, and deleting site collections
- Managing site collection quotas and locks to limit the amount of data that can be stored in a site collection
- My Site management including the enabling of My Sites and allowing My Site users to configure personalization and social networking settings
- Multi-tenancy sites management including creating the ability to partition data of shared services or software to meet the needs of multiple tenants
- Administering wikis for multiple team documentation management

- Managing file types including disabling the ability for specific file format types to be saved in SharePoint
- Administering content deployment so that users can deploy web content from an authoring platform into production
- Managing web content so that website content can be converted to different formats and deployed to variation target sites

Exam Essentials

Understanding the Various Tasks Associated with Managing Site Collections   Understand the numerous elements associated with creating, modifying, and deleting site collections; configuring quotas and locks to manage the amount of data stored in site collections; and administering social network features such as My Sites and enterprise wikis.

Understand the Activities Related to Web Content Management   Comprehend the various functions in administering web content including managing file types, administering content deployment, and enabling document conversion.

Review Questions

1. You are a SharePoint administrator for your company, and you are in the processing of planning and organizing site collections in your server farm. You are having a high-level planning session with your staff regarding site collections. In the session, you impart a number of basic points about site collections. Of the following options, which are true about site collections? (Choose all that apply.)

   A. All site collections must be created within a web application.

   B. You can create a site collection at the root (/) directory.

   C. You can create a site collection at the /collection/ directory.

   D. You can create a site collection using either Central Administration or Windows PowerShell.

2. You are a SharePoint administrator for your company. You are in the process of planning site collections in your SharePoint environment, and you want to create a connection from a site collection to a portal site so that site collection users can navigate quickly to and from the portal site. Of the following options, what are true about configuring the connection? (Choose all that apply.)

   A. You must be on the site from which you want to connect to the portal site.

   B. You must be on the portal site to which you want connect to the site collection.

   C. You must be at least a member of the site collection administrators group.

   D. You must be at least a member of the Farm Administrators group.

3. You are a SharePoint administrator for your company, and you have created a document repository site collection to centrally manage all documentation with your environment. You must create connections that will allow users on other site collections to send documentation to the repository site collection. Of the following, what is true about performing this task? (Choose all that apply.)

   A. You must configure the connection path to a specific site collection.

   B. You must configure the connection path to a specific web application containing site collections from which you want to send documents.

   C. You must configure the connection path to a specific web application containing the site collections to which you want to send documents.

   D. You must configure the connection path to the destination repository or records center to which documents will be sent.

4. You are a SharePoint administrator for your company, and you are in the process of planning your site collection strategy for your environment. You have been tasked with setting data storage limits on all site collections to conserve resources. To accomplish this, you will be using quotas and locks. In the training session you are giving to your staff, what do you say is true about quotas? (Choose all that apply.)

    A. Quotas configurations can be saved as templates.

    B. You can use the same quota template to create multiple site collections.

    C. When you modify the values of a quota template, the storage limits of all site collections previously created with the template are automatically changed.

    D. If site collection versioning is enabled, the values of the quota template used for site collection creation apply to all versions of the site collection.

5. You are a SharePoint administrator for your company, and you are in the process of planning your site collection strategy for your environment. You have been tasked with setting data storage limits on all site collections to conserve resources. To accomplish this, you will be using quotas and locks. In the training session you are giving to your staff, what do you say is true about quotas? (Choose all that apply.)

    A. A quota template will send an email notification to the relevant site administrator when the site has reached its data storage limit.

    B. Quota limits can be set at the web application level as well as for individual site collections.

    C. When configuring a quota template, you can specify who should receive email notifications regarding when storage limits are about to be reached.

    D. You can set email notifications to be sent when storage capacity has reached any value.

6. You are a SharePoint administrator for your company, and you are in the process of planning your site collection strategy for your environment. You have been tasked with setting data storage limits on all site collections to conserve resources. To accomplish this, you will be using quotas and locks. In the training session you are giving to your staff, what do you say is true about locks? (Choose all that apply.)

    A. Locks are used to restrict user access to a SharePoint site collection when the storage limit has been approached or reached.

    B. You can make sure an email is sent to any responsible party when a site collection lock has been activated.

    C. You can set the lock to different levels of access restriction.

    D. Once a lock is activated, it can be unlocked only when the site collection administrator or other responsible party reduces the level of data storage on the site collection below the threshold.

7. You are a SharePoint administrator for your company, and you are currently devising your plan for deleting unused site collections. You know that a site collection can appear to be unused but still needs to continue to exist. Best-practice states that you should contact the administrator for a site collection when the collection appears unused, but sometimes site collection administrators cannot be reached. In the planning session you are conducting with your staff, what do you say is true about the process of deleting apparently unused site collections? (Choose all that apply.)

A. By default, unused site collections are automatically deleted 90 days after creation or after last apparent use.

B. If a site collection appears unused for a long period of time and you cannot reach the site collection administrator before deleting the site collection, you should back up the site collection.

C. All site collection deletions must be performed manually to prevent an automated system from inadvertently deleting a site collection that is in use.

D. You can set site collection deletion in both Central Administration and Windows PowerShell.

8. You are a SharePoint administrator for your company, and you are currently conducting a planning meeting with your staff for My Sites deployment in your environment. This is a high-level review of My Sites. Which of the following statements you make about My Sites is true? (Choose all that apply.)

A. The My Networks page in My Sites is used to manage a person's social networking including their Twitter, Facebook, and newsfeed settings.

B. The My Content page lets users manage their own documents and photos.

C. The My Profile Page provides users an interface for maintaining their social tags and notes.

D. The My People page lets users manage their colleagues and contacts.

9. You are a SharePoint administrator for your company, and you are conducting a planning meeting with your staff for My Sites deployment in your environment and verifying that all prerequisite tasks have been performed before deploying My Sites. Of the following, which are tasks that must be performed before setting up My Sites? (Choose all that apply.)

A. You must create the User Profile service application.

B. You must assign a designated administrator for the User Profile service application.

C. You must create a trusted My Site host location.

D. You must assign a designated administrator for the trusted My Site host location.

10. You are a SharePoint administrator for your company, and you are currently deploying My Sites in your environment. As you go through the setup process, you make changes to the default configuration settings. Of the following, what are some of the considerations when changing the default My Site settings? (Choose all that apply.)

    A. When you change the default My Site host location, you create a link to the new location and provision the My Site host at that location.

    B. When you change the default settings for Personal Site Location and Site Naming Format, you do not affect any existing personal sites.

    C. Email notifications sent by My Sites may be treated as junk mail by the Microsoft Exchange Server unless you add the IP address of the server hosting My Site to the save list in Exchange.

    D. You can only link a trusted My Site Host location to one User Profile service application at a time.

11. You are a SharePoint administrator for your company, and you are currently deploying My Sites in your environment. You want to give your My Site users the ability to interoperate Office 2010 clients with their My Sites. As you review your plan for this task, of the following, what do you find is true about Office 2010 and My Site interoperability? (Choose all that apply.)

    A. Once the task is completed, when a My Site user clicks Save As in an Office 2010 application, they are presented an option to save the document to their My Site location.

    B. When a My Site user clicks Save As in an Office 2010 document, the link to save the document to their My Site location appears in Favorite Links.

    C. When a My Site user tries to save an Office 2010 document to their My Site location, they can save it in a target location such as `Document Library` if you have configured that option.

    D. To successfully complete the configuration task, you must belong to the Farm Administrators group.

12. You are a SharePoint administrator for your company, and you are currently conducting a high-level planning meetings prior to configuring multi-tenancy sites in your environment. Multi-tenancy is poorly understood by your staff but is generally known to be the ability to partition data of shared services or software to meet the needs of multiple clients without having to set up separate hardware platforms or running multiple instances of services. Of the following, what do you say is true about multi-tenancy? (Choose all that apply.)

    A. Administrators belonging to the Farm Administrators group can host multiple tenants on the same server farm.

    B. A separate administrator role called the *tenant administrator* can manage how delegated services and features are made available.

    C. Two or more tenants consuming the same service are aware of each other accessing the service.

    D. Each tenant administration site is deployed as its own site collection.

13. You are a SharePoint administrator for your company, and you've been tasked with deploying an enterprise wiki for your environment. In the planning session you conduct with your staff prior to deploying the wiki, what do you say is true about SharePoint Enterprise wikis? (Choose all that apply.)

    A. You can deploy the wiki using either Central Administration or Windows PowerShell.

    B. Wikis can be created either as a site collection or as a subsite in an existing site collection.

    C. You must be a member of the Farm Administrators group to create an enterprise wiki.

    D. When creating the wiki from a template in Central Administration, you click the Collaboration tab to locate the enterprise wiki template.

14. You are a SharePoint administrator for your company, and you've been tasked with blocking selected file types in SharePoint. You have been provided with a list of the restricted document formats and proceed to the blocking task. As you explain the task to your staff, of the following, what do you say is true about blocking file types? (Choose all that apply.)

    A. You must be a member of the Farm Administrators group to accomplish this task.

    B. You can perform this task in both Central Administration and Windows PowerShell.

    C. To add a file to the blocked list, you must select the file extension the available list in Central Administration and then click Add.

    D. When a file type is blocked, it cannot be saved or retrieved by any web application on the SharePoint server.

15. You are a SharePoint administrator for your company, and you have just been tasked with configuring content deployment settings for your environment. Content deployment allows web content to be created in one source location and deployed to destination locations. To do this, several elements must be configured. In the planning session with your staff, of the following, what do you say is true about server farm roles for content deployment? (Choose all that apply.)

    A. The authoring farm role is the source of the web content and needs to be set to export content.

    B. The planning farm role is the review platform for web content and needs to be set to import content from the authoring farm role.

    C. The production farm role is the destination for the content and must be configured to import content.

    D. The staging farm role is the management area for incoming and outgoing content and must be set to import and export.

16. You are a SharePoint administrator for your company, and you have just been tasked with configuring content deployment settings for your environment. You have already configured the content deployment settings and must next set up content deployment paths and job management. In reviewing your task plan for configuring content deployment paths, what do you find is true about content deployment paths? (Choose all that apply.)

    A. To create a source site collection for the path, you must select the Select Template Later option for the site collection template.

    B. To create a destination site collection for the path, you must select the Select Template Later option for the site collection template.

    C. To create any site for the path, you must select the Blank Site template.

    D. You can perform this task using both Central Administration and Windows PowerShell.

17. You are a SharePoint administrator for your company, and you have just been tasked with configuring content deployment settings for your environment. You have already configured the content deployment settings and must next set up content deployment paths and job management. In reviewing your task plan for content deployment jobs, what do you find true about configuring deployment job scheduling? (Choose all that apply.)

    A. You can choose to deploy only new web content.

    B. You can choose to deploy only changed web content.

    C. You can choose to deploy only deleted web content.

    D. You can only deploy all web content.

18. You are a SharePoint administrator for your company, and you have just been tasked with configuring content deployment settings for your environment. You have already configured the content deployment settings and must next set up content deployment paths and job management. Part of this process includes configuring Quick Deploy jobs. Of the following, what do you find is true about Quick Deploy jobs? (Choose all that apply.)

    A. Quick Deploy jobs are used to deploy web content outside of the usual content deployment schedule.

    B. SharePoint users must belong to the Quick Deploy users group to be able to use this content deployment method.

    C. When you create a new user content deployment path, a Quick Deploy job is automatically created and activated.

    D. By default, Quick Deploy jobs are set to run every 15 minutes.

19. You are a SharePoint administrator for your company, and you have just been tasked with configuring content deployment settings for your environment. You have already configured the content deployment settings as well as paths, jobs, and Quick Deploy. Now you are interested in configuring job history and reports. Of the following, what do you find is true about configuring and running content deployment job histories and reports? (Choose all that apply.)

    A. Every time a content deployment job runs, a report on the job status and details is generated and logged as a record for that job.

    B. To view the status of the deployment of specific content, you must specify the location of the content by URL.

    C. If a content deployment job has failed, you cannot open the Content Deployment Report page.

    D. To view a job history or job report for a content deployment job, you must select the desired job and click View History for that job in the job's menu.

20. You are a SharePoint administrator for your company, and you are in the process of enabling document converters on a web application in your environment. Document converters allow SharePoint users to convert one document format type to another either through a user interface or through an automated process such as a custom workflow. As you are going through the process of enabling document conversion, you are offered several conversion settings. Of the following, which are valid conversion settings? (Choose all that apply.)

    A. From InfoPath Form to web page

    B. From Word document to web page

    C. From Word document to macros

    D. From XML to web page

Answers to Review Questions

1. A, B, D. You can create a site collection either at the root (/) directory or at the `/sites/` directory. The `/collection/` directory is bogus.

2. A, B, C. You must create the connection from the main page of the site collection and have at least site collection administrators permissions for that site collection.

3. B, C, D. You must configure a connection a path that specifies the web application containing site collections from which you want to send documents and the destination repository or records center at which the documents will arrive.

4. A, B, D. When you modify the storage values in a quota template, the storage limits for site collections created with the template before modification remain unchanged.

5. C, D. You can make sure an email notification is sent to any party, usually the site collection administrator, when the site collection's data storage has reached any specified level, not just when it's reached the storage limit. You only set quotas using a quota template when you create or modify a site collection and not at the level of the web application.

6. A, C. There is no option to set an email notification when a lock has been activated by crossing a threshold. The farm administrator can manually release the lock for the site collection at any time but typically won't do this unless the data storage limit for the site collection has been increased or the amount of data has been reduced.

7. A, B. Site collection deletion is configured using an automated system in Central Administration. There is no option to perform this task using Windows PowerShell.

8. B, C. The My Networks page lets My Site users manage their colleagues, interests, and newsfeed settings, not their Twitter and Facebook connections. The My People page is bogus.

9. A, B, C. You do not need to assign a designated administrator to the My Site host location in the manner of assigning one for the User Profile service application.

10. B, C. When you change the default My Site Host location, although you create a link to the new location, you do not provision the My Site Host at the new location. You can add links to trusted My Site Host locations when you want to give users access to My Site websites on more than one User Profile Service application.

11. A, B, C. Once you complete the configuration task, when as SharePoint user chooses Save As to save an Office document, they will have the option to go into the Favorite Links area of the Save As dialog box and select their SharePoint My Site as a location to which to save the document. You must be an Administrator of the local server computer hosting Central Administration to successfully complete the task.

12. A, B, D. Multiple tenants accessing the same resource are unaware of each other, because each tenant's data is isolated from all other tenants.

13. A, B, C. In Central Administration, you click the Publishing tab to find the enterprise wiki template.

14. A, D. You can only perform this task in Central Administration, and to add a file type to the list, you must type the file extension in the Type Each File Extension On A Separate Line text field and then click OK.

15. A, C, D. The planning farm role is bogus. The typical scenario is that content is created in the authoring farm role, exported to the staging farm role for central management, and then exported to the production farm role.

16. B, D. You only need to select the Select Template Later option when you create a site collection for the destination location. The Blank Site template will not suffice.

17. A, B, C. You can choose to deploy new, changed, deleted, or all web content.

18. A, B, D. When you create a new content deployment path, a Quick Deploy job is automatically created but will not be activated until a farm administrator enables Quick Deploy jobs for the path.

19. A, B, D. If a content deployment job fails, you must click Failed in the Status column for the job to open the Content Deployment Report page.

20. A, B, D. Instead of from Word document to macros, the answer should be from Word document with macros to web page in order to be correct.

Chapter

11

Deploying and Managing Applications and Solutions

MICROSOFT EXAM OBJECTIVE COVERED IN THIS CHAPTER:

✓ **Deploying and Managing Applications**

- Deploy and Manage SharePoint Solutions
- Manage Site Collections

This chapter introduces how to develop and maintain restricted sandbox environments in SharePoint and how to manage the State Service, required for workflows and InfoPath Forms Services. Then the chapter builds on previously presented material by addressing the document management solutions of InfoPath Forms Services and workflows.

Sandbox Administration

A *sandbox solution* is used to restrict access of a test environment to local and network resources in order to test load balancing or to test hosted environments prior to deployment. In essence, it's running an isolated environment where you can test platforms and features prior to releasing them into production.

The majority of the material presented in this book assumes you have installed SharePoint Server 2010 directly into your production environment, but this is not the only option for running a SharePoint platform. You can also deploy SharePoint into a sandbox, restricting the scope of its reach and preventing SharePoint from impacting your current working server farm.

Sandbox solutions are contained on the site collection level, so a manager for a sandbox does not have to belong to the Farm Administrators group. While the sandbox can be run by a site collection administrator, only the farm administrator can promote the sandbox solution into production.

Reviewing the Sandbox Solution

Although you can deploy a complete SharePoint environment in a sandbox, you can also maintain a SharePoint sandbox deployment to test just certain elements, such as new web parts, custom workflows, and InfoPath business logic. Regardless of your goals, deploying a sandbox solution is a good method for testing any changes you want to make in your production SharePoint server farm. If something breaks, productivity isn't affected, and you're free to fix the problem without the additional pressure of knowing that work isn't getting done in the enterprise as a result of the problem.

Sandbox Deployment Review

The high-level overview of sandbox environment deployment involves the following steps. Each activity has to be performed only once, and each step must be performed by the farm administrator.

1. Enabling sandboxing and starting the sandboxing service on each server that will run the sandbox solution

2. Applying a load balancing scheme to all sandbox solutions in all relevant site collections

3. Setting resource quotas that cannot be exceeded by all the combined site collections in the sandbox solution

After the previous tasks have been performed, the following tasks must be done by a site collection administrator, although it is possible for a SharePoint user with full control over the root of the site collection to do the same job.

- Uploading a solution to the site collection's Solution Gallery

- Activating and validating the solution

If the solution contains an assembly, only the site collection administrator can activate the solution.

Sandbox Isolation Management

Sandbox isolation isn't an all-or-nothing solution. You can set sandbox isolation to varying degrees depending on your requirements. Of course, the greater the isolation, the more your production server farm is protected from events occurring within the sandbox. The downside of sandbox isolation is that there are specific activities that the sandboxed platform can and cannot perform:

- Cannot access resources on a different site collection within the sandbox

- Cannot access a database

- Cannot call unmanaged code

- Cannot change the threading model

- Can connect to resources on the local server only

- Cannot write to disk

All sandbox solutions must contain a file called `manifest.xml`, which is a configuration file that defines the limits of the sandbox environment described in the previous list.

Planning and Deploying the Sandbox Solution

As previously mentioned, there is more than one reason to use a sandbox, and sandboxes can be isolated to varying degrees. Depending on your requirements, you will need to establish a particular plan for your sandbox before deployment.

The first part of the plan is whether you are going to even use a sandbox. Keep in mind that a sandbox environment comes at a cost, including more worker and proxy processes than a server farm, since the sandbox uses a separate worker thread that's unable to access server farm resources. However, if security and stability are higher priorities or if you need to provide scaled deployment of solutions into production, implementing a sandbox will serve those needs.

The following are the primary reasons to choose to use a sandbox solution:

- To provide load balancing between multiple servers for customized code

- To run and test code that is not currently supported in production

- To allow hosted SharePoint sites to upload and run customized code

Using Load Balancing in the Sandbox

You can use either local or remote load balancing with which to run custom code for testing. Local load balancing will always run the solution on the same server that received the request. This option requires less administration but has limited scalability. Remote load balancing will select the server that has the most solution affinity; that is, the solution will run on the server where it has previously been loaded and been run. This option is more scalable but has a higher administration cost on more servers.

To use either option, the User Code Host service and the Sandboxed Code service must be activated on each relevant server. You must choose either local or remote load balancing. You cannot mix both types in a single sandbox. Remote load balancing is a better choice if you want better performance in a multiserver environment. Local load balancing is the better choice if you are using the sandbox as part of a development environment and need to keep the sandbox environment isolated from the production farm.

Sandbox Deployment Management

Once the farm administrator has enabled the sandbox service, a site collection administrator can deploy the sandbox solution at the root of a site collection and then use the sandbox on any site in the collection. Note that if a person is the site collection owner but not the site collection administrator, that person will not be able to deploy the sandbox environment on their site collection.

The site collection administrator can enable or disable the sandbox on a site collection by manipulating quotas. To disable a sandbox in a site collection, set the quota to 0. This allows you to fine-tune which site collections hosted on a server will and will not run the sandbox environment.

Quotas are used in a sandbox environment in a similar manner to how they're used in production. If a sandbox solution exceeds its resource quotas, the sandbox is disabled for the remainder of the day or until the farm administrator resets the solution. This is one way to determine which site collection in the sandbox is using more resources than initially anticipated and thus requires an increased quota beyond the default settings.

Sandbox Promotion Planning

Only the farm administrator can change a sandbox environment to a fully trusted production environment. Part of your plan should include the criteria for promoting a sandbox solution to production or should include the plan for promoting the elements or code you are testing in the sandbox to production. Also, is promotion going to be a single or multistep process? You can choose to promote your sandbox material to the entire server farm or only to selected additional site collections, gradually introducing the changes over time. The latter usually means adding users who will have control over the sandboxed code or elements.

Deploying the Sandbox Solution

Now that you have some background on sandbox solution environments, it's time to learn how to enable and manage a sandbox in SharePoint. A number of tasks are associated with this activity. The first task is to enable sandbox solutions on the farm. You can do this either using Central Administration or using Windows PowerShell. Exercise 11.1 shows you the Central Administration method. You must be a member of the Farm Administrators group to perform this task. By default, the SharePoint Foundation Sandboxed Code service is disabled.

EXERCISE 11.1

Enabling Sandboxed Solutions

1. On the Central Administration home page, click Manage Services On Server under System Settings.

2. On the Manage Services On Server page, select the server on which you want to enable sandboxed services in the Server menu.

3. On the subsequent page, scroll down if necessary; in the Action column next to Microsoft SharePoint Foundation Sandboxed Code Service, click Start.

4. Repeat this procedure for any other servers on which you want to enable this service.

To perform the same task using Windows PowerShell, open PowerShell as an administrator, type the following code at the prompt, and then press Enter:

```
Start-Service -Name SPUserCodeV4
```

As previously mentioned, you can select either the local or remote load balancing schemes for the sandbox environment depending on your requirements. By default, the remote scheme is enabled. To change the scheme, you need to be a member of the Farm Administrators group. The only option to perform this task is in Central Administration. Exercise 11.2 will take you through the steps.

EXERCISE 11.2

Configuring Sandbox Load Balancing

1. On the Central Administration home page, click System Settings.

2. On the System Settings page, click Manage User Solutions under Farm Management.

3. On the User Solution Management page, under Load Balancing, select either All User Code Runs On The Same Machine As Web Requests to set the scheme to local or Requests To Run User Code Are Routed By Solution Affinity to set the scheme to remote, as shown here.

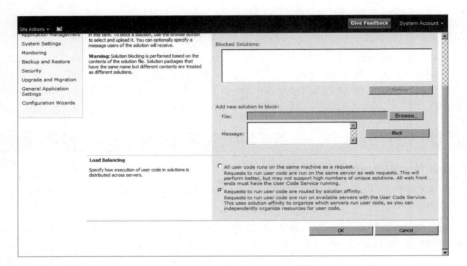

4. Click OK.

A farm administrator may need to manually block a sandbox environment, essentially disabling it, if the environment exceeds its predetermined resource limits. Exercise 11.3 shows you the process for this action.

EXERCISE 11.3

Blocking a Sandbox Solution

1. On the Central Administration home page, click System Settings.

2. On the System Settings page, click Manage User Solutions under Farm Management.

3. On the User Solution Management page, in the File field under Solution Restrictions, either type the full path of the file containing the solution you want to block or use the Browse button to navigate to the location of the solution.

4. If you desire, you can type an optional message in the Message field that will be read by users when they try to use the blocked solution.

5. Click Block to add the solution to the list in the Blocked Solutions box.

6. If necessary, repeat these steps to block other solutions.

7. Click OK.

To unblock a solution, perform the same steps to navigate to the Sandboxed Solutions Manage page, select the solution you want to unblock in the Blocked Solutions box, click Remove, and then click OK.

 Real World Scenario

Managing a Sandboxed Solution

As a SharePoint administrator for your company, you have been tasked by the CIO with planning and creating a sandboxed SharePoint environment for the general testing of different SharePoint implementations as well as specific SharePoint elements and custom code, such as customized web parts, workflows, and InfoPath forms.

The sandboxed environment must not be able to access resources on the production server farm including site collections, database servers, and even some resources in the sandbox. You must create an environment where the SharePoint implementation in the sandbox can only write to the local server. You have not been required to focus on the load-balancing aspects of using a sandbox.

If the SharePoint implementation in the sandbox becomes viable, it may potentially be promoted into production, which is a task only you or another administrator can perform, but during testing, you will enable the sandbox environment so that site collections in the sandbox can be managed by site collection administrators.

You have been tasked to limit the amount of resources site collections in the sandbox can use, and you may block the sandbox solution manually if site collection users exceed their allotted quota.

Once you've planned your sandbox deployment, you enable sandboxed solutions in Central Administration for the required servers as well as setting up sandbox solution blocking.

Managing the State Service

The State Service is a shared service in SharePoint that's used by some services and features to store temporary data across relevant HTTP requests in a SQL Server database. The InfoPath Forms Services requires the State Service as does both default and custom workflows, the SharePoint Chart web part, and some of the Visio 2010 features that do not require Microsoft Silverlight 3. This service is generally required to store session state data for forms, charts, and diagrams.

Configuring the State Service

The State Service is automatically configured when you install SharePoint as a basic deployment using the Farm Configuration Wizard, but you can also configure this service using Windows PowerShell. This section of the chapter covers both methods. Exercise 11.4 shows you the Farm Configuration Wizard procedure. If you follow these steps and the State Service check box is unavailable, the service has already been configured.

See Chapter 4, "Configuring Service Applications," for more information regarding configuring the State Service and other services in SharePoint.

EXERCISE 11.4

Configuring the State Service Using the Farm Configuration Wizard

1. On the Central Administration home page, click Configuration Wizards.

2. On the Configuration Wizards page, click Launch The Farm Configuration Wizard.

3. On the first page of the wizard, click Start The Wizard.

4. On the Services Configuration page, under Services, select the State Service check box and then click Next (if the option is unavailable, the service has already been started).

5. Complete the other configuration pages in the wizard; then, on the final page, click Finish.

Once the State Service is configured using the Farm Configuration Wizard, you can make changes only by using Windows PowerShell. You can use Windows PowerShell for the initial configuration instead of the Farm Configuration Wizard, but PowerShell is the only option you can use to make any modifications.

State Service–related tasks you can perform in PowerShell include getting information about service applications, databases, and application proxies; changing the configuration parameters for those elements; pausing and resuming the State Service databases; mounting data to a database; and removing the State Service database. You can also install the State Service schema to an existing database, create State Service service applications, and create additional State Service databases.

Remember that, just like any other shared service, the State Service application proxies are bound to web applications using proxy groups, and the State Service service application contains one or more databases.

Configuring the State Service Using Windows PowerShell

To configure the State Service using PowerShell, on the server computer hosting Central Administration, you must load the SharePoint Server module for Windows PowerShell. To do this, click Start ➤ Add Programs ➤ Administrative Tools and then click Windows PowerShell Modules. Once the modules have been loaded as indicated in the PowerShell window, the command prompt will become available.

1. To create a service application, type `$serviceApp = New-SPStateServiceApplication -Name "State Service"` at the prompt and then press Enter.

2. To create a State Service database and associate it with a service application, type `New-SPStateServiceDatabase -Name "StateServiceDatabase" -ServiceApplication $serviceApp` and then press Enter.

3. To create a State Service Application Proxy and associate it with the service application, type `New-SPStateServiceApplicationProxy -Name "State Service" -ServiceApplication $serviceApp -DefaultProxyGroup` at the prompt and then press Enter.

4. To view a list of all the PowerShell cmdlets related to the State Service, type `gcm *spstate*` at the prompt and then press Enter.

One detail to keep in mind while you're using PowerShell to configure the State Service is that you must have at least one service application for a State Service. If you have hosted deployments, although each host partition can have its own service application, it's not a requirement. However, each service application must have a unique name, so in any of the sample code, replace the example name with a unique name.

Each State Service service application requires at least one State Service database, but you may want to create additional databases if you expect a large volume of forms and charts. Like service applications, each database must have a unique name, so change the text in the example code accordingly. Also, to use another proxy group besides the one named in the sample code, change the DefaultProxyGroup parameter.

Workflow Administration

As you learned in the previous section of the chapter, one of the features in SharePoint dependent on the State Service is workflow. A *workflow* is a process that allows multiple people to collaborate and have input on documents for the purpose of managing project tasks. Workflows help impose a specific set of criteria to document creation that matches organizational requirements using a series of steps in which workflow participants can apply a status to the document at each step in order to communicate with the document's author.

When the document is created and submitted to the workflow, the workflow process sends an email from the author to the workflow approvers that the document is awaiting their review. Each approver views the document and assigns a response such as approve or reject, and, depending on the response, the document takes a different path through the workflow, either forward to the next approver or back to the author.

There are a number of workflow types, depending on the purpose of the workflow and the requirements for the document:

- Approval
- Collect Feedback
- Collect Signatures
- Disposition Approval
- Three-state
- Group Approval
- Publishing Approval
- Translation Management

In addition to workflows that come by default with SharePoint, custom workflows can be created to meet additional business needs. Customizations can be based on the default workflows or created "from scratch" using SharePoint Designer. In addition, custom activities and custom nondeclarative workflows can be created using Visual Studio.

Creating custom workflows is beyond the scope of this book and not a requirement for the certification.

Managing Workflows

Workflows are a significant portion of a user's SharePoint experience, and as an administrator, you will be responsible to activate, deactivate, modify, and otherwise manage workflows. This first set of workflow exercises will show you how, starting with activating a workflow at the site collection level in Exercise 11.5. Any workflows you activate at the site collection level will become available to all subsites in the collection. You must be a member of the Site Collection Administrators group for the site collection on which you want to activate workflows to complete this task.

You can also deactivate the feature by navigating to the Features page and clicking the Active indicator next to the feature to deactivate it.

EXERCISE 11.5

Activating Workflows in a Site Collection

1. At the top level of the site collection, click Site Actions and then click Site Settings.

2. On the Site Settings page, click Site Collection Features under Site Collection Administration.

3. On the Features page, locate the workflow feature you want to activate and click the Activate button next to the feature, as shown here.

4. When the indicator in the status column next to the feature displays as Active, close the page.

Activating the workflow feature for a site collection is just the first step. Your users still won't be able to use workflows until you add one or more workflow associations. A workflow association assigns a task or history list that will be used with the workflow. You can use the default list, select a different list, or create a new one. You can associate a number of workflows to a single list or associate separate workflows with separate lists. Choose the latter option if you don't want to experience a performance slowdown by having a large number of workflows associated with one task list and one history list.

Any workflow participant can view the task list for a workflow by using the My Tasks view of the Tasks list in Quick Launch; however, if the tasks list contains confidential or private information you do not want viewed by all participants, you can associate specific task lists to specific workflows. Then only users who can participate in the confidential workflow can see the associated tasks.

You can perform a number of different workflow association tasks. Exercise 11.6 shows you how to associate a workflow with a list or document library. The task can vary depending on the type of workflow you are associating. For instance, if you are adding a Three-state workflow to a list, you should create a Choice type column to the list and assign the column three choices. At a minimum, you must have Full Control permissions to the relevant list or library to complete this task.

Associating a Workflow to a List or Document Library

1. In the site collection, navigate to the desired site and then to the desired list or library.

2. For a list, on the List Tools tab, click List. For a library, on the Library Tools tab, click Library.

3. Under Settings, click Workflow Settings and then click Add A Workflow.

4. On the Add A Workflow page, select the workflow template under Workflow that you want to associate with the list or library.

5. Give the workflow association a name in the Name field.

6. Under Task List, specify the desired task list.

7. Under History List, specify the desired history list.

8. Under Start Options, choose Automatically or Manually to specify the start option type, select Item Update, Creation, or both to specify the event or events that will start the workflow, or select the user or users who can start the workflow.

9. If additional configuration options are available for the workflow template you previously selected, click Next to customize the settings, make your customizations, and then click OK; otherwise, click OK to apply your changes.

The history list has a tendency to grow a lot, so depending on the amount of activity you expect the workflow to experience, you may want to create a new history list, rather than using the default list or selecting another currently existing list.

Normally, any user with Edit Item permissions can start a workflow, but if you want to restrict this activity further, you can specify that Require Manage List permissions be required. Then, only users with Manage List or Web Designer permissions will be able to initiate a workflow.

Associating a Workflow with a List or Library Content Type

You can associate a workflow with a list or library content type in almost the same manner. You need to be a member of the Site Owners group for the relevant site to perform the task, though. Follow steps 1 and 2 in Exercise 11.6 to get to the List Settings or Library Settings page; then under Content Types, in the Content Type column, click the content type you want to associate. Then under Settings, click Workflow Settings. On the Workflow Settings page, click Add A Workflow; then follow steps 4 through 9 in Exercise 11.6 to finish the job.

The task of associating a workflow with a site content type is also similar but different enough to outline in Exercise 11.7. You must be a member of the Site Owners group for the relevant site to successfully complete this task.

EXERCISE 11.7

Associating a Workflow with a Site Content Type

1. In the site collection, navigate to the desired site, click Site Actions, and then click Site Settings.

2. On the Site Settings page under Galleries, click Site Content Types.

3. On the Site Content Types page, click the desired content type in the Site Content Type column.

4. Under Settings, click Workflow settings, as shown here.

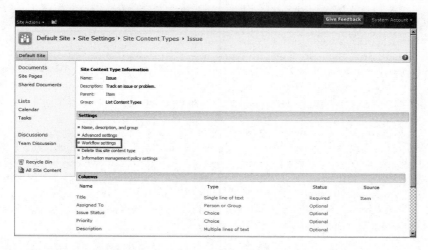

5. On the Workflow Settings page, click Add A Workflow.

6. On the Add A Workflow page under Workflow, select the desired workflow.

7. Give the workflow a name in the Name field.

8. Select the desired task list under Task List, and select the desired history list under History List.

9. Under Start Options, select the desired start options as you did in Exercise 11.6.

10. If the workflow you select has additional configuration steps, click Next and configure those steps. Then click OK to finish; otherwise, click OK to apply your changes.

To associate a workflow with a site, click Site Actions on the relevant site and then Site Settings. On the Site Settings page, click Workflow Settings under Site Administration and then follow steps 5 through 10 in Exercise 11.7 to finish the job.

Editing and Deleting Workflow Associations

To modify any of the associations that you just created, navigate to the area where you created the workflow; select the desired list, library, or workflow; and edit your settings.

To delete a list or library workflow association, navigate to the list or library settings page, and click Workflow Settings under Permissions and Management. Then on the Workflow Settings page, click Remove Workflow. You can then select No New Instances to prevent new workflows from being started but allow workflows in progress to be finished, or you can select Remove to remove all workflows immediately.

To remove associations with list or library content types, navigate to the List or Library Settings page, and under Content Types, click the name of the content type you want to remove. Under Settings, click Workflow Settings. On the Workflow Settings page, click Remove A Workflow, select the workflow, and then select either No New Instances or Remove.

To remove a workflow association from a site content type, navigate to the Site Settings page. Under Galleries, click Site Content Types. Select the desired content type in the Site Content Type column and click Workflow Settings under Settings. On the Workflow Settings page, click Remove A Workflow and then select either No New Instances or Remove. If after clicking OK, the Apply Changes To All Content Types Inheriting From This Type message appears, click OK.

To remove a workflow association from a site, on the Site Settings page under Site Administration, click Workflow Settings. On the Workflow Settings page, click Remove A Workflow and then follow the remaining steps required to remove the workflow.

Now that you've activated the workflow features and made workflow associations, you must start a workflow instance. Exercise 11.8 shows you how to set a workflow instance for a site to start automatically. You must be a member of the Site Owners group for the relevant site to successfully complete this exercise.

EXERCISE 11.8

Starting an Instance of a Workflow for a Site

1. On the home page for the desired site, click All Site Content in Quick Launch and then click Site Workflows.

2. On the Workflows page, under Start A New Workflow, click the name of the desired workflow.

3. When the Start button appears, click Start.

In step 2 of the previous exercise, if no workflow names appear, it usually means that no workflows have been associated with the site.

Manually Starting a Workflow for a List or Library

If you're a site owner, you can also manually start a workflow for a list or library. Just navigate to the desired list or library and click Workflows on the lists or library settings page. On the Workflows page, click the name of the desired workflow under Start A New Workflow. You may have to click the Start button should it appear.

If a user has the Contribute permission level for a list or library, they can manually start a workflow in either Office 2007 or Office 2010. Regardless of the version of Office being used, the user must save the relevant Office file to the list or library before you proceed with these steps.

Manually Starting a Workflow in Office 2007

Follow these steps:

1. In the SharePoint list or library, open the desired file.

2. In Office 2007, click the Microsoft Office Button and then select Workflows.

3. When the list of available workflows appears, click Start next to the desired workflow.

4. If the workflow form appears, enter the requested information and then click Start.

Manually Starting a Workflow in Office 2010

Follow these steps:

1. In the relevant list or library, open the desired file.

2. In the Office 2010 client application, click Save & Send on the File tab.

3. Under Workflows, click the desired workflow.

4. In the right pane, click Start Workflow.

5. If the workflow form appears, enter the requested information and then click Start.

In Exercise 11.8, you learned how to start an instance of a workflow. You can also cancel or terminate the instance. When you cancel the workflow, any tasks created in the workflow are lost, and the workflow is ended.

You cannot restart a workflow instance once canceled or terminated. You must start a new instance. You terminate a workflow instance when it cannot be canceled. This usually occurs when the workflow stops responding or a workflow error occurs. Exercise 11.9 shows you how to cancel a workflow instance. You must be the Site Owner on the relevant site to complete this task.

EXERCISE 11.9

Canceling a Workflow for a List or Library

1. Navigate to the desired list or library, click the document for which you want to stop the workflow, and click Workflows in the menu.

2. On the Workflows page, click the name of the desired workflow under Running Workflows.

3. On the Workflow Status page, click Cancel All <name of workflow> Tasks under Workflow Information. When prompted, click Yes.

The Cancel All <name of workflow> Tasks link will not be available if the cancel operation isn't supported or a workflow error has occurred. In that case, your only option is to terminate the workflow.

To cancel a site workflow, on the home page for the site on which you want to cancel the workflow, click All Site Content and then click Site Workflows. Then follow steps 2 and 3 in Exercise 11.9 to finish the job.

To terminate a workflow for either a list or library or site, navigate to the Workflows page as you did in the previous exercise and click Terminate This Workflow Now under Workflow Information. When prompted, click OK.

Monitoring Workflows

Once the workflow feature is active and people are using workflows, you can monitor workflow health and well being by checking workflow status and viewing workflow reports. You may also have to troubleshoot workflow errors should they occur.

Checking Workflow Status

Checking the status for a list or library workflow is as easy as browsing to the relevant list or library and, in the row for the specific item, clicking the link in the Workflow Status column. You only need Edit Items permission for the list or library in question. Then, on the Workflow Status page, you can check the status details, such as the name of the person who started the workflow, the date and time it was started, the name and link to the document or item in the workflow, the list of tasks assigned to workflow participants, and so on.

To do the same thing for a workflow associated with a site, in Quick Launch on the relevant site, click All Site Content and then click Site Workflows. On the Workflows page, you can click either My Running Workflows to view the status of current workflows or My Completed Workflows to see the status of workflows that have finished. From either area, click the name of the desired workflow, and view the available information on the Workflow Status page.

Checking Workflow Reports

To view the workflow report for the entire site collection, on the top-level page for the site collection, click Site Actions and then click Site Settings. On the Site Settings page, click Workflows under Site Administration. The Site Collection Workflows report will become available.

If you want to view reports for custom workflows, the specific parameters for the reports must be defined in the workflow template so that the reports will be generated. The designer must create these specifications while creating the custom workflow template in Microsoft Visual Studio. This will not be a task for which the SharePoint administrator will be responsible.

SharePoint generates two different reports for individual workflows as Excel documents: the Activity Duration report, which provides information about how long each activity lasts, and the Cancellation and Error report, which displays a list of the workflows that have been canceled or where errors occurred during the workflow process.

Exercise 11.10 will show you how to view an individual workflow report. Anyone with Edit Item permissions to view workflow reports can complete the following task.

Viewing an Individual Workflow Report

1. Browse to the desired list or document library.

2. Click the item or document to open the menu and then click Workflows.

3. On the Workflows page, click the name of the desired workflow under Running Workflows.

4. On the Workflow Status page, click View Workflow Reports under Workflow History.

5. On the View Workflow Reports page, locate the desired workflow association and then click either Activity Duration Report or Cancellation & Error Report.

6. Under File Location, click Browse and navigate to the location to which you want to save the report.

7. Click OK.

If no workflows are listed under Running Workflows, it means no workflows are currently active. On the View Workflow Reports page, the reports are listed alphabetically by workflow association name.

Troubleshooting Workflow Errors

The most common problems you will encounter with workflow failures are network issues, permissions issues, and problems with the design of the workflow itself. For instance, a workflow might be designed to interact with a list or library, but the list or library has been deleted; or a user may have originally had permissions to access a workflow but subsequently their permissions changed, removing that access. These are only a few examples of what might cause a workflow to fail. In actuality, the number of reasons for workflow failures is vast.

Besides receiving user notifications that a workflow is having problems, one way to determine the state of a workflow is to check its operating status. In addition to the expected Completed status of a workflow, you may see messages such as the following:

- Error Occurred

- Failed On Start

- Failed On Start (Retrying)

- Stopped

Troubleshooting workflow errors is complicated by having to accommodate the type of workflow. For a simple status message such as Error Occurred, the cause can be different depending on workflow type, including custom workflows created using Visual Studio. If you are working with the predefined, out-of-the-box workflow, using workflow history is a good starting place for diagnosing the problem. In reviewing the workflow's history, the last item in the history list will contain the error message. Although the details may not be present (by design to avoid revealing security information), look for network, permissions, and incorrect email setting problems.

If a problem occurs with a custom-made workflow and you cannot determine the cause, you may have to turn to the design team that created the workflow so they can debug the workflow. Although this issue is beyond the scope of your duties as a SharePoint administrator, you can find out more about this process by going to `http://blogs.msdn.com/b/sharepoint/archive/2006/11/30/developing-workflows-in-vs-part-6-deploy-and-debug-your-workflow.aspx` or by searching TechNet for *deploy and debug your workflow*.

Configuring Global Workflow Settings

Global workflow settings determine the behavior of workflows across all sites in a web application. The following section shows you the various tasks associated with global workflow settings.

Enabling Declarative Workflows

Classic workflows are generally good for offering process support for structured processes but do not provide much flexibility. Declarative workflows offer a balance between flexibility and support by declaring a framework that simultaneously provides wider flexibility and supports user recommendations and other process-mining diagnostics.

Although you don't have to be an expert in understanding declarative workflows, you will need to know how to enable and disable them. When you enable a declarative workflow, you can determine whether users with Design-level permissions can create and deploy such workflows using the Workflow Editor in SharePoint Designer 2010. Exercise 11.11 will show you how. You must be a member of the Farm Administrators group to successfully complete this exercise.

EXERCISE 11.11

Enabling and Disabling Declarative Workflows

1. On the Central Administration main page, click Application Management.

2. On the Application Management page, click Manage Web Applications under Web Applications.

3. On the Web Applications Management page, select the desired web application.

4. On the Ribbon, click General Settings and then click Workflow.

5. In the Workflow Settings dialog box, under User-Defined Workflows, select Yes to enable declarative workflows or No to disable declarative workflows, as shown here.

EXERCISE 11.11 *(continued)*

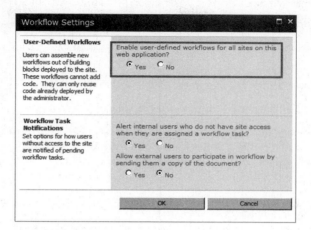

6. Click OK to close the dialog box.

Nonauthenticated Users Accessing Workflows

Although there is a risk of breaching security by allowing nonauthenticated users to participate in SharePoint workflows, you may encounter situations where it is to the company's advantage to do so. As a SharePoint administrator, you can allow internal SharePoint users who normally don't have access to a workflow to participate. You can also allow people who normally do not have access to your SharePoint environment at all to participate in a workflow.

To allow internal users to participate in a workflow, you can approve an email message being sent to the required user describing the request process. External users typically are required to sign a nondisclosure agreement or other similar document before being allowed to participate. You must be careful that such messages do not contain confidential or sensitive information the user is not entitled to possess. You must also consider what information the user may be able to access unintentionally, once allowed access to the workflow.

This feature allowing internal workers to access workflows where they are not participants is enabled by default.

Exercise 11.12 will show you how to allow an internal user to access a workflow. You must belong to the Farm Administrators group to complete this task.

EXERCISE 11.12

Allowing Internal Nonauthenticated Users Access to a Workflow

1. On the Central Administration main page, click Application Management.

2. On the Application Management page, under Web Applications, click Manage Web Applications.

3. On the Web Applications Management page, select the desired web application.

4. On the Ribbon, click General Settings and then click Workflow.

5. In the Workflow Settings dialog box, under Workflow Task Notifications, click Yes for Alert Internal Users Who Do Not Have Site Access When They Are Assigned A Workflow Task?, which will send an email to any internal user without access to the workflow, assigning them a workflow task when a site administrator makes that user a workflow participant.

6. Click OK to close the dialog box.

To allow external users permission to access an internal workflow task, follow steps 1 through 4 from Exercise 11.12; in the Workflow Settings dialog box under Workflow Task Notifications, for Allow External Users To Participate In Workflow By Sending Them A Copy Of The Document, click Yes, which allows external users participation rights by sending them a copy of the document being "workflowed" via email when a site administrator makes that person a workflow participant. Click OK to close the dialog box.

 This setting allowing external nonauthenticated users access to a Share-Point workflow is disabled by default.

Disabling Automatic Workflow Cleanup

When you enable workflows and workflows are created, a workflow task list and history list are created with the workflow. By default, these records are removed every 60 days to prevent cluttering up the system. Although the workflow history items themselves aren't deleted, the cleanup process removes the entry point to view the items on the status page for the specific instance of the workflow. You can disable the cleanup process if you need to retain access to the items beyond the default 60-day period. Just keep in mind that the longer the cleanup process is disabled, the longer the list can potentially grow and possibly affect site performance.

Exercise 11.13 shows you the steps in disabling automatic workflow cleanup. You need to belong to the Farm Administrators group to complete this task.

EXERCISE 11.13

Disabling Automatic Cleanup in Workflow

1. On the Central Administration main page, click Monitoring.

2. On the Monitoring page, under Timer Jobs, click Review Job Definitions.

3. On the Job Definitions page, under Title, click the Workflow Auto Cleanup link next to the desired web application (you may have to scroll to the bottom of the page and switch to a subsequent page to see the entry, because the list is quite long).

4. On the Edit Timer Job page, click Disable to disable the cleanup process, as shown here.

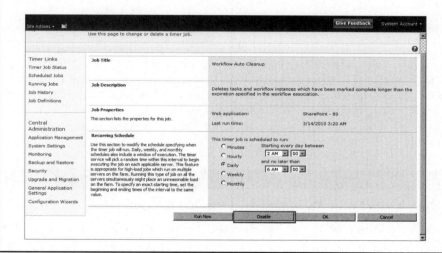

If you want to enable the process again for the web application, follow steps 1 through 4, and click Enable to enable the process.

Deploying Workflow Templates

When you or someone uses SharePoint Designer 2010 to create custom workflows, the workflows can be saved as workflow templates with a .wsp file extension. You can then use the .wsp file to deploy the workflow on different sites and site collections. This section of the chapter shows you how to work with workflow template files.

Managing Workflow Templates

When a workflow template (.wsp) file is created, it is stored in the Site Assets document library on the top-level site of the site collection for which it was created. You can download the .wsp file to a local folder and subsequently deploy the template. Exercise 11.14 describes the procedure.

EXERCISE 11.14

Downloading a Workflow Template

1. On the top-level site for the desired site collection, click All Site Content in Quick Launch.

2. On the All Site Content page, click Site Assets under Document Libraries.

3. On the Site Assets page, click the workflow you want to edit; on the menu that appears, click Send To and then click Download A Copy.

4. In the File Download dialog box, navigate to the location where you want to save the template and then click Save.

5. When the Download Complete dialog box appears, click Close.

Once you have the .wsp file saved locally, you can choose to upload it to the Solution Gallery for a desired site collection to make the template available as a feature you can then activate for the site collection. Activating the feature can be handled as a separate process or as part of the upload process. You can upload the .wsp file either using the Site Actions menu on the top-level of the desired site collection or with Windows PowerShell. Exercise 11.15 shows you the GUI method.

EXERCISE 11.15

Uploading a Workflow Template to a Site Collection

1. On the top-level site for the desired site collection, click Site Settings in Quick Launch.

2. On the Site Settings page, click Solutions under Galleries.

3. On the Solutions tab on the Ribbon, in the New box, click Upload Solution, as shown here.

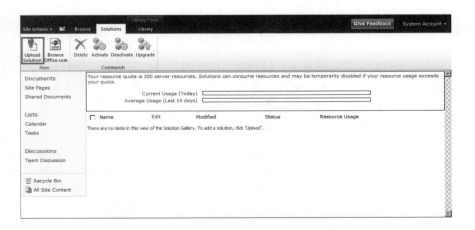

4. When the Upload Document dialog box appears, click the Browse button and browse to the location of the desired .wsp file.

5. In the Choose File To Upload dialog box, select the desired .wsp file and then click Open.

6. When the Upload Document dialog box appears, click OK.

7. When the Solution Gallery – Activate Solution dialog box appears, click Activate.

The name of the workflow will now appear in the Solutions Gallery with its Status set to Activated for the site collection.

To perform the same task using Windows PowerShell, open PowerShell, type the following, and then Press Enter, substituting the sample values with your production values:

```
Add-SPUserSolution -LiteralPath <LiteralPath> -Site <SiteURL>
```

To activate the feature for the site collection, type the following at the prompt, and then press Enter, substituting the sample values with your production values:

```
Install-SPUserSolution -Identity <Solution> -Site <SiteURL>
```

You can also activate a workflow template for a specific site using either the Site Actions menu or Windows PowerShell. To activate the template using the menu, click Site Actions on the main page for the desired site and then click Site Settings. On the Site Settings page, click Manage Site Features under Site Actions. On the Manage Site Features page, click Activate next to the desired workflow template.

To perform the same task using Windows PowerShell, type the following at the PowerShell prompt, and then press Enter, substituting the sample values for your production values:

```
Enable-SPFeature -Identity <Feature> -Url <URL>
```

Administering InfoPath Forms

The *InfoPath Forms Services* in SharePoint 2010 provides the ability to deploy an organization's forms in the SharePoint environment, allowing users to fill out any and all required forms within a web browser. SharePoint users can publish form templates to a list or form library in a site collection as long as the form does not use business logic, does not require full trust, and does not use data connections managed by an administrator. A site collection administrator can publish form templates containing code used by sandboxed solutions. Form templates requiring full trust or that use data collections must always be deployed by a farm administrator.

Configuring InfoPath Form Services and Templates

You may be called upon to manage a number of InfoPath Forms Services configuration settings including browser-related settings, authentication and connection settings, and user session settings. These settings are universally managed using the Central Administration interface.

Exercise 11.16 teaches you how to configure browser-enabled user form templates. You must belong to the Farm Administrators group to perform this task.

EXERCISE 11.16

Configuring Browser-Enabled User Form Templates

1. On the Central Administration main page, click General Application Settings.

2. On the General Application Settings page, click Configure InfoPath Forms Services under InfoPath Forms Services.

3. On the Configure InfoPath Forms Services page, under User Browser-Enabled Form Templates, select the Allow Users To Browser-Enable Form Templates check box if you want to allow users to publish browser-enabled form templates.

4. Select the Render Form Templates That Are Browser-Enabled By Users check box if you want to allow browser-enabled form templates that users publish to be rendered in a web browser.

5. Click OK to apply your settings.

If you clear the Allow Users To Browser-Enable Form Templates check box as described in the previous exercise, you will disable browser-enabled form templates for the entire server farm. If you clear the Render Form Templates That Are Browser-Enabled By Users check box in the previous exercise, users can still publish browser-enabled form templates to form libraries, but the templates that have been published to form libraries will be unable to be filled out in a web browser. Templates published to lists will be unaffected.

You can make other configuration changes on the Configure InfoPath Forms Services page including settings for HTTP data connections. These will be described in Exercise 11.17.

InfoPath Form templates can contain data connections that access data sources located outside the site collection. This feature is disabled by default, but you can choose to allow form templates to perform cross-domain data access for the entire server farm as well as performing other configuration tasks. Exercise 11.17 shows you how. You will need to be a member of the Farm Administrators group to perform this task.

InfoPath Forms Services uses the State Service to store the transient data generated while the form is being filled out by a user. This means front-end web servers remain stateless between round-trips and user session data isn't required to be sent repeatedly, consuming additional network bandwidth. You can manage a variety of user session settings for the server farm to optimize the user session and prevent the loss of user data because of premature session termination. You may have to perform these actions when the default settings are not adequate, though this should be fairly rare. If you do change the default settings, verify afterward that user form sessions behave as expected.

EXERCISE 11.17

Configuring InfoPath Forms Data Connection and Authentication Settings

1. On the Central Administration main page, click General Application Settings.

2. On the General Application Settings page under InfoPath Forms Services, click Configure InfoPath Form Services.

3. On the Configure InfoPath Form Services page, set the connection timeout under Data Connection Timeouts by typing the time in milliseconds that will elapse before timeout in the Default Data Connection Timeout field.

4. To set the maximum amount of time that can elapse before connection timeout, type the time in milliseconds in the Maximum Data Connection Timeout field.

5. To set the maximum size of responses that data connections are allowed to process, type the value in kilobytes in the Data Connection Response Size field so that any responses that exceed the set size will throw an error message.

6. Under HTTP Data Connections, select the Require SSL For HTTP Authentication check box if you want to require SSL-encrypted connections for data connections using Basic or Digest authentication.

7. Under Embedded SQL Authentication, select the Allow Embedded SQL Authentication check box if you want to allow forms to use embedded SQL Server credentials.

8. Under Authentication To Data Sources (User Form Templates), select the Allow User Form Templates To Use Authentication Information Contained In Data Connection Files check box if you want to allow user form templates to use embedded authentication data.

9. Under Cross-Domain Access For User Form Templates, select the Allow Cross-Domain Data Access For User Form Templates That Use Connection Settings In A Data Connection File check box if you want to allow user form templates to access data from another domain.

10. When you are finished, click OK.

Follow the steps in Exercise 11.18 to learn how to configure the session state for InfoPath Services. You must be a member of the Farm Administrators group to complete this task.

EXERCISE 11.18

Configuring InfoPath Forms Service Session State

1. On the Central Administration main page, click General Application Settings.

2. On the General Application Settings page, click Configure InfoPath Forms Services under InfoPath Forms Services.

3. On the Configure InfoPath Forms Services page, under Thresholds, type the maximum number of postbacks you want to allow in the Number Of Postbacks Per Session field, with 75 being the default value.

4. In the Number Of Actions Per Postback field, type the value for the maximum number of actions per postback you want to allow, with 200 being the default value.

5. Under User Sessions, type the value for the maximum session duration in minutes in the Active Sessions Should Be Terminated After field, with the default value being 1440 minutes.

6. In the Maximum Size Of User Session Data field, type the maximum session state size in kilobytes, with 4096 kilobytes being the default value.

7. Click OK to apply your changes.

As previously mentioned, depending on the form template requirements, there are some templates that users can upload without administrator approval. Forms that use business logic using managed code, that access external resources, or that use administrator-managed data connections must be granted trust to execute code and access data. This trust originates either from sandboxed solutions or from administrator-approved form templates.

Forms uploaded in sandboxed environments don't require full trust because the environment is isolated from the larger server farm. Administrator-approved templates require individual verification and must be uploaded and activated by an administrator with full trust to the domain. These forms are stored in a special document library accessible only by administrators.

The following tasks focus on activities-related administrator-approved form templates.

Exercise 11.19 shows you the process of uploading administrator-approved form templates using Central Administration. You must be a member of the Farm Administrators group to complete this task.

EXERCISE 11.19

Uploading Administrator-Approved InfoPath Form Templates

1. On the Central Administration main page, click General Application Settings.

2. On the General Applications Settings page, click Upload Form Template under InfoPath Forms Services.

3. On the Upload Form Template page, browse to the location of the desired template under Upload Form Template.

4. In the Choose File To Upload dialog box, select the desired template and then click Open.

5. Click Verify to make sure the template doesn't register any errors; if errors exist, they will be displayed in the Report Details section of the Form Verification Report.

6. After the verification is complete and no errors appear, click OK to return to the Upload Form Template page.

7. Browse to the location of the template again and choose and open the template.

8. Under Upgrade, clear the Upgrade The Form Template If It Already Exists check box if the template does not already exist on the server or if it exists but you do not want to upgrade the template.

9. If you have chosen to upgrade a template but you want currently running browser sessions to use the current version of the template, make sure the Allow Existing Browser-Based Form Filling Sessions To Complete Using The Current Version Of The Form Template is selected; otherwise, select the Terminate Existing Browser-Based Form Filling Sessions check box, which will result in all data from the current sessions being lost.

10. Click Upload to finish the process.

When you upload a form template, if the same template already exists on the server, you may receive different messages depending on the circumstances. If you try to upload an earlier version of the form, you will receive a message indicating that you already have a more recent version of the template on the server. You can either remove the form currently stored on the server, increase the version number of the new template, or cancel the upload.

If you try to upload the same version of the form as the one already on the server, you will receive an error saying that the same version exists on the server. You can increase the version number of the template you are uploading or cancel the upload.

If you are uploading a newer version of the form than the one currently on the server, you can choose to upgrade the current form while allowing currently running sessions to use the older versions. You can also terminate all currently running sessions, causing users to lose their data and forcing them to use the newer form. Additionally, you can perform a gradual upgrade, which causes the newer version to be adopted for use as a separate template while gradually removing the older template. You can quiesce the older form template prior to upgrading to the newer version, gradually transitioning the template from an active to inactive state.

You can optionally upload an administrator-approved form template using Windows PowerShell. To do so, open PowerShell as an administrator, type the following string at the prompt, and then press Enter, replacing the sample values with your production values:

```
Install-SPInfoPathFormTemplate -Path <FormTemplateLocation>
```

Once an administrator-approved form template is uploaded, you must still activate it before the form becomes available to users. The form template can be activated either from Central Administration or from the site collection features page. Exercise 11.20 shows you how to activate a template from Central Administration. You must be a member of the Farm Administrators group to complete this task.

EXERCISE 11.20

Activating a Form Template in Central Administration

1. On the Central Administration main page, click General Application Settings.

2. On the General Applications Settings page, click Manage Form Templates under Info-Path Forms Services.

3. On the Manage Form Templates page, click the name of the form template you want to activate and then click Activate To A Site Collection.

4. If you need to change to a different site location, click the Site Collection box under Activation Location and then click Change Site Collection.

5. When the Select Site Collection dialog box appears, click the URL of the desired site collection and then click OK.

6. Click OK again to activate the template.

You can also change the web application in the Select Site Collection dialog box if necessary.

To activate a form template from the features page of a site collection, click Site Actions on the top-level site of the site collection and then click Site Settings. On the Site Settings page under Site Actions, click Manage Site Collection Features. On the Manage Site Collection Features page, click Activate next to the desired form template. To verify that the form template is available, on the top-level site for the site collection, click Site Actions and then click View All Site Content. On the All Site Content page, under Document Libraries, click the Form Templates document library and make sure the desired template is in the Form Templates list.

You can deactivate an administrator-approved form template for a site collection in Central Administration. This action removes the template from any document library in the site collection, and any currently running form-filling session will be terminated, causing all form data to be lost. To prevent such a loss of data, you must quiesce the form template before deactivating the template. Exercise 11.21 shows you how to deactivate a form template. You must be a member of the Farm Administrators group to successfully perform this task.

EXERCISE 11.21

Deactivating a Form Template in Central Administration

1. On the Central Administration main page, click General Application Settings.

2. On the General Applications Settings page, click Manage Form Templates under Info-Path Forms Services.

3. On the Manage Form Templates page, click the name of the desired form template and then click Deactivate From The Site Collection.

4. If necessary, under Deactivation Location, click Site Collection and then click Change Site Location.

5. When the Select Site Collection dialog box appears, click the URL of the desired site collection and then click OK.

6. Click OK to deactivate the template for the site collection.

On the Select Site Collection dialog box, you can also select a different web application if necessary.

You can quiesce an administrator-approved template prior to deactivating it in order to prevent users from losing data during currently running browser sessions. Exercise 11.22 shows you how. You must be a member of the Farm Administrators group in order to complete this task.

EXERCISE 11.22

Quiescing a Form Template in Central Administration Prior to Deactivation

1. On the Central Administration main page, click General Application Settings.

2. On the General Applications Settings page, click Manage Form Templates under Info-Path Forms Services.

3. On the Manage Form Templates page, click the name of the desired form template and then click Quiesce Form Template.

4. On the Quiesce Form Template dialog box, under Quiesce, type the number of minutes to quiesce form sessions prior to the form template becoming deactivated, with 240 minutes being the default.

5. Click Start Quiescing, and verify that the status under Quiesce changes to Quiescing.

6. Once the status changes to Quiesced, indicating the process has completed, you can upload the new version of the form or deactivate the existing version of the form.

To completely delete an administrator-approved form template using Central Administration, navigate to the Manage Form Templates page as you've done in the previous exercises, click the name of the desired form template, and then click Remove Form. On the Remove Form Template page, click Remove.

To view the properties of a form template, click the name of the desired form template on the Manage Form Templates page and then click View Properties.

Managing Data Connection Files for InfoPath Forms

InfoPath forms can use data connection files to specify which settings to use when connecting to data sources. The main data connection is created automatically when you create a form template from a database, when you create one from a web service, or when creating a customized form. You can optionally create additional data connections to be used as secondary data connections.

Data connection files are XML documents saved as XML or UDCX files, and they contain connection information for an individual external data connection. These files are stored in a data connection library on the same SharePoint server where the forms templates are stored. They can also be centrally managed in a library on the Central Administration site. Typically developers create data connection files using InfoPath Designer 2010 or using an XML editor.

By default, data connection files in the library in Central Administration can be used only as web browser forms, although farm administrators can decide to allow for HTTP access by clients such as Microsoft InfoPath Filler 2010. Data connection files manage connections either across servers in the same farm or across server farms. Data connection types can include query data connections, database data connections, SharePoint list data connections, SOAP web service data connections, REST web service data connections, and XML file data connections.

Converting a Data Connection to a Data Connection File

Form developers create data connections and data connection files when they design form templates. Data connections can be converted into data connection files using InfoPath Designer 2010. The designer must be a member of the Site Members SharePoint group or a group with Add Items permissions to be able to perform this task.

1. In InfoPath Designer 2010, open the desired form template.

2. On the Data tab, click Data Connections under Get External Data.

3. When the Data Connections dialog box opens, under Data Connections For The Form Template, click the desired data connection.

4. Click Convert To Connection File.

5. In the Convert Data Connection dialog box, in the Specify The URL Of The New Data Connection field, type the URL of the data connection library you want to use with the filename for the data connection file such as `http://server/library/filename.udcx`.

6. Under Connection link type, select Relative To Site Collection to link to the data connection file in the same site collection.

7. Click Centrally Managed Connection Library to upload the file to the library in Central Administration.

8. Click OK.

9. Click Close in the Data Connections dialog box to close it.

Once the data connection file is created, farm administrators can upload such files into a data connection files library in Central Administration for central management. These files can then be used by any form templates that have been uploaded using the Manage Form Templates page in Central Administration. Exercise 11.23 shows you this process. You need to be a member of the Farm Administrators group to successfully accomplish this task.

EXERCISE 11.23

Uploading a Data Connection File Using Central Administration

1. On the Central Administration main page, click General Application Settings.

2. On the General Application Settings page, click Manage Data Connection Files under InfoPath Forms Services.

3. On the Manage Data Connections Files page, click Upload.

4. On the Upload Data Connections File page, under Select File, browse to the location of the desired file, click the filename, and then click Save in the Choose File To Upload dialog box.

5. Under Category, specify the desired category for the file, which can be any name.

6. Under Web Accessibility, click Allow HTTP Access To This File if you want to let client applications such as InfoPath Filler to be able to access the data connection file using HTTP.

7. Click Upload.

Managing the Web Service Proxy for InfoPath Forms

The InfoPath Forms Services web service proxy lets InfoPath forms displayed in a web browser connect to web services with credentials trusted by the web service. This also separately passes the identity of the user filling out the form to the web service to authenticate the user. If InfoPath Services didn't use the web service proxy, InfoPath wouldn't be able to authenticate to a web service on a third tier when NTLM would usually prevent user credentials from being reused. The use of symmetrical authentication between a form displayed in InfoPath Filler 2010 and the same form being viewed in a web browser would also not be able to occur.

For InfoPath to use the web service proxy, the InfoPath forms designer must create a web service connection when creating the form in InfoPath Designer 2010. Then the designer must convert the web service data connection to use settings from a data connection file and edit the file to set the useFormsServiceProxy value to True and add an Authentication element referencing a valid Secure Store application ID.

As a SharePoint administrator, you won't necessarily need to know how to perform designer tasks, unless you are also a forms designer, but you will need to know how to enable InfoPath Forms Service web service proxy and to enable server-specific authentication settings.

Exercise 11.24 shows you the former process. You will need to belong to the Farm Administrators group to complete the task.

EXERCISE 11.24

Enabling InfoPath Forms Web Service Proxy

1. On the Central Administration main page, click General Application Settings.

2. On the General Application Settings page, click Configure InfoPath Forms Services Web Service Proxy under InfoPath Forms Services.

3. On the Configure InfoPath Forms Services Web Service Proxy page, click the Enable check box for Enable InfoPath Forms Services Web Service Proxy.

4. Click OK.

Once you have enabled this feature, user form templates will be able to use this service. All administrator-approved form templates have access to the web service proxy even when you have not enabled the feature using the steps in the previous exercise.

To allow user form templates to use the Secure Store Service, these templates must be authorized to use server-specific authentication settings. To permit this, you must enable this authentication form in Central Administration. Exercise 11.25 shows you how. You must be a member of the Farm Administrators group to complete this task.

EXERCISE 11.25

Enabling Server-Specific Authentication

1. On the Central Administration main page, click General Application Settings.

2. On the General Application Settings page, click Configure InfoPath Forms Services under InfoPath Forms Services.

3. On the Configure InfoPath Forms Services page, under Authentication To Data Sources (User Form Templates), select the Allow User Form Templates To Use Authentication Information That Is Contained In Data Connection Files check box.

4. Click OK.

Summary

In this chapter, you learned a great deal of information regarding deploying and managing SharePoint solutions, including the following:

- Sandbox environment planning and deployment
- Setting up and managing the State Service to support workflow and InfoPath Forms Services
- Creating, provisioning, and managing SharePoint workflows
- Enabling and managing features related to InfoPath Forms Services

Exam Essentials

Understanding the Various Tasks Associated with Enabling and Managing a Sandboxed Environment   Understand the concepts behind planning a sandboxed environment and running a separate, isolated SharePoint platform that can be used for testing new SharePoint implementations or modified and customized elements such as web parts.

Understand the Activities Related Enabling Workflows and InfoPath Forms Services   Comprehend the various functions related to enabling the different types of workflows in SharePoint as well as enabling and provisioning InfoPath Forms Services, including their dependence on the State Service and its proper configuration.

Review Questions

1. You are a SharePoint administrator for your company, and you have been tasked with planning a sandbox solution for deployment. You are conducting a high-level review of SharePoint sandboxes, including the steps that must be performed by a farm administrator. Of the following, which steps are considered valid for preparing sandbox deployment? (Choose all that apply.)

    A. The farm administrator must enable and start the sandboxing service on each server that will run the sandbox solution.

    B. The farm administrator must activate and validate the sandbox solution.

    C. The farm administrator must apply a load balancing scheme to all sandbox solutions if load balancing is a requirement.

    D. The farm administrator must set resource quotas that cannot be exceeded by all the combined site collections in the solution if resource quotas are a requirement.

2. You are a SharePoint administrator for your company, and you have been tasked with planning a sandbox solution for deployment. You are conducting a high-level review of SharePoint sandboxes, including sandbox isolation management and resources that an isolated sandbox environment is unable to access. Of the following, what are the resources an isolated sandbox cannot access? (Choose all that apply.)

    A. Cannot access resources on a different site collection within the sandbox

    B. Cannot access a database

    C. Cannot access the `manifest.xml` file

    D. Cannot access resources on the local server

3. You are a SharePoint administrator for your company, and you have been tasked with planning a sandbox solution for deployment. You are conducting a high-level review of SharePoint sandboxes, including planning for load balancing in the sandbox. As a SharePoint administrator, you can choose between two possible load-balancing schemes for the sandbox. Of the following, which two schemes are valid? (Choose two.)

    A. Local load balancing will always run the solution on the same hard drive of the server that received the request.

    B. Local load balancing will always run the solution on the same server that received the request.

    C. Remote load balancing will select the server that the solution previously ran on and for which it has an affinity.

    D. Remote load balancing will select a different server that the solution previously ran on to balance resource load.

4. You are a SharePoint administrator for your company, and you have been tasked with planning a sandbox solution for deployment. You are conducting a high-level review of SharePoint sandboxes, including deployment tasks. You have included the relevant site collection administrators involved in the sandbox project, since they will be responsible for much of the work, once the sandboxed environment is enabled. Of the following tasks, which can be performed both in a web browser and using Windows PowerShell? (Choose all that apply.)

A. Enabling sandbox solutions

B. Configuring sandbox load balancing

C. Blocking a sandbox solution

D. Managing user solutions

5. You are a SharePoint administrator for your company, and you are planning to configure the State Service pursuant to enabling workflows and InfoPath Forms Services in your SharePoint environment. What is the most common method of configuring the State Service?

A. Using Central Administration and clicking Manage Services On The Farm

B. Using Central Administration and clicking Service Management

C. Opening Windows PowerShell and executing the relevant cmdlets

D. Enabling the State Service while running the Server Farm Configuration Wizard when you first install SharePoint

6. You are a SharePoint administrator for your company, and you are planning to enable and activate workflows in your environment. You are working with the site collection administrators who have requested that workflows be enabled for their collections. The site collection administrators want to know which tasks they can perform within their site collections. Of the following, what are the valid answers? (Choose all that apply.)

A. Enabling declarative workflows

B. Activating workflows in a site collection

C. Associating a workflow with a list or document library

D. Associating a workflow with a content type

7. You are a SharePoint administrator for your company, and you are planning to enable and activate workflows in your environment. You are working with the site collection administrators who have requested that workflows be enabled for their collections. The site collection administrators want to avoid confusion about which tasks they must perform to enable workflows and in which order the tasks must be performed. As part of your response to these administrators, what valid answers to you give? (Choose all that apply.)

A. The first task is to activate workflows at the site collection level on the top-level site of the collection.

B. Once workflows have been activated at the top-level site for a site collection, it is activated for all the subsites in the collection.

C. If workflows are activated at the web application level, they are available for all site collections in the web application.

D. Once workflows are active for a site collection, the next step is to create one or more workflow associations.

8. You are a site collection administrator who is configuring workflows for your site collection. You are associating a workflow to a document library that assigns a task list and history list for the workflow. The documents that will be processed through the workflow contain sensitive material, and you don't want all workflow participants to be able to view any task lists containing such confidential material. To prevent this, what must you do?

A. You can associate specific tasks lists to the specific workflows containing the sensitive material so that only the participants for those workflows can see the tasks lists.

B. You can set the permissions on the workflows containing the sensitive material so that only the assigned users for those workflows can see the relevant tasks lists.

C. You can create a security workflow requiring higher than normal permissions and then give the relevant participants those permission levels.

D. There is no option for isolating a task list. All workflow participants in the site collection can automatically see all workflow tasks lists.

9. You are a site collection administrator who is configuring workflows for your site collection. By default, a wide variety of SharePoint users can start a workflow, but you want to restrict this ability to a smaller number of document authors. What method can you use to limit who can start a workflow?

A. You can specify that only users with Edit Item permissions can start a workflow.

B. You can specify that only users with Manage List permissions can start a workflow.

C. You can specify that only users with Edit Library permissions can start a workflow.

D. You can specify that only users with Workflow Design permissions can start a workflow.

10. You are a site collection owner and administrator who is configuring workflows for your site collection. You have heard that you can associate a workflow with different content types, but you aren't sure of the specifics. You consult with a SharePoint farm administrator, and she tells you that you have the ability to associate a workflow with the following content types. (Choose all that apply).

A. List content types

B. Library content types

C. Site collection content types

D. Site content types

11. You are a site collection owner and administrator who is configuring workflows for your site collection, and you want to associate a workflow with a specific site content type on a particular site. Where must this task be performed?

A. Start on the Site Settings page under Galleries for the specific site.

B. At the top-level site for the site collection containing the site.

C. In Central Administration, in the web application containing the site collection containing the site.

D. The task must be performed using Windows PowerShell.

12. You are the site collection administrator for a site collection that has workflows enabled. Users for the sites in your collection use either Microsoft Office 2007 or Microsoft Office 2010 to create documents that need to enter the workflow. These users want to know if it's possible to set up the workflow so they can submit documents directly from their versions of Office. What do you tell them? (Choose two answers.)

   A. After opening the relevant list or library in the site the user wants, click Save & Send. Under Workflows, select the desired workflow on the File tab in the desired Office 2007 application. Then click Start Workflow.

   B. After opening the relevant document in the list or library in the site the user wants, click Save & Send on the File tab in the desired Office 2010 application. Under Workflows, select the desired workflow. Then click Start Workflow.

   C. After opening the relevant document in the list or library in the site the user wants, click the Microsoft Office Button in Office 2007. Select Workflows. Then, in the list that appears, click Start next to the desired workflow.

   D. After opening the relevant list or library in the site the user wants, click the Microsoft Office Button in Office 2010 and select Workflows. In the list that appears, click Start next to the desired workflow.

13. You are the site collection administrator for a collection with workflows enabled. The SharePoint farm administrator who originally enabled workflows has suggested that you regularly monitor the performance of the workflows in your site collection. You review the different ways of performing these tasks and want to view an individual workflow report. What must you do?

   A. On the desired site, browse to the list or library for the workflow, click the item or document to open the menu, click Workflows, and click View Workflow Reports under Workflow History on the Workflow Status page.

   B. On the desired site, browse to the list or library for the workflow. In the row for the specific item, click the link in the workflow status column to view the reports.

   C. On the desired site, click All Site Content and then click Site Workflows. On the Workflows page, click the name of the desired workflow to view the reports.

   D. On the top-level site for the site collection, click Site Actions and then click Site Settings. Under Site Administration, click workflows and then click the name of the specific workflow to view the reports.

14. You are a SharePoint administrator for your company, and you are reviewing your workflow deployment and maintenance strategy. Although classic workflows fulfill most of the workflow requirements for the users you support, you believe some of them may benefit from using declarative workflows, which provide a better balance between flexibility and support for user recommendations. What is the easiest way for you to enable declarative workflows?

   A. Declarative workflows are enabled automatically when you run the Farm Configuration Wizard.

   B. In Central Administration, navigate to the desired web application and click Manage, General Settings. Then click Workflows and enable declarative workflows in the Workflow Settings dialog box.

   C. In Central Administration, navigate to System Settings, Farm Management. Then click Workflows and enable declarative workflows on the Workflows page.

   D. On the top-level site for the site collection on which you want to enable declarative workflows, click Site Actions, Site Settings, Galleries, Workflows. Then enable declarative workflows by selecting the relevant check box.

15. You are a SharePoint administrator for your company, and you have enabled workflows in your environment. You have received requests from some of the site collection administrators for web applications you maintain that they would like to be able to invite non-authenticated users to participate in some of their workflows. Initially, this seems like an unacceptable security risk, but you check with the CIO, and there appears to be a business case for this activity. Of the following, which nonauthenticated user types can you allow access to SharePoint workflows? (Choose all that apply.)

   A. You can allow SharePoint users who are not normally able to access the specific workflows to participate by adding them to the access workflow list.

   B. You can allow non-SharePoint users to participate as long as they agree to the conditions of a nondisclosure agreement.

   C. You can allow SharePoint users who are not normally able to access the specific workflows to participate by sending them an email with instructions on how to request access.

   D. You can allow non-SharePoint uses to participate in workflows by creating SharePoint accounts with limited workflow access.

16. You are a SharePoint administrator for your company, and you have received requests from some site collection administrators that the workflow history items become unavailable too soon, and they'd like to have access to these records beyond the default 60 days. These links are removed as part of an automatic maintenance system for workflow. What can you do to accommodate the request?

A. At the top-level site for the site collections that want to have access to workflow reports beyond the default period, click Site Actions, Site Settings, Workflow Settings, Reports. In the Workflow Reports dialog box, clear the Automatically Delete Workflow Reports After 60 Days check box.

B. At the top-level site for the site collections that want to have access to workflow reports beyond the default period, click Site Actions, Site Settings, Site Collection Administration, Workflows. On the Workflows page, clear the Automatically Delete Workflow Reports After 60 Days check box.

C. In Central Administration, click Monitoring, Timer Jobs, Review Job Definitions. On the Job Definitions page, click Auto Cleanup and then click Disable on the Edit Timer Job page.

D. The Auto Cleanup feature cannot be disabled.

17. You are the site collection administrator for a site collection with workflows enabled. You have requested a custom-made workflow template be designed and deployed for your site collection and have just been notified that the template is now available as a `.wsp` file. What must you do you enable this template so it can be used on sites in your site collection?

A. You must first download the template from the Site Assets page under Document Libraries in the top-level site in your site collection, save it in a location on your hard drive, and then upload it to the Solution Gallery on the top-level site in your site collection.

B. You must first download the template from the Solutions Gallery in the top-level site in your site collection, save it in a location on your hard drive, and then upload it to the Site Assets page under Document Libraries in your site collection.

C. You must download the template from the Solution Gallery on the designer's SharePoint site collection and then upload it to the Site Assets page under Document Libraries in the top-level site of your site collection.

D. You must download the template from the Site Assets page of the Document Library of the designer's SharePoint site and upload it to the Solution Gallery in the top-level site in your site collection.

18. You are a SharePoint administrator for your company, and you are enabling InfoPath Form Services in your environment. You must perform a number of tasks to make InfoPath forms available to users in SharePoint. What are the first steps you must take to begin the process of performing most InfoPath-related tasks?

A. In Central Administration, click System Settings. Then under InfoPath Forms Services, click Configure InfoPath Forms Services.

B. In Central Administration, click Services on a server. Then under InfoPath Forms Services, click Configure InfoPath Forms Services.

C. In Central Administration, click General Application Settings. Then under InfoPath Forms Services, click Configure InfoPath Forms Services.

D. Configuring InfoPath Forms Services is usually done using Windows PowerShell.

19. You are a SharePoint administrator for your company, and you are enabling InfoPath Form Services in your environment. InfoPath Forms can use data connection files to specify which settings to use when connecting to a data source. You want to be able to convert a data connection to a data connection file so you can store the configuration settings in XML format. What tool or utility must you use to perform this task?

A. Central Administration

B. Windows PowerShell

C. InfoPath Designer 2010

D. Visual Studio

20. You are a SharePoint administrator for your company, and you are enabling InfoPath Form Services in your environment. InfoPath Forms Services web service proxy lets InfoPath Forms displayed in a web browser to connect to web services with credentials trusted by the web service. You have been tasked with enabling InfoPath Forms web service proxy in your environment. What must you do to accomplish your task?

A. Enable the web service proxy on the Configure InfoPath Forms Services Web Service Proxy page in Central Administration.

B. Use Windows PowerShell cmdlets.

C. Edit the service connection data file using InfoPath Designer 2010 and set the useFormsServiceProxy value to True.

D. Enable the web service proxy on the Configure InfoPath Forms Services page in Central Administration.

Answers to Review Questions

1. **A, C, D.** The site collection administrator can activate and validate the sandboxed solution as well as upload the solution to the site collection's Solution Gallery.

2. **A, B.** The sandbox must be able to connect to the local server and access the `manifest.xml` file, which contains the configuration information defining the sandbox environment.

3. **B, C.** Local load balancing will always run the solution on the same server that received the request. Remote load balancing will select the server that has the most solution affinity; that is, the solution will run on the server where it has previously been loaded and been run.

4. **A.** Only enabling sandbox solutions can be performed both in the browser and using Windows PowerShell. This task must also be performed by the farm administrator.

5. **D.** In all likelihood, you enabled the State Service as part of the SharePoint installation process when you ran the Farm Configuration Wizard.

6. **B, C, D.** All the listed tasks can be performed by the site collection administrator within the site collection except enabling declarative workflows, which must be performed by a farm administrator using Central Administration.

7. **A, B, D.** You cannot activate workflows at the web application level.

8. **A.** You can create specific lists for workflows rather than using the default list or a list already created for other workflows to isolate the list information to the participants of the specific workflows only.

9. **B.** Normally, any user with Edit Item permissions can start a workflow, but if you want to restrict this activity further, you can specify that Require Manage List permissions be required. Then, only users with Manage List or Web Designer permissions will be able to initiate a workflow. The Edit Library and Workflow Design permissions are bogus.

10. **A, B, D.** You cannot specifically associate a workflow with a site collection content type. All of the other options are valid.

11. **A.** Go the specific site where you want to make the association and navigate to the Site Settings page; then under Galleries, click Site Content Types and make the association by clicking the desired content type.

12. **B, C.** These two options show how to begin a workflow from within their respective versions of Microsoft Office.

13. **A.** Option B will let you check on a workflow's status but not view the report. Option C will let you check the status of a workflow associated with a site, and option D will let you check the workflow reports for the entire site collection but not for a specific workflow.

14. **B.** Declarative workflows must be enabled at the web application level in Central Administration. All the other options are bogus.

15. C. Internal SharePoint users can be allowed to participate in workflows they normally wouldn't be able to access by following the request procedure in the email you send them. External users can be allowed to participate in workflows upon their signing a nondisclosure agreement; however, this isn't an actual SharePoint requirement.

16. C. This feature must be disabled in Central Administration as described in option C.

17. A. Only the first options gives the correct procedure. The other options are bogus.

18. C. Only option C provides the correct procedure. The other options are bogus.

19. C. You typically will use Microsoft InfoPath Designer 2010 to open the desired form template and convert the data connection to a data connection file.

20. A. Only option A describes the correct procedure. Windows PowerShell cannot be used and, while a designer must perform the task in option C before you enable the InfoPath Forms web service proxy service in your environment, it's not part of the actual enabling procedure. Option D is bogus.

Chapter

12

Backing Up and Restoring SharePoint

MICROSOFT EXAM OBJECTIVE COVERED IN THIS CHAPTER:

✓ **Maintain a SharePoint Environment**

- Backup and Restore a SharePoint Environment

This chapter provides the core information necessary to plan and execute a backup and restore strategy for SharePoint Server 2010. You'll begin by learning the required permissions for various accounts including the Timer Service account and then proceed to SharePoint backup details. The information covers the different variations in performing backup and restore tasks, including backing up and restoring the entire server farm as well as performing similar jobs using smaller SharePoint elements such as exporting and importing a list or document library.

Configuring Permissions for Backup and Recovery

The backup and restore process for SharePoint is dependent on accounts, groups, and users having access to specific operations and directories. Accounts include the Timer Service account and the SQL Server service account. The required permissions aren't present by default, and a SharePoint farm administrator must initially configure and then maintain these permissions.

Required Services and Groups for Backup and Recovery

Both the SharePoint Services Timer V4 (SPTimerV4) and the SQL Server service account are required to perform backup and restore operations, and they both need to have Full Control permission on any folders used for backup. Also, members of both the Administrators group on the local computer and the Farm Administrators group require specific permissions to different farm components.

Managing Service Permissions

Before performing any backup and restore operations, you must create a network folder in which to store backups and then give SharePoint Services Timer V4 (SPTimerV4) and the SQL Server service account Full Control over this folder. You can add these permissions to the folder in the same way you would do so on the local computer, by using the Security tab in the folder properties dialog box to add the accounts and giving them Full Control. You must also grant Full Control to the required group accounts as outlined in the next section.

Managing Group Permissions

To perform recovery operations from Central Administration, being a member of the Administrators group for the local computer is required for backing up and restoring the farm, service applications, and content database. Being a member of the Farm Administrators group is required for backing up and restoring site collections, as well as sites, lists, and document libraries.

If you are using Windows PowerShell for backing up and restoring, you must be a member of the Administrators group on the local machine and have Full Control on the backup folder to perform these operations on the farm, service applications, and content database. To back up and restore a site collection using PowerShell, you must be a member of the Farm Administrators group and have Full Control on the backup folder. To perform these operations on sites, lists, and document libraries using PowerShell, you must be a member of the Administrators group on the local machine and have Full Control on the backup folder.

Managing Permissions to Back Up and Restore Using Windows PowerShell

Anyone who will be performing backup and restore operations using Windows PowerShell must be a member of the SharePoint_Shell_Access role on the relevant database as well as have the permissions described in the previous section. The `Add-SPShellAdmin` cmdlet is used to accomplish this task. You need to grant this permission only once to a specific user account and to all the relevant databases unless new farm components are added. The task will have to be performed again for the relevant accounts for new components.

Adding and Removing Accounts to the SharePoint_Shell_Access Role

To add a user account to a specific database, type the following command at the prompt and then press Enter, replacing the sample values with your production values:

```
Add-SPShellAdmin -Username <User account> -Database <Database ID>
```

To add a user account to all the databases in the farm, type the following command, and then press Enter, replacing the sample values with your production values:

```
ForEach ($db in Get-SPDatabase) {Add-SPShellAdmin -Username <User account>
-Database $db}
```

To remove a user account from all the databases in the farm, type the following command, and then press Enter, replacing the sample values with your production values:

```
ForEach ($db in Get-SPDatabase) {Remove-SPShellAdmin -Username <User account>
-Database $db}
```

To view the user accounts currently added to the databases in the farm, type the following command, and then press Enter, replacing the sample values with your production values:

```
ForEach ($db in Get-SPDatabase) {Get-SPShellAdmin -Database $db}
```

Managing Backup Operations

If you are responsible for a server infrastructure of any kind, you know what a backup is and what it's good for. You also know you can't live without an adequate backup plan, and you cannot ignore a substandard or absent backup solution for even one day, because that could be the day when a flood hits or something explodes.

Backing Up SharePoint Components

SharePoint's backup solution is capable of preserving your environment on a continuum, from backing up the entire farm to any of its components, right down to lists and libraries. This section of the chapter will present that continuum one element at a time, starting with its biggest piece, the whole farm, and working its way down.

Backing Up the Farm

In terms of performing a backup of the farm, you must back up both the entire contents of the farm and the farm configuration.

You can think of the farm as being made up of two large, general components: the farm content database and the farm configuration database. The content database contains all the content that comprises the SharePoint farm, including site collections, sites, list, and library content. The farm configuration database contains all the SharePoint configuration information for the server farm.

In Central Administration, when you click Perform A Backup under Backup And Restore, you can see on the subsequent page all of the components that are backed up when you back up the content and configuration data for the entire farm, including the following:

- InfoPath Forms Services and all its subsettings
- SharePoint Server State Service
- Microsoft SharePoint Foundation web application, which includes all web applications containing site collections
- WSS_Administration, which contains SharePoint Central Administration
- SharePoint Server State Service proxy
- SPUserCode, which contains the various groups of code collected for backup
- Diagnostics Service
- Global Search Settings
- SharePoint Foundation Help Search
- Application Registry Service
- Shared Services, which includes Shared Services applications and Shared Services proxies

You must perform this activity regularly to ensure that if a catastrophic failure of the farm should occur, usually because of a significant hardware failure, you would be able to restore the farm environment.

Although the farm can continue to be accessed during the backup, farm performance will be affected by this process, so it's usually done after business hours if possible. Prior to performing this task for the first time, you will need to create a folder either on the local computer or on the network to which you will back up the farm. The recommended procedure is to first back up the farm to a folder on the local machine and then transfer the backup to a remote location on the network.

Although a farm backup stores the farm configuration and the content databases, the restore process cannot be performed for these elements using SharePoint Server 2010 tools. The restore process will be covered later in this chapter.

Although the SharePoint farm backup process backs up the Business Data Connectivity (BDC) service external content type definitions, it doesn't back up the actual data source. If you intend on protecting this data, back up the data source at the same time you back up the BDC service.

Restoring the BDC service can be a little tricky. If you restore the BDC service first and then restore the data service to a different location, you must change the location information stored in the external content type definition. Failure to do so might result in the BDC service being unable to find the data source.

SharePoint backs up the remote Binary Large Object stores, also called BLOB stores, only if you use the FILESTREAM remote BLOB store provider to move data in remote BLOB stores. If you use a different provider, you are required to manually back up the remote BLOB stores. For more information on BLOB stores, see Chapter 14, "Optimizing SharePoint."

One final note before proceeding with farm backup tasks: backing up the farm does not back up any certificates used to create trust relationships. To reestablish these trusts after restoring the farm, you must make sure you have copies of these certificates before you begin the farm backup.

The beauty of using Windows PowerShell to back up the farm is that you can perform the task either manually or as part of an automated script that periodically executes the backup. Exercise 12.1 shows you the manual procedure. If you are backing up the farm for the first time, you must use the Full option. You can subsequently use the Differential option. The -BackupMethod parameter is used to indicate the desired option.

EXERCISE 12.1

Backing Up the Farm with Windows PowerShell

1. Open Windows PowerShell as an administrator.

2. At the prompt, type the following command and then press Enter, substituting the sample values for your production values and selecting either Full or Differential:

```
Backup-SPFarm -Directory <Backup folder> -BackupMethod {Full |
Differential} [ -Verbose]
```

You can perform the same task using Central Administration. You must be a member of the Farm Administrators group to approach this task. Exercise 12.2 shows you how. After you configure and start the backup, the backup process may take several seconds to begin.

You will not be able to perform farm backup and restore tasks on a single-server SharePoint deployment with a built-in database.

EXERCISE 12.2

Backing Up the Farm with Central Administration

1. On the Central Administration home page, click Perform A Backup under Backup And Restore.

2. On the page that says Perform a Backup – Step 1 of 2: Select Component To Back Up, select the farm in the available list, as shown here, and then click Next.

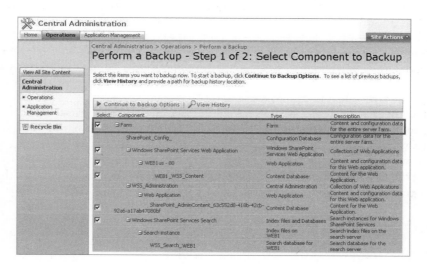

EXERCISE 12.2 *(continued)*

3. On the page that says Start Backup – Step 2 of 2: Select Backup Options, under Backup Type, select either Full if this is the first backup for the farm or Differential if you have previously performed a full farm backup.

4. Under Back Up Only Configuration Settings, click Back Up Content And Configuration Settings.

5. Under Backup File Location, type the UNC path to the backup folder and then click Start Backup.

6. Review the status of the backup under Readiness at the top of the Backup And Restore Status page and under Backup lower on the page, either allowing the information to refresh every 30 seconds automatically or manually refreshing the page by clicking Refresh. Allow the backup to complete.

Any problems with the backup will appear in the Failure Message column on the Backup And Restore Job Status page. Failure messages can also be viewed in the Spbackup.log file. You can find the file in the backup folder at the location you specified with the UNC path during the previous task.

It's possible to back up the farm using SQL Server tools but only the databases containing the farm's content. To back up the entire farm including the configuration data, you must use either Windows PowerShell or Central Administration. If you need to back up only the content databases, Exercise 12.3 will illustrate the procedure. You must be a member of the SQL Server db_backupoperator fixed database role on the database server where the database is located to successfully complete this exercise.

In your farm, you will need to perform this process again for each of the databases, including the configuration and search databases.

In the previous exercise, you saw how to use SQL Server tools to back up the server farm database but not the configuration. Although it's recommended that you periodically perform a backup of the complete farm including the configuration and the database, you can back up just the configuration using either Windows PowerShell or Central Administration. You cannot perform this task using SQL Server tools or the Data Protection Manager.

EXERCISE 12.3

Backing Up the Farm Databases with SQL Server Tools

1. Open the SQL Server Management Studio tool on your computer and connect to the desired database server.

2. In Object Explorer, expand Databases, as shown here.

EXERCISE 12.3 *(continued)*

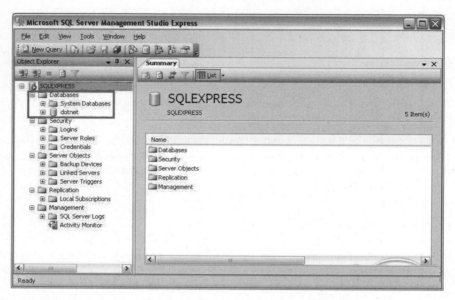

3. Right-click the desired database, point to Tasks, and then click Back Up.

4. When the Back Up Database dialog box appears, under Source, select the desired backup type in the Backup Type list based on the desired recovery model, such as Simple, Full, or Bulk Logged.

5. Under Backup Component, click Database.

6. Type a name for the backup set in the Name field or accept the default.

7. Specify an expiration date for the backup set, which indicates when this backup set can be overwritten by subsequent backup sets, or accept the default value of 0 days, indicating that the backup set never expires.

8. Under Destination, specify the location of the backup folder and then click OK.

Performing a farm configuration backup extracts the configuration settings from the configuration database. This will not be sufficient to allow you to restore service applications. You will need to perform a backup of both the configuration and content database to ensure such a restoration.

The following shows you how to back up the farm configuration with Windows PowerShell. To perform this task, either you must be a member of the db_backupoperator fixed database role on the desired database server or you must specify the value for the DatabaseCredentials parameter.

Backing Up the Configuration Database with Windows PowerShell

Open Windows PowerShell as an administrator, type the following command at the prompt, and then press Enter, substituting the sample values with your production values:

```
Backup-SPConfigurationDatabase -Directory <Backup folder> -DatabaseServer
<Database server name> -DatabaseName <Database name> -DatabaseCredentials
<PowerShell Credential Object> [-Verbose]
```

You can also back up the configuration database using Central Administration. You must be a member of the Farm Administrators group to perform this task. Exercise 12.4 will show you the steps.

EXERCISE 12.4

Backing Up the Configuration Database with Central Administration

1. On the Central Administration home page, click Perform A Backup under Backup And Restore.

2. On the page that says Perform a Backup – Step 1 of 2: Select Component To Back Up, select the farm in the available list and then click Next.

3. On the page that says Start Backup – Step 2 of 2: Select Backup Options, select Full under Backup Type.

4. Under Backup Only Configuration Settings, select Backup Only Configuration Settings.

5. Under Backup File Location, type the UNC path to the location of the backup folder and then click Start Backup.

6. Monitor the backup status, allowing the backup to proceed to conclusion.

7. Any problems with the backup will appear in the Failure Message column on the Backup And Restore Job Status page. Failure messages can also be viewed in the Spbackup .log file. You can find the file in the backup folder at the location you specified with the UNC path during the previous task.

Backing Up Applications and Services

Although it's best practice to regularly back up your entire SharePoint farm, there may be a business or technical reason to back up web applications more often. While backing up the entire farm backs up all web applications at the same time, if you want to back up just web applications, you can back them up only one at a time. As with any other backup operation, access to the farm and web applications will remain available, but the backup may affect performance, so it's best to perform the task after business hours if possible.

You can back up a web application using Windows PowerShell, Central Administration, or SQL Server tools. The following shows you the PowerShell method.

Backing Up a Web Application with Windows PowerShell

Open Windows PowerShell as an administrator, type the following command at the prompt, and then press Enter, substituting the sample values with your production values. If you are backing up the web application for the first time, select the Full option.

```
Backup-SPFarm -Directory <Backup folder>
-BackupMethod {Full | Differential}
-Item <Web application name> [-Verbose]
```

Backing Up a Web Application with Central Administration

The method of backing up a web application using Central Administration is almost identical to the previous Central Administration backup tasks you've performed. One significant difference is that on the Perform A Backup – Step 1 Of 2: Select Component To Back Up page, select the web application from the list; then click Next. Otherwise, follow the identical steps you performed in Exercise 12.2 and Exercise 12.4.

Backing Up a Web Application with SQL Server Tools

As with the server farm, you cannot back up the entire web application using SQL Server tools. You can only back up the databases associated with the application.

Backing up a web application with SQL Server Management Studio is identical with the steps you performed in Exercise 12.3. The only difference is, in step 3, you must choose the desired database for the web application rather than the database for the entire farm. Otherwise, follow the same steps.

Backing Up Search Using Windows PowerShell

Backing up search with PowerShell is substantially similar to performing other backup functions at the command prompt. Like other SharePoint features, it is optimal to back up SharePoint at the farm level, but you may have the occasion to back up just search.

If you are using FAST Search Server 2010 for SharePoint, you should also back up the Content SSA and Query SSA, which includes the People Search index, as well as backing up the FAST Search Server.

To back up search with PowerShell, type the following code at the prompt and then press Enter, replacing the sample code with your production code. If you are backing up search for the first time, use the Full option:

```
Backup-SPFarm -Directory <Backup folder>
-BackupMethod {Full | Differential}
-Item <Search service application name> [-Verbose]
```

Backing Up Search Using Central Administration

The method of backing up a web application using Central Administration is almost identical to the previous Central Administration backup tasks you've performed. One significant difference is that on the Perform A Backup – Step 1 Of 2: Select Component To Back Up page, expand Shared Services, and then expand Shared Services Applications to view the list of service applications in the farm. Select the search service application from the list of components and then click Next. Otherwise, follow the identical steps you performed in Exercise 12.2 and Exercise 12.4.

Backing Up the Secure Store Service with Windows PowerShell

Before you back up the Secure Store Service, you must first manually record the passphrase, which you will need to access the Secure Store Service once it has been restored after backup. Occasions when you would back up the Secure Store Service are when you change or refresh the master key.

Backing up the Secure Store Service with PowerShell is very much the same as the other backup procedures you've performed except that you must always use the Full option.

At the prompt, type the following code, substituting the sample values with your production values, and then press Enter:

```
Backup-SPFarm -Directory  <Backup folder>
-BackupMethod Full -Item <Secure Store Service > [-Verbose]
```

Backing Up the Secure Store Service with Central Administration

The method of backing up a web application using Central Administration is almost identical with the previous Central Administration backup tasks you've performed. One significant difference is that on the Perform A Backup – Step 1 Of 2: Select Component To Back Up page, expand Shared Services, expand the Shared Services Applications node, select the Secure Store Service application from the list of components, and then click Next. Otherwise, follow the identical steps you performed in Exercise 12.2 and Exercise 12.4.

Keep in mind that the Secure Store Service can consist of numerous components, and you must select the topmost component to ensure a complete backup.

Backing Up Databases

The single part of SharePoint that can continue growing and growing and eventually become huge is the content database. This holds all of the "stuff" that users create in SharePoint including site collections, sites, lists, libraries, list items, and library documents. For this reason, it's best if you back up the content database separately from backing up the SharePoint farm. In an enterprise environment, you will likely have multiple content databases; however, you can back up only one content database at a time.

As with prior backup tasks, you can back up the content database using Windows PowerShell, Central Administration, and SQL Server tools. Exercise 12.5 will show you the Central administration method. You must be a member of the Farm Administrators group to successfully complete this task.

EXERCISE 12.5

Backing Up the Content Database with Central Administration

1. On the Central Administration home page, click Perform A Backup under Backup And Restore.

2. On the page that says Perform A Backup – Step 1 Of 2: Select Component To Back Up, select the desired content database in the available list and then click Next.

3. On the Start Backup – Step 2 Of 2: Select Backup Options page, select either Full or Differential under Backup Type, selecting Full if you have never backed up the content database before.

4. Under Backup File Location, type the UNC path of the folder to which you will be backing up the database and then click Start Backup.

5. Allow the backup procedure to continue, monitoring its progress on the Backup And Restore Job Status page.

Backing Up the Content Database with Windows PowerShell

Using Windows PowerShell to back up a content database is similar to other PowerShell backup tasks. At the prompt, type the following code and then press Enter, substituting the sample values for your production values and selecting the Full option if you have never previously backed up the content database:

```
Backup-SPFarm -Directory <Backup folder> -BackupMethod {Full | Differential}
-Item <Content database name> [-Verbose]
```

In other backup tasks, when you used SQL Server tools, you were unable to perform a complete backup of the selected component. For the content database, this isn't so, and you will be able to perform a complete backup. Exercise 12.6 shows you how. You must be a member of the SQL Server db_backupoperator fixed database role on the database server containing the desired content database to perform this task.

EXERCISE 12.6

Backing Up the Content Database with SQL Server Tools

1. Open the SQL Server Management Studio tool on your computer and connect to the desired database server.

2. In Object Explorer, expand Databases.

3. Right-click the desired database, point to Tasks, and then click Back Up.

4. When the Back Up Database dialog box appears, select the desired backup procedure from the Backup Type list under Source.

EXERCISE 12.6 *(continued)*

5. Under Backup Component, click Database.

6. You can either use the default name provided in the text area for the backup set or type the name you want.

7. Enter the expiration date for the backup set in days to determine how long the backup set will be preserved before it can be overwritten by a more recent backup, with 0 days meaning the backup set will never expire.

8. Under Destination, specify the location of the backup folder to which you will back up the content database.

9. Click OK.

You will need to perform this set of steps for every content database you intend on backing up, which should be all the databases you depend upon in your SharePoint environment.

You can also back up databases, including content databases, by backing them up to a snapshot. A database snapshot is a read-only static view of the source database as it existed at the moment of snapshot creation. Snapshots are particularly useful in the event of a user error in a database. The snapshot can be used to revert the database to the state it was in when the snapshot was created. You can also take a database snapshot right before making a major change to the database, such as the table structure or schema. If a problem occurs, you can revert to the snapshot and preserve all your data.This task has some specific requirements. You must be running Microsoft SQL Server 2008 with SP1 and with Cumulative Update 2 Enterprise Edition. Also, you can perform this task using SQL Server tools only and must be a member of the SQL Server db_owner fixed database role on the SQL server containing the desired database.

 You cannot use a snapshot database to back up a site collection if a remote BLOB storage provider is being used.

A database snapshot is a read-only, static container of a source database as it existed at the moment you took the snapshot. This is very much like taking a photograph of a person or object, preserving the appearance of the person or object at the exact moment you opened the camera's shutter.

Any uncommitted transactions existing at the moment the snapshot is taken are rolled back in a new database snapshot. This occurs because the database engine runs recovery after the snapshot has been created. All transactions already committed are not impacted by this process.

Snapshots are stored like any other backup file, so you must have a folder already created where you want to put the snapshot, prior to beginning this task. While backing up a database to a snapshot is performed with SQL Server tools, there are some interesting differences in the steps than in exercises you previously performed with this utility. Exercise 12.7 will provide the necessary information.

EXERCISE 12.7

Backing Up a Database to a Snapshot with SQL Server Tools

1. Open the SQL Server Management Studio tool on your computer and connect to the desired database server.

2. In Object Explorer, expand Databases.

3. In the list that appears, select the desired database and then click New Query.

4. Enter the following code, substituting the sample values with your production values:

```
CREATE DATABASE <snapshot name>
ON
(
NAME=<logical name of the database file>,
FILENAME = 'c:\WSS_Backup1.ss')
AS SNAPSHOT OF <database name>;
```

Backing Up Site Collections, Sites, Lists, and Libraries

As with other SharePoint components, it's generally recommended that you back up the entire farm, but there may be occasions when you will need to back up smaller elements, including site collections, sites, or individual lists and libraries.

For backing up a site collection, if the collection's Lock Status is set to Not Locked or Adding Content Prevented, the site collection is set to Read-Only for the duration of the backup operation. This prevents SharePoint users from changing features of the site collection during the actual backup. Once the backup is complete, the site collection's status is returned to normal.

You can perform a site collection backup using either Central Administration or Windows PowerShell. Exercise 12.8 will show you the Central Administration method. You must belong to the Farm Administrators group to perform this task. The SharePoint Service Timer V4 service must also have Full Control permissions to the folder to which you will be backing up the site collection.

EXERCISE 12.8

Backing Up a Site Collection Using Central Administration

1. On the Central Administration main page, click Perform A Site Collection Backup under Backup And Restore.

2. On the Site Collection Backup page, select the desired site collection in the Site Collection list.

EXERCISE 12.8 *(continued)*

3. Type the UNC path to the backup file in the Filename field and, if you want to reuse the file, select the Overwrite Existing File check box.

4. Click Start Backup.

5. Allow the backup to proceed and monitor the backup on the Granular Backup Job Status page or on the current page under Site Collection Backup.

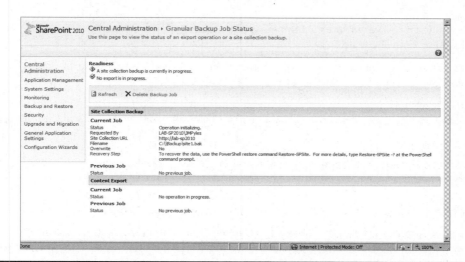

To perform the same task with Windows PowerShell, open PowerShell as an administrator and enter the following code at the prompt, substituting the sample values for your production values; then press Enter:

```
Backup-SPSite -Identity <Site collection name>
-Path <backup file> [Force] [-NoSiteLock] [-UseSqlSnapshot] [-Verbose]
```

The following exercises are equally applicable for exporting individual sites, lists, and libraries, so there won't be separate tasks for exporting each of the SharePoint components. You can use either Central Administration or Windows PowerShell for such export processes. Exercise 12.9 shows you how to export using Central Administration. You must be a member of the Farm Administrators group to proceed.

EXERCISE 12.9

Exporting a Site, List, or Library with Central Administration

1. On the Central Administration main page, click Backup And Restore.

2. On the Backup And Restore page, click Export A Site Or List under Granular Backup.

3. On the Site Or List Export page, select the desired site collection from the available list under Site Collection and then select the desired site from the site list.

4. To export a list, select the desired list or library from the List list, or ignore this step if you are exporting the entire site.

5. Under File Location, type the UNC path of the folder to which you are exporting in the Filename field.

6. If you want to overwrite a currently existing file in the folder, click the Overwrite Existing Files check box.

7. To export all the security settings and permissions for the list or library, click the Export Full Security check box under Export Full Security.

8. To specify a version of the list or library to export, in the Export Versions list, select one of the following: All Versions, Last Major, Current Version, or Last Major and Last Minor.

9. Click Start Export.

10. Monitor the export procedure on the Granular Backup Job Status page.

Exporting a Site, List, or Library with Windows PowerShell

Although you can perform this task with a relatively small command string at the prompt, there's a little more to it than that. If you are exporting a larger site, list, or library, it's better to use the GradualDelete parameter, which actually deletes the site, preventing further access to any of its content. The deletion, as the name suggests, occurs over a period of time, managed by the Timer Job, minimizing the impact on server farm and SQL server performance.

If you want to specify a version of the site, list, or library, use the IncludeVersions parameter. The default version is LastMajor, but you can specify CurrentVersion, LastMajorandMinor, or All. To include the security settings and permissions that are associated with a list or library, use the IncludeUserSecurity parameter. To overwrite an existing file in the backup folder, use the Force parameter. Using the Verbose parameter lets you see the progress of the backup operation.

It's sometimes helpful to prevent file compression during the export to conserve resource usage. You can use the NoFileCompression parameter to accomplish this; however, if you use this parameter in the export process, you must also use it in the import process.

With that in mind, to perform a site, list, or library export using Windows PowerShell, type the following string at the command prompt and press Enter, substituting the sample values with your production values and using the specific parameters that meet your requirements:

```
Export-SPWeb -Identity <Site URL> -Path <Path and file name> [-ItemUrl
<URL of site, list, or library>] [-IncludeUserSecurity] [-IncludeVersions]
[-NoFileCompression] [-GradualDelete] [-Verbose]
```

Backing Up Logs

Between backing up the SharePoint server farm environment and restoring it is a set of instructions for the restoration contained in the SQL Server transaction logs. Microsoft SQL Server 2008 R2, SQL Server 2008 with Service Pack 1 (SP1) and Cumulative Update 2, and SQL Server 2005 with SP3 and Cumulative Update 3 have transaction logs that record all the changes made to a database since the last checkpoint or full backup. Within the logs is also the information required to restore the farm.

Fortunately, these logs are automatically backed up whenever you perform a backup on the farm, a web application, or the databases using either Central Administration or Windows PowerShell. When the logs are backed up, they are automatically truncated, but the longer between backups, the larger the log becomes, affecting the time it takes to perform the backup and the impact on resources.

The transition logs are the only log files that you must absolutely back up, but they are not the only information source you can back up. Both Collect Usage Data and Archive Diagnostic Logs can also be backed up. The usage data log provides information on how websites are being used within SharePoint. The diagnostic logs record data on farm operation.

The default location for the Collect Usage Data files is on the same partition where SharePoint is installed, so if you back up the farm, these files are also backed up. However, since the files can grow to be very large, it's recommended that you change the location to a folder on a separate drive. Since the location of this log is a farm-level setting, the information will still be backed up when you back up the farm.

You can back up the diagnostic logs using Windows PowerShell in a number of ways.

To archive diagnostic logs from all farm servers, type the following string at the prompt and then press Enter, replacing the sample values with your production values:

```
Merge-SPLogFile -Path "<path to merged log file>.log" -Overwrite
```

Here's an example of what this command looks like with "real" values:

```
Merge-SPLogFile -Path "C:\Logs\MergedFiles\MyFarm_merged_05-11-2010.log" -Overwrite
```

This is a very time-consuming operation since you are merging all the log data from all the farm servers. You can merge log entries that match only a certain set of parameters by using the following string:

```
Merge-SPLogFile -Path "<path to merged log file>.log"
-Area "<Area>" -Category "<Category>"
```

Area can contain one or more parameters including wildcards, as can Category. You can also filter by Level, Correlation, EventID, Message, StartTime, EndTime, Process, and ThreadID.

In addition to archiving diagnostic logs for all servers, you can perform the same action for a specific server. The command string to perform that task is as follows:

```
Copy-Item <Log folder path> -Destination <Archive folder path> -Recurse
```

Here's an example of what that command looks like in "real life":

```
Copy-Item "C:\Logs\Files\diagnostics" -Destination
"C:\Logs\MergedFiles\MyFarm_merged_05-11-2010.log" -Recurse
```

Managing Restore Operations

Performing a restoration operation in SharePoint isn't quite the reverse of performing backup operations. The permissions and qualifications are similar but not identical, and there are specific considerations to be aware of prior to performing a restore.

Restoring SharePoint Components

Once you have backed up the farm, you have the basis from which to restore the farm to its previous configuration should a disaster occur to your SharePoint environment. Details regarding the permissions required for people and systems must be observed, and there are restrictions regarding the restoration itself. Understand the following carefully before attempting to restore the farm.

Managing Account Permissions and Conditions

To perform a restore operation using Central Administration, you must belong to the Farm Administrators group. If you intend to perform a restore operation using Windows PowerShell, you must belong to the SharePoint_Shell_Access role for the specified database. Your account must have Read permissions to the backup folders.

The database server's SQL Server account, the Timer Service account, and the Central Administration application pool account must all have Read permissions to the backup folder, and the database server's SQL Server account must belong to the sysadmin fixed server role. The SharePoint Foundation Administration Service must be started on all farm servers prior to initiating the restore operation.

To do so, on the computer running SharePoint Server 2010, click Start ➤ Run, type **services.msc** in the Run field, and then click OK. When services.msc opens, scroll down until you see the SharePoint Foundation Administration Service in the list. Right-click the service and click Start in the list that appears, as shown in Figure 12.1.

The SharePoint Foundation Administration Service is not started by default on stand-alone SharePoint installations such as the one configured for the exercises in this book, so make sure to start this service or your restore operations will fail.

A caveat for restoring SharePoint includes not being able to perform more than one backup or recovery operation at a time. After the recovery operation is complete, you may still be unable to access search for up to 15 minutes. If the system has to perform a crawl, accessing search may take even longer. You are also unable to restore one version of SharePoint to another version.

FIGURE 12.1 The SharePoint Foundation Administration Service in Services.msc

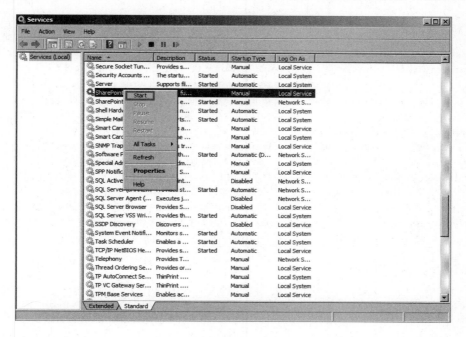

Preparing to Restore the Farm

Although regularly backing up the entire farm is the backup method of choice, you will restore the entire farm only if a disaster has brought down the whole farm environment. If only a single SharePoint component such as a web application, database, or site collection has an issue, use a restore method that applies to just the affected component.

- There are limitations regarding what restoring the farm can and cannot do.

- Although backing up the farm includes backing up the configuration and content databases for Central Administration, you cannot restore these elements using SharePoint Server 2010 utilities.

- Restoring the farm with SharePoint Server utilities does not restart all the service applications within the farm.

- You must restart these services manually using either Central Administration or Windows PowerShell. Do not attempt to use the SharePoint Product Configuration Wizard.

- Although the wizard will restart the services, it will also reprovision the services and service proxies, causing you to lose your specific configurations for these elements.

> The following sections regarding restore limitations and other aspects of preparing to restore the farm are particularly important, relative both to the certification exam and to the duties of administering SharePoint Server 2010.

The best-case scenario for restoring or reattaching a database using built-in tools is to employ the overwrite option. This allows the unique identifier (ID) for each content database to remain the same, resulting in the change logs for all databases to be retained. The advantage to this is that search continues its usual crawling schedule as defined by the crawl rules you set up prior to the system's last backup. If you do not use the overwrite option, a new ID is assigned to the restored database, and the change log is lost. When the next crawl of the database occurs, new data from the content database will be added to the index. A full crawl will be required as opposed to an incremental crawl.

You can use SharePoint restore operations to restore remote BLOB stores only if you use the FILESTREAM remote BLOB store provider to put data in the BLOB stores. If you use another provider, you will have to restore the remote BLOB stores manually.

When you perform a farm restore, you cannot use a backup from a multiple server farm and restore it to a single farm environment, nor can you use a single farm backup to restore to a multiple-server farm. You also cannot use a backup from one version of SharePoint to restore to a different version.

Restoring the Farm

You will typically perform a restore operation on the entire farm if a disaster, such as a fire or flood, has caused significant hardware damage and data loss. You can also perform a full farm restore if you need to return SharePoint configuration and data settings to a previous date or if you are moving your SharePoint deployment from one farm environment to another.

As with the farm backup, you can restore SharePoint using Central Administration, Windows PowerShell, or SQL Server tools. Exercise 12.10 will show you the Central Administration procedure.

EXERCISE 12.10

Restoring the SharePoint Farm with Central Administration

1.   On the Central Administration main page, click Restore From A Backup under Backup And Restore.

2.   On the Restore From Backup – Step 1 Of 3: Select Backup To Restore page, in the available list of backups, select the backup that contains the farm backup and then click Next, as shown here.

EXERCISE 12.10 *(continued)*

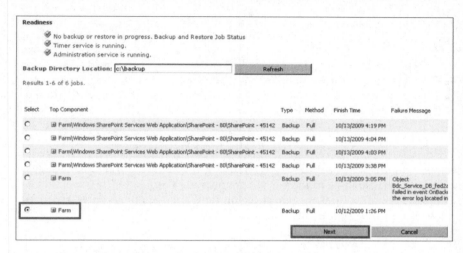

3. On the Restore From Backup – Step 2 Of 3: Select Component To Restore page, select the check box next to the farm and then click Next.

4. On the Restore From Backup – Step 3 Of 3: Select Restore Options page, under Restore Component, verify that the word Farm appears in the Restore The Following Component list.

5. Under Restore Only Configuration Settings, verify that the Restore Content And Configuration Settings option is selected.

6. Under Restore Options, select the Same Configuration option for Type Of Restore.

7. When the confirmation dialog box appears, click OK.

8. Click Start Restore.

9. Monitor the recovery job under Readiness at the top of the Backup And Restore Job Status page or under the Restore section lower on the page.

10. Once the restoration operation has finished, go to the Central Administration main page and click Manage Services On Server under Application Management.

11. On the Services On Server page, start any necessary service applications by clicking Start in the Actions column next to each application.

For step 2, if the required backup job isn't present in the list, type the UNC path to the backup folder in the Backup Directory Location field and then click Refresh.

For step 6, if the Restore Only Configuration Settings section is not present, you most likely selected a configuration-only backup. Select a backup job that contains the farm backup.

If, after you start the restore operation, you receive any error messages, review the errors in the Failure Message column on the Backup And Restore Job Status page. You can also review error messages in the Sprestore.log file located in the backup folder.

 After restarting your services, you will still need to reestablish trust relationships between farms. Review Exercise 4.9 in Chapter 4, "Configuring Service Applications," for details.

Restoring the SharePoint Farm with Windows PowerShell

You can perform the same operation using Windows PowerShell. You must be logged in with an account belonging to the Farm Administrators group. Open PowerShell as an administrator, type the following code at the prompt, and then press Enter, replacing the sample values with your production values:

```
Restore-SPFarm -Directory <Backup folder>
-RestoreMethod Overwrite [-BackupId <GUID>]
```

Here's an example of what this command looks like using "real-world" values:

```
Restore-SPFarm -Directory C:/backups/backup_folder/farmbackup
-RestoreMethod Overwrite [-BackupId 1234]
```

If you do not specify the unique ID number of the backup using the -BackupId switch, the most recent backup will be used.

To view the available backups for the farm, execute the following command, replacing the sample values with your production values:

```
Get-SPBackupHistory -Directory <Backup folder> -ShowBackup [-Verbose]
```

After the restore operation, to restart all service applications, use the following command:

```
Start-SPServiceInstance
```

To restart a specific operation, use the same command followed by the -Identity switch and the GUID for the specific service application, replacing the sample value for the actual GUID:

```
Start-SPServiceInstance -Identity <ServiceApplicationID>
```

Restoring the SharePoint Farm with SQL Server Tools

Just as you cannot perform a full farm backup with SQL Server tools, you also cannot perform a full restore. You can only restore the databases for the farm. You'll still need to use either Central Administration or Windows PowerShell to restore the farm configuration. Also, if you choose to use this restoration method, search will not be restored, and you will be required to perform a full crawl after restoring the content database.

The recommended order to perform a database restoration is to first restore the last full database backup, then restore the most recent differential backup that occurred after the last full backup, and finally restore all transition log backups that occurred after the most recent backup, regardless if it was a full or differential backup.

Prior to beginning this procedure, stop the SharePoint Services Timer Service and wait until any running stored procedures have finished, which can take several minutes. You should restart this service only after the databases have been restored.

1. Start the SQL Server Management Studio tool on your computer and connect to the desired database server.

2. In Object Explorer, expand Databases.

3. Right-click the desired database, point to Tasks, point to Restore, and then click Database.

4. When the Restore Database dialog box appears, specify the source and destination of the backup or accept the defaults and then select the desired backup set or sets.

5. Click Options in the Select A Page pane.

6. Under Restore Options, select Overwrite The Existing Database without selecting any other options in this section.

7. Under Recovery state, select Recover With Recovery if you have included all transition logs that need to be restored or select Recover With Norecovery if you must restore more transaction logs.

8. Click OK.

You will need to repeat this procedure for each database you want to restore, except for the configuration database. To restore the configuration settings, you must use Central Administration or Windows PowerShell. After restoring the required databases, you can restart the SharePoint Services Timer Service and then restart any required service applications.

As previously mentioned, if you restore the SharePoint farm using SQL Server tools, after completing the procedure, you must still restore the farm configuration. You can perform this task using either Central Administration or Windows PowerShell. You can also restore the farm configuration when there has been an incident damaging that information but not a catastrophic event bringing down the entire farm.

Using Central Administration, the process of restoring the farm configuration is identical to the process of restoring the entire farm, as shown in Exercise 12.10. Using Windows PowerShell, you can use the same cmdlet string as you did in the section "Restoring the SharePoint Farm with Windows PowerShell" when you restored the entire farm. At the end of the string, add the following parameter to indicate that you want to restore only the farm configuration:

```
-ConfigurationOnly
```

> You can use Windows PowerShell to enter a script that will record the entire server farm configuration. See Chapter 15, "Working with Windows PowerShell 2.0 Administration," for details.

Copying the Configuration Settings from One Farm to Another Farm

You might want to back up the configuration settings from one farm and then copy those settings to a separate farm for a number of reasons. For instance, you might want to develop a SharePoint test environment that has identical settings to your production farm. You might also want to use identical settings for multiple farms in your organization.

One of the ways you can accomplish this goal is to back up and recover a farm without the content databases being attached. With this method, you get the farm settings and the web application settings as well as any service applications you may choose to include. You can also choose to back up and recover configuration settings only, which gives you only the core SharePoint Foundation 2010 settings.

To back up and recover a farm without content databases, open Windows PowerShell as an administrator and follow these steps. After entering each command, press Enter, substituting the sample values with your production values.

Use the following command to document the current web application URLs and content database mappings:

```
Get-SPWebApplication | %{$_.Name;$_.Url;%{$_.ContentDatabases|%{$_.Name};
Write-Host ""}}
```

If you want to dismount all content databases, use the following command:

```
Get-SPContentDatabase | Dismount-SPContentDatabase
```

If, instead of dismounting all content databases, you want to dismount a specific content database, use the following command:

```
Get-SPContentDatabase WSS_Content | Dismount-SPContentDatabase
```

Now that the database or databases have been dismounted, back up the farm using this command:

```
Backup-SPFarm -Directory \\servername\share -BackupMethod Full
```

After the backup is complete, remount the content databases using the following command:

```
Mount-SPContentDatabase -Name <WSS_Content> -WebApplication http://servername/
http://servername
```

You can restore the configuration settings to a different farm using the following command:

```
Restore-SPFarm -Directory <Backup folder> -RestoreMethod Overwrite [-BackupId
<GUID>] -ConfigurationOnly
```

In Central Administration, you can back up the configuration settings as previously discussed and then restore them to a separate farm. The only difference is setting the specific destination for the other farm during the restore process. Any configuration settings already present on the farm to which you are restoring will be overwritten.

Restoring SharePoint Applications and Services

As in the various backup procedures chronicled earlier in this chapter, you can choose to restore the entire farm or just certain components or services. Among these specific components, you can choose to restore a web application, a service application, search, the Secure Store Service, and more. This section will start you off with restoring a web application.

You can perform this task using both Central Administration and Windows PowerShell. Exercise 12.11 will show you the Central Administration method. You must be a member of the Farm Administrators group. Make sure the SharePoint Services Timer V4 Service and Farm Database Access account both have Full Control permissions to the backup folder. You cannot use SQL Server tools to restore a web application.

EXERCISE 12.11

Restoring a Web Application with Central Administration

1. On the Central Administration main page, click Restore From A Backup under Backup And Restore.

2. On the Restore From Backup – Step 1 Of 3: Select Backup To Restore page, select the backup job containing the desired farm with the web application from the list and then click Next.

3. On the Restore From Backup – Step 2 Of 3: Select Component To Restore page, locate the desired web application, select the check box next to it, and then click Next.

4. On the Restore From Backup – Step 3 Of 3: Select Restore Options page, under Restore Component, verify that Farm\<web application> appears in the Restore The Following Component list, where <web application> is the actual name of the web application you want to restore.

5. Under Restore Only Configuration Settings, verify that the Restore Content And Configuration setting is selected.

6. Under Restore Options, select Same Configuration for Type Of Restore.

7. When the verification dialog box appears, click OK.

8. Click Start Restore.

As with other backup and recovery jobs already documented, you can review the progress of the restore operation as it happens, and if an error occurs, you can find details in the Sprestore.log file in the backup folder as well as in the Failure Message column of the Backup And Restore Job Status page.

You can perform the same operation using Windows PowerShell. Open PowerShell as an administrator, type the following command string at the prompt, and then press Enter, replacing the sample values with your production values:

```
Restore-SPFarm -Directory <Backup folder name>
-RestoreMethod Overwrite -Item  <Web application name> [-BackupId <GUID>]
[-Verbose]
```

Use the -BackupID parameter to specify the desired backup using the backup's GUID. For <Backup folder name>, type the actual name of the path to the folder containing the desired backup. For <Web application name>, type the name of the web application you want to restore.

Restoring a Service Application with Central Administration

The process of restoring a service application with Central Administration is substantially similar to Exercise 12.11. For step 4, under Restore Component, make sure the desired service application appears in the Restore The Following Component list in the format Farm\Shared Services Applications\<Service application>, where <Service Application> is the actual name of the desired application. After that, follow the remaining steps just as you did in Exercise 12.11 to complete the task.

This task can also be accomplished using Windows PowerShell. Type the following command string at the PowerShell prompt and then press Enter, replacing the sample values with your production values:

```
Restore-SPFarm -Directory <Backup folder>
-Item <Service application name> -RecoveryMethod Overwrite [-BackupId <GUID>]
[-Verbose]
```

The only difference between running this command and the PowerShell command for restoring a web application is entering the actual name of the service application rather than the web application. If you don't type in a GUID, the most recent backup will be used.

Restoring a Service Application with SQL Server Tools

Unlike restoring a web application, you can restore a service application with SQL Server tools. Like other SQL Server tool backup and restore tasks, you cannot restore the complete service application; instead, you can only restore the databases associated with the application. You can only restore the complete service application using Central Administration or Windows PowerShell. To perform this task, you must belong to the SQL Server sysadmin fixed server role on the database server containing the desired database.

1. Open the SQL Server Management Studio utility on your computer and connect to the desired database server.

2. In Object Explorer, expand Databases,

3. Right-click the desired database, point to Tasks, and then click Restore.

4. Under Restore Component, click Database.

5. Either type the name of the recovery set in the Name field or accept the default name present.

6. Either accept the default expiration date of zero days for the recovery set, indicating that it will never be overwritten, or specify a date when the recovery set may be overwritten.

7. Under Destination, specify where you want the recovery to occur.

8. Click OK.

This procedure must be performed for every database you want to restore for SharePoint components.

Restoring SharePoint Search

You can restore search using Central Administration or Windows PowerShell, but not with SQL Server tools. Like other components, you can restore just search in SharePoint; however, if your search topology uses FAST Search Server 2010 for SharePoint, the following procedures will also restore the Content SSA and the Query SSA. In this case, you'll additionally need to restore the FAST Search Server.

The process of restoring search using Central Administration is very much like the process of restoring a service or web application. You follow the steps for recovery for those tasks and, on the Restore From Backup – Step 3 Of 3: Select Restore Options page, under Restore Component, verify that the Search service application name appears in the Restore The Following Content list. Otherwise, follow the restore procedure as you did in the other recovery tasks using Central Administration.

The process of restoring search using Windows PowerShell is virtually the same as restoring a service or web application. The only difference is specifying the name of the Search service application for the -Item parameter as follows:

```
Restore-SPFarm -Directory <Backup folder> -Item <Search service application
name> -RecoveryMethod Overwrite [-BackupId <GUID>] [-Verbose]
```

Just type in the actual values for the backup folder and the GUID for the backup ID. If you don't enter a GUID, the most recent backup will be used.

Restoring the Secure Store Service

You can restore the Secure Store Service with either Central Administration or Windows PowerShell but not with SQL Server tools. The tasks are very similar to those you've already performed, but, in addition, you'll need the passphrase you wrote down when you originally backed up the service. Without the passphrase, you will be unable to restore the Secure Store Service.

The process of using Central Administration to restore the Secure Store Service is similar but not identical to other Central Administration restore tasks.

1. On the Restore From Backup – Step 2 Of 3: Select Component To Restore page, you need to expand Shared Services Applications and then select the check box next to the desired Secure Store Service application backup group.

2. Click Next and on the Restore From Backup – Step 3 Of 3: Select Restore Options page, under Restore Component, make sure the name of the desired Secure Store Service appears in the Restore The Following Component list in the format Farm\Shared Services\Shared Services Applications\<Secure Store Service name>

3. After that, continue with the steps you've used to restore other SharePoint components such as web and service applications.

After the restore operation is done, you will need to refresh the passphrase using the following steps:

1. On the Central Administration home page, click Manage Service Applications under Application Management.

2. On the Service Applications page, click the name of the desired Secure Store Service.

3. On the Secure Store Service page, select the check box next to the desired key and then click the Refresh Key button on the Ribbon.

4. When the Refresh Key dialog box opens, type the passphrase you previously recorded in the Pass Phrase field and then click OK.

The process for performing this restoration using Windows PowerShell is pretty straightforward. Type the following string at the prompt and then press Enter, replacing the sample values with your production values:

```
Restore-SPFarm -Directory <Backup folder>
-Item <Secure Store Service name> -RecoveryMethod Overwrite [-BackupId <GUID>]
[-Verbose]
```

Replace <Secure Store Service name> with the actual name of the Secure Store Service. After the restore operation is complete, you can refresh the passphrase by executing the following command, typing the actual passphrase for the -Passphrase switch.

```
Update-SPSecureStoreApplicationServerKey -Passphrase <Passphrase>
```

Restoring SharePoint Databases

You can restore a content database using Central Administration, Windows PowerShell, or SQL Server tools, but you must use Windows PowerShell to attach and restore a read-only content database.

Restoring a Content Database

To restore the content database using Central Administration, follow the steps you performed for other Central Administration restore tasks. On the Restore From Backup – Step 2 Of 3: Select Component To Restore page, select the check box next to the desired content database and click Next. Afterward, proceed as you have in other similar tasks and start the restore. If the content database check box cannot be selected, you will need to use either Windows PowerShell or SQL Server tools to do the job.

You can perform the same task using Windows PowerShell. Type the following string at the command prompt and then press Enter, replacing the sample values for your production values:

```
Restore-SPFarm -Directory <Backup folder name> -RestoreMethod Overwrite -Item
<Content database name> [-BackupId <GUID>] [-Verbose]
```

You'll need to know the name of the content database and the GUID of the desired backup. If you don't enter a GUID, the most recent backup will be used for the restore operation.

The procedure to restore the content database using SQL Server tools is similar but not exactly the same as other like procedures. Here are the steps:

1. Open the SQL Server Management Studio utility on your computer and connect to the desired database server.

2. In Object Explorer, expand Databases.

3. Right-click the desired database, point to Tasks, point to Restore, and then click Database.

4. When the Restore Database dialog box appears, specify the source of the backup set and the destination where you want it restored, or accept the default values.

5. In the Select A Page pane, click Options.

6. Under Restore Options, select Overwrite The Existing Database and no other options in this section.

7. Under Recovery State, select Recover With Recovery if you have included all transaction logs that must be restored or select Recover With Norecovery if you must still restore more transaction logs.

8. Click OK to start the restoration process.

Repeat this process for every database you need to restore.

Attaching and Restoring a Read-Only Content Database

There are a variety of reasons why you might want to restore a read-only content database including using such a database to allow users to access SharePoint during maintenance procedures. When you restore a read-only database, however, it becomes a read-write database.

To perform this task, type the following string at the Windows PowerShell command prompt and then press Enter, replacing all the sample values with your production values:

```
Mount-SPContentDatabase -Name <Database name> -WebApplication <Web application
ID> [-Verbose]
```

The Mount-SPContentDatabase cmdlet associates the content database with a web application, allowing the contents to be read. This is different from performing this task using SQL Server tools.

Restoring Site Collections, Lists, and Libraries

You can use Windows PowerShell to restore a site collection, list, or document library if you are having an issue with just those individual elements in SharePoint. The following tasks will describe the procedures.

Restoring a Site Collection with Windows PowerShell

As with other, similar PowerShell tasks, you must be logged in with an account that has read permissions to the relevant backup folder and is a member of the db_owner fixed database role on both the farm configuration database and the content database where you want to restore the site collection.

Some caveats associated with this task are that if the site collection you are restoring is larger than 1GB, you can use the GradualDelete switch to get better performance during the restoration operation. This procedure overwrites the site collection and marks the site collection as deleted, preventing any further access to the content. The data is then deleted over a period of time rather than all at once.

To restore the site collection to a specific content database, use the DatabaseServer and DatabaseName switches to specify the desired content database. Otherwise, the SharePoint system will select the content database to which the site collection is restored. To restore a host-named site collection, use the Identity switch and specify the URL for the site collection. Also, use the HostHeader switch to specify the URL of the web application that will contain the host-named site collection.

To restore a site collection using Windows PowerShell, open PowerShell as an administrator, type the following command string at the prompt, and then press Enter, substituting your production values for the sample values:

```
Restore-SPSite -Identity <Site collection URL> -Path <Backup file>
[-DatabaseServer <Database server name>] [-DatabaseName <Content database name>]
[-HostHeader <Host header>] [-Force] [-GradualDelete] [-Verbose]
```

Importing a Site, List, or Library with Windows PowerShell

The account requirements for performing this task are the same as for restoring a site collection with Windows PowerShell. Caveats include using the Identity switch to specify the template of the site or subsite you want to restore. You can use the Get-SPWeb cmdlet and pass the ID to Import-SPWeb.

Use the Path switch to define the name of the export file you want to use in the recovery operation. To specify the user security settings for the list or library, use the IncludeUserSecurity switch. Overwrite the desired list or library by using the Force switch and use the UpdateVersions switch to indicate how you want to manage any versioning conflicts.

For importing a site, open Windows PowerShell as an administrator and use the following, replacing the sample values with your production values:

```
Restore-SPSite -Identity <Site collection URL>
-Path <Backup file> [-DatabaseServer <Database server name>] [-DatabaseName
<Content database name>] [-HostHeader <Host header>] [-Force] [-GradualDelete]
[-Verbose]
```

Here's an example of what this would look like in production:

```
Restore-SPSite -Identity http://lab-sp2010
-Path C://storage/backup/backupfile -DatabaseServer sqldb_101 -DatabaseName
content_db -HostHeader hostheadername -Verbose
```

For importing a list or library, use the following sample code, substituting your production values for the example values:

```
Import-SPWeb -Identity <Site URL> -Path <Export file name> [-Force]
[-NoFileCompression] [-Verbose]
```

Remember, the NoFileCompression parameter means that no file compression is performed during the import process. If you compressed the file during export, you must decompress it during import. If you specified no file compression for export, use the NoFileCompression switch for import. Also, the Verbose switch lets you see the progress of the restore operation in the PowerShell window. Finally, recall that you cannot import a site, list, or document library that was exported from a different version of SharePoint. The versions must match.

Summary

In this chapter, you learned how to set up user and system accounts and backup directories for the purpose of backing up and restoring the SharePoint environment:

- Understanding permissions necessary for the human and system accounts required for backup and recovery operations

- Learning the various tools required to perform backups of the SharePoint farm and its subelements, including services, applications, databases, lists, and libraries

- Comprehending the different procedures for initiating a SharePoint recovery, not only of the entire farm but also of its various subelements

- Learning which backup and recovery tasks are specifically managed by Windows PowerShell

Exam Essentials

Understanding the Various Tasks Associated with Backing Up the SharePoint Farm and Its Various Components   Understand the concepts behind planning the backup strategy, including assigning necessary permissions to user and system accounts, creating a backup directory on the local computer or network, and configuring and executing backups of the farm and its various elements.

Understand the Activities Related to Restoring the SharePoint Farm and Its Various Components   Comprehend the various functions related to planning your recovery strategy, including assigning necessary permissions to user and system accounts and configuring and executing recovery methods for the server farm and its various components.

Review Questions

1. You are a SharePoint administrator for your company, and you are planning the backup and recovery strategy for your server farm. You know that certain services in SharePoint must have Full Control permissions to the folder where backups are stored. Of the following, which services must have this permission? (Choose all that apply.)

   A. The SharePoint Services Timer V4 Service

   B. The SharePoint Foundation Service

   C. The SharePoint Backup Service

   D. The SQL Server Service

2. You are a SharePoint administrator for your company, and you are planning the backup and recovery strategy for your server farm. You are developing your plan for access permissions for various accounts. A user must be a member of the Administrators account on the local computer to perform which of the following tasks in Central Administration? (Choose all that apply.)

   A. Backing up and restoring the farm

   B. Backing up and restoring applications

   C. Backing up and restoring sites

   D. Backing up and restoring document libraries

3. You are a SharePoint administrator for your company, and you are planning the backup and recovery strategy for your server farm. You are developing your initial plan for the backup directory or folder where you will back up your server farm. What is the recommended procedure for backing up the farm to a folder?

   A. Back up the farm to a folder on the local computer.

   B. Back up the farm to a folder on the network.

   C. Back up the farm to a folder on the local computer and then transfer the backup to a remote location on the network.

   D. Back up the farm to a remote location on the network and then transfer the backup to a folder on the local computer.

4. You are a SharePoint administrator for your company, and you are planning the backup and recovery strategy for your server farm. You are developing your backup and recovery strategy. Backing up the entire farm regularly is a necessary task, but not all necessary elements are backed up during this process. Of the following, what is not backed up when you back up the farm? (Choose all that apply.)

   A. Business Data Connectivity service external content definitions

   B. Business Data Connectivity data sources

   C. Binary Large Object stores when using the FILESTREAM store provider

   D. Certificates required to establish trust relationships

5. You are a SharePoint administrator for your company, and you are planning the backup and recovery strategy for your server farm including the Windows PowerShell method. Of the following, which cmdlet would you use to initiate a farm backup?

A. `Backup-SPFarm`

B. `Import-SPFarm`

C. `BackupMethod-SPFarm`

D. `AddBackup-SPFarm`

6. You are a SharePoint administrator for your company, and you are about to perform a backup of the entire farm using Central Administration. You go to the Central Administration home page and you want to click Perform A Backup under Backup And Restore, but you see the option isn't available. You notice that the Backup A Site Collection option is available. Of the following, which is the most likely explanation for this occurrence?

A. You are logged into Central Administration as a site collection administrator but not a farm administrator.

B. You are working on a single-server deployment of SharePoint with a built-in database and not a true server farm environment.

C. You must click Backup And Restore to go to the Backup And Restore page before you can see the Perform A Backup option.

D. The farm is currently in the process of being backed up, and the Perform A Backup option automatically disappears from the page during the backup process.

7. You are a SharePoint administrator for your company, and you are about to perform a backup of the entire farm using Central Administration. You are specifying the location of the backup directory. How are you supposed to indicate this location?

A. Using the web location such as `www.backup.local/backup1.bak`.

B. Using the Fully Qualified Domain Name (FQDN) such as `backup.domain.local/backup1.bak`.

C. Using the UNC path such as `//backupfolder/backup1.bak`.

D. You can input the location using HTTP, FQDN, or UNC, and they are equally accepted.

8. You are a SharePoint administrator for your company, and you are performing a backup of the server farm using Central Administration. You want monitor the progress of the backup. Of the following, what are valid options for doing so? (Choose all that apply.)

A. Review the status of the backup under Readiness on the Backup And Restore Status page.

B. Review the status of the backup under Backup on the Backup And Restore Status page.

C. Review the status of the backup under Status on the Backup And Restore Status page.

D. Review the status of the backup in the `Spbackup.log` file in the backup folder.

9. You are a SharePoint administrator for your company, and you are developing a strategy for backing up the server farm. Of the following, which tools and utilities can you use to perform a complete backup of the farm? (Choose all that apply.)

A. Central Administration

B. Windows PowerShell

C. SQL Server tools

D. Data Management Console

10. You are a SharePoint administrator for your company, and you are currently backing up the server farm using SQL Server tools. You are required to select a recovery model. What are the valid options the SQL Server Management Studio? (Choose all that apply.)

A. Simple

B. Full

C. Differential

D. Bulk logged

11. You are a SharePoint administrator for your company, and you are planning the backup and recovery strategy for your server farm including the Windows PowerShell method. You want to have the ability to back up just the configuration database using PowerShell. Of the following, which is the correct cmdlet?

A. Backup-SPConfigurationDatabase

B. Import-SPConfigurationDatabase

C. BackupMethod-SPConfigurationDatabase

D. AddBackup-SPConfigurationDatabase

12. You are a SharePoint administrator for your company, and you are planning the backup and recovery strategy for your server farm including the Windows PowerShell method. You add the -Verbose parameter to the end of the command to back up the server farm. Of the following, what do you expect this parameter to do?

A. -Verbose will print a detailed list of the actions the backup performs to the Spbackup.log file.

B. -Verbose will print a detailed list of the actions the backup performs to the Status column of the Backup And Restore Status page in Central Administration.

C. -Verbose will print a detailed list of the actions the backup performs in the PowerShell window as the backup operation executes.

D. -Verbose will print a detailed list of the actions the backup performs to the backup.txt file in the backup folder on the local computer.

13. You are a SharePoint administrator for your company, and you are planning the backup and recovery strategy for your server farm including the Windows PowerShell method. You want to have the ability to back up just a web application using PowerShell. Of the following, which is the correct cmdlet?

   A. `Backup-SPWebApplication`

   B. `Import-SPWebApplication`

   C. `BackupMethod-SPFarm`

   D. `Backup-SPFarm`

14. You are a SharePoint administrator for your company, and you are developing your backup plan for different SharePoint components using Windows PowerShell. You want to be able to back up search using PowerShell, and you use FAST Search Server 2010 for SharePoint. In addition to backing up SharePoint search, what else must you back up? (Choose all that apply.)

   A. Content SSA

   B. Query SSA

   C. FAST Search Server 2010

   D. The Bing Search add-on

15. You are a SharePoint administrator for your company, and you have backed up the entire server farm in a testing environment to evaluate the performance of the SharePoint backup and recovery tools. You now want to perform a restore of the farm using Windows PowerShell. Of the following, which is the correct cmdlet?

   A. `Restore-SPFarm`

   B. `Export-SPFarm`

   C. `RestoreMethod-SPFarm`

   D. `RestoreBackup-SPFarm`

16. You are a SharePoint administrator for your company, and you have backed up the entire server farm in a testing environment to evaluate the performance of the SharePoint backup and recovery tools. You now want to perform a restore of the farm using Windows PowerShell. How do you specify which backup file you want to use?

   A. Use the `-BackupName` parameter and specify the name of the backup such as `backup1.bak`.

   B. Use the `-BackupId` parameter and specify the GUID of the backup such as 1234.

   C. Use the `-BackupDate` parameter and specify the date of the desired backup.

   D. There is no way to specify a backup file. The most recent backup file will be used for the restore operation.

17. You are a SharePoint administrator for your company, and you are currently restoring the server farm using SQL Server Management Studio. You have included all the backed-up transition logs in your recovery, so which selection do you need to make?

   A. Recover With Recovery

   B. Recover With Norecovery

   C. Recover With Nonrecovery

   D. Recover With Transitionlogs

18. You are a SharePoint administrator, and you are planning to copy the farm configuration from your production farm environment to a testing farm environment. Your plan is to test new features and customizations in a testing farm environment that has the identical configuration settings to your production environment. This action must be performed using Windows PowerShell. What is the first cmdlet you use in this operation?

   A. `Get-SPContentDatabase`

   B. `Get-SPWebApplication`

   C. `Get-SPFarm`

   D. `Backup-SPFarm`

19. You are a SharePoint administrator for your company, and you are planning on backing up the database to a snapshot using SQL Server Management Studio. While most backup tasks performed with Management Studio follow a similar set of steps, what is significantly different about backing up a database to a snapshot?

   A. In Object Explorer, you expand Snapshots rather than Databases.

   B. After selecting the desired database, you click New Query and type in code within the Management Studio tool.

   C. You follow the usual instructions but do not have the option to set an expiration date for the snapshot.

   D. This task can be performed using either SQL Server tools or Windows PowerShell only.

20. You are a SharePoint administrator for your company, and you want to restore a particular site collection using Windows PowerShell. What parameters must you use to specify the required content database for the site collection? (Choose two.)

   A. `DatabaseGUID`

   B. `DatabaseHeader`

   C. `DatabaseName`

   D. `DatabaseServer`

Answers to Review Questions

1. A,D. The SharePoint Services Timer V4 (SPTimerV4) and the SQL Server service account must have Full Control over the folder used for backups.

2. A, B. To perform recovery operations from Central Administration, being a member of the Administrators group for the local computer is required for backing up and restoring the farm, service applications, and content database. Being a member of the Farm Administrators group is required for backing up and restoring site collections, as well as sites, lists, and document libraries.

3. C. The recommended procedure is to first back up the farm to a folder on the local machine and then transfer the backup to a remote location on the network.

4. B, D. Although the SharePoint farm backup process backs up the Business Data Connectivity (BDC) service external content type definitions, it doesn't back up the actual data source. Backing up the farm does not back up any certificates used to create trust relationships. SharePoint backs up the remote Binary Large Object stores, also called BLOB stores, only if you use the FILESTREAM remote BLOB store provider to move data in remote BLOB stores.

5. A. The `Import-SPFarm` and `AddBackup` cmdlets are bogus. `-BackupMethod` is a parameter used with the `Backup-SPFarm` cmdlet that lets you determine whether you are performing a Full or Differential backup.

6. B. The Perform A Backup link under Backup And Restore will not appear on the main page of Central Administration if you are working on a single-server installation of SharePoint with a built-in database.

7. C. Under Backup File Location, type the UNC path to the backup folder. If you attempt to use any other method, you will receive an error.

8. A, B. Review the status of the backup under Readiness at the top of the Backup And Restore Status page and under Backup lower on the page. The Status area of that page is a bogus option. You review the `Spbackup.log` file only if an error occurred.

9. A, B. You can perform a complete backup of the server farm only using Central Administration and Windows PowerShell. SQL Server tools will only back up the databases containing the farm's content. Data Management Console is a bogus option.

10. A, B, D. Although you can specify a differential backup in Central Administration or Windows PowerShell, it is not a recovery option in SQL Server tools. All the other options are valid options.

11. A. The `Import-SPConfigurationDatabase` and `AddBackup` cmdlets are bogus. `BackupMethod` is a parameter used with the `Backup-SPFarm` cmdlet but not the `Backup-SPConfigurationDatabase` cmdlet.

12. C. Using the -Verbose parameter lets you see the progress of the backup in the PowerShell window as it occurs.

13. D. You use the same cmdlet, Backup-SPFarm, that you use when you back up the entire farm. The way you specify that you want to back up only a web application is using the -Item parameter and then indicating the name of the web application.

14. A, B, C. If you are using FAST Search Server 2010 for SharePoint, you should also back up the Content SSA and Query SSA, which includes the People Search index, as well as backing up the FAST Search Server. The Bing Search add-on is a bogus option.

15. A. Export-SPFarm and RestoreBackup-SPFarm are bogus options. RestoreMethod is a parameter you can use with Restore-SPFarm to specify either a Full or Differential restore.

16. B. Use the BackupID parameter and specify the GUID number of the backup. If you don't specify the desired backup file, the most recent backup file will be used by default.

17. A. Use the Recover With Recovery option. The Recover With Norecovery option is used when you still need to restore the transition logs. The other two options are bogus.

18. B. The first action you take is to document the current web application URLs and content database mappings using the Get-SPWebApplication cmdlet. The Get-SPContentDatabase is used to dismount and later remount all content databases, and the Backup-SPFarm cmdlet is used to back up the farm configuration once the content databases are dismounted. Get-SPFarm is a bogus option.

19. B. After expanding Databases in Object Explorer, in the list that appears, you select the desired database and then click New Query. Then you enter a specific set of code similar to the following:
    ```
    CREATE DATABASE <snapshot name>
    ON
    (
    NAME=<logical name of the database file>,
    FILENAME = 'c:\WSS_Backup1.ss')
    AS SNAPSHOT OF <database name>;
    ```

20. C, D. You must use the DatabaseServer and DatabaseName parameters to indicate the required server and database name. The other options are bogus.

Chapter

13

Monitoring the SharePoint Environment

MICROSOFT EXAM OBJECTIVE COVERED IN THIS CHAPTER:

✓ **Maintaining a SharePoint Environment**

- Monitor and Analyze a SharePoint Environment

Once you have the SharePoint Server 2010 environment configured and operating as you desire, you are responsible for monitoring SharePoint, not only to determine when errors occur and when corrective action is required but to review and analyze the long-term operation of SharePoint. This allows you to see trends and to decide when changes to SharePoint, such as adding additional servers, are required based on those trends.

Understanding Monitoring Tools

In general, *monitoring* involves a collection of tools that lets you view the actions of various features and activities in SharePoint in order to establish a baseline of systems operations, determine when problems occur, and note trends that may require changes in the SharePoint hardware, deployment, and configuration settings.

Monitoring features are enabled in SharePoint by default using a collection of standard settings. As a SharePoint administrator, you may determine that monitoring settings need to be adjusted to meet your technical or business requirements. You have the ability to modify the settings for diagnostic logging and health and usage data collection.

Diagnostic Logging

Diagnostic logging is composed of a series of logs that collect data typically used in troubleshooting errors in SharePoint. Although the default settings are sufficient for most SharePoint deployment scenarios, you can adjust the configuration for diagnostic logging to more closely match your company's requirements. Changes to diagnostic logging settings are sometimes made when you require the system to collect more data more often such as when making a significant hardware or configuration change to the SharePoint environment.

Health and Usage Data Collection

Health and usage data collection is a set of monitoring tools that gather different types of data including event log data, performance counter data, and timer service metrics data. These tools use specific timer jobs to perform their tasks, and once the information has been collected, it is used to create various reports, such as administrative, health, and web analysis reports. Adjustments you can make to these features include changing the schedule for the timer job, controlling data collection, manually triggering timer jobs, and disabling timer jobs.

SharePoint Health Analyzer

The *SharePoint Health Analyzer* runs a set of predefined health rules against servers in the SharePoint farm to monitor any potential configuration and performance issues. When a rule is run and fails, the result is written to the Health Analyzer Reports list and Windows event log. The failure also triggers an alert that is sent to the Health Analyzer Reports live found on the Review Problems And Solutions page in Central Administration, so you have multiple avenues for locating and reviewing this data. If you suspect that the rule itself may be poorly configured in relation to your purposes, you can also modify the rule to result in more accurate readings.

The Health Analyzer Reports list is just like any other list in SharePoint and can be configured and modified the way you would any other list. You can also export list items to an Excel spreadsheet for further analysis or to send via email.

Actions you can modify in relation to this tool are enabling or disabling rules, modifying the schedule by which rules run, defining the scope of rules, triggering rules manually, and having an email alert sent when a rule fails.

Configuring Monitoring

This section of the chapter will provide you with the necessary information for configuring and editing all monitoring tools in SharePoint. This includes the configuration of diagnostic logging, usage and health data collection, and the SharePoint Health Analyzer.

Configuring Diagnostic Logging

Although diagnostic logging is enabled by default when you install SharePoint, you can control a number of features regarding this utility including event throttling and event log flood protection. Exercise 13.1 shows you what's involved. You will need to be a member of the Farm Administrators group to successfully complete this task.

EXERCISE 13.1

Configuring Diagnostic Logging

1. Go to the Central Administration home page and click Monitoring.

2. On the Monitoring page, click Configure Diagnostic Logging under Reporting.

3. On the Diagnostic Logging page, under Event Throttling, to configure event throttling for all categories, click the All Categories check box, select the desired event log level in the Least Critical Event To Report To Event Log list, and then select the desired trace log level from the Least Critical Event To Report To The Trace Log list.

EXERCISE 13.1 *(continued)*

4. To configure event throttling for one or more categories, select the check boxes next to the desired categories and then select the desired event and trace log levels from the lists mentioned in the previous step, as shown here.

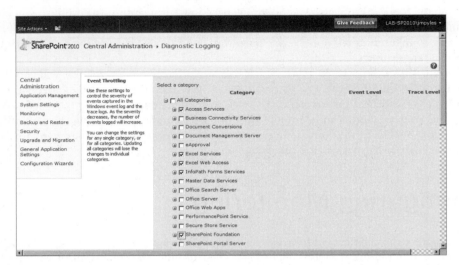

5. To configure event throttling for one or more subcategories of a category, expand the plus (+) sign next to the desired category, select the check box next to the desired subcategory, and then select the desired event and trace log levels from the lists mentioned in step 3.

6. To set event throttling for all categories back to their default levels, select the All Categories check box and then select Reset to default in both the Least Critical Event To Report To The Event Log list and the Least Critical Event To Report To The Trace Log list.

7. Under Event Log Flood Protection, select the Enable Event Log Flood Protection check box.

8. Under Trace Log, type the path to the folder where you want the logs written in the Path field.

9. In the Number Of Days To Store Log Files field, type the number of days you want logs retained, from 1 to 366, before the files are deleted.

10. If you want to limit how much disk space the logs can use, select the Restrict Trace Log disk space Usage check box and then type the number in gigabytes (GB) that you want to be the disk space limit for log files.

11. When finished, click OK.

For step 10, once the disk space limit has been reached, older logs will be deleted to make room for newer logs.

You can perform the same task using Windows PowerShell. To do so, open PowerShell as an administrator, type the following cmdlet string at the prompt, and then press Enter, selecting the desired parameters and substituting your production values for the sample values:

```
Set-SPLogLevel -TraceSeverity {None | Unexpected | Monitorable | Medium | High
| Verbose} -EventSeverity {None | Information | Warning | Error | Critical |
Verbose} [-Identity <Category name...>]  -Verbose
```

Going through Exercise 13.1 will help you understand the options available with the `Set-SPLogLevel` cmdlet. You want to select one option for `-TraceSeverity` such as Medium, one option for `-EventSeverity` such as Error, and you can use the `Identity` parameter to select one or more categories to change, such as Administration. If you want to view current settings, use `Get-SPLogLevel`, and to reset categories back to the default levels, use `Clear-SPLogLevel`.

Configuring Usage and Health Data Collection

As mentioned earlier in this chapter, the usage and health data collection system uses specific timer jobs to perform monitoring tasks and collect monitoring data and then writes data to the logging folder and logging database. Exercise 13.2 shows you how to configure this logging tool. You need to be a member of the Farm Administrators group to perform this task. Also, any settings you make are applied to the entire farm and cannot specify a smaller group of servers.

EXERCISE 13.2

Configuring Usage and Health Data Collection

1. Go to the Central Administration home page and click Monitoring.

2. On the Monitoring page, click Configure Usage And Health Data Collection under Reporting.

3. On the Usage And Health Data Collection page, select the Enable Usage Data Collection check box under Usage Data Collection.

4. Under Event Selection, select the check boxes for the events you want to be logged in the Events To Log list.

5. Under Usage Data Collection Settings, type the path to the logging folder in the Log File Location field, which is a location that must exist on all servers in the server farm.

6. Type the maximum disk space in gigabytes (GB) that the logs may use in the Maximum Log File Size field.

7. Under Health Data Collection, select the Enable Health Data Collection check box.

8. To change the health data collection schedules, click Health Logging Schedule, and in the list of timer jobs that appears, click the desired timer jobs and then either change the schedules or disable the timer jobs.

9. Under Log Collection Schedule, to change the schedules for log data collection, click Log Collection Schedule. In the list of timer jobs that appears, click the desired timer jobs and then either change the schedules or disable the timer jobs as seen here.

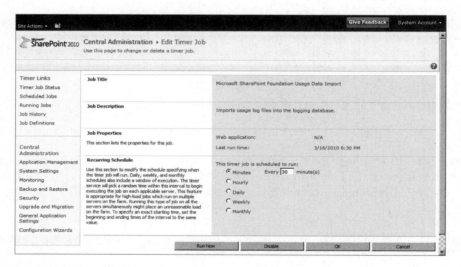

10. Under Logging Database Server, select either Windows Authentication or SQL Authentication to change the authentication option or accept the default setting.

11. Click OK when you're finished.

When selecting the events to log, keep in mind that the more selections you make, the more resources the logging system will consume. Choose to log only those events for which you need regular reports. If you are making a specific change in your system and need additional reports for those events, enable logging for them only as long as you need the information. Afterward, go back in and disable logging for the added events.

In the last step before exiting, you selected the authentication method for the logging database server; however, you cannot change the name of the database server or the name of the database used for logging. That modification can be made only using Windows PowerShell. This task will be subsequently presented in this portion of the chapter.

You can perform a number of tasks on the usage and health data collection system using Windows PowerShell, including configuring the system as a whole, as you just did with Central Administration. To do so, open Windows PowerShell as an administrator, type the following string at the prompt, and then press Enter, selecting the desired parameters and substituting your production values for the sample values:

```
Set-SPUsageService [-LoggingEnabled {1 | 0}] [-UsageLogLocation <Path>]
[-UsageLogMaxSpaceGB <1-20>] [-Verbose]
```

For the -LoggingEnabled switch, select 1 to enable logging and 0 to disable logging. For the -UsageLogLocation, type the path to the logging folder. For the -UsageLogMaxSpaceGB switch, enter a value from 1 to 20 to indicate the amount of disk space to be allowed by the logs.

Using PowerShell, you can specify a specific type of event to be logged and the number of days it will be kept before deletion. At the prompt, type the following string and then press Enter, using the desired parameter values and substituting your production values for the sample values:

```
Set-SPUsageDefinition -Identity <GUID> [-Enable] [-DaysRetained <1-30>] [-Verbose]
```

The -Enable switch turns on usage logging for the specified event, and the GUID used with the -Identity switch specifies the event to be logged. Enter a value from 1 to 30 for the number of days you want the log retained.

If you choose to log usage data to a different database than the one used by default, you must use Windows PowerShell to make the specification. At the command prompt, type the following string and then press Enter, indicating the actual name of the database server, the database, and a username and password that has rights to the server and database:

```
Set-SPUsageApplication -DatabaseServer <Database server name> -DatabaseName
<Database name> [-DatabaseUsername <User name>] [-DatabasePassword <Password>]
[-Verbose]
```

You do not have to add the username and password if the account you're already logged in with has access to the relevant database server and database.

Configuring the SharePoint Health Analyzer

A SharePoint administrator can be expected to configure both the timer jobs for the Health Analyzer as well as the rules. Exercise 13.3 shows you how to perform the timer jobs task using Central Administration. You must belong to the Farm Administrators group to complete this task. Also be aware that this configuration has a farm-wide scope. You cannot configure Health Analyzer timer jobs for just a few servers in the farm.

EXERCISE 13.3

Editing Health Data Collection Timer Jobs

1. Go to the Central Administration home page and click Monitoring.

2. On the Monitoring page, click Configure Usage And Health Data Collection under Reporting.

3. On the Configure Usage And Health Data Collection page, click Health Logging Schedule under Health Logging.

4. When the Job Definitions page opens, click the desired timer job.

5. On the Edit Timer Job page, modify the timer job schedule to the desired parameters under Recurring Schedule and then click OK.

 This task is substantially similar to Exercise 13.2, which shows you how to go in and edit or disable a timer job after initially configuring it.

The same task can be performed in Windows PowerShell using a series of command strings. To begin, open PowerShell as an administrator. At the prompt, type this cmdlet using the desired values and parameters and then press Enter:

```
Set-SPTimerJob [-Identity <name>] [-Schedule <Schedule string>]
```

For the -Identity parameter, type the name of the timer job. If you do not specify a name for Identity, all timer jobs will be affected by the schedule change. If you don't know the name of the specific timer job you are looking for, type the following at the prompt and then press Enter:

```
Get-SPTimerJob | Format-Table -property id,title
```

To see a list of the current timer jobs and their schedules, type the following at the prompt and then press Enter:

```
Get-SPTimerJob | Format-Table -property id,title,schedule
```

There are a large number of specific values you can type at the -Schedule switch. Use one of the following lines of code to set the timer job schedule you want to apply:

```
every <1-60> seconds
every <1-60> minutes at <1-60>
every <1-60> minutes between <1-60> and <1-60>
hourly between <1-59> minutes past the hour and <1-59> minutes past the hour
daily between starting from <hh:mm:ss> and starting no later than <hh:mm:ss>
weekly between starting on <day of the week hh:mm:ss> and starting no later than
<day of the week hh:mm:ss>
monthly between starting on < day number hh:mm:ss> and starting no later than <
day number hh:mm:ss>
monthly by <hh:mm:ss> on <week number> <day of week>
```

You can edit the rules for the Health Analyzer in Central Administration. You must be a member of the Farm Administrators group to complete the task. Exercise 13.4 shows you how.

When you modify a health rule, you can edit Configurable Fields and Read-Only Fields.

Configurable Fields are Title, which is the name of the health rule; Scope, which indicates which server or servers the rule runs against; Schedule, which defines the schedule for the rule; Enabled, which shows whether the rule is on or off; Repair Automatically, which if on, tries to fix any errors the rule encounters; and Version, which tracks the version history of the rule.

Read-Only Fields include Version, which only lists the version number for the rule; Created At, which shows the date and time that the rule was made; and Last Modified, which shows the date and time the rule was last edited.

EXERCISE 13.4

Configuring Health Data Collection Rules

1. Go to the Central Administration home page and click Monitoring.

2. On the Monitoring page, click Review Rule Definitions under Health Analyzer.

3. On the Health Rule Definitions page, click the desired rule under the desired category.

4. When the Health Analyzer Rule Definitions dialog box opens, click Edit Item.

5. Edit any of the rules as you desire. When you're done, click Save or click Cancel to close without saving any changes, as shown here.

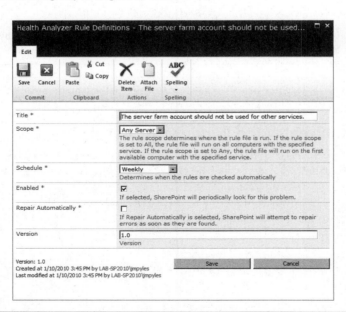

Reviewing Logs and Reports

Now that you have your environment set up to gather information, once sufficient data is collected, you are responsible for reviewing the various logs and reports that are available in SharePoint. You can review administrative reports, diagnostic logs, health reports, timer jobs, and health reports.

Reviewing Reports Using Central Administration and Windows PowerShell

Most of the report review tasks you perform are done in Central Administration, but a few can be done using Windows PowerShell. Exercise 13.5 illustrates the steps for reviewing administrative reports in Central Administration. You must be a member of the Farm Administrators group to perform the following steps.

EXERCISE 13.5

Reviewing Administrative Reports

1. Go to the Central Administration home page and click Monitoring.

2. On the Monitoring page, click View Administrative Reports under Reporting.

3. On the Administrative Report Library page, click the name of the desired report folder.

4. On the Report Folder page, click the name of the desired report.

5. If you want to filter the results on the page, make the desired filter changes and then click Apply Settings.

Filtering can help you narrow down the scope of the data you are exploring so that you can focus on the information that's most important to you.

Viewing Log Events with Windows PowerShell

Interestingly enough, you can filter diagnostic logs in a number of ways using Windows PowerShell. PowerShell can access the Universal Logging System (ULS) logs in SharePoint and, depending on the parameters used, view the raw data and apply specific filters to your views. To do so, open PowerShell as an administrator, and to view all trace events, type the following at the prompt without any parameters and then press Enter:

```
Get-SPLogEvent
```

You can use a number of parameters and values to filter your view of the event logs as follows.

To view an event log by area, type the following at the prompt and then press Enter, inserting your production value for Area at the appropriate switch:

```
Get-SPLogEvent | Where-Object {$_.Area -eq <Area>}
```

To view event logs by category, type the following string at the prompt and then press Enter, putting in the production value for Category at the Category switch:

```
Get-SPLogEvent | Where-Object {$_.Category -eq <Category>
```

To view an event log by event ID, type the following string at the prompt and press Enter, replacing the sample value with the actual event identifier at the EventID switch:

```
Get-SPLogEvent | Where-Object {$_.EventID -eq <EventID>}
```

To view an event by level, type the following string at the prompt and press Enter, entering the desired level such as warning or error at the Level switch:

```
Get-SPLogEvent | Where-Object {$_.Level -eq [Information | Warning | Error |
Critical | Verbose | Unexpected | Monitorable | High | Medium]}
```

To filter event log content by a specific text string, enter the following command at the prompt and press Enter, replacing the sample value with the actual string of text by which you want to filter:

```
Get-SPLogEvent | Where-Object {$_.Message -like "*<string>*"}
```

To filter event logs by process, type the following command at the prompt and then press Enter, replacing the process sample value with the value of the actual process property:

```
Get-SPLogEvent | Where-Object {$_.Process -like "*<Process>*"}
```

You can use Central Administration to view SharePoint health reports. Exercise 13.6 gives you the steps. You must be a member of the Farm Administrators group to perform this task.

EXERCISE 13.6

Reviewing Health Reports in Central Administration

1. Go to the Central Administration home page and click Monitoring.

2. On the Monitoring page, click View Health Reports under Reporting.

3. On the Report page, click the name of the desired report.

4. When reviewing the report, click the desired data criteria and then click Go.

5. Click the desired column name to sort data rows.

Timer jobs run specific services in SharePoint defining the schedule for these services including monitoring. You can view the status of timer jobs using either Central Administration or

Windows PowerShell. Exercise 13.6 shows you the Central Administration method. You must be a member of the Farm Administrators group to perform this task.

EXERCISE 13.7

Reviewing Timer Jobs in Central Administration

1. Go to the Central Administration home page and click Monitoring.

2. On the Monitoring page, click Check Job Status under Timer Jobs.

3. On the Check Job Status page, use the paging arrows at the bottom of the desired groups such as Scheduled, Running, and History.

4. To view the timer job status for a particular group, click the name of the group.

To view the status of a specific timer job using Windows PowerShell, type the following at the command prompt and then press Enter, specifying the timer job name at the -Identity switch:

```
Get-SPTimerJob [-Identity <Timer job name...>] | Format-Table -Property
DisplayName,Id,LastRunTime,Status
```

You can also view the history for a particular job by using the following command:

```
(Get-SPTimerJob [-Identity <Timer job name...>]).HistoryEntries | Format-Table
-Property Status,StartTime,EndTime,ErrorMessage
```

You can view web analytics, which is a collection of reports regarding site and site collection usage, in Central Administration. Exercise 13.7 provides the instructions. You will need to belong to the Farm Administrators group to perform this task.

EXERCISE 13.8

Reviewing Web Analytics in Central Administration

1. Go to the Central Administration home page and click Monitoring.

2. On the Monitoring page, click View Web Analytics Reports under Reporting.

3. On the Web Analytics Reports page, click the desired web application.

4. On the Web Analytics Reports – Summary page, click the name of the desired report in Quick Launch, and depending on the type of report, you may or may not be able to change the report settings by clicking Analyze on the Ribbon.

5. Click the desired column name to sort the rows in the data grid.

Options for modifying the settings of a report type when you click Analyze in the Ribbon are Date Range, Export To Spreadsheet, Filter, and Paging Size. You can modify Date Range and export reports to a spreadsheets for all report types. You cannot edit filter or paging size for Summary, Number Of Page Views, Number Of Daily Unique Visitors, Number Of Referrers, Number Of Collections, and Top Site Collection Templates.

 Real World Scenario

Collecting Data from SharePoint Monitoring

You are a SharePoint administrator for your company, and you implemented a Share-Point 2010 Server farm solution in your organization several months ago. At that time, you configured the various SharePoint logging and monitoring tools to gather information including diagnostic logging, health and usage data collection, and SharePoint Health Analyzer. Now you must gather information from these various tools as part of a report you are going to present to the CIO and the rest of the management staff regarding SharePoint's effectiveness.

To review these logs and reports, you will need to use a combination of Central Administration and Windows PowerShell because no one interface can access everything. You pull information from the administrative reports, health reports, timer jobs, and web analytics sections in Central Administration, but you also use PowerShell to display different views of the event logs.

You will still need to compile all this data so that it can be presented to the management team in a more narrative form supported by various graphs, but you will be able to demonstrate both the baseline performance of the server farm and any changes and trends in usage over time.

Summary

In this chapter, you learned the specifics about the different monitoring and analysis tools in SharePoint:

- The differences between diagnostic logging, health and usage data collection, and the SharePoint Health Analyzer

- How the different monitoring tools are configured

- How to access and review reports in SharePoint

Exam Essentials

Understanding How to Enable and Configure Monitoring and Analysis Tools   Understand the practices involved in setting up and configuring diagnostic logging, health and usage data collection, and the SharePoint Health Analyzer.

Demonstrating the Ability to Review Reports   Know how to access each monitoring tool and the reports it generates in SharePoint using Central Administration and Windows PowerShell.

Review Questions

1. You are a SharePoint administrator for your company, and you are currently managing the monitoring and analysis tools in SharePoint. As you perform these tasks, what do you find is true about SharePoint monitoring?

   A. All monitoring tools in SharePoint are enabled by default.

   B. All monitoring tools managed by Central Administration are enabled by default, but you must manually enable those tools managed with Windows PowerShell.

   C. All monitoring tools managed by Windows PowerShell are enabled by default, but you must manually enable those tools managed by Central Administration.

   D. All monitoring tools in SharePoint are disabled by default.

2. You are a SharePoint administrator for your company, and you are currently managing the monitoring and analysis tools in SharePoint. You want to gather different kinds of information including event log data, performance counter data, and timer service metrics data. Which of the following tools should you use?

   A. Diagnostic logging.

   B. Health and usage data collection.

   C. SharePoint Health Analyzer.

   D. Any of the available monitoring tools gathers that data together.

3. You are a SharePoint administrator for your company, and you are currently managing the monitoring and analysis tools in SharePoint. Of the following, which tool should you typically use to troubleshoot errors in SharePoint?

   A. Diagnostic logging.

   B. Health and usage data collection.

   C. SharePoint Health Analyzer.

   D. Any of the available monitoring tools can be used equally well to troubleshoot errors.

4. You are a SharePoint administrator for your company, and you are currently managing the monitoring and analysis tools in SharePoint. You are currently configuring diagnostic logging using Central Administration. Of the following, which features can you manage for diagnostic logging? (Choose all that apply.)

   A. Event Backwash

   B. Event Log Flood Protection

   C. Event Failure Control

   D. Event Throttling

5. You are a SharePoint administrator for your company, and you are currently managing the monitoring and analysis tools in SharePoint. You are currently configuring Diagnostic Logging using Windows PowerShell. Of the following, which PowerShell cmdlet should you use?

    A. SPDiagLog

    B. SPDiagnosticLog

    C. SPLogLevel

    D. SPLogSet

6. You are a SharePoint administrator for your company, and you are currently managing the monitoring and analysis tools in SharePoint. You are currently configuring usage and health data collection using Central Administration. Of the following, what is true about configuring this utility?

    A. You can configure this data collection tool to apply to a web application, a single server, a collection of servers, or the server farm.

    B. You can configure this data collection tool to apply to a single server, a collection of servers, or the server farm.

    C. You can configure this data collection tool to apply to a group of three servers or more including the entire server farm.

    D. You can configure this data collection tool to apply to the entire server farm only.

7. You are a SharePoint administrator for your company, and you are currently managing the monitoring and analysis tools in SharePoint. You are currently configuring diagnostic logging using Central Administration and want to limit the amount of disk space that can be used by the logs. When the disk space limit has been reached, what happens?

    A. You receive an error that no further information can be written to the log files until you delete currently existing files.

    B. You receive a notice that you have exceeded the disk space limit but information will still be written to the log files.

    C. The most recent log files are overwritten by the current log files.

    D. The oldest log files are overwritten by the current log files.

8. You are a SharePoint administrator for your company, and you are currently managing the monitoring and analysis tools in SharePoint. You are currently configuring usage and health data collection using Central Administration. Of the following, which task or tasks can you not perform for usage and health data collection in Central Administration? (Choose two.)

    A. You cannot change the name of the database server.

    B. You cannot change the name of the database on the database server.

    C. You cannot change the authentication method for the database server.

    D. You cannot change the schedule for timer jobs.

9. You are a SharePoint administrator for your company, and you are currently managing the monitoring and analysis tools in SharePoint. You are currently configuring usage and health data collection using Windows PowerShell. You want to specify a specific type of event to be logged. Of the following, which is the correct cmdlet to use?

A. `SPUsageService`

B. `SPUsageIdentity`

C. `SPUsageEvent`

D. `SPUsageDefinition`

10. You are a SharePoint administrator for your company, and you are currently managing the monitoring and analysis tools in SharePoint. You are currently configuring usage and health data collection using Windows PowerShell. You want to change the database used to log usage data to one different from the default. Of the following, which cmdlet should you use?

A. `SPUsageApplication`

B. `SPUsageDatabase`

C. `SPUsageDatabaseName`

D. `SPUsageService`

11. You are a SharePoint administrator for your company, and you are currently configuring the SharePoint Health Analyzer. You want to configure health data collection rules in Windows PowerShell. Of the following, which is the most correct statement?

A. You can only manage Configurable Fields for health rules in PowerShell.

B. You can only manage Read-Only Fields for health rules in PowerShell.

C. You can manage Configurable and Read-Only Fields for health rules in PowerShell.

D. You cannot manage health rules in PowerShell. You must use Central Administration.

12. You are a SharePoint administrator for your company, and you want to view log events using Windows PowerShell. There are a number of ways you can filter log event views in PowerShell, and they all begin with the same command. Of the following, which is the correct command?

A. `Find -SPLogEvent`

B. `Get -SPLogEvent`

C. `Set -SPLogEvent`

D. `View- SPLogEvent`

13. You are a SharePoint administrator for your company, and you want to view log events using Windows PowerShell. There are a number of different ways you can filter event views in PowerShell. Of the following, which are correct methods? (Choose all that apply.)

A. You can view by `Area`.

B. You can view by `Category`.

C. You can view by `EventID`.

D. You can view by `Server Name`.

14. You are a SharePoint administrator for your company, and you want to view the timer jobs for health reports using Windows PowerShell. Of the following, which is the correct command you must use to achieve your goal?

    A. `Find -SPTimerJob`

    B. `Get -SPTimerJob`

    C. `Set -SPTimerJob`

    D. `View- SPTimerJob`

15. You are a SharePoint administrator for your company, and you are currently reviewing web analytics using Central Administration. You are changing the settings for the report type. Of the following, what are valid options for this task? (Choose all that apply.)

    A. Data Range

    B. Export To Spreadsheet

    C. Filter

    D. Paging Size

16. You are a SharePoint administrator for your company, and you are currently reviewing web analytics using Central Administration. After you click Analyze on the Ribbon, you are presented with a number of editing options, but not all of these options work with all report types. Of the following, which options work with all report types? (Choose two.)

    A. Date Range

    B. Export To Spreadsheet

    C. Filter

    D. Paging Size

17. You are a SharePoint administrator for your company, and you are currently reviewing health report information in Central Administration. On the Central Administration home page, you click Monitoring. What must you click next to review timer jobs?

    A. Health Reporting.

    B. Reporting.

    C. Timer Jobs.

    D. You must perform this task in Windows PowerShell.

18. You are a SharePoint administrator, and you currently want to review administrative reports in Central Administration. You can find administrative reports on which of the following pages?

    A. A library page

    B. A list page

    C. A reports page

    D. A web part page

19. You are a SharePoint administrator for your company, and you are currently configuring the rules for the Health Data Collection tool in Central Administration. You want to set a rule that, when it encounters an error, will attempt to correct the error. Of the following, what rule applies to this task?

A. Error Repair

B. Fix Error

C. Repair Automatically

D. No rule applies

20. You are a SharePoint administrator for your company, and you are currently setting up the schedule for timer jobs as they apply to the Health Data Collection utility. Of the following, what schedule types or frequencies can you configure for timer jobs in PowerShell? (Choose all that apply.)

A. Every <1–60> seconds

B. Every <1–60> minutes at <1–60>

C. Hourly between <1–59> minutes past the hour

D. Annually between <1–366> days

Answers to Review Questions

1. A. Monitoring features are enabled in SharePoint by default using a collection of standard settings.

2. B. The health and usage data collection is a set of monitoring tools that gather together different types of data including event log data, performance counter data, and timer service metrics data.

3. A. Diagnostic logging is comprised of a series of logs that collect data typically used in troubleshooting errors in SharePoint.

4. B, D. You can configure and manage Event Throttling and Event Log Flood Protection for diagnostic logging. The other two options are bogus.

5. C. Use the `SPLogLevel` cmdlet and appropriate parameters to configure diagnostic logging in Windows PowerShell. The other cmdlets are bogus.

6. D. Any usage and health data collection tool settings you make are applied to the entire farm and cannot specify a smaller group of servers.

7. D. Once the disk space limit has been reached, older logs will be deleted to make room for newer logs.

8. A, B. You can select an authentication method, but you cannot change the database on the default database server or change the database server using Central Administration. You can only change the database and the name of the database server used by the usage and health data collection tool using Windows PowerShell. You can change the schedule for a timer job in Central Administration.

9. D. `SPUsageService` is the Windows PowerShell cmdlet used to generally configure the usage and health data collection system as a whole. The other cmdlets are bogus.

10. D. `SPUsageService` is the Windows PowerShell cmdlet used to generally configure the usage and health data collection system as a whole. The other cmdlets are bogus.

11. D. You can only manage health rules for health data collection using Central Administration.

12. B. `Get -SPLogEvent` is the correct command. All the other options are bogus.

13. A, B, C. You can view event log information by `Area`, `Category`, `EventID`, `Level`, and `Process` but not by `Server Name`.

14. B. `Get -SPTimerJob` is the correct command. All the other options are bogus.

15. B, C, D. The correct option is Date Range, not Data Range. All other options are correct.

16. A, B. Only the options for editing a date range and exporting information to a spreadsheet work with all types of reports in web analytics. You can use filtering and edit paging size for only some report types.

17. C. You can click Reporting to view health reports but must click Timer Jobs to view the timer jobs for health reports. The Health Reporting option is bogus, and you can perform this task in both Central Administration and Windows PowerShell.

18. A. Administrative reports are found on the Administrative Report Library page.

19. C. For Health Rules under Configurable Fields, select Repair Automatically so that the rule will try to fix any errors it encounters.

20. A, B, C. The option for setting the schedule annually is bogus. All other options are correct.

Chapter
14

Optimizing SharePoint

MICROSOFT EXAM OBJECTIVE COVERED IN THIS CHAPTER:

✓ **Maintaining a SharePoint Environment**

    ▪ Optimize the Performance of a SharePoint Environment

When you buy a new car, it should work great and do everything you want a car to do. Of course, with just a few modifications, it might perform even better. SharePoint is the same way. Although an "out-of-the-box" deployment of SharePoint may be just fine for your basic needs, with just a little extra care and attention, you can make it perform even better than you imagined. Optimization can take many forms. A key player in SharePoint optimization is the modification of the Remote BLOB storage and cache settings, but that's only the beginning. Areas ranging from resource throttling to mobile administration come into play, plus a lot more.

SharePoint Optimization

You can use a number of techniques to optimize SharePoint performance. Some utilize tools and methods you have already worked with in previous chapters, while others will be new to you. This section of this chapter will focus on how to use what you already know to optimize the SharePoint environment.

General SharePoint Optimization Principles

There are a wide variety of activities that can be performed to optimize SharePoint access and performance, but not all of those activities are done by a SharePoint administrator. Nevertheless, as an administrator, you should have at least some understanding of the larger realm of techniques that affect your environment.

This section will present information at a high level. It's unlikely that all this information be part of the certification exam, but you'll encounter the topics when you are actually administrating SharePoint.

Caching

Anyone responsible for managing a web environment knows that users don't have to get a fresh view of a website every time they hit the site. Depending on how you classify users and their priorities, you can assign different caching profiles for different user types, conserving SharePoint resources. For instance, if you service Anonymous or other "lesser-priority" users, you can assign them a different caching profile than authenticated users. You can also manage caching profiles by page type if it makes more sense in your environment to prioritize by content framework rather than user.

Database Optimization

Generally, what's good for SQL Server and the content databases is good for SharePoint. If SharePoint experiences performance issues, the problem may, strictly speaking, not be in SharePoint but rather be a SQL Server issue. Communicate with the database guru in your environment, and make sure you have a good working relationship. Chances are, that person wants their environment to operate just as smoothly as you want yours to, so why not work together?

Some specific issues with database servers have to do with the timely defragmentation of the databases and scaling hardware and software resources so that higher-demand databases have access to more storage and network bandwidth than lower-demand databases.

Navigation

Navigation depth is something that can be controlled by SharePoint designers. The deeper and more complex the navigation scheme, the more resources are required for SharePoint to fetch navigation menus. On top of that, users are more likely to become confused and unable to quickly find the pages, lists, and libraries they need. If this is a problem in your environment, you can ask the SharePoint designers responsible for navigation to limit the level and depth of navigation menus, keeping them within manageable parameters. What you consider "manageable" will depend on your specific technical and corporate requirements and standards.

Network Traffic

With the use of today's high-speed corporate LANs, we have a tendency to think that we won't experience bandwidth issues. Consider, though, how incredibly dependent SharePoint is on SQL Server and on databases. An untold number of calls go between SharePoint and SQL Server each time something changes on a site or site collection. Multiply that usage by thousands or tens of thousands of users, and you get an idea of just how much traffic is being exchanged between SharePoint and SQL Server. Now imagine that people are using the same network segments that SharePoint uses to communicate with its databases.

The way around this problem is to isolate the network traffic between SharePoint and SQL Server. This can be accomplished either by constructing a separate physical network for this purpose or by using VLANs.

Managing General Optimization

You can perform a number of tasks to optimize SharePoint performance. One such task is to minimize the use of application pools in SharePoint. The more application pools SharePoint must support, the more active memory on the server machines that is consumed. If you minimize the creation of service applications, you conserve memory resources.

One principle is to use a specific application pool or pools for customizations and to consolidate all other service applications under one application pool. It's also recommended by Microsoft to use a separate application pool for the administrative virtual server and to have all other virtual servers share another, single application pool.

Create as few application pools as possible and then, when creating new applications, only use pools for specific purposes, consolidating as many services into as few pools as possible. Exercise 14.1 will show you an example. You will need to be a farm administrator to complete this task.

EXERCISE 14.1

Consolidating Application Pools to Conserve Memory

1. Go to the Central Administration home page and click Manage Service Applications under Application Management.

2. On the Manage Service Applications page, click New in the Ribbon.

3. In the list that appears, click the desired selection, such as Business Data Connectivity.

4. Configure the service application as you desire and select Use Existing Application Pool under Application Pool. Then use the drop-down menu to select the application pool under which you are consolidating all similar service applications.

5. When finished, click OK.

You have already created similar service applications by performing the exercises in Chapter 4, "Configuring Service Applications," but this time, you have a better understanding of which application pool to select when creating a service application and why.

A general performance killer is the Repair Automatically feature found in the Health Analyzer rule definitions. Unless you find this feature for a rule to be absolutely necessary, you should turn it off to optimize performance. You saw how to configure these rule definitions in Exercise 13.4. Exercise 14.2 will provide a refresher with optimization in mind.

EXERCISE 14.2

Minimizing the Use of the Repair Automatically
Feature of Health Definition Rules

1. Go to the Central Administration home page and click Monitoring.

2. On the Monitoring page, click Review Rule Definitions under Health Analyzer.

3. On the Health Analyzer Rule Definitions page, review the list of rules that have Yes listed in the Repair Automatically column, as shown here.

EXERCISE 14.2 *(continued)*

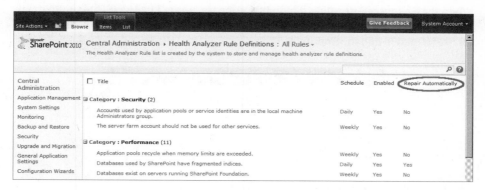

4. Click the name of a rule that has the Repair Automatically feature enabled in which you want to disable the feature.

5. When the dialog box for the rule appears, click Edit Item.

6. When the Edit Item dialog box appears, clear the check box under Repair Automatically and then click Save.

7. Repeat this procedure for all rule definitions for which you want to turn off the Repair Automatically feature.

You also have the option of improving SharePoint performance by adjusting the resource throttling settings for web applications using Central Administration. For example, the default settings run HTTP throttling every five seconds. Exercise 14.3 shows you how to change this and other performance settings.

EXERCISE 14.3

Adjusting Resource Throttling for a Web Application

1. Go to the Central Administration home page and click Manage Web Applications under Application Management.

2. On the Manage Web Applications page, click next to the name of a web application to select it, but do not directly click the name.

3. In the Ribbon, click General Settings and, in the menu that appears, click Resource Throttling.

4. When the Resource Throttling dialog box appears, under List View Threshold, if you desire, change the value of the List View Threshold field, as shown here, as required for performance enhancement.

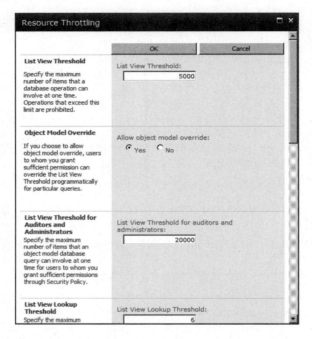

5. Under List View Threshold For Auditors And Administrators, adjust the value in the List View Threshold For Auditors And Administrators field as required for performance enhancement.

6. Under List View Lookup Threshold, adjust the value in the accompanying field as required for your performance enhancement needs.

7. Under Daily Time Window For Large Queries, to make sure large queries are performed outside of work hours to reserve resources used during work hours, select the Enable A Daily Time Window For Large Queries check box, set a start time for the large queries using the Start Time drop-down menu, and then set a direction for these queries using the Duration drop-down menu.

8. Under List Unique Permissions Threshold, adjust the number of unique permissions that a list can have at one time in the associated field to meet your performance requirements.

9. For Backward-Compatible Event Handlers, if you do not need this feature, select Off.

10. Under HTTP Request Monitoring And Throttling, select On to enable this feature, which will reject low-priority HTTP requests at times when a high number of such requests would otherwise affect web server performance.

11. Under Change Log, click After. In the associated field, specify the number of days after which entries in the change log will be deleted in order to preserve disk space.

12. Click OK.

If you are using multiple content databases in your SharePoint environment, you want to set each web application to use a specific database so that every time you create a site collection within a web application, you are using the desired content database. Depending on the size of your environment, access to resources, and your topological plan, you'll want either to use one content database for all site collections or to logically organize the site collections and specific content databases based on the size and priority of the site collection. If you need to see which content databases are associated with which web applications, perform the steps in Exercise 14.4. You will also see the instructions for how to set a default database server for your SharePoint environment.

Optimizing Content Database Usage

1. Go to the Central Administration home page and click Application Management.

2. On the Application Management page, click Manage Content Databases under Databases.

3. On the Manage Content Databases page, if necessary, click the Web Application menu and choose the desired web application.

4. Once you've determined which content database is being used for the desired web application, if you require a different content database, click Add A Content Database, enter the desired values on the Add Content Database page, and then click OK.

5. To specify which database server will be used by default, navigate back to the Application Management page and click Specify The Default Database Server under Databases.

6. On the Default Database Server page, enter the name of the server in the Database Server field under Content Database Server.

7. Under Database Username And Password, if you want to use SQL Server authentication, enter the appropriate SQL Server account username and password in the available fields. To use Windows authentication, leave these fields blank.

8. Click OK.

SharePoint content consists of two primary sources: static files for the SharePoint root directories located in C:\Program Files\Common Files\Microsoft Shared\14 for 2010 and dynamic data stored in the content. At runtime, SharePoint merges the page contents from both sources and then transmits them inside an HTTP response to the requesting user. Internet Information Services (IIS) versions 6 and 7 both contain various mechanisms for reducing the payload of HTTP responses prior to transmitting them across the network. Adjusting these settings can reduce the size of the data transmitted to the client, resulting in shorter load times and faster page rendering.

Exercise 14.5 shows you how to enable and adjust IIS compression to optimize SharePoint web page load times. When you enable static content compression, the default settings will only compress files larger than 2,700 bytes and will create a per-application pool disk space limit of 100 MB.

EXERCISE 14.5

Enabling and Adjusting IIS Compression

1. On the desired web server, click Start ➤ All Programs ➤ Administrative Tools and then click Internet Information Services (IIS) Manager.

2. In the Connections pane on the left, select the desired server.

3. Under the central pane, make sure Features View is selected. Then scroll down, if necessary, and double-click Compression under IIS.

4. When Compression appears in the main page, click either the Enable Dynamic Content Compression check box, the Enable Static Content Compression check box, or both.

5. Under Static Compression, if desired, select the Only Compress Files Larger Than (In Bytes) check box and then enter the desired value in bytes in the associated field.

6. If necessary, in the Cache Directory field, enter the path to the directory used for caching or accept the default path.

7. If desired, select the Per Application Pool Disk Space Limit (In MB) check box and then enter a value in megabytes in the associated field.

8. Under Actions on the right, click Apply.

10. Close the Internet Information Services (IIS) Manager.

Optimizing Cache Settings

In Chapter 3, "Configuring SharePoint Farm Environments," you performed a number of the basic configuration tasks for Remote BLOB Storage. In this section of this chapter, you'll see how to configure cache settings for not only Remote BLOB Storage but also cache profile settings and object cache settings. Most of these adjustments are made in the Internet Information Services (IIS) Manager.

Remote BLOB Storage (RBS) is an optional feature for Microsoft SQL Server 2008 and is designed to let you move a storage of binary large objects (BLOBs) from a database server to commodity storage solutions. This comes in handy if your SharePoint content databases grow beyond about 4 GB. You can optimize access to BLOB storage by configuring a disk-based BLOB cache or a web application. Exercise 14.6 shows you the steps in this process. You must belong to the Administrators group on the local computer to successfully perform this task.

You will need to make changes to the web.config file for the desired Share-Point web application on the computer you are using for this exercise. You should make a copy of this file and name it something like web.config_bak in case a problem occurs during the exercise and you need to restore the original web.config file. You may want to save your backup file to a different directory.

EXERCISE 14.6

Configuring BLOB Cache Settings

1. On the desired web server, click Start ➤ All Programs ➤ Administrative Tools and then click Internet Information Services (IIS) Manager.

2. In the Connections pane on the left, expand the server name and then expand Sites to view the list of web applications.

3. Right-click the name of the web application for which you want to configure BLOB disk-based caching and then click Explore.

4. In the central pane, right-click the web.config file and then click Open, as shown here.

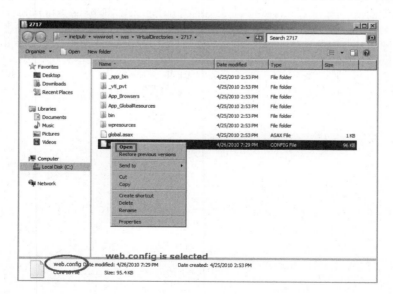

EXERCISE 14.6 *(continued)*

5. When prompted by the dialog box that appears, select Select A Program From A List Of Installed Programs and then click OK.

6. In the Open With dialog box, select Notepad and then click OK.

7. When Notepad opens, locate the line `<BlobCache location="" path="\.(gif|jpg| jpeg|jpe|jfif|bmp|dib|tif|tiff|ico|png|wdp|hdp|css|js|asf|avi|flv|m4v|mo v|mp3|mp4|mpeg|mpg|rm|rmvb|wma|wmv)$" maxSize="10" enabled="false" /` and locate the `location` attribute.

8. Change the `location` attribute to point to a directory on the computer that has sufficient disk space for the cache, preferably a directory that is not located on the same physical drive as the operating system swap files or the server log files.

9. For `path="\.`, modify the list of file extensions to add or remove extensions as desired, making sure that, if you add an extension, you include a pipe (|) right after the extension.

10. To change the size of the cache, modify the `maxSize` attribute so that the correct value in gigabytes is present, with 10 GB being the default value and using a value that is not smaller than the default.

11. Change the `enabled` attribute from `false` to `true` to enable the BLOB cache.

12. Save the Notepad file and then close it.

When you change and save the `web.config` file and then close Internet Information Services (IIS) Manager, IIS automatically cycles, causing a brief interruption in SharePoint services. This is an expected behavior, and it's best to perform this task after business hours or when SharePoint site collection usage will be light.

Output caching allows web pages to be cached based on user profiles so the amount of a cache and how long web data is cached varies depending on the user account. Output caching can be configured at the site collection and web application levels. Exercise 14.7 shows you how to perform this task at the site collection level, which is necessary before doing so at the web application level.

 For the site collection, the SharePoint publishing feature must be activated on the Site Settings page under Site Collection Administration before continuing with this process.

You must be an administrator for the desired site collection to complete this task.

EXERCISE 14.7

Configuring Output Caching in Site Collection Administration

1.   Navigate to the main page of the desired site collection.

2.   Click Site Actions and then click Site Settings.

3.   On the Site Settings page, under Site Collection Administration, click Site Collection Cache Profiles.

4.   On the Site Collection Cache Profiles page, click the Enable Output Cache check box.

5.   Use the Anonymous Cache Profile drop-down menu to select either Disabled, Public Internet (Purely Anonymous), Extranet (Published Site), or Intranet (Collaboration Site).

6.   Use the Authenticated Cache Profile drop-down menu to select either Disabled, Public Internet (Purely Anonymous), Extranet (Published Site), or Intranet (Collaboration Site).

7.   Click OK when finished.

These are the minimal actions required to enable output caching profiles. There are other specific settings you can manipulate in this interface.

Configuring Page Output Cache Profile Settings for a Web Application

If you configure the page output cache profile settings for a web application, all site collections hosted by the web applications will use those settings. The process of configuring these settings is performed using the Internet Information Services (IIS) Manager and is substantially similar to Exercise 14.6; however, the majority of attributes must be overridden by entering a custom parameter specified in the .NET Framework Class Library. Although this may be within the skill set of some readers, it is beyond the scope of a SharePoint administrator and will not be covered here.

Configuring Object Cache Settings for a Web Application

Object caching settings can also be set at the site collection level, and this feature is turned on by default. In the site collection, you can change the settings for object caching on the Site Settings page under Site Collection Administration by clicking Site Collection Object Cache and then, on the subsequent page, editing the settings according to your preferences.

To perform this task for a web application using Internet Information Services (IIS) Manager, follow the steps in Exercise 14.6 to open the `web.config` file for the desired web application, find the line `<ObjectCache maxSize="100" />`, and change the value in megabytes to the desired value. Save the file when finished and close the Internet Information Services (IIS) Manager, understanding that web applications services will be momentarily interrupted when the manager recycles.

A number of parts of the SharePoint publishing feature make queries, and the responses to those queries are cached in the object cache. The querying process is linked to the user account making the query. To optimize cache performance such as hit rate, queries must be tailored to the rights and abilities of specific user accounts such as whether the user has rights to see draft items.

For query results to get to the object cache, when a user makes a query, the query is actually not made in the user's name, but rather two queries are made by system entities: one by the Portal Super User account, which includes draft items in the results, and another by the Portal Super Reader account, which includes only published items. Once the query is made, the object cache checks the access control list (ACL) to determine the user account access and returns one of the two results in the object cache based on the user account's rights. Although this process increases the number of results returned, it conserves memory used by the cache.

For the object cache functionality to be used effectively, you must create two users, one for the Portal Super User account and one for the Super User Reader account to be used in place of the SharePoint systems accounts. The default system accounts used for Portal Super User and Portal Super Reader will not return the desired results.

To effectively use the object cache, the SharePoint administrator must perform two actions. First, object cache user accounts must be created in Central Administration that will be used in place of the default system accounts. Second, the new user accounts must be added to the web applications using Windows PowerShell. Exercise 14.8 will show you how to create the accounts in Central Administration. You must belong to the Farm Administrators group to successfully complete this task.

EXERCISE 14.8

Creating Object Cache User Accounts in Central Administration

1. On the Central Administration main page, click Manage Web Applications under Application Management.

2. On the Manage Web Applications page, select the desired web application; on the Web Applications tab of the Ribbon, click User Policy under Policy.

3. When the Policy For Web Application dialog box appears, click Add Users.

4. Select All Zones in the Zones list and then click Next.

5. Type the username for the Portal Super User account in the Users field and then click Check Names.

6. Under Choose Permissions, select the Full Control – Has Full Control check box.

7. Click Finish.

8. Click Add Users again and follow the same steps to add the Portal Super Reader account.

9. Under Choose Permissions, select the Full Read – Has Full Read-Only Access check box.

10. Click Finish.

Before closing the dialog box, you should make a note of how the two account names are displayed in the User Name column, since the display strings can be different depending on whether you are using claims authentication to access the web application.

 Real World Scenario

Optimizing SharePoint Using Multiple Techniques

You are a SharePoint administrator for a midsize retail company. You have installed and configured a SharePoint Server 2010 environment and are in the process of making it more efficient through various optimization techniques.

As part of optimization, when you were creating various service applications, you made sure you used only a single application pool. This helps conserve memory usage across your server hardware. Although you haven't needed to create any specific customizations yet, you will create additional application pools only as required for such customizations.

You are planning to adjust the settings for resource throttling for your web applications so that HTTP throttling will run less frequently than once every five seconds. You also are going to set web application throttling to make large queries starting at 7 p.m. on week-days, after most of the SharePoint users have gone home for the day, and you are going to turn on HTTP request monitoring and throttling so that low-priority HTTP requests will be rejected when web servers are receiving a high amount of traffic.

Adding Super User Accounts to a Web Application

The process of adding users to the web application involves creating a file with a `.ps1` extension, such as SetSuperUsers.ps1. To do so, open a blank Notepad document and type the following code:

```
$wa = Get-SPWebApplication -Identity "<WebApplication>"
$wa.Properties["portalsuperuseraccount"] = "<SuperUser>"
$wa.Properties["portalsuperreaderaccount"] = "<SuperReader>"
$wa.Update()
```

Make sure you change the sample values to your production values as in the following example:

```
$wa = Get-SPWebApplication -Identity "SPWebApp1"
$wa.Properties["portalsuperuseraccount"] = "PortalUserAccount"
$wa.Properties["portalsuperreaderaccount"] = "PortalReaderAccount"
$wa.Update()
```

Save the document with a name such as `SetSuperUsers.ps1`. Remember, the filename must have the `.ps1` extension. Make sure you know the location of the directory to which you have saved this file.

 At the end of adding superuser accounts to a web application, you must restart IIS. See `http://technet.microsoft.com/en-us/library/dd364067(WS.10).aspx` for how to accomplish this task.

Configuring Mobile Administration

One of the new features in SharePoint Server 2010 is the ability to interact with SharePoint from a mobile platform. Although mobile sales staff and other "road warriors" have been in existence for years, connecting with their primary offices via VPN, within the past few years, cell phones and similar devices have become widely used as tools for the enterprise. Many websites are being optimized for handheld devices. SharePoint is no different.

In SharePoint, mobile users can now subscribe to alerts on SharePoint changes using Short Message Service (SMS) so that said alerts are sent directly to their mobiles when these changes occur. In some ways, this works similarly to outgoing email alerts, which existed in prior versions of SharePoint, but mobile alerts are more akin to texting than emailing.

Another important piece to connecting to SharePoint via a mobile device is that SharePoint is commonly implemented as an intranet rather than Internet service, making it particularly difficult to contact using a mobile phone away from the main office location.

As a SharePoint administrator, you have the option of configuring a mobile account for a specific web application or for the entire farm. How wide or narrow you create your scope can be defined by priority concerns. For instance, if you configure a mobile account for the entire farm, anyone in the farm can subscribe to such alerts. This would be ideal if you needed to send organization-wide alerts to users, but you may want to organize alerts by web application, containing information to specific groups. Before you begin to configure a mobile account in SharePoint, you must make sure that the server farm account has access to the Internet so alerts can be sent. You must also acquire the root certificate for the service provider's HTTPS web address.

Importing a Root Certificate

As just mentioned, you won't be able to configure a mobile account until you import the root certificate for your service provider's HTTPS web address and then create a trusted root authority. You must perform this task using Windows PowerShell. To do this, you must belong to the Farm Administrators group and the local Administrators group on the computer running PowerShell. You must also be a member of the SharePoint_Shell_Access role for the required database.

To acquire the root certificate, open Windows PowerShell as an administrator and type the following command at the prompt, substituting the actual path to the root certificate file for the sample value in the following code string:

```
$cert = Get-PfxCertificate <ObtainedCertificatePath>
```

Here's an example of what the command might look like in production:

```
$cert = Get-PfxCertificate C:\downloads\path\location\certificate
```

Next in PowerShell, run the following command to create the trusted root authority, replacing the sample name for the actual name of the trusted root authority:

```
New-SPTrustedRootAuthority -Name <Name> -Certificate $cert
```

Here's a sample of what the command could look like in production:

```
New-SPTrustedRootAuthority -Name "RootAuthorityName" -Certificate $cert
```

Use only the root certificate to execute this task, not any of the other certificates that are present.

Configuring a Mobile Account

Now you'll be able to configure a mobile account. The task can be performed using either Central Administration or Windows PowerShell. Exercise 14.9 will show you the correct procedure for Central Administration. You will need to be a member of the Farm Administrators group to successfully complete this task.

EXERCISE 14.9

Configuring a Mobile Account in Central Administration for the Server Farm

1. On the Central Administration main page, click Systems Settings.

2. On the Systems Settings page, click Configure Mobile Account under E-Mail And Text Message (SMS).

3. On the Mobile Account Settings page, under Text Message (SMS) Service Settings, click the Microsoft Office Online link to see a list of service providers.

4. On the Find An Office 2010 Mobile Service Provider page, select the desired country or region for your wireless service provider in the Choose Your Wireless Service Provider's Country/Region list.

5. Choose the desired provider in the Choose Your Current Wireless Service Provider list.

6. When you are directed to, go to the service provider's web page and apply for the SMS service from the provider.

7. When you receive the necessary information from the service provider, return to the Mobile Accounts Settings page.

8. In the URL Of Text Message (SMS) Service field, type the URL of the SMS service, making sure you use HTTPS instead of HTTP.

9. In the appropriate fields, type the username and password that you received from your SMS service provider.

10. Click Test Service to verify the credentials.

11. Click OK.

To perform the same task using Windows PowerShell, execute the following command at the PowerShell command prompt, substituting the URL for Central Administration for <WebApplicationUrl>, the URL to the server providing the SMS service for <ServiceUrl>, the username you received from the SMS service provider for <UserID>, and the password you received from the SMS service provider for <Password>.

```
Set-SPMobileMessagingAccount -Identity sms -WebApplication <WebApplicationUrl>
[-ServiceUrl <ServiceUrl>] [-UserId <UserId>] [-Password <Password>]
```

Here's an example of what this command might look like in production:

```
Set-SPMobileMessagingAccount -Identity sms -WebApplication http://catesting:8080
-ServiceUrl https://www.smsbusiness.com/omsservice.asmx -UserId johndoe@
smsbusiness.com -Password mypassword
```

If you want to use the pipeline operator, a sample of the command as it might look in production is as follows:

```
Get-SPWebApplication -Identity http://catesting:8080 | Set-SPMobileMessagingAccount
-Identity sms -ServiceUrl https://www.smsbusiness.com/omsservice.asmx -UserId
johndoe@smsbusiness.com -Password mypassword
```

When entering the URL for the SMS service provider, make sure you use HTTPS instead of HTTP.

The previous two tasks configured a mobile account for the entire server farm. Exercise 14.10 shows you how to configure a mobile account for a web application. You will need to belong to the Farm Administrators group to complete this task.

Configuring a Mobile Account in Central Administration for a Web Application

1. On the Central Administration main page, click Application Management.

2. On the Application Management page, click Manage Web Applications.

3. On the Manage Web Applications page, select the desired web application and, on the Ribbon, click Mobile Account under General Settings.

4. On the Web Application Text Message (SMS) Service Settings page, click the Microsoft Office Online link under Text Message (SMS) Service Settings to see a list of service providers.

5. On the Find An Office 2010 Mobile Service Provider page, select the desired country or region for your wireless service provider in the Choose Your Wireless Service Provider's Country/Region list.

6. Choose the desired provider in the Choose Your Wireless Service Provider list.

7. When you are directed to, go to the service provider's web page and apply for the SMS service from the provider.

8. When you receive the necessary information from the service provider, return to the Mobile Accounts Settings page.

9. In the URL Of Text Message (SMS) Service field, type the URL of the SMS service, making sure you use HTTPS instead of HTTP.

11. In the appropriate fields, type the username and password that you received from your SMS service provider.

12. Click Test Service to verify the credentials.

13. Click OK.

In Windows PowerShell, you use the same commands as you did for configuring a mobile account for the server farm except for the WebApplication switch; you enter the URL for the web application instead of Central Administration. Everything else is the same.

To retrieve information about the mobile account, you must use Windows PowerShell. For the WebApplication switch, if you need this information for the server farm, enter the URL for Central Administration. If you need this information for a web application, enter the URL for the web application.

A production example for the farm server scenario looks like this:

```
Get-SPMobileMessagingAccount -WebApplication http://catesting/http://catesting.
```

A production example for the web application scenario looks like this:

```
Get-SPMobileMessagingAccount -WebApplication http://localwebapp/http://localwebapp
```

To delete a mobile account for the server farm, in Central Administration, go to System Settings and click Configure Mobile Account under E-mail And Text Messages (SMS). On the Mobile Account Settings page, remove all the entries from all the available fields and then click OK.

To delete a mobile account for a web application, in Central Administration, click Manage Web Applications under Application Management. On the Manage Web Applications page, on the Ribbon under General Settings, click Mobile Account. On the Web application Text Message (SMS) Service Settings page, remove all entries from all the fields and then click OK.

Configuring Mobile Views

Although mobile views are configured by default for most lists and libraries, they are not configured for customized lists or libraries or those that were created in previous versions of SharePoint and imported into SharePoint Server 2010. Mobile views allow users on mobile phones to be able to view a list or library in a manner optimized for handheld devices. Exercise 14.11 shows you how to configure mobile views for a list.

EXERCISE 14.11

Configuring Mobile Views for a List

1. Navigate to the desired site collection, site, and list for which you want to configure mobile views; in List Tools, click the List tab on the Ribbon.

2. On the Tools panel on the Ribbon, click Modify View.

3. On the Edit View page for the desired list, expand Mobile.

4. Select Enable This View For Mobile Access.

5. If you want the mobile access view to be the default view, select Make This View The Default View for mobile access.

6. Type the number of list items you want displayed in the list view for this web part in the Number Of Items To Display In List View Web Part For This View field.

7. Select Field To Display In Mobile List Simple View if you want the simple view option used.

To perform the same task for a library, navigate to the desired library. In Library Tools, click the Library tab on the Ribbon. Then follow the same steps you did in Exercise 14.11. Not all lists and libraries will display the identical configuration options, so you can use only those presented.

The previous exercises all assume that the alerts will be sent to mobile users from a company's intranet, which is normally accessible only within the organization's network infrastructure. There's an additional task if these alerts are to be sent from a SharePoint site normally accessible from the Internet and published across a firewall using Secure Sockets Layer (SSL).

As a SharePoint administrator, you must specify a cross-firewall access zone to be used to generate external computer and mobile URLs in the alert messages sent to mobile users. This allows users sent externally accessible URLs when they click the E-mail A Link button on the Ribbon.

 The ability to configure the Microsoft Forefront Unified Access Gateway for SharePoint is beyond the scope of the SharePoint administrator or this certification exam, but for more information, go to http://technet .microsoft.com/en-us/library/cc482990.aspx.

To configure a cross-firewall access zone, follow the steps in Exercise 14.12.

EXERCISE 14.12

Configuring a Cross-Firewall Access Zone for Mobile Accounts

1. On the Central Administration main page, click System Settings.

2. On the System Settings page, click Configure Cross Firewall Access Zone under Farm Management.

3. On the Cross Firewall Access Zone page, under Web Application, select the desired web application in the available list.

4. Under Cross Firewall Access Zone, select the desired zone in the Zone Select For Cross Firewall Access list.

Summary

In this chapter, you learned a variety of techniques you can use to optimize SharePoint access and performance:

- General, high-level optimization principles
- Specific optimization practices, such as HTTP throttling
- Optimizing cache settings for RBS and other features
- Configuring mobile access so that users can receive SharePoint alerts via their hand-held devices

Exam Essentials

Understanding How to Enable and Configure Features to Optimize SharePoint Performance   Be able to demonstrate how to enhance SharePoint performance using techniques such as HTTP throttling, application pool consolidation, and content database optimization.

Administering Mobile Accounts for SharePoint Interaction with Mobile Devices   Know how to enable mobile accounts so that users can receive SharePoint alerts via SMS, configure mobile accounts for the server farm and web applications, and enable mobile views of lists and libraries.

Review Questions

1. You are a SharePoint administrator for your organization, and you are in the process of optimizing SharePoint performance. You are reviewing a high-level optimization plan. Of the following activities, which one is most likely to be performed by a SharePoint designer?

    A. Configuring object caching

    B. Database optimization

    C. Controlling navigation depth

    D. Network throughput optimization

2. You are a SharePoint administrator for your organization, and you are in the process of optimizing SharePoint performance. You want to modify your use of application pools to reduce memory usage. Of the following, which is most likely to accomplish your goal?

    A. Create an application pool for each site collection.

    B. Create an application pool for each web application.

    C. Create one application pool for customizations and another for all site collections.

    D. Create one application pool for Central Administration and another for all other websites.

3. You are a SharePoint administrator for your organization, and you are in the process of optimizing SharePoint performance. A number of applications and features within Share-Point, including the Health Analyzer rule definitions, consume a great deal of resources and should be disabled if not absolutely necessary. Of the following, which health definition rule or feature should be used most sparingly?

    A. Application Pools Recycle When Memory Limits Are Exceeded

    B. Databases Used By SharePoint Have Fragmented Indices

    C. Repair Automatically

    D. Search—One Or More Property Databases Have Fragmented Indices

4. You are a SharePoint administrator for your organization, and you are in the process of optimizing SharePoint performance. You currently are modifying resource throttling for a web application. The Resource Throttling dialog box offers a wide variety of features that allows you to manage resources consumed by a web application. Of the following, which feature should you specifically turn off if not required?

    A. Daily Time Window for Large Queries

    B. List Unique Permissions Threshold

    C. Backward-Compatible Event Handlers

    D. HTTP Request Monitoring and Throttling

5. You are a SharePoint administrator for your organization, and you are in the process of optimizing SharePoint performance. You want to optimize content database usage. Of the following, which is the appropriate option for optimizing content database usage based on size and priority of site collections?

    A. Use one content database for all site collections.

    B. Logically organize the site collections to content databases for resource usage.

    C. Create one content database for each site collection.

    D. Create no more than 100 site collections per content database.

6. You are a SharePoint administrator for your organization, and you are in the process of optimizing SharePoint performance. You want to reduce the size of the payload of HTTP responses from SharePoint sites to decrease loading times. Of the following, where should you perform the task that will achieve this goals?

    A. In Central Administration

    B. On the main page of the relevant site collection

    C. In the Internet Information Services (IIS) Manager

    D. In Windows PowerShell

7. You are a SharePoint administrator for your organization, and you are in the process of optimizing SharePoint performance. You want to optimize BLOB cache settings by modifying a particular file for a web application. What is the name of this file?

    A. `blob.config`

    B. `blob.cache`

    C. `web.config`

    D. `web.cache`

8. You are a SharePoint administrator for your organization, and you are in the process of optimizing SharePoint performance. You want to optimize access to BLOB storage by configuring a disk-based BLOB cache. Of the following, what is the correct tool to use to accomplish this task?

    A. In Central Administration

    B. On the main page of the relevant site collection

    C. In the Internet Information Services (IIS) Manager

    D. In Windows PowerShell

9. You are a SharePoint administrator for your organization, and you are in the process of optimizing SharePoint performance. You are currently configuring BLOB cache settings in a particular configuration file. After finding the `BlobCache` line in the file, which parameters can you modify as part of the optimization process? (Choose all that apply.)

    A. `attribute`

    B. `enabled`

    C. `location`

    D. `path`

10. You are a SharePoint administrator for your organization, and you are in the process of optimizing SharePoint performance. You have just finished modifying a configuration file to optimizing BLOB cache settings, and you have saved the file and closed the tool you used to make your changes. What is the expected behavior that will immediately follow?

    A. All database connections will reset, causing a momentary interruption in access to site collections.

    B. Internet Information Services (IIS) automatically recycles, causing a momentary interruption in access to site collections.

    C. All output caching web pages reset, causing a momentary interruption of access to all SharePoint web pages on all site collections.

    D. To save your configuration settings, you must reboot the server on which SharePoint Central Administration resides.

11. You are a SharePoint administrator for your organization, and you are in the process of optimizing SharePoint performance. You want to modify web page output caching so that anonymous users receive cached pages when they revisit a page in SharePoint they recently visited and authenticated users access updated pages each time they visit any page. Where must you configure output caching for a site collection?

    A. In Central Administration

    B. On the main page of the relevant site collection

    C. In Internet Information Services (IIS) Manager

    D. Using Windows PowerShell

12. You are a SharePoint administrator for your organization, and you are in the process of optimizing SharePoint performance. You want to modify web page output caching so that anonymous users receive cached pages when they revisit a page in SharePoint they recently visited, and authenticated users access updated pages each time they visit any page. Where must you configure output caching for a web application?

    A. In Central Administration

    B. On the main page of the relevant site collection

    C. In Internet Information Services (IIS) Manager

    D. Using Windows PowerShell

13. You are a SharePoint administrator for your organization, and you are in the process of optimizing SharePoint performance. You are currently enabling output caching for a site collection, and you want to set the Anonymous Cache Profile for anonymous users. What are the available options for this profile? (Choose all that apply.)

    A. Anonymous Access

    B. Public Internet

    C. Extranet

    D. Intranet

14. You are a SharePoint administrator for your organization, and you are in the process of optimizing SharePoint performance. You are currently configuring object caching, and in order for the proper query results to be returned to users, you must create two user accounts to take the place of SharePoint systems accounts. Of the following, which two accounts must you create? (Choose two.)

A. Portal Super Access account

B. Portal Super Cache account

C. Portal Super Reader account

D. Portal Super User account

15. You are a SharePoint administrator for your organization, and you are in the process of optimizing SharePoint performance. You are currently configuring object caching. You must first create two user accounts to be used for object caching and then add those accounts to a web application. Of the following, what is the most correct procedure?

A. You must create the object cache user accounts in Central Administration and add them to a web application using Windows PowerShell.

B. You must create the object cache user accounts in Windows PowerShell and add them to a web application using Central Administration.

C. You must create the object cache user accounts and then add them to a web application using Central Administration.

D. You must create the object cache user accounts and then add them to a web application using Windows PowerShell.

16. You are a SharePoint administrator for your organization, and you are in the process of optimizing SharePoint performance. You have just finished configuring object caching by creating the necessary object cache user accounts and adding them to a web application. What must you do to apply your changes?

A. Restart the server on which Central Administration resides.

B. Restart the SQL server on which the relevant content database resides.

C. Restart Internet Information Services (IIS).

D. Click OK at the end of the configuration process in Central Administration.

17. You are a SharePoint administrator for your organization, and you are in the process of configuring mobile accounts in SharePoint so users can receive SharePoint alerts on their mobile phones. Before you begin to configure a mobile account, what tasks must you perform? (Choose two.)

A. The server farm account must have access to the intranet.

B. The server farm account must have access to the internet.

C. You must acquire the root certificate for your SMS service provider's HTTP web address.

D. You must acquire the root certificate for your SMS service provider's HTTPS web address.

18. You are a SharePoint administrator for your organization, and you are in the process of configuring mobile accounts in SharePoint so users can receive SharePoint alerts on their mobile phones. You can configure a mobile account at different levels in SharePoint. Of the following, which are valid levels at which you can configure a mobile account? (Choose all that apply.)

   A. The server farm

   B. A web application

   C. A site collection

   D. A list or library

19. You are a SharePoint administrator for your organization, and you are in the process of configuring mobile accounts in SharePoint so users can receive SharePoint alerts on their mobile phones. To configure a mobile account using Windows PowerShell, what command must you use?

   A. Set-SPMobileAlertsAccount

   B. Set-SPMobileMessagingAccount

   C. Set-SPSMSAccount

   D. Set-SPSMSMessagingAccount

20. You are a SharePoint administrator for your organization, and you are in the process of configuring mobile accounts in SharePoint so users can receive SharePoint alerts on their mobile phones. The relevant SharePoint site is one that can be accessed from the Internet rather than an intranet that is accessible only from within the company. What additional step must you perform to enable a mobile account?

   A. Configure Microsoft Forefront Unified Access Gateway for SharePoint.

   B. Configure a cross-firewall access zone for mobile accounts in Central Administration

   C. Open the required port in the firewall using Windows PowerShell.

   D. No additional task is required.

Answers to Review Questions

1. C. SharePoint designers can control the level and complexity of the navigation scheme in SharePoint for ease of use and to conserve resources. As an administrator, you will configure object caching; the DBA or other database server staff will be in charge of database optimization, and the IT/network infrastructure staff will implement network throughput modifications.

2. C. To conserve memory resources, use as few application pools as possible, creating one for all of your customizations and using one more for all your site collections.

3. C. For any given rule, you should disable the Repair Automatically feature unless the use of this feature is absolutely necessary in order to conserve resources.

4. C. The other options are all features that are used to conserve resources. Only use the Backward-Compatible Event Handlers feature if you expect to use legacy event handlers. If not, turn it off to conserve resources.

5. B. If you need to organize content database usage based on the site and priority of site collections, logically organize site collections that are larger or that receive more traffic to specific content databases and smaller, less utilized site collections to different databases.

6. C. You must use the Internet Information Services (IIS) Manager to enable and adjust IIS compression.

7. C. To configure the BLOB cache, you must locate and modify the `web.config` file in order to optimize access to BLOB storage for disk-based BLOB cache or a web application.

8. C. Use the Internet Information Services (IIS) Manager to locate and access the necessary file to specify a directory for the cache.

9. B, C, D. You must change the `enabled` attribute from `false` to `true` to enable BLOB caching, set the `location` attribute to indicate the location of the BLOB cache directory, and modify the list of file extensions in the `path` attribute to include or exclude the desired files for the cache. The `attribute` option is bogus. You can also change the `maxSize` attribute to change the size of the cache in gigabytes.

10. B. When you change and save the `web.config` file and then close Internet Information Services (IIS) Manager, IIS automatically cycles, causing a brief interruption in SharePoint services. This is an expected behavior, and it's best to perform this task after business hours or when SharePoint site collection usage will be light.

11. B. Navigate to the main page of the desired site collection, and make the adjustments starting on the Site Settings page.

12. C. The process of configuring these settings is performed using the Internet Information Services (IIS) Manager. The majority of attributes on the required configuration file must be overridden by entering a custom parameter specified in the .NET Framework Class Library.

13. B, C, D. The Public Internet option is used for anonymous access. The other valid option is Disabled.

14. C, D. The Portal Super Reader account can view published information in the query return but not draft information. The Portal Super User account can read both published and draft information. The other two options are bogus.

15. A. Object Cache user accounts can be created only in Central Administration, but they can only be added to a web application using Windows PowerShell.

16. C. At the end of adding super user accounts to a web application, you must restart Internet Information Services (IIS).

17. B, D. Before you begin to configure a mobile account in SharePoint, you must make sure that the server farm account has access to the Internet so alerts can be sent. You must also acquire the root certificate for the service provider's HTTPS web address.

18. A, B. You can configure a mobile account so that alerts are sent farm-wide or web application–wide. They cannot be configured at the site collection, list, or library levels.

19. B. For creating a mobile account at any level, such as farm-wide or web application-wide, you must use the `Set-SPMobileMessagingAccount` command followed by the required parameters.

20. B. If alerts are to be sent from a SharePoint site normally accessible from the Internet and published across a firewall using Secure Sockets Layer (SSL), you must configure a cross-firewall access zone for mobile accounts in Central Administration.

Chapter 15

Working with Windows PowerShell

MICROSOFT EXAM OBJECTIVE COVERED IN THIS CHAPTER:

✓ Maintaining a SharePoint Environment

In the other chapters of this book, you focused on performing a variety of tasks using multiple tools, including Windows PowerShell. This chapter will focus on PowerShell as a tool in general and how it is used in the SharePoint Server 2010 Management Shell.

Windows PowerShell Essentials

A *shell*, in the world of computing, is an interface between computer users and the operating system that gives users access to the system kernel. Although the graphical user interface (GUI) can be considered a *shell*, the term more commonly refers to the command-line shell, which serves the purpose of launching other specific programs, browsing the directory structure of the computer, and acting as an environment for scripting.

Windows PowerShell is designed to be a command-line interface specifically for administrators. It differs from previous Windows shell environments in that it does not act as a text-processing tool but rather as a utility that processes objects based on the .NET Framework. It also comes equipped with a large number of built-in commands, called *cmdlets*, and presents a consistent interface across different tools and activities. Although Windows PowerShell may seem new to you, it was initially released in 2006 and is available on Windows systems including Windows XP, Windows Server 2003, and all other, more recent Windows systems. PowerShell supersedes the `Stsadm.exe` administration tool and supports a scripting language that is optimized to, among other things, develop command-line scripts in SharePoint Foundation 2010.

Any shell environment can seem intimidating when you don't know your way around. As you likely experienced in some of the other chapters of this book, knowing which cmdlet to use to accomplish a specific task, knowing the command-line syntax, and knowing the various switches or parameters available can appear overwhelming. Familiarity and frequent use helps overcome those barriers. You may be a command-line guru, in which case you probably have already delved deep into the arcane secrets of PowerShell. If not, you can still become competent and even expert in PowerShell by using it as much as possible. Start by learning the basics.

Windows PowerShell First Steps

Windows PowerShell has a lot in common with other shell environments, so if you understand shell basics, you can probably make your way around PowerShell as well. However, if your shell skills are a little rusty, or even thoroughly oxidized, you can start learning here.

You don't have to be on Windows Server 2008 to work with PowerShell. If you have Windows XP, click Start, type **powershell** in the Run field, and press Enter. For Vista and Windows 7, click the Windows button and do the same thing. Windows PowerShell will open on your desktop computer, as shown in Figure 15.1.

FIGURE 15.1   Window PowerShell 2.0

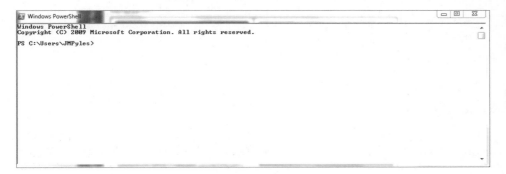

How you get PowerShell depends on which OS you are running:

- Windows XP and Windows Server 2003: PowerShell v1 and v2 versions are downloaded and installed (effectively as an OS patch).

- Windows Server 2008: PowerShell v1 is a "feature" and can be added. PowerShell v2 versions are downloaded and installed (effectively as an OS patch).

- Windows 7/Windows Server 2008 R2: PowerShell v2 is installed by default.

For the latest information on PowerShell 2.0, visit the PowerShell Team Blog (http://powershell.com/cs/blogs/windows-powershell-team/default.aspx). You can find more about how to get Windows PowerShell 2.0 for pre–Windows 7 computers here: http://powershell.com/cs/blogs/windows-powershell-team/archive/2010/06/22/windows-powershell-2-0-on-windows-update.aspx.

Some of the same common actions you're used to in other shell environments work the same way in PowerShell.

To close the shell, type **exit** at the prompt and press Enter.

To interrupt an action while it's occurring in the shell, press Ctrl+C.

Getting Help

To get basic help for commands in the shell, type **help command** at the prompt and press Enter. The help menu will appear, as you can see in Figure 15.2.

FIGURE 15.2   Help menu in Windows PowerShell

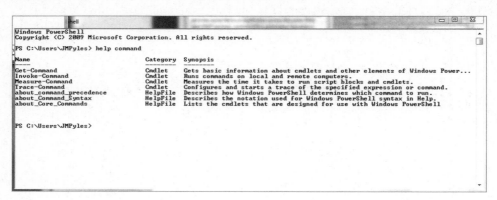

You can use wildcards (*) with the `help` command such as `help get-*` or `help set-*` if you don't know the specific `get` or `set` command you are trying to find. If you know the letter the cmdlet starts with, you can type **help get-I** and receive information about all the `get` cmdlets starting with that letter. Another example of how to get help is typing **about_*** at the prompt and pressing Enter. This will result in all the general help topics prefixed with `about` being displayed. If a long list results, use the spacebar to scroll down the list.

Keyboard Interaction

You can use a standard set of keyboard keystrokes to elicit specific results. Feel free to try any of these in PowerShell to see how they work:

- Backspace: Use this key to delete one or more characters behind the cursor.
- Ctrl+left arrow and Ctrl+right arrow: Press these keys to move left or right in the current line one word at a time.
- Delete: Use this key to delete the character directly under the cursor.
- End: Press this key to move the cursor to the end of the current command line.
- F7: To see the command history, press F7. A separate window will appear with the command history. To close the window, press Esc.
- Home: Press this key to move the cursor to the beginning of the current command line.
- Insert: Press this key to toggle between insert and overwrite modes.
- Left and right arrows: Press these keys to move left or write in the current line one character at a time.
- Tab: Press this key for command-line completion. It'll save you a lot of typing.
- Up arrow: Use this key to scroll back in the command history.

Commands

Four main types of commands are available in Windows PowerShell:

- Applications: These are Windows programs existing on the Windows system, such as executables, PowerShell scripts, or scripts written in other languages.

- Cmdlets: These are the PowerShell built-in commands written in a .NET language such as C# or Visual Basic that can be extended by loading PowerShell snap-ins.

- Functions: These are commands written specifically in the PowerShell language and are dynamically defined.

- Scripts: These are text files with a `.ps1` extension that contain PowerShell commands.

You will not likely be tested on writing PowerShell scripts for SharePoint in the certification exam, so this chapter will not go into any detail about the PowerShell language. You will be working mainly with PowerShell cmdlets.

PowerShell Cmdlets

As previously mentioned, rather than accepting text input and returning text output as previous Windows command-line utilities have, PowerShell accepts and returns .NET Framework objects, allowing for improved control as well as the ability to use completely new tools and methods, such as cmdlets (pronounced "command-lets").

At its simplest level, a cmdlet is a verb-noun pair separated by a hyphen (-) to define an action. In English, examples of this would be `Find-Fred` and `Bring-Donuts`. You've already experienced examples of using cmdlets in SharePoint tasks such as `Get-SPWebCollection` or `Set-SPMobileMessagingAccount`. When you issue a command such as `Get-SPWebCollection`, the specified object, `SPWebCollection`, is retrieved. When you issue a command using the `Set` cmdlet such as `Set-Llocation`, followed by a path, you will change your present working directory (PWD) to that location. The `Set` command is used to set session variables or parameters.

To see a list of classes in the `Microsoft.SharePoint` namespace, visit http://msdn.microsoft.com/en-us/library/microsoft.sharepoint.

Any parameters used with a cmdlet are passed as name-value pairs. Remember that cmdlets return objects in their output, and object properties display as name-value pairs, which can then be passed or piped to another cmdlet. This gives you the ability to chain cmdlets together. It's not hard from here to see how PowerShell not only serves as a command-line tool but as a new scripting language as well.

The cmdlets you use in SharePoint are based on a specific cmdlet class: `SPCmdlet`. This is opposed to cmdlets for Windows PowerShell, which are from the `PSCmdlet` class. The verbs you use in cmdlets are `Get`, `Set`, `New`, and `Remove`. In the previous chapters, you used `Get` and `Set` almost exclusively.

Although SharePoint has its own specific namespace defining the cmdlets that can be used, you can practice with some general cmdlets that will work in any namespace. Exercise 15.1 will give you some practice. You can perform this task on any Windows computer that has PowerShell installed.

EXERCISE 15.1

Using Generic Cmdlets and Commands

1. On any compatible Windows system, open the Run field, type **powershell** in the field, and press Enter.

2. When the Windows PowerShell window opens, type Get-Acl at the prompt and press Enter to see the access control list for the local computer.

3. Type **Get-Location** at the prompt and then press Enter to see the present working directory (pwd).

4. Type **help Get-I** to see a list of all the Get cmdlets beginning with the letter I.

5. Press the up arrow to toggle through the commands you previously ran until you find a command you want to run again; then press Enter to execute the command.

6. Press F7 to view a list of the commands you have run in a separate window, use the up and down arrows to toggle through the commands; then, with the desired command highlighted, press Enter to run the command.

7. Type **exit** and then press Enter to close PowerShell.

While the main cmdlets are Get, Set, New, and Remove, other available cmdlets begin with Copy, Rename, and Clear. Mkdir is also available. So, using an example from the previous exercise, not only can you use Get-Location, but you can use Set-Location in order to change the current working directory. Not only can you set the contents of a file using a cmdlet such as Set-Item, but you can also use Copy-Item to copy a file, use Remove-Item to remove a file or directory, use Clear-Item to clear the contents of a file, and use New-Item to create a new empty file or directory.

Windows PowerShell for SharePoint 2010

As mentioned previously, there is a separate namespace for SharePoint relative to Windows PowerShell. You've probably noticed that, when you've executed a cmdlet specific to SharePoint, the part of the cmdlet after Get or Set begins with SP, which of course means SharePoint.

On a desktop Windows computer, you've already invoked the Windows PowerShell console by using the Run field. On a Windows Server machine running SharePoint, you typically don't actually open this console but, rather, open the SharePoint Management

Shell instead. To open the Management Shell, go to Start ➤ All Programs ➤ Microsoft SharePoint Products, and then click SharePoint 2010 Management Shell.

The Management Shell isn't identical to the PowerShell console, but in the Management Shell, you can use PowerShell cmdlets to manage all the different aspects of SharePoint 2010 including creating service applications and proxies, site collections, web applications, and user accounts. Because you're using the SharePoint Management Shell, it isn't necessary for you to register the snap-in containing SharePoint-specific cmdlets. The registration automatically occurred when SharePoint was installed. If you try to use the Windows PowerShell console instead of the Management Shell, you'll have to manually register the snap-in before you can utilize SharePoint specific cmdlets.

To gain access with the SharePoint Management Shell and Windows PowerShell cmdlets, you must be a member of the SharePoint_Shell_Access role or the WSS_Admin_WPG local group. When you installed and configured SharePoint, you did so with an account that contains these roles. To add someone to these roles, use the Add-SPShellAdmin cmdlet.

For specific information about the Add-SPShellAdmin cmdlet, go to http://technet.microsoft.com/en-us/library/ff607596.aspx.

Opening the SharePoint 2010 Management Shell

When you open the SharePoint 2010 Management Shell for the first time, you may encounter the following error: "The local farm is not accessible. Cmdlets with FeatureDependencyID are not registered," as shown in Figure 15.3.

FIGURE 15.3   SharePoint 2010 Management Shell error

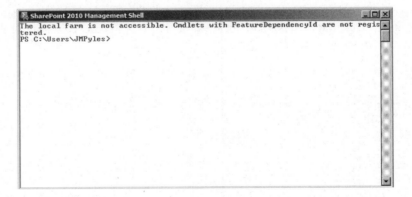

If you encounter this error, it means you are logged in as a user who does not have access to the SharePoint_Configuration database. You must belong to the SharePoint_Shell_Access role or the DB_owner role in order to have this access.

If you log in as the SharePoint administrator and then open the management console, you will have rights to the SharePoint_Configuration database, and the shell will appear as in Figure 15.4.

FIGURE 15.4   SharePoint 2010 Management Shell

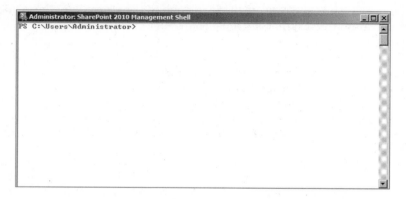

Windows PowerShell Cmdlets

As you've seen in the other chapters of this book, the number of different cmdlets that apply specifically to SharePoint seems vast. Just how are you supposed to know which cmdlets to use for specific situations? Even if you know the names of the SharePoint cmdlets that are available, how are you supposed to use them?

You saw previously in this chapter how to get general help in PowerShell. In the SharePoint Management Shell, you can use the help system to get information about SharePoint cmdlets. If you know nothing at all about which cmdlets are available, type **get-help get-*** at the command shell prompt and then press Enter. A list of all the SharePoint cmdlets and their descriptions will appear, as shown in Figure 15.5.

FIGURE 15.5   SharePoint cmdlet list in the SharePoint 2010 Management Shell

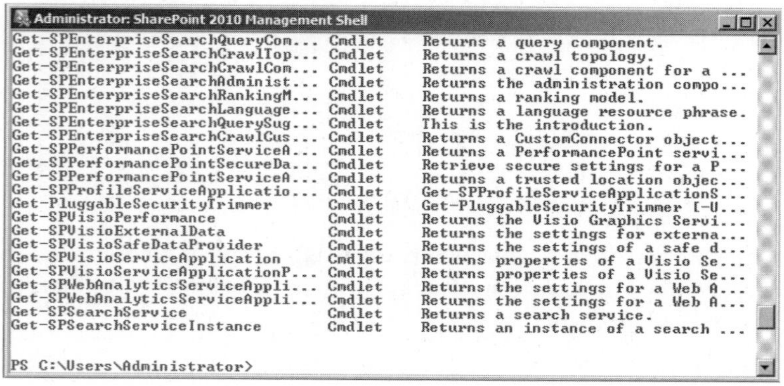

Of course, this list scrolls by very quickly, but you can type **get-help get-* | more** and then press Enter. Piping the `help` command through `more` lets you go through the list one page at a time. Just press the spacebar when you want to view the next page and keep paging through until you find what you want or reach the end of the list. Press the Q key to quit the list and return to the prompt.

Once you find the name of the desired SharePoint cmdlet, you can get help information just for that cmdlet by typing **get-help Get-<cmdlet name>** and then pressing Enter. Since the details can be lengthy, you should pipe the `help` request through `more`.

In Exercise 15.2, you'll see how to find the list of all the available SharePoint cmdlets, select a specific cmdlet, and then look up help for that cmdlet. You must be logged into SharePoint as an administrator to successfully complete this task.

EXERCISE 15.2

Getting Help for SharePoint Cmdlets

1. On a computer with SharePoint 2010 Server installed, click Start ➢ All Programs ➢ Microsoft SharePoint 2010 Products ➢ Microsoft SharePoint 2010 Management Shell.

2. At the prompt, type **get-help get-* | more** and then press Enter.

3. When the list of cmdlets appears, press the spacebar repeatedly until you locate the name of the desired cmdlet; then make a note of the cmdlet name.

4. Press Q to quit the help list.

5. At the prompt, type **get-help Get-<name of SP cmdlet>** such as **get-help Get-SPSearchService | more** and then press Enter to see help for the cmdlet, as shown here.

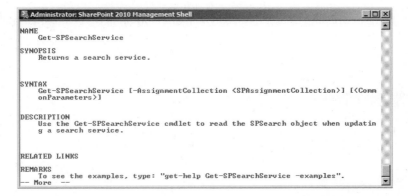

6. Read the help information and press the spacebar to page through all the information.

7. At the prompt, type **get-help Get-<cmdlet name> -examples** and then press Enter, such as **get-help Get-SPSearchService -examples** to see a list of examples for how the cmdlet is used.

EXERCISE 15.2 *(continued)*

8. Repeat the previous step but substitute the parameter –detailed for –examples and then press Enter.

9. Repeat the previous step but substitute the parameter –full for –detailed and then press Enter.

10. Repeat the process to get a list of SharePoint-related cmdlets and use the help steps presented in this exercise to discover more information about those cmdlets.

11. When you are done, type **exit** at the prompt and then press Enter to close the Management Shell.

You can use the same process to get help for the Set, New, and Remove cmdlets. Typing **help** at the prompt and then pressing Enter will show you all the different methods of help available in the Management Shell. Many of these help methods, and their results may not be specifically relevant to administrating SharePoint but may eventually help you gain more skills in Windows PowerShell as your skill sets continue to develop.

Between the general syntax information yielded by the **get-help Get-SP<cmdlet name>** command and using the –**examples** parameter, you should learn enough information about a SharePoint related cmdlet to be able to execute it in your environment.

Often, you will be logged in to SharePoint as an "ordinary user," and in it is a good security practice to only log into SharePoint as an administrator when you need to perform an administrative task. If you are logged in to SharePoint as a user and need to run a quick cmdlet in the Management Shell as an administrator, click Start, click the arrow to the right of SharePoint 2010 Management Shell, and then click Run As Administrator to open the shell with administrative rights. This is shown in Figure 15.6.

FIGURE 15.6   Opening SharePoint 2010 Management Shell as an administrator

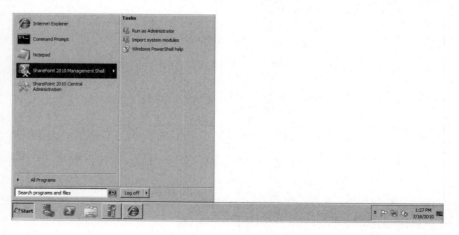

You can use this method to run help for PowerShell and to import modules if necessary. You can also click Start ➤ All Programs ➤ SharePoint 2010 Products and then right-click Microsoft SharePoint 2010 Management Shell and select Run As Administrator to achieve the same result.

Summary

In this chapter, you discovered the basics of using Windows PowerShell:

- Learning PowerShell basics
- Understanding PowerShell cmdlets
- Learning how to use cmdlets in the SharePoint 2010 Management Shell

Exam Essentials

Understanding Windows PowerShell Basics   Understand how to use common shell commands and syntax in Windows PowerShell, including how to get help.

Demonstrating Knowledge of SharePoint 2010 Management Shell   Know how to use the SharePoint Management Shell to use Windows PowerShell cmdlets that are specific to the SharePoint environment, including how to find information about specific cmdlets.

Review Questions

1. You are on the staff of a SharePoint administrator for your company, and you are learning Windows PowerShell basics as applied to the SharePoint environment. You understand the basic concept of a shell but are trying to understand what makes PowerShell different from Stsadm.exe. Of the following, what is true about PowerShell?

    A. PowerShell is a text-processing tool.

    B. PowerShell processes objects based on the .NET Framework.

    C. PowerShell processes objects written in Perl.

    D. PowerShell is the next generation of Stsadm.exe.

2. You are on the staff of a SharePoint administrator for your company, and you are learning Windows PowerShell basics as applied to the SharePoint environment. You are trying to understand cmdlets as a basic PowerShell concept. Of the following, what is true about cmdlets? (Choose all that apply.)

    A. Cmdlets are PowerShell built-in commands written in C#.

    B. Cmdlets are PowerShell built-in commands written in Visual Basic.

    C. Cmdlets are PowerShell built-in commands written in Perl.

    D. Cmdlets are PowerShell built-in commands that can be extended using snap-ins.

3. You are on the staff of a SharePoint administrator for your company, and you are learning Windows PowerShell basics as applied to the SharePoint environment. You are trying to learn more about cmdlets through the PowerShell help system and open Windows PowerShell on your desktop computer. Of the following, which command will give you help specific to Get-Command?

    A. help

    B. help command

    C. help cmdlet

    D. help powershell

4. You are on the staff of a SharePoint administrator for your company, and you are learning Windows PowerShell basics as applied to the SharePoint environment. Although you are just learning about PowerShell, it has been around for awhile in Windows systems. Of the following, on which Windows desktops would you expect to find Windows PowerShell? (Choose all that apply).

    A. Windows 2000 Professional

    B. Windows XP

    C. Windows Vista

    D. Windows 7

5. You are on the staff of a SharePoint administrator for your company, and you are learning Windows PowerShell basics as applied to the SharePoint environment. You are at a Windows PowerShell window and want to find a list of all the `Get` cmdlets beginning with the letter *J*. At the prompt, what should you type?

   A. `get-j`

   B. `help get-j`

   C. `help command get-j`

   D. `help get command j`

6. You are on the staff of a SharePoint administrator for your company, and you are learning Windows PowerShell basics as applied to the SharePoint environment. You want to see a list of the previous commands you issued in Windows PowerShell in a separate window. What should you do?

   A. Press the up arrow to toggle through the prior commands.

   B. Press the down arrow to toggle through prior commands.

   C. Press F7 and then toggle through prior commands.

   D. Press F1 and then toggle through prior commands.

7. In Windows PowerShell, you have invoked a `help` command, and at the bottom of the information that was returned you see the word `more`. How can you see the additional information?

   A. Press F1 to see the following page.

   B. Press Tab to see the following page.

   C. Press Q to see the following page.

   D. Press the spacebar to see the following page.

8. You are on the staff of a SharePoint administrator for your company, and you are learning Windows PowerShell basics as applied to the SharePoint environment. You have been practicing typing commands at the prompt and have heard that you can speed up the process of writing commands by using command-line completion. This will let you type only part of the command and then use this method to complete the line. Of the following, which method accomplishes this task?

   A. Press F1 to use line completion.

   B. Press Tab to use line completion.

   C. Press Q to use line completion.

   D. Press the spacebar to use line completion.

9. You are on the staff of a SharePoint administrator for your company, and you are learning Windows PowerShell basics as applied to the SharePoint environment. As part of your education, you have found out that there are three other main types of commands in PowerShell besides cmdlet. Of the following, what are those commands? (Choose three.)

   A. Applications

   B. Functions

   C. Scripts

   D. Variables

10. You are on the staff of a SharePoint administrator for your company, and you are learning Windows PowerShell basics as applied to the SharePoint environment. You are trying to learn cmdlet basics. At its most fundamental level, how is a cmdlet structured?

   A. A cmdlet is a verb-noun pair such as `Get-Fred` or `Set-Item`.

   B. A cmdlet is a noun-verb pair such as `Fred-Get` or `Item-Set`.

   C. A cmdlet is a verb/noun pair such as `Get/Fred` or `Set/Item`.

   D. A cmdlet is a noun/verb pair such as `Fred/Get` or `Item/Set`.

11. You are on the staff of a SharePoint administrator for your company, and you are learning Windows PowerShell basics as applied to the SharePoint environment. You have been working extensively in Windows PowerShell on your desktop, navigating through various directories, and you aren't sure where you currently are in the directory structure. How do you find out?

   A. At the prompt, type **path**.

   B. At the prompt, type **directory**.

   C. At the prompt, type **Get-Directory**.

   D. At the prompt, type **Get-Location**.

12. You are on the staff of a SharePoint administrator for your company, and you are learning Windows PowerShell basics as applied to the SharePoint environment. You are at the Windows PowerShell command prompt and want to change your current working directory to `C:\Users`. What command must you issue?

   A. `Set-Location:Users`

   B. `Set-Location:C:\Users`

   C. `Set-Location C:\Users`

   D. `Set-Location \Users`

13. You are on the staff of a SharePoint administrator for your company, and you are learning Windows PowerShell basics as applied to the SharePoint environment. You are at a computer with SharePoint 2010 Server installed, and you want to open the SharePoint 2010 Management Shell and practice using Windows PowerShell cmdlets. When the Management Shell opens, you receive an error that states, "The local farm is not accessible. Cmdlets with Feature-DependencyID are not registered." What has happened?

   A. You need to register the SharePoint snap-ins for the Management Shell before you can use Windows PowerShell cmdlets specific to SharePoint.

   B. You are logged into the computer without sufficient privileges.

   C. You cannot use Windows PowerShell cmdlets in the SharePoint Management Shell.

   D. The SQL Server database server containing the database for the local farm is offline.

14. You are on the staff of a SharePoint administrator for your company, and you are learning Windows PowerShell basics as applied to the SharePoint environment. To expect the Management Shell to open without errors, you must log in as the SharePoint administrator or as what other roles? (Choose all that apply.)

A. You must log in as a user who is a member of the DB_owner role.

B. You must log in as a user who is a member of the SharePoint_Shell_Access role.

C. You must log in as a user who is a member of the SharePoint_Central_Administration role.

D. You must log in as a user who is the administrator for the local computer on which SharePoint 2010 Server is installed.

15. You are on the staff of a SharePoint administrator for your company, and you are learning Windows PowerShell basics as applied to the SharePoint environment. You have opened the SharePoint 2010 Management Shell and want to find a list of Windows PowerShell cmdlets that are specific to SharePoint. Of the following, what command will accomplish this?

A. `help-get get-commands`

B. `get-help get-commands`

C. `help-get get-*`

D. `get-help get-*`

16. You are on the staff of a SharePoint administrator for your company, and you are learning Windows PowerShell basics as applied to the SharePoint environment. In the SharePoint 2010 Management Shell, you want to get an example of how to use the command `Get-SPTimerJob`. Of the following options, which will accomplish your goal?

A. `get-help Get-SPTimerJob -example`

B. `get-help Get-SPTimerJob -examples`

C. `get-help Get-SPTimerJob -sample`

D. `get-help Get-SPTimerJob -samples`

17. You are on the staff of a SharePoint administrator for your company, and you are learning Windows PowerShell basics as applied to the SharePoint environment. You are in the SharePoint 2010 Management Shell, and you want to learn the correct syntax and all possible parameters for the command `Get-TimerJob`. Of the following options, which will accomplish your goal?

A. `get-help Get-SPTimerJob`

B. `get-help Get-SPTimerJob -examples`

C. `get-help Get-SPTimerJob -syntax`

D. `get-help Get-SPtimerJob -variables`

18. You are on the staff of a SharePoint administrator for your company, and you are learning Windows PowerShell basics as applied to the SharePoint environment. You have been using the help system in the SharePoint Management Shell to get information about the Get cmdlet, which is one of the common cmdlets used both in PowerShell and in SharePoint. Of the following, what other help commands return information about common PowerShell cmdlets used in SharePoint? (Choose all that apply.)

A. get-help set-*

B. get-help new-*

C. get-help remove-*

D. get-help send-*

19. You are on the staff of a SharePoint administrator for your company, and you are learning Windows PowerShell basics as applied to the SharePoint environment. You are logged into SharePoint as an "ordinary user" and want to execute a quick cmdlet in the SharePoint Management Shell as an administrator. How can you do this?

A. Open the Management Shell, click in the upper-left corner of the shell window, and then click Run As Administrator.

B. Click Start ➢ All Programs ➢ Microsoft SharePoint 2010 Products, and then click Run SharePoint 2010 Management Shell As Administrator.

C. Click Start ➢ All Programs ➢ SharePoint 2010 Products, and then Microsoft SharePoint 2010 Management Shell.

D. Click Start ➢ All Programs ➢ SharePoint 2010 Products, right-click Microsoft SharePoint 2010 Management Shell, and then click Run as Administrator.

20. You are on the staff of a SharePoint administrator for your company, and you are learning Windows PowerShell basics as applied to the SharePoint environment. You are using the help system in the SharePoint Management Shell to learn more about cmdlets using to manage SharePoint. Some of the lists that output are very long, and you want to go through them a page at a time. What should you pipe the command through to accomplish this?

A. Pipe the command through more.

B. Pipe the command through less.

C. Pipe the command through page.

D. Pipe the command through toggle.

Answers to Review Questions

1. B. While `Stsadm.exe` processes text, Windows PowerShell processes objects based on the .NET Framework and is not the "next generation" of `Stsadm.exe`.

2. A, B, D. Cmdlets are PowerShell built-in commands written in a .NET language such as C# or Visual Basic (but not Perl) and that can be extended by snap-ins.

3. B. Although the other options will yield help information, using the `help` command will provide specific help about `Get-Command`, `Invoke-Command`, and `Measure-Command` in the cmdlet category.

4. B, C, D. Windows PowerShell made its advent in 2006, and the earliest Windows desktop environment on which it is available is Windows XP.

5. B. You will receive an error message if you use any `help` command other than `help get-j` to try to accomplish your goal.

6. C. You can press the up arrow to toggle through prior commands, but this will not occur in a separate window. If you have toggled through prior commands, pressing the down arrow repeatedly will let you toggle through commands subsequent to the one you are currently viewing. Pressing F1 under certain conditions will return the command you previously typed one character at a time.

7. D. Pressing the spacebar will take you to the following page, and you can review subsequent information one page at a time using this method. Pressing Q will quit the view of the help information. The other options produce no result.

8. B. Pressing F1 will yield no results. Pressing Q will add the letter Q to the line you are typing, and pressing the spacebar will add a space to the line you are typing. Pressing Tab will complete the line you are typing.

9. A, B, C. Valid PowerShell commands are applications, such as executables; functions, which are commands written in the PowerShell language; and scripts, which are text files with a `.ps1` extension containing PowerShell commands. Although variables can be part of a function or a script, they are not commands.

10. A. A cmdlet is a verb-noun pair separated by a hyphen. In English, it might be expressed as `Get-Fred` or `Bring-Donuts`.

11. D. You can also type **pwd** or **location**, which will also return the current working directory or your location in the directory system.

12. C. Options A and B will produce an error, and option D will only return the prompt without changing your working directory.

13. B. If you encounter this error, it means you are logged in as a user who does not have access to the SharePoint_Configuration database. You must belong to the SharePoint_Shell_Access role or the DB_owner role in order to have this access. Log in as the Share-Point administrator and then open the management console; you will have rights to the SharePoint_Configuration database, and the shell will appear without the error message.

14. A, B. A member of either the DB_owner role or the SharePoint_Shell_Access role has access to the SharePoint_Configuration database, which is necessary in order to open the Management Shell without errors.

15. D. `help-get` is an improper method of getting help. You need to issue `get-help`. Typing `get-help` commands will cause an error because `commands` is not a valid command option.

16. B. Typing `-examples` after the `help` command will return at least one example of how to use this command in a production environment.

17. A. When you execute `get-help Get-SPTimerJob`, the `Syntax` section of the results will show all the possible variables and correct syntax for the command. Although adding the `-examples` variable to the `help` command will yield a practical example of the cmdlet, there is no guarantee that the example will include all or even any of the variables.

18. A, B, C. Although all these commands will yield valid results, the `send` command is not a common cmdlet used in the SharePoint Management Shell, and that `help` command will only yield information about a single cmdlet rather than a list.

19. D. The first two options are bogus. If you open the Management Shell using the third option, you will only be able to use it with the rights of the user account you used to log in to SharePoint, and this method may cause an error.

20. A. Issue the command such as `get-help get-*  |  more` to be able to view long lists a page at a time. Although piping through `less` works in other shells, such as the BASH shell on Linux, it isn't available in the SharePoint Management Shell. The other options are bogus.

Appendix

About the Companion CD

IN THIS APPENDIX:

✓ What you'll find on the CD

✓ System requirements

✓ Using the CD

✓ Troubleshooting

What You'll Find on the CD

The following sections are arranged by category and summarize the software and other goodies you'll find on the CD. If you need help with installing the items provided on the CD, refer to the installation instructions in the "Using the CD" section of this appendix.

Sybex Test Engine

The CD contains the Sybex test engine, which includes the two bonus exams.

Electronic Flashcards

These handy electronic flashcards are just what they sound like. One side contains a question or fill-in-the-blank, and the other side shows the answer.

PDF of the Book

We have included an electronic version of the text in `.pdf` format. You can view the electronic version of the book with Adobe Reader.

Adobe Reader

We've also included a copy of Adobe Reader so you can view PDF files that accompany the book's content. For more information on Adobe Reader or to check for a newer version, visit Adobe's website at `www.adobe.com/products/reader/`.

System Requirements

Make sure your computer meets the minimum system requirements shown in the following list. If your computer doesn't match up to most of these requirements, you may have problems using the software and files on the companion CD. For the latest and greatest information, please refer to the ReadMe file located at the root of the CD-ROM.

- A PC running Microsoft Windows 98, Windows 2000, Windows NT4 (with SP4 or later), Windows Me, Windows XP, Windows Vista, or Windows 7
- An Internet connection
- A CD-ROM drive

Using the CD

To install the items from the CD to your hard drive, follow these steps:

1. Insert the CD into your computer's CD-ROM drive. The license agreement appears.

Windows users: The interface won't launch if you have autorun disabled. In that case, click Start ➢ Run (for Windows Vista or Windows 7, Start ➢ All Programs ➢ Accessories ➢ Run). In the dialog box that appears, type `D:\Start.exe`. (Replace *D* with the proper letter if your CD drive uses a different letter. If you don't know the letter, see how your CD drive is listed under My Computer.) Click OK.

2. Read the license agreement, and then click the Accept button if you want to use the CD.

The CD interface appears. The interface allows you to access the content with just one or two clicks.

Troubleshooting

Wiley has attempted to provide programs that work on most computers with the minimum system requirements. Alas, your computer may differ, and some programs may not work properly for some reason.

The two likeliest problems are that you don't have enough memory (RAM) for the programs you want to use or you have other programs running that are affecting installation or running of a program. If you get an error message such as "Not enough memory" or "Setup cannot continue," try one or more of the following suggestions and then try using the software again:

Turn off any antivirus software running on your computer. Installation programs sometimes mimic virus activity and may make your computer incorrectly believe that it's being infected by a virus.

Close all running programs. The more programs you have running, the less memory is available to other programs. Installation programs typically update files and programs; so if you keep other programs running, installation may not work properly.

Have your local computer store add more RAM to your computer. This is, admittedly, a drastic and somewhat expensive step. However, adding more memory can really help the speed of your computer and allow more programs to run at the same time.

Customer Care

If you have trouble with the book's companion CD-ROM, please call the Wiley Product Technical Support phone number at (800) 762-2974.

Glossary

Glossary Terms

Active Directory Federation Service (AD FS)   This is an industry-supported web services architecture designed to assist the single sign-on (SSO) service to authenticate users to multiple, related web applications over a single online session, securely sharing digital identity and entitlement rights across security and enterprise boundaries.

administration reports   This is a set of documents you can view in Central Administration that reports on the health and functioning of different aspects of search.

audience   This is a collection of users defined by their membership in a group such as a distribution list and used to target information to specific groups based on their profile information.

authoritative web pages   In search, you can configure web pages as authoritative indicating they contain the most relevant information.

business intelligence   Generally refers to the various applications, practices, and technologies used to support business decision making.

claims-based authentication   This is a method that uses attributes possessed by an individual, such as group membership and age, to make "claims" about the person that, when verified, grant the party access to resources and that personalize the session.

cmdlets   These are built-in Windows PowerShell commands using different PowerShell-specific namespaces and processing commands as verb-noun pairs.

content deployment   This is the process of moving content from one site collection to another, usually across two or more server farms.

crawl databases   These are used by a specific search service application to store information about the location of content sources as well as crawl schedules and other crawl operation–related data.

crawl rules   These are rules you can apply to crawls that include or exclude specific paths in a URL from being crawled as well as specifying authentication accounts.

crawler impact rules   These are rules you can apply to crawls that minimize the impact of crawls on server resources.

diagnostic logging   This is composed of a series of logs that collect data typically used in troubleshooting errors in SharePoint.

differential backup   This is the type of backup that backs up only the portions of the platform or component that have changed since the previous backup operation.

document converters   These tools let users migrate documents from one format to another, either through a UI or through an automated process such as a custom workflow.

enterprise wiki   In SharePoint, this is a site or site collection that allows collaboration and coauthoring of content in a single location and allows for the discussion and management of such data relative to team and group-level projects.

federated locations   This is a method of allowing SharePoint search to crawl external content sources such as Google news.

folksonomy   A system of classification related to the practice and method of collaboratively creating and managing tags to categorize content.

forms-based authentication   This method presents the party wanting to authenticate with an editable form that credential data is entered into and processed, allowing the party access to resources.

full backup   This is the process of backing up the entire platform or component such as the farm or a web application, regardless of whether anything has changed in the platform or component since the previous backup.

health and usage data collection   This is a set of monitoring tools that gather together different types of data including event log data, performance counter data, and timer service metrics data.

index partition   These are groups of query components that are used to contain a subset of the full-text index that returns search results.

InfoPath Forms Services   This service provides the ability to deploy an organization's forms in the SharePoint environment, allowing users to fill out any and all required forms within a web browser.

Kerberos   This authentication protocol allows nodes communicating over a nonsecure network to establish their identity in a secure manner, based on the client-server authentication model. In SharePoint, nodes must have access to an Active Directory domain.

lock   This is also known as a *site collection lock*. The lock prevents SharePoint users from accessing a site collection that is near or has reached its the data storage limit set by the quota template.

metadata   This term refers to "data about data" and describes the characteristics of the information as used to catalog said information.

metadata property mappings   This process is used to map properties taken from crawled documents and managed properties that users employ in search queries.

Microsoft SQL Server 2008 Reporting Services (SSRS)   This is a complete, server-based platform designed to provide a wide variety of report types, allowing organizations to gather relevant data and apply it across the enterprise.

monitoring   In general, this is a collection of tools that lets you view the actions of various features and activities in SharePoint in order to establish a baseline of systems operations, determine when problems occur, and note trends that may require changes in the SharePoint hardware, deployment, and configuration settings.

multi-tenancy   This refers to the ability to partition data of shared services or software in order to meet the needs of multiple tenants, as opposed to setting up separate hardware platforms or running multiple instances of the service.

object caching   This allows the return of query information to be set by user permissions so that, in response to queries, users can view published information or published information plus draft documents depending on their permissions.

output caching   This allows web pages to be cached based on user profiles so the amount of a cache and how long web data is cached varies depending on the user account. Output caching can be configured at the site collection and web application level.

PerformancePoint Services   Formerly a separate product called PerformancePoint Server 2007, this service is not fully integrated into SharePoint Server 2010 and provides interactive dashboards and display key performance indicators (KPIs) to aid in business intelligence decisions.

profile synchronization   The process of linking, exchanging, and matching data between the SharePoint profile store and other profile stores, such as those in Active Directory Domain Services (AD DS).

property databases   These contain the metadata associated with crawled content and can be added to or removed from SQL Server database servers.

quota template   This contains the storage limit values that determine how much data can be stored in a site collection.

Report Viewer web part   A specific web part for SharePoint installed when the SQL Server 2008 Reporting Services (SRSS) Add-in is installed; it can read report definition (.rdl) files generated by SRSS.

sandbox solution   This environment is used to restrict access to local and network resources to test load balancing or to test hosted environments prior to deployment.

scopes   These are used with scope rules to limit search queries to specific content and property types in order to return more accurate search results.

search service application   The specific service application in SharePoint responsible for providing search functionality.

Secure Store Service   This services replaces the Microsoft Office SharePoint Server 2007 single sign-on feature and is a shared service that provides storage and mapping of credentials to allow connections to external systems.

Security Token Service (STS)   This is a specialized web service used to respond to requests for security tokens and to provide identity management.

service application connections   This is used to associate service applications with web applications.

service applications   Services that are deployed in SharePoint and provide resources that can be shared across sites in a farm or between multiple farms.

service principal name (SPN)   This is a name that uniquely identifies an instance of a service among multiple services running on a computer. An SPN consists of the service name, the computer host name, and the port number.

SharePoint Health Analyzer   This utility runs a set of predefined health rules against servers in the SharePoint farm to monitor any potential configuration and performance issues.

shell   This is an interface between the computer user and the operating system kernel.

social features   These are components that authenticated SharePoint users can access and utilize in their My Site websites, such as ratings, social tags, and Note Board.

term store   This is a container for terms, which are words or phrases that are associated with a particular item in SharePoint.

unattended service account   This is a shared domain account that is used for accessing PerformancePoint Services data sources.

User Profile service   This is a shared service in SharePoint that lets you create and manage SharePoint user profiles that can then be accessed from sites and site collections.

User Profile service application   A central location in Central Administration from which you can manage personalization settings such as audiences, My Site settings, and profile synchronization.

Visio Graphics Service   This is a service application that allows users to share and view Visio diagrams directly in SharePoint provides data connections between diagrams in the Visio application and those published in SharePoint.

web analytics reports   This is a set of documents you can review in Central Administration that provides information about how the amount and type of search requests for different pages and sites in SharePoint.

web.config   This is a configuration file accessed with the Internet Information Services (IIS) Manager that, when edited, allows the administrator to configure BLOB and object cache settings.

Windows PowerShell   This is a command-line interface that processes objects based on the .NET Framework.

workflow   This is a process that allows multiple people to collaborate and have input on documents for the purpose of managing project tasks.

Index

B

Q

S

The Absolute Best MCTS: Microsoft SharePoint 2010 Configuration Book/CD Package on the Market!

Get ready for your Microsoft Certified Technology Specialist: Microsoft SharePoint 2010, Configuration certification with the most comprehensive and challenging sample tests anywhere!

The Sybex test engine features the following:

- All the review questions, as covered in each chapter of the book

- Challenging questions representative of those you'll find on the real exam

- Two full-length bonus exams available only on the CD

- An assessment test to narrow your focus to certain objective groups.

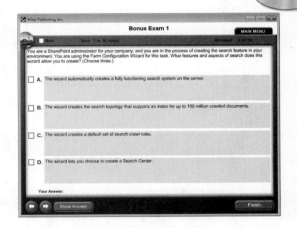

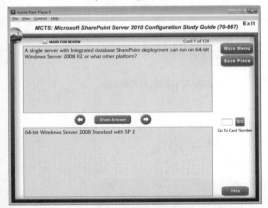

Use the electronic flashcards to jog your memory and prep last-minute for the exam!

- Reinforce your understanding of key concepts with these hardcore flashcard-style questions.

- Now you can study for the MCTS: Microsoft SharePoint 2010, Configuring (70-667) exam any time, anywhere.

Search through the complete book in PDF!

- Access the entire *MCTS: Microsoft SharePoint 2010 Configuration Study Guide* book, complete with figures and tables, in electronic format.

- Search the *MCTS: Microsoft SharePoint 2010 Configuration Study Guide* chapters to find information on any topic in seconds.

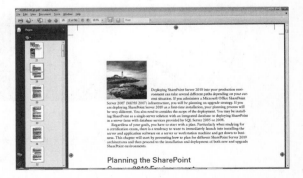

Get real!

Get *Real World Skills* from Sybex and take your career to the next level. These books not only help you on the job, they also help you prepare for your next certification exam.

Get real. Get Sybex!

For more information, go to www.sybex.com/go/realworldskills